Contemporary Authors

Autobiography Series

ISSN 0748-0636

Contemporary Authors

Autobiography Series

Adele Sarkissian
Editor

volume 4

GALE RESEARCH COMPANY • BOOK TOWER • DETROIT, MICHIGAN 48226

EDITORIAL STAFF

Adele Sarkissian, *Editor*
Christopher J. Momenee, Mark Zadrozny, and Donald E. Zurack, *Assistant Editors*
Marilyn O'Connell, *Research Coordinator*

Mary Beth Trimper, *External Production Supervisor*
Art Chartow, *Art Director*
Vivian Tannenbaum, *Layout Artist*
Darlene K. Maxey, *External Production Assistant*

Laura Bryant, *Internal Production Supervisor*
Louise Gagné, *Internal Production Associate*
Sandy Rock, *Internal Senior Production Assistant*

Alan Dyer, *Indexer*
Donald G. Dillaman, *Index Program Designer*

Frederick G. Ruffner, Jr., *Publisher*
Dedria Bryfonski, *Editorial Director*
Ellen Crowley, *Associate Editorial Director*
Christine Nasso, *Director, Literature Division*
Adele Sarkissian, *Senior Editor, Autobiography Series*

Contents

Preface

Each volume in the *Contemporary Authors Autobiography Series (CAAS)* presents an original collection of autobiographical essays written especially for the series by noted writers. *CAAS* has grown out of the aggregate of the Gale Research Company's long-standing interest in author biography, bibliography, and criticism, as well as its successful publications in those areas, like the *Dictionary of Literary Biography, Contemporary Literary Criticism, Something about the Author, Author Biographies Master Index,* and particularly the bio-bibliographical series *Contemporary Authors (CA),* to which this *Autobiography Series* is a companion.

As a result of their ongoing communication with authors in compiling *CA* and other books, Gale editors recognized that these wordsmiths frequently had "more to say"—willingly, even eagerly—than the format of existing Gale publications could accommodate. Personal comments from authors in the "Sidelights" section of *CA* entries, for example, often indicated the intriguing tip of an iceberg. Inviting authors to write about themselves at essay-length was the almost-inexorable next step. Added to that was the fact that the collected autobiographies of current writers were virtually nonexistent. Like metal to magnet, Gale customarily responds to an information gap—and met this one with *CAAS.*

Purpose

This series is designed to be a congenial meeting place for writers and readers—a place where writers can present themselves, on their own terms, to their audience; and a place where general readers, students of contemporary literature, teachers and librarians, even aspiring writers can become better acquainted with familiar authors and make the first acquaintance of others. Here is an opportunity for writers who may never write a full-length autobiography (and some shudder at the thought) to let their readers know how they see themselves and their work, what carefully laid plans or turns of luck brought them to this time and place, what objects of their passion and pity arouse them enough to tell us. Even for those authors who have already published full-length autobiographies there is the opportunity in *CAAS* to bring their readers "up to date" or perhaps to take a different approach in the essay format. At the very least, these essays can help quench a reader's inevitable curiosity about the people who speak to their imagination and seem themselves to inhabit a plane somewhere between reality and fiction. But the essays in this series have a further potential: singly, they can illuminate the reader's understanding of a writer's work; collectively, they are lessons in the creative process and in the discovery of its roots.

CAAS makes no attempt to give an observer's-eye view of authors and their works. That outlook is already well represented in biographies, reviews, and critiques published in a wide variety of sources, including *Contemporary Authors, Contemporary Literary Criticism,* and the *Dictionary of Literary Biography.* Instead, *CAAS* complements that perspective and presents what no other source does: the view of contemporary writers that is reflected in their own mirrors, shaped by their own choice of materials and their own manner of storytelling.

CAAS is still in its infancy, but its major accomplishments may already be projected. The series fills a significant information gap—in itself a sufficient test of a worthy reference work. And thanks to the exceptional talents of its contributors, each volume in this series is a unique anthology of some of the best and most varied contemporary writing.

Scope

Like its parent series, *Contemporary Authors,* the *CA Autobiography Series* aims to be broad-based. It sets out to meet the needs and interests of the full spectrum of readers by providing in each volume twenty to thirty essays by writers in all genres whose work is being read today. We deem it a minor publishing event that more than twenty busy authors are able to interrupt their existing writing, teaching, speaking, traveling, and other schedules to converge on a given deadline for any one volume. So it is not always possible that all genres can be equally and uniformly represented from volume to volume. Of the twenty-two writers in Volume 4, about half are novelists and half are poets. Like most categories, these oversimplify. Only a few writers specialize in a single area. The range of writings by authors in this volume also includes books of nonfiction as well as work for movies, television, radio, newspapers, and journals.

Format

Authors who contribute to *CAAS* are invited to write a "mini-autobiography" of approximately 10,000 words. In order to give the writer's imagination free rein, we suggest no guidelines or pattern for the essay. The only injunction is that each writer tell his or her own story in the manner and to the extent that each finds most natural and appropriate. In addition, writers are asked to supply a selection of personal photographs, showing themselves at various ages, as well as important people and special moments in their lives. Barring unfortunate circumstances like the loss or destruction of early photographs, our contributors have responded graciously and generously, sharing with us some of their most treasured mementoes, as this volume readily attests. This special wedding of text and photographs makes *CAAS* the kind of reference book that even browsers will find seductive.

A bibliography appears at the end of each essay, listing the author's book-length works in chronological order of publication. If more than one book has been published in a given year, the titles are listed in alphabetic order. Each entry in the bibliography includes the publication information for the book's first printing in the United States and Great Britain. Generally, the bibliography does not include later reprintings, new editions, or foreign translations. Also omitted from this bibliography are articles, reviews, and other contributions to magazines and journals. The bibliographies in this volume were compiled by members of the *CAAS* editorial staff from their research and the lists of writings provided by many of the authors. Each of the bibliographies has been submitted to the author for review. When the list of primary works is extensive, the author may prefer to present a "Selected Bibliography." Readers may consult the author's entry in *CA* for a more complete list of writings in these cases.

Each volume of *CAAS* includes a cumulative index that cites all the essayists in the series as well as the subjects presented in the essays: personal names, titles of works, geographical names, schools of writings, etc. The index format is designed to make these cumulating references as helpful and easy to use as possible. For every reference that appears *in more than one essay,* the name of the essayist is given before the volume and page number(s). For example, W.H. Auden is mentioned by several essayists in the series. The index format allows the user to identify the essay writers by name:

For references that appear *in only one essay,* the volume and page number(s) are given but the name of the essayist is omitted. For example:

Stieglitz, Alfred   **1**:98, 99, 104, 109, 110

CAAS is something more than the sum of its individual essays. At many points the essays touch common ground, and from these intersections emerge new mosaics of information and impressions. *CAAS* therefore becomes an expanding chronicle of the last half-century—an already useful research tool that can only increase in usefulness as the series grows. And the index here, for all its pedestrian appearance, is an increasingly important guide to the interconnections of this chronicle.

Looking Ahead

Each of the essays in this volume has a special character and point of view that set it apart from its companions. Yet these life stories take on an added significance as the reader comes upon them grouped together. Echoes reverberate from one essay to another: events, people, places, ideas that are common to many of these memoirs. Fellow writers often cast a long shadow. Robert Lowell, for instance, is recalled here by several poets whose lives or work he touched: Fred Chappell, Peter Davison, Robert Pinsky, and Louis Simpson. Other essayists, like Ben Belitt and John Wain, offer distinctive and differing perspectives on the academic profession. And many of the contributors to this collection pinpoint some of the special influences that they perceive in their work. For example, Rudolfo Anaya acknowledges the unique oral tradition he inherited as a Mexican-American: "From Spain, from the Mediterranean world of Catholics, Jews and Arabs, from the borrowing of medieval Europe, . . . into the Mexico of the Americas with Cortez, to be enhanced with the serious magic of the pre-Columbian Indians, north into the heart of New Mexico, . . . a rich world view came to sustain the people. In the *cuentos,* in the oral tradition, the view of the world was kept alive, and it was fed to us with *atole* and *tortillas,* filling us with the wonder of creation." Peter Davison recognizes more immediate influences: "It is no wonder, perhaps, that much of my writing is concerned with the implications of inheritance. A Jewish mother, something of an apostate, living in Colorado but loving New York. An Anglican father [poet Edward Davison], who, having fled his own land, yearned for its language and literature.... And, as though these contrasts did not concern us, at every opportunity my family had trekked somewhere else, winter or summer, like ants whose nest had been kicked." For Michael Hamburger the distinctive element in his personal history is "that I was born in Germany into a German-speaking family, uprooted at the age of nine, but began nonetheless at the age of fifteen to turn into a British poet . . . . My early need to translate must have sprung from my own translation from one country, one language, to another. Ever since, translation has been so much a part of my work that for long stretches it displaced my own writing, and I have translated far more poems than I have written poems of my own." In James Kirkup's memoirs, the sea is a special presence. "From my earliest infancy, the sea was always there. It lay a few steps from our street in South Shields, in the North East of England." Years later when he reached Japan, Kirkup found, " . . . my life was transformed. As soon as I set foot in Japan, I felt that I had come home. And this new home, like my old one, was forever within sight and sound of the sea." For Elie Wiesel the Holocaust has indelibly marked his life and his work. "Sighet: my home town, a special place, an inhabited setting that haunts the memory. I return to it often in my imagination. A search for landmarks? Perhaps for certainties? This permanent obsession nourishes my writing . . . . If, in my books, I return so often to my childhood, my purpose is to describe its death. I return to Sighet to confirm the disappearance of its Jews, myself included."

These brief examples can only hint at what follows in this volume. The essays will speak differently to different readers; but they are certain to speak best, and most eloquently, for themselves.

Acknowledgments

A special word of thanks to all the writers whose essays appear in this volume. They have given as generously of their enthusiasm and good humor as of their talent. We are indebted.

Authors Forthcoming in *CAAS*

Jonathan Baumbach (novelist, short story writer, and playwright)—An experimental writer, Baumbach uses innovative narrative structures, dreams, and hallucinations to delineate the nightmarish aspects of society. Among his works are *A Man to Conjure With* and *What Comes Next.*

Philip Jose Farmer (science fiction novelist and short story writer)—A three-time winner of the Hugo award, Farmer introduced innovative themes and techniques to the sci-fi genre in works like his "Riverworld" and "World of Tiers" series.

Leslie Fiedler (critic, novelist, poet, and editor)—Fiedler is one of today's most distinguished, and often controversial, literary critics. His well-known writings include *Love and Death in the American Novel* and *The Last Jew in America.*

George Garrett (novelist, short story writer, poet, critic, and editor)—Although each of Garrett's works is a deliberately new venture in subject and form, all of them share the viewpoint of a Christian moralist. Garrett's works include *Do, Lord, Remember* and *Death of the Fox.*

Nikki Giovanni (poet and essayist)—In verse collections like *My House* and the recent *Those Who Ride the Night Winds,* Giovanni creates poetry that mirrors her life-long concern for the rights and dignity of black people.

Carolyn Kizer (poet, translator)—Employing adroit technique, Kizer casts an impassioned yet stoical eye on the harshness and serenity of life and love in such critically praised volumes as *Knock upon Silence* and *Mermaids in the Basement.*

Jessica Mitford (essayist, journalist)—Her *American Way of Death* and *Kind and Unusual Punishment* are muckraking masterpieces. Equally renowned for her autobiographies, Mitford is a writer of good humor, profoundly concerned with civil liberties.

Jon Silkin (poet, critic, and editor)—A former unskilled laborer in London, Silkin now lets the skilled imagery of his poetry work for him. Collections such as *The Peaceable Kingdom* and *Nature with Man* reveal the poet's unusually keen sensitivity toward nature and human relationships.

David Wright (poet, essayist, and editor)—Born in South Africa and deaf at the age of seven, Wright asserts his special identity in his poised yet powerful poetry. His works include *Monologue of a Deaf Man, Nerve Ends,* and *A South African Album.*

Contemporary Authors

Autobiography Series

Rudolfo A. Anaya

1937-

Rudolfo A. Anaya

Womb of Time

What is it I remember about the first stirring of my imagination? I pause and listen, and I hear the wind blowing across the empty stretches of the plains of eastern New Mexico. This harsh but strangely beautiful land is my home; it is a land dotted by ranch houses, herds of cattle, flocks of sheep, the tough vegetation of the plain, gnarled juniper trees, cactus, mesquite bushes. By day, the wind plays a sad and mournful symphony across the land. By night, the wind is a lullaby, a fitting accompaniment to the surge of blood which flows around me, nurtures me, speaks to me, as I grow in my mother's womb. I hear her voice as she speaks to the children around her, siblings who have preceded me into the world of sun and wind.

Her name is Rafaelita. She is the daughter of Liborio Mares, a farmer from the Puerto de Luna Valley, a small village nestled along the Pecos River just south of Santa Rosa. They are farmers, a Spanish-speaking people who have been in the valley for over a hundred years. They came from the Rio Grande Valley, to farm, to raise their families, to adore their Catholic God and venerate His Blessed Mother, as their forefathers had done in Spain and Mexico before them. They speak Spanish to the few Anglo settlers who begin to come into the valley from the east. The Anglos learn the rudiments of the language of Spain. All settle into the life of the valley. They grow their crops, they raise pigs and sheep for meat, cows for milk. The horse is their beast of burden, their means of travel, the status symbol of the *vaquero*.

There are no pretensions on this land. The effort to survive cuts through all that, for this is not the land of milk and honey. My mother's family works from sunup till sundown. Life in the small village is difficult, but the joys of the *fiesta* sustain them. The feast day of the patron saint of the village, *Nuestra Señora de Refugio*, is celebrated. The men gather to clean the irrigation ditches that bring the water from the river into the fields. The harvest is abundant, the crops are gathered. They make *chile ristras*, the women boil jams and jellies, the men butcher their pigs to make the lard of winter, they store the meat in the *soterranos*, the cool earth pits. A good harvest sustains the isolated village through the winter.

My mother left the river valley to marry a man from the *llano*, a *vaquero*, a man who prefered to ride horseback and work with cattle, not a farmer. My mother's first husband was Salomon Bonney. She bore him a son and a daughter. He died only a few years after their marriage. The land was not always kind to my people. A mistake can be final, a frightened horse that rears and throws its rider can kill even the best *vaquero*. A winter storm roaring across the empty *llano* exempts no one, even the innocent shepherd caught unawares may freeze to death.

A widow with two small children has no time for a long romance. She married Martin Anaya, a man without pretensions, a man who knew how to work the cattle and the sheep of the big ranchers. The myth of the *caballero* courting the daughter of Spain was just that, a myth. For the workers of the *llano* there was survival. A man needed a wife, a woman needed the warmth and safety of a home to raise her children. Out of that union in the small village of Pastura, my brothers and sisters came, and in 1937 I was born.

My father, too, was married before he married my mother. He had a daughter from that marriage. Later I will know her as a sister; I know nothing about the first woman in my father's life.

A family was born to Rafaelita Mares and Martin Anaya, my older brothers, Larry and Martin. I came sandwiched between the younger sisters. Edwina, Angelina, me, then Dolores and Loretta. My brothers were models for my manhood, but they were young men of sixteen and seventeen when World War II swept away the young men of the small towns of eastern New Mexico. I was in the primary grades while they fought the war. Awaiting their return, I grew up surrounded by sisters.

Why do I remember the dreams of life in my mother's womb? Is it possible I felt the sting of the sun, heard the mournful cry of the wind, the lullaby of my mother's songs as she carried me in her womb? Why do I think I heard the cry of the *coyotes* at night, the bleating of goats and sheep? In that small village of my birth, Pastura, why do I remember the dim light the kerosene lamps cast on the adobe walls, the aroma of smoke from the wood stove where my mother cooked? Why do I remember the voices of the old women of the village as they visited my mother in her kitchen, drank coffee, smoked cigarettes, talked about the impending birth. The date was October 30, 1937, almost the eve of All Saints Day.

"You were born with your umbilical cord tied round your neck," my mother was to say many years later. "*La Grande* was there to help in your delivery . . ."

La Grande. That name will haunt my childhood. She was a woman of power, a power born of understanding. An intelligent woman who knew the harmony in nature. Some say she was a *curandera*, a woman who knew how to use her power and herbs to cure sickness. All my life I will meet such people, people who understand the power of the human soul, its potential. If I am to be a writer, it is the ancestral voices of these people who will form a part of my quest, my search. They taught me that life is fragile, that there are signs given to us, signs that we must learn to interpret.

That is why, if I am to write these short chapters of my life, I must go to the beginning. For me, it began there, with the blood of a farmer's daughter and a *vaquero*, commingling in the womb, to create a child who will come strangling in his own umbilical cord, pulled into the world by the strong hands of an old woman who understood life.

My father and his *compadres* got drunk that night and shot their pistols into the frigid night air of the empty plain. My mother groaned and made the sign of the cross. One more son was born alive. Strange signs were in the air. The owls hooted in the hills and flew away at the sound of gunfire. The *coyotes* lay quiet. Overhead the Milky Way was a river of sperm, a river of life shining down on the lonely planet earth. I will always wonder about the first stirrings of that journey to earth. Whence? Wherefore?

"When you were still a baby," my mother said many years later, "we sat you on a sheepskin on the floor. We put different things around you. Your father put a saddle. I don't remember who put a pencil and paper. Perhaps it was me, because I had always yearned for an education. I had a bright mind, but in those days the girls remained at home. Only my brothers went to school. Anyway, you crawled to the pencil and paper . . ."

A silence fell between me and my father. Why? Did the familiar story tell him that to his way of life his youngest son was lost?

The Child Rebels

In my childhood world the power of prayer was supreme. God listened. The saints came down from heaven to comfort those who needed comforting. The Virgin Mary would always intercede on behalf of those who needed help. But the demonic powers of the devil were also a truth in the world. The devil came to men, whether they had done evil or not, to tempt them and claim their souls. Witches rode across the open plain disguised as balls of fire, disguised as owls or *coyotes.* They could appear at any time. Their power was equal to the power of the saints. Only the Cross of Christ could save one.

We moved from that small village of Pastura to Santa Rosa when I was a small child. Our new home was perched on the edge of a cliff, below flowed the Pecos River. The wind blew around the edges of the house, along the dreary and lonely cliff. Here I first heard the cry of *La Llorona,* the tortured spirit of a woman who had once murdered her children and gone insane. Now she was a witch who haunted the cliff of the river. With eyes burning with fire, clawlike fingernails, hair stringy, and her clothes torn and tattered, she came at dusk to haunt the river. Her cries were carried by the wind around the corners of our house. I felt a terror I had never felt before. *La Llorona* wanted me, she wanted my flesh and blood, she wanted my soul. She wanted to take me deep into her lair where she would consume me, as she had consumed her own children. I fled in fear into the arms of my mother.

Not yet a man, I found safety only in the arms of my mother. Later she, and the priest at the church, would move me one step further along the road to salvation. They would teach me that if I made the sign of the cross, *La Llorona* and all the witches and demons of hell could not harm me. Armed with the sign of the cross I could go out into the world and fear no evil. Ah, to be innocent again and to believe those foundations of faith which protect us from harm.

If I am going to look squarely at the forces which have formed my life, then I need to look at the church. My mother was a devout Catholic, but I was never sure about my father. Although he prayed and came along to mass, I always suspected he was a rebel. He rebelled in his silence, he drank, the settled life seemed to torment him. He had lived life on the open *llano,* those men of cattle and sheep were his only real friends. Now he was a *vaquero* without a horse. In many respects, a broken man.

I understood that streak of the skeptic in him years later when I read Angelico Chavez's book on New Mexico families. There is a story of an Anaya who had a strong argument with the parish priest. His crime was serious enough to cause him to be sent to Mexico City to be tried before the church fathers. He was made to recant, to apologize, then he was sent back home to New Mexico. Upon returning to his village, he dressed in a most outlandish costume, probably to imitate the cassock of the priest, and he rode his horse down the village street. Sipping drinks from a bottle of *aguardiente,* I am sure, boasting to the people that he had never apologized.

Many years later, while I was traveling in Spain, a guide who studied genealogy told me that Anaya was originally a Basque name. It means something like "brotherhood" or "brothers of a clan." Knowing the anarchistic and independent nature of the Basque people has provided me as much of a clue to my father's nature as all the years I knew him. Perhaps I remember all this only because it sheds light on my nature. There is something of the rebel and the anarchist in me.

My mother taught me catechism in Spanish. I grew up speaking Spanish at home, as far as I knew all of the world spoke Spanish. Even mass at *la iglesia de Santa Rosa de Lima* was said in Spanish. I was taught that the church was in charge of my salvation, that I needed the sacraments. I was molded into a good Catholic, insofar as any Anaya can be molded into one. I kept asking the sisters and the priest uncomfortable questions, questions which had to do with the nature of the Trinity and the geography of heaven. "You must have faith" was not an adequate answer for my inquisitive mind. I was breaking the chains of dependence, but I still feared the devil and his demons.

Years later when I read Dante's *Divine Comedy,* I discovered that his inferno was like my hell. I was thoroughly fascinated. If the sisters of Santa Rosa had read Dante, they would have been able to answer my questions about the geography of hell.

Life in Santa Rosa was good. I had friends, I played all day. We wandered into the open plain country, hunting. We spent entire days along the river, fishing and swimming. We made our own toys, boats and wagons and airplanes and wooden guns. I went to school and learned English. Moving from a world of Spanish into a world of English was shocking. I had very little help, except for the teachers at school. I don't know how I survived. A lot of my classmates didn't.

The Voices of Childhood

The seasons of the *llano* are distinct. In the spring the wind blows, the dust clouds are thick, the tumbleweeds roll across the land. In the years of the late thirties and early forties I remember sandstorms that blocked out the light of the sun. Imagine, a small boy coming from school, leaving the warm safety of the school and entering the terrible windstorm that obliterated every familiar landmark. Down the town streets and toward the river, across the bridge and up the rocky path I struggled to reach the safety of home.

Outside the storm raged and tore at the tin roof, but inside was safety, warmth, hot *tortillas* with butter. Maybe I played paper dolls with my sisters, Edwina, Angie, Dolores, and Loretta, or I took out my marbles and trucks and played alone. Maybe I sat in the kitchen and asked my mother a lot of questions. Where does the wind come from? Where does it go? She always said I asked a lot of questions, that I was destined to go against the current of life.

The Chávez boys were my neighbors. We grew up like brothers, playing hide and seek, tag, football, fishing, swimming in the river, sitting around campfires at night where we told stories, sometimes fighting and swearing and tearing at each other like little animals. The town boys feared us. The battles we fought with them were fierce. Luckily no one was ever killed. I accidently shot Santiago Chávez in the eye with a bee-bee gun during one terrible battle. It is a bad memory that haunts me still. I saw one boy's eye smashed by a rock from a slingshot. A bloody mess.

How strange that I could grow up gentle and in a loving home, and outside the home I lived very much the life of a little savage. I grew tough and brown in the summer sun. No shoes, except for the movies in town on Saturday. My dog Sporty by my side, I feared no one. No one, that is, until the sounds and shadows of the ghosts in the bush reared their heads. I hated to travel alone along the river. In the deep brush lurked *La Llorona.* I heard her, I felt her, I saw her. As I cut wild alfalfa that grew by the river to feed my rabbits, it

would suddenly grow dark, and I was alone, far from home, in a world full of strange powers.

Summer was the most joyous season. We could go into town and play baseball with the town boys, or go fishing in the lakes, streams, and rivers around the town. The town is unique in this part of the country, because it lay in a natural depression. Many springs and lakes are born out of the underground water. Clear, precious jewels of water in an otherwise arid plain. Some of these lakes had beautiful golden carp in the waters, all were haunted by sirens, frightful fantastical sisters of *La Llorona.* To fish in the day along the rivers and lakes was fine, but no one was brave enough to be caught there at night. Nothing is as lonely or frightening as one of those lakes out in the middle of the desolate plain, at dusk, when the bats and nighthawks begin to fly. Even the friendly shapes of cows became shadows of ghosts, and to get home one had to cross the cemetery.

An aunt who had come to live with us died of cancer. I had grown very close to her. My father made her coffin from pine planks we bought at the lumberyard. We placed her in my mother's parlor, *la sala,* where the rosary was said at night and the family and friends gathered to pray. Coins were placed on my aunt's eyes, because they would not close. When the rosary was done a little girl and I were awarded the coins, and after that I had the gift of finding coins.

Death lurked in the bud and flower of summer. We accepted death as a fact of life. Like our destiny, it was there, waiting to manifest itself. It was a mystery, as the winds of spring were a mystery, but it was nonetheless a part of life.

There were only half-a-dozen *familias* on our little hill. I remember the Chávez family, my cousin Fio and his wife Amelia, the Giddings, the Gonzalez family. George Gonzalez and I became good friends. His father, who had been the sheriff of the small town, was tragically killed. George became a man at a young age. He had a ranch to run, and I spent summers with him there, helping as best I could. The ranch was a terribly lonely and deserted place, but the experience helped me along my road to manhood. Only by looking back do we see how crucial are the steps that separate us from our mothers.

School was not difficult for me, but I was learning that I saw things in a different way. I would be running home and stop suddenly because I had heard a voice calling my name. I would stop and turn slowly around in a circle, looking for the source of the voice but seeing only the brilliant sunset, the red and gold and mauve which filled the large sky, the whirl of the nighthawks, the flutter of dusk. Who? I would ask. The sound would slowly fade, and I was alone, weak, wondering. The sun set, the clouds turned grey, the owl called on the hill. Was it the call of *La Llorona* along the river? Was it the call of my mother calling me to hurry home? Was it the mournful pleas of my dead ancestors asking me to remember them? Awakening from the brief trance, I would run home, still full of the mystery of that voice that called my name so clearly.

Winter on the plains is severe. The storms whip down from the northwest, there are no mountains to break their intensity. Sliding down the eastern slope of the Sangre de Cristo mountains they gather momentum, and by the time they reach Las Vegas and Clines Corners and Santa Rosa they are bellowing bulls of winter. The snows drift, the ice freezes everything solid, the trees along the river are transformed into ice palaces.

But the enchantment doesn't last long. The cold brought reality with it and the hardship of life. Our feet bundled in several pairs of socks and warm shoes wrapped in burlap (there was no money for the galoshes), we trudged to school. My mother was fanatic about school, not one day was to be lost. She knew the value of education.

A New Life

I attended school in Santa Rosa until the eighth grade. It was then that the gang of boys I had known began to fall apart. Some had moved away from the small town. Some began to fight with each other. Prejudices I had not known before appeared. We who had always been brothers now separated into Anglos and Mexicans. I did not understand the process. I had always known I was brown, that I was *mejicano* in the language of my community, that we were poor people. But those had been elements of pride, and now something had come to separate us.

We moved to Albuquerque in 1952. In a way I was glad to escape the confines of Santa Rosa. But how could I escape it? Being fifteen was the same in most places, the process of finding a new identity as young men is the same anywhere. The pain in the blood and the flesh is a joy, a new awareness.

Albuquerque in the early fifties was a great place to be. The war was over, the boom was on. Cheap sand hills near the mountain became new and instant housing additions. The city was a young woman growing into womanhood, and I a young man ready to take her. We lived in the Barelas *barrio,* at 433 Pacific. There in the heart of the *barrio* I met new friends, and I quickly learned the rhythm of survival on the streets.

As before, life was easy, safe, sure, if I kept to the corners I knew, near the people I trusted. My brother Larry lived in Barelas, and he knew the people and the

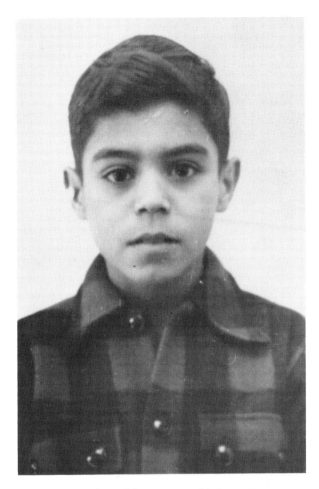

Rudy, about thirteen years old, Santa Rosa Grade School

street gangs. He was respected, so I had no trouble. Still, life for my discarded and poor people was tough. Country people were entering the city in search of work. On the streets, the gangs of *pachucos* were vicious, deadly. Small drug traffic. Baseball in summer in the park, football in fall. My friend Robert Martinez and I cleaned lawns in the Country Club for spending money. We stayed clear of the gangs, the *tecatos* on dope, but when we had to fight, we fought.

I attended Washington Junior High, later Albuquerque High School. Cars came into our lives, without a car you were nothing. Games, bebop dances in the gym, James Dean, the State Fair in the fall and wild rides with wild girls, after-school rumbles, Bill Haley and His Comets, Fats Domino, customized '48 Fords, learning to French kiss and always wondering about going all the way, *macho* men, fifties-cool dress, ducktails, tapered denims and black shoes with double soles. . . . We were all pretending, growing up and pretending we were cool as Jimmy Dean. We pretended to know everything, and we didn't.

Not My Time to Die

There are events that change one's life forever. Each experience causes a perceptible change in the rhythms of the soul, and the ripples which flow outward measure the degree of the change. Slight or serious, the spirit adjusts and goes on.

It was a beautiful day, warm and carefree. The water of the irrigation ditch came through a culvert and created a deep pool. We had been there before, we knew the place. Laughing and teasing each other, we headed for the water, and I dove first. Then the world disappeared. The doctors would later explain that I had fractured two vertebrae in my neck and I had gone into instant paralysis. I could not move a muscle.

I floated to the top of the water, opened my eyes, saw the light of the sun shining in the water. I tried to move, I couldn't. Face down, my shouts for help were only bubbles of water. I felt a panic I had never felt before. Death was coming for me, and I could not move in protest. I struggled violently to move, to kick, to swing my arms, to turn upside down so I could at least breathe and keep from drowning, but I could not move. The panic closed around me, I knew I was about to drown. But my instinct for survival had been sharpened too well for me to give up without a struggle. It was not my time to die!

I held my breath, but I knew I could not hold my breath forever. Panic turned to dread, then into a strange acceptance of my fate. I began to breathe water, felt it sting my lungs. A strange peace came over me, I prayed, surrendered my soul to God. My soul seemed to ascend into the air. Beneath me I could see my friends jumping and swimming in the water. Then I saw Eliseo tentatively approach my floating body. He thought I was playing, but I had been down a long time. He turned me over. I remember smiling and laughing at him, and with that I returned to earth. I had pulled away from the first step toward death.

I have not spoken or written about this accident before because I learned during the ensuing years that pity did not help rebuild my world. I learned that indulging in confession did not really help me. Perhaps it was that I withdrew too much into myself and refused to share that experience with others, perhaps I learned too quickly that most people really do not possess the sensibility we call empathy. Most people are too much in their world, they find it difficult to understand the world of others, they do not have the sensibility to understand the feelings of others.

In later life I would meet friends and acquaintances who did not know my past and thus could not know or guess my pain. We learn very well to hide our disabilities. It is only when we are asked to do something we cannot do, like play baseball or volleyball or run, that we are painfully reminded of our limitations, and worse, because we have learned to live with those limitations, we are reminded how little our friends know us, how cruel the simplest invitation may sound. We learn to hide our pain, to live within, to build a new faith inside the shell of bones and muscle.

For the following weeks fever and fantastical monsters filled my tormented days and nights, leaving in the wake of pain the scars I still carry. But I lived, and I vowed to move again. I found slight movement in my fingers, worked from there to regain the use of my legs, then my arms. I spent that summer at Carrie Tingley Hospital, and when I returned home I was walking with a cane, stiffly, but walking. Most of those with similar neck injuries never regain any movement. I had been saved for a new role in life.

One of the first things I did on my return was to go down to the YMCA, alone. I waited until the pool was deserted, then stepped to the edge of the pool. I did not know if I could swim. My muscles were stiff, very weak. But I dove into the water, floated to the top, smiled, dog-paddled out, got out as well as I could, sat panting on the side of the pool. I had conquered one fear within.

I walked stiffly through those following years, turning into myself, protecting the soft spot within. I learned the true meaning of loneliness, that is, how it feels to be alone. I had the support of my family, my mother nursed me through the worst part of the paralysis, daily massaging the stiff limbs back to life, and my friends never wavered. But I was alone, alone and wondering: Why me?

But I was so strong, or had been so strong, that I survived. I exercised, swam, reentered the rough and tumble of life. I accepted no pity, and really moved out determined to do more than my more abled friends had ever done. I fished, scaled the mountains of Taos, hunted with Cruz from the pueblo, finished high school, entered the university, married, and began to travel. I climbed mountains and crossed oceans and deserts in foreign places my old friends back home didn't know existed. So who is to judge whether an adversity comes to crush us or to reshape us.

Self-Discovery

I attended Albuquerque High School and graduated in 1956. I did nothing to distinguish myself at school. My grades were good, but there was little to challenge the imagination. Reading the *Readers Digest* during free period in English class doesn't make for producing a writer. Anyway, a writer learns to live beyond his circumstance, he learns to be in touch with a stream of active imagination which is fed from deeper, internal sources.

The fifties, as we are being told by the historians of popular culture, were a great time. They were. We had the king, Elvis. John Wayne was still shooting them up at the Kimo theatre every Saturday afternoon. Stolen hubcaps adorned our cars. Rock-and-roll and bebop liberated us musically. *The Blackboard Jungle* and *Rebel Without a Cause* reflected part of our youth. We rocked around the clock, hung out at Lionel's, the local drive-in, and went to dances at the community center, always following the sweet fragrance of blossoming girls. But all times come to an end, and even heroes die.

Yes, the fifties were a good time, but one has to remember that historians do not see everything. There are huge pockets of people whose history, at any given time, is never told. The large Mexican-American population is a case in point. Moving through high school without purpose, never seeing Mexican teachers, never reading the history or the literature of the people, created in us a sense of the displaced. We knew our worth. It was reflected in our families, in the *barrios*, in the cities and ranches. We knew there was a long history of the Hispanic presence in the Southwest United States, but the education we received did not reflect this. Society's melting-down process was at work, but the idea of the melting pot was a myth. Society did not accept, as equals, the black and brown people of the country. Prejudice did exist, racism was thriving.

Small wonder any of us entered professional fields. People ask me why I became a writer. My answer is that I became a writer in my childhood. That is why that time has been so important to me. The characters of my childhood, the family, friends, and neighbors that made up my world, they and their lives fed my imagination. All cultural groups develop an oral tradition, and the tradition of the Mexican-Americans is immensely rich. The stories of characters, fanciful and real, constantly filled my life. In the circle of my community, my imagination was nourished.

There is something in the Mexican character which, even under the most oppressive circumstances, struggles to keep art and its humanizing effect alive. I have seen this in the simplest details carved into door frames, the brightly painted walls, the decorative altars in the home, the gaiety of the music, the expressive language. The Mexican possesses a very artistic soul; I am heir to that sensibility.

My discovery of my past should not seem so pro-

found, but it was, because nothing of that past had been intimated in the schools. We studied no Mexican history or art, no Indian religious thought or art. Even during my undergraduate days at the University of New Mexico, not a word or a suggestion that the cultures of these two groups existed. Of course I could have studied in the Spanish department, but in those days those scholars were *too* Spanish. Their concern was for the literature of another time and place, and rightly so, for every discipline needs its scholars. But in their assistance or encouragement, there was no sense that they either understood or cared about our needs.

I cannot say I found a more welcoming home in the English department, and yet, taking Freshman English as it used to be taught, as the building block of a liberal education, I was suddenly turned on to literature. It was not easy. I had attended business school for two years, I was good at the work. More study and a CPA could have been my vocation. Even that would have been more than many from my neighborhood aspired to in those days. But the study of business was unfulfilling, so I dropped out and enrolled in the university. I didn't have the money, but I worked every odd job imaginable. I kept books for a neighborhood bar, I worked for a state agency, anything to pay my way. Long hours of work by day, fitting classes into the schedule, and reading into the night became a way of life.

On the surface there was nothing new here in the life of a student, but there was a difference for us. We were Mexican students, unprepared by high school to compete as scholars. We were tolerated rather than accepted. The thought was still prevalent in the world of academia that we were better suited as janitors than scholars. English was still a foreign language to us; I had to work hard to dominate its rules and nuances. Even in university classes, I was still corrected for allowing my Spanish accent to show. We were different, and we were made to feel different. It was a lonely time; many of us did not survive.

A Faith Shaken

The friendship of other Chicanos helped me survive in the university. Dennis, who later became my *compadre,* was there. Jimmy, who was studying Spanish and Latin American literature, was there. On weekends we got together, went out drinking, played pool, met girls. Dennis and I fished a lot up in the Jemez Mountains. The *barrios* of the city were always there to welcome us home. We knew we were moving out into a bigger world, but it was the old world we knew which provided our stability.

Reading created a new, turbulent world with

ideas that challenged the foundations of my faith. I began to write poetry to fill the void. It is a terrible thing when the foundations of faith fall apart. A great vacuum opens up, one wanders lost in that void. There is little meaning to life. Suicide becomes a perverse companion. I felt betrayed. Life and the church had betrayed me. I lost faith in my God, and if there was no God there was no meaning, no secure road to salvation. All this may sound like the retelling of the crisis of faith which many young people experience, but it is important to verbalize these feelings. The depth of loss one feels is linked to one's salvation. That may be why I write. It is easier to ascribe those times and their bitter-

will not snap. Love is such a thread. Forgiveness is another. The will to *be* in the face of nothingness. The will to reconstitute the faith. Something in the stream of my blood and the blood of my community gave me the strength to begin my search anew. I can rebuild the foundations of my faith, I said. A realization slowly arrived at, one that came out of the difficult years.

I began to write novels of young people caught in the same despair which seemed to drown me. I wrote exclamatory poetry. "Man is born free! But everywhere he is in chains!" Reams of manuscripts. One novel, I remember, ran nearly a thousand pages. I burned all those old manuscripts. It was a necessary

The author on the terrace of his West Mesa home, Albuquerque, New Mexico

sweet emotions to my characters.

Love is most poignant when we are young. I fell in love with a young artist at the university, but in the tradition of that beatnik generation which was moving around the country, she moved away. I was shattered. My religious beliefs were being assaulted from every side. I think it is precisely those two elements which are the most difficult for young people to deal with: the loss of love and loss of faith.

What saves us? Something in the fiber of the soul will suffer the loss of meaning, be dragged to the depths of despair and depression, and still find threads which

phase for the budding writer, but no need to trouble the world with pure emotion regurgitated.

I received my degree and accepted a teaching position in a small town in New Mexico, later I taught in Albuquerque. So, I still had not left home except for brief journeys to New York, into the south, to St. Louis. Always in search of something, something I thought the eastern part of the American continent could give me but did not.

I married a woman from Kansas. Patricia. I think she was the one person who truly believed I could be a writer. Her encouragement was a new pillar in the foundation I was building. She became a good editor who could read my work and respond to its strengths and weaknesses.

Every writer needs a relationship with an editor, a sort of mentor. In our formative years especially we need to see our work reflected in the eyes of another person. That person somehow represents our eventual readership. If he knows our desire to write, that person will quickly go to the strengths and the weaknesses, saving the writer time by focusing on areas that need revising.

For many writers, marriage is difficult. It seems to add to the storm of emotion which is the baggage of our work. I have needed a stable base from which to write, so for me marriage and home have been positive. Two miscarriages were the most difficult experiences of my married life. The flushing of one's own blood hurts more than anything I know. But time softens the memories and images and teaches us to forget and forgive. Still, the image of that loss remains sharp and clear in my mind, painful. Perhaps the writer or artist is a person who is damned not because he or she writes, but because those sharp and poignant images of joy and pain remain so clear in our blood and soul that we must flee into writing to assuage the pain.

In the sixties I had thrown out all my old work and I began work on my novel *Bless Me, Ultima.* I would teach by day, come home and write in the afternoons and into the night. It was a simple story, the story of a boy growing up in a small New Mexico town. I was still haunted by the voices of my childhood, and I had to capture the memory of those times and people. But I was still imitating a style and mode not indigenous to the people and setting I knew best. I was desperately seeking my natural voice, but the process by which I formed it was long and arduous.

Literary historians have not been kind to the literature of the Mexicans in this country. In many ways, history has cheated us. It has not reflected the true accomplishments of this cultural group. This slight we are just now setting right. But in the sixties I felt I was writing in a vacuum. I had no Chicano models to read and follow, no fellow writers to turn to for help. Even Faulkner, with his penchant for the fantastic world of the south, could not help me in Mexican/Indian New Mexico. I would have to find my way alone. I would have to build from that which I knew best.

Ultima Appears

I was working late one night, trying to breathe life into the novel that would one day be known as *Bless Me, Ultima.* The *curandera* Ultima had not yet entered the story. One light was on, a desk light near the typewriter. I heard a noise and turned to see the old woman dressed in black enter the room. This is how Ultima came to me, deep in that process of creativity, while I was struggling with the story. Old and bent, the fragrance of sweet herbs clinging to her dress, wrinkled but with the fire of truth and wisdom burning in her eyes, she moved toward me.

Que haces, hijo? the old woman asked. I am writing a story, I said. Her presence in the room was strong, palpable. She laid her hand on my shoulder and I felt the power of the whirlwind. I closed my eyes and saw into the heart of the lake, the deep pool of my subconscious, the collective memory and history of my people.

One thing should be made clear about my meeting with *Ultima.* Those who don't know me may smile and suggest perhaps I had a little too much to drink, and in a state of weariness I was hallucinating. No doubt about it, I do enjoy good bourbon or scotch. Most writers I know are hooked on something or other, or it may be that writers just acquire a little bit more of public fame and think they have to keep up their notoriety. A bit of the *enfant terrible* syndrome. But I trained myself from the very beginning never to drink when I am writing.

In the process of writing, the serious writer enters planes of vision and reality that cannot be induced with alcohol or drugs. And in that stage of creativity, when the juices flow and the story begins to write itself, the soul of the writer seems to enter the story. The trance can only be explained as a kind of spiritual high. The writer's materials may be from the world of the profane, but in breathing life into those materials the writer enters the world of the sacred. Even the most simple and mundane story might at any moment transport the writer into that flow of creativity which seems to connect him with the world of the story. At that moment everything is in balance, in harmony. The mind and the body keep pace with each other, the words flow, the story grows. I feel that connection right now as I write these ideas down. The flow is natural. Life itself.

I respect my work. I want nothing to get between me and the natural, creative high I discover there. So it was the night Ultima appeared. I told her about the story I was writing, the setting, the characters. I told her I wasn't satisfied with the story, that it lacked soul. I could imitate the writers I had read, but I couldn't write like me, Rudolfo Anaya, a *Nuevo Mexicano, hispano, indio, catolico* son of my mother and father, son of the earth which nurtured me, son of my community, son of my people. Ultima opened my eyes and let me see the roots of my soul.

I worked for seven years on *Bless Me, Ultima.* The process of discovery continued. Those realizations we later see so clearly actually came in small steps, and that's how it was for me. I began to discover the lyric talent I possessed, as the poet I once aspired to be, could be used in writing fiction. The oral tradition which so enriched my imagination as a child could lend its rhythm to my narrative. Plot techniques learned in Saturday afternoon movies and comic books could help as much as the grand design of the classics I had read. Everything was valuable, nothing was lost.

The First Novel Is Born

The sixties were turbulent years. The war in Vietnam created a national debate which tested the nation, tested communities and families. Most of the people I knew in education opposed the war. I circulated petitions to end the war, and I worked hard to organize the first teachers union in the Albuquerque school system, an alternative voice to the lame classroom union that was in place. Around us the winds of the Chicano movement which were later to sweep me up blew across the land. In California César Chávez led the first organized *huelgas,* the farmworkers union was born. In New Mexico Reyes Lopez Tijerina led a group of private citizens to the courthouse in Tierra Amarilla, a small town in northern New Mexico. They went as private citizens to arrest the district attorney. A shooting incident erupted, the now famous Tierra Amarilla courthouse raid became a national incident around which Chicanos rallied, especially those who knew the meaning of having lost the ancestral lands of the old Mexican and Spanish land grants. Corky Gonzalez organized the Crusade for Justice in Denver and La Raza Unida Political Party was born in Texas. Bobby Kennedy broke bread with César Chávez. The political activity of the Chicano Movement was spreading. The assassination of President Kennedy was deeply felt in the Chicano community. Black Friday was viewed as a symbolic striking back of the reactionary forces which guarded the power in the country, a power they did not want to share with the oppressed.

In the midst of these turbulent years, I struggled to learn the intricacies of writing a novel. I wrote incessantly, exhausted though I might be, I pushed myself to develop a strict schedule of writing. I knew the only difference between me and the other young writers of my university years was that they wrote sporadically, when the spirit moved them. I wrote every day. I created my own spirit.

I completed *Bless Me, Ultima* and began to circulate it. I started the only way I knew how, a slave to that American myth which deludes us into thinking that the only place for a young writer to begin is with the big publishers of the east. Little did I know that many of the old giants of the publishing world were dying, that American publishing was changing, that the small presses of the country were on their way to creating a publishing revolution. I went the old route, with dreams of New York, Boston if need be, sure that *Bless Me, Ultima* was a good novel, perhaps a great novel.

I approached dozens of publishers, the result was always the same. I collected enough form letter rejections to wallpaper the proverbial room, but I was undaunted. Sometime in 1971 I was reading a literary magazine published in Berkeley. It was *El Grito,* a Chicano magazine, one of the first and finest of the early Chicano movement. It was founded by professors, students, and writers in the Bay Area, and it called for manuscripts. So I sent the editors a letter. Would they like to see my novel? Months later they responded. They wanted to publish the novel. Months later came the crowning achievement. My novel was to be awarded the prestigious Premio Quinto Sol Award for the best novel written by a Chicano in 1972. I went to Berkeley and met Octavio Romano, Herminio Rios, and Andres Segura, the movers behind the fledgling Quinto Sol Publications. *Bless Me, Ultima* became an instant success.

It was a fabulous time to be alive. I was a novelist, a novelist whose work had been awarded a literary prize, an honor which carries great distinction in the Latino world. Everywhere I went I was lionized. It was a moveable feast! This sense of being destined to complete a purpose in life, the sense of being chosen, need not be as egotistical as it sounds. Every person who develops a healthy sense of self feels important, unique, chosen. Those who begin to do important work in life have the feeling of destiny heightened.

Bless Me, Ultima had touched a chord of recognition in the Mexican-American community. Teachers and professors were reading it, but most rewarding of all, the working people were reading it: "I gave it to my aunt, my uncle, my cousin." "I gave it to my neighbor." "The bus driver was reading it at the stop." "I saw it in a bookstore in Alaska . . ." My novel was moving out into the world. Most of the Chicanos who had lived the small town, rural experience easily identified with it. Everybody had stories of *curanderas* they had known in their communities. The novel was unique for its time, it had gone to the Mexican-American people as the source of literary nourishment. It became a mirror in which to reflect on the stable world of the past, a measure by which to view the future. I traveled all over the country, from California to Washington to Texas and Colorado, into the Midwest in Ohio and Michigan, and everywhere I found large communities of Chicanos. The Chicano Movement and the artistic work we were producing united us all and gave us a sense of worth and destiny.

I had made my connection to the Chicano Movement. The winds of change which before had only been felt as the stirring of the storm were now a gale of commitment to our people. The Mexican-American people, long suffering under their economic, political, and educational oppression were moving to change their destiny. In the universities, Chicano Studies classes and programs were created. Never again would we be denied a study of our history, literature, and culture!

The farmworkers organized across the Southwest. Years of frustration erupted in riots, some of our people died. But their efforts, the efforts of all, were to be rewarded. The movement changed the destiny of the Chicanos, changed in small part the way the society looks at this cultural group. The country was not completely changed, but a significant beginning was made. A feeling of renewed pride flowed in the people. Everywhere I went, the message was the same: It is good to be a Chicano!

The Search for Aztlán

During the sixties I was teaching junior high school, then later, high school in Albuquerque. My wife's parents had moved from Kansas to Taos where they built their retirement home. I had been to Taos, had stayed in the pueblo with Cruz and Tonita. I learned to hunt with Cruz in the Taos mountains. I was also doing a lot of fishing in northern New Mexico. Growing up in rural New Mexico I had hunted rabbits, *coyotes,* small game, but with Cruz the hunt took on a deeper meaning. The deer was a source of nourishment for the pueblo, the deer is also a brother. The hunt is a ceremony involving the energies of life: man and animal. I had been privileged to understand the delicate balance of nature from Cruz, something which bordered on the sacred. More important, the time I spent with him began to reveal to me the vibrations of my Native American soul.

Patricia and I began to take trips into Mexico. At first we went as tourists, down the western coast to Mazatlán and Guaymas and later into Mexico City. As we became drawn to the country, the tourist baggage dropped away. I was on the trail of clues or roots which seemed to speak to my identity. We had no family in Mexico, the Anayas had been in New Mexico for centuries. My father's father had been one of the incorporators of a land grant in Albuquerque: *La Merced de Atrisco.* So our roots were New Mexico, but now I was making my connection to other, more distant roots in Mesoamerica.

The land grant which my father's family had helped incorporate consisted of a huge area of land stretching for miles along the Rio Grande in Albuquerque's south valley, and then for miles west into the desert as far as the Rio Puerco. The land grant had always been a bone of contention between my parents. My father, as heir to the land grant, had received some lots in the forties and sold them very cheap. My mother, having that peasant *Nuevo Mexicano* instinct and love for the land, saw the land grant as a source of our values. Take care of the land and it takes care of us. She believed that someday we would all own a piece of that land grant which had been handed down for generations. The real history of the Spanish and Mexican land grants of New Mexico would prove her wrong. Most of the big land grants were stolen away from the true inheritors.

It was part of those themes which I incorporated into my second novel, *Heart of Aztlán,* a novel about people living in the Barelas barrio in the early fifties. It was an exploration of the relationship the *Nuevo Mexicano* of New Mexico has to the land. How did the relationship change as the old communal villages lost their sons and daughters to the cities? How were we affected by the symbols and knowledge of Mesoamerica which the poets and artists of the Chicano Movement were finding in Indian Mexico? I knew I was discovering an association to Indian Mexico. At the height of the Chicano movement the myths, legends, and symbols from Aztec pre-Columbian Mexico began to be a very important ingredient in Chicano poetry and thought.

The artistic arm of the movement also aligned itself with the farmworker who became the symbolic hero of the young activists and artists. The three-headed figure of the *mestizo* appeared in posters everywhere. The eagle of the farmworkers became the flag of the movement. The Teatro Campesino used people and experiences from the farmworkers' community to reflect the reality of people's lives. Everywhere there was a feeling that the artist had to return his art to the people, to the pueblo.

From the cave man, whose art on the wall of the cave is partly inspired by the need for communal food, to the priests past and present who pray to the gods for the community's spiritual well-being, man has developed his spiritual and artistic self as a reflection of the group's needs. Writers have always reflected on their life in the group. By extolling the virtues of the heroes of the group or by challenging the pettiness of restrictive group rules, they have been the mediators between what is and what can be.

But all social and political and artistic movements have shortcomings. All movements have individuals within their ranks who want to dictate the role of each person in the context of the movement. Within the Chicano Movement there was a small band of Marxist-Leninist critics who insisted that Chicano writers had to follow their ideology. The struggle was of a working people against capitalistic oppression, they said, so the role of the arts was to present that theme and nothing else. That, to me, was a limited perception of what I felt to be the creative spirit. *Bless Me, Ultima* was attacked by the Marxist critics as having no relevant, social value to the working class. Yes, I had many defenders of my work, but I also had to face the few detractors.

In *Heart of Aztlán* my inclination was to follow the symbols I was encountering. The concept of Aztlán began to dominate my thoughts, and the novel reflected this obsession. By now I was reading about the Indian history of Mexico. I had visited the ruins at Tenochtitlán, Cholula, and Monte Albán. I was discovering the grandeur of power which those ancient people had felt in their relationship to each other and to the mystery of the cosmos.

I was in Mexico City in the summer of 1974 when I received a call from the chairman of the English Department at the University of New Mexico. Would I come and teach creative writing for them? I left to take up my new position, but I would return to renew myself in my spiritual homeland.

Tortuga, A Trilogy Completed

The seventies were busy but rewarding years for me. I traveled extensively throughout the country, lecturing, reading from my work. Patricia and I traveled twice to Europe. Our world was growing, and we loved and appreciated it. At the university I worked hard to help develop the creative writing program, and I helped to found a state-wide writers association. Those were good years, the writers in the state and the region came together. We sponsored conferences and readings, we developed a summer writing workshop. The Rio Grande Writers grew. We looked seriously at the problems inherent in distributing small press works, and we began a distribution project.

In 1974 I was invited to serve on the board of the Coordinating Council of Literary Magazines (CCLM), whose office is in New York. It was an excellent opportunity to serve the community of writers I knew and had faith in, the small-press editors and writers of the country. I met a very important group of writers, writers like Ishmael Reed, Ron Sukenick, Toni Cade Bambara, many others. Twice a year the board held regional workshops around the country, so I not only got a good sense of the country, visited places I normally might not have known, but I also got to know many writers and got a good feel for the grassroots writing of the country. From the Carolinas to Atlanta, from Seattle to Los Angeles, from Buffalo to Albuquerque, we took our show on the road and became a very active part of one of the most phenomenal literary movements in the country: the small-press revolution.

In retrospect, it seems I have been at the right place at the right time to see at least a few literary movements born. Certainly, the small-press movement of those years changed the course of publishing in this country. As more and more of the older, established publishers went under or were lost in the mega worlds of the multinational corporations, the small presses established themselves as logical heirs to publish the serious first works of many of the country's young writers.

Before I joined CCLM I had taken part in a conference held in Ellensburg, Washington. Frank Chin, Lawson Inada, Leslie Silko, Mei-Mei Berssenbrugge, Ishmael Reed, Victor Hernandez Cruz, and others were there. We were there to discuss minority writing in America. The ever-growing number of writers in the Native American, Asian American, Black, and Chicano communities was a phenomenon destined to change the face of American literature. We were the vanguard of something new and exciting, as was the women writers movement. Many of us would remain friends for life.

During those years I was working on *Tortuga*, the third novel which I felt would complete my trilogy. *Tortuga* was my hospital story, and thus a very difficult novel for me to write. Yet I believe it to be one of my best works. The novel is loosely based on my experience in a hospital, but it quickly became more than that. The theme of healing still occupied my thoughts. How do people get well? I looked around and saw that we had created a society that was crushing and mutilating us. People were sick, physically and spiritually. How could those people be helped? The hospital I created became an existential hell, symbolizing our own contemporary hell.

In *Tortuga* I took my characters to the depths of despair and human suffering, and they find in their hellish existence the faith they need to survive in the world. Perhaps I was finally bringing together my own foundations of faith, finally regrouping from an existential wasteland and giving form to my own credo.

Heirs to the Dream

My discipline as a writer evolved from early training. I would write every morning, and I still do. I traveled to explore the world and ventured out to do readings, but I would always return to home base. The old *Hispanos* and Indians of New Mexico knew that to be without a land base is to be cut away from the center of the universe. I feel the same about my home. In New Mexico I can connect to the people and the sustaining energy of the earth. We built an *adobe* home on the west *mesa* of the city in 1974. From there I can watch the Sandia and Manzano Mountains across the valley, I can watch the seasons change the character of the Rio Grande Valley below. I can watch as my city grows.

I embarked on a long novel, a novel about the city. In the meantime I had followed other threads. I had been writing short stories throughout, somewhere in between novels I squeezed out short stories. I also did translations of old Southwest Hispanic folktales, and these *cuentos* were published in 1980. Working with the old oral materials which had been collected by folklorists renewed my connection to that exciting and magical stream of the oral tradition. The magical realism, which the Hispanic writers of the region were weaving into the soul of their writings, was the historical inheritance which gave those *cuentos* life.

For those who had lived close to the oral tradition of the people, the literary inheritance was clear. From Spain, from the Mediterranean world of Catholics, Jews, and Arabs, from the borrowing of medieval Europe, from the dozens of waves which swept over the peninsula of Spain to evolve the characters of those groups, into the Mexico of the Americas with Cortéz, to be enhanced with the serious magic of the pre-Columbian Indians, north into the heart of New Mexico, north up along the Rio Grande, a rich world view came to sustain the people. In the *cuentos,* in the oral tradition, the view of the world was kept alive, and it was fed to us with *atole* and *tortillas,* filling us with the wonder of creation. The old people respected the mystery of the universe, the awe it inspired in the individual, and they passed some of that wonder down to us.

But the inheritors of this fantastic world view and heritage were most often at the bottom of the socio-economic system. We resolved, in those years, always to fight to better the life of the Hispanics and Mexicans of the Southwest. That is why we called ourselves Chicanos. To be Chicano was a declaration of independence, to be free to create our destiny, to announce to the world that we would not live intimidated under injustice and prejudice. That movement we created is now a historic ripple in the stream of our time. Perhaps to declare to be Chicano, with that pride which we felt in the sixties and seventies, will pass away and the contemporary generation will move to join the mainstream culture of this country, but certainly the ideals of our movement will never be forgotten.

My interest with Mexican thought continues to grow. I will not rest until the people of Mexican heritage know the great cultures and civilizations they are heirs to from that country to the south. I've written a few stories with Mexico as the setting, and the story of *La Llorona* I also placed in Mexico. To write her story I went back to the Mexico of Cortéz and the conquest of Mexico. The heroine becomes Malinche, a young Indian woman who befriends Cortéz and is later betrayed by him. Using the scant details of legend, I wrote a novel about Quetzalcóatl, one of the most interesting deities of Mesoamerica. A redeemer and savior, Quetzalcóatl is the one who brings wisdom and the arts to pre-Columbian Mesoamerica. He represents the wise men and philosophers of Mexico, perhaps a new age of awareness, perhaps a god who walked among men, as Christ walked in Jerusalem.

And now, how do I summarize this short, autobiographical view into my life? How can one truly explore, in such short space, the details of sights and sounds and moments of poignant love and sadness? I wish I could acknowledge all the people who have helped me in my journey, those who have affected my life. The list would be long. I wish I could allow the reader into other corners of my heart, those darker niches where the view would be more profound and complex. Each of us is neither all good nor all bad, we share the natural human emotions. A writer is no different from the vast swarm of mankind, only in us, something is heightened, that vibration of creativity forces us to look closer into the lives of our brothers and sisters.

I am now spending more time writing plays, learning the techniques of writing drama. I also allow time to edit the work of other writers and to try to encourage and guide those young writers who are developing. I continue to read from my works and to lecture around the country; the public continues to be interested in my work and in Chicano literature. Quite recently my wife and I returned from a trip to West Germany, where we met the publisher who is publishing German editions of my novels.

I traveled for a month in China in 1984 and the University of New Mexico Press is publishing my journal, *A Chicano in China*. During the past few years trips have taken me not only to Canada and Mexico but to China, Brazil, Israel, and to Peru where I visited the incredible Machu Picchu. My interest in exploring the world continues.

My writing is ongoing; it fills my life. I have many projects and planned novels, and teaching continues to be rewarding. I am forty-eight, and now time is the most valuable element; there is so much to do in life. Day-to-day relationships become more important, what one shares and gives is more important than the

Anaya, 1984

taking. One's autobiography does not end, it simply moves into a new, and one hopes exciting, plane of living.

BIBLIOGRAPHY

Fiction:

Bless Me, Ultima. Berkeley: Tonatiuh-Quinto Sol Intl., 1972.

Heart of Aztlán. Berkeley: Editorial Justa, 1976.

Tortuga. Berkeley: Editorial Justa, 1979.

The Silence of the Llano (short stories). Berkeley: Tonatiuh-Quinto Sol Intl., 1982.

Nonfiction:

A Chicano in China (travel journal). Albuquerque: University of New Mexico Press, 1986.

Plays—Selected Productions:

The Season of La Llorona, first produced in Albuquerque, 1979.

Screenplays:

Bilingualism: Promise for Tomorrow. Bilingual Educational Services, 1976.

Translator of:

Cuentos: Tales from the Hispanic Southwest. Santa Fe: Museum of New Mexico Press, 1980.

Editor of:

Cuentos Chicanos: A Short Story Anthology, with Antonio Márquez. Albuquerque: University of New Mexico Press, 1980.

A Ceremony of Brotherhood, 1680-1980, with Simon J. Ortiz. Albuquerque: Academia, 1981.

John Arden

1930-

John Arden, 1978

I am far too young to write an autobiography. Ideally it ought to be written ten years after my death: then I could put all my life into it, plus a fierce rebuttal of the smears and inaccuracies contained in obituary notices and subsequent critical reappraisals ("Arden, an exploded myth"; "Arden, the long decline," and so forth). But early this year my mother died at the age of eighty-nine, and in 1979 my father had died aged eighty-eight; also this year my youngest son (of four sons living) achieved his twenty-first birthday (and has now become the father of a son

of his own): so maybe 1985 does represent some sort of watershed. Also, the week I am writing this, Robert Graves died. I never knew him, though I did once get a very friendly letter from him, answering a query I had made to him about an ancient Irish saga he had treated in an essay: and all his work—particularly *The White Goddess*—has always been of immense importance to me ever since I first read *I, Claudius* when I was a schoolboy. *His* obituary notices were up to standard, right enough. "He considered he was one of the very few who knew what poetry was, and such pretensions did not seem justified by the quality of much of his large output" . . . "Anthropologically and mythographically, it *(The White Goddess)* is, partially, unsound". . . . As he himself wrote:

> To evoke posterity
> Is to weep on your own grave . . .

I am thinking about Graves particularly because for a crucial chunk of his life he was living with, writing with, and inseparably (until the separation, if indeed it ever occurred) connected with, a woman poet, Laura Riding. In 1955 I met Margaretta D'Arcy, an actress from Dublin. She was the first professional theatre-person I ever got to know: and through her I met many people without whom my career as a playwright could never have got off the ground. Two years later we were married. She was closely involved with the most progressive aspects of the theatre of that time, aspects which I knew nothing of, with my limited Shakespearian provincial orientation and my academic (and indeed pompous) attitude towards the stage. She gave me a copy of Brecht—a writer I had only heard of: she introduced me to the works of Beckett, Strindberg, Toller, Behan . . . Her name now appears, sometimes first, sometimes second, together with mine, upon a great deal of published work which nonetheless the male critics, managements, publishers, and broadcasters, will insist upon referring to as "Arden's." Or, worse, as "the Ardens'." It also appears on work of her own, but this did not appear until after the collaborative pieces. It would have been different if I had collaborated with a man called Hiram Hinks, or even with a woman called Evadne Pershore (assuming that she was known already as a professional author, and *not* known to be married to, or living with, me). In that case, the *Arden-*

Hinks opus, or the *Pershore-Arden* volumes, would be perfectly acceptable concepts, just like Beaumont-and-Fletcher or Hart-and-Hammerstein. Graves's difficulty, like mine, has been that his name was to an extent before the public as a writer before he began publicly to collaborate with his female partner: and the female partner was known to have a personal/sexual companionship with him—with me—before the artistic one became apparent. D'Arcy was indeed known in theatre before I was, but as a performer, not a playwright. By swopping one discipline for the other, she did not make things easier as far as *recognition* was concerned: though it should not have mattered a damn. What did matter was the nature of the collaborative work, after 1968 anyway. Before then the problem had been but slight: because our plays were fairly conventional in form and content. After 1968 their political dimensions became less and less acceptable to the British cultural establishment, which has its own very decided notions of what liberties may be taken with the Imperial traditions: and can unfortunately influence other peoples abroad to respect these notions as examples of British liberalism and tolerance. (Also, neither in our case, nor in the Graves-Riding case, was the work light-comedy or musical-showbiz, where joint scripts are so common as to cause no comment.)

If it is too early to write a proper autobiography, it is also too early for me to write accurately about my partnership with D'Arcy, which must be taken "as read" throughout the following pages. It is still very much in progress, and its shape changes from day to day, from sequence to sequence of completed work, and I might as well try to define a rainbow as the clouds move across the sky. But D'Arcy herself has set down some of her thoughts on the subject: her thoughts of what she thinks *my* thoughts might be if I were to write them. I won't either contradict or confirm them. She presents me as it were a character in a play, thus:

ARDEN *(sol):*

I think all men must find it difficult to be objective when writing about their partner, especially if it is a woman. We could say it is modesty, or that the woman is so precious to us that we don't want other predatory males stealing her away, or that she is so wonderful that we don't want to appear vulnerable in the eyes of our partners, we don't want to *wear our heart on our sleeve.* There is nothing that belittles one more than the notion that one is "uxorious." Ken Tynan, in reviewing a *Macbeth* in London where the actor-manager's wife played Lady M., wrote that the casting was "the ultimate in uxorious

Margaretta D'Arcy

David Hone

miscalculation": he didn't object, however, to parading with *his* wife, Elaine Dundy, a known writer in her own right, through the foyer of the Royal Court theatre on first nights, like Justinian and Theodora receiving the homage of the Byzantine eunuchs, while George Devine (who ran the theatre so courageously from one crisis to another) had to return their nonchalant waves and hope that between them they could decide on a review—to be printed under the Tynan name alone—that would not kill both play and theatre in one swoop. The Tynan-Dundy double-act on these occasions was one of the wonders of London theatre in the hothouse 1950s. But somehow the "obscenity" of working with one's own wife undermines the whole concept of personal creativity. Firms of solicitors, "Widgey and Wellock," drapery-shops, "Death and Son," these are OK-symbols—heredity, families, patriarchal amalgamations: but "Widgey and Mrs. Widgey," "Death and Wife" . . . ? No. Is it the fusing of new blood with old, the mixing of cultures, or is there something deeper? Certainly in western culture artists' wives are fair game for all sorts of offensive innuendo—consider the cases of D.H. Lawrence, or Thomas Hardy. As far as D'Arcy and myself are concerned, there seems even to be a public accusation that I have gone over to the "enemy." What enemy? Well, D'Arcy is Irish: and has expressed herself hostile to British political and cultural policies. So have I: I have gone so far as to go and live with her in Ireland itself. But Ireland is not itself "the enemy." There is no state of war between the British monarchy and the Irish republic. Well, not really . . . don't all the British know it is only "the troublesome Irish quarrelling amongst themselves"? When I asked Martin Esslin, then head of drama for BBC radio, if he would commission a radio play from me, he specified to my agent that it must be "genuine Arden." The meaning was unmistakeable, no joint-work with D'Arcy, and nothing about Ireland. Have I broken a very ancient taboo and allowed myself to "be held in thrall" by

the Witch-wife? And thus am in need of rescue, protection? That seems to put me in a very wet, wimpish role. And who are my protectors, then? What are their fantasies? One very blatant critic actually speculated about what we said to each other in bed. Our pillow-talk could not, he deduced, have been very happy, or we would not have written a play which satisfied him so little. The extreme interpretation of this gratuitous comment would be that he, the critic, really wanted to be in bed with me himself. That's it, of course. The post-religious society elevates artists into sacrificial gods, and critics are the new priesthood with their celibate sexuality directed solely towards dreams of the godhead in passionate love. In our regular religions, Christian and Jewish at least, God is not married: and when he *was* married (Zeus and Hera, Woden and Frija), this was only because he had already conquered the Great Goddess who had once been Mother of All Things (including himself), and made her subject to his will. I doubt very much if any of this would now be so clear to me if Margaretta D'Arcy had not been so clearly established by so many commentators as the Serpent in my garden. Laura Riding

The Arden children: Adam, Neuss, Finn, and Jacob—in the 1960s

was, let us not forget, an American, a re-volted ex-colonist of renegade British stock (whether her forebears had emigrated from Britain or not, that is what Americans, subli-minally, *are* . . .): Yoko Ono was a Jap. The British Empire—cultural rather than politi-cal these days, but still an Empire—does not say any "thank-yous" to those who have said to it "no thank you" . . .

I won't write here anymore about my present life, in-deed about my life as an adult. I prefer to continue now with a series of snapshot pictures of those whom I lived with as a child. They are not complete, and do not pretend to be. More like the odd memory which seems to have some relevance to what I am today, and what my work contains. Suggestive rather than pre-cisely narrative. And I will not draw any specific con-clusions. Readers who know my work can, if they will, draw their own.

M y life began among Aunts. My father had ten sisters and no brothers. My mother had four sisters and only three brothers. At the time of my birth my father's mother and father were living, and my mother's mother was living. My mother's sisters were unmarried (though one was a widow), and of my fa-

Father, Charles Alwyn Arden, as a Sergeant Major in World War I

ther's sisters only four of them had husbands. Three of my father's sisters lived with their parents: and all my mother's sisters lived with their mother.

I was an only child. Our small household was therefore little more than an outshut (to use a north-of-England term—it means a small building attached to a greater one, a 'lean-to') for two awe-inspiring, lower-middle-bourgeois, matriarchal establishments. That one of them contained a grandfather did not make any difference. He thought he was a patriarch, but he wasn't: he was a lazy old man who was kept by his active females in a passive state of indulgent luxury until his time came to surrender his kingdom. Signifi-cantly, he died before his wife, as had my maternal grandfather. All three households were, geographi-cally, quite close. All in Yorkshire. My parents lived in Barnsley—a coal-mining, glass-blowing, linen-manu-facturing, dirty town. My mother's mother (Granny Layland) lived at Otley, twenty-seven miles away: and the Arden Grandparents at Beverley, fifty-two miles away. Yorkshire is an important county, it is more im-portant to be Yorkshire than English. Anyone can be English: to be a Yorkshireman is to have been *chosen*. By whom, and for what? The question is unanswer-able. So is the other question: why say Yorkshire*man* when, by all my own experience, the place was ruled by women? These are contradictions which I have never been able to resolve. Subconscious reactionary atavism, but . . .

The Laylands however were not really Yorkshire at all. They came from Lancashire, to the west, less than fifty miles from Otley, but on the far side of the Pennine Hills, which pyschologically were mountains, Alps, Rockies, Andes. The Woodhead Railway Tunnel that pierced them was a structure of gruesome legend, how many lives had it cost to build, how many train-wrecks and murderous falls of rock had taken place in it since its first building? I shuddered to travel through it and had to be calmed with barley-sugar.

So, as the Beverley family were more "authentic," ethnically, than the Laylands, and as I preferred, for other reasons, to go on visits to Beverley rather than Otley, I'll talk about Beverley first.

Christmas dinner at Beverley. I was the only child present (perhaps four years old). All the Aunts round the long table, Grandfather at one end, Grandmother at the other. Only Auntie Mary, who had had, I think, polio, and could not use an ordinary chair, lay on a couch to one side. Not enough chairs for everyone, so two Aunts, Olive and Florance, Twins, sat on high kitchen stools between me and my Grandmother. At my Grandfather's elbow, Great-Uncle Charlie. My Grandfather had a white beard and I confused him

Mother, Annie Elizabeth Arden (extreme left), with fellow students at college, about 1914

with King George V. Great-Uncle Charlie had gold spectacles and was clean-shaven and plump, I confused him with Mr. Pickwick. There was a picture of Mr. Pickwick on the wall, among an array of portraits, from the seventeenth century through to the nineteenth, some of them Ardens, some of them other families married-in to the Ardens, oil paint, water colour, pastel, silhouette, large and small, wigs and cravats, widow's-caps, mobcaps, serious Christian people, very still and ceremonious for the godlike judgement of the provincial face-painter contracted at so many shillings per square inch of human feature.

My Aunts, for digestive reasons, drank warm water with their meal. It was poured out of a special glass jug with a silver cover and spout. There was also wine, which my Grandfather sold for a living. It was not the blood-red wine but the virginal digestive water that caused the strange noises. One by one my Aunts rumbled, as the eating came to its end. I turned my head left and right, following the sound with wide eyes, like a plumber tracking a fault in a pipe. I began to giggle. I *made a comment.* It was a comment upon *personal noises.* It brought about the most dreadful silence. Aunt-eyes, censorious, bore in upon me. My Grandmother's Ro-

Arden's grandparents, his father, and the Aunts

Young John Arden with his father and grandfather, 1931

man profile turned sharper, even more marmoreal. My Mother, half the height of any of them, attempted desperately to catch my attention before it was too late, she was angry at me and angry in defence of me against her husband's people: and she *was* too late.

My Father was looking worried; my Grandfather was sucking in his red wine, oblivious; Great-Uncle Charlie was the first to speak. He was a lawyer in real life when he wasn't being a courtier (with an indefin-

ably disreputable past) in his sister-in-law's house: and, as he crumbled a portion of dry cheese onto biscuit, his voice was his professional voice, reluctantly concurring with the magistrate's view of the worthlessness of his client. "Yes, I do think that John is the—worst-behaved boy I have ever—ah—had occasion to observe." One of the Twins said, "Yes." The other Twin said, "Yes indeed." Auntie Ruth, the Aunt Whom I Loved, said, "Poor John." And she took me swiftly out of the room. Across the hall, in the sitting-room, she sat me down with one of my Christmas presents, a book about ancient Greeks, and launched into a story: King Odysseus and various monsters. Pallas Athene helped Odysseus at all his most dangerous moments: and Auntie Ruth was Pallas Athene—she even looked like the picture in the book.

Beverley was a classic Olde English town, almost a toy-town. It had two shining white limestone Gothic churches, one of them (the Minster) a thirteenth-century pocket-cathedral, more exquisite though less formidable than the much larger real cathedral in nearby York. Dedicated to St. John the Evangelist, the Minster contained the tomb of a local saint of the same name, Anglo-Saxon John of Beverley, who had cured deaf-mute children in the Dark Ages, and to whose grave-slab the schoolchildren even nowadays bring annual offerings of daffodils. My father or Auntie Ruth would bring me into the Minster choir to look at the grotesque oak-carvings under the tip-up seats: a hairy

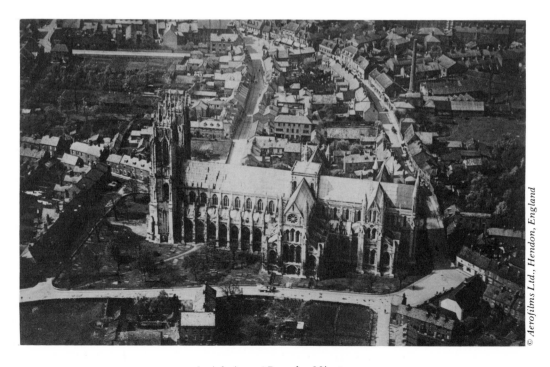

Aerial view of Beverley Minster

34

devil carrying away to hell the wicked man who cut wood on the Sabbath, or two knights fighting in front of a toy castle full of fair ladies (aunts?) in horned headdresses, or another devil playing the bagpipes— except that they weren't bagpipes, but a fat little dog held upside down under the devil's arm, he bit the dog's tail, the dog's four legs stood up in the air like the pipe's drones, and the dog's open mouth howled and squealed. I found it hard to believe that these carvings were five-hundred-years-old. They seemed neither older nor younger than the Wren-style market cross with its curling baroque roof-dome and its ring of doric columns, or the two conical stumps of windmills on the great greensward common that bounded the entire west of the town (my Grandparents' house opened onto it through a private gate).

Nor did the north gate (the Bar) of Beverley—all that remained of the town's fortifications—with its battlements and narrow arch, particularly bring to mind King Henry V, in whose reign it had been built. Double-decker blue buses went through it, and I vaguely thought that the Bar and the buses had been made for each other. In fact the East Yorkshire bus company had designed its double-deckers with special coved roofs to fit the Bar. I found out later that they had done this reluctantly: they had first put all possible pressure on the town council to get the ancient Bar torn down to accommodate their progressive transport-business. I think Great-Uncle Charlie, who had been Mayor, was instrumental in resisting this pressure.

A number of old Ardens had been instrumental in various ways in Beverley throughout the nineteenth century. One of them had prohibited the Beverley Football Game, some time towards the end of the life of Thomas Jefferson, or the start of the life of Abraham Lincoln. The Football Game was in fact an annual legalised riot in which every hooligan in the town took part. There was but one goal, the Bar itself, and the hundreds of players divided themselves into those who would kick the ball from the common through the arch and those who would try to keep it out. Whoever won or lost, windows were broken, shops looted, heads cracked, women assaulted, and public-houses wrecked during the evening and night following the Game. When Dr. Arden (Mayor no less than nine times) decided this picturesque tradition was only fit to be forgotten, he sent the Town Constable onto the common to seize the ball as soon as it was kicked off, throw it to a Deputy on horseback, who was then to ride away with it at full speed and deliver it to Dr. Arden in the Mayor's Parlour of the Town Hall. There being only one ball, it was assumed that this brilliant strategy (worthy of Captain Queeg of the USS *Caine*) would prevent all football violence for evermore. It didn't

The North Bar, Beverley, built during the reign of King Henry V

work: the devoted Constable indeed seized the ball, but was immediately himself seized by the infuriated multitude, and dragged through a quickset hedge until his eyes were almost out and the ball was dropped to the ground. Play recommenced, and the riot was far worse than in any preceding year. Next year, Dr. Arden, still in the Town Hall, called out the military: and that did work.

Also, the same Dr. Arden, nine-times Mayor, refused to give a bull to be baited in the marketplace. All the Mayors of Beverley had always given bulls—or paid for bulls, if they were not themselves farmers. How did a man with such disdain for the people's Olde English pleasures get himself elected so many times?

No need to look far for the answer. All inns in those days had political connections, and Dr. Arden, who combined liquor-sales with medical practice (he wouldn't be allowed to do it in England today), owned the Beverley Arms, a known Tory house. Inside this

The Marketplace, Beverley

inn was an unusual hatchway, between the main entrance and the bar-parlour. It did not open into the back of the bar for quick sales, as might have been thought, but into a small office, only used on election days. The voters, coming in from different parts of the town and suburbs, and pausing for refreshment before going to their democratic duty, would each in turn insert a hand into the hatchway. When they removed the hand again, it would have a golden sovereign miraculously in it. Nobody saw the bribe given, nobody stated for what it had been given, nobody saw who gave it. But everybody knew that the chief Liberal inn could only provide half-a-sovereign.

Later on, in the full respectability of Queen Victoria's reign, Anthony Trollope was the Liberal parliamentary candidate for Beverley. A good political novelist but an ineffectual politician: he lost his contest of course. His defeat was sufficiently blatant as to cause enquiry to be made. The historical accounts of this enquiry do not mention the Arden family. They were hatchetmen rather than bosses, and great survivors, first-class at closing ranks and keeping the name out of things. But the corruption uncovered *was* undeniable, and for several years disgraced Beverley was forbidden to have a Member of Parliament at all.

Much earlier, before any Ardens lived in Beverley, the local Member had been a man called Topcliffe, chief persecutor of Roman Catholics for Queen Elizabeth. He was a Reagan-Thatcher kind of operator: his

torture chamber in Smithfield, London, was a privatised concern, with some sort of government license to be sure; but, as torture was illegal, no one could say

An early nineteenth-century Arden

that he had been officially ordered by the State to perpetrate it. In those days the Ardens lived in Warwickshire, were themselves Catholics, managed to steer clear of Mr. Topcliffe's private enterprise: and one of them, Mary, became the mother of William Shakespeare. There was another Shakespearian connection with Beverley. An ancient knight's helmet hung on a pillar in the Minster. It was said to have belonged to Harry Hotspur.

The old Arden of Trollope's time—I think, my Great-Grandfather—was presented, by a grateful Conservative Party, with a magnificent clock, in token of all his "years of service." (I daresay he had been covering up more names than his own.) This clock was a brass fret-work construction about two-and-a-half feet high, representing the front of a twin-towered Gothic church. I always used to think it was Beverley Minster, though in fact it was of German make. On the hour and the quarter-hours little shining hammers visibly rang bells in a gallery between the towers. It stood on the Grandparents' side-board, and then, after my Grandmother's death, on a table in my Father's house. Every fifteen minutes it sang and chimed away, a most haunting tone, which has remained in my ears ever since.

A brief word about the other old church in Beverley, St. Mary's, completed in the reign of Henry VIII. It had a most glorious roof, flat wooden panels, black with age, and then, in the 1930s, amazingly restored. Some of them all blue with silver and gold stars, moons and suns. Others with a series of allegorical portraits of the Kings of England, starting with the legendary Brutus, great-grandson of Aeneas the Trojan refugee, and running through Lear, Cymbeline, William the Conqueror, Edwards and Henrys, up to Henry VI. One of the more mythical ones, whose name proved indecipherable, was repainted as King George VI, who had just come to the throne. His naturalistic clean-shaven features were pale and unimpressive alongside all his farouchely-bearded forerunners. His presence, though patriotic, did rather spoil the fairy-tale quality of the whole. Constitutional Hanoverian monarchs necessarily look unwilling to cut people's heads off, which is what all the other kings, each with his huge broadsword, seemed to think was their main raison d'être. I was anyway disappointed in George VI: just after the Coronation of 1937, he came on a formal "progress" around his kingdom. I was at school, in Barnsley, and all the children were marched out of town to a place on the main road where we would see the king in his car arrive. It was a very hot day, we had to walk about three miles, we were all tired and ill-behaved, and the teachers were totally losing patience. And we waited

and we waited and we waited. *The king was an hour or two late.* At last, when he came, all we saw was about four black limousines, driving very fast behind motorcycle police outriders. In which car was the king? In every car there were men in top hats and ladies in flowered hats. No doubt the queen was there too, but she was as invisible as he was. We had gone all that way, sick with loyal excitement, and all for nothing but a sort of speeded-up funeral. So much for constitutional monarchs. One of the Beverley church-roof kings would have come in on a horse with trumpets on either side of him, and we would have known for sure it was him because his varlets would have struck at us with clubs to make no doubt that we knew. It would not have been pleasant: but at least it would have *happened*.

Also in St. Mary's was a row of pillars in the nave, each of which had been erected by donors who had their names written up to prove it. "Thys Pyllar made the Minestrals": the Minstrels' Guild of Beverley, famous throughout Europe; they left behind a carving, painted and gilded, of themselves playing late-mediaeval instruments and wearing thick gold chains. "Thys Pyllar made Gode Wyves": the rich ladies of the parish. A man's head, in a Tudor beret, presumably referred to " + lay and his wyffe" who "made"—over the next capital—"these two Pyllars"—and then, over the half-capital abutting on the end wall of the nave—"and a haffe." Mr. Crossley, solid citizen of the 1530s, was evidently addicted to silly word-play. East Yorkshire jokes have always been fairly rudimentary, like the tale of "th'owd man as sat near t'door: he nivver spoak in aall his life but th'yah time *(one time)*." You are supposed to ask what it was he said, expecting some great word of wisdom. "Why, he nobbut towd 'em to shet t'door . . .": pay-off. A solemn pursed mouth and an appreciative grunt will amply repay the comedian. West Yorkshire people (Otley and Barnsley were *West* Yorkshire, there's a deal of difference) speak far more rapidly and raucously, and do expect a noisy response to their one-liners.

When I stayed with Grandmother Arden, St. Mary's was the church I was taken to, surrounded by Aunts, for Sunday service. My crippled Auntie Mary, a very sweet-natured person, became confounded in my mind with the dedication of this church. I used to call it *Auntie* Mary's Church, and was rebuked for my profanity.

I must mention the Great-Aunts. They were Sarah and Gertie, my Grandmother's sisters, unmarried: they lived next door to her and shared a front garden, so that to go from one house to the other you did not need to go all the way down the path, out at the gate, and in at the next gate. American readers will not find

Aerial view of St. Mary's Church, Beverley

this strange: in England dividing fences between bourgeois front-gardens are an absolute essential. In England, people *mind their own business:* the Anglo-Saxons came in their pirate ships, fought battles, took root: and immediately built fences round their individual homesteads so that *their own business* could be very severely minded. The Great-Aunts seemed older than the Grandmother. Their name was Stephenson: Stephensons were tall and blonde, Ardens were shorter and darker and had big noses. Their house was a treasure chest of eighteenth- and nineteenth-century curios; miniature Chinese gardens, built to the last pagoda and mirror-glass boating lake in porcelain fruit-bowls; cigarette boxes made of whitey-brown porcupine quills; carved ivory games of spillikins or chess; and an array of Samurai swords, razor-sharp—"For heaven's sake, Ruth, keep that child's fingers to himself!"—East Indian blowpipes with real poison on the tips of the darts; and a regular tiger-skin stretched along the wall, with the tiger's head, teeth, and claws, all in place. A male Stephenson had been an engineer of imperialist renown, building railways, bridges and harbour-works all over the Orient.

There was also a mysterious cupboard full of toys dating from the Great-Aunts' own childhood—I guess sometime in the 1860s. German toys, mostly: strange puzzles, stereoscopes, little dancing men, and picture-books. I was, under supervision, allowed to play with them. You have to play with toys, even though you risk

breaking them. They cannot live, as museum objects. I remember the savage book of *Struwwelpeter,* still in print; though frowned upon by modern child-psychologists, for the cruelty of the fates that befall the naughty children in it. Little Johnny Head-in-Air (me, according to Aunts), who fell in the river and nearly drowned: Fidgety Phil who wouldn't Sit Still (me again), *he* pulled the entire contents of the dinner-table, boiling soup and everything, all over himself by dragging at the cloth: the Suck-a-Thumb boy whose thumbs were gorily cut off by the Great Long-Legged Scissorman (this one did not scare me, thumb-sucking was not my vice): and the very wicked boys who laughed at the black man in the street and were therefore plunged into an inkwell by Tall Agrippa, a sort of schoolmaster, until they themselves were as black as the object of their racialism.

Great-Aunt Sarah became very tremulous. I amused her, and scandalised some younger Aunts, by asking once, as she poured out tea, did she make the stream of tea shake on purpose so that we could all see how clever she was at never spilling it?

Great-Aunt Gertie was given a radio, by her nieces. This was in the early days of broadcasting, but after the crystal-set had become obsolete. The new bakelite box, with all its workings flush inside the smooth moulded envelope, and only the control-knobs, dial, and decorative trellis over the speaker, to break the functional outline, was regarded as a most progressive novelty. Some weeks after the gift, the Aunts asked her was it giving satisfaction? "Oh yes," she said, "but there is far too much interference. It is very difficult to hear the programmes sometimes because of all the crackling and other noises. For instance," she said, carefully pointing to the bottom left-hand corner of the box, "there is a wretched little man just *here,* who will keep jabbering away in German whenever I am trying to listen to a symphony concert." Could she have meant Hitler? He was very much in evidence in those days, interfering with everyone's programmes: a pleasing fancy, that he might have been confined in the bottom of a radio like a genie in an Arabian bottle. But even so, some fool would have let him out.

I mentioned York Minster, a larger and coarser version of Beverley's elegant church. York is not a lucky Minster. In 1984, for instance, it was severely burned by lightning. The superstitious (and it's amazing how many of them there are in an allegedly secularised country) attributed this to God's wrath against the consecration there of the new Bishop of Durham, a man of good sense who has been accused of heresy by the "Moral Majority"—or so they call themselves, stealing an up-to-date mendacious Americanism to dignify their age-old English nonsense. The real problem with the Bishop of Durham has been that he—to an extent—supported the coal-miners against Mrs. Thatcher when she compelled them into a year-long strike, but that is by the way . . . The recent York fire, however, was as nothing compared to the one that gutted the building about 160 years ago. It was lit, not by God, but by an arsonist surnamed Martin. He believed indeed that he did the work of God. He had written pamphlets denouncing the "great height" of the bishops and their pagan pride, and stating that their palaces and churches must be destroyed, in fulfilment of listed prophecies. When the pamphlets were ignored he broke into the Minster by night, piled the stools, benches, and hymnbooks in the middle of the floor, and applied a lucifer-match. His bonfire shot up flames so high as to enkindle the timber vault. When he was caught, he made no attempt to protest his innocence: and was consigned to the madhouse, from which he continued an uninterrupted flow of pamphlets. He had a brother, almost as mad, but not certifiably so. This was John Martin, an artist, and, for a time, a highly fashionable one. He specialised in enormous canvases of flood, death, battle, destruction, doom, Belshazzar in Babylon, Noah and the Deluge, Moses engulfing the hosts of Pharaoh. His best-known work: a series of highly-excitable engraved illustrations to *Paradise Lost.* Gustave Doré out-dramatised him in the same line of country, and largely replaced him in public esteem.

The Martins (there was a third brother, a sailor, also a visionary of sorts, who had *experiences* in ocean storms) were ancestral connections of my Uncle Guy, who married Dorothy, one of the Beverley Aunts. There was a book of John Martin prints, either in his house or my Grandmother's, which for a time strongly affected my view of world history, which I saw as having been broken at irregular intervals by huge and hysterical catastrophes, involving hundreds and thousands of terrified people, earthquakes, electric tempests, and the annihilating rage of a deity out for blood.

When my Mother married my Father she was much smaller than the Arden Aunts, of a different religion (brought up a Methodist, though now confirmed into the Church of England), from a different part of Yorkshire (indeed not really from Yorkshire at all), and from what the Arden Aunts regarded as a slightly lower social class within the bourgeoisie. That is to say, her father had sold insurance and not wine. An important distinction in the north of England. She was a schoolteacher in Barnsley. When she first became employed there, at a primary school where the children were the sons and daughters of "rough" coal-miners or of embittered and impoverished unemployed, she wore her hair down her back in a tail. Her slight figure, conducting games in the playground, gave rise to protest from the parents: "That's no right teacher you've got in charge of our Ethel; she's nowt but a schooil-lass hersen: even though we are on t'welfare, we've got an entitlement to a grown-up teacher! I shall complain at t'Town Hall!" She had, not surprisingly, something of an inferiority complex, particularly among what she called the "bossy" Arden women: she made up for it by a determination to disapprove of rather too many people and institutions; and, after her marriage, and more so during her widowhood, to retain a set of social and domestic standards of cleanliness, taste, and propriety which I always found overstated and needless, though impossible to refute. Any argument, she'd simply set her stubborn mouth: "No, I've had my say. I say no more. . . ."

When she was very young, her father, who was a Liberal activist, busied himself in support of the coal-miners from South Wales who were on strike. Two of them came up to Otley to appeal for funds at a public meeting, and he entertained them in his house. My Mother was astonished to hear them talking Welsh to one another: she could not believe this language. She asked one of them to put out his tongue. Surprised and amused, he did so. She touched it with her finger. She could not, she said, get over the fact that it was as wet and red as her own . . . On another occasion, her father brought home a young woman whom he had met at the railway station. She had a little girl with her, about the same age as my Mother, and was exhausted and depressed. She had travelled from the far end of England, following her husband, who had gone to Otley to find work. When she arrived, she discovered that he had failed in his desperate search and had moved on to another town; and if she were to go after him, she would have no money left for a bed that night. My Grandfather Layland invited her home with him. He must have had a winning manner; invitations of that sort, late at night, on railway stations, from strange men, were justly suspect, then as now. But she came: and was given tea by my Grandmother, who served boiled eggs. "The strange lady" accepted one egg only (the Layland children were all, as usual, helping themselves to two each), and carefully divided it, half for her little girl, half for herself. "Oh do give the child a whole egg, my dear!" said my Grandmother. And she did. And then, after persuasion, two. But my Mother said she thought about it for years afterwards, only slowly realising that there were people so poor that they automatically shared eggs, even when eating at someone else's table . . .

She was about twelve when she came under the influence of a new young teacher at the Otley school. This teacher, very vigorous and beautiful, talked to her class about rather more than the prescribed syllabus. My Mother came home and announced in the middle of tea that "Women ought to have the Vote." Her father was appalled. He beat his fist on the table and asserted that he "would have no militant suffragette in *this* house!" Given his undoubted Liberalism in politics generally, indeed his *radicalism,* toward certain causes (for example, opposition to the colonialist Boer War), this may appear to have been an inconsistent aberration: but not so. His political hero was David Lloyd George: Lloyd George was against women's suffrage, partly perhaps because in his own sexual life he was a promiscuous pasha, and partly because his strength in parliament depended on an uncertain coalition of interest-groups. The Women's Lobby was not yet strong enough to take first place: so his meetings became the continual scenes of feminist interruption, disruption, and what the press called "petticoat hooliganism." My unwitting Mother was threatening to bring all this into her family home: hence her father's indignation, and the sudden rebuff. After it she tended to keep her political feelings more closely within her own breast. Nonetheless, she was clearly on the Liberal side of the nation—not as far to the left as the newly-formed Labour Party—but far enough to incur the unspoken disdain of all those Tory Ardens. On one occasion, at Beverley, there was a cousin of my Father's present, who had been living in Egypt. She spoke with enthusi-

asm of a day of riot in Cairo, when the British colonial authorities had successfully sent British troops into the "native quarter" to overawe the nominally independent Egyptians. My Mother incautiously asked, "But why *should* our troops go in? Isn't it the Egyptians' own country?" This remark was not well received.

Her feminism suffered a diminution in later years, though it was never actually denied by her—she and my Father used to argue good-humouredly about it: did female suffrage in fact come because of the women's militance, or was it a natural constitutional development which (as my father maintained) was only delayed by the militance? She disliked Mrs. Thatcher as Prime Minister—not because Mrs. Thatcher was a roaring Tory, but because a "bossy" woman is always a menace, whatever her ideology. She warned me, when I got married, never to lose control of the household. And her vocabulary has caused my cultural subconscious an amount of difficulty now that revived feminism is seeking to change the male-dominated word. One example will suffice: she came back home from the shops one evening during the war, very angry because she had been accused unjustly of queue-jumping by a female of obnoxious manners and low social status. My Mother said of her: "She was standing there swearing at me, a very large and virulent lady—no, not a lady, she was a *woman*—I won't even call her a woman, she was definitely a *person,* and a *most* unpleasant one!" This was not up-to-date speech, even by the standards of West Yorkshire gentility forty-five years ago. I think it really belonged way back in Jane Austen's time: my Mother's mother had been brought up by *her* grandmother, and the entire cultural development of the family was accordingly retarded by the space of a complete generation, in a very interesting, but sometimes embarrassing way.

The Layland household in Otley carried a totally different atmosphere from that of the Beverley Ardens. I don't remember Grandmother Layland very well, she died when I was quite small. I do recollect a kind and gentle old lady, short, just like my Mother, and easily tired. She stayed with us once in Barnsley and took me out shopping. Unwise of her. On the way home I got tired of keeping pace with her small legs, and ran on ahead to play *ambushes,* pretending to be a "savage," hiding behind gateposts and corners, and leaping out on her just as she came up with me. She endured this with great patience. I became overambitious, and ran too far ahead. I waited and waited in my chosen hideout, behind a corner. But she never came. I could not look round the end of the wall to see how close she was—I feared she would be so close that my ambush would be spoiled of its drama. I concluded, at

John, about 1933

last, that she had taken an available side-turning and had gone home by the back streets. She would thus be already at my Mother's doorstep, triumphantly waiting to ambush *me*. So I ran for home as fast as I could go. I rang the bell, my mother opened the door, and looked at me in horror. "But, John, where is Grandma?" "Hasn't she come? She left me in Victoria Crescent to come the other way and get here first." "John, you are not telling the truth: she cannot have left you!" My Mother must have thought that Grandma had been taken ill in the street, she appeared so alarmed. And then, suddenly—"Oh, there she is!" A small trudging figure in black, with a large black straw hat, bent by the weight of her shopping bags, wearily turning into our road a hundred yards away beside the mailbox corner. "Naughty naughty boy, and a *lying* boy as well, you ran away from poor Grandma and left her to walk home all by herself, how *could* you be so unkind?" And when Grandma reached us, she was not at all in the spirit of the game: all she could say was how scared she had been when she lost sight of me altogether. She had imagined I don't know what— everything from motor-accidents to kidnappers, I suppose . . .

I had the impression that the Otley ladies were always slightly scared of something. A feeling there of a hostile world full of danger and offence, which was precariously kept out of their house: but which at any time

might come insidiously (or violently) in. Methodist preoccupation with Sin had much to do with this. So did the sudden death of Grandfather Layland from heart failure in 1914 when he was still under fifty. His children were all young and not settled in the world. Such unexpected bereavements must always leave the survivors with a sense of general insecurity. I do know that at Beverley I was often made conscious of my capacity for naughtiness: whereas at Otley I tended to feel guilt even when I had not discernably been naughty. This must have been due to recollections of my Uncle George, whom I never knew, but who was regularly being held up to me as having been a very naughty, nay wicked boy, who brought such great disgrace and distress to his parents and all Laylands generally. As a child I was not given details: except the Quarry Story. The Otley house was on a steep hillside, overlooking the narrow gray stone town that clustered with its woollen-mills along the green valley of the River Wharfe. Behind the house reared the Chevin, a long brooding ridge, now wooded, but at one time, I guess, as bare and bleak as Wuthering Heights. There were stone-quarries near the top. My Uncle George, as a school-boy, had once climbed, with some wicked friends, up to the quarry (a forbidden place), and, moreover, on the Sabbath day. They got to playing with a crane, which the off-duty quarrymen had left unattended and unsecured. Somehow the boys managed to wind up the cable, and then, unable to control it, let it run with a load of rock straight onto George, shattering his leg.

His later adventures illustrated even more plausi-

Arden's parents (right) with two of his Layland aunts in the 1920s

41

bly the way the Lord pursues Sin (and Sin, alas, pursues the Lord). With a good deal of parental influence, he found employment in a local bank. To be a bank clerk was then the ultimate in middle-class provincial respectability, and you needed as good a public character as a Hollywood movie-star in the days of *morals-clauses*. But before long the restless spirit of George was bringing him out at night on the town. It is hard to imagine what exactly was to be found of soul-destroying intensity at night on such a town, but whatever there was, he found. Liquor, for a start. His father was now dead, or you can be sure his stumbling ascent of the bedroom stairs long after everyone else was asleep would not have been put down so easily to "extra work overtime" and fatigue. His elder brother, a lawyer, knew quite well what was going on, but he did not live in Otley, and he was unable to be at hand when the crisis came. The crisis was the altering, forging, fudging in some way, of a cheque, or bank statement, or some other paper of trust, to enable George to pay off a gambling debt. Or so at least I understand the story, which I have never heard fully told. My Mother had always been a great raconteur, as indeed was my Father, but the George business was genuinely painful, and was evaded as far as possible in subsequent reminiscence. Anyway, there was no prosecution: but George had to go to Australia, where he died about the end of World War II, having apparently got married out there. I never met his wife and I do not know whether they had any children. The whole tale has a strangely anachronistic flavour, as though it had been composed by a popular Victorian novelist, left among his papers, and printed for the first time today by a contemporary publisher who had been led to believe it was an unpublished Scott Fitzgerald . . .

The Layland Aunts were mostly teachers and tended to treat me like a tiresome pupil. The eldest one, Nessie, was not a teacher, and was a complex person. She had been a real beauty when young. Her photographs recall Burne-Jones's paintings of maidens in Arthurian forests, tied up for dragons to ravage, and awaiting rescue by melancholy but courageous knights. During World War I she married a young soldier who was killed in France immediately after the honeymoon. She was very brave and refused to give way to grief. Instead, she opened a hat-shop, to be quite independent of her (fatherless) family, and also to provide for her mother-in-law who was, it seems, penniless. By the 1930s she had soundly established herself: but in so doing had tightened and repressed any outgoing elements of her character—at least, as far as her response to me was concerned. She was invariably kind, but kind in such a way that all the time one was aware she was only doing her duty by me, a melancholy duty,

and that lively small boys ought not ideally to have formed part of it. Of course I did not realise she had already had one small boy to deal with, and that she loved him so much that any others were redundant.

This was the youngest Layland, my Uncle Harold. Only a schoolboy when his father died, he had been brought up by his sisters more than his mother. He gained an Oxford scholarship from the Otley grammar school, and at at Oxford had been a great academic success. He had also run up a large amount of debt, and Nessie had bailed him out, at considerable personal sacrifice. He then married a young woman from the North of Ireland and went to live in Belfast to teach modern languages at a most illustrious Protestant boys' school there. I saw him but rarely: but my mother was very fond of him, as indeed were all the Laylands, and he was constantly in correspondence. When I was eight he sent me a present, which greatly excited my mind: a book of Irish legends, Cuchulain and the Red Branch Heroes. I knew already the Greek and British (Arthurian) mythologies. But these Gaelic tales were something new. They struck at my heart, with their unpronounceable names; their combination of battlefield butchery with hallucinatory landscapes, druid-haunted bogs, bare mountains, bottomless pale lakes; their alarming women, Morrigan the death-goddess, Scatha the war-goddess, Deirdre the self-willed man-stealer, Maeve of Connacht filled with unslakeable rage for the loss of her prize bull. And also the sense of death: Cuchulain reluctantly killing Ferdia his friend in the middle of the river with the one battle-trick Ferdia had never mastered, Cuchulain himself strapped to a pillar-stone so that he would die standing while none of his enemies dared come any closer to his deeply wounded but still dangerous body. I had of course no notion of the recent Irish rebellion and the relevance of these tales to it: but there was an odd political irony associated with my Uncle's gift. The parcel arrived very late: weeks after his letter saying he had posted it. The reason was an IRA bomb in the Belfast Post Office which had thoroughly disordered the due process of the mails . . .

Uncle Harold was a man of mischief. I remember him, in the 1940s, mildly distressing the strait-laced Nessie by a defence of Charlie Chaplin's sex-life, at that time the subject of salaciousness in the tabloids. Harold maintained that the "greatest comic genius since Molière" had been abominably abused by mean-spirited prudes, not because he was really to blame, but as a cover for reactionary American capitalists who were in fear of his radical humanism. To the morality of Methodist Otley these opinions were almost as nerve-racking as they would have been in the U.S. Bible Belt.

He got into trouble in Belfast during the war. As a

teacher of German he became well known among a circle of Bohemian friends for his imitations of Hitler. He also spoke Irish: a language not favoured in the British-ruled North of Ireland, where it immediately suggested Catholic "Fenian" Nationalism and pro-Nazi gunmen. He could do Hitler in Irish as well as German, he could do Churchill in both languages. His friends, insofar as they were Ulster Protestants, were drawn from that fast-waning area of true Protestant radicalism which had set afoot the Insurrection of 1798 with all its French-Revolution republican principles. Insofar as they were of Catholic origin, they were determinedly anti-Fascist and would have supported that section of the IRA which sent volunteers to fight against Franco in the Spanish war. Anyway, the police were told that meetings of "German spies" were taking place in Harold's flat. He and his late-night guests were thereafter followed about by detectives, whom they encouraged by pretending to pass secret messages in public places, scratching their eyebrows at one another, cocking their hat-brims, and generally behaving like B-movie foreign agents. It is a wonder he was not interned . . .

He had a cottage in the Mourne Mountains, just a few miles north of the Irish Border, where the people, mostly Catholic, still spoke Irish as their everyday tongue. Cuchulain's fort had been at Dundalk, in the immediate vicinity, and the area was steeped in ancient history and legend. One day, about seven years after the war, he was staying in this cottage with his wife, daughter, a sister, and a colleague from Belfast. On an impulse he asked his fellow schoolmaster to go up the mountain with him for a walk before bed. It was a moonlit night, but there was cloud-mist higher up, and the slopes of rock were slippery. Harold lost his footing and, before his friend could catch him, fell to his death hundreds of feet below. I was spending my own summer holidays with my parents on the Isle of Arran, between Scotland and northern Ireland, when the news came. Arran has its own place in the old Gaelic poetry. It seemed appropriate I should have been there to hear of Harold's end: the landscape, common to both isle and mainland, has been well-recorded by a twelfth-century Irish writer:

> Arran of the many stags, the sea reaches to its shoulder; island where companies were fed, ridges where blue spears are reddened. Wanton deer upon its peaks, mellow blaeberries on its heaths, cold water in its streams, nuts upon its brown oaks . . .

Had it not been for Harold, I might never have become acquainted—at least not for many years—with that particular aspect of European literature. It is now

inseparable from my imagination.

Otley as a town had no great resonance for me, as opposed to the very powerful historical undercurrents of Beverley. Probably because the Laylands had anyway only lived there for a half-generation. The Laylands did not on the whole have much to say about their own family story: but my Mother always, and rather irritably, assured me that it was quite as ancient and distinguished as the Arden pedigree. She said that there had been a Layland family tree, but one of her Aunts had taken it away with her when she got married, and now no one could remember exactly who was in it. John Leland, topographer and antiquary to King Henry VIII was allegedly included . . . In any event, my Mother was never to be persuaded that the Ardens were in any way a better class of family than the Laylands. Of course, they thought they were, they did have a family tree, and it ran far back to the days of the Norman Conquest, to before the Norman Conquest, to before even the Anglo-Saxon invasions. They could not claim it ought to be actually *believed:* it had presumably been cooked up for some member of the Arden family in the eighteenth century by an officer of the notoriously venal College of Heralds (which is what happened with most Olde English genealogies). But the very fact that an Arden had had sufficient pull to get a Herald to do the cooking for him was in itself suggestive of the worth of the family. Provincial north-country wine-merchants, true: but sometimes one would have thought they entertained a secret claim to be Kings of England.

My mother's personal pride often led her to "stand no nonsense." One day, in Barnsley, in appalling winter weather, when the thawing snow had been scooped by the municipal work force into mounds of black slush completely covering the sidewalks, she found she could not walk into town without getting her short legs soaked to above the knee, and her boots full of snow. The other pedestrians were apparently prepared meekly to submit to this discomfort. But not Mrs. Arden. She stepped off the curb into the middle of the road, and marched on into town as though she were heading a parade. Very soon she did head one: a line of motor-traffic, angrily piling up behind her, unable to overtake her either to left or right because of the snow-mounds, and all hooting, honking, and calling out abusive epithets. She led them at her own pace for maybe a mile: her own pace in the slippery conditions being about 2½ mph. After a while, other people followed her example, until the ascendancy of the motor-car (on what was indeed the main throughfare into Barnsley from the north, a very busy highway) was completely demolished. If the police saw her, they wisely decided to take no action. They knew it was neither the time nor place to be partisan in defence of internal combustion.

During World War II she worked as a volunteer in the Citizens' Advice Bureau: largely concerned with bewildered people who could not understand the ludicrous embellishments of wartime bureaucracy and its tyrannical regulations. As Barnsley was not bombed by the Germans, her work was perhaps lighter than had she been doing it in Liverpool or London, but it was taxing enough. For instance, evacuees had been brought into the town from the blitzed areas. A nervous maiden-lady, elderly, living alone in a small house, would heroically offer to accommodate two persons. The evacuee-billeting officer leaves six adults and four children on her doorstep. When she states neither she nor the house can cope with such a number, she is shown a docket or chit authorising her home to accept twelve: and told that two more children, without parents, will be arriving the next day. Clearly a clerical error, 12 for 2: but it has passed all sorts of official desks where it has been stamped and countersigned. How to set it right? Undoing such a muddle might well take all day. Meanwhile the ten evacuees will also have turned up at the Advice Bureau, complaining that they have been put to live with a woman who refuses them entry, and the billeting-officer, run off her feet, has abruptly told them it is now *their* problem, and has left them in the street to sort it out for themselves. Finding a roof for them before nightfall has automatically doubled the load . . . Barnsley was run by a self-perpetuating mafia of Labour Party Demagogues. Their ideology was humane and excellent (and was to prove itself the genuine choice of the people in the General Election of 1945): but we lived in a pocket of highly complacent local politics, where socialist-jobs-for-the-socialist-boys had been the watchword ever since the failure of the great Coal (and General) Strike of 1926: defensive barriers had been set up against whatever Tory government ruled in Westminster, and a mule-headed obstinacy took the place of intelligent and imaginative administration. The Citizens' Advice Bureau, as a national non-party voluntary organisation, was highly suspect to the local ward-heelers in the Town Hall. The Bureau's chairperson was the Church of England Rector, instead of being a trade-union hack: and many of the Bureau workers were thought to vote Tory or Liberal. So, in a dispute like the one I have outlined above, you could be sure that Town Hall would be highly obstructive. My mother always brought these problems home with her and worried about them all week. At the end of the war she received a letter, from the infuriating Town Hall itself, telling her that in view of her sterling war-service, she had

been recommended for a national medal. She was enraged: not that she did not think she *deserved* a medal: but it was altogether too much that the King should be giving it her merely on the say-so of the incompetent half-wits who had done their level best to prevent her sterling service having any sort of practical effect. She replied with what she called "a strong letter, a snorter," refusing the medal, and explaining why . . .

In their old age my parents moved into the North Yorkshire countryside. They had never owned a car, and were dependent upon the local bus-service (expensive and irregular) or a taxi (expensive) if they wanted to go anywhere outside their village. My Mother was an active member of a church ladies' group. After some years—she would have been in her late seventies—she saw this group being taken over, slowly, by a number of younger members, wives of newcomers to the parish; or, more precisely, of newer-and-wealthier-comers than my Father. There was an amount of ill-feeling, genteelly expressed, but no open hostility. Just a self-augmenting undercurrent of Byzantine shiftings of alliance, and a sense of lurking confrontation. Then suddenly, the occult struggle became overt. A deputation of the younger ladies waited on my Mother. Over her coffee and cakes they temporised like old-fashioned Arab sheiks about to negotiate oasis water-rights. Their eventual request: would my Mother please make one of her famous trifles for a joint-meeting, the following week, with an affiliated ladies' group in the parish of M—, twenty miles away. Is *trifle* a dish known in America? In the north of England it is the sine qua non of any formal tea. It is made in a large bowl, layers of cake, biscuit, fruit, jam, jelly, custard, cream, pieces of chocolate and so on, and necessarily takes a long time to prepare: each layer must set solid before the next one is added. My Mother spent the next few days planning her masterpiece, special journeys into the market-town to buy the ingredients (returning home by costly taxi because the parcels were more than she could manage on the bus), intermittent worries about what she should wear for the trip to the joint-meeting, and her assured triumph there. It seemed to her the hidden intriguers were at last coming to terms with her status in the group.

On the morning of the great day the great trifle was complete: a vast yellow mixing-bowl, filled to the brim with rich sweetness, almost more than she could lift, covered in plastic film to prevent it slopping over. She would carry it in Mrs. B—'s car, balanced upon her knee: she would guard it with her very life. Mrs. B—at the door, fur from head to foot, her polished car humming at the garden-gate. In the car, a clump, copse, thicket, of ladies' best church hats. "Oh, Mrs.

Arden's mother, about age seventy

Arden, what a beautiful trifle! Exactly what we'd expected!" And then: shockingly: "How are you going to get to M—?" My Mother was speechless, for was she not going in Mrs. B—'s car? She was not. "I do have a carful, you see: just room for the trifle on the back seat with Mrs. C—, but we're so sorry, not for you. We really thought you had your own transport . . ." My Mother could have rung for a cab: expensive, yes, but not impossible. But she disdained the expedient. She stood on her doorstep and watched her trifle carried off in the car, like a little fat princess taken to the ball amidst sycophantic ladies-in-waiting. As far as she was concerned, declaration of hostilities had been unilateral, on *their* part, not *hers*. They must remain unilateral. She gave up all connection with the ladies' group: and evaded all efforts by the clergyman or by other well-wishers to involve her ever again . . .

My Father began his life defeated by women. One son amongst all those daughters, and his parents always favoured the daughters. They went to college: they received paternal influence if their careers needed it (except for those who did not have careers—the Twins, for instance, must stay at home to do the house-

keeping): but my father at Beverley Grammar School was only allowed to stay there till he was sixteen, and then he was told to earn his own living. He was not even groomed for the wine-merchant business. The old Grandfather may or may not have disliked or despised him, I don't know: probably he enjoyed so much deference from his more dependent daughters that he preferred to make the independent ones so finally independent that they would not interfere with his complacence, while a son in the Arden counting-house would only expose his own commercial incompetence. So my Father went to work as a junior clerk in local government: and then went to war, returning home in 1919 as a Sergeant Major, happily unwounded, but with his health severely impaired. His clerkship in the County Hall had not been kept for him—the postwar government did not place veteran's rights high on its political agenda—and he had to look outside Beverley for a new career. He did ask his father, could he not come into the wine-business? This was run from an atmospheric mediaeval vault, an ancient monument indeed: but the traditional clientele (East Yorkshire country gentry) had fallen on evil days, and sales were badly dropping off. How to restore the business? My Father made an unwise, though commercially sound, suggestion: diversify, turn the vaults into a regular wine-bar, and establish a restaurant upstairs. But this, to my Grandfather, was *quite out of the question:* it was incredibly vulgar American-style "hustling," and under no circumstances, this time-honoured family enterprise, under *no* circumstances would he allow, etc., etc. . . . In fact he understood he could not organise such a development himself, and he greatly resented any possibility that his son might be seen to outpace him in Beverley society . . .

So my Father found a place as a trainee-manager in a glass-manufactory in Barnsley. Eventually he became works-manager, and had a perfectly dreadful time. His owners were a family of exceptionally neurotic capitalists, and inept into the bargain. Their approach to labour relations verged on the permanently hysterical. The worst of them all was an elderly lady known as "Auntie," who had a controlling interest in the firm without any technical knowledge to support her vehement prejudices. Whenever there was a dispute between the trade union and the bosses, my Father (who, as manager, was supposed to support management) found himself siding with the employees and their grievances. This in spite of his strongly felt ancestral Toryism. Of course, the authentic old-English Tory was always in danger of gravitating towards radical anarchism in defence of human liberty; principles and grass-roots practice became inextricably mixed-up.

There was a traumatic day, just after the end of World War II, when a woman, absolutely distraught, telephoned our house an hour or two before breakfast. She was the wife of one of the glassblowers, and the police had just completed a dawn raid on her home, hauling her husband off to jail, and ransacking the whole place. It emerged that a malicious person, never discovered, had sent an anonymous letter to the cops, accusing this man, and several other of the firm's work force, of theft from the factory. There was, at the time, much press-agitation about a supposed local crime-wave, and the men-in-blue were under pressure for results. They did not check their information, but swooped with macho enthusiasm. In every house they raided, they assembled all the family glassware, and demanded to see the receipts for the purchase of each item. Well, whoever can produce a receipt for a set of beer glasses bought fifteen years ago? As it happened, the glassblowers were, by common custom, allowed to take home at nominal cost any items that were found to be *flawed* after cooling. A *flaw* might be a slight bubble in the glass, scarcely visible to the naked eye, but it nonetheless rendered the piece unsuitable for public sale. Our own home was equipped with items of this sort: receipts were never given for them, they were a perquisite of the work and it was all well-understood. About half-a-dozen workers, in handcuffs, in the sight of their terrified families, had been imprisoned all in one morning. My Father was furious: I had never seen him so upset. These men could not "ring for their law-yers," workers in a town like Barnsley simply didn't have any lawyers. He rang for one, right away: and—in case the lawyer failed to turn up—went himself, in great haste, down to the courthouse to offer evidence for the defence. As soon as the magistrate had heard what my Father had to say, he stopped the case, refused to let the police-prosecutor add another word, and told the police that their action was a disgrace to Barnsley law-and-order. I suspect there was good luck involved: this particular magistrate was Labour Mayor of the town: and whatever may be said about the Labour Party in unchallenged office, their members on the bench of justice had some thought for the underdog. Had it been a Tory politico, things might have gone badly for the accused . . . Certainly, when my Father got back to the factory, having been missing most of the day, he received an angry tongue-lashing from one of the directors of the firm—"Good God, Charles, I'd had a conference here this morning, I'd expected you at it, we needed your report; damn it, man, what on earth were you doing *in court?* Auntie was in a terrible rage: she says if those chaps hadn't stolen the glassware, she's damn sure they'd been up to *something.* She's usually right, you know. No smoke without fire. That letter-writer must have known *something.* J— and K—" (two of the arrested men) "have always been trouble-makers, you shouldn't be so damn ready to believe everything they try to tell you . . . Are you losing your touch, or what . . . ?"

John Arden and Margaretta D'Arcy, in the 1960s

It is likely that some details in what I have written are not exactly accurate. I have made a point of not checking my memories. And many of the things I have written are known to me only by hearsay. It is not so much a question of what really took place, as what I grew up believing took place. There is no such thing as true history, anyway. We all, individuals, nations, classes, religions, make up our own particular biographies (separate or collective) to suit the needs of what we are doing now, or what we mean to do next. To take a very simple example: Julius Caesar was assassinated by Brutus, Cassius and others, on the Ides of March, 44 B.C. It took place before witnesses and is established as a proper historical fact. It is assumed that whatever the reasons for this killing, Caesar was thereby cut off short just before he really got into his stride as the new ruler of Rome: and what he would or would not have done, had he lived, is treated by historians as a matter of consequence. But suppose he would have done nothing, because he could think of nothing to do: and because he could think of nothing to do, he therefore deliberately allowed himself to be murdered? Such an interpretation would not contradict the ascertainable facts. He *is* supposed to have ignored several attempts to warn him, and so forth . . . Reading back from the Ides of March, it is an interpretation that must alter absolutely any view we may have formed of Caesar's career and intentions prior to his taking of power. The point is, one can not possibly *know*. Assumptions must be made, without verification: and they are made. In the interests of those to whom Roman dictatorship, Roman republican "democracy," carry political lessons for today.

I do not know why I am, who I am, or why I have written what I have written. I don't know, either, whether anyone else can make any better guesses at it than I can, in the long run. But simply to be asked by an editor to think about it prompts a number of recollections, to be added-to or subtracted-from, according to the available space. The space is now filled: and there you are . . .

BIBLIOGRAPHY

Plays:

The Business of Good Government, with Margaretta D'Arcy. London: Methuen, 1963; New York: Grove, 1967.

Ars Longa, Vita Brevis, with M. D'Arcy. London: Cassell, 1964.

Three Plays (includes *The Waters of Babylon, Live Like Pigs,* and *The Happy Haven*). Harmondsworth: Penguin, 1964; Baltimore: Penguin, 1965. (*The Happy Haven* written with M. D'Arcy).

Ironhand. London: Methuen, 1965.

Left-handed Liberty. London: Methuen, 1965; New York: Grove, 1966.

Plays One (includes *Serjeant Musgrave's Dance, The Workhouse Donkey,* and *Armstrong's Last Goodnight*). London: Methuen, 1967; New York: Grove, 1977.

The Royal Pardon, with M. D'Arcy. London: Methuen, 1967.

Soldier, Soldier and Other Plays (includes *Wet Fish, When Is a Door Not a Door?* and *Friday's Hiding*). London: Methuen, 1967. (*Friday's Hiding* written with M. D'Arcy).

The Hero Rises Up, with M. D'Arcy. London: Methuen, 1969.

Two Autobiographical Plays (includes the *True History of Squire Jonathan and His Unfortunate Treasure* and *The Bagman*). London: Methuen, 1971.

The Island of the Mighty, with M. D'Arcy. London: Methuen, 1974.

The Non-stop Connolly Show (five volumes), with M. D'Arcy. London: Pluto Press, 1977-78.

Pearl (written for radio). London: Methuen, 1979.

Vandaleur's Folly, with M. D'Arcy. London: Methuen, 1981.

The Little Gray Home in the West, with M. D'Arcy. London: Pluto Press, 1982.

The Old Man Sleeps Alone (included in *Best Radio Plays of 1982*). London: Methuen, 1983.

Fiction:

Silence among the Weapons. London: Methuen, 1982; also published as *Vox Pop.* San Diego: Harcourt, 1982.

Nonfiction:

To Present the Pretence: Essays on the Theatre and Its Public, with M. D'Arcy. London: Methuen, 1977.

Ben Belitt

1911-

FROM THE BOOKLESS WORLD: A MEMOIR

I

Prolog: From the World of Books

In the ontogeny of the poet, the individual talent is expected to move from influence to affluence, in a bell-shaped curve, over a corpus of books and mentors whose natural habitat is the School and the Library. Books beget books beget books; schools beget schools; mentors beget prentices and disciples. The proliferation of writers is accomplished by *other* writers, or whole libraries of antecedent talents, which perform phylogenetic marvels and battle for survival by natural selection. For some, the prospect is Darwinian in its ferocity; for others, it is cabalistical in its compounding of "anxieties" and requires an elaborate midrash of scribal interpretation by the elect. In either case, the result is a table of "influences" like a table of elements in chemistry: the critic is then at liberty to compile a library of "sources" out of the "elements"—to dig for the poet's library card, as anthropologists dig for a skull. *Cherchez la bibliothèque!*: it is there that one is likely to uncover the cranial past in all of its phases: the child's skull, the prentice's skills, and then, the total circuitry of the master, advancing the history of his species.

Presumably, that is the true business of the literary autobiographer: to furnish posterity with an authorized inventory of his reading and apprenticeship to the Word. A writer's "sense of the Past" is not a cup of hot tea and a madeleine: in philosophical terms, it is the record of an invasion or a seduction professionally identified with letters rather than living. All writers are presumed to have it, like the watermark for a talent—a nexus of literary texts which establishes his accountability to a jury of mentors, a mapping of hermeneutical shocks which adds to our stockpile of viable sources.

If so, *The Words* by Jean-Paul Sartre is exemplary in its impassioned commitment to authors, titles, mentors, libraries, tomes—the complete incunabula for a literary genealogy. Although Sartre's chronicle *stops* at

Ben Belitt, 1960

the age of ten, his precocity is such that Futurity need go no further: in the beginning was The Word, and the Beginning is All. The result is a bibliographical pageant that is multicultural in its scope and Alexandrian in its recovery of a founding Library. A riffling of the pages is enough to suggest the magnitude of Sartre's portrait of the artist as polymath and boggle the mind with its sophistications:

> I began my life as I shall no doubt end it:
> amidst books. In my grandfather's study
> there were books everywhere. . . . Though I
> did not yet know how to read, I already re-
> vered those standing stones: upright or lean-
> ing over, close together like bricks on the
> book-shelves or spaced out nobly in lanes of
> menhirs. . . . In my grandmother's room, the
> books lay on their sides. . . . I did not yet
> know how to read, but I was pretentious
> enough to demand to have *my* books. . . . I
> wanted to start the ceremonies of appropri-
> ation at once. . . . Frightening sentences
> emerged . . . : they were real centipedes, they
> swarmed with syllables and letters, stretched
> their diphthongs, made the double conso-
> nants vibrate. . . . Perched on a cot, I pre-
> tended to read. . . . I would climb up my cot
> with Hector Malot's *No Family,* which I knew
> by heart, and, half reciting, half deciphering,
> I went through every page of it, one after the
> other. When the last page was turned, I knew
> how to read. . . . The library contained little
> other than the major French and German
> classics. There were grammars, too, a few
> novels, de Maupassant's *Selected Stories,* some
> art books—a *Rubens,* a *Van Dyck,* a *Dürer,* a
> *Rembrandt.* . . . But for me, the Larousse Ency-
> clopedia took the place of everything. . . . I
> reread the last pages of *Madame Bovary* twenty
> times and ended by knowing whole para-
> graphs by heart. . . . I had found my religion:
> nothing seemed to me more important than a
> book. I regarded the library as a temple. . . .
> I had to be told about authors. My grandfa-
> ther told me, tactfully, calmly. He taught me
> the names of those illustrious men. I would
> recite the list to myself from Hesiod to Hugo,
> without a mistake. They were the Saints and
> Prophets. . . . In my sight they were not dead;
> at any rate not entirely. They had been
> metamorphosed into books. . . . Flaubert was
> a cloth-bound, odorless little thing spotted
> with freckles. The multiple Victor Hugo was
> on all the shelves at once. . . . Voltaire and
> Corneille were familiar acquaintances. . . .
> Alone in the midst of grownups, I was a min-
> iature adult and read books written for
> adults.

Recognizably juvenile, in that congress of book-
bearing immortals, however, is the child's primer of
derring-do, to which Sartre also bears witness: the *faux-*

naïfs of Jean de la Hire's *The Three Boy Scouts,* Arnould
Galopin's *Around the World in an Airplane, Captain Grant's
Children, The Drunkard and his Wife, Puss in Boots, Michael
Strogoff, The Adventures of a Paris Urchin, Nick Carter, Buf-
falo Bill, Texas Jack, Sitting Bull, A Crime in a Balloon,* etc.
Thereafter, the muses come down in a body and ar-

*Belitt (left) with Pablo Neruda at a Grove Press
reception, New York City, 1966*

range themselves punctually and providentially
around the nine-year-old and provide the ambiance
proper for the author of *La Nausée, L'Être et le Néant,*
and *Huis Clos.* There are parties at the Modern Language Institute at which his mother plays Chopin; his
grandfather decides to "write and stage a patriotic play
with ten characters"; precisely at the right moment he
is given a rhyming dictionary and "becomes a versifier." There are family junkets to the "boulevard
houses": the Kinerama, the Folies Dramatiques, the
Vaudeville, the Gaumont Palace where "I saw *Zigomar,
Fantômas, The Exploits of Maciste, The Mysteries of New
York*"; piano recitals of Schumann's sonatas, Franck's
symphonic variations, the overture to *Fingal's Cave* (two

of which furnish the autobiographer in 1963 with surrogates for deity and the numinous life): "Schumann's sonata would finally convince me [*aetat:* nine years old]: I was both the creature who despairs and the God who has always saved him since the beginning of time."

Into this pantheon of imminence (which now includes Goethe, Schiller, Molière, Racine, La Fontaine, Heinrich Heine, Victor Hugo, James Fenimore Cooper, Byron, and Dickens) God and the prentice leap at a single bound: "I confused literature with prayer. I made a human sacrifice of it. . . . I decided to write for God with the purpose of saving my neighbors. . . . I accepted the loathsome myth of the Saint who saves the populace because, in the last analysis, the populace was myself." By the age of nine, *reading,* for Sartre, has metamorphosed entirely into *writing:* "I discovered that in belles-lettres the Giver can be transformed into his own Gift, that is, into a pure object . . . I could appear to the Holy Ghost as a precipitate of language." The resultant transfiguration into ink and paper accomplishes a latter-day miracle of the loaves and fishes; and, presumably, the Canon of Jean-Paul Sartre is on its way, at the age of ten: "My pen raced away so fast that often my wrist ached. I would throw the filled notebooks on the floor."

Here, the wary Sartrian will doubtless wish to balance the scales with that deflationary grain of salt which is due Sartre as ironist, philosophe of the queasy palate, and trickster of negative hyperbole. Sartre is the first to admit: "What I have just written is false. True. Neither true nor false. . . . I have reported the facts as accurately as my memory permitted. . . . That already sounds false, since, at the same time, I remained a child. I am claiming that I was guilty. That's how it was, and that's that." However, the probity of all such retrospective searches for sources, "portraits," "educations," and intellectual histories is not the point of my concern. I wish only to suggest that Sartre's autobiography of The Word seems to constitute a kind of paradigm for all such ventures, in that it moves from "reading" and "writing" to "the word" with a minimum of autobiographical dalliance and at once strikes for the Book, the Library, the Mentor, and those meshings of "tradition" with "the individual talent" laid upon us by Eliot. For Sartre, *all*—absolutely all, without stint or remainder—is *literature.*

It is otherwise with Vladimir Nabokov's equally volatile assault upon Mnemosyne, *Speak, Memory.* Building upon a "cornerstone" of "maps, time tables, a collection of match boxes, a chip of ruby, and the view from my balcony of the Geneva Lake," Nabokov loads every rift with anecdotal ore, to the limit of affectionate

recall. Not until Section V of Chapter V—80 pages into his *recherche*—do the italics of bibliographical discourse occur in sufficient abundance to constitute a significant cluster of literary references. Even so, the disclosures are minimal: "We got it all: *Les Malheurs de Sophie, Le Tour du Monde en Quatre Vingt Jours, Le Petit Chose, Les Misérables, Le Comte de Monte Cristo,* many others." More important to Nabokov is the roster of governesses and tutors, of which the anomalous purveyor of Verne and Hugo, addressed only as "Mademoiselle," is only one of many. For Nabokov, the priorities of Mnemosyne are familial rather than bibliographical: as mother of the muses, Memory must address the matriarchal lozenge of his family shield: childhood illnesses, games of skill and gambling, hobbies like "the very Russian sport of *hodit' po gribï* (looking for mushrooms)," dachshunds, a summer *soomerki* ("the lovely Russian word for dusk"), and "a bewildering sequence of English nurses and governesses."

Thus, Chapter III—one of the longest in the book—is totally devoted to an almanach of Nabokovian Begetters "rampant, regardant, arrogantly demonstrating the unfortunate knight's shield" from 1494 up to the present. For those who cannot muster a similar avidity for parenthetical dates and *noms de noblesse,* the successions of privilege and territorial aggrandizement are likely to appear numbing. The pages teem with retrospective digressions on the hobbies and avocations of a writer on leave of absence from his Muse: lepidopterology, magic lanterns, politics, heraldry, bicycling, soccer, courtship, the "dreamy flow of punts and canoes on the Cam," arboretums, crossword puzzles, and the "quasi-musical, quasi-poetical, or, to be quite exact, poetico-mathematical, process of thinking up a chess composition." To be sure, by the conclusion of its tour, Memory has also summoned up a small cadre of literary predilections: *Les Malheurs de Sophie,* Captain Mayne Reid's *The Headless Horseman,* and James Fenimore Cooper, for the youthful Nabokov; Pushkin and Tyutchev for the fifteen-year-old versifier; Hofman and the Grand Duke Nikolay Mihailovitch's *Mémoires* for the lepidopterist; and Gogol, Tolstoy, Blok, Tsvetaeva, and Sirin ("the author that interested me most") for the émigré of Berlin and Paris.

But—what of the Library, the Mentor, the Book, the Tradition, The Word? In the volume inscribed in her name, none strikes a dominant chord in the byplay of Memory. The voice is the voice of the patrician and the solipsist, and the theme, the nostalgias of exile rather than the ontology of a talent or a medium. Unlike Sartre, Nabokov does not appear to have found The Library a "temple" and tutelary sibyl; it does not assume the afflatus of a paternity or a divinity. Instead, library and tutor alike are taken for granted as *droits du*

Stanley Kunitz, Ben Belitt, and Howard Nemerov at a poetry symposium, Skidmore College, 1973

seigneur of the manorial way, and occur only twice in this portrait of the artist as a young aristocrat: once, as an addendum to the defections of "Mademoiselle": "My father's library, not her limited lore, taught me to appreciate authentic poetry"; and again, as the bravado of a dandy at large on the quads of Cambridge:

> Not once in my three years at Cambridge—repeat: not once—did I visit the University library, or even bother to locate it (I know its place now), or find out if there existed a college library where books might be borrowed for reading in one's digs. I skipped lectures, I sneaked to London and elsewhere. I conducted several love affairs simultaneously. I had dreadful interviews with [my tutor] Mr. Harrison. I translated into Russian a score of poems by Rupert Brooke, *Alice in Wonderland* and Romain Rolland's *Colas Breughon.* I might as well have gone to the Inst. M.M. of Tirana.

At the other end of the spectrum, of course, we have Dickens as laureate of the artist-as-waif, foundling, disinherited orphan and adoptive castaway, moving toward the Word by skewed but irresistible degrees, in a picaresque progression of alternating solitudes and restorations, devoid of heraldic privilege: Dickens as Copperfield. Here, due allowance must be made for the priorities of fictive procedure and its baggage of episodes and personae that often render the autobiographical objective barely visible behind the multiplications of plot and the swarming of contingent "characters." With good reason, the artist-as-novelist, in comparison with the artist-autobiographer, yields to the momentum of his fiction, rather than the longueurs of bibliography. The priorities of plot, entertainment, narration, favor the fabulist, not the scholarly historian.

In the case of Copperfield, the fable, as we know, is notoriously gothic in its baroquerie: episodes, anecdotes, labyrinthine contrivances, ironies, private and public vendettas, melodramatic digressions, diminishments, aggrandizements, histrionics—the whole of that repertory which thickens the plot to the peculiar consistency required by Dickens, writing at his characteristic best and worst. Given the general seethe and *busyness* of the fictive compost in *David Copperfield,* there is reason to wonder whether the hard-working protagonist will ever proffer his library card to the Librarian at

Belitt (right) with Bernard Malamud at commencement ceremonies, Bennington College, 1981

any phase of his saga, despite our assumption of his accountability for an artist-hero who will one day answer to the name of Charles Dickens. However, The Library, with its full complement of sources, is indeed present, in a form considered classic by bibliophiles, as early as Chapter IV. In a personal epic that runs to more than 800 pages, it is Copperfield the runaway, the casualty of dispossession chafing beneath a stepfather's deprivals, who furnishes all that the prodigal Nabokov does *not*, in explicit detail:

> My father had left a small collection of books in a little room upstairs, to which I had access (for it adjoined my own), and which nobody else in our house ever troubled. From that blessed little room, Roderick Random, Peregrine Pickle, Humphrey Clinker, Tom Jones, the Vicar of Wakefield, Don Quixote, Gil Blas, and Robinson Crusoe, came out, a glorious host, to keep me company. They kept alive my fancy, and my hope of something beyond that place and time—they, and the *Arabian Nights* and the *Tales of Genjii*— and did me no harm, for whatever harm was in some of them was not there for me; *I* knew

nothing of it. It is astonishing to me now, how I found time, in the midst of my porings and blunderings over heavier themes, to read those books as I did. It is curious to me how I could ever have consoled myself under my small troubles (which were great troubles to me) by impersonating my favourite characters in them—as I did—and by putting Mr. and Miss Murdstone into all the bad ones— which I did too. I have been Tom Jones (a child's Tom Jones, a harmless creature) for a week together. I have sustained my own idea of Roderick Random for a month at a stretch, I verily believe. I had a greedy relish for a few volumes of *Voyages and Travels*—I forget what, now—that were on those shelves; and for days and days I can remember to have gone about my region of our house, armed with a centrepiece out of an old set of boot-trees—the perfect realization of Captain Somebody . . . . This was my only and constant comfort . . . reading as if for life.

Here, with a single stroke of the pen, we have it all—a critic's Baedeker to the works and days of Charles

Dickens, in the image of a book-hungry child.

But it is to the *Portrait of the Artist as a Young Man* that all quests for the compleat autobiographer are likely to lead in this century of the omnipresence of Joyce. In the *Portrait* we have a modern epitome of the metamorphic spirit distilling life into letters, invoked in the language of Ovid himself, as the epigraph for an artist's accountability: "*Et ignotas animum dimittit in artes.*" ("And launches his spirit in unknown arts.") Unlike Dickens', however, Joyce's plunges into contingency are of the sort that create black holes in a Daedalian cosmos and compel every episode to yield autobiographical returns beyond the chartable orbit of Memory and The Word. For Memory is not the point of the *Portrait,* and The Word is not its limit: and though mentors and "artificers" are abundantly present, no Library, familial or institutional, is capable of confining them to a shelf or a reference number. The streaming of consciousness is no respecter of Dewey decimals or due-dates. In the *Portrait,* books appear and disappear like planetary scintillations: Byron, Newman, Ovid, the Catholic Missal, Thomas Aquinas, Yeats, Shelley, Horace, Victor Hugo, as well as the memory of vanished mythologies: Greek, Irish, Egyptian. Time and again the Word is weighed, as both Sartre and Nabokov have weighed it: *suck, kiss, belt, toe in the rump, tower of ivory, ivoire, tundish, God, Dieu.* The swish of a soutane or the smack of a pandy-bat are registered within a decimal point of their visceral frequencies, along with whole sermons on Hell-fire and eternity; but Joyce's assault upon the "Unknown" presses on beyond autobiography and narrative to the kingdoms of Thoth and Dionysus, where "the ineluctible modality of the visible" turns into the invisible.

In that kingdom, it is the filial archetype, rather than the Library, that presides: Daedalus as "old father" and maker of mazes, Icarus as "flyer of the nets" or their later incarnations as Odysseus and Telemachus, Simon and Stephen, Stephen and Leopold Bloom—each of whom creates not a bookshelf, but the very poetics of tale-telling as such. It is significant, for example, that the *Portrait* begins with a child's formula for the fairy story—"Once upon a time"—rather than a Homeric or Miltonic invocation to the Muse, as though the urgency of his fiction had forced Joyce back to the atavisms of the secular and infantile life. Simon Dedalus, remembered, appears to the child in the role of the Nurturer, telling the *once*-told tale of Baby Tuckoo and the Moocow without rubric or precedent. Stephen Dedalus, as listener, feels himself privileged, engrossed, aroused, at large "on the road where Betty Byrne lived," heroizing a world that tastes of lemon platt, within a verbal artifact that incorporates the particulars of a morning's experience. The hearing and the telling are full of recognitions: "His father told him that story: his father looked at him through a glass: he had a hairy face." But the recognitions are not those of the bibliophile rehearsing a hieratic literature of Cuchulain and Conchubar or Red Riding Hood—which Simon might have summoned for the occasion: they are the primordial intimations of identity and kinship itself. "Every telling," Joyce instructs us in a canto of *Finnegan,* "has a taling, and that's the he and the she of it."

In short, Identity, and not Mnemosyne, is the Muse's intent in Joyce's *Portrait:* it is to this end that the Father-Artificer fashions for his son a primitive esthetic experience which makes the "taling" of the story indistinguishable from the *being* of the listener: "*He* was baby tuckoo. The Moocow came down the road where Betty Byrne lived: *she* sold lemon platt." What Sartre has called the "ceremonies of appropriation" have already begun: "*He* sang that song. That was *his* song." At the same time, deep within the plasm of utterance itself, the genius of Repetition is at work, laboring to retrieve the whole patrimony of language and song—epic, lyric, instrumental and vocal music, measure, dance—in their primitive guise as "tale," along with the fivefold repertory of the sensorium: all are engaged by Joyce in the opening paragraphs as the child's invocation to a spiritual conquest of the "unknown." There, waiting to be summoned by the Teller, or Hammerer in the Smithy, lie the long ancestry of his "clan," the "uncreated conscience" of his race, the tabula rasa of his "art," the protocol of the House of Dedalus, the scheme for a universe written on the flyleaf of a geography book, and the nurturing lilt of that Irish washerwoman's jig which gives its tune to both the child's fairy story and the labyrinthine plainsongs of Anna Livia Plurabelle. The *booklessness* of Joyce's world, thought to be unutterable, is made one with the people of his book. The Hammerer in the Smithy is metamorphosed into the Flyer of the Nets. The Library, the Mentor, the reading and writing of The Word, in which telling and taling are *all,* are on their way.

II

The Bookless World: Orphanage

Perhaps the first thing to be said for the first decade of my life is that my childhood had no interpreters for the *booklessness* of the world. My childhood was a surrogate world of the parade field, the public "asylum," the institutional regimen, without possessions or

Ben Belitt, age ten, Hebrew Orphan Asylum, New York City

portfolio—the Orphanage, where, in the extremity of their need, my mother and father had placed me. The Hebrew Orphan Asylum, quite the most massive of its species in the City of New York, occupied a prominent plateau of upper Manhattan: a dense pullulation of cinderpaths and bricks, rising like a Mayan enclave, on an enormous platform shored up on three sides by a slope of graded masonry four blocks deep, on 137th Street and Amsterdam Avenue, just across the street from the old Lewisohn Stadium and the City College of New York. Seen from the street, its entrance, a baronial crescent sweeping grandly to a porched and pillared doorway, feigned two rows of tulips institutionally pruned and enlarged to an anthracite cheerfulness. Five stories into the mid-city grime and glare of the avenue, a belfry with a monitory clock struck the hours and the half-hours; but my memory of it is relentlessly nocturnal, as my mother and I, climbing the steps from the subway kiosk after one of my rare visits home, scanned the illuminated dial to see whether the pointers had not already converged upon IX, the absolute

curfew of return.

Doubtless, the books and the libraries were also present, somewhere in that warren of dormitories and underground playing fields. In the protocol of orphanage, tribal indoctrination went hand in hand with the gratuities of eleemosynary life: bed, board, instruction in basic Hebrew, graham crackers and milk in a blind man's cup at four in the afternoon, a week of midsummer camping in Southfield, New York, for the durable and the diligent, Sunday night movies in a courtyard where we straddled the steel of a fire escape in dizzying tiers over a cyclone of triangulated incandescence, Visiting Days with mothers and uncles stooping under the weight of their brown-bagged cornucopias. Sacred and secular mentors were also plentiful at all levels of elementary and secondary literacy—teachers, rabbis, superintendents, governors, counselors, monitors—but I remember only the paradigm from our Hebrew primer, rust-red on black, with its accompanying illustration: *Al gog sol: On the roof is a basket*—precarious perch!

The true text of my childhood was not a literature or a grandfather's library, but a life devoid of scribal transformations from an avuncular past: *things done* in institutional sequences to an accompaniment of bells, with adults and adolescents to assemble and dismiss us in hierarchical units designated by a letter and a numeral—F-1 through F-6 for the girls and M-1 through M-6 for the boys. There was the Girls' Side and the Boys' Side; and only siblings in good standing were permitted to cross over on authorized afternoons. None of us owned a book. We slept, ate, showered, answered to our last names in congeries, like grackles; we groped toward our identities in swarms and formations; we mustered in squadrons and drilled on the playing fields, making squared circles in the crude orthography of the conscript. These were our daily "sentences," our "handwriting" like the ovals and pushpulls in the exercise books, our semiotic signals, our grammar. All was public, behavioral, secretive, and solitary—chapters with no turnable pages, as though written in concrete and cinder with the soles of our feet, a rhetoric of ordered displacement, actions without alphabets, unvoiceable, consentless. Six decades later, all that remains of that "literature" are pure states of being, legible only in their unalterable immediacy, textless transfigurations vaguely or explicitly sexual—a Poetics of Orphanage which has served me as both a paradigm for the military life, with its massive regression to Booklessness, and a tutelary theme for my work as a whole: they are equally present in the *School of the Soldier* (1943), and the autobiographical sequence of poems called *The Orphaning,* published in 1970.

I made book out of a riffle of sensations: a sum-

The Hebrew Orphan Asylum, New York City
(Photograph courtesy of the Jewish Child Care Association of New York.)

mons from my underground games, to learn of the death of my father (my birth certificate calls him a "cloak presser") from the lips of my mother in 1918; the moment of abandonment when my mother turned her huge back and surrendered me to the Orphanage barber some months before; an ambiguous spanking in full view of a "bin-room" detail, administered bare-bummed over the knees of an unhurried monitor of the dormitory laundry, like a love affair or a prolonged caress, rather than the barrel-head justice of a discipli-narian; a lesson in elementary percussion on the lap of a sixteen-year-old Drum Captain whose soldierly cha-risma made him the object of institutional envy, in a squad room full of bugles and windows and drums, which was also my induction into the endearments of male adolescence. From this waif's "library" of as-sorted perils and derring-do, with no help whatever from Smollett or Dumas or Jules Verne, I transcribed the literature of pure presence into stories, poems, con-fessional subtexts, after a providential change of venue brought my mother from a candy store in Manhattan, to Lynchburg, Virginia, as bride of a master-tailor, adding her own three orphans to a household of eight reluctant Fogels on 821 Madison Street. There, in a

kind of midnight magic, stories and rhymes crystallized suddenly like manna in a desert of booklessness. I com-peted for purses donated by the city Chamber of Com-merce, won a state medal for a reminiscence of Or-phanage life, and, in my senior year at Lynchburg High School, was summoned to Charlottesville to read a prize-winning story called "Mended Armor" at the Cabell Hall Auditorium of the University of Virginia before a diorama of Raphael's *School of Athens* and the doting witness of my mother and English teacher.

In High School and throughout my undergrad-uate years at "The University," retrospective realism went hand in hand with Byzantine fantasy: orphanage stories with titles like "Little Davy's Goblins" and "The Door Swings Wide," Oriental parables like "The Shah Lemai's Vision" and "The Bronze Image," pub-lication in Harriet Monroe's *Poetry, Scholastic,* the *New Outlook,* and the old *Midland Magazine,* and finally my professional bow in *Weird Tales* at the age of nineteen with "Tzo-Lin's Nightingales," a tale of the Fourth Di-mension in the style (I thought) of Stevenson's "Sire de Malatroit's Door" and Poe's "Cask of Amontillado."

The stories came first because the fantasy came first. Prose was the domain of fantasy; but poetry was already preparing the way for those terser penetrations of identity which go by the name of the actual. In my reading of Poe, it was the hashish of style, rather than the plottings of horror, which elicited my first imitations: the "high style" of mandarin narrative at once sinister and anachronistic, which constituted both a theater of light and sound, and a prosody of the grotesque. In poetry, I opted for closure, meter, declamation, the clean-cut, Presbyterian line of A. E. Housman and Elinor Wylie, turning chaos into epigram, and giving me a scrubbed sense of placement—that bonding of ego with the intoxicating materiality of language that turns discourse skeletal as well as magisterial. No one ever proctored me in sonnet during my high-school days, or recommended it as a calisthenic for the tenderfoot; but in my bedroom with a cracked bedstead and a leaning wardrobe that preempted every inch of habitable lebensraum, I wrote a sonnet every night before retiring, in borrowed rhetoric too big for me by several sizes. When I was fifteen and sixteen, they came easily to my bedside perch, like a hallucinogen or a ritual of undressing:

Bombastic Man, slow, dense, you weary me
With your conceit and vulgar gasconade.
Peacocklike, you seek the sun's publicity
To preen your feathers in, and shun the shade.
Heavy with the weight of false ideals,
Burdened with borrowed creeds and mouldering
    lores,
You munch fat creeds and fling away the cores,
Enticed by drab and mercenary zeals . . .

My removal to Lynchburg also brought with it a lifting of institutional purdah: I was free to add mentors and libraries to the solitude of the orphan's conception of his destiny. The Jones Memorial Library on Rivermont Avenue is separated from the township itself by a natural chasm bridged like a portcullis or a castle-keep, breathtaking in its depth and topographical dishevelment, from which sudden gouts of flame are periodically visible on a scarred horizon; and my sense of borrowing books—*The Girl of the Limberlost, The Scarlet Pimpernel,* Edna St. Vincent Millay, Poe—is one which still smells of gases and blast furnaces lining a causeway for dragons and paladins. It was also the scene of a providential encounter with the first of my mentors, a published poet and incumbent novelist, who frowned at my armload of rubbish and asked me disdainfully if I had ever read Keats's "Ode to a Nightingale."

Two brothers, of good family and some parochial eminence, undertook to sophisticate my tastes, in the semidarkness of a miniscule bookshop on Church Street. Since they plied their little franchise with no regard for profit or desultory custom, I was free to come and go in the twilight of a lending library where all seemed transfigured into the celluloid of a green eyeshade, and meditation was Stygian. From Abe and Murrell Edmunds I learned that the calling for which my scribbles were preparing a way in the desert was Isaianic, and that triviality—to which they relegated their whole stock of circulating stereotypes—was universal. So great was his contempt for the pedestrian that *Abe* became *Craddock* Edmunds—a Christian name of considerable panache in Lynchburg—midway in his career. It was Abe who sent me back over the blast furnaces of Beck Bridge to exchange the Baroness Orczy for Robert Browning, Ben Johnson, the tragic plays of William Shakespeare, and William Ellery Leonard, a sonneteer whose autobiographical sequence entitled *Two Lives* he regarded as the masterwork of an undeserving epoch. His insistence on the high style, the solitary option, and the mordant encompassment of the tears of the things was reflected in his own choice of subject matter: a lengthy narrative poem of World War I called *Five Men,* a sequence of dramatic monologs called *The Renaissance,* including Leonardo da Vinci, Cellini, and the Sistine Michelangelo, a meditation on Shakespeare ("He Walks from His Tavern to an Inn"), which I still read with profit as pieces of quality and passion now obliterated by an altered mandate for the memorable. His demotic paraphrases of Dante, Villon, the medieval lute songs of the troubadours, the paroxysms of Hamlet and Lear, forced me out of my depths while I still dabbled in the shallows, and gave to the whole perspective of the Past a glory that turned me into a voyeur of the dumbshow of letters.

Such was not the case, however, during my eight years of undergraduate and graduate study at the University of Virginia. The fault was not the fault of a perfectly durable faculty of English Literature skilled in the prevailing routines of multiplying masters of the arts, but the Teutonic bent of American universities charged with the certification of competencies and the indoctrination of potential college professors. The pedagogical mission at Virginia, as elsewhere, was identified with the cloning of scholars, rather than the enlistment of journeymen for the risks of pastoral reflection of the inexhaustibility of letters. Though the Past lay all around me as I moved from the undergraduate's reading lamp in Mr. Jefferson's Rotunda, to the stacks packed like the seeds of a pomegranate to the very dome, to the carrels under the dome where the youthful scholar amassed his bibliographical treasures in the fine italic of footnotes, it pressed on me as a syllabus rather than a "sense."

For the writer caught in the act of writing, it may be that the Past is never a "sense": the sound of his pen on the page is a sense, the emergence of a word from the ink is a sense—but the sense is that of Time Present moving ruthlessly into the Future. The Libraries had come, only to remind me that I was in deadly peril of their Pastness and to lay an insatiable mandate upon me; but the exchange was undemonstrative, usurious, unrequited. My erudition constitutes no material addition to this chronicle of Past Time; what clung to me was the overlay of languages—French, German, Greek, Anglo-Saxon, Middle English—in which I alternately froze and burned as in an ongoing safari. My most memorable accomplishment was to charm an improbable 100 out of James Southall Wilson ("Julien Green was my only other student to receive one!") who let me rail at an "unvolant" Wordsworth or profess my private predilections in orphic final examinations, opened the pages of the *Virginia Quarterly Review* to my sonnets, sent me on monthly junkets of book-reviewing to Richmond's Station WRVA as "Peter Quince Book Reviewer," and approved an unorthodox Master's Thesis on Katherine Mansfield and Anton Chekhov.

The most unobtrusive mentor of them all, whom I last visited in a small nursing home in Lynchburg in the summer of 1947, was a high-school teacher who might have sat for one of Dickens' Benefactresses and furnished him with the epitome of a name. Evelina Wiggins, a senior member of the English faculty with a peculiarly trapezoidal reflex of tugging at her hemline and rearranging a sleeve at the collarbone, carried me off in her teeth as a cat carries off a reconnoitering kitten, after an assignment in autobiographies. Bemused, confidential, unnerving, in her little shed of an office under the stairway to the assembly hall, she probed for the child under the polysyllables and opened the way to a lifetime's collaboration of equals. She began with flowering plants, which she taught me to identify with their God-given seasons, instead of linking them together for their sounds, thereby acknowledging that the providence of nature precedes the providence of language. There were seasonal inspections of her garden on 8 Vista Avenue, which sloped into tractable terraces toward some middle region whose center must have been Edenic, when I was made to repeat each species after her in a calendar for gardeners—zinnias, peonies, violets, hydrangeas, amaryllis, foxgloves, lilacs, and the special treasure of her squills, for which she also taught me the Latin name of *Scilla siberica.* I thinned them down when they crowded the terraces, in bouquets for the provident husbandman. Making a sound like a top under the frosty coiffure of a "bob" considered by some inappropriate for a

maiden lady of her years and institutional obligations, she showed me the Van Bokkelyn glassware crammed with dogwood and flowering judas on her living-room shelves, interpreted the sunset from an upper sundeck from which the whole sweep of her garden was visible in the shifting light, like some lucky turn in a child's kaleidoscope, and left me to chatter with her extortionate mother over a cucumber wedge and a tumbler of iced tea while she wadded an armful of flowers in wet newspapers and waved me back to Madison Street with a bounty "for Mother." Later came the poets: A. E. Housman for cherry trees, Alfred Noyes, as laureate of Kew Gardens, for lilacs, Amy Lowell for squills, Sandburg for fog, Keats for waning autumns, Edna St. Vincent Millay for apocalyptical horizons. On the ill-fated afternoon when she learned of the untimely death of a nephew, she called me to her office under the stairs and told me the detailed story of Maeterlinck's *Bluebird* until we could no longer see each other's faces in the darkness that smelled of closed doors and the janitor's disinfectant.

To all of these confidences I replied with poems, or whole fascicles of flower-pieces for which the word "anthology" was originally invented. Each flower in her cornucopia of wet newsprint had its lyric, written in the urgency of its manifest perishability, and then retyped on gray drawing paper for safe keeping. There was a sonnet in pentametric hexameters devoted to the resurrection scene in Maeterlinck when

A bird, blue-feathered, would sing with all his might
From his bright nest built in celestial eaves

with the most monosyllabic couplet I have ever written, to mark my return to gravity:

Full well I know that this—all this—is so.
You taught me once and I have learned. I know.

Miss Wiggins is the heroine of two of my published short stories—one of them an autobiographical account of a visit to 8 Vista Avenue during a summer recess from the University of Virginia (*Midland Magazine,* 1930), in the manner of Katherine Mansfield and Virginia Woolf, with a title out of Keats: "Not to Lethe," the other devoted to precisely the opposite premise, the suicide of a gardener to whom a premonition of winter burial was intolerable, entitled "The Flower Garden" (*Scholastic Magazine,* 1930). Both marked my deliverance from a "bookless" world to a sensible Past where mentors and languages mingled with a memory of books and characters of my own choosing, and telling and taling were one. Miss Wiggins, in the person of Esta Strange, is summoned from her garden, pruning shears in hand, to reflect on "the prodigality of the absurd" in the opening pages of "Not to Lethe":

> The screen door was like fire to the touch when Esta, swinging the hot frame after her, came into the house. She stopped on the stairway and leaned against the bannister. In the front hall the sun exploded noiselessly: hats, umbrellas, broken arcs, half-stars— nothing was familiar or credible. She cupped a hand across her eyes. Feeling the coolness of stems against her arm, she was reminded of the pear cuttings, still wadded in folds of wet newspaper under her arm. They should have gone in the jardiniere in the front hall; stupid of her to have forgotten that! Five years ago, she'd have remembered. Perhaps Ceebee was right and one did merge into a sort of dotage at thirty-seven . . . Oh, the prodigality of the absurd! Dead animals with laces, for the feet, dead flowers, dead grasses, inked, for scarves and dresses; tridents of metal to carry dead animals, flowers, grasses, to the mouth! Nonsense! Madness! Nothing had meaning except nothingness! Sunlight on wicker chair- forms and through windows: blue, little hills crouched a hundred miles away . . .

The playgrounds of the Hebrew Orphan Asylum rea- rise for David and Emily in "The Door Swings Wide":

> The afternoon shook itself drowsily like an old woman, settling its great belly and draw- ing the heavy sunlight closer about its shoul- ders. Behind him, David could hear a razzle- dazzle creak throatily, and the regular pound and thump of seesaws bouncing one after an- other into the dry, hot clay and up again. Some F-6 girls were playing jackrocks under a tired-looking maple tree. Scrawny caterpil- lars, their files of legs rippling lazily, moved across the canyons of hot bark and up and down among the bleached and dust-covered leaves . . . From across the baseball field, balls cracked and thudded smartly, and feet, hidden to the hips in dust the fineness of pow- der, scuffled the gravel diamond from base to base. Molly Opinitsky, skipping rope by the greasy-pig, called out to Emily in a high, shaky voice; her face was flushed like a peach, her hair and dress flew out with each upward lunge and sweep downward. The rope whirled over her head and beneath her feet, slapping up dust and sometimes the fragment of a leaf.

> *"On the mountain stanza la-d-e-e-e,*
> *Who sheyis I do not know . . . "*

I had found my song. I sang that song. That was my song.

III

Toward a World of Books: The Mentors, the Grandfathers

Where do they come from—those overarching depth-sounders and bailbondsmen who deliver us from booklessness, to the libraries of our "grandfa- thers"? When do storytellers turn into poets for whom words work prosodical miracles on all that was merely fictive, autobiographical, and quotidian? Writing po- ems in a triple bronze borrowed from the armories of A. E. Housman and Elinor Wylie with my left hand, and stories in the make-believe and hindsight of the solipsist, with my right, in my senior year at Virginia I dispatched a sheaf of poems to Eda Lou Walton, whose reviews for the *New York Times Sunday Book Section* and the *Nation* were well-known to my generation. I re- ceived the following reply under the letterhead of 61 Morton Street, New York:

Oct. 10, 1932

> Dear Mr. Belitt:
>   I want to tell you that your contribu- tions to *College Verse* are the best poems I've seen in quite some time. I want to feature your work this month, and I am keeping all of them. May I say that I think you are very authentically a good poet, and they are ex- tremely rare these days. I was much moved by your work. I wonder just how you come to be at the University of Virginia, for the feel- ing of your work is certainly not that of a Southerner. Do go ahead with some trust in yourself. I am afraid of praising young people too much. But I'm inclined to believe you will not be affected by praise, but only by what is necessary to yourself.

Four years later, I was occupying a Greenwich Village apartment at the opposite end of Morton Street and sharing an office with that construer of deserts and Schubert Alley premieres, Joseph Wood Krutch, as Assistant Literary Editor of the *Nation,* through the in- tervening magic of Miss Walton, who was determined to oust me from Mr. Jefferson's Rotunda and depasto- ralize my vision:

> If you could uproot yourself from your sur-

roundings and spend a winter here, you'd come to know things differently (she wrote me). You'd find what Yeats found: that reality is more important than daydreaming, that human beings are more important than roses. One can look at the present day scene, the complete inner disturbances that all people are going through. One can keep one's pen on the facts and project the vision from the facts. You cannot live your childhood much longer. I see in your work the first glimpse of something new from youth. And I'd like to uproot you from peace.

All at once, I found myself in the library of my "grandfather," "reading," as Dickens has said, "as if for life," and straining to keep attentive in the eerie pandemonium. The reading laid upon me by Miss Walton was unprecedented in its mind-boggling contradictions: Hart Crane, William Butler Yeats, Léonie Adams, W. H. Auden, Burke's *Attitudes toward History,* Strachey's *Coming Struggle for Power,* Caudwell's *Reality and Illusion,* Gerard Manley Hopkins. In my weekly chores as *Nation* reviewer and in occasional pieces for the *New York Times Book Review,* the *Virginia Quarterly Review, Poetry,* and *Story,* I was confronted with the latest offerings of Thomas Mann, Wallace Stevens, Carl Sandburg, W. H. Auden, Stephen Spender, E. E. Cummings, William Carlos Williams, Allen Tate, H. G. Wells, Katherine Mansfield, Katherine Anne Porter, and William Empson. I shared my luncheon or my midday walks to the Battery with visiting contemporaries like Theodore Roethke and David Schubert; winced at the incendiary exhaustion of André Malraux on a combat mission for embattled Spain as special courier to the *Nation;* added postscripts on the Federal Theater of Orson Welles's *Dr. Faustus* or Ibsen's *Enemy of the People,* wrote articles on "vanity publishing" and American documentary filmmakers like Paul Strand and Leo Hurwitz for the weekly chronicles of the *Nation* on special assignment; revived the annual *Nation* Poetry Prize in 1936 with awards to Wallace Stevens and John Peale Bishop; ogled the cages of 20 Vesey Street for the unpredictable materializations and disappearances of Louis Fischer and John Gunther in the twilight of the Foreign Correspondent; published the first English translations of the murdered García Lorca and the latest ventures of a new generation of poets at the bidding of a benevolent and permissive Senior Editor, pasted dummies of the Books and the Arts Section in weekly rites of Procrustean "bed-making." By that time, the Crash of '29 had peaked to its first decade of Rooseveltian Depression, in a largesse of muralized post offices, WPA guidebooks to the lore and logistics of the forty-eight states, soup kitchens, road crews and Conservation Corps, International Brigades to republican Madrid, and mandates for a proletarian literature in the name of Abraham Lincoln and *la condition humaine.* Reality took on the balance of a feather as a century was "uprooted from its peace."

Already adept in the polity of Orphanage, I was easily absorbed into the labyrinths of 61 Morton Street, 107 Waverley Place, and a host of cindery retreats in suburban New Jersey that were the summer provenance of Eda Lou Walton as Imaginary Jewess, university intellectual, and wife of David Mandel, for whom labor law and forensic metaphysics cut a pendular path over the years from Perth Amboy to New York City, from libraries and art galleries to picket lines, courtrooms, and trade union forums. At 61 Morton Street Miss Walton convened a special pantheon of begetters, like voices in a cloud, reading the morning's headlines like a binnacle or scanning the barricades for an Armageddon of united and divided fronts—card-carrying communists, avowed or clandestine, fellow-travellers, russophiles and voyeurs of the "liberal" persuasion, zealots committed to the utopias of Trotsky or Marx or Franklin Delano Roosevelt, "non-political" *examens de conscience* in the manner of Thomas Mann or the hermeneutical calculus of Caudwell and Kenneth Burke.

I now think of Eda Lou Walton as a Protectress engaged in a search for *protegés* in the Gallic sense of that word—vulnerable and beseiged talents in their nonage or orphaned state. For years prior to our meeting, her impassioned choice had singled out Henry Roth at the age of nineteen and removed him from the East Side ghettos of his parentage to the privileged environs of 61 Morton Street. In 1936 I found him ambiguously installed as foster-son and prentice-prodigy, completing the final pages of a work of genius, *Call It Sleep*—a first novel of astonishing verbal splendor and intensity concentering all that I had thought irreconcilably divided: the worlds of the foundling and the castaway princeling, the fabulist and the poet, the *voyant* and the *voyeur,* in a legendary conflagration of hebraized Americana. As she explained to me, early in 1935:

> I took Henry away from his native environment when he was nineteen. I have enabled him to live his own life. He was the most inhibited and shyest and inarticulate of youngsters. He has learned to be exactly what he is to the full. His people are very poor, almost illiterate peasants, Jewish, of course. He turned back to them for his material, but by that time he had his own perspective. His parents have understood with a kind of sim-

Eda Lou Walton, 1935

ple imagination what I was intending: they are enormously proud, if a little bewildered. Of course, he has outgrown me, too: that was inevitable. Now he can pick and choose what, as an artist, he will need. He has the full-bloodedness and the health, even the joy in natural vulgarity, along with sensitivity in the extreme, that a novelist needs.

As in Gide's myth of reversal, the center of the labyrinth led, not to a tangle of passional and political threads, or an ideological monster of blood sacrifice, but a haven of fellowships which deepened over the years into a fostering kinship. Eda Lou Walton, no bigger than a wren or an ember in a hearthbed, with a phoenix's tolerance for combustion, had long ago come to a hard decision which drew her to Ishmaelites like myself and Henry in search of their patrimony: as she explained in one of her many unstinting confidences:

A complete nervous breakdown left me facing myself and I knew then that I had to

understand people, to go out to them or go quite mad. I found my way out and my sanity through making use of contacts the classroom afforded me, first, I came to realize that I wanted to understand people more than I wanted anything else and with almost too great an emotionalism got inside those students. I had learned that too much intensity on my part, could harm, that I'd know more of people if I left them quite free of myself, at the same time, of course, going out to them, as you say, "quietly." From that time on I have not been afraid of life. If people are not life, what can life be?

In response to my insistence on her own merits as a poet of daemonic celebrations and valedictions, whose New Mexican landscapes glowed like forges or anvils— the rebellious daughter of a Silver City senator assuring her father, in love, that "I am more / Than ever he bargained for"—she added:

I'm a better critic than a poet. I see my own failings all too clearly. Once long ago I gave up piano playing very abruptly and violently, learning that my hands were too small for any greatness. I hate mediocrity. And I distinctly remember a major operation, with a month in the hospital when I didn't give a damn about outcomes. I didn't care to live, and was not roused until someone brought me a maidenhair fern, and it, sitting in the window, seemed suddenly as frail and yet brilliant as a symbol of life itself.

I dwell on the priorities of Henry Roth because it seems to me now that we lived as castaway brothers, rather than waifs and wards of Eda Lou Walton, during our years on Morton Street—he, at No. 61, I, at No. 48, tandem, but curiously aloof in our comings and goings, watchful of all that bonded and divided us politically, temperamentally, philosophically, biologically, ethnically. Henry's posture to me, as latecomer to the laral sanctities of a household in which I was only a vacationing visitor, was always affectionate, ironic, probational, peripheral: but as we moved from our opposite corners to a center of mutual recognitions that can only be called *linguistic,* the symbiosis became total. On the occasion of a little poem bearing a title from A.E. Housman, "Tarry, Delight" and later rechristened "The Enemy Joy," Eda Lou wrote me:

Henry says you're a "skunk" cheerfully because you've got part of the powder which he wants to use to blow up the world in this poem, and part of his idea and he is going to steal the word "humors" from you right this minute. The truth is the powder he is using is all over the place, like gas in a mine, and the mine is ready to explode . . . You and he, in your separate ways and with your very different temperaments, are really like brothers walking toward the same word.

So long as Henry remained the preoccupation of a lifetime for Eda Lou, the "fierce contentions of friendship" enjoined by Blake as redemptive "contraries" of "spiritual warfare" wrought periodic paroxysms of separation and return. There were confrontations, disasters, Dostoevskian "lacerations," insanities, deflections, rebellions of the most intricate and tormented profundity. I trailed behind, as companion and beneficiary, very near to her heart and her hearth, till she fled to California in a wreckage of litigious divorce proceedings, taking with her the last of her adoptive sons: an adolescent offspring of a trade union provocateur promised posthumous shelter by David Mandel. In the end, as she foresaw, all that she touched turned desert-like, immolative, lapsarian: "Sleepless nights and constant dreams of loss, of *houselessness,* form a distinct symbolic story of how much this has hurt me," she wrote me from California. "I don't know what the next move will be. The story remains sordid and neurotic." And then—characteristically: "*I might even have a room for you if Tom and I take a house.*" One letter later, Eda Lou Walton, in December of 1961, exhausted to the marrow, died of a heart attack. One of her many valedictory pieces will serve as signature for a lifetime:

> We cannot live
> Or give consent
> To the cut, the shut
> And the fugitive.

But "room" had been made: three decades after her first, cautionary letter to me, Eda Lou Walton, with "hands too small for any greatness," had given me all. The "houses" of Eda Lou Walton, for all their antipodal removals and reversals, had as many mansions as the bivouacs of the Hebrews: "desert-mated" as she was to "the cut, the shut, and the fugitive," she lived in perpetual exodus and brought with her no single god of volcanoes and covenants, but a nomad's terrain of promises and diasporas, like the old Semites. To 61 Morton Street she brought an enclave of friends who became the intellectual and spiritual monitors of a lifetime, opened a way to the profession of letters and teaching, and penetrated my identity with a journeyman's longing for self-excess. To name them now is to summon up a cachet of urban and contemporary intelligences like an essence with the same distinctiveness

Hopkins associated with the smell of camphor or the taste of alum: Henry Roth, Kenneth Burke, William Troy, Léonie Adams, Louise Bogan, Horace Gregory, David Greenhood, Morton Dauwen Zabel, and James T. Farrell. With them I can begin a novice's inventory of that "sense of the Past" never given to me as a promissory Jew, a university scholar in the protocol of English Literature, or an amateur of end rhymes and fictions. Their pastness remains *sensuous,* like their minds, because they have stayed with me over the years as part of my accountability for all that is extant, antecedent, and imminent in the contemporaneous, and constitute a presence. I remember the commanding, Hibernian nose of William Troy and the confrontational charge of his glance quite as much as his mythopoeic lunges into the visionary arcana of Virginia Woolf, Thomas Mann, Flaubert, Stendahl, James Joyce, W. B. Yeats, D. H. Lawrence, Hart Crane, and Paul Valéry. I think of the humors of Léonie Adams, turning a conjecture over and over in her forepaws, like a squirrel positioning a chestnut, tossing piquancies in every direction, under her Parisian hairline cut *en frange* across the tilt of her forehead. I see Louise Bogan, Italianate in her squared balance and theatrically looped necklaces, commanding the perspectives of a sumptuous verbal exchange like gold leaf framing a portrait. I hear Kenneth Burke, that prestidigitator and monologist of purest Possibility, with the high frequency of Coleridge, mingling volleys of solitary laughter with Zarathustrian sorties of the most quizzical and recondite incandescence.

But the Morton Street symposia of Eda Lou Walton could never be regarded as a Bohemian preserve over which she presided as duenna or collectionist: on the contrary, she herself tended to disappear in the miscellany of tastes and identities she convened, as listener and bystander, as though her abhorrence of mediocrity had rendered her transparent. Not only did she open up for me the inner sanctums of the *Nation* at a time of shifting editorial priorities; but I owe her, by every direct and indirect accident of contact, my half-century at Bennington College where I was constantly forced to reinvent myself through eight presidential changes, as the protegé of Léonie Adams and William Troy.

IV

A Making of Books: A Thicket for Metaphysicians

Bennington College was ice-bound in the midwinter of my arrival for the "spring" semester. The year was 1938: the first year of an untried apprenticeship to a profession for which I had little reason to consider myself destined: the profession of teaching an undetermined segment of English Literature, by procedures as yet undetermined, to a campus of progressively determined young ladies. I was invited to share an apartment with a member of the Drama Faculty in Franklin House, where the tundra opened on an unobstructed view of Mount Anthony; or I could settle for a boarding-house in North Bennington. I looked one way at the ashen clapboard Americana of provincial Vermont; and the other way, at an indigo blue wall, with

Ben Belitt at Franklin House, Bennington College, 1939

its terra-cotta complement of ceramics, textiles, and Mexican pottery, and decided for Mr. Lauterer. Drama's Mr. Lauterer proved to be long-faced, leggy, and reclusive—a compulsive insomniac, rarely to be seen between his daylong sessions in backstage classrooms and tool shops, and his nightlong meditations over a drawing board: cordial, anonymous, inaccessible, under a thatch of graying hair, holding his chin on the bracket of his thumb and forefinger, like a surveyor's tripod, squinting markedly under the horn of his eyeglasses as though a stage light had been ill-placed or a gelatin had suddenly disfigured what it was intended to disclose. Then the new term of Bennington opened all the way, like a jet from a blowtorch.

I date my acquaintance with Arch Lauterer with the accident of a poem called "Charwoman: 20 Vesey Street," which made its appearance in Franklin House in a belated issue of the *Nation* on February 18, 1938.

Thereafter, our talks, timed to the obsessions and insomnias of my housemate, were always of stages and poems. In as much as Arch Lauterer's knowledge of poetry was not a knowledge, merely, but, like all matters close to his interest, a frenzy, we spoke of poems as often as we did of stages or dances or theaters: of a dance-drama bringing nothing less than the whole of Hart Crane's *The Bridge* to the Bennington College stage in the fall of the following semester. As incumbent collaborator, I was introduced—it was the most sumptuous of his gifts to me—to Martha Hill, to whom all orders and degrees of contemporary dance are massively in debt, and attended the Thursday workshops in the second-floor attic reserved for that purpose. I watched from the sidelines while Lauterer prodded, interpreted, emended, dilated, as though theatrical space were a plane map, like an oceanographer's chart, crossed by invisible zones of latitude and longitude, by tidal pulls, meteorological densities, weathers, magnetic forces—a system of soundings through which the dancer moved like a mariner on an inexhaustible voyage of discovery. I saw his architect's light narrow on his solitary drawing board, watched his pencil trace out the Braille of a dancer's floor plan, his T-square divide and subdivide the spaces, calibrate the relative depths and intensities of a movement, and turn all into a science of radiances. That June, I followed the Summer School of the Dance to Mills College as prentice choreographer in poetry and dance, and was eventually swept into the phantasmagoria of *The Bridge* in the autumn of '38. It was this double commitment to poetry and dance that led to my later collaborations—or collisions—with the art of Martha Graham, and resulted in the addition of four titles to the repertory, or iconography, of contemporary American dance: *Errand into the Maze, Diversion of Angels, A Canticle for Innocent Comedians, A Look at Lightning.*

But other "re-inventions" were at work in the general ferment of a college completing the first decade of its love affair with the untried and the improvisational. A mood of heady empiricism, of collaborative "doing," without program or precedent, rendered all things molten, indivisible, interchangeable, outside the classroom as well as in it, affecting students and faculty equally. In that vat of impetuous interaction, all departmental lines were written in quicksilver, and trespass was habitual. Dance hurtled toward poetry, and both plunged toward a common pedagogical center by *fait accompli* rather than by fiat. At the same time that I was drawn to the prosody of the stage by Arch Lauterer, I was engaged in a two-year tutorial in contemporary French poetry with Wallace Fowlie, who took a major part in *The Bridge,* working backward from Hart Crane to Rimbaud, Baudelaire, Corbière, Valéry,

At work in Shingle Cottage, Bennington College,
1939-40

Mallarmé, and Apollinaire.

I was drawn to the translation of Rimbaud—and then, to García Lorca, Neruda, Machado, Alberti, Borges, Guillén, among others—as a greedy amateur, for my own instruction and pleasure because existing translations, nondescript or incorrigible, forced me all the way back to their originals. My knowledge of French was such that, although I could imagine what the tension and weight of the idiom was in French, I could not get close enough to the excitement of the sound without touching it with English and, as Keats says, "proving it on my own pulses." It takes a poet to catch a poet, a language to trap another language; and, as often as not, a poet comes by a new language—Spanish and Italian, in my own case—or a distant country because he needs to discover precisely where the mind and the ear of another poet fell in his initial choice of the progressions that gave him his poem. That impulse, that originating *enablement,* happens only once and is unique to the language and composition of the original. In the Beginning was, not a Word, or even a Passion, as Coleridge contended, but a pre-verbal urge to *transfer relations:* the relationships between one object and another (which would presumably give us metaphor); between objects and the ideas and feelings to which they give rise (which might give us "metaphysics" or "literature"); between an inner world of the self and an outer world where, in the words of Pablo Neruda, "the hostile and alien begins: all the names of the world/outposts and frontiers/the noun and its adjective that my heart never summoned."

In this sense, *all* is "translation" and all poets constantly translate. An English glossary of words which appear to match those of the foreign original is only one step of which any sophomore with a dictionary and a thesaurus is capable: it is neither faithful nor unfaithful, true nor untrue. It is merely descriptive. Poet-translators, grubbing and spading in the wake of their originals, are constantly surprised by pockets of possibility abandoned by the poet, just as translations often serve to remind the poet of what he thought he had discarded. Though critics and classroom exegetes presume to tell us where poems begin and end, poets and translators never do: the illusion of completion is the first casualty of translation, which has no choice but to place its original in jeopardy. At times it has seemed to me that translation militates against the function of poetry itself; that the poet sends out his words as Jehovah sent out his patriarchs, with the injunction: *Be fruitful and multiply!* while the translator is compelled to divide and conquer. Certainly translation is no vocation for celibates: but the marriages over which the translator presides are not made in heaven. Translation is the language of the Fall. My own translations, based on what George Steiner has called the "radical

Ben Belitt, Pvt., Military Police Battalion, U.S. Army,
Camp Gordon, Georgia, 1943

indeterminacy of language" and the enigmatic nature of all knowing, have been provisional, exuberant, expendable. They have asked the question: "What does a poet know, and how has his language been made to know it?" It has been my premise that all literal translation of poetry is antipoetic, and that word by word and line after line, translation remains insatiable, approximate, apochryphal.

Bronowski, in his essays on the history of science, tells us that Heisenberg invoked what he called an "Uncertainty Principle" in the name of the electron and argued that "no events, not even atomic events, can be described with certainty." Bronowski (who wrote a fine book on Blake) went on to commend another atomic physicist, Niels Bohr, for his twofold role as "founder-father of twentieth-century physics" and "consummate artist"—an "artist" because, says Bronowski, his approach allowed of no ready-made answers. He used to begin his lectures by saying to his students: "Every sentence that I utter should be regarded by you not as an assertion, but as a question." Keats claimed a similar option for "the man of genius, especially in poetry"—the option of remaining negative, raising doubts, enhancing rather than dispelling mystery, cultivating his uncertainties—to all of which he gave the misleading name of "Negative Capability." In doing so, he discovered for all aspects of the poetic transaction— the writing of it, the reading of it, the translation of it—what Heisenberg and Bohr discovered for twentieth-century physics: the volatility of inconclusiveness.

Among the "re-inventions" of Bennington I would also place the upheavals of taste and pedagogical hazard forced upon me from the very beginning by a college upon whose charter the ink had never been allowed to dry. At Bennington, it is customary to speak of a "Golden Age" of the forties and fifties and call up the precursors who rendered it golden: Genevieve Taggard, William Troy, Léonie Adams, Francis Fergusson, Arch Lauterer, Martha Hill, Erich Fromm, Kenneth Burke, Theodore Roethke, Stanley Kunitz, W. H. Auden, Ralph Ellison, Martha Graham, Otto Luening, Stanley Edgar Hyman, Howard Nemerov, Shirley Jackson, Paul Feeley, Clement Greenberg, Bernard Malamud. All shared in the thrust and momentum of an American epoch, in their private character as talents; all reinvented both the modernities and the pastness of a disquieting educational premise as teachers and colleagues at Bennington. Landslide has followed landslide, assessment has undermined assessment, in a progress which has remained skeptical rather than evangelical. During my five decades at Bennington, I have felt their pressures, singular as well as collective,

In Santa Fe, New Mexico, 1947

in the shifting balances of an unappeasable vocation: as teacher, poet, translator, and as destroyer and retriever of an invisible syllabus of literatures and beliefs. The so-called "competencies" of traditional collegial procedure which come ready-made, with the mortarboard and reversed tassels of the "expert," and render their "professors" invulnerable, have constantly yielded to the amateur's surmises and his intimations of things to come. At Bennington the approach has been Faustian rather than fustian: the Doctors have renounced the complacencies of Wittenberg and succumbed to the ravishments of "magic"; the autodidact has transcended the Academy. Time and again, the classroom has served as threshing floor for works in progress, poems or books in the making, possibilities in search of a rationale. Poems, treatises, dances, paintings, avocations, have run their courses, over the years, as mice and mythological champions run their mazes, and returned to the studio or the scholar's study bearing the collective imprimatur of student and teacher. Whole works, such as Fromm's *Forgotten Language,* Stanley Edgar Hyman's *Iago: Some Approaches to the Illusion of His Motivation,* Kenneth Burke's meditations on

Belitt conducting a tutorial with student Susan Wheeler, Bennington College, 1976

rhetoric and motives in Biblical discourse, Wallace Fowlie's "readings" of the French moderns, Francis Fergusson's *The Idea of a Theater*, William Troy's essays on Virginia Woolf and Thomas Mann, were once untried additions to the syllabus of an educational venture. Given that long leash, teachers were constantly impelled to exceed rather than recycle themselves, and students, for a four-year interval, raised their sights like a pole-vaulter's crossbar, to measure their tolerance, and overleap it. Both took away glimpses of self-excess which turned into works of imagination or credentials for a personal identity.

Looking backward toward Bennington, I can perceive a Past taking shape like a wasp's nest or a thicket for metaphysicians, in the image of Marvell's Garden—a sixth sense or aroma of antecedence, "annihilating all that's made / To a green thought in a green shade." It is a landscape exactly fitted to my shadow, full of joinings, cave scribbles, channelings, cat's cradles, transfers of pattern and fingerplay, interstices, entrapments—an integumented web-work of papery leavings moist with my spittle and visceral geometry. In it are libraries, mentors with book-bags, planters and mowers, grandfathers, begetters, adolescents with poised pencils and astonishing improvisations, rabbis of

the fabulous. Classrooms and curricula flicker like swamp fire or planets; chairmen, departments, presidents, courses, pedagogical trial balances are planted and plowed under. Plainest of all is a canon of poems over my signature, calling to Keats, Dostoevsky, Blake, Hopkins, Kafka, Kierkegaard, Shakespeare, Forster, Neruda, Machado, and Crane. All rings like a tuning fork: at long last I have put away booklessness for an edifice of the word and its phantasms. Smerdyakov, Alyosha, Esmiss Esmoor, Prospero, Cleopatra, Job, and Thoreau move through the foliage because they once inhabited a classroom and spoke for a schoolteacher's obsessions. In the distance are Italy and Spain and the gorges of Mexico, because their language and poetry are there. I am what I have taught, teaching as I please because the outcome is incalculable and I think of myself as a work in progress.

BIBLIOGRAPHY

Poetry:

The Five-Fold Mesh. New York: Knopf, 1938.

Wilderness Stair. New York: Grove, 1955.

The Enemy Joy: New and Selected Poems. Chicago: University of Chicago Press, 1964.

Nowhere But Light: Poems 1964-1969. Chicago: University of Chicago Press, 1970.

The Double Witness: Poems 1970-1976. Princeton, N.J.: Princeton University Press, 1978.

Possessions: New and Selected Poems 1938-1985. Boston: Godine, 1986.

Nonfiction:

Adam's Dream: A Preface to Translation (essays). New York: Grove, 1978.

Literature and Belief: Three "Spiritual Exercises" (essay). Bennington, Vt.: Bennington College, 1986.

Translator and Editor of:

Poet in New York: Federico García Lorca. New York: Grove, 1955, 1983; London: Thames & Hudson, 1956.

Selected Poems of Pablo Neruda. New York: Grove, 1961.

Juan de Mairena and Poems from the Apocryphal Songbooks, by Antonio Machado. Berkeley: University of California Press, 1963.

Selected Poems of Rafael Alberti. Berkeley: University of California Press, 1966.

A New Decade: Poems 1958-67, by Pablo Neruda. New York: Grove, 1969.

Splendor and Death of Joaquin Murieta, by Pablo Neruda. New York: Farrar, Straus, 1972; London: Alcove Press, 1973.

New Poems, 1968-1970, by Pablo Neruda. New York: Grove. 1973.

Five Decades: Poems 1925-1970, by Pablo Neruda. New York: Grove, 1974.

Translator of:

Four Poems by Rimbaud: The Problem of Translation. Denver: Swallow, 1947; London: Sylvan Press, 1948.

Skystones: The Selected Poems of Federico García Lorca, translated with others. New York: New Directions, 1955.

Cántico: Selections, by Jorge Guillén, translated with others. Boston: Little, Brown, 1965.

Selected Poems, by Eugenio Montale, translated with others. New York: New Directions, 1965.

A la pintura, by Rafael Alberti. West Islip, N.Y.: Universal Art Editions, 1972.

Selected Poems, 1923-1967, by Jorge Luis Borges, translated with others. New York: Delacorte, 1972.

Las Piedras del cielo, by Pablo Neruda. Easthampton, Mass.: Emanon Press, 1981.

Sound Recordings:

The Poetry of Ben Belitt. New York: J. Norton, 1974.

Outside the Firehouse, North Bennington, Vermont, 1977

Belitt is also the author of numerous articles published in periodicals, including these autobiographical writings:

"A Reading in Kierkegaard." *Quarterly Review of Literature* 55, no. 1 (1947): 67–78.

"In Search of the American Scene," In *Poets on Poetry,* 48–57. New York: Basic Books, 1966.

"The School of the Soldier." *Quarterly Review of Literature* (30th Anniversary Prose Retrospective, 1975): 24–54.

Interviews:

"The Antipodal Man: An Interview with Ben Belitt" (on poetry). *Midway* 12, no. 3: 19–40.

"Words for Dancers, Perhaps: An Interview" (on dance). *Ballet Review* 8, nos. 2 and 3 (1980): 200–42.

"Ben Belitt: An Interview" (on translation). In *The Poet's Other Voice: Conservations,* 57–78. Amherst: University of Massachusetts Press, 1985.

Special issues devoted to Belitt's work:

Voyages 1, no. 1 (1967).

Modern Poetry Studies 7, no. 1 (1976).

Material quoted in this essay is taken from the following publications:

Quotations on pages 50-51 from *The Words* by Jean Paul Sartre. Published by Random House, 1981.

Quotations on pages 51-52 from *Speak, Memory* by Vladimir Nabokov. Published by The Putnam Publishing Group, 1970.

Quotations on page 53 from *David Copperfield* by Charles Dickens. Published by the New American Library, 1962.

Quotations on page 54 from *A Portrait of the Artist as a Young Man* by James Joyce. Published by the Viking Press, 1956.

Marie-Claire Blais

1939-

It has always been very hard for me to talk about myself. As we know, writers of fiction do not necessarily invent but take the reality which they have lived or observed and imbue it with their subjectivity. Often their characters are disguised aspects of themselves, like the fragmented selves which confront and challenge each other in dreams. Even in a novel or a short story it is difficult to write in the first person because the choice of this narrative form (the only true one, according to certain writers and critics) requires a face-to-face meeting with the narrator, which inspires as much terror and bravado as a love-tryst, for it requires absolute honesty. And talking about oneself seems more arduous because one can't take refuge in the role of detached witness faithfully transcribing what an impartial observer might have remembered.

This kind of self-exposure frightens me and it extends beyond my writing to every kind of interview and questionnaire. I think that my reticence remains from an education that taught me that it was as rude to talk about oneself as to help oneself before others. Modesty and reserve were taught me, just as they were taught, more or less successfully, to all young girls of my age. The result is that when people talk endlessly about themselves I associate the habit with vanity or an absence of discretion. But there is also an element of vanity in the decision *not* to talk, though in my case it comes from my wish to remain a witness and to hear what other people have to say.

To talk about oneself is to bring to life times that lie deep in our subconscious memory. Remembering that somewhere in a dusty box were hidden photographs of my childhood, I found them and laid them out at random on a table. I looked at them curiously and saw familiar faces and objects that recalled, like a fragrance or a musical phrase, the faded memories of a past without precise boundaries. I saw again my mother's laced boots, a scarf she sometimes tied under her chin, my grandmother's muff, and then, huge and rounded, my father's first automobile. He is sitting very straight, proudly gripping the wheel, and I am kneeling on the backseat, smiling timidly, one of my hands bent against my chin in an almost worldly attitude, surprising for a five-year-old child. In fact, all the photographs of this period show a strangely serious little girl. In one, dressed in my Sunday-best, I am smiling,

Marc Drolet, Montreal

Marie-Claire Blais, 1985

but my smile doesn't soften my severe look; in another, muffled in a snowsuit on a dismal winter day, I'm walking with a troubled gaze beside my grandmother, a woman with a strong, almost masculine bearing, straight and proud. In still another, my father and I are standing side by side in a shallow lake; my blond childish pigtails are in strange contrast to the grave, fixed expression in my eyes, a tranquil sadness. It wasn't caused just by the unpleasant sensation of cold water on my bare body, for I hated strenuous games and physical exercise when I was little. There was another cause; for as far back as I can remember, I was tormented by metaphysical anguish and by a morbid fear of death, so that I never shared the happy carelessness of other children. When I notice this same anguish in certain children, I wonder how it is that they have the power to imagine suffering so far beyond them and face it as they do in a state of complete moral solitude.

Our life was certainly not an easy one, and perhaps without knowing it my parents conveyed their own anxieties to me. I was born October 5, 1939, at the

mind, he studied refrigeration techniques at a school in Saint-Hyacinthe, then moved to Quebec City and found a job in a factory for the manufacture of dairy products; there, he was responsible for the maintenance and repair of the machinery. At that time, Quebec was in the midst of an economic slump, jobs were rare and salaries low. Many bosses took advantage of the situation by making their employees work long hours for inadequate pay and without overtime, and held the threat of dismissal over their heads. My father worked hard and earned very little, clinging to his

Marie-Claire with her grandmother, about 1941

Marie-Claire and her mother, Véronique, about 1944

beginning of World War II, when the economy was struggling out of the Depression. My father, Fernando Blais, came from a family in Saint-Paul-de-Montmagny, a village close to the American frontier. The Blais family land descended, according to the custom in Quebec, from father to son, most often the eldest son. My father was one of seventeen children with many brothers ahead of him, so he had no hope of inheriting the family farm. Besides, like so many young people of his time he dreamed of living in a city, where, he said, "there was a future." He was bored by farming and the country. He decided to learn a trade with the hope of eventually running his own business. With this in

dream of his own business and considering himself lucky to have a job at all. It was just at this time that he met my mother.

Véronique Nolin was the daughter of a Quebec City carpenter and had always lived in the city. "Your mother lived in the Upper City," said my father proudly. This was the more prosperous part of the city, as opposed to the Lower City. Véronique was a schoolteacher who dreamed of marrying and having children. She and Fernando met in church at Vespers, which isn't surprising to anyone who knows about the link between the history of Quebec and its powerful Roman Catholic Church. I remember that my mother often described the scene of their meeting with a mocking look in her lively, intelligent eyes and added, "Your father has always been faithful to the Church." As for her, she wasn't too fond of priests and pious people and had sworn to herself that her house would never be invaded by frocked clerics sermonizing over one of her good meals. Of course she was a believer,—it was inconceivable not to be at that time,—but less so than my father. His temperament combined with religion made him a fatalist who did not permit himself to be angry or rebellious. He was (and still is) tolerant

Marie-Claire and her father, Fernando, about 1942

and magnanimous and because of this he endured resignedly an exhausting job that gave him hardly any free time. His boss required him to be on call day and night. My mother was outraged by this but swallowed her resentment, and it was only much later when the workers formed a union and went on strike, that she enjoyed the sweet taste of revenge.

I was the eldest of five children: two brothers and three sisters. Since my father was always at work, my mother had the whole task of bringing us up. We didn't see Father much but we knew that his hard work kept the wolf from the door. He had to put aside his dream of being his own master because my mother

thought it would be too risky and that he should wait for a more propitious time. It never came, either because my mother argued him out of it or because, tired of waiting, he gave up the whole idea.

When I emerged from my stubborn or melancholic silence I was a very talkative child, my mother tells me, and I loved having long conversations with the grocer, the telephone operator, and the plumber. Like all children, I loved to have an audience, to dazzle the grown-ups. When I was three or four years old and the adults were chatting in the living room, I used to bring in several volumes of the encyclopedia and pretend to read them with great interest. (I remember a similar scene in Sartre's *Les Mots*.) Enchanted by my precocity, the adults predicted a brilliant career for me.

I was sent to the parish elementary school and then to the Saint-Roch convent where, at my request, I was a boarder for a few months. I was delighted to be rid of household chores and the noisy, importunate presence of my little brothers and sisters, but also because I was surrounded by unfamiliar beings whose lives seemed more fascinating because they were so different from ours. But my exile as a boarder didn't last long for I fell sick and my mother decided that I should live at home, so I became a day-student.

In the course of those years at the convent I discovered literature and the world outside the convent gates and fell in love with books. By a combination of willpower and trickery we could secretly get hold of books we were forbidden to read: Baudelaire, Rimbaud, Verlaine, Flaubert, Balzac, Proust, and later, Zola, Gide, Lautréamont and the Surrealists. I wrote poems for the *Journal du Couvent*, and drafts of novels, and I began to dream about having a career as a writer. The same determined ruses that had enabled me to get books that I wanted was useful when I decided to broaden my culture by studying music. We didn't have a piano at home and my parents had no intention of buying one, so it seemed absurd to my mother that I kept insisting on having lessons. When I saw that she wouldn't give in I pleaded my cause with one of the nuns at the convent, who telephoned my mother to beg her to change her mind. She succeeded without difficulty (I was standing next to her, which infuriated my mother), not because my mother agreed with her argument but because she didn't want anyone to know that we couldn't afford it. I had counted on her pride for the success of my little strategy and my victory filled me with joy—and terror, since I knew what was in store for me at home. The piano was bought and took its place in the living room, and for a few months inspired my frenetic devotion. But I quickly got tired of finger exercises, just as my mother had anticipated, and the piano fell silent except when some visitor arrived who could play it. But this incident which my mother still recalls with annoyance as one of the innumerable examples showing my stubborn and inflexible character, was a valuable lesson which convinced me that if only I were clever, strong-minded, and tenacious enough I could have anything I wanted.

But it was much less simple to persuade my parents that I needed a university education. They had four young children and they wouldn't hear of it. Moreover, they didn't take my passion for literature seriously and dreamed of my having a secure future, assured by my taking a secretarial course. So, much against my will, I had to learn how to type and take dictation. My years at the convent had given me a taste for study and discipline and I still kept my love for the pagan beauty of Roman Catholicism. Perhaps my admiration for Simone Weil, Georges Bernanos, Paul Claudel, and François Mauriac was born of the swarming aesthetic emotions which I think of as my religious feeling. But I hated the Catholic Church, its clergy, the nuns, and the ostracism of all those who were judged to be deviant. Much has been written about the crushing power and omnipresence of the Church in Quebec; the overthrow of the Church's power and the triumph of the laity is still recent enough, I think, to remember the courageous struggle which had its climax in the Quiet Revolution. But I am afraid that we are threatened all over again with a rebirth of a mediaeval kind of religion and that we will be victims again of the same intolerance and bigotry, which in the name of morality once forbade my books to be sold in bookstores. I still have a vivid recollection of the poverty of intellectual life in Quebec at the time when I came of age and I hope never again to see a time when the same kind of religious hysteria will trample on works of art.

Les Manuscrits de Pauline Archange, published in 1968, tells of the struggle of a young woman in this bigoted society to win her freedom as a writer; the three novels which compose it are the story of a painful search for knowledge in an ignorant world which violently rejects everything unfamiliar. I had seen how the efforts of a young immigrant doctor, who lived with his family in our parish, to set up a kind of literary meeting-place, were perceived as suspect and dangerous. He had probably been alarmed by the cultural void he saw around him and foresaw the sad fate that threatened the gifted young people who were being suffocated by a society which frowned on books and ideas. He wanted to make it possible for them to come together, exchange books and read their work. I went enthusiastically to these meetings until, at the instigation of the parish priest, the well-meaning parents forbade their children to go.

And yet it was to a priest, Père Georges-Henri Lévesque, that I owe the publication of my first novel. Père Lévesque had founded the School of Social Sciences at the Laval University and was an admirably progressive man who had done much for the intellectual life of Quebec. With my usual determination, I began to pester him by sending him letters, poems, short stories, and novels, convinced that he would end by being moved, if not by my talent (of which I had no doubt) then by my persistence. At this time I was still living with my parents and had had various jobs: as a clerk in a biscuit factory, a cashier in a bank, a salesgirl in a department store—all with an absence of enthusiasm that exasperated my employers. Seeing that I was determined to write, my mother had fixed up a little worktable in her room where the sound of my typewriter was less likely to wake up the other children, but I always had to stop working when my father wanted to sleep. Since I worked in the daytime and wrote at night, the situation became impossible. I dreamed of an attic room like Balzac's and waited patiently for Père Lévesque to notice me.

Finally, thanks to Père Lévesque, I had the means to rent a room in Old Quebec; it was small and ugly, and freezing in winter but it was "a room of one's own," and just what I needed. I was enchanted by my new domain and surprised by my parents' unhappy reaction, for they thought of it as futile misery that I imposed on myself in the name of a dream of glory, and that it could only lead to defeat and poverty. In vain, they tried everything to convince me—didn't I want a family, children, a decent life?—and then tried to make me more comfortable. On Sundays they came with the children, bringing blankets, clothes, and food so as to be sure that I stayed alive and well, and this with a touching solicitude which my brother Michel remembers to this day. And he remembers his big sister whom he hardly knew, who seemed unique and far away.

My first novel, *La Belle Bête,* was published in 1959 when I was nineteen. In general, the reviews were crushing. The book occasioned a dispute which pitted those who liked it against the others, the more numerous, who claimed to be horrified by it. But it didn't stop me from writing and when I had time I took courses in literature and philosophy at Laval University. But if the severe judgement of *La Belle Bête* didn't completely discourage me, it did frighten me a little and calmed the violence of the mental images I dreamed of using in my work. *Tête Blanche,* which was published a year later, shows this restraint. *La Belle Bête* was an adolescent nightmare brimming with passion and vitality about the erotic love of a mother for her handsome retarded son and the jealous hatred felt for him by his ugly sister. *Tête Blanche* was closer to the classic novel form; it was a study of a gifted young delinquent boy and of his surroundings, his school, and his family. After all the sound and fury of *La Belle Bête* this was a relatively calm book, a little the way *L'Insoumise* would be after the stir caused by *Une Saison dans la Vie d'Emmanuel*.

At the time *Tête Blanche* was published I was still living in Quebec. Exasperated by the narrow provincial life of the city I suddenly decided to leave, and for another reason—that I had fallen in love with a filmmaker who lived in Montreal. I told my parents that I had found a job there and they encouraged me to go, convinced this time that I'd made the right decision. I rented a room in a boardinghouse on Prince Arthur Street and perhaps for the first time in my life had the feeling that I was really free. I was twenty-two years old.

My life in Montreal was composed of writing, reading, music, and German language courses which I took at the Goethe Institute. Now and then I worked in the City Archives, under the wing of Louise Myette who was studying German with me and later became my literary agent. A grant from the Canada Arts Council then allowed me to go to France and there I made enduring friendships. But the thing that really changed my life (and it was something many writers hoped for even if they didn't admit it) was praise and understanding from the great critic, Edmund Wilson.

One summer evening I got home to find a note for me saying that a Mr. Wilson had tried to reach me on the telephone. A few days before that Père Lévesque had told me that a great American critic was coming soon and that it was important for me to meet him. Ironically, I didn't know who Edmund Wilson was, so Père Lévesque hastened to tell me about his work and his great influence and suggested a few books for me to read before his arrival. At that time I was familiar with French literature but had read only a few American writers: some Henry James, Melville, Fitzgerald, Hemingway, Faulkner, and Steinbeck, but I had to read much more, I thought, to be worthy to meet Edmund Wilson. So I rushed to a bookstore to find books to fill the vacuum and began to read as anxiously as if I were preparing for an oral examination.

Edmund Wilson was at that time making a study of Canadian literature (*O Canada,* published in 1965) and he wished to meet some of the writers whose work he was studying. He arranged for us to meet at the Ritz-Carlton where he was staying with his wife, Elena. I had never set a foot in the Ritz, had never even imag-

ined crossing its dazzling threshold under the eyes of the man in uniform, as so many people did with complete indifference. But ever since that first time I've felt a superstitious attraction to the slightly faded charm of the Café de Paris. Its heavy dark blue velvet curtains seem even in the daytime to cast a warm shadow, lit softly by lights which suggest the whispering intimacy of a boudoir. But when I was getting ready to meet Edmund and Elena I was preoccupied by my clothes: a blouse and skirt and a long raincoat which was much too hot for that August afternoon; I felt awkward, ignorant, and timid and I was sure in advance that I was going to disappoint them, for they undoubtedly expected to meet a learned, brilliant, and graceful young woman.

I had counted on having a drink to get me over my shyness but since the waiter thought I was a minor he refused to give me one. I had to dig into a worn little handbag I'd been trying to hide to find my card proving that indeed I had come of age. Edmund found this incident, which happened again several times, very amusing, and couldn't resist mentioning it in his book.

Edmund was very kind to me that day but it was Elena whose smiling gentleness put me at ease. Of my meeting with her that day I remember best the extraordinary brilliance of her blue eyes. Edmund expressed his admiration for my work and promised to recommend me for a grant from the Guggenheim Foundation, which would allow me to write full-time. After we had shaken hands I went off in a state of ecstatic joy and hope, reeling with dreams of the future.

Two long months went by without news and I was sure Edmund and Elena had forgotten me completely. I was even more impatient then than I am now and the delay seemed intolerable. It was the terrible autumn of 1962, when for endless hours we faced the imminent possibility of nuclear war. I remember that people I saw in the street, far from being petrified by the thought that the Soviet Union might not withdraw its missiles from Cuba, went to work as though their changeless routine would prevent the catastrophe and ensure a connection between yesterday and tomorrow. "Worse than dogs, they didn't imagine their own death," wrote Céline about the young soldiers who were about to die on the front, torn to pieces by a shell, but in the meantime, ate, drank, and slept just as usual. Sometimes I think that the indifference and scepticism of many people in the face of the nuclear threat, as though they are hiding their heads in the sand or passively accepting the inevitable, comes from their inability to imagine the horror of it. My books are haunted by my own anguish; in my most recent novels—*Visions d'Anna, Pierre ou la Guerre du Printemps '81*—I have written about the mutilated lives of characters whose *joie de vivre* has been shattered by the piercing light of their vision of disaster. They are enclosed in their state of painful lucidity, unable to feel pleasure which seems futile beside the death of our planet. The young people in these books are no longer fictional characters, but real human beings struggling to survive, broken by their own visions.

A few days after we heard that the Soviet Union had withdrawn its missiles from Cuba I got a friendly letter from Edmund saying that I would certainly get the Guggenheim grant. He also sent me the poems of A.E. Housman and Edna St. Vincent Millay. As he had foreseen, the grant came and in the month of July 1963, I moved to Cambridge, Massachusetts. I found a little apartment which I moved into without even taking the trouble to furnish it properly, for I was in a hurry to begin work on what was to become *Une Saison dans la Vie d'Emmanuel.*

After *Tête Blanche* I had written two books: *Les Voyageurs Sacrés* and *Le Jour est Noir,* half-novels, half-poetry, which because of their lyrical quality seem to me to betray my immaturity then as a writer. But in spite of its weaknesses, *Les Voyageurs Sacrés* still touches me when I reread it because it is a daring attempt to combine music, poetry, and sculpture in a lucid, aesthetic unity, symbolised by the converging paths of the three lovers who meet and embrace each other in various European cities.

Edmund Wilson said that *Le Jour est Noir* re-

Marie-Claire Blais, about 1965

minded him of Walter de la Mare, whose work I had not yet read. With its publication, my reputation in Quebec as a "somber" writer was firmly fixed. From then on, it was customary to speak of me as a depressing writer who loved misery and felt at home in a morbid, ugly world—Ugliness with a capital *U* being the opposite of Beauty, like Good and Evil, in the minds of people who distinguished so easily between virtue and vice. Some of them even said that I used "blackness" as a device to help me write my novels. I was particularly exasperated by this view after the publication, in 1965, of *Une Saison dans la Vie d'Emmanuel;* its biting humor and uncompromising irony were completely ignored by a chorus of reviewers who angrily denounced its falseness and the depravity of the characters. It has often been said that the children in my books have revolting habits, and above all, that I talk too much about them. This way of stigmatizing a book makes me indignant both because it is unjust (I shall say more later about this) and because to me it is a form of literary terrorism which denies an artist the freedom to explore his chosen world. Nevertheless there were certain critics, like Jean Ethier-Blais, who wrote enthusiastically about my book, and I got a favorable reception in the United States and in France, where it won the Prix Médicis in 1966.

In Cambridge I worked on the first draft of my novel and in my free time I discovered the exciting life of an American university-town in the sixties. Edmund had said in one of his letters that he wanted to introduce me to some of his friends in Wellfleet and he brought one of them, Mary Meigs, to Cambridge where the three of us had lunch together. I felt intimidated and fascinated by this tall, thin woman with graying hair and bangs cut just above her blue eyes. I liked her immediately, and was drawn by her uncertain laugh and quick smile, by her grace, and by a sort of elegance in her conversation. Not long after our lunch together, I went to Wellfleet and saw the house where she lived with Barbara Deming, an old house on a hill, with locust trees surrounding it and the pine woods behind. The house and studio were full of books and of her paintings and drawings, and I discovered in her a very good painter who was to introduce me to a world of form and color which until then had been unknown to me. She invited me to work in her studio and to use her brushes and paints, and I discovered an inexhaustible world where I could take refuge and abandon myself as one would to a game without penalties and without any rules. I got into the habit of illustrating my notebooks and the margins of letters, and I quickly took over this new space, a place of repose where my anguish and agitation as a writer, the tangle of emotions that threatened to choke me, were soothed

Mary Meigs (left) and Barbara Deming, 1966

and dissipated.

When Mary invited me to live in her house, I left Cambridge for Wellfleet, a haven of peace, where I looked forward to being able to do some good work. Mary and Barbara led a healthy and disciplined life which by contrast to my own—disorderly and impulsive—seemed almost monastic. They lived a kind of golden mean, without any excesses, went to bed early and got up early in order to work. I did my best to imitate them, partly because I didn't want to disturb their working times, and also because I felt vaguely ashamed of my restlessness and imprecise schedule when I felt that I was under their ascetic gaze. I also felt that for the time being their rigor was good for me and would help me in my work. It seemed to me that I was being shown the way of most writers, which was to shut oneself up in one's room and work for a certain number of hours every day. I worked "like an angel," Mary said in her book, *Lily Briscoe: A Self-Portrait.* And in fact, I did a tremendous amount of work during those years in Wellfleet, which I might not have done as well in other circumstances, particularly since I wasn't in good health. But now I don't practice that kind of discipline anymore. I need to be in perpetual motion, travelling, writing as I go, wherever my needs or my phantasy tells me to go. My writing has come to need this kind of movement; it has taken on its color and is reflected in long sentences like ocean waves with hardly any punctuation to slow their rhythm.

In Wellfleet, even if I was an exemplary disciple, I needed to get away from my too-calm life and dive into the delicious excitement of a city. I needed streets swarming with complicated lives, bars full of slightly crazy or melancholy people, the feeling of living dangerously. This need, which I have had since I was a small child, reminds me of one of Colette's heroines, Minne. Sometimes it would get me into situations that were really dangerous, but most of the time it helped to sharpen my imagination which proceeded almost without my knowing it to create a danger that wasn't really there. I laugh when I think about it now; nevertheless my ventures into unknown worlds gave me valuable impressions which I would use in the novels that were already beginning to take shape in my mind.

Our life in Wellfleet, in spite of its happy moments, was difficult for me because I had no place in that closed little society, and I spoke hardly any English. Our happiest times were spent together. I remember the hours we spent reading out loud and I can still hear Barbara's grave voice reading Ibsen's *The Wild Duck,* which, along with *The Doll's House,* is the Ibsen play I like best.

Barbara (who died in 1984) was an extraordinary being who was ready to give her life for the causes she believed in. Once she had committed herself she never wavered and she always remained loyal to her beliefs. She was active in the pacifist and civil rights movements which became more radical in response to the violence unleashed against the non-violent demonstrations of Martin Luther King, Jr. and his followers. If a political action ended in prison Barbara saw it out to the end. She was in prison many times and spent a month in the Albany, Georgia, jail, an experience which inspired her beautiful book *Prison Notes.*

The pacifist movement became more powerful with the increased involvement of the USA in Vietnam. Sometimes, members of the New England Committee for Non-Violent Action would gather in our house to discuss strategies, which included fasting and non-violent actions. Neither Mary nor I was capable of living with Barbara's fervor and we continued our work as artists, but with feelings of guilt. Almost every day I wrote down my reflections on the day's events, on the activists who came to the house, and I smile now at my scruples of conscience, exacerbated by the indomitable courage of Barbara. As I leafed through these notebooks full of watercolors and crayon drawings, I came on a newspaper clipping about an American Quaker who set himself on fire on the steps of the Pentagon as a protest against the war. The horror of this

Mary Meigs, about 1981

was quickly forgotten in the flood of atrocities committed in Vietnam, but it made a profound impression on me. François Reine, one of the characters in my novel *David Sterne,* kills himself in the same way, and his friend David is deeply troubled by François' intransigence, his insistence on a sacrifice that will do nothing to stop the war, on his own useless death. "Cursed be the martyrs, who are loved neither by God nor men!" says David Sterne. "Whether it be heaven or hell, whether the flame rises straight and pure into the sky or races across the dry plain, what difference does it make to us, François Reine? Aren't our bodies embers extinguished in the same way? Don't we always rediscover the same void, the same nothingness at the moment of death?"

During those troubled days I kept on working as hard as ever. *Une Saison dans la Vie d'Emmanuel* had won the Prix Médicis and my editor, Jacques Hébert, decided that Les Editions du Jour would do a deluxe edition with Mary's illustrations. I had been amazed by the richness of imagination of her drawings which were unlike anything else she had done and gave me the feeling that I was in real communication with another artist. When I wrote the book I intended it to be tender and humorous, casting an ironic eye on the tragedy and cruelty of humble lives. It is true that the setting is one of extreme hardship but the characters are full of life, of sensuality, and friendship. And it is in a comic spirit that Jean-Le-Maigre, le Septième, and even Héloïse, who leaves her convent to enter a brothel, try to survive and rebel against destiny. Far from being lugubrious, the book is brimming over with vitality and ferocious humor, and a rebellious dignity and grace are shown in Jean-Le-Maigre's refusal to give way to sadness and bitterness. Mary gave form to all my beloved characters.

After *Une Saison dans la Vie d'Emmanuel* I wrote *L'Insoumise,* an impressionistic book in softer colors, in which the characters are imprecise sketches of people which suggest how opaque and impenetrable human beings are to those who try to discover their mysteries or understand the fragile links which hold them together. They are unsuccessful and wander anxiously in uncertainty and doubt, holding tight to their own secrets and their own suffering. In *Visions d'Anna,* published in 1982, there is another kind of invading fog, induced by drugs; it has almost an autonomous existence which threatens Anna's life. She is helpless to get rid of it and sinks into a comatose state which affects everything she experiences. *Visions d'Anna* for me is about life as a dream shown in a succession of fugitive images bound by a steady rhythm, as regular as that of sleep.

At the time I was writing *L'Insoumise* I was also

Mary Meigs in her studio in Kingsbury, Quebec, 1980

working on a play, *L'Exécution,* the hero of which, Louis Kent, was to find his full stature in my latest novel, *Pierre ou la Guerre du Printemps '81.* The play was produced in Montreal by the Théâtre du Rideau-Vert, directed by Yvette Brind'Amour. At about the same time, a film version of *Une Saison dans la Vie d'Emmanuel,* which had been made in France by Claude Weiss, also was shown in Montreal. I came often to Quebec in connection with my work as a writer and spent a couple of summers in a somewhat flimsy prefabricated house Mary and I had had placed on a piece of land I bought near the beach in Grande-Vallée, in the Gaspé Peninsula. The house was battered by storms even in summer and was blown down by a particularly ferocious gale one winter. We had also acquired a big piece of land in Val-David and had had a sugaring-house rebuilt and insulated so that it served as a refuge, a place of silence and peace. It is still there among the old maples, and a jungle of young spruces and maples has grown up around it. I still have a dream of transforming the land into an artists' colony.

In 1970, Mary and I moved to France and lived for four years in an old house in Brittany—La Salle en Sulniac—and in a succession of apartments in Paris, where I went to see friends, to work and to absorb the life of the city. It was both in Paris and in Montreal that I found material in the streets and in bars for my two books which study homosexual love: *Le Loup* and *Les Nuits de l'Underground;* Lali, in the latter, and Sébastien, in the former, live only for love and sex, drawn to the beings they meet "in the warm shadows of a bar." The characters in both books talk about homosexual love with complete naturalness and simplicity, without guilt-feelings, at times denouncing the hypocrisy of people who lead a double life which they think they are hiding when they noisily condemn what they are living in secret: ". . . as fathers they punish what they cherish as lovers." Lali and Sébastien celebrate their freedom to love while living lives that hold little promise of happiness.

Two other novels are the result of my shuttling between two continents and come out of the meeting of

Marie-Claire Blais and Mary Meigs at La Salle en Sulniac, Britanny, 1973

two worlds which are slowly coming together in Quebec and France. *Un Joualonais, sa Joualonie* reminds us by its title of the inebriating awakening in Quebec, when we glorified for a while our impoverished French, called *joual*, in a rebellious attempt to be different from the mother-country, or to have an identity of our own. *Une Liaison Parisienne*, on the other hand, is about a naïf young poet who falls in love with a bourgeoise Frenchwoman and then lives her life of perverse refinement, scented with the perfume and culture of old France. This woman, Madame d'Argenti, has nothing in common with Florence, the heroine of *Le Sourd dans la Ville*, who breaks all her ties to her bourgeois milieu to engage in a solitary journey towards death. I wrote this book while I was alone in the Alps and in a little inn in Hudson, Quebec; this relentlessly lucid book which perhaps seems sharp and hard, is nevertheless my favorite. In the book, people, animals, even a chair which falls over in an empty room, are invested with radiant life and the most despairing characters know that nothing is more precious than the lives that they may lose.

After several years of exploring Mexico and the

Caribbean Islands, where I met the young people I wrote about in *Visions d'Anna* and in *Pierre ou la Guerre du Printemps '81*, I decided to live for a few months of the year in Key West, at the end of the Florida Keys, a little town full of light, of sweet-smelling flowers and tropical plants; as a northerner deprived of sun and warmth in winter, I never cease to be delighted by it. I've become deeply attached to "my" island and to my friends there. I spend hours watching the ocean and the milky transparency of the water that slides up the beach. I think of Tennessee Williams who lived and worked there such a short time ago as I silently watch his cousin, Stella, reading my hand, her head bent over misfortunes she sees and would like to wish away. Barbara Deming, too, only two years ago was still working on her own nearby island, Sugarloaf Key, struggling bravely and unsuccessfully against cancer. I think of "Grass," the first poem in James Merrill's *Late Settings:*

> The river irises
> Draw themselves in.
> Enough to have seen
> Their day. The arras

Also of evening drawn,
We light up between
Earth and Venus
On the courthouse lawn,

Kept by this cheerful
Inch of green
And ten more years—fifteen?—
From disappearing.

Time goes so swiftly. We write to survive, to escape death—that was the aspiration of Pauline Archange, who had the pretentious naïveté of her years. At forty-six, having lost most of my illusions, wouldn't I say that one writes because life is unbearable without the solace of writing? I am sitting on the beach beside a child who is carefully torturing his soldier-toy without the least desire to hide his cruelty, and my mind is already busy with the task of describing the somewhat terrifying aspect of this little being lost in primitive fantasies. I try ceaselessly to plumb the depths of human nature, extract heavy ore which I have to turn into something light and fluid. I have a book about Virginia Woolf on my knees, and read what she repeated herself: "Sacrifice nothing to the clarity of my vision." I have the painful task of creating a limpid, transparent style which will carry the subjects which obsess me. I tirelessly pursue this fugitive idea, indefinable, which,

like love, is like a mirage that draws me toward the horizon forever, in pursuit of something intangible. But isn't it this vision of the ideal, like the vision of the beloved, which spurs us on and sometimes even recalls us to life?

BIBLIOGRAPHY

Fiction:

La Belle Bête. Quebec: Institut Littéraire, 1959. Translation by Merloyd Lawrence published as *Mad Shadows.* Toronto: McClelland & Stewart, 1960; Boston: Little, Brown, 1960; London: J. Cape, 1960.

Tête Blanche. Quebec: Institut Littéraire, 1960. Translation by Charles Fullman published as *Tête Blanche.* Toronto: McClelland & Stewart, 1961; Boston: Little, Brown, 1961; London: J. Cape, 1962.

Le Jour est Noir. Montreal: Editions du Jour, 1962. Translation by Derek Coltman published as *The Day Is Dark.* New York: Farrar, Straus, 1966.

Une Saison dans la Vie d'Emmanuel. Montreal: Editions du Jour, 1965. Translation by Derek Coltman, with an introduction by Edmund Wilson, published as *A Season in the Life of Emmanuel.* New York: Farrar, Straus, 1966; London: J. Cape, 1967; Toronto: Bantam, 1976.

L'Insoumise. Montreal: Editions du Jour, 1966. Translation by David Lobdell published as *The Fugitive.* Toronto: Oberon, 1978.

Les Voyageurs Sacrés. Montreal: HMH, 1966. Translation by Derek Coltman published as *Three Travelers* in *The Day Is Dark* [and] *Three Travelers.* New York: Farrar, Straus, 1967.

David Sterne. Montreal: Editions du Jour, 1967. Translation by David Lobdell published as *David Sterne.* Toronto: McClelland & Stewart, 1973.

Manuscrits de Pauline Archange. Montreal: Editions du Jour, 1968. Translation by Derek Coltman published as *The Manuscripts of Pauline Archange.* New York: Farrar, Straus, 1970; Toronto: McClelland & Stewart, 1982.

Vivre! Vivre! (second book of *Manuscrits de Pauline Archange*). Montreal: Editions du Jour, 1969. Translation by Derek Coltman published as the second part of *The Manuscripts of Pauline Archange.* New York: Farrar, Straus, 1970; Toronto: McClelland & Stewart, 1982.

Les Apparences (third book of *Manuscrits de Pauline Archange*). Montreal: Editions du Jour, 1970. Translation by David Lobdell published as *Dürer's Angel.* Vancouver: Talonbooks, 1976.

Le Loup. Montreal: Editions du Jour, 1972. Translation by Sheila Fischman published as *The Wolf.* Toronto: McClelland & Stewart, 1974.

Un Joualonais, sa Joualonie. Montreal: Editions du Jour, 1973. Translation by Ralph Manheim published as *St. Lawrence Blues.* New York: Farrar, Straus, 1974; London: Harrap, 1975.

Marie-Claire Blais in Kingsbury, Eastern Townships, Quebec, 1981

Une Liaison Parisienne. Montreal: Stanké/Quinze, 1975. Translation by Sheila Fischman published as *A Literary Affair.* Toronto: McClelland & Stewart, 1979.

Les Nuits de l'Underground. Montreal: Stanké, 1978. Translation by Ray Ellenwood published as *Nights in the Underground: An Exploration of Love.* Toronto: General Publishing, 1979; New York: Beaufort Books, 1983.

Le Sourd dans la Ville. Montreal: Stanké, 1979. Translation by Carol Dunlop published as *Deaf to the City.* Toronto: L. & O. Dennys, 1980.

Visions d'Anna. Montreal: Stanké, 1982. Translation by Sheila Fischman published as *Anna's World.* Toronto: L. & O. Dennys, 1985.

Pierre ou la Guerre du Printemps '81. Montreal: Primeur, 1984.

Published Plays:

L'Exécution. Montreal: Editions du Jour, 1968. Translation by David Lobdell published as *The Execution.* Vancouver: Talonbooks, 1976.

Fièvre, et Autre Textes Dramatiques. Montreal: Editions du Jour, 1974.

L'Océan [suivi de] Murmures. Montreal: Quinze, 1977. Translation published as *The Ocean.* Toronto: House of Exile, 1977.

La Nef des Sorcières. Montreal: Quinze, 1977.

Selected Productions:

La Roulotte aux Poupée, Quebec.

Eleanor, Quebec.

L'Exécution, Montreal, 1967.

Poetry:

Pays Voilés. Quebec: Garneau, 1963. Translation by Michael Harris published as *Veiled Countries* in *Veiled Countries* [*and*] *Lives.* Montreal: Vehicule Press, 1984.

Existences. Quebec: Garneau, 1964. Translation by Michael Harris published as *Lives* in *Veiled Countries* [*and*] *Lives.* Montreal: Vehicule Press, 1984.

Editor of:

The Oxford Book of French-Canadian Short Stories, with Richard Teleky. New York: Oxford University Press, 1980.

Brigid Brophy

1929-

A CASE-HISTORICAL FRAGMENT OF AUTOBIOGRAPHY

Brigid Brophy, with Darius, 1978

On the last day of 1979 I was ambushed by my closest ally. I experienced catastrophic grief.

The psychological and many of the social constructs through which I had been negotiating my environment trembled. Chunks of my history threatened to tumble into the limbo of nonvalid concepts. Doubt and malfunction attended all that was disclosed to have rested, for longer than a decade, on my mere gullibility towards lies and masquerades systematically thrust on me.

In the impact of shock, my personality, always mildly lacking in the narcissism that a psyche needs if it is to hold together, looked likely to fly apart.

I was saved by the love, wits, and wit of Michael Levey, my husband, who was himself not unscathed by an act that he, too, had conceived to be inconceivable and that forced us to redraft in haste both the design and the hour-to-hour logistics of our life; and by another fellow writer, who, despite the turmoils that beset her at the time, extended me unconditional love and wit.

I sought psychotherapeutic advice. Friends, including Michael's and my daughter, Kate Levey, took my wreckage in tow and tugged me towards a regained conviction that my work and existence might be, in no matter how nugatory a sense, worthy of pursuit.

At night I still grieved and puzzled. My night thoughts shaped a curious metaphor, by which I was curiously obsessed: without committing any crime the laws would recognise, my assailant had yet contrived to maim and incapacitate me permanently.

By November 1982 I was tolerably sure of not inflicting tedium on them if I accepted invitations from my friends for meetings less snatched than encounters at committees.

Towards the end of the month I spent a morning tending by telephone some of the concerns of the authors' collecting society of which I am one of the founders, dashed through some minimal shopping, and went in the afternoon to a committee of writers' trade unions. That evening I left Michael, who is a gifted cook, to his own vegetarian supper and the completion of an article he was writing. In the dark I set out again from our flat in SW5, found a cab, and had myself taken to NW1, there to visit Elizabeth Jane Howard in her newly acquired house.

Pleasingly decorated and dressed by Jane, it is a smallish unit of the admirable 1790-to-1840ish architecture of that part of London.

When I had thoroughly seen and taken pleasure in the house, Jane and I walked round to the main road, where she had chosen an Italian restaurant for our dinner, because that would not impose it on Jane but would without fuss cater for my veganism.

It was already lateish, by the standards I observed, on a sharply but handsomely cold night. In minor anxiety I silently bade myself make no delay after dinner about seeking a cab for my return. Michael could not keep late hours because he went off early on weekday mornings, and I had never mastered the skill of sliding into our flat and bed without disturbing him.

At dinner Jane and I talked happily: about the Writers' Guild, our trade union, on whose elected council we have both served, and about politics, which a politick rule in its constitution prevents the Guild from having but which Jane and I both have—on opposite sides, as if to demonstrate why a union of writers must eschew party, but amusingly often in agreement.

We paid the bill for dinner, I fumbling over the numerical and social arithmetic of the tip, and initiated our departure.

There a barrier bisects my memory.

In the next scene to enter my awareness, Jane was absent and Michael present. I questioned him and he

Sir Michael Levey, Director, National Gallery, London, 1973-1986

replied that Jane was well and had done better than well but he had urged her home because it was beyond two in the morning.

While we held that conversation I was lying on a trolley in the casualty department of University College Hospital.

It was evident that something had not unspectacularly falsified my hopes alike of not perturbing Jane and of not disturbing Michael, but I had no idea what.

A doctor arrived and told me that my skull had been X-rayed and shewn to be intact, that he was about to stitch up the gashes, of which I had been until then unaware, in my face, and that I could eventually seek the removal of the stitches from my usual local doctor.

I was advised to stay overnight in the hospital for fear of concussion. Michael managed, however, to summon a hired car by telephone and to persuade the doctor at the hospital to let him take me home in it.

My first action during the next ten days was to thank and apologise to Jane.

For the rest, I had no concussion and made visits to my doctor's surgery, on the last of which I was relieved of the stitches.

By rehearsing in my mind the events of that day I

discovered that I had detailed and continuous memory up to the point where Jane and I were on the verge of quitting the restaurant. The transactions at the hospital informed me that I must have been knocked out by some bang to the head. My memory included nothing that could be a preliminary to that. I deduced that the bulk of my blacked-out interval represented time when I was unconscious but that a section of it was the product of retrospective amnesia, which had crept backwards from whatever the event was that had induced it.

Forgivingly, Jane offered, when I telephoned her, to relate to me what she knew of the incident I could not remember.

Jane told me this.

On leaving the restaurant we decided that the most likely place for a cab was the intersection of the main road we were on, which runs downhill, and the other large main road of the area, which crosses it at the bottom of the hill. Staying on the right-hand pavement, we set off to walk there.

Expressly to contradict in advance any figments

Elizabeth Jane Howard

to which I might seek to ascribe what happened a minute or two later, Jane told me that we were definitely sober and that, as we walked down the road, we talked "amicably."

Before we had walked far I suddenly and without explanation detached myself from Jane's company and ran "very fast" across the road, which was virtually empty of traffic. When I reached the curb at the opposite side I must, Jane considered, have tripped, though she did not see me do so. What she did see was that I fell down and lay unmoving. "I thought you were dead," she told me, but when she crossed to me she found me no more than unconscious and bloodied. She did her best to succour me. In doing so she saw and picked up from the gutter or the pavement a ring that had slipped off my finger as I fell.

Jane managed to attract the attention of a policeman, which cannot have been easy at that empty time of night. He walkie-talkied for an ambulance while Jane returned to the restaurant we had just left, whence she telephoned Michael.

Jane then argued her way into the ambulance with me and sat inside it holding my hand. When the ambulance divulged, by arriving there, which hospital it had taken us to, she again telephoned Michael and told him where to come. When he arrived she gave him my ring.

In that narrative the items that impressed me most but least surprised me were those that incarnated Jane's efficiency and the imaginative quality of her kindness.

A little of what she found inexplicable I could reconstruct, conjecturally, by extrapolation from knowledge and from what I did remember of the evening, particularly my anxiety to reach home before Michael should be asleep.

Many years before, I had lived in that neighbourhood. My sense of direction is deeply deficient. Even so, I must have given informed assent to the idea that the likeliest place for a cab was the main intersection. Equally, however, I will have known that as we walked towards it we were walking away from another intersection, from which, though less probably, a cab might approach.

I think that, on a night virtually empty of traffic noise, my ear, which has the acuteness acquired by a nondriver much dependent on cabs, heard the distinct diesel sound of the motor of a London taxicab somewhere in the distance behind us. There was no guarantee that it would come in our direction or be free if it did, but I conceive that I crossed the road in order to be well-placed to hail it on the side of the road it must, if it came at all, drive down. I left Jane abruptly, I think, in a resolution to secure the cab first, should it present itself, and make my explanations and farewells afterwards.

That I ran, by Jane's account, very fast was not odd. No champion sprinter went to waste in me, but I could run short distances tolerably fast. Doing so gave me intense and exhilarating pleasure. Few opportunities to run occurred in the life of an urban intellectual and I was often inhibited by fear of dishevelment, but I took what opportunities or pretexts I socially could. Grandmaternity, which vested me earlier in 1982 and gave me a personal delight I had never expected from something that required neither effort nor even volition on my part, seemed no reason to drop the habit.

My taste for running contrasted with my distaste for walking. True, brought up by parents who walked for fun, I walked ten miles of the Lake District in a day when I was three. The exploit was much cited to me later, but by way of reproach. As soon as I emerged from the compliance and passivity of prepuberty I discovered that I was bored by walking. I never learned Bernard Shaw's technique of thinking while doing it. In adulthood I evaded walking whenever I could. When it was not to be evaded I did it at a pace that disconcerted most companions except Michael, not because I liked walking fast but with the same motive that made me do most chores at top speed, namely, to have it done with as soon as might be.

Whether the cab I think I was planning to hail truly did come down that road that night I do not know. Jane thought not but understandably, given her preoccupations to my benefit, could not be sure. My conjecture had in any case to stop with my resolve to have it if it did. What happened when my run took me to the opposite side of the road I could not even conjecture, and seven months passed before I became able to.

E arly in the June of 1983 Michael and I dined with Francis King.

Francis was already a friend of long standing when, in 1972, he, Michael, and I were three-fifths of the posse of five writers who created WAG (Writers Action Group). Braving multifarious wrath, we invited writers of all types to join and campaign for publicly funded annual payments to authors in proportion to the annual number of loans of their books from public libraries. Seven years of tumultuous struggle later, WAG achieved the passage of the Act of Parliament we sought. We had argued justice to a prime minister and many ministers; we had demonstrated to civil servants the electronic and statistical methods that could compute each author's tally of loans. Even after the Act of 1979 WAG had, through me, to negotiate with the civil servants the administrative machinery they were to set

up, and only in 1982, when the machinery was poised, could I write the last of WAG's newsletters to its members and signal WAG's autodestruction.

It was thus a tidy decade of my life that was chewed and eaten by my function as co-organiser of WAG. In *A Guide to Public Lending Right,* a book I wrote in response to an enterprising commission, I recount the history of the quest in Britain, where it was initiated by my father. In keeping with the anti-autobiographical temperament I am at this moment trying to defy, my account is compact and tucked at the end of a volume the bulk of which is a multinational conspectus of rationale and technique. In the title of my book I had to accept and use, since I had failed to shift it, the name which the entitlement and the payments bear in English-speaking countries and under which they were legislated into being in Britain. The name is non-self-explanatory and perhaps positively misleading. It is in fact a fossil, dumped on the official mind by a discarded idea. Canadian PLR, announced in 1986, has a more sensible name: Payment for Public Use.

For my devotion to the struggle I have happily received thanks, praise, book dedications, and two awards from literary bodies, most of them shared with the other organiser of the campaign. Although I was indeed a happy recipient, the truth is that nothing I did could have been done but for the generosity and patience of Michael, and that the whole experience was a grand adventure, exhausting, perilous, and heartwringing but almost always instructive and always completely absorbing.

Francis's dinner party was the occasion of Michael's and my first meeting with him after the triumph and the dissolution of WAG. Francis had assembled Isobel English, Neville Braybrooke, and Kay Dick, all of them writers and warriors in WAG's cause, and Penelope Hoare, whose history as a publisher had several times intertwined with mine as a writer and whom Michael and I had last met at a celebration in connexion with a book whose text is by me.

All his guests were old acquaintances of Francis, of Michael and me and, for the most part, of one another. The evening was memorably delightful by reason of those reunions and also through the flexible hospitality as well as the flexible conversation of Francis, who possesses a gift I take to be rare in writers: in talk with him you encounter the tones and themes you enjoy in his novels. He talks about people and does not shroud his acute insights but there is never a suspicion of malice because he is so intently interested in the people concerned. I sometimes think that Francis feels towards his whole human acquaintance and many of the dogs and cats who engage his affection the unresting and unflinching concern that a novelist feels towards his char-

Francis King

Miriam Nicholas

acters.

My enjoyment of Francis's dinner party veiled for a time a minor episode I experienced on Michael's and my way there.

Our taxi from our part of Kensington to his took us along one of the quiet and domestically attractive roads north of the High Street until its route was crossed by the road that contains Francis's house. At the crossroads our driver paused, pushed back the communication panel and asked us if he should turn left or right. I had visited Francis more recently than Michael had and felt convinced that his house was a couple of doors down to the left. From experience in many cities Michael knows that such a conviction on my part argues a high probability that the truth lies up to the right—but not the infallible certainty that would transform my frailty into a useful gift. As it turned out, I was on that occasion correct. Michael made, however, the rational decision and told our driver that we would dismount at the key crossroads he had brought us to and walk the rest. We got out. While Michael stood paying the driver, I strolled the couple of intervening paces to the pavement, where I intended to wait for Michael. When I reached the curb I found it impossible to raise my foot in order to step up.

I waited, deliberately relaxing my muscles, and then stepped onto the pavement without trouble.

I was, however, curiously shaken by an inability of a kind I had never encountered before. On the inner side of the pavement, conveniently just in front of me and conveniently low, there was the wall of someone's front garden. I sat on it for a minute. When Michael had paid the cab-driver, who drove away, he joined me; I told him briefly what had happened and he waited sympathetically until I was enough myself to indicate that we should go on to Francis's.

The pleasure of the dinner party, plus work to be done, hid the significance of the episode from both of us for some days. Then I recognised that I had felt shaken because I had, in fact, experienced something of the kind before, although I could not remember doing so. On the evening I happily spent with Elizabeth Jane Howard I ran full tilt across the main road. I naturally could not stop dead. If, when I reached the curb opposite, I found myself unable to raise my foot and step onto the pavement to wind down my run there, then it was inevitable that I should lose balance and, rather in the manner of a stalled aircraft, tumble headlong.

Within a few days the episode on our way to Francis's proved to be no—as I thought of it—*hapax legomenon*. Beautiful and useful items from my classical training have fled from my memory, but that scholarly tag in ancient Greek, whose meaning is "one-off," adheres to the idiom of my thoughts. I expect it is a memorial to my deep unsatisfactoriness as a scholar both of Greek and of my college at Oxford. The college gave me, and I was glad to have because it virtually relieved my parents of fee-paying, an unusual scholarship that was awarded, at no regular frequency, to an "exceptional" candidate, who might be reading any subject whatever, whenever one cropped up in the entrance examination. From the moment I set green foot in Oxford I was technically the senior scholar of my college. I did not take the status seriously, considering it only a kindly excuse for giving me money. A natural egalitarian, I thought it would be impolite to go round slapping the tails of my scholar's gown in the faces of colleagues more experienced than I was, and I declined or ignored most of the privileges extended me. Only by disaster did I learn that my conduct was construed as cavalier disregard of my responsibilities.

A persistent though sporadic difficulty in moving about fell on me that high summer of 1983 while I fulfilled two commissions, both greatly to my liking. In the first half of June I was to lecture to a copyright conference in London. At Oxford I had pursued the "special subject" of formal (Aristotelian) logic, which has given form though not formality to my thinking and arguing ever since and from which I borrowed some of the code names that medieval scholars devised for types of syllogism to use in my novel *In Transit*. At Oxford logic was considered a mere way-in to philosophy, the end destined for undergraduates who began by reading classics. As I had neither aptitude for philosophy nor any belief in its value to anyone, my hope was to swerve from the orthodox route and progress from Latin and Greek to a congenial subject. I explored my chances of becoming a psychoanalyst, resting my case on Freud's advocacy of lay analysis, but the route was of course blocked by the compact in Britain under which the psychoanalytic movement agreed that its practitioners should be people who had qualified in medicine. I did not persist because even my interest in psychoanalysis was outdone by my vocation for writing. I needed, however, something that would let me take a degree without philosophy, and perhaps my inability to find it made the disaster of my academic career inevitable. Logic would have suited me splendidly but for its being linked to philosophy. The immediate practical good I had of it was the mechanical and relaxed delight of doing its puzzles, which served me as, I imagine, knitting serves some of my friends. Only when, as a chairman of a committee of the Writers' Guild, I decided that someone ought to become knowledgeable about copyright, did I discover a second type of intellectual knitting, and I have enjoyed few of my tasks so much as my vice-chairmanship of the British Copyright Council.

My lecture that summer was on the subject of Public Lending Right; and the nub of what I had to tell a copyright conference was that in Britain there is no connexion whatever between PLR and copyright—for the cardinal reason that British copyright law, unlike West German, does not invariably make the copyright in a work the property in the first place of the creator of the work and, even when it is his, does not make it inalienable from him throughout his lifetime.

The end of June and the beginning of July I spent as I have done every summer of my adult life: watching, nowadays on the television screen, Wimbledon. That I should have done in any case. That year I did it the more happily because the residue of the bourgeois work-ethic or of nonconformist conscience that can still smoulder in my socialist and atheist breast was tranquilized. Giles Gordon, my friend, fellow writer, fellow member of WAG and literary agent, had, not for the first time, secured me a commission to write about the championships. In pursuit of it, he helped me acquire tickets, so that one day of the championships I spent sitting not before the television but, in Michael's company, above the Centre Court.

Even so, I sat uncomfortably. There had developed a stutter in my gait, sometimes, though not always, when I wanted to step onto a pavement. I could find no correlation with any particular circumstance. I slowed down my habit of doing everything at top speed and walked cautiously. I had a number of tall, slim umbrellas in a number of colours. I took to taking one

with me whenever I went out. Though it was a fine day, I took one to the copyright conference and leaned on it while I lectured. I felt more foolish still when I did the shopping in a shower and I persisted in carrying an inviolably furled umbrella.

Much as I enjoyed Wimbledon, I found the journey there by underground and bus perilous to my disturbed sense of bodily balance. Soon I found household chores perilous and left many of them to Michael, who had always done his share of them and more. I was incapacitated for days at a time by a sensation I likened to an experience I have, to my regret, never in literal reality had, floating, among up-and-down currents of air, in an airship.

My doctor, whom I invoked, plausibly suspected that my ability to walk was impaired by arthritis and sent me for X-ray to a local hospital. The X-ray disclosed no more arthritis than was "to be expected" at my age, which was then fifty-four. Before July was quite out, I kept an outpatients appointment at a big general hospital. I was given a thorough-going physical examination by the head of the unit whose clinic I was attending and afterwards questioned by several of its doctors. I did not expect but should not have been surprised to meet prejudice against my vegan diet, but medical fashion had changed. No disapproval met me. I was asked to prepare a two-days' list to shew in practice what I did eat. I went home and typed one, a task for which I had served a long apprenticeship in complying with frequent requests from strangers for recipes or menus for inclusion in "celebrity" cookery books. I took my list to later visits to the clinic, but it was never asked for. I did, however, politely resist the doctors' description of my airship-like symptom as "dizziness," because I had no illusion of spinning. I thought that, if I insisted on an exact description of the symptom, one of the doctors might recognise it from a previous encounter and be set on the trail of what the trouble might be.

The trail the doctors pursued first was a false one. At my next visit I was interrogated, in a manner one might expect were one a subversive in a police state, about my drinking habits. Those were and had been for many years desultory, hedonistic, and not abstemious but not addicted either. My replies, which were honest, were noted down with presumably deliberately transparent scepticism. I silently wondered whether the medical profession had been seized with a nostalgia for the eighteenth century and was ascribing my difficulty in walking to gout. Eventually, on one of my visits, which I made at intervals of, variously, a fortnight, a month, and three months, a doctor agreed with me that that trail was false. I had by then surrendered what seemed to be litres of blood for analysis. My blood vessels and my very blood retreated from the needle and I always had to explain to the nurse deputed to seek another batch that my reason for averting my gaze from her repeated attempts was squeamishness.

After giving up the false trail, the hospital identified fairly quickly an abnormality in my blood: a deficiency of thyroid function. Early one morning Michael and I went to the hospital and collected a prescription for replacement tablets, of which, the doctor impressed on me, I was to take one a day "forever." From the moment I began to do so, I had no more sensations of being in an airship. The doctors assured me that my ability to walk would be restored as soon as my thyroid level was.

After participating in the organisation of PLR and the campaign for it, I observed with curiosity the organisation of the outpatients clinic I attended. Six patients would be given an appointment for an identical time with the same doctor. He would see perhaps two of them, and then a further six, with appointments for a half-hour later, would arrive. As the closing time of the clinic approached, the backlog increased. The method was systematic and deliberate. Evidently the patients were meant to perceive as well as endure its operation. I concluded that it was designed to deliver to them the message, which I found particularly infuriating as I waited two empty hours with a deadline to meet, that the time of doctors was so precious that they could not afford to risk a moment's delay were a patient not there when his turn came up. Yet there cannot have been any frivolous or merely hypochondriac patients waiting, since an appointment at the clinic could be secured only if your doctor had referred you to the hospital.

At the hospital I attended, there was a purposely designed waiting room for the patients. In style it was like a rather shabby airport lounge. You arrived there and were required to present your appointment card at the desk. When you had gone through those formalities, you were at once moved on from the waiting room and told to sit on a random row of benches and ruined chairs that was cramped along one side of a corridor, with the doors of the rooms the doctors occupied opening opposite it.

The room designed as a waiting room was thus kept empty apart from the transients about to be sent to the corridor.

On one occasion, when the doctor with whom I had an appointment kept it after I had waited nearly three hours, I mentioned to him the distresses of such a wait. He replied that it could not be helped.

I could discern only two possible purposes in the system. Either the free health service, funded by obligatory taxes, was set up with such political acumen that it was impossible for those who sought to do so to abolish it and they had found it easier to foist on it a system that uttered to its patients a propagandist inducement to use and pay for, in addition to their taxes, private medicine instead; or the system was intended to burnish the egos of the doctors. A doctor whose door opened to admit the next patient would see facing him something resembling the chorus in *Idomeneo:* the miserable and ravaged people had assembled to beg their king to relieve their afflictions. It disturbed me to conjecture that only by such methods could the doctors maintain the self-confidence doctors undoubtedly need if they are to carry their serious responsibilities of action to preserve life or to pronounce it officially extinct. I had hoped that their medical expertise was prop enough.

My perilously halting gait made me go no further alone than to our local shops, and squeamishness beset me in relation to hospitals. I was on all my visits to outpatients, at each of which I was given an appointment for the next, accompanied either by Michael, when he could make time free from his directorship of the National Gallery, or, which happened more often, by Shena Mackay. Her company was freely and affectionately accorded, even though she fulfills many responsibilities, including those to her three daughters, and, since she is a nondriver who lives in the philistia of the home counties, my requests doomed her to the unloveliest of rail journeys, on the Southern Region.

Shena Mackay, 1984

It was, all the same, a philistine use to which I put the finest architect of literary baroque, funny and tragic, and the most Firbankian master of surrealism now extant in the English language.

I cannot excuse myself except by need of, precisely, her gifts. Only a great baroque imagination could make acceptable to me the comic and tragic occasions paraded while we waited. The abrasions the system inflicted on my rationality could be balmed and surmounted only by the gift of a great surrealist.

It was about six weeks from my first visit to the outpatients clinic to the hospital's identification of a shortage of thyroid in the blood I had yielded with physiological reluctance. Three months after that, when December 1983 was just into double figures, I made another outpatients visit and was told that the replacement tablets had brought the thyroid level of my blood up to normal.

I reported myself gratefully free of floating sensations ("Oh yes, your dizziness") and asked whether I should presently be able to walk. "Yes," I was told, "you'll soon be running about like a spring chicken."

In the new year of 1984 Michael and I met Iris Murdoch, a friend of ours for three decades, for luncheon in the neighbourhood we share with her when she is in town. The only restaurant that could offer us a table was up a flight of stairs. Iris robustly put her hand beneath my elbow and hoisted me up it. All the same, I believed the hospital's forecast that I should soon be able to follow what I still thought of as my usual way of living. I went with Shena Mackay to an exhibition of pictures. The rules, mindful no doubt of what suffragettes once inflicted at another gallery on the Rokeby *Venus,* forbade me to take my umbrella into the exhibition rooms. I found myself at a loss. I sat on a sofa in sight of a painting I particularly liked and waited while Shena went round alone.

In February the Writers' Guild gave a party, in a suite in a high building in central London that I knew to be accessible by lift, where the minister for the arts, who was then Lord Gowrie, was to present to some writers selected by the two trade unions their first cheques for PLR. Leaning on my umbrella, I managed to advance to receive the first and to say the two public sentences needed.

It was the first-fruits of WAG. A further vindication was to follow. The government had set PLR in motion under a scheme containing many flaws, of sense and practicality, which I had been unable to avert. I published my criticisms. I already knew enough, however, to praise its appointment of John Sumsion as Registrar and writers already had occasion to applaud his common sense and friendliness. After operating its

flawed scheme for a time, the government put itself to the legislative bother it could have avoided in the first place and amended the scheme into conformity with what WAG had advised all along. By 1986 only two of WAG's original requirements were not yet in operation. One needs only an adaptation of what is done in Sweden; the other will take more radical thought and negotiation to introduce.

To friendly enquiries at the Guild party I answered what the hospital had told me, that I was on my way to recovery. My belief in that prognosis was sincere but it could not much longer hide from me that the stutter in my movements was becoming worse.

The doctors and the thyroid level in my blood pronounced me virtually cured. Yet I could not walk either fast or with ease. I therefore asked myself whether my disability might be an hysterical symptom. I could trace a plausible aetiology for such a symptom in my distaste for walking, my relation to my mother, who had wanted me to walk for pleasure, and the fact that my pretend-ally turned assailant had robbed me of my favourite means of avoiding walking.

I bent on the problem all the rationality I commanded, together with my not unknowledgeable acquaintance with the likelihoods of my own psyche. I concluded that my failure to walk was not hysterical but somatic.

One tiny nexus that conformed with my conclusion was that hysterical symptoms are inclined to mimic true diseases or somatic conditions, in garbled shape if the patient's apprehension of the model is garbled. I was, for a literate person, exceptionally ignorant of medical facts. I had been almost pathologically healthy all my life. I was also squeamish. I did not read even the medical articles and reports in the papers. I could not have named and I could not remember that I had ever seen an example of any condition that my unconscious might have been, even through a garbling scrambler, mimicking.

In March 1984 I went, again in Shena Mackay's company, to the outpatients clinic. I explained to the doctors that I was having increasing difficulty in walking.

They asked whether, in the incipiently spring evenings, I went for a stroll.

I tried to explain that I was incapable of strolling even had I been willing.

"This has been going on a long time. You've lost the habit of walking. You must practise walking."

When the taxi that took Shena and me from the hospital left us outside the house where Michael and I live, I said to her:

"The doctors say I must practise walking. Will you come with me to do some food shopping at the shops on the other side of the road?"

She did. I leaned on my umbrella and from time to time clung to the railings at the front gardens of houses.

Shena carrying my shopping, we crossed back to my home, which is in a handsome stuccoed building, once, I imagine, a posh town house and now divided into flats. A minor portico leads up five or six steps to the communal front door. Through that you enter a communal hall. Staircases lead from there to the flats on other floors. The front door of Michael's and my flat faces you across the ten or fifteen yards' extent of the communal hall.

By heaving on the railings, I mounted the outside steps. Shena took my key and opened the communal front door. Pressing on my umbrella, I mounted onto the final step of the portico and went into the building. I sank onto my hands and knees. Shena, hung about with my shopping bags, could not raise me. I crawled on all fours through the communal hall, wondering whether the occupant of some other flat would at that moment come down the staircase or, having begun to do so, would retreat thinking, "There's that eccentric Lady Levey crawling across the hall."

Having helped me through an episode she might have invented for one of her fictions and into my flat, where I managed, by heaving on the furniture, to rise, Shena insisted I telephone my doctor.

When I managed to make contact, my doctor came to see me and I implored her to urge the hospital doctors to stop concentrating exclusively on the thyroid content of my blood and to turn their attention to the actual symptom. She undertook to do what she could.

While she was trying, the Persian cat who shares Michael's and my life and bed fell ill. He loves and is loved beyond description. He was a stray whom someone found in her basement, mistook at first for an owl and eventually brought to our daughter who was then living with us.

Because I could barely move, I had to seek a home visit from our masterly vet, to whose skill and expertise I wished I could confide my own case. After a week Darius was happily mended. We had to ask Shena, whom he knows and loves, to fetch him home.

By the second week of April my doctor had managed to procure me an out-of-regular-order appointment at the outpatients clinic. Michael added his entreaties to our doctor's influence by writing to the head of the unit.

Quite as though my difficulty in walking were a recalcitrance on my part, I was told that I was causing great worry and the next stage would be a wheelchair.

I was advised to enter the hospital as an inpatient. I was naturally not anxious to do so, but no other way was suggested for the symptom to receive scrutiny. So I agreed and agreed to wait for a telephone call to tell me when to come.

Michael received a letter from the head of the unit in response to his appeal. It said that I had repeatedly been advised to go into the hospital as an inpatient but had always refused.

Until my last, irregular visit, which I had made only thanks to my doctor, no one at the hospital had ever suggested to me that I should or even could become an inpatient.

Patients cannot afford to antagonise their doctors, but neither did I want a myth entered in the records of my case. I wrote as peaceably as I could to the head of the unit, saying that Michael had shewn me his letter and that I had never been advised to become an inpatient.

When I was indeed an inpatient, he treated me affably. He never referred to the letters in our triangular exchange.

The relation between Michael and me is one of perfect confidence but my fiction-writing imagination conceived a story, which I have never written, about a couple who lived on the edge of mistrust and were pushed over it when one of them received a letter telling untruths about the other that was written by a figure in authority whose scientific exactitude in relation to facts was taken for granted.

My experience of hospital was of pervasive kindness, including the poignant kindness of patient to patient.

A large public ward runs to a timetable apparently designed to keep all the patients short of sleep. Shortage of food may be added. These days a menu sheet is distributed on which you may tick the box that allows you to opt for a vegetarian meal. The system does not work if you were not present the day before to make your future option or were undergoing medical treatment elsewhere when the sheets were distributed in the ward. In any case, carnivores and vegetarians alike found the food disgusting.

The deprivations visited on the patient reduce his emotional stamina for his dealings with the most rigorously hierarchical society to be found in Britain since the Middle Ages. The most cheerful social layer is the next-to-lowest, only just above the patients: the ancillary workers, who reign alone at meal times. Their kindness shewed up a social defect I have known of all my life. Neither with nor in its vegan version without milk do I like tea. The English and Irish tea ceremony—and, I suspect, the Russian—is more stately and more inscrutable than the Japanese. Only the context discloses whether "Would you like a cup of tea?" signifies "I am sorry for you," "I apologise for being rude," or "Let us be friends." To decline is to slap the face of a well-intentioned enquirer. To ask for coffee instead, as I did in hospital through an addict's need, is to administer a double slap, forehand and back.

I spent five days in the hospital I had visited as an outpatient, with several trips, by sit-up ambulance with a nurse to escort me, to other hospitals, and was then transferred ("We'll lay on an ambulance") to another large hospital. ("The doctor who was to book the ambulance has gone off for the weekend. Could your husband go to the main road, find a taxi, and take you there?")

A thin thread of identity was kept alive in me by the constant visits of the people I most closely love, who braved every private inconvenience to keep faith. On my last day in, Anne Graham Bell, whom Michael and I have held dear since we met her when she was working for a firm that published some of my early books, brought me, as she does every year (though this, she said, was a second, later, and bonus crop), a clutch of the stout staves which, in her Hampstead garden, miraculously bear camellia flowers, fleshy, vivid, exotic, and delicate.

From the daily ritual of weighing the patients, in a chair-scale for those like me who could not be free-standing, I observed that I was becoming thin, a result I should have earlier been glad to have so effortlessly.

Indian files of medical students practised their gavel technique one by one on the reflexes of my knees. Swarms-at-a-time of medical students settled about my bed. I was asked to walk about the ward for them, which I did leaning on the umbrella I had taken into hospital, and they were asked to note that my way of walking was "highly characteristic." I did not know what of.

I was rushed through a series of tests: of the responses of my nerves, of my vision; electrodes were glued to my scalp; I was dunked in a brain scanner.

I went home for a fortnight and returned to the same ward and the same bed of my first hospital for a lumbar puncture. It was done, by a kind doctor, without pain to me, without provocation to my squeamishness, since it all went on behind my back, and without fear since the doctor acceded to my request and told me in advance each act he proposed to perform. The hospital averted the dire headache other patients have suffered as a result of the procedure by keeping me lying flat for twenty-four hours. Then I was allowed to go home.

A better read patient would, I dare say, have

guessed what tentative diagnosis the tests were designed to confirm or deny.

I was told that I had multiple sclerosis: or, rather, that the results of all the tests thoroughly conformed with my having it—a presumably legalistic formula that reminded me of my sending down. My college wrote during a vacation to say not that I had been sent down but that I should be if I attempted to return to Oxford when the new term began.

The remnants of my ancient Greek told me that sclerosis was a thickening. I did not realise that the thickening in question was of the very nerves. Neither did I know that the cause of the disease is one of the puzzles of medicine. I asked the doctors what caused it. "You had a very severe illness in childhood." "No. I didn't." "You mean you don't remember. You were too young at the time." "I mean I specifically and explicitly remember that I was exceptionally healthy as a child and that my parents repeatedly and specifically told me that that was so from the moment I was born."

In the search for the cause of multiple sclerosis and other mysterious diseases, and for a means of curing them, it is vital that no animal, human or nonhuman, be tortured or killed.

That, which I have given a good chunk of my life to saying in print, I now say with the authority of a person with a personal stake in the matter. It is not my personal stake that makes my antivivisectionist argument correct, but unless you can cite it you are open to emotional challenge by the emotionalists who support vivisection.

Human society has consistently asked itself the not-to-the-point question, "What is the life of this rat or the freedom from terror and agony of that monkey worth to us?" The pertinent question is what they are worth to that monkey or this rat. His life is the only one that is open to him. His awareness, which you can so easily suffuse with torment, is the only one he can experience.

The vivisectionist fallacy is a wilful and antiscientific denial of the unique singularity of each individual sentient animal. To persist in asking the wrong question is fascism. You convince yourself that the life and happiness of this socialist, homosexual Gypsy-Jew, whatever it may be worth to him as a unique possession, is worth nothing to you.

Vivisection would still be a fascist atrocity even did abandonment of it, as its advocates pretend, place on you the responsibility of abandoning the hope of solving puzzles and discovering cures.

In reality, however, the method, in which society

has invested not only millions of lives but millions of pounds and man-hours, has produced results far from commensurate with the investment. Adherence to an expensive, luridly impressive and old-fashioned orthodoxy inhibits scientific imagination.

The answer to some cardinal puzzles about multiple sclerosis is likely to emerge from an imaginatively used computer—an instrument that is, in many of its aspects, an automated version of a formal logician.

In Britain I have found only one enquiry into the disease that explicitly forswears the torture of animals and thus makes itself the only organisation to command the allegiance of antifascists: the Naomi Bramson Trust, which operates at Newcastle-on-Tyne.

It was there that my antifascist daughter was examined and learned that, although it clusters in families, the disease is not directly inherited (a dictum I half understand thanks to the tuition of statisticians on the subject of PLR) and that, to our relief, she is extremely unlikely to contract it.

To find the cause of that or another puzzle-disease, it is necessary first to compile comprehensive statistics: the number of extant persons in Britain with the disease, properly broken down according to their age when they experienced the first symptom, which may be recognisable as such only by hindsight, their sex, and where they live. Only when those facts are gathered can an accurately representative sample be chosen, to whom you can put questions, starting with the most likely and working down, if need be, to the seemingly irrelevant, so that by computer-sifting of the replies you can eventually isolate a factor common to all the cases. It will, of course, be necessary to listen to the replies rather than assume you know better.

As a multiple sclerosis case I refute one medical myth I heard before my case was diagnosed, namely that people are safe from the disease once they have passed forty.

I conceive that it would be possibly useful to ask the subjects in such an enquiry whether they were precocious, late, or average developers; whether they have reason to think they have any specific natural immunities to infectious diseases; and whether they had, as children and as adults, good or mediocre health up till the time they contracted the disease.

I am not sure whether my own experience suggests to me that it would be worth asking, "In the five years before you contracted the disease did you undergo a major emotional shock?" The answers would be difficult to evaluate, since one person's shock is another's frisson. Given the chance, my assailant no doubt would have wished the disease on me; but I find it impossible to believe that it can be induced by malign wishes or witchcraft. The answer to the question of what does

induce it may well drop out of the accumulated and sifted replies to a question as seemingly wayward as, "Do you like blackcurrants?"

Kate Levey and her son, Roland Gurney, 1986

When my night thoughts were obsessed by the metaphor in which my assailant had maimed me, the disease that did in reality maim me had not yet produced a single symptom apprehensible by me, let alone by outside observers. The metaphor gave expression to my realistic recognition that the fury I suddenly encountered was, in psychological content, murderous, though it did not issue in a literal murder. For that perception I might have found a dozen different metaphors. Yet my thoughts returned to and dwelt on that single metaphor every night.

Although there were no symptoms of it, I find it easy—indeed, almost obligatory—to believe that the disease was already attacking me and carrying out its stealthy work in my body. I find it possible, though no more, to believe that the clandestine actions the disease was provoking were accessible to me by sensations that I was not consciously aware of, just as a person may perhaps unknowingly keep track of his digestive processes. I find it hard to believe that my subterranean awareness of clandestine processes was accessible to my unconscious, which framed the metaphor. I think I find it virtually impossible to believe that the metaphor thus framed was one that contained an objectively correct account of the results the disease had not yet made manifest. Before it was diagnosed in me, I heard the disease named once, in connexion with the medical myth about the age at which it attacks; I had probably read the name once or twice in passing; I had no concept of its symptoms. My obsessive metaphor was perhaps occasioned simply by my obsessive and fearful state of mind, but I do not think it entirely unthinkable that intimations from my body were alerting my mind to facts it did not know.

If it is random bad luck to be struck down by the disease, it is random comparatively good luck to be struck down in a welfare state.

My umbrellas are returned to the umbrella stand. The DHSS (Department of Health and Social Security) lends me a device that resembles the mythical monsters whose existence Lucretius shewed cogently and mellifluously to be impossible: its upper half is like the handlebars of a scooter and its lower half like the wheels of a tricycle. By leaning on it, I quasi-walk about our flat. At noon on weekdays I go to the next room, climb into the electrically motivated wheelchair, whose batteries Michael recharges for me weekly, and drive to the kitchen where he has left Persian-cat-food ready in the fridge.

The wheelchair, which the technicians who delivered it to me called by the lethal name, "the electric chair," pays me out for having written a novel with the title *Palace without Chairs*. Only in a palace without furniture of any kind, instead of in our narrow-corridored flat, could its virtuosity be fully used. I was given the loan of it in exchange for an undertaking never to take it out of doors, though I am allowed to seek special permission to take it abroad. How I could do that without taking it out of doors I cannot work out unless the entrance to the Channel Tunnel were to lead through our floorboards.

The occupational therapist has had a discreet handrail placed in our portico. By clasping it with one hand and leaning on one of the tripod sticks I have on loan, I can follow the system the physiotherapist coached me in and descend the stairs. A companion carries down the nonautomated wheelchair that is allowed to go out and that folds. Michael or Shena pushes me out for an airing or loads the chair and me into a cab, which, on the strength of my GLC (Greater London Council)-invented taxicard, will take us at subsidised rates to an exhibition of paintings and which is of all vehicles the easiest for a cripple to climb into. I do not visit operas and concerts; even if there were dispensation for my wheelchair, there could not and should not be any for my need to move about after ten minutes' immobility; but music is, happily, available

to me at home.

That I can work—and do, constantly, for understanding editors and publishers who do not nag me for delivery—I owe to friendship. In addition to her novels, Gillian Freeman writes scripts, which are often exigent about format. In her exploration of word processors she saw a portable one so small that she divined that I should be just about able to transfer it to and from a mobile worksurface. Since she is one, she knew what a writer would want of such a machine, and she put me in touch with the firm from which I bought it.

My doctor, who sends me prescriptions by post when I ask, has passed on to me word of my being allowed to visit the outpatients clinic should I need to. I have made only one visit, soon after the diagnosis. I was told there was no pressure on me to comply but I was asked to spend a day at the hospital standing or sitting by to serve as a specimen for students taking exams. The service was asked of me, but I could not have given it without passing on the burden to Michael or Shena. So I said no.

That is the chief curse of the illness. I must ask constant services of the people I love most closely, of whom I require my three meals a day and constant water and eternal coffee, by vacuum flask when I am alone. I cannot do any service to friend or stranger without passing on the burden of doing it to the people I love. They must buy me the card and the stamp before I can reply by polite postcard to a stranger's letter.

Sporadically it is, in its manifestations, a disgusting disease. Also sporadically, it has another antisocial result, wrapping one suddenly in an inexorable fatigue like a magic cloak of invisibility. Its sporadicness destroys the empiricism by which normal people proceed without noticing they are doing so. The fact that yesterday I sat on the edge of the bed and managed to open the drawer that faced me argues nothing predictable, in either direction, about my chances of doing exactly the same action today or of falling to the floor and staying there for a quarter of an hour before I can lever myself up.

In the limbs worst affected, which for me are the legs, it induces a strange, unnatural numbness, which does not preclude pain or even the further numbness of cold but makes one inhabit a surrealist world. As I sit in a chair or lie in bed at night, I cannot tell whether I have crossed one ankle over the other unless I look to see.

It is an illness accompanied by frustration. Writing, even by shorthand, has always been slower than thought. The time lag is unimaginably magnified by the delays of crippledom. The reference I must check is in a green book on the left of the shelf to the right in the room next door; yet, though I can slowly limp through to its vicinity, I cannot reach it and could not carry it away with me if I could. That makes another service I must ask of someone I love. That ornament is askew. I cannot reach that either. That makes two further services I must ask.

It is an illness that inflicts awareness of loss. The knowledge that I shall never be in Italy again is sometimes a heaviness about me like an unbearable medallion that bends my neck.

Yet the past is, except through memory and imagination, irrecoverable in any case, whether or not your legs are strong enough to sprint after it. All that has happened to me is that I have in part died in advance of the total event.

The obverse of the medallion that weighs me down is my luck in having the opportunity, and my wisdom in taking it, to know so much of Italy. While my going was good I visited the Soviet Union; I have been in Samarkand in a blizzard. I have been in the incomparable city of Lisbon; in Prague; in Reykjavik; in Budapest. When Michael prepared his book on Ottoman art, I went with him and perceived that the form of the mosque is one of the great inventions of architecture, the twin to the baroque.

I am the granddaughter of an architect, but I never met him and I do not think it is through heredity that architecture moves me. The raw intellectual material of architecture is the relation of one space to another. How have I so great a sense of architecture when I have so little of direction?

I have set foot in places that are, and not only to classical scholars, holy.

The three of us stood on the plateau of wind-racked grass at the top of the site of Troy. To one side were the quasi-terraces cut by the excavation to disclose the layers of the successive cities.

Perhaps because we were three in number, three Turkish—three Trojan—children circled us at a distance. The oldest was a girl of perhaps eight or nine. Walking slowly, with an almost processional dignity, they approached us direct. They were seriously beautiful, without a touch of the urchin, and seriously serious. Unspeaking and unsmiling but with courtesy they gave us three long-stalked vermilion poppies plucked from among the grasses. They were keeping the oldest social rule of Greeks and Trojans alike, that you must give an hospitable welcome to strangers, a rule still in observance in countrified parts of both countries. I thanked them in a couple of sentences of formal English, whose sense I knew they would not understand but whose tenor I hoped they would. We realised that we were involved in another high Homeric custom, an exchange of gifts between notables. We rapidly discussed whether we should give the children money but hesitated because of the seemingly lunatic generosity we had already noted to be a debonair matter of self-respect in Turkey, especially among people who could patently not afford it. The only givable alternative we had with us was a great assembly of boiled sweets, big cellophane-swathed ovals in the deep, not quite transparent colours of jewels which we carried as protection from thirst on the dusty drive through Asia Minor. None of us could be sure that the sweets were the right choice. I gave some clutches of them to the children. They accepted them with a demeanour of courtesy and seriousness. They withdrew a little way, presumably to indicate that they were not seeking more from us, and looked at us courteously. After a couple of minutes they walked with slow dignity away.

I am the ancient Greek ghost, sent down in the ultimate sense, who on meeting Charon proffered a boiled sweet as the price of the ferry passage.

Copyright © Brigid Brophy, 1986

BIBLIOGRAPHY

Fiction:

The Crown Princess and Other Stories. London: Collins, 1953; New York: Viking, 1953.

Hackenfeller's Ape. London: Hart-Davis, 1953; New York: Random House, 1954.

The King of a Rainy Country. London: Secker & Warburg, 1956; New York: Knopf, 1957.

Flesh. London: Secker & Warburg, 1962; Cleveland: World, 1963.

The Finishing Touch. London: Secker & Warburg, 1963.

The Snow Ball. London: Secker & Warburg, 1964; published with *The Finishing Touch.* Cleveland: World, 1964.

In Transit. London: Macdonald & Co., 1969; New York: Putnam, 1970.

The Adventures of God in His Search for the Black Girl. London: Macmillan, 1973; Boston: Little, Brown, 1974.

Pussy Owl (for children). London: BBC Publications, 1976.

Palace without Chairs. London: Hamish Hamilton, 1978; New York: Atheneum, 1978.

Nonfiction:

Black Ship to Hell. London: Secker & Warburg, 1962; New York: Harcourt, 1962.

Mozart the Dramatist: A New View of Mozart, His Operas, and His Age. London: Faber & Faber, 1964; New York: Harcourt, 1964.

The Rights of Animals. London: Animal Defence & Anti-Vivisection Society, 1965.

Don't Never Forget: Collected Views and Reviews. London: Cape, 1966; New York: Holt, 1967.

Fifty Works of English and American Literature We Could Do Without, with Michael Levey and Charles Osborne. London: Rapp & Carroll, 1967; New York: Stein & Day, 1968.

Religious Education in State Schools. London: Fabian Society, 1967.

Black and White: A Portrait of Aubrey Beardsley. London: Cape, 1968; New York: Stein & Day, 1969.

The Longford Threat to Freedom. London: National Secular Society, 1972.

Prancing Novelist: A Defence of Fiction in the Form of a Critical Biography in Praise of Ronald Firbank. London: Macmillan, 1973; New York: Barnes & Noble, 1973.

Beardsley and His World. London: Thames & Hudson, 1976; New York: Harmony Books, 1976.

The Prince and the Wild Geese. London: Hamish Hamilton, 1982; New York: St. Martin's 1983.

A Guide to Public Lending Right. Hampshire, England: Gower, 1983.

Plays:

The Burglar (first produced in London in 1967). London: Cape, 1968; New York: Holt, 1968.

David Caute

1936-

Stoking myself up to write this, my first, rash essay in autobiography, I run alongside the Thames in one of its most beautiful reaches, the slow, wide curve between Hammersmith and Barnes. It's an immaculate, cloudless day in autumn and already the old towpath on the south side of the river is lightly dusted with fallen leaves and conkers. A rowing eight smoothly glides upriver, pursued by a single skuller. My children enjoy riding bicycles here, pausing to gather conkers from beneath the horse chestnuts, but this Monday morning they are in school and I—a free man, a writer, apparently master of my own timetable—run alone.

We moved into this flat, riverside area of London ten years ago and since that time Oxford have beaten Cambridge in the annual boat race every year. It cannot be a coincidence. Now at last relieved of the threat of serious flooding by the great barrier at Greenwich, Hammersmith can settle down to fulfill (or not) the pastoral destiny mapped out for it in William Morris's utopian tale, *News from Nowhere*—a title I intend to borrow for the long novel I am now completing after three years' labor.

Running beside the Thames under a cloudless sky, forty-eight years old, married, with two sons and two daughters, all of whom give me great happiness, I ought to be poised to recall my life in a spirit of celebration. Yet abruptly I find myself running through a dark and private tunnel.

At a certain age, we are confronted with the frightening repetition of our daily thoughts and routines as time runs out. I observe my shadow in motion along the towpath and see, unmistakably, the clumsy, heavy tread of a stranger whose limbs and lungs are palpably in decline. I also know that I never will be as good a writer as I had hoped to be—merely an obscure footnote of transitory interest, one of life's quarterfinalists. The truth oozes from the deep wound of self-knowledge, then settles like the old Thames fogs in the paintings of Claude Monet, forcing me to abandon the fool's perennial prayer, "Next time, next book."

My mother's family and my father's were of incompatible background and culture, yet as far as I can tell Edward ("Teddy") Caute got on very well with Mother's five brothers, two or three of whom

David Caute

shared his love of sport and all of whom appreciated his quick wit. Mother's parents were Jews from Galicia, from Hapsburg Poland, who settled in north London some time during the 1890s. Rabbi Asher Perlzweig was a noted musician. His wife Sarah bore him eight children. I can just remember the old man, a small, gentle patriarch, but Grandmother Perlzweig had been dead ten years before I was born.

My father's parents were a complete contrast. Jean Caute, a French peasant from Angoulême, had emigrated to the south coast of England and set up as a barber (also in the 1890s) before marrying Mary Kelly, an Irish maid and devoted Roman Catholic. He was a great miser who wore cardigans smelling of mothballs, lived in a bungalow in Bournemouth, and offered a plain biscuit to visitors, including his grandson. I was christened a Catholic to please the living grandmother but neither of my parents were believers, indeed my mother's outlook was entirely secular, rational and scientific.

I am myself an atheist who regards religion as a tragic superstition at best and a fraud at worst. The Papacy is a long-running racket, and its official position on birth control, when set against the vast misery engendered by the population explosion in the developing world, is unforgiveable. But if the mumbo-jumbo of the creed and cult, of counting beads, murmuring prayers, lighting candles, burning incense, and offloading confessions into the skulls of bigoted priests brings comfort to the ignorant, the sick, and the dying (as it did to Grandmother Caute) then one must recognise that we are ill-equipped to confront our own mortality.

My father was a Colonel in the Army Dental Corps. I remember him with a choking love, a short square man, rather keen on boxing, which he tried in vain to teach me, but without proper gloves. "Come on, hit me," he urged, but I was timid and afraid, which infuriated him, particularly as the boys from the posh schools like the Edinburgh Academy, which I attended from 1946 to 1950, were regularly waylaid by

Colonel Edward Caute, 1946

Rebecca Perlzweig (back row, left) with her two sisters and three of her five brothers, about 1912

the working-class ruffians, the "keelies," who duly snatched the silver-braided caps from their curly, shampooed heads. My father admired the manly virtues and despised snivellers; I was eager to match his standards and gain his admiration—which is by tradition what fathers are for. He pulled one of my teeth in his army surgery in Edinburgh Castle on top of that vast, granite rock; on that occasion I didn't wince.

During the first year after the war I used to spend the school holidays in a state akin to bliss. My father was at that time working in Edinburgh at the head of a team of dental mechanics in a large, suburban house of solid stone with a generous garden. Here the mechanics would make model aircraft for the Colonel's son and I spent hours cultivating vegetables in my own patch of the garden. Father was making up for the war, the years of parting. His humour was insistent though not profound. At certain moments he would repeat "So what?" in response to anything I said. I retain a sharp photographic image of sitting with him on the top deck of one of the old purple trams as it climbed the Mound and crossed the ancient High Street which runs from Edinburgh Castle down to Holyroodhouse Palace. The dialogue ran as follows:

ME: You're late for work this morning.

HE: So what?

ME: *(grinning)* You'll be court-martialled.

HE: So what?

ME: *(laughing)* Then reduced to the ranks.

HE: So what?

ME: *(spluttering helplessly)* Then shot!

HE: So what?

He chain-smoked. I would find him smoking at seven in the morning in his dressing gown, on his knees, shovelling the cold ash from the fire in what we called "the blue room." (It was a most beautiful flat, with generous, high-ceilinged rooms, large, handsome windows, a balcony overlooking magnificent wild gardens which descended into the frothing gorge of the Dean river. We played regular tennis, despite the Scottish weather, at the Dean club down the road, of which my mother was Ladies' Singles Champion and I the junior version.) My father cleaned out the fire because it was man's work, but as he did so cigarette smoke was already curling up into his eyes. Then he lathered his face to shave and again there was a cigarette in his mouth, dripping ash into the basin. Fearing that he would die of lung cancer or the pneumonia which had almost killed him in 1944, Mother nagged him about his State Express 555 cigarettes until he and she ended up sitting in separate rooms of the house, with me acting as go-between. I hug this memory jealously, the knowledge that they could quarrel, because in later years my mother regularly compared me unfavourably to my father in every aspect of character and behaviour.

The Dental Corps had a soccer team. My favourite dental mechanic was Lance-Corporal McKenzie, a man of great charm who treated me with kindness during my school holidays and pared down a willow to make me a cricket bat of suitable size. McKenzie also played goalkeeper for the soccer team. On Saturday mornings I used to go with Father to watch the football matches. He was a bit too keen on winning and there was a noticeable abatement in the "So what's" on the way to the sports field. One day I was standing with him behind "our" goal when McKenzie, wearing his fabulous canary-yellow jersey, hesitated or fumbled or something—anyway the other team scored and my father was livid. He began to bawl at McKenzie—needless to say the social and authority gap between a Colonel and a Lance-Corporal in the British Army is formidable. I had one of my attacks of "socialism," and crawled away, ashamed that this grown man should be thus humiliated in front of me. I felt that Father was abusing his authority and I couldn't comprehend why winning a mere game meant so much to him, but I realise now that what he cared about was effort, commitment, courage—win or lose. Twenty-five years later, again on Saturday mornings, I found myself bellowing at my own sons if they flinched a tackle while playing soccer for their primary-school team. During the interval I had been bellowed at by a succession of schoolmasters—the gift of violence, like the gift of music, transmits itself with the effortlessness of a virus.

In September 1947 my mother and I visited my father, who was by now serving with the British Army of the Rhine. Though ten years old, I had never during my conscious life been outside of Britain (being born in Egypt didn't count), and now I was to inspect the nation which had rained bombs down on us, murdered six million Jews, and brought tyranny and destruction to Europe.

Our visit to Germany was the occasion of a crucial moment in my intellectual development. To understand it, one must remember the intensity of patriotism possessing a boy who had grown up in a time of war—I ought to have been prepared to swallow unblinkingly the general philosophy of British officers and their wives: that "the Hun" is arrogant in victory, sycophantic in defeat, respects only strength, and will take a mile if you give him an inch. That we should be stuffing ourselves on veal and cream cakes while the Germans went half-hungry was no more than they deserved—never forget the posture of these meek people a few years ago in France and Poland!

The ten-year-old boy visiting Germany (including a fascinating interlude in Berlin, where the Soviet troops guarding Hitler's ruined Chancery saluted my father) did not dispute the culpability of the whole

Young David Caute

David, about age six, in his "best clothes"

German nation. Yet a worm of doubt about the attitude of the victors began to form in his mind. Eight years later, as a second lieutenant serving in one of Britain's African colonies, I immediately recognised the same spectrum of attitudes. *They* were not to be trusted; respected only strength; mistook too much kindness for weakness; licked your boots but would rise and stab you at the first opportunity. But *they* were no longer the conquerors of Europe and the tormentors of the Jews, *they* were Britain's innocent black subjects in the Gold Coast and Nigeria.

One episode in Germany made a particularly acute impression on me. We had reached Hamburg, a city of rubble as far as the eye could see, a devastation that probably exceeded anything inflicted on Britain. Miraculously untouched stood the Atlantic Hotel. Naturally it had been expropriated by the British officers. There we stuffed ourselves as ragged German kids pressed their pale, smudged faces against the windows, until some officer began barking at the waiters, who hurried out to kick the kids away. The scene lodged like an arrow: I knew that on any scale of responsibil-

ity I could not be judged pure and innocent while those German boys, some younger than myself, were guilty. I was ashamed.

Memory runs like a river, sometimes subterranean and forgotten, then gushing out with a great display of foam. During the years of growing up, every day is a motion forward, a grasping at the next rung on the ladder, a rejection of yesterday's smaller, weaker child. The plays, stories, and "novels" I wrote when fifteen, seventeen, and twenty drew on freshly acquired experience—one finds in them no trace of Hamburg 1947. Yet at the age of thirty-six I began writing a radio play which drew heavily on that episode. In short, the man seeks the child who is father to the man.

In 1971 the Junges Theater, Hamburg, staged a German version of my play, *The Demonstration,* first performed at the Nottingham Playhouse. During rehearsals the director took me to lunch to meet the local Rotarians who supported his theatre, a rather respectable occasion for which I was required to wear a necktie. By coincidence the lunch was held in the Atlantic Hotel and for all I knew some of these prosperous German businessmen and lawyers now lunching off groaning tables had been the filthy orphaned boys begging for scraps at the kitchen door in 1947. As for the devastated city of Hamburg, it had of course been rebuilt and the hotel itself was now surrounded by perfectly executed replicas of the old buildings destroyed by the USAAF and the RAF.

The episode brought back my childhood and I was soon at work on a radio play, *Fallout.* In the sequence quoted below Frank accompanies his uncle, the nuclear physicist Karl, a refugee from Nazi Germany, on a visit to Hamburg after the war:

KARL: Wherever there are airtight pockets, you will find undecayed corpses.

FRANK: Those boys are following us.

KARL: You have nothing to fear from them.

FRANK: Are their parents dead?

KARL: Probably. *(Pause.)* They deserved a lesson.

FRANK: Do the boys deserve to be orphans?

KARL: You should have seen their fathers strutting about the streets in their black and brown shirts with their medals and swastikas. This race . . . one day they stamp on your face, the next they lick your boots.

(Karl and his nephew enter the Atlantic Hotel, brushing aside a woman begging for a cigarette, and join Colonel and Mrs. Peters for lunch.)

KARL: Franz, examine the menu and stop staring out of the window.

FRANK: Those boys, the ones who followed us in the street . . . they're watching us through the window.

MRS. PETERS: Oh, it's too intolerable.

COL. PETERS: Waiter! Herr Ober!

WAITER: Magnifizenz?

COL. PETERS: Senden Sie . . . Karl, you tell him.

KARL: Weg mit den Jungen hinter dem Fenster! [Get rid of the boys behind the window!]

WAITER: Sofort, Magnifizenz! [Immediately, sir!]

(Mrs. Peters and her husband have been holidaying in the beautiful Harz mountains—as the Caute family did in 1947. She displays a set of coloured champagne glasses acquired for a mere pound of coffee, at which point her husband says):

COL. PETERS: They're natural black marketeers, the Germans.

This remark touches the essence of the conqueror's "false consciousness"—some would settle for the simpler word, "hypocrisy." Resorting to naked force to enslave black West Africans, the slave traders naturally "discovered" that force is the only message "your black" is capable of understanding.

In December 1947, three months after the trip to Germany, my father was due back in Edinburgh for Christmas leave. He didn't arrive. Grandfather Caute, as we later discovered, was too miserly to squander the cost of a telephone call on notifying us that Father had fallen seriously ill in Bournemouth while visiting his parents. I came home from school on my eleventh birthday to be told by Mother that we were catching the night train south. After a chilling, sleepless journey we arrived at King's Cross Station at 7:00 A.M. on a winter morning. Mother went to a telephone box. I watched her through the glass. She turned away, to shield her face from my gaze. Then she walked towards me and said something I can't remember; she couldn't bring herself to tell me the truth.

An hour later we were having breakfast in my uncle's flat opposite Harrod's, London's most famous department store, when I suddenly blew my top: "Why are we sitting here like this? Why aren't we hurrying down to the hospital in Bournemouth?" My half-sister Cynthia, an auburn-haired beauty in her twenties, began to cry and Mother hurried me from the table. Later that morning we drove down to Bournemouth with an uncle and an aunt. While Mother went to the hospital, I was taken by my aunt to choose a new bicycle, with drop handlebars, for my birthday. I look back with horror on my compliance in succumbing to this calculated distraction. As I admired the gleaming handlebars my mother was staring at my father's sunken face, which she at first protested to the nurses did not belong to her husband. "This isn't him." They assured her it was. He was only fifty-one.

Not long after he died painful quarrels broke out in the family. My grandfather wrote Mother a letter which began not "Dear Bob" (as she was called) but "To Mrs. Caute." In it he announced that he broke off all relations with her and me (though I, as the only son of the only son of this intensely patriarchal figure had previously incarnated all his hopes that the name of Caute would achieve in England the bourgeois dignity it had apparently not possessed in France). We never saw him or my grandmother again. Even worse, there was litigation between Mother and my half-sister (daughter of Father's first marriage) over the miniscule inheritance Father left, the result being that Cynthia and everyone else related to my father were wiped from the slate of my life.

I was sent to Wellington, a public school in Berkshire, as a direct result not only of Father's profession but also of his death. Founded in memory of the Great Duke a century before my entry, Wellington College offered nearly one hundred "Foundation" places to the sons of deceased officers, the fees being adjusted to the widow's means (in our case, virtually nil). It's worth recalling that when he died as a full Colonel with the prospect of impending promotion to the rank of Major-General, my father's salary was about one thousand pounds a year and all he could afford in terms of the internal combustion engine was a Ford 10. (To assess the real value of that salary in 1986 one should multiply by ten.)

Wellington was a school with an army tradition and its Cadet Corps commandant regularly reminded us that we were "the finest in the world." I suspect that Colonel Roy had not read Anatole France's satire, *Penguin Island,* where one learns that "every army is the finest in the world." Nor had I. A high proportion of Old Wellingtonians passed straight into the Royal Military Academy, Sandhurst, only a few miles away, but I never considered the army as a career. Both literally and figuratively, my head was egg-shaped.

I grew up in solitude, reading, writing, dreaming—an introspective, self-sufficient boy who (like Sartre, as I discovered years later) dreamt of an erotic yet platonic relationship with a non-existent sister. Mine was a twin who was very good at sports but not as good as I was because I was a boy. I've forgotten her name. She felt about me rather as Leni feels about Franz in Sartre's play *Altona:* "I need you, you, the heir to our name, the only one whose caresses stir me without humiliating me."

Such was my self-sufficiency that I could play a wide variety of games "against" myself, arranging glass marbles into two soccer teams, the most favoured appearing for the normally victorious Glasgow Rangers, manipulated by my right hand, while the doomed

Celtic received unconvincing prods from my left. I did this for hours. At the end of much cunning endeavour I would rise from the thick blue carpet with grey knees—in those days long trousers were unheard of for pre-adolescent boys.

Alone, I read and wrote, mesmerized by the glory of authorship. But let me mention, also, the impact of BBC radio drama, which fascinated me in the 1940s and 1950s. If I may sound like an after-dinner speech, it was a moment of some pride for me when the fine actor Norman Shelley, whom I had first heard in the children's serial "Toy Town," took a small part in a radio play of my own. Why do the New Year's Honours lists, which so frequently transform stage actors and actresses into knights and dames, so rarely acknowledge the services of the BBC Repertory Company, whose performances still reach a million people in this age of television.

This boy-reader developed very ordinary tastes: action, adventure, exotic journeys, haunting mysteries, the great struggle between Good (us) and Evil (them), all pleasured him. C.S. Forester's "Hornblower" series, describing the naval battles of the Napoleonic wars, reinforced by Arthur Ransome's tales of mock-battles between "Swallows" and "Amazons" in the Lake District, clearly carried my authorial mind across the seas. I quote from the breathtaking climax of one of my own early novels (spelling and grammar uncorrected):

> The Japanese fleet sped accross to-wards the apparently "anchored" Settlement fleet. Meanwhile the fleet in their turn sped accros to close the gap into the sea. A flash was seen. It came from the settlement Battleship. It mist it target and fell harmlessly into the water. Just to creat confusion, the two settlement destroyers sped into the Jap fleet, shooting here and there. Captain Hawthorne went down with battleship, but he did his duty to King and country . . . .

The ten-year-old author of this masterly passage enjoyed historical settings and wrote several historical sagas and dramas of his own, filling hard-covered notebooks with a regular little script written with much-loved fountain pens. "A Year and a Day" was the story of a fourteenth-century serf's son who escaped from his feudal servitude, avoided detection for the statutory year-and-a-day, became apprenticed to a craft guild, and . . . I got no further. The epic began as follows:

> A faint wind moned his sorrows, so as to bring the dreary trees and hedges to life. Something stirred in the hedge now: yes; the dirty, tired, worn, thin face of a little boy of

about 12 years of age showed it-self. That little boy was John Wyland, a rough country urchin, whose father was a serf, and worked for the Lord of Brayle. His father Wat Wyland was a thin man, with hollow cheek bones, dark black eyebrows and dark hair. He would turn round with a leer. He had a scar over his forehead, which made his appearance all the more terrible. As I said, he leered round, and then looked away again . . . .

(I have an affection for the narrative mastery of that, "As I said.") John suffered frequent beatings, too:

> . . . stroke after stroke, groan after groan, pant after pant as Wat struck the poor helpless boy. Then it was all over. "That'll learn ye."

Turning the page of the notebook, I find that the novel ends there and gives way to page 50 of a different one. There are many page 1's in this notebook:

> My name is Jim Farmer. I was borne in Devon, but I am a scout of the army of Lord Hall, a man of Yorkshire breed. Now I kept a notebook and put down notes of my travells, as I went. Note the latter, for you will notice this story is written in the present tense . . . .

If the reader will accept a twenty-year interval, he will find that these primitive examples of the "alienation effect" were later developed in theory and practice in my trilogy consisting of *The Occupation*, a novel, *The Illusion*, an extended essay, and *The Demonstration*, a play.

Maturing rapidly, I passed on to the battle of the sexes, a war which lasts a lifetime. The setting of the next "novel" is tropical (perhaps influenced by Somerset Maugham, or by my mother's tales of colonial India, where she had worked as a teacher in the 1920s, before accompanying my father to semi-colonial Egypt, where I was born):

> "Miss Downes," I quoted. "If you were walking out there in the sand, which do you think I would find more fascinating? you or the Arabs?"
> "Well—" she started.
> "Evasive!" I warned . . .

(Now the sex war hots up. Miss Downes I discover to be "sarchastic." She even laughs bitterly and says, "You're most complementary." This drives me crazy and I let her have it):

"Look here" I fumed "You needn't think that I can sit here peacefully while you use me as a guinea pig to experiment with your stupid, so-called philosophy. You think you're a terrificly deep thinker with all your stupid rotten twaddle. As it is you're probably suffering from an inferiority complex or something . . ."

"Or something?"

"Oh shut up!"

(The row ends with a highly erotic reconciliation beside the Suez canal):

"Cecilia" I declaimed, "might I kiss you?"

"N- no."

"Please, Cecila: can you stop me?"

"Y- yes," and I kissed her soundly.

Of course that passage gives it all away. To kiss a woman "soundly" is to beat her, for only beatings and hidings are "sound" when administered by lords and lairds to foreign spies, women, children, and recalcitrant natives. It will also be noticed that I took her by force, though with her consent, a very satisfying combination, adopting the rule-of-thumb still prevalent among English judges: When she says No she means Yes.

Pathos was important: I shed tears on behalf of David Copperfield and Mowgli (at whose side I fought the cruel tiger Shere Khan in the Indian jungle), while rich veins of sentiment and sentimentality drew me to Walpole's *Judith Paris*, Margaret Mitchell's *Gone with the Wind*, Richard Llewelyn's *How Green Was My Valley*, and James Hilton's *Lost Horizon*. I brooded for hours in bed about what I had read.

I consumed history, upmarket and down, romance and allegory, with an undiscriminating appetite: Alexandre Dumas's *Count of Monte Cristo*, Anthony Hope's Ruritanian romances *(Rupert of Hentzau)*, Helen Waddell's wonderful *Peter Abelard*, the novels of Alfred Duggan, and Bernard Shaw's *Saint Joan*.

I was a shameless plagiarist. Leafing through the old notebooks, I can often detect which author I had been reading. But while "originality" is of course a crucial quality in a writer of any age, so, too, is passionate mimesis. Art begins with the imitation not only of life but of art itself. The novelists I lapped up in my early adolescence were the English and American social realists, Dickens and Galsworthy, Bennett and Sinclair Lewis, Wells and Priestley.

Reading these notebooks today, the scenes and dramas of a childhood constantly disrupted by war hurry across my vision: a little girl called Wendy I loved in Reigate, the brutal noise of bren gun carrier tracks on the streets of Dorking, the gathering of soldiers for the Normandy landings, the "Yanks" in their fine uniforms handing out candy and chewing gum, the snarl of aerial dogfights, Spitfires and Hurricanes against Heinkels and Messerschmitts. I smell again the close, damp-brick odour of the garden air-raid shelter, I see the comic gasmasks which made us look like elephants, and I remember standing on Yarnell's Hill outside Oxford watching Göring's armada pass overhead to smash Coventry, the deep growl of bomb-loaded planes, the higher snarl of those which had discharged their cargo and were running for the coast, for home.

My early childhood was bound up with this passionate physical involvement in the war; as a Jew my mother was in no doubt what would befall us if the Germans succeeded in crossing the Channel and now, more than forty years later, I still point out to my own children the concrete "pill-boxes" among the sand dunes of the south coast. I have also inspected their German counterparts along the north coast of France, the killing beaches, the vast war cemeteries, which remind me of "my" war. I used to move flags around maps of Europe to mark the progress of the Allied Armies. From my mother I derived a passionate attachment to the Red Army; not only did I compose an epic poem in honour of General Montgomery, victor of El Alamein, I also dedicated poems and eulogies to Generals Zhukov and Rokossovsky. In 1947 I first saw the Red Army in the flesh, in East Berlin. Eighteen years later I again visited the German Democratic Republic with a more jaundiced eye, but the great Soviet war memorial continued to move me.

Socialists are now regarded in America as quaint relics of the pre-postindustrial age, rather like Fifth Monarchists, dreamers, vegetarians, and the bearded fruit-juice drinkers derided by Orwell. I came to socialism via Shaw, Wells, R.H. Tawney, and the Left Book Club volumes on my mother's shelves. On my way home from the conservative, rather anti-intellectual boarding school I attended, I regularly committed two types of thought-crime, one of them standard practice among sex-starved victims of puberty, but the other unique among the 700 boys of Wellington College.

The orthodox crime I committed as I passed across London from Waterloo station to King's Cross was to buy *Paris Vedettes,* a girlie magazine, and to visit at least one film featuring such lush dream-beauties of the era as Gina Lollobrigida (my favourite) and Françoise Arnoul. The unorthodox crime was to visit Collet's bookshop in the Charing Cross Road and pick up a clutch of Soviet propaganda pamphlets extolling the advances of Soviet Woman, Soviet Housing, Soviet Education, as well as the latest issues of the periodical *Soviet Literature,* featuring socialist-realist stories of heroism and Stakhanovite reconstruction. How well I came to know the cheap shiny paper and small print of the Moscow Foreign Languages Publishing House! I also discovered the work of N.G. Chernyshevsky, a nineteenth-century Russian materialist philosopher. Armed with a load of Stalinist statistics and the Marxist dialectic, I used to take myself back to school to argue it out with those few sons of the English officer-class who were prepared to listen.

Now this was an odd situation and should have led to my immersion in one of the large and beautiful lakes which grace the extensive grounds of Wellington College. What saved me from the dawn firing squad was a compensating quality—in certain crucial respects I was a conforming officer and gentleman (though only an imitation one), demonstratively keen on games and good at some of them, which just about atones for anything at an English public school. Moreover, I subscribed to the "loyalist," hierarchical values of the institution, became a prefect, head of my "dormitory," a keen member of the Cadet Corps, and the school's best quarter-miler in the seasons of 1953 and 1954. In short, Caute (the standard manner of reference in such a school is by surname alone, though sixth-formers thaw out into first names) was, in more senses than one, a performer—not a bad actor either, particularly in female roles, though there was a disastrous moment when, as Shakespeare's Jessica, I was invited by my lover to sit down "upon this grassy bank" under the moon, whereupon the "grassy bank" collapsed noisily into its component parts, setting up howls of joy from the philistines who had occupied the front row of the theatre in the hope of just such a disaster.

What brought me to socialism was not merely Shaw, Wells, J. B. S. Haldane, and the Marxist historiography of Christopher Hill. Youthful idealism and indignation, a quest for justice, and an ardent rejection of the cynical materialism of the adult bourgeois world all played their part, but equally attractive was socialism's simple framework of explanation for human discord. My essays used to disturb, even shock, my teachers and tutors. I gained the psychological satisfaction of the rebel posture while greedily harvesting such conventional rewards as school prizes and an Oxford scholarship.

I remain a member of the Labour Party, occasionally attend branch meetings, and turn out at election time to canvas from door to door on behalf of the Parliamentary candidate. I'm still inclined to identify with the workers, or their union, in any conflict with the company or the state, yet I have broken the sacred rule of Labour by sending my children to private, fee-paying schools. I long ago abandoned my illusions about Soviet Communism but I remain hostile to the Cold Warriors of the West and to the proponents of the nuclear arms race. I regard the United States' involvement in Vietnam as one of the major crimes of the century and have opposed every attempt by the old colonial powers, Britain and France, to resist the process of national liberation in Africa. I support unilateral nuclear disarmament for Britain and am wholly behind the brave women who have besieged Greenham Common air base, where American cruise missiles are now installed.

On the other hand I'm a much less severe critic of capitalism than I was twenty years ago. That private enterprise will rapaciously exploit workers unless checked by social legislation and strong unions is undeniable. That Marx was right about the nature of "alienation" in a social system where money and property relations govern and deform human relations is also undeniable. But the real choices we have are those offered by a highly imperfect world. No one can doubt that if the famous Iron Curtain were lifted, if free movement became possible, there would be a great migration from east to west and scarcely any movement in the opposite direction. Knowing as I do, not only the Soviet Union, East Germany, and Czechoslovakia, as well as Cuba and some of the new states of Africa, I am forced to the conclusion that liberal democracy in Western Europe and America is a rare and extraordinary historical achievement which deserves to be defended—but not with atomic weapons.

My evolving style as a writer was partly influenced by an early passion for films (I dreamed of being a director, but never did anything about it). In particular I soaked up the work of Carol Reed (particularly the magical *Third Man,* with Joseph Cotten and Orson Welles), as well as the postwar renaissance of the Italian film industry (de Sica, Rossellini, Visconti). The script of *The Third Man* was unmistakably Graham Greene's—probably Greene as novelist was the strongest influence on me in the immediate run-up to my first, published novel which I wrote at the age of twenty, while a second-year History student at Oxford. By that stage things were getting serious and I had been hit by Dostoevsky, Joyce, and Faulkner. Enter now the subconscious and the "stream of consciousness." The sheer variety of literary influences, and my own joyful plagiarism, ensured that my first novel was like a calico bag stuffed with brightly coloured patchings of cloth—realism, naturalism, filthy soldiers' talk

Caute in the British infantry, West Africa, 1956

(see Mailer's *The Naked and the Dead*), free verse, stream of consciousness, the lot.

Military service had intruded. I applied to attend the crash-course in Russian, was not accepted, and ended up, after basic training and officer-cadet school, as an infantry subaltern in the Gold Coast (Ghana). I arrived on that exotic, malarial, slave coast, once known as "the white man's grave," the land of cocoa and Kwame Nkrumah, in December 1955, a few days before my nineteenth birthday. The year that followed was an enthralling experience involving long journeys through Nigeria and French West Africa, the hot politics of decolonization, intimate dealings with the various tribes to which our infantrymen belonged, unforgettable curries, surfing on the Atlantic breakers, visits to the old Portuguese and Dutch slave forts, haggling with the redoubtable market women—all the stuff of which novels are made.

Out of it—and my long childhood apprenticeship as a writer—tumbled my first published novel, *At Fever Pitch*. Drawing on the copious notes I had taken in West Africa, I started writing after my second term at Oxford, splashed £22 on an Olivetti portable typewriter, and began poking the keys with two fingers—indeed two still suffice today.

I did not tell my tutors at Oxford that I was writing a novel. At the turn of the year 1957-58 I delivered the typescript to Joyce Weiner, who was not only an old friend of my mother but also a literary agent. Highly literate, herself an Oxford graduate, warm, possessive, a bit of a snob, very fat, a reluctant spinster, Joyce invested huge resources of unspent motherliness in her brilliant young men (Mordecai Richler was another), then accused them of ingratitude when they could take no more of it. Recently I came across the letters she wrote me immediately after she first read the novel, which I had entitled "Colossus in Ebony," then "The Face on the Coin," before finally settling on *At Fever Pitch*.

"My dear boy—I like it all and dislike it all. The theme, the characterization, the background are all potentially first-class, even great and haunting [the latter phrase added in the margin]. With very few exceptions, they are choked with detail, a lot of it of a most insignificant kind. There are repetitions, vulgarities (and by that I don't mean obscenities only), and a duplication, I feel, of characters and obsessions with certain ideas."

Too true! With the help of detailed editorial work from Joyce, I began to wrestle with my repetitions, vulgarities, and obscenities. She sent the typescript to André Deutsch, Hungarian-born publisher of Norman Mailer's *The Naked and the Dead*, a novel which I regarded then, and still regard, as one of the finest of our time. André said yes! He even offered an advance of £100. I was summoned to his office in Great Russell Street and there I also met his colleague Diana Athill, who was to become the editor of all seven of the books I published with Deutsch between 1959 and 1971. She is a magnificent editor, alert, sensitive, painstaking, and a fine writer herself.

On one occasion, blushing for my sake rather than her own, she ventured to point out that I had consistently misspelled a four-letter word. This word is of course used more often than chewing gum or condoms by working-class males, not least when in khaki uniform, and its unexpurgated appearance in Mailer's *The Naked and the Dead* had caused a fine storm in England. I had spent my first night in the army in Kingston Barracks, mainly among fellow-conscripts from the East End of London, and if I heard that f-f-famous word once that night I heard it a hundred times. Yet I somehow (Diana Athill now pointed out) managed to misspell it throughout my novel as a five-letter word beginning with "ph."

Some months later a parcel arrived containing six complimentary copies of the finished novel. I gazed at them enchanted and quivering with pride; such pristine moments cannot be repeated. With trembling hands I opened the newspapers on 30 January 1959 (which must have been a Thursday) and again the following Sunday. Most of the reviews were good. The

Daily Mail came down to photograph me riding through Oxford in my flowing scholar's gown.

When *At Fever Pitch* was published the most famous of Oxford bookshops, Blackwell's, did me proud, filling its largest street window with two titles: mine, and a novel called *Doctor Zhivago* by an obscure Soviet writer, Boris Pasternak. My distinguished tutor, Lawrence Stone, must have gone out and gallantly purchased a copy of my book; when I arrived suitably gowned for a tutorial on Oliver Cromwell, he surprised me by devoting the first five minutes to "reviewing" *At Fever Pitch.*

"You obviously believe it's sex that makes the world go round," he said. "It isn't—it's money."

I suppose 1959 was "the time of my time." After the novel came a "first" in the History finals, then a graduate scholarship to St. Antony's College, finally a Fellowship of All Souls. I began the year an ordinary student occupying humble "digs" and ended up dining under a portrait of Lord Curzon and passing the port clockwise in the company of my fellow-Fellows: Lord Hailsham, Dr. A. L. Rowse, Sir Isaiah Berlin, Professor Max Beloff, Stuart Hampshire, Sir Keith Joseph, Professor R. C. Zaehner, and others. I occupied a handsome suite of rooms in the Hawksmoor quadrangle, with a view of the Radcliffe Camera from my window. A black-jacketed "scout" brought me tea and my mail in bed every morning, I ate my meals free of charge, and I began to earn modest sums of money tutoring. (The rate was then one pound, ten shillings an hour, the equivalent of two hardcover novels at that time.)

At Fever Pitch was awarded two literary prizes. All in all, 1959 was a hard act to follow.

In 1965 I resigned my Fellowship of All Souls College as a gesture of protest against the decision of the Fellows to abandon a major reform designed to transform the college from the "rotten borough" of Oxford into a viable institution of research and graduate studies. I cannot go into the issues here: my full report can be found in the March 1966 issue of the magazine *Encounter,* reprinted in my collected essays, *Collisions* (1974). Suffice it to say the process of leaving All Souls is much easier than entering it: two fellowships are offered each year on the basis of a competitive examination taken mainly by those who have just graduated with first-class honours in the various "schools," or faculties, of Oxford. In 1959, when I gained admission, All Souls (the "souls" in question were those of soldiers who died during the Hundred Years War between England and France) was distinguished not only by its immense wealth but also by its unique distinction in having no students, graduate or undergraduate. Being a Puritan Roundhead by inclination rather than the

laughing Cavalier, I regarded this state of affairs as intolerable. The other smiling incumbents did not: today, twenty years after I resigned, the College is still without students and the port continues to circulate clockwise.

Although criticism of All Souls was widespread in Oxford, most of the university's dons disapproved of my action because I followed up my resignation by publishing a long account of the internal battle within the college, using confidential documents and accounts. The first commandment in England is "thou shall not be in breach of confidence," and it is for this reason that a Freedom of Information Act as far-reaching as the American one is unlikely ever to reach the statute book in Britain. We hate disclosure. "Private and confidential" are holy words. Next month, for example, I am invited to attend a Foreign Office conference on Zimbabwe, in the company of some thirty-five other persons, none of whom may be named, quoted, or attributed.

I paid my first visit to America in 1960, crossing the Atlantic on the old Cunard liner *Queen Elizabeth,* to spend a year at Harvard, where I pursued my Ph.D. thesis, purchased an old Buick from a shouting Irish-American dealer ("D'ya want the car or don'tya?), wrote my first stage play, fell in love with my future wife, Catherine Shuckburgh, travelled south to Washington, the Carolinas, and Georgia, and returned to

Steven Trefonides, Boston

Caute, 1960

England to resume my life in All Souls College and marry—as Marxists tend to do—an ambassador's daughter. (Oddly enough, I have always been congratulated rather than despised for constantly breaking my own professed principles—the habit, I suppose, is taken as evidence of maturity and sophistication. But at least I succeeded in upsetting my future father-in-law by refusing to marry in a church.)

By the time I returned to America in 1966 much had changed. Catherine and our two small boys, Edward and Daniel, didn't accompany me, and the marriage was clearly on the rocks. The *Sunday Express* and several other newspapers telephoned to ask why. I had nothing to say about it then and have nothing to add now. America, too, had changed. When I arrived at Harvard in 1960, I spoke of socialism like a missionary from another planet; five years later the campuses were in revolt, the students were dodging the draft, Che Guevara was the standard hero, and my lectures on Marxism were boycotted by the radicals as reactionary. The mid-sixties were a fabulous era. The place was awash with money. I was invited by Professor Conor Cruise O'Brien to join his new "Albert Schweitzer" team at New York University (with George Steiner and John Arden); we occupied luxurious offices at 1, Fifth Avenue. The money I collected from Macmillan for my novel *The Decline of the West*, plus my NYU salary, as well as convenient sums picked up for teaching courses at Columbia and Indiana, rendered me financially secure for the next four or five years and partly contributed to my decision to resign from Brunel University in 1970 and risk the hazards of a fully freelance existence.

I found myself teaching summer school in Bloomington, Indiana, to an excellent class partly consisting of nuns. I had been invited to spend the summer at the Austin campus of the University of Texas and was nastily surprised when I was invited to sign a "disaffiliation oath," a relic of the McCarthy era. I refused, though of course I had never belonged to any of the excellent parties and organizations listed. A colleague, a scholar with an international reputation who has written repeatedly about the Holocaust, urged me to swallow my distaste for the Texas political test: "Don't forget you have a family to support," he told me. "And don't forget that I went to some trouble to arrange that invitation for you."

Some of my books have involved extensive travel, others contemplative immobility. *At Fever Pitch* was the product of military service in West Africa, with an obvious debt to Greene, Mailer, and some others. My second novel, *Comrade Jacob,* the story of a communistic peasant settlement which lasted a year on a Sur-

rey hillside in 1649-50, was of course born out of reading and imagining, though I did, naturally, visit St. George's Hill, only to discover that the "common land" for which the Diggers had fought was now covered in prosperous homes and warning notices: "Private. No Entry." This novel became the object of a minor cult on the Left which persists to this day. Soon after publication it was adapted for television by Christopher Williams. In 1969 John McGrath's stage adaptation became the opening production of the Gardner Arts Centre at Sussex University.

Finally, in 1975, Kevin Brownlow and Andrew Mollo produced the film version they had laboured on for years, *Winstanley.* I had written the script but asked for my name to be withdrawn when I realised how little of my own version remained. In my perspective Gerrard Winstanley, the leader of the Diggers, was not only an early communist but also a Puritan mystic, a visionary, a man whose dreams and trances are vividly reflected in his writings. Brownlow, however, is essentially a documentary film director whose passion is social and historical detail, and he wanted none of Winstanley's torrential visions, only the class struggle. The film became a cult among London's urban squatters in the mid-seventies, for Brownlow and Mollo shrewdly introduced seventeenth-century squatters (or "Ranters" as they were called) to irritate Winstanley's worthy, hard-working early communists.

Communism and the French Intellectuals, my first work of nonfiction, was in origin an Oxford D.Phil. thesis. I found excellent material on the early history of the French Communist Party in the Widener Library, Harvard, where I was a graduate student, but such a project obviously required visits to France and long hours in the Bibliothèque Nationale. The book was later translated into French and published by Gallimard. *The Left in Europe since 1789* and *Essential Writings of Karl Marx* were both undertaken to educate myself and involved very little original research. The same applied to *Frantz Fanon,* one of the first titles of Professor Frank Kermode's "Modern Masters" series.

The Decline of the West, a novel written on an epic scale, whether one likes it or not—and I would stamp on some of the purple passages were I rewriting it today—drew on sources and experiences so diverse that I cannot itemise them. Much of it was written during an idyllic four-month sojourn on the island of Hydra, in Greece. I would write from eight in the morning until one, have a light lunch, sunbathe, accompany Catherine and our infant son Edward by boat to the rocky coast, swim in warm blue lagoons, return for drink and food, then wish that the rented house had electricity, because I cannot write by gas lamp or candle. This was the only period when I have led the kind of existence one reads about in the memories of wealthy novelists who seek tax exile along the coastlines of the Mediterranean or Caribbean.

Peter Ritner, of Macmillan (New York), had already taken an interest in the project and while I was on Hydra a contract of commission arrived offering an advance of $1,500. I put it aside and when my agent sent him the finished work, all 240,000 words of it, a year later, Ritner came up with a contract for $15,000. In 1965 that was equivalent to a full professor's annual salary. Ritner was a hulk of a man, a son of the Great Depression and hungry for success; warm, aggressive, manic, hugely supportive to his authors until he dropped them. History was one of his passions. In the end he went over the top into the never-never land of the higher executive, and we parted company in the most expensive restaurant on Park Avenue after he had turned down *The Occupation*, he trying to recover the affections of his estranged wife while boasting how he could "smell" the best books in China even though he couldn't read Chinese—a bizarre evening. Peter slid into partial oblivion, wrote a thriller about the Shah of Iran, then fell to his death from the window of the Riverside Drive apartment where I used to stay, in

Caute, 1969

distant, better days, soaked in his magnificent hospitality. Another of my favourite editors, Tony Godwin, died in New York at about the same time.

Such was my wealth after Ritner's generous roar of greeting to *The Decline of the West* that I bought an Adler manual typewriter to my own keyboard specifications for the princely sum of £42. Everything I wrote for the next twenty years came off that gallant machine, but now I've been unfaithful to her, lured by the charms of a young word processor with expensive tastes. I also hired a secretary for a couple of months. The poor woman was confined to the tiny, unused "bachelor" bedroom attached to my study in All Souls, completely alone and with not a living soul to talk to, despite the many dead ones. I've never had a secretary since, relying on free-lance typists whenever a book is ready for the publisher. One of the Oxford typists whom I set to work on *The Decline of the West*, a solid matron, went crimson with indignation about certain sexual passages when I collected the text. From that time on I have taken the precaution of warning typists in advance; this accords them due honour while greatly exciting their interest.

The Occupation, a novel which is both a sexual comedy and an experiment in alienation techniques, involved perhaps the most enjoyable kind of "research" I know of. It was conducted on an entirely unplanned, haphazard basis in New York and London, with interludes in Paris, Florence, and Prague, during the years 1966-70. Those years were among the most vivid of my life, involving rapid alternations between high pleasure and despair, and culminating in a breakdown which rendered me both amnesiac and useless at the turn of 1969-70 (though I noticed how "sane" I became during the three-week rehearsal of my play *The Demonstration* at the Nottingham Playhouse. This play drew on my personal experience of campus revolutions in Britain and America in the late sixties).

After a recuperative visit to Israel and the recently occupied West Bank of the Jordan, I returned to London and began writing *The Occupation* in an effort to restore my sanity. I am not naturally a comic writer but on that occasion I found an idiom which was sound enough to carry the whole novel on a consistent note both sweet and sour. Indeed it should have been called "Honey and Lemon."

Later I adapted the novel as a stage play, *The Fourth World*, which received an excellent Sunday-night production at the Royal Court in March 1973. The director was the brilliant Buzz Goodbody, still in her twenties and the rising star of the Royal Shakespeare Company. We got on marvellously while working on the text until she suddenly decided, before rehearsals began, that she didn't want me in the theatre, though as far as I was aware there was no friction between us. I wasn't having it and we soon became close friends again. Six months later I saw her production of *As You Like It* at Stratford-upon-Avon. In April 1975 I happened to turn on the radio while washing the car on a country road outside our cottage in Wiltshire and was stunned to hear of Buzz's death. She had taken her own life.

The exclusion of the author from rehearsals is almost standard practice in television studios (except for the preliminary read-through), as I discovered when the late Robert Vas told me, on the first day of rehearsal of my BBC documentary drama *Brecht & Co.*, that he wanted me to go home. As with the Royal Court, I appealed successfully to higher authority. Robert was a greatly gifted documentary producer, a refugee from Communist Hungary, who turned out to detest Brecht on political grounds. We were thus in fundamental conflict over both my script and the emphasis of the production (which I wanted to be celebratory of Brecht's genius).

Cuba, Yes? was the product of a tour of Cuba that my future wife, Martha Bates, an editor at Weidenfeld and Nicolson, and I made in 1972. *The Fellow-Travellers* followed a tour of the Soviet Union in 1971, during which she and I visited Moscow, Irkutsk, Tashkent, Alma-Ata, Bukhara, and Samarkand (though the book's foundation resides in archival and literary research). This may be the moment to write a few words about the woman who has shared my life for the past fifteen years.

Martha Caute, 1982

The Caute family, 1976: Daniel, Martha holding Anna, Rebecca, and Edward

I first met her in 1970 when I was at a low ebb physically and mentally. What struck me immediately was not only her gentleness but a beauty and tranquillity worthy of a portrait by Vermeer. A passion for travel was only one of many forces pulling us together. Martha can ride my rages better than anyone I've met. In her presence, and under her immediate influence, I am almost civilized. She is not only the ideal mother to our daughters Rebecca and Anna, but also established a harmonious relationship with Edward and Daniel—I've never heard a sharp word between them. But praising one's wife or celebrating a happy family is not an interesting (or even convincing) literary enterprise, and I've said more than enough.

The Great Fear, a long, detailed study of the anticommunist campaign in America under Truman and Eisenhower, involved massive research, spread over five years, and rapidly diminishing financial resources, since Martha stopped working temporarily to have our first child and by that time I held no university post. I had to travel widely in the USA in search of both archival material and interviews (New York, Boston, Detroit, Los Angeles, San Francisco), with only a three-week stint as Regents' Lecturer at the Irvine Campus of the University of California to support me. Every grant-donating body in America I applied to turned me down, including the Rabinowitz Foundation. May they all grow hair in the wrong places. Life became no easier when the commissioning editor at McGraw-Hill departed, was replaced by someone equally sympathetic, who then departed, and was in turn replaced by a man whose treatment of me provided a monumental example of the American editor as philistine hatchet-man. Rejected by him, *The Great Fear* became the main selection of the History Book Club. May all his hair fall out.

Occasional journalism for the London *Sunday Times* had meanwhile taken me to Israel, Iraq, Kuwait, and the Persian Gulf states. I also set out with a photographer to interview President Tito for the same paper, but we became entangled in byzantine Yugoslav bureaucracy and ended up with Tito in his mountain retreat near Sarajevo as he entertained the entire leadership of North Vietnam and their wives—but no interview! A different kind of potentate—but not entirely different—was Henry Ford II, whom I interviewed in Detroit while writing a chapter for the *Sunday Times*'s series, "Great American Families." Accompanied by Lord Snowdon, I visited the Ford family home for a group photograph of Henry, his brothers, his mother, and his sister. I was of course given the full treatment by the Ford publicity men, enjoyed every moment, and duly wrote a piece ungratefully demonstrating that hospitality can be wasted. Well, they knew that anyway.

Most writers—certainly most British ones—would rather "come clean" about sex than about money. They'd rather admit who they've slept with than how much they've earned. Reading Graham Greene's autobiography a few years ago, I was struck by his failure to say how much he had earned from each book or each film. (Are we afraid our earnings were too much or too little?) Ninety percent of writers want very badly to earn a decent living from their writing and most of us are envious of those who earn a lot.

As far as I'm aware I have never altered or gilded a sentence, paragraph, scene, or chapter in the hope that I would thereby make more money. However, "never" is a treacherous word and such a claim requires its confession of sin. On two occasions I have written "thrillers" under the pseudonym John Salisbury solely in order to make money. The strategy is not only to offer an exciting story, a skilfully woven plot, exotic settings, lovely ladies, and copious bloodshed, plus well-researched documentary material, but also to shorten paragraphs, abbreviate sentences, eliminate any fancy phrases, divest characters of an inner life, and mould them into desirable stereotypes. However, the same rule applies to "downmarket" thrillers as to romances: to be really good at it, and really successful, you need to be almost as illiterate and philistine as the "mass market" whose dollars you want.

The first thriller I wrote, *The Baby-Sitters*, was sold

to Secker and Warburg, and Arrow in the UK; Atheneum and Dell in the USA (the American paperback edition appeared under the title *The Hour before Midnight*). It was also sold to publishers in France, Germany, Italy, Holland, Japan, Sweden, Spain, and Latin America, bringing me a total income of about $120,000 and enabling us not only to take our first holiday since Rebecca and Anna were born (Alexandria, Cairo, Luxor), but also to pursue my rather expensive reporting of the war in Rhodesia.

Predictably corrupted by this experience (I also *enjoy* writing thrillers), I produced another, *Moscow Gold*, which eventually sold 60,000 copies in paperback in the UK. The plot of the novel concerns the defection of the Soviet Union's leading female pentathlete to the United States during the year before the Moscow Olympics of 1980. Soon after the novel was completed reality most inconsiderately intervened to throw the

Martha and David Caute in the Valley of the Kings, Egypt, 1977

entire plot into disarray: President Jimmy Carter decided to boycott the Moscow Games.

In the late 1970s I began to return to Africa, immersing myself in Rhodesia's bitter, rearguard war against the nationalist insurgents. My reports appeared in the *New Statesman* and the *Observer* at a time when Conor Cruise O'Brien (my boss of ten years earlier at NYU) was editor-in-chief, and in the New York journal, the *Nation*. Out of successive visits to Zimbabwe (formerly Rhodesia) came *Under the Skin: The Death of White Rhodesia,* the novel *The K-Factor,* and the BBC radio play, *The Zimbabwe Tapes.* Zimbabwe is again the inspiration of a long essay, "Marechera and the Colonel," published in book form early in 1986 alongside a study of two Official Secrets Act prosecutions which took place in Britain in George Orwell's 1984.

One of those prosecutions involved extraordinarily discreditable behaviour by the editor of the *Guardian* newspaper, Peter Preston. I discovered that great investigative newspapers do not enjoy being investigated—and in the UK press we have no counterpart to the American ombudsman. My report, "Sarah Tisdall and the *Guardian,*" appeared in the Cambridge magazine, *Granta,* in August 1984. The book is called *The Espionage of the Saints.*

For two years I edited the literary and arts pages of the weekly magazine, the *New Statesman.* When the new editor, Bruce Page, approached me in January 1979 I had no thought of such a job and agreed to do it only on the basis of thirty weeks a year, imagining that I would thereby leave myself time to research and write the book that was later published as *Under the Skin: The Death of White Rhodesia.* It was a serious miscalculation. Not only must the literary editor survey at least one quarter of the 40,000 books published in the UK every year—and arrange for about 500 of them to be reviewed—he is also responsible for coverage of theatre, film, art, ballet, opera, music, architecture, television, and radio. It falls to him to allocate space to regular critics ravenous for column inches.

Even when I was supposedly enjoying my annual twenty-two-week sabbatical I discovered that the job was constantly preoccupying me. Had we reviewed this book, should we cover that festival? Well aware that my editorial policies and priorities were welcomed in some quarters but sharply opposed in others, I was wary of delegating responsibility. What I set out to do while at the *New Statesman* was to make certain connections. I tried to demonstrate that the "front half" (politics, society, the world) and the "back half" (culture) are not separate, watertight compartments. I encouraged longer, thematic review-articles of, say, four or six books, despite the opposition of the advertising manager who pointed out that this meant reviewing many books long after publication date, which in turn alienated book advertisers. I tended to avoid or expel the regular, "clever boy" reviewers who produced the same urbane, witty, sardonic, value-free prose wherever they reviewed, replacing them with playwrights and novelists and university lecturers and (sometimes) politicians who might be less professional but were more likely to have something of importance to say.

In recent times authors have tentatively begun to combine in guilds and unions, and in 1982-83 I served as Co-Chairman of the Writers' Guild in Britain. We published a survey of the standard printed contracts issued by sixty British publishers, analysed them clause by clause, and demonstrated the extraordinary, anarchical variety of terms and conditions offered. What is needed throughout the industry is a Minimum Terms Agreement between publishers and unions, establishing a code of practice and a "Magna Carta" for writers. Such an Agreement, already negotiated in Britain with a very few leading publishers like Hamish Hamilton, Faber and Faber, and the BBC, governs individual contracts without, of course, preventing an author from obtaining a seven-figure advance or a 20 percent royalty if his position commands such privileges. As Chairman of the Writers' Guild's Books Committee, I was able to bring the Guild and the Society of Authors into collaboration, so that the Agreement they now offer to publishers represents both unions. But it's too civilized a document for the taste of most publishers.

During those years British writers did achieve one major victory, the arrival of Public Lending Right on the statute book. All that is now required is for the Government to put a meaningful amount of money into the scheme—one penny per borrowing is hardly that.

Active membership of the Guild had its snags. As soon as writers become seriously involved in union business they begin to imitate the politicians—posturing, indulging in rhetoric, forming cliques and barking, "Mr. Chairman, point of order!" like characters in their own novels and plays. Faction-fights abound; the losers sulk, walk out, resign, often on the most obscure issues. (A well-known television playwright insisted that the Guild condemn not only the London zoo but all zoos.) When I was Co-Chairman I was the target of a motion of censure by my opponents merely because I had circulated a memo to three members of the Society of Authors who sat on a joint Guild-Society working party—we were deep into that kind of triviality and madness. It was time to quit. Writers do themselves no good when they start behaving like lawyers or politi-

Anna, Martha, Rebecca, and David Caute at Table Bay, Cape Town, South Africa, 1984

cians.

Let me conclude by making a wish for the world: to dispose of all nuclear armaments. It won't happen. And a wish for myself: to write a novel as good as Patrick White's *Riders in the Chariot.* That won't happen either.

BIBLIOGRAPHY

Fiction:

At Fever Pitch. London: Deutsch, 1959; New York: Pantheon, 1959.

Comrade Jacob. London: Deutsch, 1961; New York: Pantheon, 1962.

The Decline of the West. London: Deutsch, 1966; New York: Macmillan, 1966, Ballantine, 1967.

The Occupation. London: Deutsch, 1971; New York: McGraw-Hill, 1972.

The Baby-Sitters, under pseudonym John Salisbury. London: Secker & Warburg, 1978; New York: Atheneum, 1978; published as *The Hour before Midnight.* New York: Dell, 1980.

Moscow Gold, under pseudonym John Salisbury. London: Futura, 1980.

The K-Factor. London: M. Joseph, 1983.

Nonfiction:

Communism and the French Intellectuals, 1914-1960. London: Deutsch, 1964; New York: Macmillan, 1964.

The Left in Europe since 1789. London: Weidenfeld & Nicolson, 1966; New York: McGraw-Hill, 1966.

Fanon. London: Fontana, 1970; published as *Frantz Fanon.* New York: Viking, 1970.

The Confrontation, trilogy consisting of *The Demonstration* (play), *The Illusion* (essay), and *The Occupation* (novel). London: Deutsch, 1971.

The Illusion. London: Deutsch, 1971; New York: Harper, 1972.

The Fellow-Travellers: A Postscript to the Enlightenment. London: Weidenfeld & Nicolson, 1973; New York: Macmillan, 1973.

Collisions: Essays and Reviews. London: Quartet Books, 1974.

Cuba, Yes? London: Secker & Warburg, 1974; New York: McGraw-Hill, 1974.

The Great Fear: The Anti-Communist Purge under Truman and Eisenhower. London: Secker & Warburg, 1978; New York: Simon & Schuster, 1978.

Under the Skin: The Death of White Rhodesia. London: Allen Lane, 1983; Evanston, Ill.: Northwestern University Press, 1983.

The Espionage of the Saints: Two Essays on Silence and the State. London: Hamish Hamilton, 1986.

Plays:

Songs for an Autumn Rifle, produced in Edinburgh, Scotland, 1961.

The Demonstration, produced in Nottingham and London, England, 1969; Hamburg, Germany, 1971.

The Fourth World, produced in London, England, 1973.

Television scripts:

Brecht & Co, BBC-TV, 1979.

Radio plays:

The Demonstration, BBC Radio, 1971.

Fallout, BBC Radio, 1972.

The Zimbabwe Tapes, BBC Radio, 1983.

Editor of:

Essential Writings of Karl Marx. London: MacGibbon & Kee, 1967; New York: Macmillan, 1967.

Sound Recordings:

Nineteenth-Century European Socialism, with Ralph Miliband. Santa Monica, Calif.: BFA Educational Media, distributed by Holt Information Systems, 1972.

Fred Chappell

1936-

On August 2, 1959, I married Susan Nicholls. She was just eighteen and I was twenty-two years old. I had been introduced to her some years before by my sister, Rebecca, and we had both attended Canton High School in the mountains of western North Carolina. I am still married to Susan, and though we now reside in the middle part of the state, the Piedmont, it is still North Carolina. These facts may give some indication of what a quiet, not to say circumscribed, life I have led.

It has been mostly my choice to lead a generally uneventful life. Unvarying routine is important to me, as it is to many writers, because it provides an opportunity to schedule writing time as an inevitable part of the day. I cannot say that I live to write, and I believe that my writing is important to very few people indeed, but I can say in all honesty that my days seem incomplete without some working hours at my desk, whatever the eventual result of those hours.

It is not a matter of discipline, as my friends seem to imagine. I cannot call myself disciplined, so many times failing to quit cigarettes, so many times failing to bring a writing project to the point of attainment I had aimed at. It is instead a matter of enjoyment: I like writing, I like books, I like long studious hours with Aristotle, Homer, Virgil, Shakespeare, Balzac, and all the worthy literary totems which have dominated my sensibility since childhood. The itch to write—Horace's *cacoëthes scribendi*—has finally become a need, perhaps out of no more cause than habit. It was, after all, by means of habit that Sir Francis Galton taught himself to experience feelings of sanctity about a broken watering can.

But these habits could have become ingrained only after the date of my marriage, which marked a new life for me. Before then, I was a regrettable mess, living haphazardly, drinking to excess (a problem which continued for two decades afterward), pursuing luckless and chimerical dreams, obnoxiously flaunting a sleazy cleverness. There are many parts of my life in which I take little pride or none; but then I feel little remorse either. That was the person I was; if I could have been a different person, I would have followed a different career.

A month after the wedding, we moved to Dur-

Fred Chappell, with Drummond, 1985

ham, where I hoped to finish my undergraduate degree and eventually to attend graduate school. I had been thrown out of Duke University at the beginning of my junior year because of a typical college-boy scandal too mindless to recount here. But now I had a wife and real responsibilities, and I was determined to do the thing right this time. By the date of our first anniversary we also had a son, Christopher Heath, more responsibility than I had counted on and another solid undergirding for my determination. I went at it with a kind of angry ferocity, took my B.A., and was awarded a National Defense Education Act fellowship for graduate English studies.

Fred Chappell, the mascot in the sailor suit, with the graduating class of Bethel High School, about 1940

I had chosen Duke in the first place because I wanted to write books, though I couldn't say what kind. Poetry, fiction, criticism, scholarship—anything would be dandy. And at Duke resided the highly reputed teacher of writing, Dr. William Blackburn. A fair amount has been written about this remarkable man (William Styron's account in *This Quiet Dust* is pungent and memorable), but there is probably no way to do him real justice.

He was, first of all, a physically imposing person. Six feet tall or taller, with obvious though rarely used strength, he drew every glance when he entered a room. His ruggedly distinguished face, the lines and angles emphasized by black horn-rimmed glasses, was formidable even when he wore—as he mostly did—a pleasant or abstracted expression. He dressed habitually in dark three-piece suits and it was almost shocking to find him in summer in a colorful blue sports shirt. He was the man in whom a young and desperate writer stood in awe, no one could quite say why.

Even now, no one can really say why. In his literature courses, Renaissance and seventeenth century, he lectured elegantly and read the material aloud with grave dramatic conviction. But his creative writing class was an abyss of midnight silence. He would read a student's story (he wouldn't teach poetry composition, lacking—he said—confidence) in a subdued but resonant voice and then put it down. Then it seemed hours before anyone dared speak a word. Dr. Blackburn

would sigh, clear his throat now and again, but mostly stare into vacant interlunar space with a sad and defeated air. It wasn't just that something was wrong with the student's story, something was wrong with the mind that had produced it; and something was dreadfully wrong with the universe that had allowed this mind to survive so long with graceless impunity.

He was not a severe critic. He was actually as tactful as he could be and would always, sooner or later, say something pleasing about the work at hand. But he could not disguise his final estimate; this story had failed his standards; in fact, it had not approached near enough to get them in sight. The student had tried, surely he had tried valiantly—an instructor must suppose that much, at least—but the student had failed. It was simply more evidence of the Sophoclean injustice of the world.

That was Dr. Blackburn's view of things, always the darkest possible. His outlook might be characterized as stoic Christian fatalist, in keen congruence with the views of Donne and Samuel Johnson. He had no faith in human kindness and liked to imagine catastrophes and conspiracies. For decades he had been at odds with the university administration and with the English Department, and he imagined that he had enemies. "If you don't watch out," he would say, twisting a pretended knife in your ribs, "they'll get you right *here*." Or, "I've taught here for twenty-five years and I'm the lowest-paid full professor in this university."

Probably that was true. He was a humanist in the old sense and distrusted the heavy influences of the physical and especially the social sciences upon education. Nor did he gleefully suffer fools, and he never bothered to hide his contempt for some of his colleagues. An honest man, but not an easy one; and he paid the price of his honesty—but not without complaining.

But he was successful. When he found a student who showed talent, he could not heap him with enough praise and encouragement, and he would pester book and periodical editors with the sometimes callow efforts of young writers for whom he foresaw bright futures. A few years before my arrival, his efforts had been vindicated by the brilliant debuts of William Styron and Mac Hyman *(No Time for Sergeants).* Among the students there during my time he identified as surefire prospects Reynolds Price, Tom Atkins, James Applewhite, Wallace Kaufman, Anne Tyler, and myself.

It is easy now to say that he was not wrong. They have all achieved notable careers, but that is never simple to predict. Reynolds Price, though, was not exactly contemporary. He had returned to Duke as an instructor, having taken an Oxford degree as a Rhodes scholar. He was hard at work on his fine first novel, *A Long and Happy Life,* which so quickly placed him in the front ranks of American writers.

Reynolds decided to put together an informal writing class of these writers and he managed to get us university credit for meeting, usually at my house on Onslow Street, to drink beer and talk about our stuff. Those were happy evenings and we produced some good work, Anne Tyler the most as well as the best. Wallace Kaufman, Jim Applewhite, and I were interested in poetry, and Reynolds—unlike Dr. Blackburn—encouraged it.

In fact, Reynolds was a better instructor than the good Dr. B. He had written fiction (as our elder mentor never had) and could talk about technique. He was unerring in finding exact faults of structure, exact infelicities of phrase. He had an enormous learning, which he carried lightly, even jokingly. Sometimes he was wrong, but then—because of his youth and easy demeanor—he could be argued with, as Dr. Blackburn never would be. What he lacked was that weighty and weary moral authority, that voice of the monumental centuries. As much as we loved Blackburn, it was rather a relief to work with Reynolds.

I don't clearly remember anything I wrote in those years except a single one-page short story called "January," which may well stand as the best thing I ever wrote. I scratched it down, almost without correction, on the day my son was born, just after returning

"Glamorized senior photo for the high-school yearbook"

from the hospital to visit him and Susan. It came to me all unbidden, as a few other pieces have done, and with only one error—which Anne Tyler pointed out to me. "January" was not only the germ, but the pivot, of my first novel, *It Is Time, Lord.*

It had appeared in the Duke student literary magazine, *The Archive,* where Hiram Haydn, who was visiting the campus as a Literary Figure, saw it. Hiram was a solid scholar and novelist, and now an editor at Atheneum, which was then a fledgling publishing company. At the time he saw my story, he had just published Reynolds' novel to wide acclaim and financial success. Perhaps he was thinking that he might net another trophy fish from the same pond. At any rate, he sent a note from his publishing office to inquire if I were interested in writing a novel.

It is hard to believe now that I responded coolly to this suggestion. Partly I did so because I felt my first allegiance was still to poetry, but also because I could not see how I would possibly have time to work on a book. For by this time I had been awarded my scholarship to graduate school where "creative" effort was looked upon with a prim and crusty skepticism. In short, I was simply afraid that I might injure my chances at a college teaching career. It seemed sensible to try to get that first, and then to pursue my writing with security in hand.

I had chosen as my period of specialization eighteenth-century English literature for two reasons. The

On the ABC network program "Meet the Professor": left to right, Dr. William Blackburn,
Fred Chappell, William Styron, Reynolds Price, and Mac Hyman

first was the charming and inspired teaching of the undergraduate course by Dr. Oliver Ferguson; the second reason was that I'd heard that there was a shortage of eighteenth-century scholars and that finding a job would be relatively easy. I had it all mapped out. For my M.A. degree I would produce a concordance to the English poems of Samuel Johnson, and I would then use the concordance as a tool for my doctoral dissertation on Johnson's poetic diction. My scholarship ran for three years; I figured on taking two years to prepare the concordance, one more to write the dissertation.

I actually did produce the concordance. It may well be the world's longest master's thesis, 1,111 pages of usage entries. I worked on it four hours a day every day for nearly three years, reading straight through Johnson's poems twenty-four times and copying out words and their contexts on index cards. Nowadays, with a computer, the job would take how long? Two hours? Fifteen minutes? . . . But that is another matter I do not regret. I learned a great deal about words and about patience, and I learned not to be cowed by large tasks.

Yet there were other things going on. I was taking the regular courses, and in one of them I was personally charged by the professor to turn out a published paper. I still do not understand how this requirement came about or why I acceded to it. But I did so, and

was invited to read the unauthoritative pages about Shakespeare's *Coriolanus* at a Renaissance conference. In the audience was Dr. Joseph Bryant, then chairman of the English Department of the University of North Carolina in Greensboro. After I presented my paper, he approached to offer a job in his department. I still had two years to go in graduate studies, but I accepted on the spot. That gave me one less worry.

I could use the breathing space. We found that my scholarship, generous as it was for the times, was insufficient to support us during the summer months. We were broke. So I wrote to Haydn, offering to write a novel if he was still interested. Hearing that he was, I sat down and wrote it. In six weeks it was finished and I sent it off. The writing had actually taken five weeks; I wrote then, as I still do, in longhand and for one week my hand was too sore to hold the ballpoint.

Atheneum accepted the book and gave me $1,000 for it, and the money got us into our second year of grad school. There were changes to be made, of course; there always were with Hiram Haydn, who took a perhaps overly paternal interest in editing. He invited me to New York to discuss them, and I knew that I had to go, though the travel made quite a hole in our budget. I met with Haydn and his warm family in Westport, agreed to the changes, and returned to Durham tipsy and exhilarated. It had only just been borne in upon me that Yes, friends, this was the big time, I was publishing a novel with a high-class New York firm, I had even had a couple of accidental drinks with the actor George Grizzard at Jimmy Ryan's bar next door to the theater where he was appearing in the early performances of *Who's Afraid of Virginia Woolf?* I actually had one unsteady foot on the Yellow Brick Road.

I have occasionally heard the thought expressed by New York writers that southern writers, having achieved some measure of success, return to the south so that they can be big frogs in small ponds. That's not the way it is or was or ever shall be. Dr. Blackburn was joyous at the news, my friends were happy for me, we all celebrated. But except for my personal friends no one else in the university or in the community was much impressed or even interested, even when the book finally appeared. (Of course, a graduate student is not really a member of the local community.) This fact did not disturb me even at the time, but I noted it with some surprise and have kept it faithfully in mind. Whatever the actual value of his work, a writer is unimportant in the daily scheme of things—as he should be. When he begins to imagine otherwise, he becomes a sycophant or a demagogue.

It Is Time, Lord was pretty well received, if I remember correctly, though not by the New York papers. But I gratefully recall nice notices in *Saturday Review* and the London *Times Literary Supplement*. What has since become my favorite notice I ever got—a highly unfavorable one—appeared in a Virginia newspaper with this descriptive headline: "Weakling beats his chicken breast." I don't know if that is an accurate précis of the novel, but I admire its confidence of judgment.

Between the time the novel was accepted and the date of its appearance—about eight months, I think—I lived in fright. When it finally did appear, I stewed about the reviews. I wasn't worried about sales or hot-stuff money; I knew already that I had not written a popular book and that I never would, but I did want it to be respected on its own terms. I didn't mind a commercial failure, or even an artistic one (though that would be disappointing), as long as it was clear that my effort was honorable.

What utter silliness. An author formulates his own notion of honor; it cannot be explained to the world at large, or to anyone else. If he has accounted himself honorably, he is the only person who can know. If he has not, or does not desire to, this shortcoming will sooner or later make itself manifest in his personal character and he shall become a lesser person. That is a price the writer may pay without ever knowing it.

Publication brought about some unforeseen consequences. My friend George Garrett recommended the book to M. Maurice-Edgar Coindreau, the celebrated French translator of Faulkner, Hemingway, Steinbeck, and so many other well-known American writers. M. Coindreau liked the book, and in France it did very well indeed. This was the beginning of my much too vaunted "French reputation," which has since died a quiet death. It is true that my third novel, *Dagon,* was given the prestigious Prix de Meilleur des Livres Etrangers. But (and I have tried to explain this many times) the Académie Française was not particularly interested in my book; they wanted to reward M. Coindreau for his lifetime of devoted accomplishment. It was a well-deserved gesture, and I only wish they could have chosen a better-known American writer to represent him. Susan and I liked him immensely; a supremely intelligent man with a demonic expression, he was sympathetic, humorous, and a wonderful raconteur, telling stories about literary figures who were to us (and are still) only legends. He was then in his late sixties, or early seventies, and bemused by the youth of the authors he was now translating. When he watched our son Heath in diapers, crawling the floor of our apartment, he remarked wistfully, "Of course, I won't be translating *his* books." But if Heath wrote books, M. Coindreau could have translated them; he lived and worked well into his nineties. He advised us to come to France for publication of the book, "before all the good restaurants disappear," but we could not go then and have never gone.

We were still broke. Susan took a secretarial job and Heath began to toddle. We bought him a playpen which he couldn't abide, so while I baby-sat I sat in the playpen where he couldn't get at me and finished my concordance and began writing my second novel. The typing of the concordance—1,111 pages on the required thesis paper—was beyond our physical resources. I had now acquired an agent, Harold Matson, who would like, he said, to see some short fiction. So one rainy afternoon I went down to Mayola's Chili House, our local beer joint haunt, and wrote a short story. Mr. Matson sold it to the *Saturday Evening Post* and we used the nine hundred dollars to get the thesis typed. I turned it in to my advisor, endured a grueling and embarrassing three-hour oral examination, and came out with a Master of Arts degree.

But it had taken a year longer than I'd planned. Now I would have to teach for a few years, save my money, and then return to complete work for the Ph.D. Also I would have to learn German (Duke having decided that in my case French and Latin were not sufficient), and I would have to begin writing the dissertation as soon as possible. I looked upon this prospect with bleak dread. I would also, in the meantime, have to learn how to teach.

Susan Chappell

Even so, I felt the weight of a coliseum lifted off me. I was free of the thesis, free for a time of the grad school grind. It was with real joy that I sat in the playpen—which Heath, having learned to throw, showered with pebbles and toy blocks—and wrote *The Inkling,* an allegorical novel of Desire and Will, distantly based upon the unhappy story of the French symbolist poets, Rimbaud and Verlaine. Though the subject matter and style had to be very different, my larger ambitions for the second novel were the same as for the first: to produce a daring and even experimental novel which would not look or feel experimental, and to keep a story going with such force that a reader would be led on from first paragraph to last whether he actually liked the book or not. I must admit that in my early work, my design was as much to harrow my reader as to entertain him.

The Inkling was another, and almost the last, work that came to me as a whole, almost as a vision. In my mind's eye, I could see the book in print, a perfect novella, and even the words on the pages. Short and savage and serious, a book that took no prisoners. Again, I wrote it in five weeks, under deadline this time of our move to Greensboro, fifty miles away. I was well aware that it would be impossible to find time to write during my first year of teaching freshman composition courses for $5,500 per annum. I turned it in to Atheneum and in due time it was published, and that—as far as I can recall—was that.

Well, it *was* translated into French, and I'm sure it must have been reviewed, but by this time I was over-

taken by the attitude that still informs my behavior toward the fate of my books. Frankly, my dear, I don't give a damn. Perhaps it would have been nice to be rich and famous—but I knew that I was not going to be. It would be cozy to be understood and admired, but after that happened, then what? Already I noticed that when I was introduced to someone as a novelist, a vaguely disbelieving and faintly contemptuous expression came over his face. If I was a novelist, why hadn't he heard of me? Most of the few newspaper interviewers I talked with seemed to take it for granted that I was trying to write like Irving Wallace, with miserable lack of success. A few people asked my mother how much it cost to get my books published.

Probably the adolescent hankering for wealth and notoriety died soon because I came to understand it as foolish. But merely because I saw it as foolish didn't mean that others did. They had, of course, to measure my achievement by their own standards. If anything rankled me, it was the fact that I couldn't find opportunity to explain what *my* standards were. Except to Susan, who must have listened to my harangue some thousand-score times.

Anyway, it was almost enough to be teaching at Greensboro, where Robert Watson and Randall Jarrell and Peter Taylor taught. It was probably due to Peter's influence that I was moved into the writing program of the department, which was just now accepting its first students for a Masters of Fine Arts program. The literary reputation of UNCG was unassailable. Earlier, Allen Tate had taught here, and Caroline Gordon, and, during one semester in 1938, Ford Madox Ford. Robert Penn Warren, Robert Lowell, Elizabeth Hardwick, Jean Stafford, Eudora Welty, and many other shining lights, had been frequent visitors. I thought of it as the best possible place for a serious writer to teach, and probably I still think so.

I was earnest about my classes and worked hard at them. Teaching has been such an important goal to me that it took me twenty years to understand that I don't do it very well. I am not patient with my thoughts when I try to speak them and cannot articulate them with sufficient logic. My respect for the books I teach amounts to something like reverence, and I tend to become irritated with those students for whom Twain and Chaucer and Milton mean little or nothing. I have usually tried to teach in a variation of the Socratic method, drawing out the students by process of dialogue. But often I cannot make my intentions clear, so that the students think I am merely badgering them, trying to make them look foolish. In short, I have never learned to relax properly in teaching and probably communicate more anxiety than substance. But I still try, and this profession is still the one I would like to

Chappell with his grandmother and his parents, Anne and J.T. Chappell

succeed in.

I have been speaking of teaching academic courses, American literature and so forth. With creative writing courses—detestable term!—it is a matter of blind instinct, to be tempered with a gentle honesty. But what I have mostly got across is the blindness.

Even so, I have discovered the secret of successfully teaching creative writing. You simply stay in one place and teach for a long time, and gifted writers will fall out of the sky and land in your classes. In our very first years of the M.F.A. writing program, we had such students as Angela Davis-Gardner, Harry Humes, Thomas Molyneux, William Pitt Root, Kelly Cherry, Robert Morgan, and others too of fine talent who have made distinguished careers. And talented students are generally a forgiving lot; they tend to respect their teachers even as they recognize their liabilities. It is probable that the serious student already knows well the difficulties of literary endeavor and is not inclined to expect too much. If we have had a respected writing program at UNCG—and I think we can fairly claim that we have—it is because our students have been understanding and commiserating.

During these years, the mid-sixties, things went pretty well for Susan and me, though our lives were darkened by the death of Randall Jarrell in 1965.

It seemed plain to me that I ought to be able to write at least one novel a year, since I only had to spend six weeks or so at the task; and then I could teach and write poetry, enjoy my family, and listen to the welkin ring with bluebirds.

But of course it didn't happen that way. *Dagon*, my third novel and the shortest of my books of fiction, gave me trouble from which I never quite recovered. Though I was willing to harrow readers with my books, I never expected one of my books to harrow me. *Dagon* was designed as a horror story, tenuously and ironically connected to that tradition of horror fiction initiated by H.P. Lovecraft, the Cthulhu mythos. I had all sorts of strange ideas about the book; it was to be pop art metaphysics, for one thing, in which the garish conventions of pulp horror stories accurately depicted the terrors of contemporary civilization; it was to be rooted in a posited secret American history, an underground religion operative since colonial times; and it was to retell the Biblical story of Samson in modern dress.

All right, nothing so difficult about all that. My little books were used to having arcane purposes and hidden ambitions. But the horror of the story began to work in me, to shape my daydreams and nightmares and to poison even the most ordinary concerns of life. I had always drunk too much, and now I began to drink more. The drinking didn't help, and only made the situation more complicated and unhappy. I wrote at *Dagon* almost every day, usually tearing up the pages when I finished. I couldn't complete the story and it wouldn't allow me to discard it. And this painful stalemate went on for three years.

Finally though, it was done, and I shipped it to Hiram Haydn.

Hiram was still my editor, and the only one I've ever known in New York. But he had left Atheneum to go to Harcourt Brace Jovanovich, and it was with this firm that I had published *The Inkling.* Now he provisionally accepted *Dagon*—reluctantly, as it seemed to me. He wanted a great many changes. I made some of the changes he required; two of them were especially germane and necessary. But when I sent the manuscript back, he wanted still more. He wanted particularly to lighten the book, to make it less gloomy, and I wasn't willing to do that.

I felt great sympathy for Hiram. His position at HBJ was not explained to me, but it was obvious that he lacked the autonomy he had enjoyed at Atheneum. He seemed to admire my work and to have faith in my future as a writer, but there was pressure on him to bring out books that would sell a respectable number of copies. (I'm only guessing at this point, but I do remember my impressions of the situation.) It was clear to both of us that I wasn't going to sell Alpine ranges of books, and the question had to be whether he could afford to keep me on. And now I had sent him this agonizing little work, obscure and disturbing.

He wanted changes and he wanted to see me, to discuss the book in person. We had not met together in four years and I didn't want to meet him now. I knew pretty well what he was going to say, I knew that I disagreed, and I didn't want to get into an argument I knew I would lose. Hiram was enormously persuasive, and I also felt for him almost the same affection I felt for Dr. Blackburn. The whole thing could only be distressing.

No, I said, I wouldn't come to New York. He spoke of "neutral ground"; we would meet in Philadelphia. No, not Philadelphia. When he suggested Washington, D.C., I countered by saying that he should write out all his ideas and I would follow them to the letter and get the book back to him in six months. For I had realized that Hiram as an editor had to read tons of manuscript and that he also liked to feel that he was shaping a writer's book. So when he sent his letter, I simply laid the manuscript on the shelf, waited six months, retyped it just as it was, and sent it back to him, telling him that I had found his suggestions quite helpful.

It didn't entirely work; he wasn't completely satisfied. But he accepted it and, in about a year, published it.

I received the galleys in Florence, Italy, where Susan and Heath and I were spending a year by courtesy of a Rockefeller grant. The grant had come as a marvelous surprise. Peter Taylor and Robert Lowell had recommended me for it, but I didn't know that. (In fact, I had never heard of the Rockefeller Foundation.) The grant was, by any standard, generous in most cases. The Foundation paid the grantee his normal salary for a working year and gave a matching amount to his employer to hire a replacement. The trouble was that I was making now $9,000 a year, and even in 1967 it was inadvisable for a family of three to try to live in a European city on $9,000.

What the hell, it was glorious, the whole thing. We never learned to live within our budget, but what tourist has ever managed that? We spent so freely, in fact, that we had no money to return home on, and if I had not received another grant at the end of the year from the National Institute of Arts and Letters, just

Chappell and son, Heath, about 1967

enough for our passage, we might still be in Italy, hawking English lessons to Hungarian engineers.

There had been nothing like this stay in our experience, maybe not in our imaginations. And there can never be anything like it again. We wore out pair after pair of shoes, walking the streets, the galleries, the museums, the cathedrals. We made friends with American graduate students, cynical Communist waiters, surly Latin American poets, bartenders, fishermen, and a few genuine Starving Artists. There was a strong but merely faddish flavoring of anti-American sentiment in some of the people we knew, but we learned to ignore it and after a while it went away. Our Italian friends never learned to understand our way of life and thought and we never learned to understand theirs. But we learned to like and to respect each other; that was easy.

At night I tried to teach myself Italian by means of a translation of Shakespeare's sonnets. This plan didn't work too well, mostly because the city was too exciting for me to spend much time in language study. We got enough to read the newspapers and to carry on primitive conversation, sufficient for our modest purposes.

Mostly we looked at the art. Looked and looked and looked again. The wealth of it is at first chaotic, then burdensome, and then—after a long while—necessary to one's serenity of spirit in that town. Neither Susan nor I had ever studied art, but now we began to read up a bit. Mostly we just looked. Heath learned to hate the sound of those words, *chièsa* and *musèo*.

For most of the year I wrote nothing. How was I going to write after seeing Heath off to the second grade in his pernicious English school, lingering over coffee and pastry in a plaza cafe till ten, visiting the Pitti Palace, taking lunch at a friendly, unclean eatery called Angiolino's, napping, visiting the marketplaces or a church in the afternoon, and reading Dante or Milton in the evenings? Such overawing firsthand encounter with European culture served to make my own work seem flimsy and irrelevant, but it also taught me to live cheerfully with the knowledge of that fact.

Nevertheless I began to feel that I must do something to justify my stay in Italy and in late spring I wrote a novel. Once more, I was able to write it in a few weeks, on the backs of my galleys of *Dagon*. This was the first and last time I tried to write what I considered a more or less conventional novel with a gallery of recognizable characters and in the mode of ordinary American romantic realism. My other books had been cobbled together the best I knew how out of psychic necessity, philosophical mandate, and artistic desperation. They resembled usual fiction only by a nice leniency on the reader's part. It had occurred to me that

I had actually published three novels without having faced the ordinary problems of fiction. I had had to solve other problems, but not those of plotting, characterization, observation of mores, and details of verisimilitude. I wanted too to produce something with a much lighter tone than my stories of tragic or pathetic horror. So I wrote *The Gaudy Place* and my agent—now Peter Matson, Harold Matson's nephew—sent it to HBJ.

Hiram was glad to see this new departure in my work. He was not pleased with the last section; neither was I, and I was content to try to rewrite it. He was never quite satisfied with the ending and I have always been distinctly unhappy with it. It presents a structural problem I probably could not solve even now, but I gave it my best shot and the book was published, my last volume to be published with a major trade company.

I don't know how well the book performed commercially. My experience has been that publishers simply don't tell an author unless he specifically asks them, and I have always been too embarrassed to inquire. I really didn't want to hear the awful truth. At any rate, *The Gaudy Place* must have sold abysmally, for Hiram wrote a few months later to tell me that I was dropped from the HBJ list. I was very busy with schoolwork when his letter arrived and had no opportunity to answer for a while. A truly considerate man, he wrote again in a couple of weeks to inquire how I had taken the news. He may well have been anxious I had cut my throat. When I replied at last that I quite understood his position and that I was not upset in the least, he expressed in a final note his gratitude.

That was the end of our correspondence. We had undergone the usual argumentative ordeals that occur between author and editor, but never with bitterness or rancor. Whenever I think of the man I think of him fondly and I was darkly saddened by his death. In the last year of her struggle with terminal cancer, Mary, Hiram's widow, began to send me letters and poems. The old warmth had never extinguished and never shall—until I do.

In truth, I was not downcast about being cut loose. In the first place, I never entirely credited it. I figured that if by some weird quirk of fate I woke up one morning and wrote a novel of clear artistic merit and undeniable commercial potential, Hiram would read it and publish it. Publishers are in the business of publishing books, after all, and an author always has a chance of writing one that will do them proud. I wasn't going to, but if I did, he wouldn't reject it out of hand. And in the second place, I had an opportunity to publish poetry.

This chance came about in the oddest and most natural way. At the deservedly legendary Hollins Writing Conference in 1970 (an interesting book could be written about *that* one), George Garrett, Leslie Phillabaum, and I were standing in the sunny campus one afternoon when Leslie mentioned that he had recently moved from Chapel Hill to Louisiana State University Press and that he was looking for suitable manuscripts for their new poetry series. "Fred has a fine manuscript," George said—having not the faintest notion whether I had one or not. "Is that true?" Leslie asked. "Yes," I said, lying in my teeth. "I'll send it to you when I get back home."

So when the conference was over I went home, wrote a book of poems in a couple of weeks, and sent it to Leslie.—No, that's not really true, of course. Poetry has been my first allegiance for ever and ever. I had written hundreds of poems and had published a fair number in periodicals. But when I gathered them into a bundle and read them through, I was chagrined to find out how poor they were. This experience was especially devastating in light of the fact that I'd spent much of my life pontificating to others—and not only my students—how they should write their poems.

I was able to salvage perhaps a dozen or so of my earlier efforts, but the rest of the book I actually did have to write more or less on the spot. It cannot be supposed that I turned out a superior manuscript in this fashion, and I hope that my publisher will tolerate my admitting here that *The World Between the Eyes* is simply and frankly weak in conception and execution. I wrote the best that I could, but I was more interested in the opportunity of entering into a serious career in poetry than in producing a really good book. I figured—correctly, as it turned out—that if I could once get the first collection into print, I would be welcome to publish others.

L.S.U. produced the book rather handsomely, as I thought, and it even won a prize. And though I had no confidence in the work between those olive-colored covers, I was happy. Now for the first time I could begin to think directly about the most important intellectual and artistic endeavor in the world: the composition of poetry.

Like most young poets (old as a writer, at thirty-five years, but only beginning as a poet), I knew better what I didn't want to write than what I did want. So it was a question of starting almost at ground level. I needed proficiency in all the forms and meters, I needed ease with tropes and syntax, I needed genuine subject matter that I knew well.

One day I wrote a rather florid free-verse aubade. Didn't think much about it. When a little magazine called *Monmouth Review* wrote to request a poem, I sent it to them. (By this time I had formulated a strategy I still work by and which has made my life simpler: I submit, with rare exception, only to magazines and publishers who request my work.) When after a few months it was published and I read it in print, it struck me as being full of possibilities. It seemed too that I had written this poem at some earlier period in my life, and that I was now only recalling it. An odd sensation—which began to plague me.

A few days later, and the conception for the whole of *Midquest*—a four-volume poetic autobiography—had thrust into my mind. The hardest decision was about whether to undertake it or not. The amount of concentrated labor it would require was staggering and the technical command still beyond my grasp. But I determined to go ahead with this fictional tetralogy which was to be organized around the classical four elements of earth, air, fire, and water and to take place during one twenty-four-hour period, the speaker's birthday, May 28, 1971. I figured that by the time it was complete I would be forty. I was forty-four.

The project was—for me, at least—very ambitious, and the large ambition was bolstered by smaller designs. I will quote here a couple of sentences from a preface I wrote at editorial request when the four volumes, *River, Bloodfire, Wind Mountain*, and *Earthsleep*, were gathered into one.

> Free verse and blank verse predominate, are the basic "stitches," representing different states of mind, but we have also terza rima, Yeatsian tetrameter, rhymed couplets, syllabics, classical hexameter variation, elegiacs, chant royal, and so forth. The structural forms too are various, with dramatic monologue, interior monologue, epistle, a playlet, elegy, and other sorts. With this variety of form I hoped to suggest a kind of melting-pot American quality, and in fact my model was that elder American art form, the sampler, each form standing for a different fancy stitch.

The writing was difficult. There were many errors, much wasted motion, several hopeless cul-de-sacs. A couple of times I came near giving up in the middle—and I am not saying so to make myself look good. On the other hand, I have never experienced such unalloyed joy in the act of writing, and rarely in life itself, as when working on this poem. I fancied that I could actually feel physically an expansion of my faculties, a growing strength of expression, as the lines went on the page, to be marked through and replaced and then replaced again. The most alert moment of my existence may well have been when I paused in the middle of a poem one June afternoon to go out onto the porch to take in a spectacular rainstorm. There were powers in the air abroad, there were powers in my thought and feeling. If so much as the least of them lightly brushed my lines for a moment, they would most certainly glow like light-bulb filaments. I was happy and innocent.

These are not the moments that keep a poet going; if he is truly a poet he will go on with them or without them. But they are blessings that come at times, and for which the writer is worshipfully grateful. Perhaps they are no more than self-deluding, mild hallucinations. So what? The work itself is the thing that matters, and if experiences like these aid the author in accomplishing his work, then they need no other value or justification. It is part of the writer's job to try to arrest on paper the most subjective of feelings and, this being so, he had better experience some intense ones now and then. These brief hours were like some of the intoxicated moments of being in love. It is good for the writer to be in love with his work; it is best of all when the work loves him.

The gray shingle roofs of the neighborhood houses seemed to melt in the downpour, handfuls of young sweet gum leaves fluttered down. Then there was a shatter of milky blue lightning and an oaken crack of thunder and then the sky cleared blue in only a minute or two, as if wiped by a blackboard eraser, and I knew for the first time that I would complete *Midquest,* whose title had just occurred to me . . . I won't claim this as a mystical experience, it was too egocentric for that. But it was a complete experience, involving body and mind, and it was alien and comforting at the same time. It was the unlooked-for reward.

It didn't solve the many puzzles that every line and stanza presented, though. There is an unfunny, decrepit joke which might apply here. An orange packer visits a psychiatrist. She says, "Doc, I got mental problems." "Tell me," he says. Sez, "All day long these oranges come rolling down the chute and I got to put the little ones in one box, the middle-sized in another, and the big ones in another box." "So what's the problem?" "Oh Doc," she sez, "all day long, *decisions decisions decisions.*"

By the time I reached the middle of *Earthsleep,* the final volume, I was tired. I determined to push on through and to take a bit of vacation at the finish. That vacation has yet to arrive. The curse as well as the blessing of writing is that there is no vacation from it. The mind is always at work, observing detail, absorbing dialogue, fashioning phrases, discovering metaphors, testing rhythms. And when one can take no more of the surfeit of raw material the world pours out, there are the books to be read, the books by friends and strangers, the books one meant to read oh decades ago

now, and the books that need to be thoroughly mastered if one is to make the least pretense of being a cultivated citizen. What would a writer describe as a vacation? My friend Hilary Masters claims to hate them and I do not doubt his sentiment.

Midquest appeared in its one-volume edition in 1981, and in 1983 James Tate asked me what the reception had been. I was startled to realize that, as far as I knew, there had been none at all. No magazine or newspaper reviews, not even in the *Greensboro Daily News.* I wasn't disheartened, only surprised. That has since changed and now there has probably been more critical comment about it than is good for me. But when Jim inquired, I had no notion that there would ever be any. I think that I took a perverse pleasure in that state of affairs.

The year before *Midquest* I had published a volume of short stories. A friend and former student, Nancy Stone, had founded a publishing firm, The New South Company, located at first in Charlotte but soon removed to Los Angeles. When she hinted that she would like to see a manuscript, I could offer only a collection of stories culled from the forty or so I had published over the years. I think that we both spoke of how meager the commercial prospects were for such a book, and that has surely proved to be the case. Even so, *Moments of Light* may well be my favorite child among my books of fiction. I chose the stories and arranged them according to a secret design that I was confident would never be discovered. But when Annie Dillard sent her introduction to the book, I found that she understood and outlined in cold print my every best intention. I was exhilarated but a little dismayed too. With an introduction so perceptive and charming as Annie's, who would need the book?

But then the book became worth publishing for the sake of her introduction.

Of all the forms I have attempted, the short story is the most difficult. (I have not tried the epic poem or the philosophic dialogue.) Why should this be so? It is the form I am most accustomed to reading, especially in the guise of student work. It is the prose form I most admire. It is the one whose shape and purpose I am able to know before composition begins. Yet it is the hardest to get right.

I compounded my trials with the form by attempts in that rare genre, the historical short story. *Moments of Light* contains stories about Judas, Benjamin Franklin, and Franz Joseph Haydn, and I have written others about Linnaeus, Offenbach, Maupertuis, and Ludwig Feuerbach. Fresh characterization of familiar figures, convincing contemporaneous-sounding dialogue, accurate and trenchant detail—these are some of the necessities this particular type of story imposes, and there is the final problem of making a broadly general narrative which does not damage too much the actual historical facts. And all these things must be achieved within the straitened limits of the short story. I recommend this kind of story to any writer who no longer feels challenged in writing the usual contemporary short story.

One drawback, though, is that it has a limited audience appeal. Readers of short stories have—or so I am told by editors—little taste for history, and especially for historical scientific figures. That is probably true. In fact, the reason I first began writing stories of this sort was that I needed a pedagogical tool. Lecturing to my sophomore students in American literature, I discovered that they had absolutely no feeling for the texture of eighteenth-century life and, that while they could recognize Dr. Franklin as a name in a textbook, they could form no dimmest conception of him as a human being. And so I wrote a story about Franklin and his wife Deborah. I planned to read it to my class to try to give a human dimension to the man. Like most of my teaching experiments, this one failed. The students resented that I was forcing upon them material which was not in the textbook and which, as I had admitted, had no chance of showing up on an exam; and they suspected that I was reading my own material merely in order to show off. They may have been right on this latter score. But the possibilities of the historical story intrigued me and I pursued it and hope to pursue it in future efforts.

The three stories in *Moments of Light* I most often recommend to prospective readers are the title story and "Broken Blossoms" and "Blue Dive." I certainly cannot describe them as classics of the form, but they are the closest I have ever come to satisfying the imperious demands this discipline imposes. I have published experimental stories also, some of these so perverse, or maybe only so silly, that every now and then I still get an angry letter about some of them . . . Though none so intimidating as the letter I got about my first novel, in which a lady gave me to know that she had sliced the book into strips with a razor blade and fed it to her hogs. She must have had an ugly grudge against those hogs.

So far as I know no one has tried *Moments of Light* as hog fodder, but if anyone thinks it a viable idea, there are still plenty of copies in print.

Now that *Midquest* was completed, I wanted to try something different, but I didn't know what. Another kind of poem, something with an air of strangeness about it.

So I woke up one morning at 3:30 and went into the kitchen and set down every line of a poem that was in my head. It seemed to be in strict rhyme and regular, though varying, meter, something like an operatic text for Monteverdi. As the poem wrote itself out on the pages, I found that it was a dramatic monologue spoken by a homunculus, a miniature artificial person who lived in a fairy-tale castle sometime—perhaps—during the early Renaissance. That was all I knew about him or about the setting or about anything else.

It took three years for me to discover the rest of the story and to bring *Castle Tzingal* to completion. I still think of it as a sort of chamber opera, though now the imaginary music for it in my mind's ear sounds more like Mahler than Monteverdi. But it makes, I think, its own independent music, and it has all the strangeness about it that I could ever wish for, and sufficient allegorical undertone to give it some heft.

I have mentioned that in writing *Midquest* I made many missteps; many of the attempted poems had to be discarded, and there was other material that never quite fit into the design. Some of these aborted poems had been fashioned into short stories, and now when I looked at them I saw that they could be linked together, if a lot of new material were added, into a deliberately episodic novel something like *Winesburg, Ohio*.

What I really wanted to write was a novel about an American scientific or literary figure. I had in mind Steinmetz or maybe Muriel Rukeyser. But it is difficult for me to switch back and forth between writing fiction and writing poetry. I try to ease back into fiction by treating material that I am very familiar with, that requires more memory than invention. So I began to toy with the short stories generated by *Midquest* and struck upon the notion of a quartet of novels which would balance the *Midquest* tetralogy, surrounding that poem with a solid fictional universe. I was back in the novel business after a hiatus of ten years or so.

After twenty years of publishing books a writer ought to have acquired some instincts. So I knew pretty well that if I could bring off this introductory novel it would have some humor and charm as well as a tragic undertone. For the purposes of the quartet it needed to fit solidly into the American tradition of frontier humor, with lots of eccentric characters and practical jokes. The four novels were to be progressively sophisticated in technique, a little model of the history of modern fiction.

I also knew that I could place it with a New York trade publisher where it would sell about 15,000 copies, more than all my other books together. But that seemed unfair to L.S.U. Press which had been so faithful in bringing out my poetry with no hope of making money or even of recovery costs. Partly out of gratitude, partly out of simple friendship, I offered *I Am One*

Chappell at his workdesk

of You Forever to L.S.U. I figured that they would be able to sell about 5,000 copies and nearly get back their expenses on my poetry. And this is more or less what has taken place, I think. Out of an amused curiosity, I have kept up with the career of this novel. The reviews have been favorable and I have received a lot of amicable mail. But it is an enjoyable book, I believe, and the other three to come—if they ever get written—must necessarily be less so, if I stick to my plan.

When I can find time to do so, I labor at the second novel in the series, *Brighten the Corner Where You Are,* but mostly I work at poetry. A collection of mostly lyric verse, *Source,* appeared in 1985, and I am now taking great pleasure in writing *First and Last Words,* poetic prologues and epilogues to other literary works and works of art, and a kind of tribute to Reynolds Price.

Scribble, scribble, scribble, eh, Mr. Chappell?

To most healthy people it must seem a dour and

grubby existence to swot your life away at a desk while the world outside goes off incandescent in all directions like a skyrocket. But I don't regret a single hour of the author's life, not even the most agonized one.

Writers are commonly supposed to write for money or fame or to attract the love of women—or for posterity. I write partly in order to maintain my self-respect and to obtain respect from my friends. ("That's the same thing as posterity," Peter Taylor once told me.) I think that I mostly write out of a mingled sense of indebtedness and longing. I want to recreate in myself the sense of excitement and reverent discovery I felt when I first read Shakespeare as a child (and forever after) and Ray Bradbury when I was twelve and Thomas Mann and Tolstoy in my teens, Faulkner in my twenties, Chaucer in my thirties, Proust in my forties. And all all all the others. The act of writing refreshes those sensations.

The literary life has made me skeptical, tolerant, humorous, paunchy, absentminded, and fairly patient.

It has sharpened my attention to other interests: science, history, film, music, art, sports, animal welfare, philosophy. It has introduced me to so many fascinating and helpful friends that one authentic way to write an account of my life would be simply to list the names of all the people from whom I have learned, to whom I owe, so much. These are the things that matter; a writer learns soon enough to discount the praise and the prizes. One would like to refuse the latter, if it didn't seem such a churlish thing to do. But perhaps the writer should be honored, since he gives up his life in order to honor the world and all its creatures and whatever else he believes in beyond that. I used to be amused by Stravinsky's dedication to his *Symphony of Psalms,* "To the greater glory of God and The Boston Symphony Orchestra." Now it seems entirely appropriate, and I think that I could inscribe my own work to the prevailing God Who gave so many of us a childhood.

Fiction:

It Is Time, Lord. New York: Atheneum, 1963; London: Dent, 1965.

The Inkling. New York: Harcourt, 1965; London: Chapman & Hall, 1966.

Dagon. New York: Harcourt, 1968.

The Gaudy Place. New York: Harcourt, 1973.

Moments of Light (short stories). Los Angeles: New South Co., 1980.

I Am One of You Forever. Baton Rouge: Louisiana State University Press, 1985.

Poetry:

The World Between the Eyes. Baton Rouge: Louisiana State University Press, 1971.

River. Baton Rouge: Louisiana State University Press, 1975.

The Man Twice Married to Fire. Greensboro, N.C.: Unicorn Press, 1977.

Bloodfire. Baton Rouge: Louisana State University Press, 1978.

Awakening to Music. Davidson, N.C.: Briarpatch Press, 1979.

Wind Mountain. Baton Rouge: Louisiana State University Press, 1979.

Earthsleep. Baton Rouge: Louisiana State University Press, 1980.

Driftlake: A Lieder Cycle. Emory, Va.: Iron Mountain Press, 1981.

Midquest (includes *River, Bloodfire, Wind Mountain,* and *Earthsleep*). Baton Rouge: Louisiana State University Press, 1981.

Castle Tzingal. Baton Rouge: Louisana State University Press, 1984.

Source. Baton Rouge: Louisiana State University Press, 1985.

Peter Davison

1928-

I was born in Lenox Hill Hospital in New York on June 27, 1928, unremarkably, as far as I know, and came home on Independence Day to my parents' rented town house in Brooklyn Heights. My father, Edward Davison, on the very edge of thirty, was a tousle-haired English poet, about six feet tall, and possessed of more than enough charm to hold a crowd. Already the author of three published books of poetry and a book of critical essays, he edited a weekly contributors' page in the new *Saturday Review of Literature* and had developed sufficient reputation to excite demand on the womens' club lecture circuit.

My mother, Natalie Weiner Davison, twenty-nine, was buxom, auburn-haired, convivial, glowingly beautiful. Her childhood, unlike my father's, had been privileged, sheltered in an affluent and assimilated Jewish home with a younger sister on the upper West Side of Manhattan. My grandfather, Joseph Solomon Weiner, had come to New York at seventeen, in 1887, from his birthplace in Trenĉín, in what is now Czechoslovakia, leaving home like thousands of others to avoid Franz Josef's military conscription. He followed his elder brothers to New York and before long found prosperity as their partner in Weiner Brothers, of Spring Street, Cotton Goods. This made him eligible to claim, and win, the hand of Charlotte Herzog, a visitor from St. Louis, who with midwestern simplicity insisted on being called Lottie. Theirs was a classic American middle-class marriage, one in which the newly arrived male immigrant finds himself a genteel and acculturated wife, whose father had immigrated a generation before and found himself a genteel and acculturated wife, *und so weiter*.

Lottie Herzog's father, Herman (a man determined enough to have deserted from both sides in the Civil War, the Union side first), had married Bella Cullman soon after the War in Memphis, where, with his wife's brothers, Herman put in some good years in the tobacco business but did not choose to follow the Cullmans back to New York. (Too bad for him. Cullman Brothers later turned into Philip Morris.) Herman Herzog had to be content with respect, if not eminence, in wholesale dry goods in St. Louis. He hated the business, and he turned it over to his son Fred in 1918. His wife too longed to join the Cullmans in New York, which she did after Herman's death. In the meantime,

Lottie and Joseph Weiner with Rabbi Stephen S. Wise (center), about 1938

their daughter Lottie liked St. Louis well enough in the era of its World Fair. She taught German and French kindergarten there for a while. As a member of the St. Louis Ethical Culture Society she seems to have felt confident that she would seldom be stigmatized as a Jew. My own mother's decision, a generation later in 1925, to marry a gentile, a foreigner, a poet, and a bastard (for so my father in his pathetic moments chose to label himself), must have also risen out of some deep self-assurance that she and hers would not be rejected by America, that she was entitled to equity and prominence.

Childhood photographs of Natalie Weiner show a well-fed, lightly starched young woman, accustomed to a town house with maids. Her family lacked little in the material sense. Natalie was chauffeured from 375 West End Avenue to the Ethical Culture School, where she absorbed a moral imperative distinct from Judaism, tinged with a strong meliorative impulse, and developed a desire, which owed little to any specific religious doctrine, to improve the condition of her fellows. She learned languages and played on a lovely Steinway A-model grand piano bought for the purpose in

1915, when she was sixteen. She was given a floor of her own in the Weiners' house, furnished with the piano and with a new suite of walnut furniture, stained blue and upholstered in blue plush. The fall of 1917 saw her into Barnard College, where she made friends with bright girls whose marriages would scatter them across the country from Louisville to Milwaukee. When the World War and influenza epidemic were safely over, she travelled to Europe with her friend Marie Mayer, a thrilling journey described to us in later years with all the innocent flapper foolishness of Cornelia Otis Skinner's *Our Hearts Were Young and Gay*.

The socially conscious young woman found herself one job as a cub reporter on Walter Lippmann's New York *Daily World,* and another with the New York State Department of Labor, whose Secretary, under Governor Al Smith, was the redoubtable Madam Frances Perkins. And she fell in love, not suitably—not with one of the nice Columbia boys like Bennett Cerf or Dick Simon or Harold Guinzburg, who were founding publishing houses—but with a married man. The affair had nowhere to go; it stopped, and my mother had a collapse. Colitis was diagnosed. Psychotherapy (Jungian) was called for. After a few months my grandfather took my mother to Europe To Forget, and they embarked on a tour of family and friends in Vienna, Karlsbad, Trenĉin, Rothenburg, and the cities of the Rhine. When my grandfather felt able to leave Natalie on her own, she went on to attend the Fabian Society School in Sussex. Through a mutual friend in London she met Edward Davison, employed at the time as the business manager of an Anglican Church weekly paper, *The Challenge*.

Teddie Davison, twenty-six years old in late 1924, had already been living in London for several years and, like Natalie Weiner, stood at a crossroads. During his bright postwar career at Cambridge University he had been regarded by some as the successor to the poetic mantle of the martyred Rupert Brooke. In 1920, still an undergraduate, he had published his first volume of poems. In London he had shared quarters for a while with J. B. Priestley, critic, budding novelist, and playwright-to-be, who like Teddie had come up to Cambridge after the War. Only my father's closest friends had been vouchsafed the truth: that Teddie was the illegitimate son of a gentlewoman named Evelyn Davison, who as governess to the Leeds family of a burgher named Edward Shields, had been seduced in Edwardian fashion and then kept for years in a succession of modest lodgings in northern English cities. Though my father was born in Glasgow, on the fly, in 1898 (followed by his sister Amy in 1902), his mother did not marry Shields until 1917, after she read in the papers that the first Mrs. Shields was dead. It is odd to think that somewhere I must have a whole tribe of English cousins two-and-a-half times removed, all unknown to me as I am unknown to them.

My father was sometimes given over to the care of foster mothers, but for much of his childhood he grew up with his mother and his sister, and no father, in South Shields, 17 Porchester Street, Tyne Dock, in a four-room house without indoor plumbing or, of course, central heat. His voice proved his salvation—his voice and the Church of England. He became a chorister and learned through the Church—that traditional educator of the poor—how to pronounce the English language "properly": how, by walking an acceptable tightrope of vowels, to take his place in the middle class beside his genteel mother. He left school at the age of twelve, employed now in an office, now in a factory, and finally as a ticket-taker in a music hall;

Edward and Natalie Davison on their wedding day, April 27, 1926

but his voice brought him a little fame and a little money and confidence, as he sang solo anthems in South Shields and Newcastle and even as far afield as Durham Cathedral.

When the Great War broke out my father was sixteen. He lied about his age and volunteered for the Navy. Once again his voice came to the rescue. Young men with proletarian accents who, like him, had enlisted in the Royal Naval Division, were shovelled into the ranks. My father's enunciation won him an office job and a warrant-officer's commission, while his fellows spilled their blood to realize Winston Churchill's strategies on the beaches of Ostend and Gallipoli. For five-and-a-half years Teddie clerked in London at Royal Naval Division Headquarters in the Crystal Palace. In 1919 he qualified for a National Scholarship to St. John's College, Cambridge, despite his lack of secondary education. He was already publishing poems in the *London Mercury* and had fallen under the protectorship of its brilliant but undependable editor, J. C. Squire. Squire promised to help my father through Cambridge, encouraged his expectations, and showed him by example what few have to be taught: to live beyond his means. By the time my mother arrived in London Teddie was already deeply in debt, and he had begun perhaps to suspect, in an age of poetry that was already beginning to tilt toward T. S. Eliot and Ezra Pound, that his moody lyrics and greensward ruminations might be edging out of fashion as well.

Edward Davison met Natalie Weiner at a party at the house of their mutual friend Milton Waldman, an Anglo-American Jewish publisher and scholar, in December of 1924. Each had, I think, arrived with someone else, but they walked home through the dark streets together. My father sang. They enjoyed several weeks of intense courtship, and then my mother sailed for home. Teddie followed her the next summer, and they were married by Rabbi Stephen S. Wise in a hotel in New York on April 27, 1926. Their wedding picture shows them sitting on a blue-walnut, plush-upholstered daybed which eventually became my own, and then my children's.

To inherit a daybed is easier than to make your own life. After both my parents were dead I anatomized their marriage in a self-castigating memoir entitled *Half Remembered: A Personal History*. It began: "Home was the compartment of music and discord, the vessel of my mother's influence, the rostrum for my father's voice." I started with dangerous diseases in early childhood, when life seemed to threaten, rather than welcome me. My earliest memory is of Mill Pond House, a place my family rented from 1931 to 1933 near Peekskill, New York, on the side of a modest hill where my father wrote in a shanty in a meadow, and where he taught me to read. Indoors I often lay ill, but outdoors, beyond a ruined gristmill and above its mill-dam, lay a pond with a small boat house and a decaying skiff. My early childhood was watchdogged by a Viennese nurse, worthy of a Freudian case study, whom my family had hired while abroad on a Guggenheim Fellowship, a *Kinderschwester* who seemed to me the personification of witchery. Though my happy memories of Mill Pond House call up sunlit meadows and reflections on the water, my more sinister recollections revolve around bedroom, bathroom, and kitchen, where Schwester slapped my *bupsch* and scolded my sister and me in vile German. Fortunately Schwester, soon enough, left us.

We moved again when I was five, closer to New York, into a large house which my grandparents helped my parents to buy, on Pinesbridge Road in Ossining, then as now in nearly open country. The house is immense, as I recently confirmed after half a century—far larger even than my childhood memories of it. I recall a snowy winter with sleds; a vast vegetable garden planted in the spring by a hired man with a horse and harrow; chickens in a coop and ducks on a pond. I still lament the tragedy of a coveted gift, a green tricycle, which I carelessly left in the driveway, where the car backed over it and left it a twisted wreck before noon on Christmas Day.

After only a year in Ossining we moved on for a winter to Coral Gables, where my father, in the Great Depression of 1934–35, needed the official teaching job offered by the University of Miami to pad out the increasingly puny lecture engagements that were being offered. The spring of 1935 took us far across the dust-blown Great Plains to Boulder, Colorado, which turned out, surprise, to be our hometown for a decade to come. Somehow we never made it back to Ossining at all. After several rentals in Boulder we settled, when I was ten, in a roomy granite house at 1313 University Avenue, near the edge of the University of Colorado campus. The house is the one I will always remember as home. The ground floor was where guests entered, where the piano sat and my parents made music and I practised it, where the Latino maid, Beatrice Tafoya, cooked the meals. On the second floor, surrounding a trafficked central hallway, lay four bedrooms: one for my parents, one for my sister, one for the frequent house guests, and one for me. On the third floor, yet another circle toward heaven, lay my father's study, where he wrote his lectures, entertained students at evening seminars, and, when the fit was upon him, spoke of composing poems. Alas, the fit grew increasingly rare, and even a child could sense that more attention went to the social festivities of Floor One than to the creative exercises of Floor Three.

Every summer for three weeks the house lay open during the Writers' Conference in the Rocky Mountains, which my parents directed every year between 1935 and 1942. During those red-letter weeks guests came and went at all hours—Robert Frost, Robert Penn Warren, Thomas Wolfe, Ford Madox Ford, Katherine Anne Porter, Elmer Rice, Ralph Hodgson, Wallace Stegner, Robert Lowell, Jean Stafford, and dozens of other writers, old and young. Even in the

Peter Davison in Boulder, Colorado, 1937

winter months visiting lecturers or artists would often occupy the guest room—the pianists Josef and Rosina Lhevinne, Harold Bauer, and Percy Grainger, the mime Angna Enters, the painter Charles Hopkinson, the poet Carl Sandburg, the basso Alexander Kipnis, members of the Trapp Family Choir, and other literary or performing artists from somewhere to the East of us.

My father's third-floor library offered Melville, Scott, Cooper, Mark Twain, Dickens, Walter De La

Mare, and a thousand other authors; and my father's voice, quoting out of a fathomless memory lines from Shakespeare and Burns, Campion and Tennyson, Keats and Wordsworth, enriched the print of poetry with the thrilling dimensions of sound. My mother, who gave herself at this stage to the rearing of children, to the entertainment of guests, to the cultivation of flowers, and to the study of piano, made the house a center of conviviality. In the afternoons it became a locus for committees of the League of Women Voters, the Association of American University Women, and, later on, Finnish War Relief and Bundles for Britain.

My life outside the house was spacious, adventurous, competitive. I studied clarinet and piano and German. I rode my bike everywhere in Boulder's hills. I learned to hike in the mountains behind the Flatirons. I took up swimming and tennis and skating. I experienced the rigors of a climate starving for moisture by seeing to the watering of our own lawn and flowers. Colorado's air was clear and bright after the Dust Bowl years, as it is less often now that hydrocarbons have darkened it. As I grew older I ascended higher into the mountains on skis, and I was swiftly promoted in school. By twelve, I was ill-at-ease with my pubescent classmates of fourteen and fifteen. In 1941, none too soon, I was sent to Colorado Springs, to board at the Fountain Valley School, an Eastern oasis of learning, as it regarded itself, on the Western Plains.

It is no wonder, perhaps, that much of my writing is concerned with the implications of inheritance. A Jewish mother, something of an apostate, living in Colorado but loving New York. An Anglican father, who, having fled his own land, yearned for its language and literature. A beloved younger sister, gay and uninhibited, whose laughter diverted itself into rhymes and song. A paradisal hometown from which I was banished to a boarding school where the boys (no girls) wore blue serge suits to dinner and white shirts with detachable collars. Home and school alike lay at the foot of wild dry mountains and depended on artificial irrigation for their survival. And, as though these contrasts did not concern us, at every opportunity my family had trekked somewhere else, winter or summer, like ants whose nest had been kicked. I developed chronic car-sickness in the back seat of our blue Chevy on journeys between New York, Florida, Colorado, Arizona, Utah, Mississippi, Louisiana, California, New Mexico, and Wyoming, tires rattling over thousands of miles of pre-war ribbed concrete highways. In 1943, when my father volunteered for his second wartime of armed service—this time in the U.S. Army—we drove East again and ceased our family travels at last in Washington, where my parents spent the rest of the war while I rode out my last two years of boarding school in Colorado Springs, travelling back and forth on the raucous day-coach trains of wartime.

The War, for boys like me, threatened the very idea of home and the prospect of a future. My classmates accelerated their schooling to make ready for induction. I myself, on summer vacations in Washington, took civil service jobs—in 1944 as a page in the United States Senate, where I reported for work on the day President Roosevelt's armies invaded Normandy. I spent the summer watching Senator Harry S. Truman

lenging and even dangerous mountain climbing, and had learned enough mathematics and science to fit me for the next stage of expectation.

But Harvard was not what I had expected: it was not what anyone had expected. Within ninety days after my matriculation in 1945 the buildings and classrooms filled to bursting with war veterans returned from the Murmansk Run, from New Caledonia, from the Apennines. Though my early friends at Harvard were teenagers like myself, still damp from Exeter or

Coral Gables, Florida, winter 1934: Peter Davison, Robert Frost, Natalie, Edward, and Lesley Davison

turn into a vice-president; and in 1945, as a supervisor on a public, but still segregated playground, I heard President Truman announce the first news of Nagasaki. By the time I graduated from Fountain Valley I had developed competence in Latin, had picked up smatterings of French and German, had learned to act in plays and sing Gilbert and Sullivan, had heard the poetry of e. e. cummings and T. S. Eliot and Archibald MacLeish read aloud by a redoubtable English teacher who was the husband of MacLeish's sister; had proved myself in track and basketball, had done some chal-

Middlesex or Belmont Hill, the second wave were much older men, veterans of the Burmese Highlands or B-24 air raids over Europe, making ready to become writers or composers or publishers or college presidents. So far it had sufficed to observe and emulate the adult world, to listen to the conversation of an authoritative older generation. The new, older, Harvard men had been initiated in a way I could hardly emulate; but they accepted me as a friend nonetheless. The Radcliffe women were no older than I, as confused by the war's upheavals as I had been, and they were even further confused by the urgent demands of the grown men who wooed them.

Harvard after the war, nearly at once, burst out into the arts. The Veterans' Theatre Workshop, later to develop into the Brattle Theatre repertory company, presented Shakespeare and Shaw; the Harvard Glee Club, which lent its members to the Boston Symphony Orchestra for choral performances under Koussevitsky, Bernstein, Monteux, and others, enabled me to sing in works by Beethoven, Brahms, Bach, Stravinsky, Mahler. A tide of young poets (Kenneth Koch, John Ashbery, Robert Bly, Donald Hall, and, not yet known to me, L. E. Sissman) was flowing through Harvard, but to me the writing of poetry was still a pursuit reserved for "adults." Like my father. Like Robert Frost.

Frost had long been a family friend. My mother had attended Barnard with Frost's daughter Lesley (who would lend her name to my sister Lesley and in turn to my daughter Lesley), and J. C. Squire had given my father a letter to Frost when Teddie left London. While we lived in Coral Gables Frost had come for a visit, and I can still remember the glare of the sun in my eyes as the photographer snapped his shutter. Passing through Cambridge soon after I arrived at Harvard in 1945, my father took me to visit the old poet at home. I was immediately entranced with his way of talking, his irreverence for academic authority, his playful skepticism about the very education I was slavishly pursuing. Throughout my undergraduate years and later on, when I returned to Cambridge as an editor, Frost welcomed me to his house for an occasional afternoon or evening or would come to my house for a meal. He had a genius for friendship. I saw little—not nothing, but not much—of the jealous and self-serving careerist so vengefully portrayed by Frost's biographer Lawrance Thompson, who somehow managed in his three-volume book not to convey the most vivid fact about the living Frost—his amazing physical presence. Frost's body could remain absolutely still in a chair for hours at a time, feet planted flat on the floor, while he talked and paused and talked, his hands describing the gestures of wood-chopping, or of brushing away cobwebs, or other such motions from the world of work, while his voice took the surges of his mind and turned them into play, something witty, rhythmic, exploratory. His talk was always in motion. Even when he repeated a story or idea you had heard before, he seemed to be chivvying it for something new.

Though my years at Harvard did much to make me "well educated," my studies did little to make me a poet. Abbott Lawrence Lowell was reputed to have burbled, "When we find a spark of talent at Harvard, we water it." But I must not blame Harvard over-

much. I was much frightened of poetry, living poetry, perhaps because for years I had been watching my father lose touch with his gift. I listened to I. A. Richards lecture, with wizard brilliance, on the interactions between poetic statement and poetic meaning; I relished Walter Jackson Bate's passionate anatomization of the poetic techniques of Pope, Johnson, Keats; I pored over the cadences of Matthew Arnold and Thomas Hardy and W. B. Yeats. But all the while I learned more about the nature of poetry by listening to the words of song while singing: the way poems and prayers took to the air gave me more vital understanding of the liveliness of the art than any college course. Poetry didn't seem to me—in some ways it still does not—to be at home in college, and I have never, then or now, given or taken a course in the writing of poetry. I was abetted in my distrust by Frost's subversive patter, which often recounted, with glee, how he would advise discontented students to "quit ye like men," to drop out and go away. Since my best friends were composers and musicians, I learned from them. When I finished Harvard in 1949 I knew more than I knew but less than I thought. As though my unconscious were telling me that the time had come for me to begin living, my handwriting had changed radically and no longer looked like that of a child.

At Harvard, 1948, dressed for a choral concert

I spent the summer after my graduation in Italy, much of it listening to harpsichord music in the master classes at Siena, where my Harvard friend Douglas Allanbrook, having studied composition with Nadia Boulanger, was now studying harpsichord with Ruggero Gerlin. Italy was just what my stifled emotions needed, and I went on, in October, to a year of residence at St. John's College, Cambridge University, with my senses awakened, a hundred experiences behind me and a thousand to absorb, and no longer, what a relief, a virgin! In the academic sense Cambridge proved as inhibiting as Harvard, though here mercifully the student was encouraged to take his education less *from* the faculty than *with* his fellow students. My luckiest friendships were with the fascinating Peter Shaffer, not yet writing plays but already showing alarming signs of theatricality, and the prodigious James Mossman, brooding over the study of history, who later became an excellent television journalist but ended a suicide in 1971. We lunched, drank, dined, argued, walked and laughed. I have never laughed so hard as at Cambridge: the margins of my lecture notes are festooned with irreverent caricatures.

Oh how I longed to get away from schooling and into Life! I toyed with the thought of running away to London or Paris, but I had never yet lived in a metropolis for more than a few weeks. In the Easter vacation of 1950 I ventured out on an old bicycle to pedal north along the west coast of Britain from Cornwall to the Lakes. It was my first extended venture into the open air since leaving Colorado five years before, and it reawakened a part of me that had slept restlessly indoors all this time. Along my way I composed a sequence of clerihews on the names of English towns and villages and sent them, with comically clumsy drawings, to my parents in New York (where they had settled at last) as an anniversary gift. Poetry, I began to realize, could very well come to me from the outdoors and from rural talk. I would not learn this lesson at once and would spend nearly a decade making good the loss of a sense of place, of identity with landscape, that I had lost on leaving the plains and mountains of Colorado.

In 1950, after a second European summer spent in Paris and Bavaria—a summer darkened by the coming of the Korean War—I said my goodbyes to my father's friends and relations in England (his sister Amy and his friend J. B. Priestley had been particularly generous) and, lifted on my way by an exultant and joyously impassioned love affair in London, returned to New York, where I had got an appointment as first reader at the distinguished publishing house of Harcourt, Brace. Along with Scribner's, Harper's, and Macmil-

lan's, it was one of the last WASP publishing houses, now suffering increasingly stiff competition from the newer houses (Random House, Simon and Schuster, and the Viking Press) founded in the 1920s by my mother's Columbia friends. Harcourt in 1950 was known as the publisher of all the Bloomsbury eminences (Keynes, Forster, the Woolfs, Strachey, *et al.*) as well as some Catholic writers (e.g., Thomas Merton), and many poets and pillars of English departments: T. S. Eliot, Robert Penn Warren, John Crowe Ransom, I. A. Richards, Cleanth Brooks, William Empson, Carl Sandburg, Robert Lowell, Richard Wilbur, and Randall Jarrell.

I would spend the next five years at Harcourt, Brace, less two years of service in the Army at locations in Massachusetts, Kansas, Texas, and North Carolina. My assignment, most of the time, was as a non-commissioned officer in the Second Loudspeaker and Leaflet Company, training for "psychological warfare" against an undetermined foe. I was discharged in March 1953, the day after the death of Joseph Stalin.

I have always looked back at two pleasures in my Army experience: the actual basic military training, which, rigorous as it was, mostly took place in the open air; and the rich variety of American speech I encoun-

The soulful soldier on leave in New York, 1951

tered from all over the nation in cooks, ministers, professors, truck drivers, printers, refugees, urban blacks, bar girls, rural blacks, fellow-choristers, and all the mad variety of a peacetime war. In addition, while in Kansas among the clement limestone hills around Fort Riley, I finally confronted the actualities of religious faith. All the years in which my mother had dodged religious issues, all my years of singing in choirs and hearing the incantatory resonances of the Church of England now took me, one October weekend, by surprise. I felt, quite literally, as though God had spoken.

> But as I rav'd and grew more fierce and wilde
> At every word,
> Me thoughts I heard one calling, *Childe:*
> And I reply'd, *My Lord.*

The English side of my ancestry now stated a powerful claim. I could never acknowledge with equal allegiance my Jewish side, even though by Jewish law I will always be regarded as a Jew. To be Jewish, it is said, is not a matter of choice but of destiny; to be Christian is to consent and embrace a faith. To the bemusement of both religions, I believe I belong to both; but when I am honest with myself I have to acknowledge the truth that I cannot limit myself to the Old Testament. I would rather be a bad Christian than a bad Jew. For several years after my Kansas baptism and confirmation I remained conscientious in my churchly kneeling and singing; but the attitudes of prayer eventually found their way permanently into my poetry, and particularly into the title *(Praying Wrong)* of my 1984 selected poems.

After my discharge and return to New York and Harcourt, Brace in 1953, I lost my pleasure in the city and the Company. My father became President of the Poetry Society of America and Dean of General Studies of Hunter College; my mother became professionally active in Americans for Democratic Action and in New York reform politics. I settled in with a series of roommates, beginning with my sister, in a charming apartment in a Murray Hill brownstone; but my two principal activities were both voracious: learning about publishing and chasing girls. Overdoses threatened in both departments. At the end of 1954 Harcourt, Brace's management changed dramatically when William Jovanovich, a tall, imperious man, whom I remembered as a University of Colorado student, became president. His management caused the resignation of most of the editors and the departure of many of the authors who had brought me there; and a lucky recommendation soon enabled me to move back to Cambridge, as assistant to the revered Thomas J. Wilson, Director of Harvard University Press. I was not sorry to put some distance between me and my

family, nor to abandon the metropolis, nor to say goodbye to the woman with whom I had formed my first extended love-relationship, nor even to part with my few New York friends outside publishing circles. New York was not the place for me. At twenty-seven I had found a profession and had decided where to live, but I had not decided how. The years 1955 and 1956 began to cancel my postponements.

My new job at Harvard was interesting but not very difficult. I had a little apartment all to myself. In the search for new female companionship I telephoned Sylvia Plath, newly graduated from Smith, where I had met her the previous spring on the recommendation of Alfred Kazin, her teacher. Sylvia was summering with her mother in Wellesley and preparing to go to Cambridge University in the fall. There was a lot she wanted to know about publishing; but as it turned out she taught me more about poetry than I could teach her about the book trade. Sylvia was already devoured by literary ambition and was assiduously in training to achieve it. She had written dozens of poems, those that now fill the juvenilia of her *Collected Poems,* and I read, or heard her read, many of those sedulous villanelles and acrobatic caprices. I was far less impressed by the poems she was actually writing at that time than by the furious intensity of her preparation. She had studied contemporary poetry like coastal charts before a voyage, and she enthused about makers I had never heard about—Isabella Gardner, George Barker, Theodore Roethke. She also had a tale of her own to tell, the story of breakdown and attempted suicide and recovery that can be read in *The Bell Jar.* The version I heard in 1955, only two years after the actual event, was a tenderer, less sardonic narrative. Whatever the meaning of this confession, she soon seemed to regret having made it. After a dinner at her mother's house, only a month after the beginning of our affair, she took me for a walk and spoke in such a way as to retract any tenderness that had infused our lovemaking. She was on the lookout for a man whose strength and gifts would anchor her instability, and I was at best a leaky life preserver. After arriving in England she would find those qualities in Ted Hughes, who—no matter how things ended after their marriage—understood her gift and her nature better than anyone else has.

Soon after Sylvia left Boston, I gravitated to the Poets' Theatre in Cambridge and auditioned for their production of Molière's *The Misanthrope.* In this play, in Richard Wilbur's first verse translation, I played the part of Alceste, at once the most notable and the most ridiculous of heroes. I spent most of the autumn rehearsing and performing this role and learning my way

At Martha's Vineyard, 1955: Roger Baldwin, Eleanor Besse, Peter Davison, and Sylvia Plath

around Wilbur's shimmering and supple verse. An actor reimagines his lines onstage every night, and I could not have devised a more thorough training in poetic technique. The reviews and the audiences were admiring. My father, after a trip to Boston to watch, wrote me to say that I was a good actor, but he thought I could become a better writer. It was my father's blessing. A prohibition had been lifted.

It was now December 1955. This crowded year had left me crestfallen and dejected, so deeply that I sought help in psychoanalysis—for the first time, but not, alas, for the last. Over the next three years the care of M. Robert Gardner would gradually free me from the compulsions of my erotic trifling and enable me to start writing poetry at last. And, as advertised, psychoanalysis taught me how to love and how to work.

In late 1956 I yielded to the repeated invitations of Seymour Lawrence, an old friend, to join his staff at the Atlantic Monthly Press. I remained at work there, serving both the book publishing arm and its body, the *Atlantic Monthly*, for the next twenty-nine years. I fell in love with Nell Halsted, granddaughter of my family's friend Charles Hopkinson, the painter, and I often visited their beautiful family estate on the North Shore in Manchester-by-the-Sea. By late 1957, and I do not at-

tribute it to coincidence, I began to write poems. On a late summer day I was sitting on the screened porch of my Cambridge apartment reading, in manuscript, the *Selected Poems* of Stanley Kunitz—knotty, disturbing, uningratiating poems. They upset me: I did not like them, but they would not leave me alone. I walked indoors, sat at my desk, and wrote the first lines of a poem: *I hear a child inside / Crying to be let out.* It seems I had to become part of New England, part of its very landscape, to write poetry. The desire had walked unacted with me in the Colorado mountains, had ridden with me along the roads of Devonshire and Gloucestershire, had lain with me on Army bivouacs and maneuvers. Like my master Frost and so many other American writers, I found myself as a writer in a land far to the east of my origins.

The *Atlantic* celebrated its centennial in 1957 while the Atlantic Monthly Press was still glowing in the aftermath of three 1956 best-sellers: *The Last Hurrah* by Boston novelist Edwin O'Connor; *The Nun's Story* by Kathryn Hulme; and *Much Ado about Me* by the great Boston comedian Fred Allen. The elegant and magisterial Edward Weeks, at fifty-nine, was at the peak of his career as editor of the *Atlantic;* Seymour Lawrence, only thirty, was building his reputation as a fiction pub-

Davison as Alceste in The Misanthrope, *1955*

writing my way into my work through the back door of grief—an all-too familiar route. I showed some early pieces to Ted Hughes and Sylvia, who gave generous advice, and to Robert Frost, who said little but asked to see more. May Sarton spoke very encouragingly of my early poems, and colleagues at the *Atlantic* were positively and perennially supportive. Weeks asked me to write an annual review of new poetry and printed some of my own. But the lion's share of my time was spent editing books for the Press for publication by Atlantic-Little, Brown.

In late 1958 I learned that my mother, in New York, had cancer; and on a visit to see her a few weeks later, I met Jane Truslow, whom I knew within hours I wanted to marry. As Joan Didion wrote me about Jane many years later: "I met her when [we were] twenty . . . and she was the smartest and most sensible and funniest and kindest and generally the most enchanting girl I had ever met. She seemed to have exactly the right angle on everything and everyone . . . and she suggested by her example that everything could be all right. . . . This sense I had of her never changed." Jane had a way of transforming the mundane into the witty with a conniving sparkle of her blue eyes, a rueful grimace, a wave-it-off wisecrack. She was instantly adorable, and, as much for her diffidence as for her charm,

lisher while directing the Atlantic Monthly Press; and Arthur H. Thornhill the elder was steering Little, Brown and its Atlantic co-publisher to prosperity. Boston was about to become, for a few years, a peerless arena for poetry. Nowhere else in America were so many good poets working. A mere handful of those who were resident in the late fifties includes: Robert Frost, Archibald MacLeish, Adrienne Rich, Robert Lowell, Sylvia Plath and Ted Hughes (newly returned from England), Maxine Kumin, Anne Sexton, Richard Wilbur, and George Starbuck. V. R. Lang and the Poet's Theatre were staging dramatic productions by John Ashbery, Kenneth Koch, W. S. Merwin, James Merrill, and poetry readings by dozens of others. Harvard, under the benign curatorship of John L. Sweeney, paid more attention to new American poetry than it had in a century. It was not the worst time and place for a poet-come-lately to be sniffing the air.

My poetry grew, in my own eyes at least, beyond apprenticeship exercises and became a hot necessity of life after my relationship with Nell died out and she married another man. I mourned, loonlike, for months,

Stettner Photography

Jane and Peter Davison, March 7, 1959

promptly adored. My Boston friends fell for her the moment I brought her up from New York. Even my parents were delighted. I was grateful as a puppy that I had finally, at thirty, found the only woman I had ever unhesitatingly wanted.

Jane and I were married within weeks of our meeting. She left her job in New York publishing and took another in Cambridge as assistant editor of the John Harvard Library reprint series under my old professor Howard Mumford Jones, who lent us his Vermont farmhouse for our honeymoon. Soon after our marriage, in the summer of 1959, my mother relapsed and died, slowly, painfully, and horribly of cancer which metastasized from kidney to spine to brain and left her suffering, speechless, and, mercifully, at long last, lifeless a day beyond her sixtieth birthday. I wrote a suite of elegies, "Not Forgotten," before and after the actual event. Like so many elegies, they said more about the poet's grief than the loved one's loss.

The focus of my emotional life shifted for the next twenty years and more to Jane, while the pattern of my days settled increasingly into the calendars of the publishing trade. My work became more assiduous and administrative after my promotion to Executive Editor of the Press in 1959, and I began gathering a following of authors: Farley Mowat the Canadian, Dan Jacobson the South African, Harry M. Caudill the Kentuckian, and Robert Coles, the Massachusetts child psychiatrist who was already at work at the beginnings of his "Children of Crisis" series. I got interested in books on architecture (*The Architecture of America* by John Burchard and Albert Bush-Brown), psychology (I persuaded C. G. Jung to make a little book of an *Atlantic* essay, and *The Undiscovered Self* is still in print after nearly thirty years), anthropology, politics, history, and biography; but the larger portion of my time was spent in managing the schedules of books for other editors until, in 1964, Seymour Lawrence resigned as Director of the Atlantic Monthly Press, and Edward Weeks asked me to take over.

Jane and I now had two children: Angus, born in 1960, and Lesley, born in 1963. We owned a red clapboard house on an unremarkable Cambridge side street. Our friends were mostly professional Cambridge types—attorneys, publishers, writers, psychiatrists, scholars. I continued my poetry reviews for the *Atlantic* and elsewhere, and I wrote music reviews, mostly of choral concerts, for the weekly Boston *Jewish Advocate*. More centrally, however, poems had bloomed out of the fertile ground of my marriage. In April 1961, just as the United States was invading the Bay of Pigs, I drove with George Starbuck and Anne Sexton to a literary festival at Cornell, where I gave my first public

Angus, Jane, and Lesley Davison, 1966

poetry reading with Anne. In 1963 I completed my first book, *The Breaking of the Day*, which to my delight Dudley Fitts chose to win the Yale Series of Younger Poets Competition.

This success came at a strange juncture—hard after the deaths, two weeks apart, of Robert Frost and Sylvia Plath. My last contact with each poet had been in December 1962. Sylvia had sent me, from England, a group of her late poems, dealing with beekeeping, two of which I'd eagerly persuaded Ted Weeks to accept for the *Atlantic*. They were published shortly after the shock of her death. Jane and I stared at one another after reading *The Bell Jar* later in the spring. Both Jane and Sylvia had lost their fathers and had been sent to Smith College by widowed mothers. They both lived in a scholarship dormitory called Lawrence House, both majored in English, both studied with Alfred Kazin. Both had been guest editors at *Mademoiselle*. Both, too, had broken down under psychic strain, and both recovered to graduate with high honors in 1955. Sylvia belonged to us both, and when Jane turned to writing, in *The Fall of a Doll's House: Three Generations of American Women and the Houses They Lived In* (1980), she would write about their common inheritance, as I would write about Sylvia in *Half Remembered* and in poems like "The Heroine."

Jane and I had last seen Frost just before his last hospitalization, when he stayed up half the night at our house quizzing Alastair Reid about his Scottish childhood. I had already asked Frost whether I might dedicate my first book to him. In the event, a year after his death, he shared the dedication of *The Breaking of the Day* with my father.

One could infer, from the posthumous careers of these two, how deeply poets could be misunderstood. Frost, the more tempered, accepted the omen during his lifetime when he growled one night, "I want people to understand me; I want them to understand me wrong." Sylvia, hesitating as she did between ladies' magazine fiction and the volcanoes of poetry while struggling as wife and mother, threw herself at last into the crater, but first she wrestled openly in her poetry, where some day all might read. Both poets had, as young people, sacrificed more than most others do to alter their way of understanding themselves, and both would be, as Keats had written, "among the English poets at my death." Sylvia could never have guessed at the extent to which her concluding gesture might be vulgarized for propaganda purposes, just as Frost could not have guessed how his chosen biographer would distort the tone and tenor of his entire life. I suppose the fate of these friends suggests that there is no way to control reputation. As Keats wrote, "That which is creative must create itself." Poetry is a gift, not a role. "Admit," I would write later on in reflecting on another suicide, John Berryman's: "that poetry is one of the dangerous trades." Anyone who writes in such as way as to epitomize the self must anticipate the confusion that readers will make between what one *is* and what one has *made*. Neither reader nor writer can be certain what is fact, what is fancy. We are divided; we are not divided.

Jane and I learned from experience that the world was a dangerous place. I worked each year in the 1960s a little harder at publishing, and it became each year a little harder to squeeze out the time for poems. On weekends I would walk with friends and watch birds, animals who know how to fly away from danger. The poems, however, in their mysterious way kept arriving, and so did the collections embodying inner division: *The City and the Island* in 1966 and *Pretending to Be Asleep* in 1970, like all my subsequent poetry published by Atheneum. But my props began to creak after 1968, a year in which a whole series of deaths at the *Atlantic* and in my family and among older friends (to say nothing of Martin Luther King, Jr. and Robert Kennedy) began to undermine the convictions of youth and

bring on the anxieties of middle age. Finally, in early 1970, my father died of cirrhosis of the liver and, only two weeks after him, Arthur H. Thornhill of Little, Brown, a beloved protector of mine, died too. I spent my free time in the summer of 1970 sorting my father's papers and writing "Dark Houses," an "inverse biography in verse."

I was more than tired. I wanted to get away from New England now for a while. Jane agreed to the adventure and persuaded the children it would be exciting. Garth Hite, the *Atlantic*'s new publisher (who had, as it happens, been my father's student at Colorado) and Bob Manning, the editor, agreed to my request for a year's leave without pay. We decided to spend a year in Rome beginning in the autumn of 1971. I applied for a Guggenheim Fellowship and was refused. We lived on savings, on a most welcome award from the National Institute of Arts and Letters, on the money from a small coincidental inheritance, and the Rockefeller Foundation took me in for a month at the Villa Serbelloni at Bellagio. Jane began to explore the history of architecture, which after our return to Boston she would take up professionally. And I found Rome—to the surprise of many—an ideal place in which to

In Italy, 1972

work. The net result was *Half Remembered: A Personal History,* published by Harper and Row in 1973 and by Heinemann in London in 1974, where it appeared simultaneously with my fourth book of poems, *Walking the Boundaries,* the book in which I think I hit my stride as a poet and began, as one well might in one's forties, to gather together the strands of my life.

On my return from Italy in 1972 I had accepted, in addition to my editing work, the job of choosing the poems for the *Atlantic* as its poetry editor. As director of the press I had administrative responsibilities that had increased since Rome. Yet I knew that, whatever else happened, a part of me was dedicated to my farm in West Gloucester. When my mother's uncle Fred Herzog, the last of my St. Louis family, died in 1968, he left me enough to buy a yellow Greek-Revival cottage and some beautiful acreage by a salt marsh a mile or two from the sea. My father's ashes had, at his earnest plea, been scattered there after his death, as my stepmother's would be after hers. While I worked in Italy dreams of Gloucester had kept visiting me and instigating a new kind of poem. The aspect of my imagination that surrendered only to outdoor air ("The Two of You") had taken Gloucester as its soul's country. Increasingly, back in America, I found the Gloucester experience and landscape pushing in as foreground or background for my poems. I wrote a series of longish pieces, *Walking the Boundaries,* as a tour of my property's seasons and edges. My poetry began fastening on a tree, a rock, a field, a stream, a bird, and endowing these "natural things" with sacramental importance.

In 1974 I pushed this trend farther when writing a centenary paper about Robert Frost for delivery at the Library of Congress, trying to imagine how Frost, coming from the West, invented New England for himself in 1911-1912. In 1975, further exploring myself, I began farming in a small way, keeping pigs, then sheep, with the partnership of my neighbor Kim Bartlett. Something had altered forever as a consequence of my sojourn in the Eternal City: a unification of sensibility which took my work beyond the agonies of "encounter and struggle," as Dudley Fitts had characterized some of my earlier writing. From *Dark Houses* (written in 1970) for the next decade and a half, nearly all my poetry would take its beginning or end from Gloucester's sparse and stony landscape. The migration of my sensibility had been fulfilled. After a 1974 business trip to London (still, as I write this, my most recent visit there) I found myself composing poems of farewell to England. I also managed to return to Colorado every year, and each of these visits brought me back again to touchstones of my childhood, in poems like "Creatures of the Genitive" and "Atmospheres," to mention only two.

During the 1970s my publishing career, like my writing, took on a bit more depth. I seem to have learned to take some confidence in my judgment, enabling me to predict, if not what the masses, at least what educated readers, might value; and some of the books that emerged from the Atlantic Monthly Press as the result of my sponsorship found their way into the mainstream. A sampling of these hundreds of books may give a sense of my interests: *Eskimos, Chicanos and Indians* and *Privileged Ones* by Robert Coles; *A Whale for the Killing* by Farley Mowat; *Beautiful Swimmers: Watermen, Crabs, and the Chesapeake Bay* by William W. Warner; *The Poems of Stanley Kunitz, 1928-1978; The Kennedy Imprisonment* by Garry Wills; *A Dangerous Place* by Daniel Patrick Moynihan; *Blue Highways: A Journey into America* by William Least Heat Moon; and *American Primitive: Poems* by Mary Oliver, are all books which found critical acclaim and wide audiences. Most won prizes.

Jane moved, in the seventies, toward a new phase of her own. As our children grew up and prepared to leave home she began preparing herself to launch out, at long last, into writing. In 1973 she edited a successful cookbook, *The Romagnolis' Table.* In 1974 we wrote a piece jointly for the *New York Times Magazine* on adolescent rites of passage. When a subsequent invitation came from the *Times* she wrote it alone, and the assignments proliferated into an impressive series on renovated architecture, much of it in Boston during the era of the restoration of the Faneuil Hall Market Place. By 1977 we had moved out of our house in Cambridge—our friends there thought us so brave!—to live in a mixed-income housing project on the new Boston waterfront. I published *A Voice in the Mountain* at just this time, and I also edited *Hello, Darkness,* the collected poems of my friend L. E. Sissman, who had died in 1976. Jane began a book about the lives and homes of three generations of American housewives, which she would entitle *The Fall of a Doll's House* (1980), sharing its title with one of my poems. Jane's book, however, would also encompass an aspect of our lives together which I never had the insight to describe, the ways in which men depend on women and women accept the weight of the dependence. Her book is, as John Updike described it, "a polemic of rare good humor."

After two years on the waterfront Jane finished her book, and in a hard but loving reassessment of our lives we decided not to look back to Cambridge. Both children had finished school there. The town we had loved, a college community in the 1950s, had in two decades taken on a glossy operational affluence which embodied all the distorted ambitions of the Kennedy and Nixon years. America had changed, and so had we: it was with a sense of renewal that we sold our

The house in Gloucester, Massachusetts

Cambridge house and determined to move full-time to the country in June of 1979.

Our next two years would be both our most intimate and our most harrowing. In the same week as we moved to Gloucester Jane found a lump in her breast. She had, as it transpired, just two years to live. She rented a pied-à-terre on Commonwealth Avenue where she could work during the day, and most mornings we boarded the commuter train from Gloucester to Boston together. She continued writing through the months of chemotherapy and of remission and wrote a second book, *This Old House,* based on a popular public television program. It was published in 1980, only a few months after her first book. (In the years since, *This Old House* by Bob Vila and Jane Davison has sold more copies than all of my own books taken together.) In this same year I published an anthology of selections, with preface, from the works of an old friend and Atlantic Monthly Press author entitled *The World of Farley Mowat.*

My life and my work cannot be separated from Jane's during these last years. In late 1979, after four years of earnest entreaty, the Press allowed me to relinquish the directorship, which passed to my longtime associate Upton Birnie Brady, and this allowed me to concentrate my responsibilities upon my own books and authors. I was writing the poems of country matters published in 1981 as *Barn Fever and Other Poems;* I would soon write the anxious sequence called "Wordless Winter"; and I was doing what I could to nurse Jane through her illness. In the fall of 1980, just before its darkest phase, we were able to travel together to Sicily and Umbria, to visit our beloved friends Shirley

and François Caracciolo in Todi and to return to Gloucester for the last act. Jane set up a screened tent in the meadow to ward the sun off her chemotherapy-sensitized skin, and in that beautiful place sat out the lengthening days of spring, receiving farewell visits from friends, setting her house in order, and watching the unchanging rocks and changing woods of Gloucester until she slipped away on July 4, 1981, just fifty-three years after the day I first came home from the hospital to my first home in New York. She was forty-nine.

James Dickey, reviewing my *Praying Wrong* in 1984, wrote: "Davison himself is a man with a great capacity for loving and a terrible apprehension over losing it, over the loss or straying of the beloved." For a while in 1981 it seemed to me as though I might lose everyone and everything, even though it was not so. My daughter Lesley had just graduated from boarding school and had settled on college in California, as a way, no doubt, of distancing herself from the sorrows of home. My son Angus had already settled into his working life in Belmont, Massachusetts, and seemed bound for engagement and marriage, which happily ensued. Jane's mother, one of the dearest women on earth, showed us an example of survival and dedication. I had to make a new life. I was reeling with grief.

As Jane's disease had worsened, and even before, I had yet again sought the challenges and consolations of psychoanalysis, this time with a gifted and kindly young Finnish doctor named Gunilla Enlund Jainchill, who knew and admired Jane. She helped me through the heaviest convulsions of mourning and the new

*Davison speaking at the memorial service
for Jane, July, 1984*

course thereafter. I found help from men and women friends alike. In Gloucester, where the children and I buried Jane's ashes not far from all the others, and where, obedient to her instructions, I had conducted her memorial service, I found myself posing like Orpheus with his lyre, making the trees to move. It could easily have turned into too luxurious a grief. To counter that temptation I threw myself into extra work, fund-raising for Yaddo in New York, serving the National Endowment for the Arts in Washington. I travelled whenever possible—to Nova Scotia to visit Farley and Claire Mowat; to Texas, Utah, and California for poetry readings; to Japan and Hawaii out of curiosity; to Italy again and, more happily to Portugal and Spain, where Lesley spent her junior year of college.

Eight months after Jane's death I began keeping company with Joan Goody, a beautiful and gifted architect, whose husband and partner Marvin Goody had died a year before Jane. The two women had met once; Jane had admired Joan's housing designed for the elderly; Joan came to admire Jane's books; I came to love what Marvin had done for Joan. Time, as we

warily sized one another up, brought Joan and me gradually, then more swiftly, together. At length we decided to join our lives, and we began when Joan redesigned my house in Gloucester and her own house in Boston, not only to accommodate herself and me, but to lay some of our ghosts. We would divide our time between the two places.

On August 11, 1984, Joan and I were married in Cambridge, in Agassiz House, a beautiful college building which Joan had renovated for Radcliffe and where I, thirty-six years before, had acted a role in George Bernard Shaw's comedy *Getting Married.* My sister Lesley, her husband, Forrest Perrin, and their children Wendy and Scott, made the music for us; friends made speeches; I recited poems and sang "Drink to Me Only with Thine Eyes." Several months later I published *Praying Wrong: New and Selected Poems, 1957-1984* with a last dedication to Jane, my beloved companion of nearly all those years. In the poems that have come to me since my second marriage I detect a new dedication in every sense.

Therefore at the end of 1985 the time came for me to sever my connection with the Atlantic Monthly Press after twenty-nine years and to strike out on my own as an editor. Though I would continue to choose the poetry for the *Atlantic,* I would turn to editing "Peter Davison Books" for Houghton Mifflin Company, the alert yet venerable publishing house which has long stood directly across the Boston Common from the *Atlantic,* and which had even, for much of the nineteenth century, owned the magazine. But from now on, after a career of allegiance to institutions, I would be working for myself and would, I imagined, move toward the pleasures of old age responsible to no one but myself, my wife, my terrain, and my poetry. "Best ask for gifts," as I had written twenty years earlier, "as though I had none coming."

BIBLIOGRAPHY

Poetry:

The Breaking of the Day, and Other Poems. New Haven: Yale University Press, 1964.

The City and the Island. New York: Atheneum, 1966.

Pretending to Be Asleep. New York: Atheneum, 1970.

Dark Houses (1870-1898). Cambridge, Mass.: Halty-Ferguson, 1971.

Half Remembered: A Personal History. New York: Harper, 1973; London: Heinemann, 1974.

Walking the Boundaries: Poems, 1957-1974. New York: Atheneum, 1974; London: Secker & Warburg, 1974.

Peter Davison and Joan Goody at their wedding, August 11, 1984

A Voice in the Mountain. New York: Atheneum, 1977.

Barn Fever and Other Poems. New York: Atheneum, 1981; London: Secker & Warburg, 1981.

Praying Wrong: New and Selected Poems, 1957-1984. New York: Atheneum, 1984; London: Secker & Warburg, 1985.

Editor of:

Hello, Darkness: The Collected Poems of L. E. Sissman. Boston: Atlantic-Little, Brown, 1978.

The World of Farley Mowat: A Selection from His Works. Boston: Atlantic-Little, Brown, 1980; Toronto: McClelland & Stewart, 1981.

Thomas M. Disch

1940-

The Disch family, circa 1900. "My great-grandparents (he was a tailor in southern Germany, who came to the States around 1850) and their children. My grandfather Thomas is the one in the middle."

I was born on February 2, 1940, in Des Moines, Iowa, the eldest son of Helen and Felix Disch. I was named for my paternal grandfather, who ran a corner grocery store in Minneapolis. He died before my memory was operational, and my only recollection of that Thomas Disch concerns the very fine strawberry ice cream cones that were to be had at his store. My grandmother, his wife, was a crippled, mean-spirited, small-minded German Catholic. Of her my earliest memory is the dread I felt at having to kiss her wrinkled, powdery cheek at the end of a visit. Another vivid memory of Grandma Disch comes from the early '50s, when she had a choking fit as a result of swallowing a baked bean. As she choked, all the children at the dinner table—me and my three younger brothers, Greg, Jeff, and Gary, but not Nancy, who would still have been a baby then—laughed uproariously, think-

ing that our grandmother had swallowed her false teeth. After her husband's death, Grandma Disch (rarely did anyone address her by her first name, which was Maggie) was supported by her captive daughters, Aurelia and Cecelia, who worked as secretaries. A third daughter, Lorraine, escaped her sisters' fate, first by enlisting in the war effort, then by marrying. She was promptly exiled from Grandma Disch's presence forever: Lorraine's husband was a divorcé, and *we* were Catholics.

My mother's people were subsistence farmers in the Mille Lacs area of central Minnesota. Their lives and land were poor enough that they could fairly be called peasants. They cut their own firewood and the blocks of ice for the icehouse, got their water from a hand pump, and shat in a privy. Grandpa Gilbertson lived in a mangey leather rocker, a vastly fat, grouchy

Grandma and Grandpa Gilbertson, about 1910

"My parents with Grandma Disch, in the early forties"

man who'd been crippled in the Spanish-American War. From that fixed position it was his joke to hook me by the neck with the crook of his cane whenever I ventured too near the rocker. He had heroically stubborn prejudices. My mother's favorite tale of him was that when taken to see a traveling circus he refused to believe that the lion, tiger, camel, etc. were real; he insisted that they were people in costumes. His wife, Emma, was the salt of the earth, a good-tempered, robust, bustling countrywoman right out of a Brueghel painting. Her people, the Bricks, were Norwegians, like the Gilbertsons. She was utterly capable, much loved, an archetypal cook, an unstoppable gossip, and a compulsive game-player, though in her last years her religious convictions, or her faltering attention span (she was very long-lived), required her to give up playing Hearts and take up the less sinful pastime of Rook. It was stipulated that there was to be no booze at her wake.

My father was a traveling salesman. He met my mother, the farmer's daughter, in the late '30s, in Minneapolis, where he was heading a crew selling *Collier's Magazine* (and she was working at a drugstore soda fountain). After they were married, she traveled with

his crew, which is how I came to be born in Des Moines. The earliest home I have any memory of was a downstairs duplex in St. Paul, where, being forbidden to cross the street, a colored boy and I played with each other in pantomime from our opposing curbstones. There too, grazing on neighborhood lawns in emulation of *Bambi,* an early role model, I came down with a bad case of oral poison ivy.

Before I entered kindergarten we'd moved across the Mississippi to Bryant Avenue in Minneapolis. There on Saturday mornings I would sit staring into the single green glass eyes of our radio, listening reverently to "Let's Pretend." There I marshalled two sets of bowling pins (children and grown-ups) in enactments of my own fairy tales (the big pink pin was a witch; the little blue pin was me). There, at night, I would cross my eyes, stare up at the ceiling, and watch self-projected home movies in wide-screen color (sad to say, I can no longer regulate my phosphene activity so purposefully).

Through the summer of 1946 there was a polio epidemic and my mother kept me indoors. To keep me occupied she taught me to read, and this led to my being skipped ahead to second grade when I entered

Incarnation School in the fall, to which rupture in the natural order I ascribe much of my later overweening. Yet even in kindergarten I'd found ways to distinguish myself: the nun in charge told my parents she believed I was possessed by a devil—because (if memory serves) I refused to pretend to be taking a nap after our milk and cookies, as tradition then required.

I continued at Incarnation only through third grade. Then my Gilbertson grandparents decided the farm was too much for them, and so for five months I was to live in that hand-me-down Eden. The raspberry bushes, flower beds, and senile orchards; the sagging barn and haunted chicken coop; the icehouse with the woodpile stacked against it; the bats in the attic, the wrens in the birdhouse, the snakes in the grass; the wood range in the kitchen, the grates in the floors of the upstairs bedrooms, which were their only source of heat (and a wonderful way to eavesdrop on the grown-ups): no other place in my childhood remains so distinct in memory or so dear as that house, the fields and woods and swamps about it, the great reedy lake just down the road. We Disches enjoyed that borrowed splendor for the summer and fall of 1948. We brought in and canned one harvest of vegetables—and then my father's new job, selling insulation and quonset housing, brought us to Fairmont in the prosperous corn belt in the southwest corner of the state.

I attended St. Paul's Convent School in Fairmont from fourth through eighth grade. There were twenty-three girls and eight boys in that class, and three social classes: the farm children, who were brought in by school bus, had the poorest clothes, and got the lowest grades in class; and a lower (manual labor) and lower-middle (shop-owning) class from the two sides of the railroad tracks. Already by the fourth grade the lines of

The Gilbertson farmhouse in early 1973. "I took the photograph when I drove up from Minneapolis looking for what was left of my personal past."

social demarcation were drawn as immutably as if we'd been blacks and whites in South Africa. I started school as a boy from the wrong side of the tracks, but as the family expanded and the quonset business peaked, we moved across the tracks to a brand-new four-bedroom house, supplied by my father's employer (and, I would one day discover, my mother's lover), Mr. M. W. Miller.

Fairmont tried hard to live up to the standards set for small-town America by the covers of the *Saturday Evening Post* (my father's favorite magazine), and the nuns who taught at St. Paul's Convent School were doing their best to carry on in the tradition of *The Bells of St. Mary's* and *Going My Way*. Ours was a sanitized All-American Catholicism cleansed of ethnic influence, and blind to history. Though I would come in time to recognize in Christopher Durang's Sister Mary Ignatius the sum of all the nuns who drilled me in the *Baltimore Catechism,* it would be ungrateful to write off my debt to the individual women who taught me as no more than early instruction in theories of sin and guilt. The nuns of St. Paul's ran a tight ship, and from them I learned to diagram sentences accurately and to sit relatively still behind a desk for hours at a time, essential skills for any writer. If I did not learn to read music, it wasn't for want of instruction (St. Paul's did a brisk trade in 8:00 A.M. requiem Masses, and no one was exempted from choir duty). Chiefly, the nuns were alive to a sense of beauty that expressed itself partly in the stage-management of the liturgy (seeing to candles, incense, and good linen, and drilling us altar boys in Latin pronunciation) and partly in a fondness for the

"My parents with my sister, Nancy, 1951"

"Our house at 706 North Main in Fairmont, Minnesota, summer of 1949." Tom standing behind his brothers, Jeffrey, Gary, and Gregory

alternative realms of the imagined, the visionary, the conjured-up.

In those same years, from age nine onwards, I began to earn my living, delivering the *Minneapolis Star* and the *Tribune* to those more cosmopolitan folks not content with Fairmont's own *Sentinel*, and, more lucratively, selling greeting cards and various household novelties from door to door. My father instructed me in the arts and wiles of salesmanship, and in the summers he often took me on the road with him to nearby towns, especially after he'd eased out of the quonset housing business and begun selling *Britannica Junior*.

Being allowanceless, I needed my earnings then (and now) for movies, books, and restaurants. My very first mortal sin was going to see Cecil B. deMille's *The Greatest Show on Earth*, which the dread Legion of Decency had given a B rating because James Stewart portrayed a mercy killer in it—sympathetically! To this day I feel an immediate complicity with mercy killers on the Evening News, and have, half-plotted, a novel on that subject that I hope may set the Legion of Decency clucking all over again, assuming it's still in business.

My reading, by contrast, was relatively unpatrolled. I read through my mother's stacks of Perry Mason paperbacks until they got to be too solvable, the serials in the *SatEvePost*, all the animal adventures and sea stories in the children's section of the library, as many Hardy Boy adventures as I could buy or borrow. Comic books, too, of course, with a special appetite for Dick Tracy, Kerry Drake, and Classics Comics. E. C. Comics, the *bêtes noires* of Dr. Wertham I prudently did

not buy for myself but read them, reverently aghast, at my best friend's house.

It was through the same friend, Bruce Burton (who attended public school at the other end of the universe from St. Paul's), that I made the acquaintance of science fiction. SF became my ruling passion during seventh and eighth grades; SF—and the Theater. For I'd exhausted the children's section of the library (where Bruce's sister Beverly had been librarian) and discovered, upstairs, an alcove stuffed with twenty years of Broadway hits. The script of a play can be read almost as quickly as a comic book, and the dialogue is often better. A critic in the *New York Times* has written, in disparagement of my too-developed treatment of character in a SF novel, that it was as though I'd inserted "one of O'Neill's family dramas . . . into a play by Brecht." At the age of twelve I had yet to discover Brecht, but already my concept of total literary sublimity was a bipolar model with *Strange Interlude* to the north and *Brave New World* down under. Though I've added other role models over the years, I still think that represents a fairly worthwhile ambition and a good plan for the reform of science fiction.

Just before I entered high school, my family—seven of us now—moved back to the Twin Cities. The Fairmont area had been milked dry of encyclopedia prospects, and I suspect there were problems with our landlord, Mr. Miller. From being one of eight boys and twenty-three girls in my grade school class, all known quantities, I became one of unknown hundreds in a brand-new suburban high school. Try as I might, which was not very hard, I never managed to be popular, though I never stopped believing I ought to be. (My career in a nutshell.) The next year, at my own request, I switched to Cretin, a Catholic military high school named for a former bishop of the diocese. Cretin's Christian Brothers accelerated my departure from the faith of my childhood and from Cretin, and one man in particular, Brother Anthony, should get credit for rousing me from latent to overt rebellion. Brother Anthony resumed his duties as biology teacher twelve weeks late in the school year, having been recovering from an earlier nervous breakdown. He was fanatically obsessed on two subjects: his hero Joe McCarthy (the Army-McCarthy hearings were then in progress) and the dangers of fluoridated water. By way of demonstrating the latter, he rigged experiments in his biology classes that resulted in lots of green scuzz and scum growing in the fluoridated water. We did not take to each other, and the day came when, after being cuffed about the face for whistling in class, I was ejected from the biology classroom. As I refused to apologize, I had to spend the second hour of each school day in the library, where I read smuggled-in copies of books by

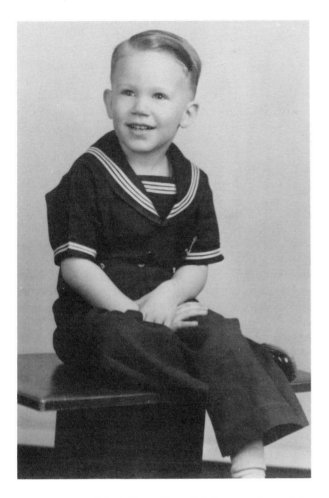 

Disch "in uniform": left, at age four; right, at age fourteen, at Cretin Military High School

Thomas Paine and Voltaire and other authors on the Church's Index of Forbidden Books.

Indeed, I was on fire with reading that year, having begun the serious business of checking off my autodidactic progress on the catalogue of Modern Library titles printed inside the cover of each of their books (which I bought, used, for seventy cents from Harold's Book Shop in downtown St. Paul). Thomas Hardy understood my problems, and Shakespeare lighted the world like a sun, and not just Shakespeare but all poetry, and not just poetry but classical music, which I checked out from the downtown library and played on my own squalling 33⅓ record player, erecting a sonic barrier between myself and my television-viewing family.

But I had still to come to the Rubicon of my adolescent rebellion. It came, or I came to it, in summer of '55, when, after being dragooned from my job as a library page in order to provide an audience for a lecture no one had shown up for, I fell in love with the lecturer and her subject. That fall I started taking ballet classes from Mrs. Andahazy, formerly of the Ballets Russes de Monte Carlo. It was the next best thing to running away with the circus.

In retrospect those two years of ballet classes and rehearsals (for the Andahazy production of *Aurora's Wedding,* in which I was a member of the corps) strike me as having been the major defining (and enabling) experience of my teenage years: in part because they required obstinate self-definition as (at best) a nonconformist; in larger part because by their means the spirit of art became fused with body's fiber. Most men are obliged to rely on sports for that confirmational, or transubstantive, benefit. I think I had the better bargain. Surely it is Mrs. Andahazy, more than to any other teacher I've had, to whom I feel most deeply beholden.

My twig was bent, and the branches pruned, in various other ways in my high-school years. From older fellow students at the Andahazy school I picked up the rudiments of a political radicalism that would not be chic for another decade. I discovered the not very well-hidden secret of my mother's liaison with Mr. Miller and deduced from that the character of my father's long-outstanding debt to his old employer, and after only a little *Sturm und Drang* I, too, learned to look the other way. Basically I was counting off the days on the calendar. Meanwhile I worked hard at assimilating the elements of a culture not mine by birthright, thought myself miserable (though happy as a colt in a spring meadow), and as soon as I had my diploma from Central High School and a bit of cash saved from a summer job as a trainee structural steel draftsman, I took off for New York City like an iron filing to a magnet.

It was just like its movies. I shared a 1½-room apartment on West Eighty-eighth Street with three dancers from the Andahazy school, Alan, Kay and Judy, who'd come to the city with traditional high hopes of breaking into show biz. Though I knew I wasn't destined for a dancing career, I was able, with the help of another ex-Andahazy dancer, Warren Ruud, to get a job as a "super" at the Metropolitan Opera, where I appeared with Fonteyn in *Swan Lake,* as a slave in the Bolshoi's *Spartacus,* and as a black-amoor in a new production of *Don Giovanni* with a Eugene Berman costume tailor-made for me as I then was, six-foot-two, 175 pounds. I got a job at the Marlboro book store on Fifty-seventh Street next to Carnegie Hall, and lied my way to another night job at the *Daily Mirror,* and then a month or so shy of my eighteenth birthday I lost my cherry to an English actor, who conducted the procedure with clinical despatch, and that was that. Except that it wasn't: I went into a belated tailspin that took me, by Greyhound bus, to New Orleans (I had some hope for a scholarship at Tulane), where, being both destitute and dismayed by my sexual destiny I thought to solve both problems by enlisting in the army.

Four or five weeks into basic training I realized that I did not want to spend the next three years in the army (which was *not* like its movies), and happily the English actor had provided me with an exit visa. The sin that dare not, spoke its name, and when the army doctors didn't at once eject me, I went AWOL, hitchhiked back to New York, and turned myself in just before AWOL became desertion and a serious matter. I got sent to an ancient dungeon on Governor's Island, and from there, after some not too sincere threats of suicide, to a combination prison and mental hospital in Valley Forge, Pennsylvania, where I had, actually, a splendid time. The food was good and the company vivid; there was a heated swimming pool, a sufficient library (once I'd twice read through the copy of Dostoevski's *The Idiot* that I'd clutched all the way from New York like a security blanket), and a virginal set of oil paints in the physical therapy room. Only when the doctors declared that the price of my continued residence would be shock treatments did I agree to declare myself of sane mind and got shipped to the brig. But the army had decided I was more trouble than I was worth, and sane or not, they discharged me that May.

I returned to New York, my future unshadowed by the draft, and found, through people I'd met in my days of supering at the Met, a plum of a sublet on West Sixteenth Street and an ideal (i.e., minimally demanding) job, working the checkroom at the Majestic Theater and selling orange juice at the intermission, a job I left and returned to many times over the next few years during the extended runs of *The Music Man* and *Camelot.* In the days I read mass quantities of books and practiced drawing in preparation for the entrance test to tuition-free Cooper Union, where in pursuit of the daydream I'd formed in senior year of high school (it was too hazy to be called an ambition) I meant to study architecture. I passed the test and entered Cooper Union—but left it even faster than I had the army, for the ostensible reason that I couldn't find a part-time job that left me time enough to study, but really, I suppose, because the steam had gone out of the dream.

For the next year I bounced around the job market. (Jobs were so easy to get back then, and there were genuine cold-water flats available for a pittance. The world's become, if not colder, costlier since 1958.) I inherited (from the last of the three Andahazy dancers to depart New York with her hopes revised) the back two rooms of a partitioned railroad flat on Thompson Street that rented for $32 a month, a rent that sometimes got halved when I took in a roommate. There I built my first set of bookshelves and settled in.

In the summer of '59 I took a job at the Metropolitan Life Insurance Company that paid half my tuition for evening classes, and that fall I started to attend NYU's Washington Square College. This time I didn't funk out. I got good grades and took advantage of NYU's traditional apathy to become the editor of the evening student newspaper and president of the evening student council. The result was a full-tuition scholarship to the day school, where, as a point of honor, I refrained from all further extracurricular activities. I returned to the Majestic checkroom, and for the next year and a half I wrote term papers (and a few short stories), took tests, and checked hats and coats at an even keel.

Then, just before finals in May of 1962, I had what we called in those days a nervous breakdown. That's to say, I'd decided to leave NYU but didn't know how to do so other than by claiming dementia. (It had worked to get me out of the army, after all.)

Over the first weekend of this "breakdown" I stayed indoors and wrote what I figured I now *must* write, by way of earning the luxury of a breakdown—a story I could sell to a magazine. Two long months later, Cele Goldsmith, the editor of *Fantastic,* bought "The Double-Timer" for 1½ cents a word, or $112.50. I didn't study for my make-ups, and I didn't return to NYU. I was now, officially, a writer.

There is a great mystique attached to being a writer of fiction or poetry, and by the very fact that I am preparing this sketch of my life for a series of writerly autobiographies I am contributing to that mystique. Although there may be a basis for pronouncing, as Carlyle did, that writers are the prophets of a secular age and for making other heroic comparisons, the practical bases for the prominence of writers are surely simpler. For one thing, such prominence is mostly a matter of writers writing about other writers when they're not writing about themselves, which might be called the frog-pond effect. More important, writing represents a possible escape from, in extreme cases, a life of poverty, and, for almost anyone, from the demands of the job market—the need to clock in at nine o'clock, to follow orders, to be immobilized and bored for hours at a stretch, to cajole customers, and generally to serve time. For most hired workers prison is a resonant metaphor for their condition, and writing often represents, literally or figuratively, an escape from prison. It surely did for me.

Writers, being exempted from the common fate, are inclined to make much of the splendors and the miseries of the profession by way of justifying the exemption. We proclaim our significance antiphonally, and kvetch about low pay, nepotism ("What about that *David* Updike then!"), and writer's block. Rarely do we speak of the pleasure of writing, or the further blessedness of being paid for our pleasure. No doubt those of my colleagues who complain of the pain it costs them to wrench the right words from the void of the unwritten are offering sincere testimony and not practicing trade unionism. Temperaments differ.

One further ironic generality on the subject, and then back to a proper chronological order. The "freedom" of a career in literature is only to be had by recreating all those constraints and routines that made the workaday world seem so prison-like. Hence, the emphasis in all those *Paris Review* interviews on the need for diligence and regular hours. In the twenty-four years since I sold that first story, I've written over a dozen novels (two in collaboration), five collections of stories, seven of poems, and one of criticism. Most of the last year was given over to writing a computer-interactive novel called *Amnesia.* There has been, as

well, a fair amount of work that was published ephemerally or died a-borning. All the work has been through at least two drafts. That all adds up to a very sedentary, officey life, and when I speak of the "pleasure" of writing it is the craftsmanly pleasure of seeing the things one is making locking into the right shape, step by step, from clay through kiln. The pleasure, for instance, of handling once again that ancientest of metaphors for creation and thinking how variously apt it can be: in the process's wonderful susceptibility to repetition—another pot, another poem, and then another; in the different, but parallel, relation of the potter and his audience toward his creations; and in the boredom that an onlooker experiences witnessing the artist pottering about his job.

So, with that note of caution and apology, back to the age of twenty-two, and the beginning of my apprenticeship. Since I was a fresh college dropout it wasn't that hard to get jobs, though I wasn't that good at keeping them. Usually before I was fired for tardiness I would quit out of impatience, having saved enough to buy myself a month or two of full-time writing. There was a job at another insurance company, and one as a teller at a savings bank in Flatbush, and finally a job at the National Industrial Conference Board, where I learned to do proofreading and copy-editing. Meanwhile, at night or on weekends or between jobs, I wrote stories, which for that first year sold to Cele Goldsmith or not at all.

In October '63, with some coaching and an introduction from David Leddick, the friend of supering days from whom I'd sublet the Sixteenth Street apartment and who was now a rising advertising executive, I

Disch as a trainee copywriter in the office of Doyle Dane Bernbach, 1964

got a job as trainee copywriter at Doyle Dane Bernbach, the company famous for selling Volkswagens to America. It paid $100 a week, and I stuck to the job for over a year, making no larger a success of it than my minimal effort deserved. But I did increase sales of Nikolai Vodka enormously in Pennsylvania by posing the question of why, if vodka, by its legal definition, could not possess a "characteristic taste, odor, or aroma," anyone should pay more for a "prestige" vodka. I also made my first and still my only appearance in *The New Yorker*—a double-page spread for Hartmann Luggage. And, partly through the need in ad copy to aim for high compression without any sacrifice of naturalness, I began (at long last) to write viable poetry. Indeed, the *Minnesota Review* had already accepted a single, stiff, three quatrain poem written in the fall of '62, "Echo and Narcissus," and it would be a few years—not till 1968—before I had the knack (for me the essential knack of poetry) of being able to recognize the *occasion* of poetry, the phrase or the formulation that can be grown into a poem.

Meanwhile, I knew that if I was to reach escape velocity as a professional writer I would have to write a novel. Early in '63 I had made one long false start in that direction, *A Game of Armageddon,* which was aborted at eighty pages, and a year later I tried again, producing two chapters of a stillborn SF novel, *The Freedom Years of R. B. O'Meara.* Those chapters served as my presentation piece when, in the the summer of 1964, I attended my first Milford SF Writers' Conference, where I had my first heady experience of meeting other professional writers *en masse,* all my seniors in the business, and most with novels already to their credit. Before Milford I had sampled the social milieu of science fiction at a couple of New York conventions, and felt such a horror of hotel corridors thronged with drunken teenagers dressed as hobbits as only a twenty-four-year-old aspirant to a Brooks Brothers charge account can know. But Milford was another matter. Milford was home, complete with sibling rivalry (Harlan Ellison, the reigning *Wunderkind,* considered me a usurping presence), an adopted father, Richard McKenna, and mother, Judith Merril, and Damon Knight's somewhat baronial Victorian house as a setting representing the Old Manse every would-be foundling imagines himself an heir to. (Indeed, four years later I would sublet that very house and dwell in the myth of it a full six months.) But the sweetest fruit of Milford was my contract from Berkley Books (for whom Damon Knight acted as talent scout) to write my first novel, *The Genocides.*

To make my money go farther and from a simple appetite to see the world, I went to Mexico to write my novel, renting a villa that had been previously rented by the editor of the *Magazine of Fantasy and Science-Fiction,* Avram Davidson. It was in the town of Amecameca, situated an hour's bus-ride south of Mexico City between the two volcanoes Popocatepetl and Ixtacihuatl. Aside from two Mormon missionaries who shared the same walled garden with me, I was the only American in the town. I arrived speaking no Spanish and learned little. I wrote until my typewriter broke down, and then I bought another Olivetti from one of the missionaries (equipped with a cedilla *c* and pinon *n*). The book that had been contracted as *The Long Harvest* became *The Harvest Is Past, the Summer Is Ended.* It took me about ten weeks' work, with a week off for Christmas in Vera Cruz. The finished manuscript was mailed off to New York just as I reached my twenty-fifth birthday. I celebrated by becoming, briefly, a beach bum on one of the Pacific beaches, and there took up with a wonderful con-man-cum-adventurer and his girlfriend who were taking a van to British Honduras, where they hoped to trade it for a sailboat. I went with them through Guatemala, basking in the reflected glory of their raffishness, sailed up a jungle river on a concrete barge, got taken up by a Pentecostal missionary, and rounded off my rite of passage with a visit to the Yucatán penninsula. At last I'd entered the '60s (though really it was more the case that at last I'd entered my twenties). It seems to me that such an itinerary is no longer one of the options open to the young—unless they decide to become mercenary soldiers.

The news, returning to my mailbox, was that except for a change of title and the circumcision of its first too-arty paragraph, my novel—now called (by my own suggestion) *The Genocides*—was okay. I abandoned my self-made Trappist cloister in Amecameca and sampled the official "artists' colony" of San Miguel de Allende, but though there were plenty of people there who spoke English, and a few who claimed to be writers, none of them seemed at all appreciative of the fact that I was a bona fide novelist. Enough of such drunks and wastrels! Enough of Mexico and Spanish irregular verbs! I booked passage on a passenger liner and sailed back to New York in triumph, a man whose name would soon appear on the cover of a book, albeit a science-fiction paperback.

While I'd been in Mexico, I had been subletting my Thompson Street apartment to a friend I'd made on a visit back to Minnesota in the summer of '63. John Sladek had gone off to Europe to write *his* first novel, had done so, and then lost it in a trunk misrouted or stolen by the railroad. He'd returned to New York just as I was leaving and was happy to be the curator of my bookshelves. During the time I was away John worked at a nightmarish office job and revenged himself on his job by writing a superb absurdist no-vella, "Masterson and the Clerks." I praised the wit of "Masterson," John returned the compliment, we collaborated on assorted short stories (including a dead-pan, brain-damaged imitation of James Bond, "The Floating Panzer," which may be the absolutely trashiest thing either of us has ever written), and we decided to collaborate on a larger scale—and tour Europe at the same time.

I spent the summer and fall of '65 working at an ad agency for what seemed to me the dangerously seductive salary of $250 a week (lest I become unmanned by luxury, I refused to expand my business wardrobe beyond the minimum daily requirement of a single Haspell suit) and drawing up outlines of new novels. By October my then-agent, Bob Mills, had got me contracts for four paperback originals: a gothic to be written (collaboratively) as Cassandra Knye; an expansion, for Ace Books, of "White Fang Goes Dingo," a comic SF novella I'd written immediately after "The Double-Timer," which Ace would retitle *Mankind under the Leash,* but which since has been restored to what I wanted to call it, *The Puppies of Terra;* and two more SF novels for Berkley, *Echo Round His Bones* (also based on an earlier, unpublished novella) and *Camp Concentration.* Besides these four John and I had already plotted out and set to work on a draft of a mystery/thriller called *Black Alice,* which we intended to write on spec and hope for a hardcover. (I also, that summer, wrote a story, "Problems of Creativeness," that would become the basis for the book *334.*)

All five projected books got written within the next fifteen months, the gothic first during the voyage by freighter to, and month-long sojourn in, Casablanca. Then we rented an off-season villa on the Costa del Sol, where I let out the hem of "White Fang Goes Dingo." Then, as a consequence of eating seafood fished from the polluted waters of the Costa del Sol, John and I simultaneously came down with hepatitis. The available medical care was minimal in the town of Fuengirola, and the disease was so debilitating that a two-block walk to the corner grocery was a major effort. For a month we slept, ate mashed potatoes, and every day, at one o'clock, injected our thigh muscles with hypodermic needles (that seemed big as syringes) of gamma globulin, a cure at least as horrible as the disease. We also went on writing: John did a second Cassandra Knye gothic set on the romantic Rock of Gibraltar, and I wrote what is, by reason of these associations, the novel least dear to memory, *Echo Round His Bones,* a resolutely cheerful science fiction adventure as traditional in all its trappings as a khaki fatigue uniform. When we had the strength for it, we packed our bags onto a P & O boat stopping at Gibraltar on

its way from Australia to London, where we arrived in the spring of '66. In London, we took separate lodgings to recover from the frayed tempers of our shared convalescence. I finished my share of *Black Alice,* which involved some further fraying of tempers, but in London there was plenty of remedy for that. Through Judy Merril, who was an expatriate there herself, I had introductions to various SF writers, most of them connected one way or another with the magazine *New Worlds.* For the first time in my life my social calendar brimmed over.

In a full-dress autobiography I would have to do cameos of the entire New Wave (as we came collectively to be called): there was Brian Aldiss, living the life of a don in a *thatched* cottage just outside Oxford; there was Jimmy Ballard in the first flush of his notoriety as a *romancier maudit;* there were the Brunners, John and Majorie, with their weekly at-homes in Hampstead; and above all, there was the editor of *New Worlds,* Michael Moorcock, who was the very model of a modern major general, a big, brassy extravagance of a fellow, with the beard and long hair of the new era and clothes from the racks of Carnaby Street, which then was a synonym for the new male glitz mandated by the Beatles. Mike was also a good writer in his own

With John Sladek (left) in Amsterdam, 1966

right *and* a charismatic editor, which meant, in practical terms, being the host of a perpetual tea party/smorgasbord/drinking bout, in the course of which the magazine got put to bed once a month.

When summer came, I set off on a tour, planned months earlier, with my former boss at Metropolitan Life. From Amsterdam we drove through Germany, Switzerland, and the Austrian Tyrol. At the end of the trip I met up with John Sladek and we again rented off-season quarters—in the modest ski resort of Reutte, just south of the German border in the Tyrolean Alps. There he started work on his most ambitious novel to date, *The Reproductive System,* and I began *Camp Concentration.*

Reutte wasn't quite the isolation booth that both Amecameca and Fuengirola had been, for I'd studied German all through college, but even so my German never amounted to a social asset. Indeed, it didn't serve to get me through the daily paper. Since high school I have tried my tongue at five different languages, yet never have I become proficient enough in one of them to conduct any but the most utilitarian conversation or to read a novel for pleasure. Partly, no doubt, it's sheer laziness, and partly it may be a natural incapacity, especially at ear/mouth coordination, but the real problem has always been a lack of full-time intellectual commitment to the task. My ROM memory banks are usually taken up with the Work-in-Progress, and that is always in English. True polyglots have a more generous spirit than mine. Yet I may, for all that, finally overcome my torpor and get either my German or Italian into functional shape, since (as this memoir so much reminds me) some of the happiest times of my life have been those stints of writing in the estranged solitude and strange excitement of a foreign country, where the whole world becomes (as it would be, even at home, if one were sufficiently attentive) a congeries of riddles.

I took off from Reutte and from my novel, in order to see *Tristan* and *The Ring* at Bayreuth, and, when I placed a short-short with *Playboy* for $1,000 (as much as I'd got for an entire novel from Ace!), to celebrate my good fortune by seeing Paris for the first time. With such riches of experience raining down on me, it was only natural that the novel I was writing should convey some sense of giddy repletion and intellectual jubilation, feelings that set up an interesting interference pattern with the book's darker themes. At the age of twenty-six death is not usually much to the forefront of one's thoughts, but I had just recovered from an illness that had seemed at the time to take me within shouting distance of my own death, and then in the fall of '66 my mother died of throat cancer and the effects of chemotherapy, a death made more bitter for her and for those who had to witness it by her ever-worsening alcoholism. I did not have to witness it, and I decided not to return to Minnesota for the funeral.

In November, as the fogs and rains of autumn settled over the Tyrol, I returned to London but continued to work on *Camp Concentration* in spate. John and I found a dismal flat in far-off Temple Fortune, but more and more we spent our time in the lavishly cluttered Camden Town quarters of Pamela Zoline. Pam was the friend, since their high-school days in Winnetka, Illinois, of my friend from NYU days, John Clute, and for most of one year, from fall of '62 through spring of '63, we three had shared an apartment on Riverside Drive. Then Pam had gone to London to study at the Slade. She was a marvelously gifted painter, but no better a student than I had been, and by 1966 she'd long since dropped out of the Slade. Pam and I passed beyond simple friendship to a passion of mutual admiration, which led to an understanding, though not a formal engagement, that some day. . . .

But another day dawned sooner. A week or two short of my twenty-seventh birthday and the completion of *Camp Concentration* I fell in love. Lee Harwood was a poet, indeed a Penguin poet, the same age as I. Though he had a wife and son, he'd also recently had an affair with a senior American poet, exquisitely memorialized in Lee's book *The Man with Blue Eyes.* My memory insists that his complexion (pale with hectically flushed cheeks) was of equal significance with these other facts. For not more than six weeks love was requited, and then Lee explained, firmly but kindly, that our romance was at an end since he was returning to heroin. For a few months I knew an ecstasy of unrequited love that quite dwarfed the fledgling affair that had preceded it, and had "nervous breakdowns" successively in Ireland, Friesland, and Istanbul, where toward the end of '67 I'd gone to study Turkish by way of preparing myself to write a travel book about the Pontine Mountains of northern Turkey. Why the Pontine Mountains? I've no idea, except that they represented the ends of the earth. I sightsaw, was dumbfounded by my first (and only) encounter with a non-Indo-European language, became very lonely, and for the first time found that I could not start my writing engine by the *Fiat lux* of sitting down at the typewriter, even though in April and May I had made a promising beginning at a new novel, *The Pressure of Time* (which is still in-progress), inspired by the pangs of despised love and the earlier trip through Ireland. Finally I admitted defeat and returned to London long enough to write some short stories, including what I think was my best up to that time, "The Asian Shore." Then in summer of '68 I sailed back to the States.

There the first thing I did was check in at the

Milford Conference. The Knights were about to move to Florida, and I undertook to rent the "Anchorage" from them, sharing the house with Jim and Jane Sallis. Jim I had met in London, where he'd become involved with *New Worlds,* and he remained in London for some time, while Jane and I (strangers till that moment) and four-year-old Dylan Sallis took occupancy of the old manse. It was very pleasant, having, as though by magic, all the accoutrements of middle-class life: wife, child, house, car, but once Jim joined us the idyl began to fizzle as it became clear that I was on the sidelines of a marriage that was breaking apart. The Anchorage itself was sold by the Knights, spent some years tenant-less and falling apart, and then burned to the ground.

In New York, in spring of '69, I found a studio apartment on Sheridan Square and bought a big mahogany rolltop desk (I am sitting at it as I write this on a KayPro 2), and then, even before I'd put up bookshelves, I fell in love again, and again got ditched four weeks out of the starting gate. Clearly, I had a Problem, and in New York, in 1969, the solution to a Problem was Therapy. My new therapist (there had been others before: I was a glutton for therapy) was of the school of Alexander Lowen and had me doing isometric exercises to channel my cosmic energies from my overenergized head to the southern, underdeveloped regions of my body. At the same time I was encouraged to get out and fuck more. I followed my doctor's orders and had a memorable summer, though, if the poetry that got written then is any indication, it may be I directed too much of my cosmic energies from my head. Or it may be that I was trying too hard to be

laid-back after the manner of the second generation "New York School" poets then operating out of St. Mark's Church, among whom I'd been granted a provisional visa (long since lapsed and never renewed). For whatever reason, my poetry was off and the only fiction I'd written for the past year were two novelizations, one of *The Prisoner* TV series, the other of a movie that flopped into instant oblivion, *Alfred the Great.*

On September 20, 1969, I met Charles Naylor, and this time love was here to stay. He moved in the next day, and we've been together over sixteen years. Beyond the general observation that our strengths and needs dovetailed like mortise and tenon, I won't attempt to account for my many-anniversaried good fortune, nor will I chronicle it at much length, and this for three reasons: (1) Charlie is jealous of his privacy, (2) so am I of mine, and (3) it's all there in the poetry for anyone who's that curious. Not that my poetry is particularly diaristic or confessional, but among the poems in the four collections of poetry between 1981 and 1984 and the two more assembled and waiting in the wings, the circumstances of our lives together are pretty thoroughly documented. (The first collection, from 1972, *The Right Way to Figure Plumbing,* consists of poems from 1967 or earlier and was meant from the first to be

"On my green BMW, 1969"

Charles Naylor in Minneapolis, 1973

counted as juvenilia; but I can't resist a parenthetical footnote to account for its title. From time to time, after I'd published my first book, I would peek into the catalogue of the New York Public Library to see if my name had been entered onto a filecard to be placed in one of those beautiful oak file drawers, but no, for years the only Disch the Public Library knew of was Emil Disch, who had written the *fin de siècle* classic, *The Right Way to Figure Plumbing*. The title of my first book of poetry was my revenge on Emil Disch and a joke to be shared with imaginary cataloguers.)

An immediate result of connecting with Charlie was that my cosmic energies again got redistributed. My poetry came into focus, and my fiction got back in gear. Within only a couple months I had taken up the task I'd been avoiding almost for a year, continuing my projected novel *334*, a neo-realist portrait of New York City circa 2023, a book that I consider my best work to date in the genre of science fiction, and that owes its distinctive tone to the fact that I was writing for a new non-ghetto audience, Charlie. Among the mortise-and-tenon correspondences I can be thankful for not the least has been Charlie's acumen as critic, editor, and de facto first reader (but not till a work is finished; nor will he let me add the gloss of reading it aloud). He's knowledgeable about poetry at both the astronomic and molecular level, and his complete in-difference to science fiction as a field (and as a social experience) has been a useful counterweight to my ego's natural impulse to glory too much in the triumphs of the frog pond—or (more to the point) to agonize over its frustrations. In 1979 my friend John Clute summed my career up for *The Science Fiction Encyclopedia:* "TMD is perhaps the most respected, least trusted, most envied and least read of all modern sf writers of the first rank: his reputation can only grow. He has won no awards." The judgment has been quoted verbatim more times than I care to think, and it is nearly as true in 1986 as it was in 1979. I confess that "least trusted" galls and somewhat puzzles me, unless the supposition is that every writer is presumed to have made a bargain with his audience to flatter, soothe, or console them, and that to do otherwise is to betray a trust, and that it is a worse betrayal yet to discuss the bargain, as I have tended to do in writing criticism. A couple of years ago I sat on a panel discussing SF criticism, and one of the panelists, a SF writer with many subtrashy bestsellers under his belt, argued precisely that—that critics should never say what might be wounding to a writer (from which it would follow, as a corollary, that writers should never write anything that might ruffle their readers' feathers). For the one bumpkin guileless enough to express such a wish, there must be a dozen savvier hacks who nevertheless believe it, and so I must be grateful to

"My first oil painting," completed at the "Anchorage" in Milford, Pennsylvania, 1969

Charlie for the example of his own unremitting standards of judgment. It is the one thing we argue about most often, whether and how gladly fools and rogues should be suffered, and while I consider the question still moot in many cases, overall Charlie's verdicts have carried the day and my life has been the better for it.

One natural result of domesticity is that, except for explicating my bibliography—where this or that book got written, what editor bought it, etc.—there has not been much autobiographical "news" during the last sixteen years. Some friendships suffered attrition, some new friendships were made, and the best held steady. The major blips on the chart rarely represent a change of course. Thus, in the winter of '73 I returned to Minnesota to teach a course in fiction-writing for one semester at the University of Minnesota, and again in the summer of '75 I taught a course in SF at Wesleyan in Connecticut, but on the whole I've been pre-

served from the temptation of teaching by lack of even a B.A.

I've more often been tempted by the lure of Stage and Screen, and still am, but so far the only tangible results of having yielded to the temptation were two operas by Gregory Sandow for which I wrote the libretti, the one-act *Fall of the House of Usher* and the three-act *Frankenstein.*

My one genuine mid-life crisis (so far) came in 1979, after Charlie and I had returned from London and had finished *Neighboring Lives,* our collaborative novel about Victorian Chelsea. Turner, Whistler, and Rossetti were among the *dramatis personae* of that novel, and having written so much about painters and painting, and being at the end of a particularly long and hard haul and accordingly weary of writers and writing, I signed on for classes at the Art Students League and started to paint. For almost a year I did nothing

Charles Naylor. Drawing by Tom Disch, Rome, 1972

Tom Disch. Drawing by Charles Naylor, Rome, 1972

else. I studied first with the late Robert Philips, and then with Knox Martin, and when I was not at the League painting the life models, I would paint still lifes at home in the bathroom. After a while, however, two things became clear: (1) there was no more room anywhere in the apartment for my paintings, and (2) I was never going to be another Gauguin. I still fantasize of having a place in the country with a Studio, but I'm resigned to considering painting a hobby rather than a second string to my bow.

As to the first string, since 1970 my writing has gone on at a fairly steady pace without any system of daily quotas and with only such fallow periods as the soil required. Even in those periods I usually kept my typewriter exercised with reviews or short stories or the odd piece of nonfiction (like this). The circumstances under which some of the books got written were straight out of *La Bohème: 334* was finished in a cold, damp workingman's cottage on a dairy and pig farm in Surrey, with a living room that overlooked the pen the cows used as their waiting room before being milked (but that neglects to mention the nightingales); the studio apartment at Sheridan Square was ludicrously small (but we coped with that by installing a ping-pong table in the middle of the room by way of using *all* the space), and our present digs still probably wouldn't qualify as middle-class. On the other hand we have also lucked into some palatial (or idyllic) sub-lets,

especially the penthouse in Rome of the composer Vittorio Rieti (found through an ad in the daily paper) where we spent the winters of '71-'72 and '73-'74 and where I wrote most of what was to be my most commercially successful novel, *Clara Reeve*—(though that book was never publicly "mine," since at the insistence of Knopf it appeared under a pseudonym).

Success is no doubt the subtext of such considerations as how well or poorly I've lived, and as friend Clute's quote (cited above) would indicate, I can not be rated a great success in the marketplace of science fiction, nor have my ventures outside the ghetto yielded rewards proportional to the effort expended. *Neighboring Lives,* for instance, though it garnered some good reviews did not go into paperback; to keep Scribner's from selling the paperback rights for zilch I bought them myself for half of what we'd been paid as an advance. *The Businessman: A Tale of Terror* got good reviews, was never advertised, and never went into paperback, and to prevent Harper and Row from letting a second novel on the contract die the same death, I sacrificed the better part of my advance in order to buy my freedom. My grievances against Knopf are of a different nature, and I wouldn't care to risk a libel suit to air them, but that was not ultimately a happy experience either. Richard Howard once remarked to me that he found it surprising that I did not feel more bitterness about my career (though he was referring to

In Bermuda, 1970

my career as a poet), and I was pleased to think that I could give that impression. For of course I do feel bitter about any number of things, and envious often enough, but nature has blessed me with a naturally high endorphin level, and usually I can deal with the "adversities" of my career by developing a *theory* of adversity to account for them. After all, to have such worries at all is a form of good fortune. As well be bitter about the way the garage has nicked the chrome on one's Rolls Royce.

A more legitimate source of fretfulness is the way of all flesh, which is the way of entropy as well. Philosophy isn't much help on this score, unless it is a philosophy that gets one to the gym and promotes a prudent diet, but Aquinas', Luther's, and my own experience show that philosophy can have far other effects. Right now I tip the scales at forty pounds more than I'd wish to tip them at, but I'm trying: a year ago I weighed my all-time worst, 275 pounds, and I'm down forty pounds from that. My blood pressure is high, but not yet high enough that medication is called for. Usually I can run a mile in nine minutes, and on my better days I've done two miles nonstop. If all this pulse-taking smacks of the '80s and the "Culture of Narcissism," I'm happy, considering the alternatives, to be, however half-heartedly, part of such a time and culture. Of all my role models Thomas Mann has long been my main man, and Mann led a steadily productive life to the age of eighty. My father, and Grandma Gilbertson, both lasted that long or longer, and were lucid almost to the end. Maybe, if I can keep my weight down, I can live to be an elder statesman.

I can't seem to keep from sounding a valedictory note: a chronological memoir necessarily confronts that blank space after the one-en dash that follows the birth date. But let me try to end with an account of what is, in fact, my primary concern—the situation here and now. I am writing this at the end of December '85 on Union Square, where we've been living without any major change of scene since October '78. Next spring Doubleday will be bringing out my first children's book, *The Brave Little Toaster*, which I wrote in London early in '78. The first copies are stacked beside the toaster who provided the model for my hero. The book could not be sold *as* a children's book until film rights had been sold to Disney and it was in production as a feature-length cartoon. At the same time Doubleday was to have brought out, in a single volume, three books of poetry that have already been published in England (the last of which, *Here I Am, There You Are, Where Were We,* having been a Poetry Book Society Choice in 1984), but Doubleday has informed me that that book has been indefinitely postponed. You win some, you lose some.

Doubleday is also presently in contractual possession of three other novels: *A Troll of Surewould Forest: A Post-Modern Pantomime for the Reading-Impaired,* which I wrote in 1982 in five and a half months of manic self-delight and which, for the pleasure it gave me, I must account my own personal favorite among the novels I've written; *The M.D.: A Horror Story,* which is set in the same meta-Minneapolis as my earlier fantasy novel, *The Businessman: A Tale of Terror,* and which now exists as a portion of 100 pages and an outline that represents, probably, another year's work; and the ever-procrastinated, constantly-accumulating SF novel, *The Pressure of Time* (60,000 words completed in a near-final draft, at least as many more to go). Meanwhile, I've completed a computer-interactive novel, *Amnesia,* which should appear from Electronic Arts in May of 1986. For a while it was touch-and-go whether *Amnesia* would ever exist. Harper and Row Software contracted for it in the fall of '83, and then a year later, when the project was halfway to completion, Harper and Row dissolved their software department before it had put a single product on the market, a decision dictated by considerations of accounting (they'd just sold off an educational division, and the loss from the abortion of the software department could be written off against the profits from the sale). Shortly after Harper and Row scuttled that boat, Doubleday did the same thing with their Dial subsidiary, with whom I'd

Thomas M. Disch, 1984

157

just signed the five-book contract referred to above and where I'd found at long last my ideal editor in the person of Phil Pochoda. All this might be thought to be unsettling, and I did for one unmanly moment break down into tears of hopelessness and self-pity in a Boston movie lobby while waiting to see, what else, *The Bostonians.* But I was all right by the time the feature started and came away thinking that Vanessa Redgrave was splendid and Christopher Reeve more than just okay. Better, certainly, than he'd been as Superman. I returned to New York and proceeded to write the first section of *The M.D.,* because it is, after all, a book *I* want to write, whoever ends up publishing it, and then when Electronic Arts took over *Amnesia* I returned to work on that. And now that's done, and now this is done, and tomorrow I can go out and shop for Christmas presents.

BIBLIOGRAPHY

Fiction:

The Genocides. New York: Berkley Publishing, 1965; London: Whiting & Wheaton, 1967.

Mankind under the Leash. New York: Ace Books, 1966; also published as *The Puppies of Terra.* London: Panther, 1978; New York: Pocket Books, 1980.

One Hundred and Two H-Bombs (short stories). London: Robert & Vinter, 1966; New York: Berkley Publishing, 1971; also published with a new arrangement of stories as *White Fang Goes Dingo and Other Funny S.F. Stories.* London: Arrow, 1971.

The House that Fear Built, with John Sladek under joint pseudonym Cassandra Knye. New York: Paperback Library, 1966.

Echo Round His Bones. New York: Berkley Publishing, 1967; London: Hart-Davis, 1969.

Black Alice, with John Sladek under joint pseudonym Thom Demijohn. Garden City, N.Y.: Doubleday, 1968; London: W. H. Allen, 1969.

Camp Concentration. London: Hart-Davis, 1968; Garden City, N.Y.: Doubleday, 1969.

Under Compulsion (short stories). London: Hart-Davis, 1968; also published as *Fun with Your New Head.* Garden City, N.Y.: Doubleday, 1969.

The Prisoner (novelization; based on the television series created by Patrick McGoohan). New York: Ace Books, 1969; London: Dobson, 1979.

334. London: MacGibbon & Kee, 1972; New York: Avon, 1974.

Getting into Death: The Best Short Stories of Thomas M. Disch. London: Hart-Davis, 1973; also published with a new arrangement of stories as *Getting into Death and Other Stories.* New York: Knopf, 1976.

Clara Reeve, under pseudonym Leonie Hargrave. New York: Knopf, 1975; London: Hutchinson, 1975.

On Wings of Song. London: Gollancz, 1979; New York: St. Martin's, 1979.

Fundamental Disch, edited by Samuel R. Delany (short stories). New York: Bantam, 1980; London: Gollancz, 1981.

Neighboring Lives, with Charles Naylor. New York: Scribner, 1981; London: Hutchinson, 1981.

The Man Who Had No Idea (short stories). London, Gollancz, 1982; New York: Bantam, 1982.

Ringtime (short story). West Branch, Iowa: Toothpaste Press, 1983.

The Businessman: A Tale of Terror. New York: Harper, 1984; London: J. Cape, 1984.

Torturing Mr. Amberwell (novella). New Castle, Va.: Cheap Street, 1985.

Amnesia (computer-interactive novel). San Mateo, Calif: Electronic Arts, 1986.

The Brave Little Toaster (for children). Garden City, N.Y.: Doubleday, 1986.

Poetry:

Highway Sandwiches, with Marilyn Hacker and Charles Platt. Privately printed, 1970.

The Right Way to Figure Plumbing. Fredonia, N.Y.: Basilisk Press, 1972.

ABCDEFG HIJKLM NOPQRST UVWXYZ. London: Anvil Press Poetry in association with Wildwood House, 1981.

Burn This. London: Hutchinson, 1982.

Orders of the Retina: Poems. West Branch, Iowa: Toothpaste Press, 1982.

Here I Am, There You Are, Where Were We? London: Hutchinson, 1984.

The Tale of Dan De Lion (for children). Minneapolis: Evening Coffee Editions, 1986.

Libretti:

The Fall of the House of Usher, music by Gregory Sandow (opera), 1975.

Frankenstein, music by Gregory Sandow (opera), first produced at the Lake George Opera Fest, 1982.

Editor of:

The Ruins of Earth: An Anthology of Stories of the Immediate Future. New York: Putnam, 1971; London: Hutchinson, 1973.

Bad Moon Rising: An Anthology of Political Foreboding. New York: Harper, 1973; Hutchinson, 1974.

The New Improved Sun: An Anthology of Utopian Science Fiction. New York: Harper, 1975; Hutchinson, 1976.

New Constellations: An Anthology of Tomorrow's Mythologies, with Charles Naylor. New York: Harper, 1976; London: Hutchinson, 1976.

Strangeness: A Collection of Curious Tales, with Charles Naylor. New York: Scribner, 1977.

Michael Hamburger

1924-

Michael Hamburger

There was a time, in my teens and twenties, when nothing came more easily to me than writing about myself. All those long letters I used to write my friends about what I felt, thought, believed about this and that! Autobiography, though, is something different. One is supposed to write it in retrospect, as near the end of one's life as possible, out of an awareness of the totality of a life and in the knowledge of what mattered in it, what did not. Yet the older I have grown, the harder it has been for me to write about myself, let alone sum up that totality or be sure what in my life was mine, what was anyone's, what I made of my life, and what life made of me.

I came up against some of those difficulties when, before the age of fifty, I wrote a book of "intermittent memoirs" called *A Mug's Game*. The memoirs were intermittent because, even then, my memory was selective, "like a sieve"; and the meshes in that sieve have grown larger since. Even then, too, it became clear to me that recollection is inseparable from imagination—and so from invention. Mnemosyne, Memory, was the Mother of the Muses. Whether we like it or not, autobiography—as distinct from merely factual chronicles—is a kind of fiction. Since I had no wish to write fiction about myself, I made my book of memoirs as drily factual as I could make it, incorporating diary entries and assorted documents that had no emotive or literary appeal, because they gave no scope to imagination. This procedure may have been forced on me by a puritanism or purism that has inhibited me throughout my life. In the book of memoirs I traced it to my upbringing, and especially to the character of my father, a scientist—pediatrician and professor of medicine—in whom moral intransigence and extreme conscientiousness were combined with strong artistic leanings which, most of the time, he had to sacrifice to his many obligations. Strict truthfulness was one of the demands my father made on himself and on his children.

A Mug's Game dealt with my life only up to the age of thirty. In spite of that it could not tell the whole truth, and not only because one doesn't know the whole truth about oneself but because what I did know of the truth about myself involved other people whose private affairs I had no business to make public. Despite the reticence imposed by that restriction, I had to conceal the identity of several persons, and omit all reference to events or relationships that were part of my life. Yet the writing of that book precipitated a break with one of my oldest and closest friends, whose memory or imagination contradicted my version of our earliest meetings and of his circumstances at the time.

Ever since, I have wished to write a complement to that book of memoirs; not a chronological sequel, though, on the same documentary lines. Not only have I ceased to keep a diary of events and meetings which, without one, I can no longer place in any sequence, but later experience has set up new misgivings about the decency and usefulness of chronicling my own life.

I took the title for my book of memoirs from this remark by T.S. Eliot: "As things are, and as fundamentally they must always be, poetry is not a career but a mug's game. No honest poet can ever feel quite sure of the permanent value of what he has written: he may have wasted his time and messed up his life for nothing." By the time he wrote these words, Eliot had received ample confirmation from others that what he had written was of "permanent value"; but, because a poet can place no reliance at all on how other people judge his work at any one moment—even if those judgments amount to a consensus, and they rarely do—that remark struck me not as a personal confession of Eliot's, or gesture of humility on his part, but as a general and incontrovertible truth about being a poet.

If I tell the story of my life, though, without wishing to write fiction, I assume that either my life was representative enough for others to identify with my experiences, or that my life was so exceptional as to be of interest to others for that reason. The second assumption would rest on the belief that my work is of "permanent value." If it isn't—and I have no means of knowing whether it is or not—that would leave only the career I never wanted and succeeded very well in warding or breaking off before it could carry me away.

Well, my life has been representative in some ways, in that I had to undergo an education, serve as a soldier in a war, earn my living in various ways, worry about those I loved, work very hard to keep up the mug's game of my choice; and it was exceptional or freakish in at least one regard, that I was born in Germany into a German-speaking family, uprooted at the age of nine, but began nonetheless at the age of fifteen to turn into a British poet. That oddity must have been my main incentive to write a book of memoirs; to explain it to myself, in the first place, by retracing the stages; though clearly in the hope—not confirmed by the immediate reception or sales of the book—that the story might be of use or interest to others.

That work has been done, and need not be done again except for a few improvements, corrections, and excisions I should like to make if and when the book is reprinted. The complement I have in mind now is no more a reiteration than a sequel. It has to do not with the facts of my life and work—which can be found in reference books like *Who's Who*—but with themes pushed out of *A Mug's Game* by its linear and austerely factual structure. One reason why the facts and events of my life are receding from my awareness now is that I care less and less about what I have done or failed to do, more and more about the conditions in which those things were done or not done. Drastic changes in the world at large, and in my own country, have called in question even the ambition of "permanent value" that has always underlain the poetic mug's game, where it wasn't played only out of vanity. In the present state of affairs "permanent" has become too big a word. I prefer the word "durable"; but even durability, in products of any kind other than those made for the very rich to remind them that they are different, is no longer a value in the societies I know. Built-in obsolescence and instant consumption have replaced it. If that seems inapplicable to the arts, every sort of "pop" or "camp" art proves that it isn't. So do the personality cult and the cult of instant success, with their built-in obsolescence. These are exact counterparts and concomitants of the ethos of salesmanship that has replaced the value of durability.

As for any of the careers that were open to me, they have come to look like a luxury and a self-indulgence, when the most I can wish those I care about is survival in an environment worth surviving in, and employment of any kind. In the thirteen years or so that have passed since the writing of my memoirs, these have become the realities that confront my three children and await my four grandchildren, if they are allowed to grow up.

This much had to be said before I could set out on any new ego-trip or only re-exhibit some of the data brought back from the first. To dig up and set down those data once was an exploration. To string them together once more—as one is asked to do again and again for the obligatory biographical and bibliographical notes in periodicals and anthologies—is a tedious chore, if only because an unwritten law forbids writers to repeat themselves. Up to the age of thirty, the data I can exhibit here are the same as before, though I shall have to reduce them to their bare bones. If anything has changed, it is the perspective and the presentation.

I was born in Berlin just after the runaway inflation that was like an economic prelude to the political monstrosities that followed a decade later, and part of the destabilization brought about by Germany's defeat in the First World War, in which my father had served as a medical officer, winning the Iron Cross for some act of gallantry he never talked about. Both my father's and my mother's families were of Jewish descent, but had become culturally assimilated for at least three generations before mine. Of my grandparents, only my father's mother, who was born in Poland, went to a synagogue, which she called "the Temple"—but never once took us four children there. We grew up in complete ignorance of the Jewish religion and of Jewish traditions. One of my great-uncles, an industrial man-

Mother, Lili Martha Hamburg, before her marriage

Father, Richard Hamburger, before the First World War

ager and "gentleman" show jumper, had taken assimilation to the point of marrying a non-Jewish wife of the Junker class. I have an edition of the works of Klopstock—the "German Milton" and author of *The Messiah*—published in 1782 and stolen by my mother in girlhood from the library of a grandmother she disliked; and a Latin text, a Sallust, studied by a maternal great-grandfather, Ludwig or Louis Hamburg, Jr., at the Gymnasium of Mainz in 1847. On my father's side, his grandfather N. Hamburger received his royal licence as a teacher in the Prussian educational system in 1835 at Oppeln in Silesia. His son, my grandfather Leopold, was a writer, sometimes under the anagram Burghammer, who was in touch with Alphonse Daudet and Emile Zola in Paris, where he wrote literary criticism for German periodicals before moving to Poland, marrying there, then settling in Berlin. Like my father after him, that grandfather had to give up the occupation of his choice for a career. He died brokenhearted and bankrupt soon after my birth, and had ceased to speak or write in his last years. A family tree drawn up for my maternal grandfather suggests that his family came to Mainz from Spain in the seventeenth century. Other documents suggest that Hamburger and Hamburg, my father's and my mother's surnames, were only variants of one name—and a certain degree of inbreeding in my descent. My mother's mother came from a village in Baden-Württemberg that has since been incorporated into the city of Heidelberg.

My father was an agnostic. My mother became a Quaker after his early death. They had met shortly after the end of the First World War, at the Berlin hospital where my father worked as a doctor, my mother as a temporary nurse, though her family, unlike my father's, was rich enough for her to have no need to work. Some years before our emigration we had come to divide our time between our apartment in central Berlin and a house in the village of Kladow, on the river Havel, that my mother's father had had built for his extended family. This country place, rather than the seaside holidays we had taken in earlier years on the Baltic coast, established the preference for rural surroundings that made me a "nature poet" amongst other things. Music, which both my parents played and my father would have liked to make his mug's game, and animals were my first loves, though even before the age of nine I had fallen in love with at least one little girl. In early childhood, too, I became a voracious reader, mainly of natural history; so much so that my parents thought I was sure to turn into a naturalist of some sort. (That I should not turn into a musician became apparent when I gave up my violin studies as soon as school work gave me an excuse, while at my prep school in London. I continued to improvise by ear on the piano, harmonium, and other instruments, as my father did before me and my son after me.)

My extreme introversion in childhood, even before the trauma of the months before our emigration, is explained in *A Mug's Game*—in so far as it can be explained—as a reaction to the regimenting by a governess the four of us suffered from infancy, because my father was kept too busy by his duties as a hospital consultant, teacher, and family doctor, my mother by her ministrations to my father's domestic and secretarial needs, for more than minimal attention to ours. It was not till the harm was done, in his last London years, that my father took up psychology, in response to a lack he had come to feel in his work as a physician, but also, I think, out of a realization of what had gone wrong in his own home. His mentor was Alfred Adler, whom I remember seeing and having to kiss, not Freud—though we were also friendly with Freud's son Ernst, his daughter-in-law Lucy, and their three sons, who were patients of my father's. I call my introversion extreme—though I could come out of it when the coast was clear—because it could turn into trance-like states of withdrawal, in one of which I almost died by drowning when I lost my balance on our Kladow landing-stage, dropped into the water like a stone, and made no

attempt to swim, though I was a strong swimmer. I was rescued by a governess who, unlike her predecessor, was not strict but sadistic, and whose power over us had almost certainly driven me into that state.

Almost immediately after the National Socialist victory early in 1933 my father decided to leave for Edinburgh, where he had to qualify once more as a doctor, in a foreign language, so as to be allowed to practise in Britain. It was in the next few months, before we were removed from school and went to live at Kladow while my father made preparations for the family to join him in Edinburgh in November, that our lost Jewishness came home to me with a vengeance at school, as a threat and a curse, by the shock of being suddenly picked on, segregated, and having the separateness rubbed in, physically at times, by teachers and fellow pupils. When my best friend's big brother whipped me with a length of wire on the way home we had always shared, the physical pain hurt me less than the betrayal. Yet when my father gave up his consultantship and professorship at the hospital, the Charité, members of his nursing staff burst into tears and im-

Michael with his mother, Edinburgh, 1934

plored him to stay.

Despite the uprooting and the parting from relatives and friends, especially from my father's widowed mother, who felt too old, ailing, and set in her ways to begin a new life, but survived long enough to be murdered in an extermination camp—and the confiscation, at the English port, of my grandfather's two pet budgerigars, which I loved—I must have come out of those traumatic shocks with a new competitiveness and self-assertiveness. For the first time in a city—after escapes at Kladow from supervision and outbursts there of our repressed energies—we were left to our own devices—even on what I think was the very first day, when my younger brother and I had to make our way to a new school through streets we did not know, vainly asking for directions in a language we had not yet learned to speak. My brother was in tears by the time we found a schoolmistress from that school, George Watson's, who showed us to our classrooms. My father, under pressures of every kind and much more deeply shattered than his children had the capacity to be, scarcely left his room while preparing for the examinations—special ones set up for immigrant doctors—that would permit him to set up a new practice in London within a mere year and a half, while living on borrowed money. My mother, as ever, supported him by learning to cope with domestic chores that had previously been left to servants. She had never so much as cooked, though she soon did so excellently, let alone laid a coal fire or cleaned a grate. Within a term or so at school, I won a book prize for an English essay, established my standing by what looked like feats of daring in the swimming pool, but were nothing but my familiarity with water, and was even invited to join a gang of classmates who roamed the streets for ritualized fights with boys wearing the uniforms of other, rival, schools. This kind of aggressiveness and pugnaciousness was to be needed until almost the end of my school years in England, though only in rare emergencies later, when, outside the boxing-ring, I resorted to it only when attacked, taunted, or challenged. My face is still scarred by an injury received when two Westminster enemies ambushed me on my bicycle, seized the handlebars, and made me dive off head first on to a tarmac road. What astonishes me now, though, is how little time it took me to adapt to and feel more or less at ease in all the successive institutions—from George Watson's in Edinburgh, the Brighton and Hove Grammar School (briefly), The Hall, Hampstead (my prep school in London), Westminster School, Christ Church, Oxford, to the British Army—in which I spent most of my working life from the age of nine to the age of twenty-four.

The next blow was my father's death in 1940, af-ter hard years of struggle in London, where pediatricians rarely practised as family doctors, as in Germany, and no major hospital appointment was forthcoming, notice from the International Red Cross of his mother's transportation, and the damage done to his practice when he was ordered to leave London to await bombing casualties at Hitchin, Hertfordshire. (We had become British subjects before the outbreak of war.) By then, at the age of sixteen and at the third of the successive places to which Westminster School had been evacuated from London, so that day-boys like myself became boarders, I had begun to write and translate poems consistently enough to think of myself as a writer. The loss of my father, with whom I shared most of my interests and who read my early literary attempts, at once desolated me and propelled me to action once more, by putting a sudden end to my adolescence. I persuaded my mother, guardian, and headmaster to let me leave school early, won an Exhibition to Christ Church, Oxford—but for which any further education would have been more than my mother could afford—and managed to get to Christ Church when I was barely seventeen.

The relative freedom of my first stay at Oxford—a mere four terms—gave me time to write poems and do the translations of poems by Hölderlin, with their long and rambling introduction, that became my first book, finished by the time I was eighteen and published when I was nineteen, in 1943. The book appeared when I had just become an infantryman or foot-slogger. Through the English Club at Oxford I had come to know a good many eminent writers, who talked or read there, and some of them became my friends, as well as fellow undergraduate poets like Sidney Keyes—who was to die soon after as an officer in the same regiment I joined—and Philip Larkin. Other poet friends made at Oxford were John Heath-Stubbs and David Wright, both of whom also frequented the Soho pubs that became my "second university" when in London—most regularly while I was waiting for my call-up from the late summer of 1942 to the early summer of 1943. Dylan Thomas, whose host I had been at Oxford, narrowly missing being "sent down" in consequence, was the centre of attraction in those pubs. It was there, too, that I met my first publisher, Tambimuttu of *Poetry London*. A few early poems appeared in miscellanies of Oxford and Cambridge writing in those years, so that I started out as an insider, becoming an outsider later, when I was an "established" writer—more and more so over the decades.

From 1943 to 1947, my army years, I published very little, but managed to work on another little book of translations, from Baudelaire's French in 1944, while stationed in the Shetland Islands, a wild outpost and garrison where regular army routine, with its "square-bashing" and "fatigues" and "bullshit," was suddenly in abeyance, and boredom also drove me to getting myself the job of braving the high winds on the moors to walk from camp to camp with a portable gramophone, "entertaining" my fellow soldiers with classical music very few of them wanted to hear. There, too, I fell in love with a married woman, a pianist from London staying at Lerwick with her Shetland relatives while her husband was serving abroad. The poems I wrote about that and other things remained unpublished at the time. Very few of them got into my first collection.

It was not until 1945 that I succeeded in being sent overseas, and that only by having myself downgraded medically so that I could be transferred from my infantry regiment to another occupation—that of interpreter. As such I was posted to Naples—though I had only begun to teach myself Italian with a bilingual Dante small enough to carry about in my kitbag. After having all my personal possessions, other than the Dante, stolen while I was in my hammock on the troopship, my papers also proved to have been lost at the transit camp in Naples. Since I received no pay for the extraordinary fatigues I did there, I was reduced to selling part of my cigarette ration on the black market. The "fraternization" that let me in for helped to make my Italian slightly more up to date than Dante's. In the course of moving by stages through Italy to Austria I contracted hepatitis and almost died of it, by drinking myself into a coma with a bottle of Italian cognac given to me by the ambulance driver who was to have taken me from hospital to a convalescent home, but chucked me out on to the roadside when I had lost consciousness. My punishment for this breach of medical orders was not the disciplinary action that ought to have been taken by the Commandant of my new unit in Austria, but abstinence from alcohol for the rest of my life.

The climate, landscapes, and cities of Italy were a powerful experience of that period, since we had never travelled beyond the British Isles before the war. In Austria it was the alpine scenery of my first posting, Lienz in the Dolomites, but also the impact of the collapse of a civilized order—already felt while roaming the streets and alleys of Naples. These experiences went into my sequence of poems "From the Notebook of a European Tramp," though soon all leisure and privacy for writing became so scarce that I did not finish the sequence until after my demobilization and brief return to Oxford.

At Lienz I worked with German prisoners of war employed in my unit, a store or "dump" of captured enemy equipment, some of which they found a way of smuggling out to civilians for cash over the barbed wire fence. An investigation of that smuggling ring, with cross-examinations I had to interpret, was one of my more unpleasant, but revealing, duties. Another was the murder trial of a British soldier, involving his Austrian girl friend. A German groom taught me to ride horses there, some of which had been captured from the Cossack Army that fought on the German side. The method was simple, on the same principle as teaching someone to swim by throwing him into the water, and within minutes I had learned to keep my seat. To that initiation I owed my long solitary rides through the mountainside woods on my favourite Cossack mare (which I could have bought when the unit was dissolved, but had to leave behind).

No longer needed as an interpreter, when the prisoners were repatriated, I joined the Royal Army Education Corps, taught at an Army school for British soldiers in Carinthia as a sergeant, suddenly received an "emergency commission" and was posted to the GHQ in Graz as an educational staff officer. When both the city and the office work proved uncongenial to me, I returned to the Carinthian lakes to find myself appointed headmaster of a coeducational boarding school for the children of military and civilian administrators in the British occupation zone of Austria. That proved to be the most exacting responsibility I have taken on in my life, and one that was too much for me at the age of twenty two. When my seven-day-a-week, all-day work was also subverted by the opposition of members of the staff to my unconventional notions of how a school should be run—by persuasion, not coercion or punishment—I developed a fever that was the alternative to a nervous breakdown, and was given a short leave in England. When I returned it was as "second master" to an older, more experienced, and less libertarian head, a schoolteacher in civilian life, who also had the advantage of higher military rank in his dealings with our remote controllers at HQ. The school, an unprecedented experiment and showpiece for the Army, was inspected by Field-Marshal Montgomery amongst others.

It was during my last months there that I was given leave, but no official passes, for a very brief trip to Berlin, to visit my surviving relatives. It was a strenuous and exciting journey across the different occupation zones, helped by a dress uniform, complete with campaign ribbons and insignia, lent to me by the new headmaster, Captain Murphy, in place of my battledress and lieutenant's pips. Despite or because of that imposture, there were no hitches. I found my relatives—two great-uncles and their families—in the ruins of West Berlin, was able to deliver the gifts of food I was carrying, and even managed to make my way back to Carinthia before my leave had expired.

I was demobilized in the summer of 1947. Concessions to returning ex-servicemen enabled me to pack my remaining degree course at Oxford into one year. I duly graduated in Modern Languages, German and French, but was too impatient to get out at last into the "real," uninstitutionalized world to stay on for a doctorate and likely appointment at Oxford. In the vacations, and for some time after that, I lived at my mother's house in London, where for the next four years I earned a living of sorts as a free-lance writer and odd-job man, contributing poems and book reviews to periodicals like the *New Statesman* and the *Times Literary Supplement,* writing occasional broadcasts for the Third Programme of the BBC, but also tutoring for an agency, teaching French at Pentonville Prison, or conducting parties of foreign visitors on tours of London for the British Council. My earnings from all these activities became just enough to pay for a one-room apartment, at a time when the rent was one pound a week, with something left over for very rough travels in Italy and France out of which I concocted the one novel I ever wrote, but had the sense to withdraw before my agent had placed it. At the same period I wrote a stage play that was also spared publication and performance. I made short stories out of parts of the novel, and had to reprint them twenty years later in my book of memoirs, because the fictions had overlaid the realities on which they were based. What I remembered were the fictions, not the facts; and my documentary rigour could not undo that process.

After marrying in 1951, and with a first child on the way, I had to look for a more secure income, and was offered an assistant lectureship at University College, London. We were able to move again, from a two-room flat in Hampstead to three or four rooms on

Claire, Mary, and Richard Hamburger, 1966

two floors near Holland Park. After three years there and the birth of a second child, I moved to a lectureship at Reading and we acquired our first house in the then still rural outskirts—the former servants' quarters of a large Victorian mansion that had been divided into three parts, still leaving more land for us than I had ever dreamed of owning. There I began to garden in earnest, grew fruit and vegetables, and became a specialist in apples, thanks to a fine old orchard that belonged to our plot.

There, too, our three children spent their formative years—much happier and freer ones, we did our best to insure, than those of their parents, though at the end my son contracted an illness that crippled him for a year and changed his character. After nine years at Westwood Lodge, our home, and at the university, my wife, the actress, musician, and poet Anne Beresford, became so unhappy there that I decided to give up my Readership, move back to London and put an end to the full-time teaching that should have been my career, but had begun to clash more and more with my writing projects and commitments. Bought as a "country house" by a speculator, our home was demolished and the garden bulldozed, all the work I had put into that in nine years utterly erased. That was in 1964, when I

Westwood Lodge, Tilehurst

was forty.

A Bollingen Foundation fellowship helped me to work on my book *The Truth of Poetry,* prepared over a period of ten years out of reading that went far beyond my specialization in the German literature I had taught. Between 1965 and 1977 I also spent a great deal of time in America, as a visiting professor at various universities and colleges, never for longer than one semester at a time, so that I could return to my writing in between, or on tours that took me from New Hampshire to southern California, from South Carolina to Montana. America became the setting or theme of quite a few of my poems, including parts of the long sequence *Travelling* written between 1968 and 1976.

The strain of family life in unfamiliar surroundings at Mount Holyoke College and my frequent absences on tour during my semester there, while Anne had to cope with our unsettled and disturbed children, led to the break-up of our marriage after our return to London in 1967. We were separated or divorced for seven years—years of acute loneliness for me, bungled new relationships, and one intense new passion "begotten by Despair / Upon Impossibility." At the worst times I was on the verge of collapse through undernourishment, not because I couldn't afford to buy food but because I couldn't be bothered to buy or cook it. In fact our bonds proved stronger than our differences, and Anne never moved far from our South London house, even when the children had gone to live with her. After wretched muddles and complications, involving others, we entered into a second marriage on my fiftieth birthday.

I now wish that I had kept a diary of my comings and goings, adventures, encounters, impressions, and discoveries in those critical and troubled years. Since I didn't, and have lost all sense of chronological sequence, I cannot recapitulate them other than as fiction without laborious researches and reconstructions from scattered documents and tatters of recollection. Only a few of them come back to me from poems of those years.

In 1976—with the children grown up and Anne now prepared for a life away from London—we moved to Suffolk in East Anglia, one of the most "backward," least industrialized parts of England, into a house that began more than four centuries ago as a cottage and is so far from being practical after its last enlargement and conversion in 1920 that "only a madman would have bought it," as a former village rector was tactful enough to tell us. As I write this, my fingers are numb with February east winds coming in from the North Sea, blowing right through the flimsy walls of the newer parts of the house and the warped window-frames. Snow has dislodged a pane glass from the top

Anne Beresford, about 1952

of our unheated lean-to greenhouse, threatening the plants I grew from seed collected in Mexico, Colorado, California, and the State of Washington, on trips in 1981 and 1984. As I type this, water has poured through a ceiling on to a bookcase, drenching the books. Here Anne directs an amateur drama group and puts on plays for the villagers, amongst other occupations; I divide my time between my writing-table and cultivating our three-and-a-half acres, though half of them remains wild marshland reserved for the local flora and fauna. Pheasants, partridges, moorhens, and mallard ducks breed there. Herons, snipe, kestrels, a marsh harrier, and a barn owl are among the visitors. On the other half I have planted flowers, shrubs, many kinds of trees, including the New England hemlock, vegetables, soft fruit, and a second orchard of mainly obsolescent varieties of apples.

Two of our children with their families have chosen to settle near us. Until her recent death at the age of ninety, Anne's mother lived with us, writing her first book, published when she was eighty-eight, and devotedly nursed after that by her daughter Jane, who still shares the house with us. My mother, too, lived to see the first of her great-grandchildren, though she could visit us only once—and that against doctor's orders—before her death in London at the age of nearly ninety-three. For a time, four generations could be brought together under the four roofs, built over four centuries, of our conglomerate house, most of whose worst leaks, most of the time, we have been able to stop over the years.

So much for the bare bones of a life. These bare bones were fleshed by the thousand things around them, bound up with persons and places, scenes and situations, moments and continuities of which my factual account has stripped them. It is because the bare bones of biography are dead and meaningless that one takes up the mug's game of writing poems. Compared to narrative fictions, lyrical poems may be a sort of shorthand, but they can catch the live moments. Put together, they can also trace the continuities both of an individual life and of human life generally. So if my real and essential life is registered anywhere, it is in my poems. I write "if," because of what Eliot wrote about the mug's game; and because, when I put together my collected poems for my sixtieth birthday, I had to reject most of those in my first and second collections. Those were poems that did not catch the live moments; and the reason is that I was literarily precocious long before I was anything like emotionally mature. Since I could not know that at the time, I published too soon, though a single marginal comment in the script of early poems of mine that Eliot himself was patient enough to read became a pointer to my worst failings at the time—bombast and generalization. "What kind of birds?", Eliot wrote against one of the symbolic or apocalyptic creatures that filled my lines. In my introversion I had not yet learned to trust my senses, least of all my eyes.

As for "messing up" one's life for the sake of the poems that may or may not have grown good enough, I did that too, inevitably, though not perhaps in the spectacular way that would make me posthumously attractive to the biography-reading public. Even my close escapes from death—and I had as many lives as a cat, the animal so dear and near to me that it would be hard for me to live without one—were private and unsensational, as when I swam back to my wife and small daughter on a Bay of Biscay beach in a gale, against a back-tow so strong that I progressed by inches, and thought I wasn't progressing at all; or the series of motor accidents that began when the army driver of a jeep I was in ran head-on into a rock escarpment in Austria at 50 mph or more. No, the messing-up was that of the monomania one needs to keep up the writing of poems for a lifetime—at the expense of everyone and every-

Michael Hamburger, about 1974

thing else, one's "human" self and its needs included; while for others that occupation is a harmless hobby at best, a "career" only in retrospect, at best, when all the prices have been paid and the messed-up life is over. Not that I regret the price I paid, or the things I might have done instead. That was my choice from the start, and I have been able to stick to it much of the time for forty-five years. What hurts is the price that those I love have had to pay.

The first book I published was a book of translations—so inadequate, too, that I had to spend another thirty years and more on the same poet, Hölderlin, trying to improve my translations and adding to them. As I found out much later, even that inadequate juvenile attempt was of some use to others, by providing a first key to a difficult and incomparable poet. My early need to translate must have sprung from my own translation from one country, one language, to another. Ever since, translation has been so much part of my work that for long stretches it displaced my own writing, and I have translated far more poems than I have written poems of my own. In the minds of many readers, too, my translations have displaced my poems. The bearing of this anomaly on the mug's game is that, with rare exceptions, translations can have only a very limited life span, so that for them not even the possibility of "permanent value" can be entertained. Part of their value, then, must lie in their being useful; and being useful, of service, is also the only good reason I know for having a career. Translating and the critical writing which, for me, was akin to translating in being a form of mediation, made up for the career the writing of poetry could not be.

Unlike Eliot's work as a publisher or the jobs most poets have to do to subsidize their work, these occupations of mine were hardly more remunerative than the mug's game itself. So they, too, had to be subsidized—by teaching, lecture and reading tours, and the like. Translating was also the next best thing to writing poems of my own, since it involved a related grappling with the same medium, language, a related search for the right word, right rhythm, right image in the right place. Because a translation called for all my concentration, once I was immersed in it, I made a principle of not accepting commissions to translate long works, like novels, except in the few instances where the commissions coincided with plans and preferences of my own—as with Beethoven's letters or the Goethe verse plays that cost me a full year's daily work as recently as 1982. The writing of even the shortest poem takes much more time than most people think; not so much because that poem may go through many drafts before its is finished—most of my later poems do not—but because the poem cannot get through at all in the first place if the writer's mind is preoccupied with matters that compete with it, as it has to be when translating. Idleness of a sort, though not physical idleness, is a prerequisite for the writing of poems. Outdoor labour, on the other hand, was not only congenial to me in its own right—because I am an introverted outdoor man—but the sustenance of many of my poems. Walking, sculling, swimming, or horse-riding took the place of physical labour when I had no plot to cultivate, but was exempt from the team games and other sports—football, cricket, tennis, boxing, and rowing—compulsory in my school years.

Strangely enough it is an indoor game I had played only once or twice in my adolescence, in blacked-out London during the war, at the house of a friend, that gave me the imagery for one of the early poems I could and did salvage from my first book of 1950, because there was something in it beyond its literariness, even a prediction that came true:

A Poet's Progress

Like snooker balls thrown on the table's faded green,
Rare ivory and weighted with his best ambitions,
At first his words are launched: not certain what they mean,
He loves to see them roll, rebound, assume positions
Which—since not he—some power beyond him has assigned.
But now the game begins: dead players, living critics
Are watching him—and suddenly one eye goes blind,
The hand that holds the cue shakes like a paralytic's,
Till every thudding, every clinking sound portends
New failure, new defeat. Amazed, he finds that still
It is not he who guides his missiles to their ends
But an unkind geometry that mocks his will.

If he persists, for years he'll practise patiently,
Lock all the doors, learn all the tricks, keep noises out,
Though he may pick a ghost or two for company
Or pierce the room's inhuman silence with a shout.
More often silence wins; then soon the green felt seems
An evil playground, lawless, lost to time, forsaken,
And he a fool caught in the water weeds of dreams
Whom only death or frantic effort can awaken.

At last, a master player, he can face applause,
Looks for a fit opponent, former friends, emerges;
But no one knows him now. He questions his own cause,
And has forgotten why he yielded to those urges,
Took up a wooden cue to strike a coloured ball.
Wise now, he goes on playing; both his house and heart
Unguarded solitudes, hospitable to all
Who can endure the cold intensity of art.

I wrote that poem in 1949, when I was twenty-four or twenty-five, an age by which some poets have done their best work. For me, with at least two cultures to bridge before I began to write, then cluttered with more book learning than I could digest—not to mention skills like telegraphy, radio, semaphore, morse, and cable-laying I had to acquire when I became an infantry signalman, on top of rifle, hand grenade, machine-gun, assault course, bayonet, and other training—the hardest thing was to work my way through to directness, plainness, and immediacy. Those came later, if they came at all. Yet this poem's house and heart that are unguarded solitudes remain valid for me now that I have indeed withdrawn from the London-based literary life so important to me in youth and middle age, shedding even the "best ambitions" of that poem. These have been driven out by concern about all the other games being played outside, on a playground far more evil and lawless than that snooker-table. To do my own thing to the best of my ability is still a self-evident requirement; but I now know that my mug's game could turn out to have been a waste of time not because I wasn't good enough at it, but because there will be no one left to invite into my "hospitable" solitude, even if it hasn't vanished without a trace like our house and garden at Tilehurst.

Those concerns are most explicit in poems that are not my best—those I have called "owls' pellets, gobbets of matter so coarse that they couldn't be assimilated poetically, only regurgitated"—about the madness of our automatized and automated technologies, industrial, commercial, and military. Less directly they also inform my critical writings, because literature, however autonomous that may try to be, cannot be sealed off from the things going on around it. My special interest in German literature—though I have also translated from the French, Italian, and some other languages—springs not only from what remains of my German roots but from what can be learned from the violent extremes that have clashed or interlocked in German life and writing. My latest critical book, to be published in 1986, comes closer than earlier ones to being a sort of history, of the postwar period. Out of the same concerns I have translated work by the most diverse German-language writers of this century, West German, Austrian, Swiss, and East German. It is the last of these, and the poets above all, whose individual voices and needs have been brought up against the tightest corporative restrictions—and prevailed against them in many cases.

A British anthologist placed my poems in a section allotted to "Influences from Abroad," meaning not that the poets in that section were influences from abroad but that they were open to such influences. In a note on my work he wrote: "Curiously enough, his own poetry remains more 'English' in flavour than that of some of his collaborators, such as Christopher Middleton."—meaning those born in Britain, but represented in the same section. My early poems were influenced more by French poets—Baudelaire and the Symbolists—than by German ones, except for Hölderlin, a contemporary and coeval of Wordsworth, and perhaps Rilke and Trakl. Later it was American poetry, above all, that shook me out of the rhymed stanzaic forms of my early verse. If my poems did remain "English in flavour," it must have been because I adapted so thoroughly to British assumptions and ways—possibly with the excessive fervour for which converts are notorious. Someone who had experienced only the little I experienced of Nazism could respond to British civility with an appreciation more keen than that of people who had taken it for granted from birth.

Before the erosion of that civility, rapid and conspicuous in the past ten years, I had no reason not to take my assimilation for granted; least of all during my army years, when my German name and birth were never so much as alluded to by a single fellow soldier, any more than differences of race or class, though I spoke the English of the public schools and of Oxford in barrack-rooms shared with working-class men. My oddities and awkwardnesses at first were not only tolerated, but accommodated with a delicacy and helpfulness I shall never forget. In the first weeks of intensive infantry training I was marched into the Company Commander's office for what I thought must be a reprimand or punishment for inefficiency. It turned out that he had received a letter from the Poetry Society in London asking me to give a reading and talk to celebrate my newly published Hölderlin translations. Never having done such a thing before, and too conscious of the incompatibility of those two worlds, I asked to be excused, but he ordered me to "represent the regiment" at that celebration of a German poet in the midst of a war against Germany. This was the British civility, British magnanimity, which often went with a seeming innocence or ingenuousness, I thought worth fighting for, and dying for, if it came to that. The reason why it did not come to that may well be that the same authorities kept me out of the fighting as a special case. I never found out why I was not drafted to Burma with other soldiers in my regiment and intake, most of whom did die there, and posted instead to a battalion on home duty in Lancashire.

The same British civility and magnanimity may have made the country uncompetitive in the postwar world, after the loss of empire and the wealth that empire had brought. Because, to me, the civility and magnanimity are incomparably more precious than success in the international power and money arenas—and even that success has not come with the monetarist brutalities that are destroying the old decencies of the nation—it is in the last years that I have been beset by the most acute doubts and difficulties as a writer, often to the point of feeling that it is time for me to give up. Yet, as I wrote somewhere, "the poem knows better than the poet . . ." Somehow or other, the poems still get through my worst despondencies, demanding to be written. Even translations, a few, still demand to be done—as from Paul Celan, whose poems were wrested from a deeper trauma than any I have suffered—though in the end it pulled him down into the death by drowning from which I was saved in childhood. So does the prose I write to bear witness to those things or get closer to an understanding of the conflicts and tensions out of which all imaginative work is produced.

Thanks to the vanishing civilities and magnanimities, as well as my father's prescience more than half a century ago, only one member of my family fell victim to the combination of ideological atavism and technical efficiency that was National Socialism. Since my maternal grandparents emigrated when we did and died in England, and two great-uncles and their families survived in Germany, it was easier for me than for many others to recover from childhood traumas and build those bridges without which I could not have functioned as the poet, translator, and critic I became. For a few years, at school before the outbreak of war, all things German were almost lost to me, and I was reluctant to speak the language. In a satirical sketch we performed at Westminster I took the part of Hitler, published a political sonnet—about the annexation of Czechoslovakia—in a school magazine and, at the age of fifteen, sent my first submission to a national magazine in the form of an allegorical story with an anti-Nazi moral. Yet I could not hate the Germans as a whole without falling into the very racism to which some, not all, of them had succumbed; and a return to Judaism, when I had had no grounding in it at any time and only racial descent was left of that heritage, would have come up against the same interdict, besides demanding an immense effort of deliberate reclamation for which I had no opportunity and no time, either at a school attached to Westminster Abbey or a college attached to the Cathedral of Oxford. Though theology and nature study—not biology—were the two poles of my earliest concerns, and all the others flickered in between, I chose to remain outside all the religious communities—a pagan or a heathen, outwardly and officially at least.

That choice, too, goes back to my school years, I think, beginning with the Creed that is part of the Church of England liturgy. Faith, it seemed to me, is something other than belief. My beliefs could be shaken by experience or knowledge, and they changed over the years. My faith did not change, because it lay beyond experience and beyond reason. That Creed worried me, for it seemed to have less to do with wor-

ship than with religion in its most literal sense—a binding together, and a binding together *again*, implying that there had been a separation; and that separation did indeed take place as soon as people were not at church. In that sense, religion was a closing of ranks. I could not reconcile that with the lone voices of prophets or the Passion of Christ.

In later years another stumbling block was the anthropocentric fixation of the same religious tradition, Jewish as much as Christian. Had Noah saved the animals for their own sake, or only because we need them, or some of them? Unlike Greek pantheism, some of the Far Eastern religions, and most "primitive" ones, our theological tradition seemed to posit a world made only for human use. St. Francis of Assisi was the one glorious exception known to me—and I always wondered how he had escaped excommunication as a heretic. When Christianity was secularized, in the so-called Enlightenment of the eighteenth century, so was this emphasis on the utilization and exploitation of the non-human world. Not content with the botching of our own earth, the twentieth century has carried the same processes into outer space.

Not that I longed for any regression to a stud farm or gut tribalism, when the Third Reich had taught me that every merely biological or racial classification of human beings is barbarous and pernicious. City and countryside, civilization and culture, were prototypes, also going back to antiquity, to which my poems returned again and again, before I had found a third paradigm, wilderness, and all three of them had to meet and clash. I have tried not to falsify the hardships and cruelties of any of these orders, whatever my personal preferences. In interhuman affairs, both experience and faith convince me, gentleness is stronger than assertiveness, mercy and magnanimity are stronger than retribution. Yet when the long-suffering, exploited, and oppressed are exasperated into violence, I am on their side.

What I have almost left out of my account are the loves and friendships that meant quite as much to me throughout my life as anything I could write about here. A few of them are recorded in my book of memoirs, and other tributes or recollections will follow in another book. In some cases friendships impinged on my translating and critical work, too, though I have tried to keep them out of essays and book reviews, and made a principle early on of not writing about the work of British fellow poets in their lifetime, just as I kept out of groups, movements, and cliques of every sort, for related reasons. If the same prohibition didn't apply to foreign writers, including a few American ones who were friends, it was because I was in less danger of getting entangled in their literary politics, and friendships did not conflict with the job of mediation that was part of my work. Though I have written few "love poems," all poetry is love poetry, no matter what it is about; even the ugly or harsh verse I called "observation, ironies, unpleasantries," about things opposed to my loves and loyalties, which are implicit in my rejection of those things. (Robert Graves called the two kinds "poems of the right hand" and "poems of the left hand," aware that the same force moves both hands.)

Nor can I attach enough importance to the occasional gratifications and persistent setbacks of my professional life to write about them. Parts of my work have been kept in print for thirty or even forty years, and that is as much as a writer can hope for, short of "permanent value." The rest has been an unremitting struggle against pressures and frustrations, with help at times in the shape of awards or prizes. Holidays became a habit we had to break when I dropped out of full-time teaching, but invitations to read, lecture, take part in poetry festivals or the regular sessions of the three German academies of which I am a member have provided me with as much travelling as I can cope with, now that I have come to hate tourism, hotels, and airports. The walks I owe to some of these events, and meetings with friends I could never have expected to see again otherwise—even at airports in some instances, or in hotels—were the rewards of those travels in many parts of Europe and America.

It is to America mainly that I owe my discovery of wilderness, as distinct from the cultivated countryside in most of Europe. Very early one morning I wandered from Antioch College into a small valley where every step I took was a revelation; and that was only one of more such "epiphanies" than I can list or place. The wild animals, birds, and wildflowers of America are as much a part of me now as those I grew up with or those around my house. That goes back to my first stay in Massachusetts. It was there, much later, that my friend Peter Viereck told us that, as far as he was concerned, there are "three kinds of birds—big birds, little birds, and seagulls." Near Austin, Texas, where I stayed with my friend Christopher Middleton, we counted more than fifty kinds of birds at his feeder—mainly little ones, down to the hummingbirds—and I got so close to an armadillo that I could have grabbed it. On a South Carolina island racoons took food from my hand. The chickadees that did the same for Robert Francis outside his hermit's cabin at Amherst went into a poem I wrote for him and into the title of an interim collection of poems; but images from Brooklyn—my very first American scene—Manhattan and Boston had to counterpoint those near-idylls, as did the first supermarket I had seen in my life, before shopping in supermarkets

had become as inescapable and unremarkable a thing in England as it was in America by the mid-sixties.

That kind of naivety—a sense of wonder that can also turn into a sense of outrage—seems to be a characteristic of poets, and a condition for their persistence in the mug's game. This naivety can go with a good deal of sophistication and worldly wisdom, though not, I think, with a cynical accommodation to things as they are. If the wonderment and the outrage dry up, so does—or should—the poet. To many, therefore, poets are freaks who would become formidable monsters if they were ever taken seriously; and they could be taken seriously because such a core of naivety, even of childishness, lies hidden in most people, however mature they think themselves and are taken to be—very much as an old cat, grown staid and dignified, will revert to kittenish play from time to time. That would be one reason why the lonely mug's game of poetry, played for no calculable audience in a world obsessed with other matters, is not the obsolete pursuit which, sociologically, it was judged to be long ago.

As a poet, though, it is not my business to ask why or how I go on, how or why my work appeals or does not appeal to those who read such work—a tiny minority at the best of times—whether or not it will prove to have been worth the price paid for doing it. My business is to remain true to the wonderment and outrage as long as they recur, always unexpectedly, always in a way I can neither plan nor choose; and to keep quiet when there is nothing that wants to use me to make itself heard.

Hamburger in his Suffolk garden, 1982

© *John Beilby*

SELECTED BIBLIOGRAPHY

Poetry:

Flowering Cactus: Poems, 1942-49. Aldington, England: Hand & Flower Press, 1950.

Poems, 1950-51. Kent, England: Hand & Flower Press, 1952.

The Dual Site. London: Routledge & Kegan Paul, 1958; New York: Dodd, Mead, 1958.

Weather and Season. London: Longmans, Green, 1963; New York: Atheneum, 1963.

In Flashlight. Leeds, England: Northern House, 1965.

In Massachusetts. Menomonie, Wis.: Ox Head Press, 1967.

Feeding the Chickadees. London: Turret Books, 1968.

Penguin Modern Poets 14, with Alan Brownjohn and Charles Tomlinson. Harmondsworth, England, and Baltimore: Penguin, 1969.

Travelling. London: Fulcrum Press, 1969.

Travelling I-V. London: Agenda Editions, 1972.

Ownerless Earth. Cheadle, England: Carcanet Press, 1973; New York: Dutton, 1973.

Travelling VI. London: I.M. Imprimit, 1975.

Travelling VII. Erpeldange, Luxembourg: 1976.

Moralities. Newcastle-upon-Tyne, England: Morden Tower, 1977.

Real Estate. Manchester, England: Carcanet Press, 1977.

In Suffolk. Hereford, England: Five Seasons Press, 1981.

Variations. Manchester, England: Carcanet Press, 1981; Redding Ridge, Conn.: Black Swan Books, 1981.

Collected Poems 1941-1983. Manchester, England, and New York: Carcanet Press, 1984. Corrected edition, 1985.

Nonfiction:

Reason and Energy: Studies in German Literature. London: Routledge & Kegan Paul, 1957; New York: Grove, 1957. New, enlarged edition. London: Weidenfeld & Nicolson, 1970; also published as *Contraries.* New York: Dutton, 1970.

From Prophecy to Exorcism: The Premises of Modern German Literature. London: Longmans, Green, 1965.

The Truth of Poetry: Tensions in Modern Poetry from Baudelaire to the 1960s. London: Weidenfeld & Nicolson, 1969; New York: Harcourt, 1970. New edition. Manchester, England: Carcanet Press, 1982; London and New York: Methuen, 1982.

Hofmannsthal: Three Essays. Princeton, N.J.: Princeton University Press, 1972.

A Mug's Game: Intermittent Memoirs, 1924-1954. Manchester, England: Carcanet Press, 1973.

Art as Second Nature: Occasional Pieces, 1950-74. Manchester, England: Carcanet Press, 1975.

A Proliferation of Prophets: Essays on German Writers from Nietzsche to Brecht. Manchester, England: Carcanet Press, 1983; New York: St. Martin's, 1984.

Translator of:

Poems of Hölderlin. London: Nicholson & Watson, 1943.

Twenty Prose Poems of Baudelaire. London: Editions Poetry, 1946. New edition. London: J. Cape, 1968.

Letters, Journals, and Conversations, by Ludwig van Beethoven. London: Thames & Hudson, 1951; New York: Pantheon, 1951. New edition. London: J. Cape, 1966; Westport, Conn.: Greenwood Press, 1978.

Decline, by George Trakl. St. Ives, England: Latin Press, 1952.

Hölderlin: Poems. London: Harvill Press, 1952; New York: Pantheon, 1952.

Hofmannsthal: Selected Plays and Libretti: New York: Pantheon, 1963; London: Routledge & Kegan Paul, 1963.

Selected Poems, by Günter Grass, translated with Christopher Middleton. London: Secker & Warburg, 1966; New York: Harcourt, 1966.

Poems and Fragments, by Friedrich Hölderlin. London: Routledge & Kegan Paul, 1966; Ann Arbor: University of Michigan Press, 1967. New, enlarged edition. Cambridge: Cambridge University Press, 1980, 1986.

Journeys: The Rolling Sea at Setúbal and The Year Lacertis, by Günter Eich. London: J. Cape, 1968.

Poems for People Who Don't Read Poems, by Hans Magnus Enzensberger, translated with Jerome Rothenberg. London: Secker & Warburg, 1968; New York: Atheneum, 1968.

Leonce and Lena; Lenz; Woyzeck, by George Büchner. Chicago: University of Chicago Press, 1972.

Selected Poems, by Peter Huchel. Manchester, England: Carcanet Press, 1974.

In the Egg and Other Poems, by Günter Grass, translated with Christopher Middleton. London: Secker & Warburg, 1977; New York: Harcourt, 1977.

Texts, by Helmut Heissenbüttel. London and Boston: M. Boyars, 1977.

Poems, by Franco Fortini. Todmorden, England: Arc Publications, 1978.

Paul Celan: Poems. Manchester, England: Carcanet Press; New York: Persea Books, 1980.

An Unofficial Rilke. London: Anvil Press, 1981; also published as *Rilke: Poems 1912-1926.* Redding Ridge, Conn.: Black Swan Books, 1981.

The Garden of Theophrastus and Other Poems, by Peter Huchel. Manchester: Carcanet Press, 1983.

Goethe: Poems and Epigrams. London: Anvil Press, 1983; also published as *Goethe: Roman Elegies and Other Poems.* Redding Ridge, Conn.: Black Swan Books, 1983.

Selected Poems, by Marin Sorescu. Newcastle-upon-Tyne, England: Bloodaxe Books, 1983.

Editor of:

Poems and Verse Plays, by Hugo von Hofmannsthal. London: Routledge & Kegan Paul, 1961; New York: Pantheon, 1961.

Modern German Poetry, 1910-1960, with Christopher Middleton. London: MacGibbon & Kee, 1963; New York: Grove, 1963.

East German Poetry. Manchester: England: Carcanet Press, 1972; New York: Dutton, 1972.

German Poetry: 1910-1975. Manchester: Carcanet Press, 1977; New York: Urizen Books, 1976. Corrected edition. New York: Persea Books, 1977.

Sound Recordings:

Poetry of Michael Hamburger. New York: J. Norton, 1966.

James Kirkup

1918-

From my earliest infancy, the sea was always there. It lay a few steps from our street in South Shields, in the North East of England. That was where I was born, though I had been conceived in Edinburgh, Scotland, during my parents' honeymoon towards the end of the First World War.

Through all my days and nights, at home and at school, the sea was never far from my thoughts. I was an only child, and much given to daydreaming. As soon as I wakened, I could tell from the distant sounds of the sea what kind of day it was going to be. The music of those northern waves breaking upon our long, smooth sands or against the cliffs or the mile-long pier would be soft and lulling on a summer morning, inviting pleasant visions of bathing and picnicking, or hunting for shells, pretty pebbles, or tiny crabs in the calm sea-pools, or fishing from the seaweed-carpeted rocks in the many sheltered coves along the coast.

Father, James Harold Kirkup, as a young man

James Kirkup on his favorite rug, age six months

The spring storms and autumn gales produced wonderful orchestras of sound, all resonant tympani and screaming, inland-flying gulls and terns. That was the sort of weather for a walk to the end of the long, curving pier, where the waves crashed in suspended caves of glittering spray over the massive stone blocks of its firm defences. Or after dark, walking along the empty promenade, my parents and I would listen to the soughing of the trees in the locked North Marine and South Marine Parks, while the red or white eyes of lighthouses blinked and flashed as if tormented by the wind, and their sweeping arms of light cut the dark clouds above the North Sea like scimitars.

But it was the sea in winter I loved most of all.

Mother, Mary Kirkup, as a young woman

Especially at night, after my father had read the newspaper to me—I preferred that to fairytales—and my mother had tucked me into bed with a tender goodnight kiss, I would lie awake in the darkness, listening intently to all the sounds of our maritime winter. The foghorns would be hooting lugubriously at regular intervals, their hoarse voices lingering and echoing among our seaside streets and up the banks of the River Tyne. There would be the less predictable thundering of gigantic waves pounding on shuddering beaches and in resounding cliff caverns. Ships in distress would send up signals—a hollow boom—and there would be the sound of men's booted feet hurrying along the street as the volunteers of the lifeboat crew turned out in flapping, glittering black oilskin capes and sou'westers. And through it all, the fainting or swelling notes of the Town Hall clock chiming eight o'clock, nine o'clock, its noble bell sounds carried on the wind like the ripples of thrown stones in a vast sea of cloud and mist.

Or I would wake early, aroused by the unnaturally clear radiance of a sudden overnight snowfall, when the whole town lay in a hushed sleep and the winter waves sprang their detonations undisturbed, a massive drumbeat, clear and strong, with every seventh beat exceptionally powerful. That natural, subtle rhythm entered my blood, flesh, and bones, and made

my poetry move and pause and swoop. . . . Then I would run to the curtained window in my pyjamas, my bare feet rejoicing in the cold feel of the bedroom canvas, our linoleum floors, and for hours I would gaze entranced at the steadily falling snowflakes as they slanted their lace curtains this way and that across the grimy brick facades of the row of houses opposite. I would fall under a spell, so that it was not the snow that seemed to be falling, but rather the whole house, and me with it, that seemed to be rising, rising, soaring into the low-hanging skies of grey and white.

Mornings came with the rat-tat-tat of the knocker-up, the man who was paid a small sum to come and rattle the door-knockers of those houses where the men had the good fortune to be employed, and had to get up before dawn to travel to distant coal mines, shipyards or building sites. When the workman lived in an upstairs flat, the knocker-up would rap on the upstairs window with a long bamboo pole. Warm in bed, I would wake and shiver at the sound of those scattered knockings, growing nearer and nearer along the dark street, as unpredictable as fate: one could almost tell which houses had men who had been laid off, and which men had got taken on for new jobs. Sometimes the knock would come to our own front door, and I would hear my mother and father getting up in the next room, lighting the coal fire in the kitchen, putting on the kettle for tea, preparing sandwiches and a slice of cake or pie for my father's "bait" or snack. I would lie and gaze at the strip of yellowish gaslight falling through the half-open kitchen door upon the wallpaper of the passage. My own door had to stay open all night: I felt that if I were shut in for sleep, I should never wake up again, or that my parents would creep out of the house and leave me there for ever alone. Always I would get up as soon as the coal fire had "taken hold," and go and drink a cup of tea in the kitchen with my father before he left for work. He was usually gone by six o'clock, and instead of going back to bed I would sit up reading by the fire. It was in those early morning hours that I taught myself to read and study, and first grew to love books and writing.

Then my mother would make my breakfast of salt porridge, toast and jam, and it would be time to go to school. I liked to leave in good time, so that I could spend half an hour on the beach, always empty at that time of day. There were generally all kinds of strange objects cast up by the winter storms—sea-smoothed bits of green bottle-glass, worn branches of trees from who knew what far-off Scandinavian shore, dead seabirds, broken toys, odd small coins or keys—once I even found a silver sixpence! That was a memorable occasion, for my parents were poor, and I never had much pocket money. My father was an excellent crafts-

The corner shop at Cockburn and Robertson Streets in South Shields. Kirkup was born in the room above the shop, his Grandmother Johnson's flat.

man, a carpenter and joiner, but he was often out of work through no fault of his own. We were living through a period of economic depression, and in England our north-east corner always seemed to be the region that was worst-off. At times, it resembled a hopeless ghetto of unemployed coal miners, shipyard workers, labourers, and even men with good trades like my father's. But I can remember no depression in our house. My sweet, cheerful mother kept things neat and clean, and we were never short of food. My father must often have felt sad and frustrated during his periods of unemployment, but he never showed me anything but a smiling face. He spent his leisure well, reading books and studying history and biography. He had really wanted to be a seaman, so he was always reading to me volumes of discovery or arctic exploration. I learned more from him than from all my classes at school, which I hated with all the passion of a lonely, only child.

And always there was our marvellous town to entertain us. It was just an ordinary small industrial, coal-mining, sea-going place, but for us it was the most interesting and romantic town in the whole world. I tried to describe some of its peculiar magic in one of my earliest poems, a view seen from the old Victorian letter-box at the top of steep Beach Road, just outside the gates of the North Marine Park:

View from the North-East

Across the end of every street the piled-up sea,
the sky and the indelible horizon stretch
like some faintly-stirring backcloth, in front of
    which
the pillar-box, the street lamp and the tree
    detach
their elemental shapes with spectral poignancy.

Against a background of breakers that detonate
with soft explosions over the damp-stained
    beaches,
and throw up gulls like clouds of spray; the
    churches,
roof-tops, waterfront and salt-cellar lighthouses,
ruins, a deserted bandstand, a broken fort

James, age three, in the doorway of his grandmother's house, where he was born

glide like cut-out toys over panoramic lakes.

A child moves like a ghost across the pink-
 cemented promenade,
and drags her solitary shadow like a lifeless
 weed
along the wave-ribbed edges of the sea, where
 hard
cirrus sand-shapes blanch at every step she
 takes.

I attended infant, elementary and secondary schools from the age of five to eighteen. I cannot say my schooldays were the happiest days of my life. I wonder who first propounded this patent untruth. Probably some guilty schoolmaster or schoolmistress, subconsciously trying to atone for all the pain and misery inflicted on helpless children—and getting paid good wages for it, too!

Infant school and elementary school were passed in a kind of daze: I never really seemed to know what was going on. I always felt out of things. This was possibly because I was a sheltered, only child: I was badly equipped to face the outer world, the wilderness of life that was not home. I think I just retreated into a

protective shell during those early years. I was well ahead of all the other children in reading and writing, but arithmetic appalled me—I could just not see the point of it. I found all the classes stiflingly dull and boring, and I disliked my conventional, unkind, and useless teachers. Despite my excellent writing and reading skills, I was always somewhere near the bottom of the class, where I was quite content to vegetate: if that was education, I was having no part of it. Yet I suffered feelings of distress, frustration and humiliation at being dumped among the duds, because I knew that I was not one of them.

I got into my stride a little better when I started attending Westoe Secondary School around the age of eleven. There were a few sympathetic teachers there, mostly women, who taught me French, German, Latin and Greek, and gave me my first inklings of the beauties of classic and modern literature. But the rest of the staff simply terrified and terrorized me.

My main problem was that I have never liked crowds: I tend to become panic-stricken when surrounded by masses of people. School was, for me, the nightmare of some vast, unorganized political demonstration or sporting occasion, in which I would feel my poor little weak self submerged and utterly lost in enor-

Grandmother, Anna Maria Kirkup

Grandfather Johnson, "my Irish grandfather"

(hideous!) like everyone else becomes marked for life as an outsider, a freak to be bullied and beaten into hateful sameness.

I always resisted that. I refused to be cowed. Looking back now, I see that, unknown to myself, I must have possessed infinite courage, infinite powers of endurance. I never gave in. Beneath my timid exterior, I must have been tougher than most, certainly much tougher than I am now in old age, when I avoid any kind of confrontation, or just ignore unpleasantness. But as a child, as an adolescent whose growing-pains were somehow incredibly prolonged and distasteful, I steadfastly remained my own unalterable self, despite every unkindness and cruelty.

I associate my schooldays mainly with sensations of pain and shame. I felt ashamed of so many things: of my very difference most of all. Why could I not be like the rest of the school? Why could I not help standing out? I felt shame at my rapidly growing and coarsening body, my ungovernable animal desires and impulses. I felt shame at being lonely, without a single friend in that hostile environment, in which I could hardly learn anything but languages and literature. (That was quite enough for me, but not enough by far

mous mobs of undisciplined and cruel creatures falsely known as "human" beings.

The building itself was like a tall, grim, brick-and-stone penitentiary, a Kafka-like prison of scrubbed wooden floors, pitiless cement playgrounds, narrow stone or concrete staircases in which the seething throngs of savage children struggled up and down, pushing and shoving, shouting and punching, between classes or at lunch times or the end of afternoon school. Such daily experiences were absolute torture for me, after the quiet and Spartan comfort of my only-child's existence with a loving, careful and civilized father and mother. I felt that every day at school was a battle against the barbarians.

In class, too, I felt swamped by numbers of strange children who were in no way like myself. I soon knew I was a being apart. They soon noticed that, and made me suffer for it, following the example of most of the teachers, who also did not tolerate any kind of exceptions. Children are very right-wing little monsters: they insist on custom and conformity, and anyone who wears the wrong clothes or who has a strange accent or a birth defect or who refuses to wear the school cap

Grandmother Johnson, at Berwick upon Tweed

for examinations.) The lessons in other subjects were so utterly tedious, I used my old technique of taking refuge in daydreams. I simply could not see the purpose of learning algebra or trigonometry or history or science: those subjects wearied me to tears. Yet I felt ashamed of not being able to perform the simplest calculations, which other boys and girls could polish off in minutes. I became a sort of passive rebel against education. I think it was this kind of experience which made me feel so sympathetic towards the postwar, nuclear-age children I was to teach in London, at Southgate Grammar School. I lasted only a couple of terms. I simply could not keep order, for the simple reason that I didn't want to. I was on the side of the children against the rest of the adult world. Being children, and unscrupulous, they took advantage of my sympathy to make my life hell. Even so, I loved and admired them, and they inspired one of my first poems about education and students:

In a London Schoolroom

Arms in cool dresses shine, boys' throats are
    bare,
the murmuring blackboards quiver in a haze of
    chalk.
Summer has come, but will not enter
these open windows that the sunlight
blinds with heat and shutters with despair.
The tree of hands and faces tosses in the gales
    of talk.
A flashing desk-lid like a bomb explodes,
spelling disaster, the final tree of dust.

These are the children bred by war, whose lives
fret at their ignorance of peace. There is no
    answer
to the question they have raised no hand to ask,
no cloudless holiday that would release
life that is sick, hope that was never there,
no task make plain the words they cannot learn
    to trust.
Not we, who fail to understand, but only time
    can teach
a lesson they will not forget, and educate with
    pain
these last pretenders of an innocence they know
    is vain.

These were the first of the "No Future" generation we encounter everywhere today. But when I was a child, we were not allowed to believe there could be no future for us, though Mussolini, Hitler and Franco were huffing and puffing themselves up on our horizons like enormous hectoring bullfrogs. They were to destroy our world. But in the meantime, we had to pass

examinations. The teachers seemed to be either unaware of the political climate of the times, or else were fervent admirers of Mussolini and Hitler. Indeed, our German mistress, a kind, admirable woman, made no secret of her passion for Hitler, and in German class the first song we learned was the "Horst Wessel Lied":

Die Fahnen hoch! Die Reihen fest geschlossen!
SA marschiert, mit ruhig-festem Schritt . . .
Kamaraden, die Rotfront und Reaktion erschossen
Marschieren im Geist, in unseren Reihen mit! . . .

She was what one might have called in those days "a good Fascist"—as if such a monstrosity could ever exist. But the majority of the male teachers were natural Nazis. I was punished time and time again by insensitive brutes of teachers. I still dream about them, and in my dreams they often wear Fascist jackboots.

I was always being stood out in front of the gloating class to have my upraised palms severely beaten by a cutting bamboo stick, that would whistle through the air as it descended from on high above the master's black-gowned shoulder and whipped across both hands, six times on each hand.

I refused to show any signs of pain or grief over these punishments. Again, I feel I was brave in those days, for I endured daily pain with an indifference that would be impossible in me today. I am proud to this day of the fact that other boys, particularly those supposed to be manly and good at sports, when punished thus, would return to their seats crying real tears, bawling and sobbing, with their stinging hands tightly tucked under their armpits in useless attempts to stem the burning agony, whereas I would simply lower my swollen hands and walk calmly back to my seat, without cries, without tears.

Every year, I could expect to be beaten on Empire Day, after our jingoistic school parade, for refusing to salute the Union Jack, our national flag that from my earliest childhood filled me with a sense of colonial domination and unjust exploitation of conventional sentiments of dutiful patriotism. It may seem strange that such a young boy should demonstrate his contempt for blind nationalism in such a way. But it was a reaction that had inexplicably been born in me. I just could not do as everyone else did, and salute that hated flag. Again, it was partly a reluctance to do as everyone else was doing.

Naturally, I did not tell my parents about these punishments. In secret, I pissed on my martyred hands—this was the traditional remedy schoolboys employed to alleviate the pain and heal the wounds and bruises of the masters' bamboo torture-sticks. The punishments filled me with deep shame, and so I kept silent about them at home. In my first teaching post in that awful London grammar school, I was often urged by my fellow teachers to beat the unruly boys—and not on their palms, but on their bare bottoms. I did so only once, when I felt I was at the end of my tether, and had to beat a particularly obnoxious adolescent boy. I felt sick for days after that, and I never beat anyone again. For one thing, it brought back all too keenly the memories of my own beatings at school. And I could see that beatings did no good, at least when I held the rod: though the beating I gave that boy created a curious bond between us, which helped us to understand one another for the first time.

Nor did I tell my parents about the bullying inflicted upon me at school. The physical bullying was not so bad. I could endure having my hair pulled out

really feel it. I had learnt detachment and indifference at a very early age. I think that is why I was able to understand oriental philosophy and art in later years.

The most agonizing form of bullying came from a tough boy from what must obviously have been a very deprived family, perhaps one with a criminal reputation. For one long term of misery, I shared a desk with him at the front of the class. As well as having to put up with his physical cruelties, like burning me with cigarettes or sticking the sharp points of compasses into my bare thighs, I had to counter his demands for increasingly expensive material things.

It began when he threatened to choke me to death if I did not bring him all my comics: I read various weekly comics, and always kept them in pristine condi-

School class photo: James (front row, third from right) about age seven

or my nose punched out of shape, or my ears boxed until I was deaf. I did not mind being kicked black and blue. I did not care when I was tied up with ropes to the school railings and indecently assaulted by both boys and girls. The most damaging bullying was mental and emotional. I was constantly humiliated by children and teachers, who called me degrading names. One young maths teacher I hated in the depths of my heart, and have never forgiven, for calling me "Paleface" and "Goldilocks." I felt this was most unjust. How could I help having a pale skin and ash-blond hair? The boys were just as bad, tormenting me with names like "Knock-knees," "Banana-legs," and plain "Cissy." But I never showed anger. Perhaps I did not

tion, never tearing or defacing or dirtying them as other boys did. My desk companion used to extort these comics from me, and sell them. Then he demanded my school tie. I had to lie to my mother that I had lost it.

But even worse, he began demanding money—at first, only a penny at a time, which I could usually supply from my small pocket money, in those days never more than sixpence a week. Then he started to force me to provide him with ever-larger sums—threepence, fourpence, sixpence. To my utter shame, I had to resort to stealing these sums from my mother's purse, from my father's trouser pockets. Once I was lucky enough to find a shilling lying in the street. I had been trained by my parents never to pick up anything that did not belong to me. But I took the shilling. It gave me a temporary relief: it kept my blackmailer at bay for a week.

My shame was such that I dared not tell my parents about what was happening. I could not complain to my unsympathetic teachers, who would only have laughed at me. The idea of approaching the police never entered my head. At times, my anguish was so great, I could not sleep. I contemplated committing suicide by dropping in front of a local train from a

ing to do anything in unison with the rest of the class or the school. I did not even like singing in the choir. This was partly the result of my dislike of being with crowds of people: I felt my privacy and individuality were threatened, that my very personality and uniqueness were being invaded and destroyed by mindless group activities. I despised "team spirit" and *esprit de corps*. Even at the age of six or seven, I steadfastly refused to be dragooned into the Cubs; and at a later age, I adamantly rejected all attempts to enrol me in the Boy Scouts or the Army Training Corps.

The graduating class of 1934, Westoe Secondary School, South Shields. Kirkup is in the middle row, second from left.

bridge.

But somehow, I endured. I just gritted my teeth and lived through those long weeks of unremitting agony. There came the blessed interval of the Easter holidays. On my return to school, I found that my classmate had been arrested for shoplifting and sentenced to a reformatory. For the first time in that dreadful school, I felt happy. I was freed at last from my evil tormentor. But for many years afterwards, I used to meet him in my nightmares.

My other great problem at school was that I detested with all my being any form of organized games, or indeed any form of regimented activity. I hated hav-

So I was deliberately bad at games. I loathed with the utmost passion of disgust sports like football, cricket, and rugby, and only took part in them with the most undisguised reluctance. In football, I would just stand at the edge of the field and refuse to move or run or kick the ball. If I did manage to kick it, the ball would fly off in the most unexpected directions—sometimes, to my secret delight, full into the face of some hated master or schoolmate. That such behaviour made me unpopular did not bother me at all: I was not interested in the opinions of others.

I never learned to swim or dive. The only things I liked were running and cycling, because I could practise these on my own. This attitude profoundly affected my later life, when I refused to take part in the Second World War, refusing to be conscripted into the Forces, and appearing several times in court to be judged and condemned by pompous patriotic magistrates to hard labour in the wartime labour camps of Britain. They, too, were like school—pitiless prisons inhabited by demons and deviates. I began to feel that the whole of life must be like school. But in those camps, I was to meet at last a few souls with ideas similar to my own. My conscientious objection to all war and regimentation had started when I was just a little boy refusing to salute the national flag on Empire Day. It was to become the pattern of my whole life.

University life at King's College, Newcastle upon Tyne, part of Durham University, was a bitter disappointment to me. The teaching was disgracefully bad, and I had a professor of French who was a sadistic pedant. I made only two or three friends there, and the friendships did not last. I was glad to leave the place.

It was not until I started teaching in foreign countries that I began to realize my potential, both as a teacher and a writer. I spent years in various European lands before being invited by the Japanese Ministry of Education to go and lecture at the University of Tohoku in 1959. From that time on, my life was transformed. As soon as I set foot in Japan, I felt that I had come home. And this new home, like my old one, was one forever within sight and sound of the sea.

J apan was for me a completely new way of life. I adapted to the strange living conditions very quickly, with surprising ease. It was as if I had lived there in a former existence, and so found nothing unusual in even the most exotic scenes and tastes. I loved the harsh north, with its snowy mountains and wild, stormy seas. I travelled everywhere, usually completely alone, and at first with almost no knowledge of the language. Yet I was always happy. I felt secure and welcome everywhere I went, and I was accepted with kindness everywhere. For the first time in my life, I made many friends.

The smells, tastes and sounds of my new world were a perpetual fascination to me:

Geisha Dancing
to Katsura at the Toyo Kan

To the small music of a samisen,
Balancing your pale face and lacquered wig
like too-heavy burdens on your child's thin
     neck,
you gently stamp your attitudes,
working the air with an orange fan
that the orange lining of your wide sleeves

echoes, an occasional surprise.

Your ribbed fan beats the drum of air,
half-closes, and is stretched
open by a finger-tip, so,
like a bird's translucent wing
whose springy feathers softly clatter,
flash across your face's quiet moon,
the oblique eyes of a petted cat.
I sit and watch the mask of your face,
trying to read in it again
the message you gave me with your eyes
when you knelt before me to serve the wine,
but find now no answering glance.
Your blank-powdered face compels me
to watch only the movements of the dance.

It was not so much the people that fascinated me: after all, they were human beings just like myself, and despite differences in appearance I had at once felt an affinity. Their neatness and darkness made me feel unusually conspicuous. For a long time, I wanted to be as they were, with jet-black hair and those lovely, expressive eyes the colour of dark treacle toffee. Why did some of them want to change the shape of those tilted eyes by cosmetic surgery? Indeed, I wondered if the surgeon's knife could make the lids of my too-round Western blue eyes like theirs: but the surgeon I visited advised against it, for the effect would be irreversible, even though I could easily remove the dark-brown contact lenses I planned to wear, and the brushlike dark nylon wig. The Japanese, I realized, would always be beyond my reach—more beautiful and more attractive than I could ever be.

But their country was an open book. There was nowhere I could not go, nothing I could not do. The language of Japan fascinated me because it was so mysterious, and I preferred to leave it that way, an eternal enigma. Thus I could enjoy from an entirely aesthetic point of view the bold Chinese characters and the more angular signs of the other syllabaries. They looked elegant in black ink on white handmade paper. I had lessons in calligraphy, often without knowing the meaning of the noble shapes my loaded brush was producing. I wrote *haiku* in Japanese, copying from a book. The act of grinding the block of Chinese ink in water and producing ink was something I found infinitely soothing: the very name of the exquisitely carved slab of fine slate on which I patiently ground my inksticks was an enchanting whisper—*suzuri*. I wrote poems in English, too, both in modern verse forms and in vain imitation of the three-lined, seventeen-syllable *haiku* or the five-lined, thirty-one-syllable *tanka*. One of my first poems written in Japan was a tribute to the art of calligraphy:

Brushes and Ink

Lift the lacquered lid
decorated with gilt
bamboo trellises and
formal plum-blossom.

The ink-block lies within.
Pour fresh water from
the ferny china jar
into its shallow depression.

Then gently scrub
the block's smooth slate
with ink-cake, mixing
its midnight with the light of water.

How soothing it is
to grind the ink-cake
against the ink-block,
making new ink!

When the ink is made,
not too weak, not too thick,
dip your brush in its blackness.
Draw the first, perfect stroke.

I had my own Japanese house and garden, and these were a never-ending source of wonder and delight. I slept on the cool, matted *tatami* floor, in *futon* that had hung drying in the sun all day long: it was like dreaming in a field of summer clover. I woke to the light of dawn staining the sliding paper windows above my head. There I would lie for a while, my head on a pillow of rice-husks, watching the crimson rays grow lighter, until the first sun cast black shadows of bamboos or winter camellias—shadows as intense as the shapes drawn by my brush—across those snowy paper windows on their light wooden frames. At night, my lamps played upon them with a subdued golden glow that looked warm and inviting among the dark green foliage of my formal garden, with its guardian stone lantern by the brushwood gate.

At first, my only heat came from a simple, earthenware charcoal brazier. So, as the Japanese did, I would warm my body on chilly evenings by taking a long, hot bath in the big round tub of cypress planks, heated by a small fire of wood and coal beneath. Here is the poem I wrote about it:

O-Furo

The simple fragrances of this primitive bath
are those of nature: the autumn snatch
of woodsmoke and the reek of slowly-burning
    leaves,
the fume of the small fire humming under the
    tub

that scents the homely water it contains
with a whiff of pine, essence of planks fresh-
    planed,
bouquet of reeds, rice-straw, bamboo, a rare
    infusion.
—And from the scorching water curls
white steam, a briny incense,
sharp with the tang of weed and spume and
    spray
or the tranquil, mossy breath
of old stones in amber lakes.

I dip the bucket bound with copper hoops
into the brew of earth and sand and snow,
and willingly unleash their dark libations
over my naked head and body, in wild
storm after storm of grilling rain,
in long and ritual purification,
a formal greeting to and from the gods
before their final, furiously hot embrace,
closer and more complete than any lover's,
when I climb into the tub that is their temple
and crouch like an elemental in its wooden
    womb
while the flame of hidden altars tans my bones.

Inside the house, I wore traditional Japanese clothes: in winter, a padded kimono and jacket, in summer, light, indigo-dyed cotton *yukata* with a narrow silken sash. On my feet, I wore house slippers or the close-fitting, digitated sock-shoes called *tabi*: these were snug and warm on cold mornings. But it was some time before I dared venture outside, into the little lane on which my house stood, just off Kozenji-dori, to practise walking in my first formal kimono. It was so difficult to keep the thonged straw sandals on my feet: most Japanese have a large gap between the big toe and the next, formed through constant gripping of the cord or thong of *zori* or the clumping wooden *geta*. Even after only five minutes strolling slowly from one end of the lane to the other—causing a newspaper delivery boy to fall off his bicycle with shock at the sight of me—I was exhausted. But I gradually picked up the knack of moving with smaller steps than I would use in Western clothes, and of keeping the intricate garment and under-garments in order:

First Kimono

I put on my first formal kimono
today, the winter solstice.

It is dark brown and plain,
with a grey sash of crepe silk.

My under-kimono is also grey
silk, edged with dark amber brocade.

Kirkup outside his house in Tokyo, 1969

My sleeves are full, and as wide
as the wide sleeves of the long jacket.

The jacket is tied in front
with a silken knot of plaited brown cord.

On my feet, dark brown sock-shoes,
split-toed, thonged sandals of straw.

Snow moves aside like
a sliding paper window.

I leave the garden house
under my umbrella of oiled paper.

When with small steps I first walked out
in the busy street, and crossed the road,

I felt weak with the strangeness,
and utterly naked.

Mejiro

I was living all alone, in a strange land, yet I never felt lonely. As an only child, I had long since learned to live with myself, and to take pleasure in my own company and interior conversations, rather than in the mostly empty chatter of acquaintances. I was happy and at ease in Japan for the first time in my life. There was no hostility here, only natural kindness and formal courtesy that suited me well: even though it was usually only of the formal kind, it was nevertheless courtesy. In human relationships in Japan, people held themselves at a modest distance from each other: there was no intimate heart-searching or soul-baring. Again this attitude seemed to correspond perfectly to the needs of my own emotional life. I began to learn oriental acceptance, and would sit for hours on the floor beside my brazier, thinking contentedly of nothing:

At Home in Japan

A house all sliding doors and walls:
a paper cupboard becomes a room,
a rush-matted floor becomes a bed,
the bed a square cushion that is a chair
and that I turn over politely
to offer a sudden visitor.
The cushion is flat
and lies by a low table
where the tea is pale green in a brown cup.
I live by lantern light, behind torn screens.
The tiled roof
is grey waves, regular
as a wood-block sea.
A hawk hangs over it,
the tips of his wings

like my frayed gloves.
The front doors run on rails.
No lock: only a thread
of twisted metal holds them shut.
Long windows shuffle open to the quake of
    trains.
I am alone in an open house
yet sleep in peace. There is nothing to steal.

In the working street
the chime of wooden pattens on stones,
smoke from the bath-house, a man selling
    bamboos,
the sweet-potato cart's steam whistle,
the blind masseur in a black kimono,
his white stick tapping my wooden walls.
There is no telephone,
no snakes, only one quiet spider
and kind people who pretend
to take no notice of me.
I cannot speak their tongue, nor they mine:
ignorant of the language barrier,
we do not erect it.
They leave me alone in my set of boxes
with the bare wooden ceilings.
The charcoal in the blue-glazed brazier
makes the iron kettle hum. Spring again.
I sit in silence, thinking happily
of nothing, warming my empty hands.

Yes, for the most part, the people of Japan left me alone, to my own devices. This was really an unusual privilege, because the Japanese always make an unnecessary fuss over Westerners, a fuss that is at first welcome, but soon becomes tiresome. We lived together quite simply, in mutual respect.

Of course, I did have visitors from time to time. They were always careful to announce their arrival by letter or telephone—using the neighbour's phone. The visitors were always prompt: indeed, sometimes too prompt—they would arrive half an hour before the agreed time, and find I was out shopping, or in my bath. Every Wednesday afternoon, I was "at home" to my students. We would chat together in English over tea and cakes, and sometimes *sake*. Those informal meetings with students and teachers were among the most delightful memories I have. They never seemed to get over the fact that I was living all alone in my own house, for living space is scarce in Japan, and most people live in very crowded conditions. They were also awed by my complete independence from the many social obligations imposed upon the Japanese, and longed to live as I did, in complete freedom. In those hours of relaxed English practise, we talked about all

subjects under the sun. Naturally, the boys were deeply concerned about getting a good position in life with some big company like Mitsubishi or Sony. The girls, too, wanted to find good, interesting jobs: but they knew that they would be marrying in a few years' time, so the only positions they could hope for were modest office jobs—"Office Ladies" or "O.L." as they are called in Janglish—or part-time work as assistants in stores. But in order to obtain even the most modest situation, they had to have a university graduation diploma. It often seemed to me an unnecessary waste of an expensive education, when I met girl shop assistants who had laboriously and painfully composed long graduation theses on Faulkner or Somerset Maugham, or a taxi driver who had majored in French with a thesis on Samuel Beckett. I knew a dental technician who had written his graduation thesis on Graham Greene, which he pronounced "Grim Grin"—very apt, I thought, considering his profession and the wry humour of some of Greene's writing. Many of those students still keep in touch with me, occasionally visit me or send me New Year cards with poetic good wishes.

As a change from the writing of academic essays in stiff literary English, I tried to make my students attempt more free and creative forms. So we used to try writing *haiku* in English, often with delightfully quaint results. Their inventive use of English, using to the best of their ability the small vocabularies at their command, never ceased to amaze and entertain me. The unusual English often contained true flashes of poetic wit and insight.

I practised writing these short poems myself. Of course, it was impossible to reproduce all the technicalities and ambiguities and linguistic formalities of the Japanese *haiku*, but sometimes I felt it was possible to capture a hint of their almost untranslatable qualities:

Winter nights. Starlit
spiders patiently repair
frost-shattered windows.

and:

Summer gale stirring
the weary green of willows—
and their reflections.

and:

Waving handkerchief—
the lake steamer departing—
seagull lost in mist.

I travelled widely, in all the regions and islands of Japan. I was usually alone. I have always felt that it is best to travel on one's own: that way, one sees so much more, with fewer distractions or breaks in concentration. Everywhere there was the sea of Japan, for the country is as much water as land. Whether by the pounding breakers of the Pacific or the thunderous, snowy waves of the Japan Sea, or on the ferry crossing from Honshu to Hokkaido, I took the waters of Japan to my heart, with all the passion I had felt for the northern seas of my childhood. The first part of my poem sequence, "Japan Marine," combines modern free verse with formal *haiku:* the sequence won First Prize in the International Literary Competition organized by the Japan PEN Club. The first section is entitled "The Sea Outside":

Sea creature,
barnacled with peaks, castled with ice;
trembling legend
of green islands, girders,
temples, dynamos and rice;
You sprawl—cratered with stadia, crowned with
    highways,
garlanded with foam and archipelagoes
like some authentic dragon from primordial
    rocks—
your long mythologies across the present's bitter
    peace.

Cicadas chant cool
sutras in temple pinetrees:
warm stars' throbbing gongs.

Fantastic swimmer,
the sun's first castaway,
those stilled explosions, your capitals
of neon, concrete, plastic, steel and glass
govern your shaking sands with rafts of dreams,
dark scaffoldings of iron on a dawn of green.
The floating mountain
suspends in winter its canopy of snow
on mist, water, ice, a ghost of earth.

Last summer lanterns.
Corncobs grilled at street corners:
dirty paper fan.

Thrown at random,
energetic sleeper, across
the longitudes of your divine geographies,
taut athlete with the curving spine,
you breathe like a wave
under the mats of weed,
captured alive in nets of salt and spray;
or like a naked child, new-born,
twist in a basket of straw your world of brine.

Windbell, tired child's cry:
paper poem hangs faded,
but still it's summer.

Those intercalated *haiku* are in my usual style, that is, following strictly the 5-7-5 syllable count, as Basho nearly always did. Those rebellious to the form kept breaking away from it, and today most modern poets prefer a "free" and vaguely impressionistic *haiku*, striving for the effect of "lightness" (*karumi*) beloved of Basho and his disciples, and suggesting—not always successfully—the swift strokes of a brush painting. But I find the strict form liberating in a way the looser one is not. For me, the seventeen syllables are a kind of washing-line, on which I daily peg my words, thoughts, and images. Yes, I write *haiku* as a kind of spiritual jogging. My motto is: "A *haiku* a day keeps the doctor away." Those neat, sharp lines can also have beneficial physical effects upon one's system, like acupuncture needles. I like to inscribe *haiku* on bits of rice paper and eat them.

Japan is one of the most crowded countries on earth. How did I, who always hated crowds, cope with life in big cities like Tokyo and Osaka? I learned to swim with the current, to flow with the throngs, never to hurry, but to adopt the pace of the general movement. It is only those who try to run and rush who seem out of step in Japan—and one often sees Japanese running full-tilt in streets, crowded basement arcades, department stores, and subways. Even waitresses hurtle between tables in restaurants, in their eagerness to serve one. Little old ladies in kimono battle their way in brave beelines for whatever destination they have set their sights on, and woe betide anyone who gets in the way, especially a foreigner—though the inevitable collisions are always apologized for with hasty bows. On the other hand, groups of ladies leaving a tea ceremony or flower-arrangement class will block the pavements, bowing repeatedly to one another with low, deep, respectful bows that shove out the big knots at the backs of their sashes, giving an almost bustle effect under the kimono coat or *haori*: one has to negotiate these little human islands of age-old courtesy as delicately as one can in the frantic rush of the modern city.

I came to Japan from my home in the elegant, tranquil British city of Bath, all cool classicism and spacious dignity. The contrast with Tokyo was almost indescribable. Yet I enjoyed the rush-hours, the densely-packed commuter trains and subways, with their "bottom-pushers"—brawny young men whose job it was to push as many people into the already overflowing trains as possible, before the closing of the automatic doors. The crush inside often became intolerable. People fainted, and windows were shattered with the pressure of bodies. So now the bottom-pushers are often employed in pulling people out of the trains rather than cramming them in. My experience of Japanese rush-hour crowds is expressed thus:

Shinjuku Station Rush Hour

People and people and people,
people like smoke, ghosts or water
people like strokes of an ink brush
people like drowning swimmers
people like a mad lake
people all with black hair
people in trains like meat in sausages
people alone, people together
people meeting, people parting
people drunk with smiling
people bowing, hearing poem-announcements
people going underground
people like sighs, people like dying breaths.

In the train I am in an egg packed with blood
I am inside a python, devoured alive,
the muscles of its long stomach crush my bones,
　　slowly,
as it digests me hurriedly from station to
　　station.
It swallows me at Takadanobaba
and evacuates me at Ikebukuro.

People, people everywhere,
nor any stop to think . . .

Nevertheless, it is sensational, dynamic.
I feel at last involved with life
and have relationships, if only in passing,
with human beings.
We are all food for the python trains
and we eat each other also.

I am a people-watcher.
I am a people-pusher.
I am a people-eater.
In the rush hour, everyone is a cannibal.
People and people and people!
(Excuse me please, I want to get off here.)

Gradually, I became so accustomed to all these ordinary yet unusual things that I was constantly looking for newer, fresher sensations. Fortunately, Japan is a country that always provides new visual pleasures. At night, I never tire of the fantastic scenery of neon signs that splash the skies with fireworks of winking, cascading characters. Then I am thankful I have not learnt to read, otherwise my pure aesthetic pleasure in the spectacle would be corrupted by the sad realization that I was gazing at an advertisement for washing-up liquid or soy sauce or "instant" noodles. The well-dressed crowds of Japanese hardly seem to bother to contemplate these visual wonders: presumably they hold no mysteries for the native. But how sweet-smelling those throngs of revellers are! This is a fact first noticed by Lafcadio Hearn. Constant bathing makes the Japanese not only the cleanest but the most delicately fragrant people to be squashed up against in a crowd. The faint scent of pomade also floats on the air, with a suave but light freshness. Those pomaded heads of hair, so thick and rich, make some people look like expensive lacquered cabinets of the utmost refinement and art.

My happiest memories of life in Japan date from the late fifties and early sixties, just before the 1964 Tokyo Olympics and the start of the great "economic miracle." Both of these changed Japan, and the Japanese, not always for the better. I felt they had gained the whole world, but lost the precious fragrance of their immortal souls. Materialism and pragmatism prevailed, instead of contemplation and the spirit. The Olympics always change whatever city they are held in. From 1964, Japan became denatured. I felt no longer the same love and admiration for its people. Perhaps I became disillusioned by all the striving for material success. Until around 1967, I hated to leave Japan for holidays in Britain, Europe, America, or S.E. Asian lands. But slowly I began to feel that if I did not get away from Japan at regular intervals, I should go mad. So I travelled to Singapore, Malaya, Hong Kong, Cambodia, Laos, Vietnam, Thailand, Burma, and South Korea. It was that last-named country that received the heart I had once lost to Japan. I found that the Korean people were much more open and outgoing than the Japanese. They are generous hosts, kind and welcoming to strangers. Their dances, music and festivals are intoxicatingly vivid and vital. The country itself has a kind of misty, ethereal beauty, and of course the sea is everywhere there, too. In some strange way, the Koreans reminded me of the people of the North-East of England, the Tynesiders (affectionately nicknamed "sand-dancers") among whom I had grown up. I still often return to Korea, though the preparations for the 1988 Olympics in Seoul are beginning to have the same effects on the capital, and on the general population, that they did in Tokyo in 1964. But the true heart of the Korean people can never change, as the Japanese heart has seemed to do during the last twenty years. Here is one of my poems about Korea, written some years ago, at a time when the curfew was still in force: it shows Seoul as I would like to remember it today:

Seoul

At almost midnight
just before curfew,

none but foreigners abroad—

I wandered round the empty
Central Station plaza, awaiting
the arrival of non-existent trains.

*

In the first light of dawn
just after curfew ended
the blacked-out streets awoke

with an old man
dragging a cart piled with cabbages
across the empty plaza of City Hall.

While I was in Japan, I had the good fortune to be invited twice to America, first to take up the post of Visiting Poet at Amherst College, and later to accept the Morton Professorship in International Literature at Ohio University. Both Amherst and Athens, Ohio are delightful small towns, and I was very happy there. In the late sixties, I felt the full force of student revolt at Amherst, admirably controlled by our Presi-

dent's civilized expedient of a "moratorium," in which there were some lively debates and encounters between staff and students. I shall never forget that true example of democracy intelligently and very effectively at work, at the height of the Vietnam confrontations and protests.

I loved Amherst for other reasons. It had been where Frost had lived, and where another great American poet, perhaps my favourite after Whitman, Emily Dickinson had resided. I often visited her grave there, among the faded, fluttering flags on graves of soldiers of so many wars. Here I wrote many poems about Emily:

In the House of Emily Dickinson

At this small table, hardly
bigger than a checkerboard,
she told with birdlike hand
the coming of the word.

Over the square-paned casement
a muslin curtain, bright and still.
A hedge away, the country lane,
the fields, the railroad of the will.

She could see out, but they
could not see in. The heart's long mile
was all she trod, her world a room.
It did not cramp her style.

A spirit here was not confined,
but wandered high and far,
from yards of death to leagues of life,
from slowest candle to the quickest star.

These were the first American students I had taught, and I found them very receptive to the way I taught literature, especially poetry and the short story. I always teach these subjects from the point of view of a professional practitioner: I can show students just how things work, or how to make them work, and how the poets of the past, and myself, made them work. We issued an irregular little typed magazine called, significantly, "Workings." These highly intelligent and privileged youths were exciting to teach and to argue with, after the passivity and silence of most Japanese students. Some of them were already accomplished writers, and there was little I could teach them. The main thing was to encourage, to be positive in my reactions, whether good or bad, and to say exactly what I thought. I found they had great interest in oriental literature and poetic forms, so I was able to open a path for many would-be poets in that direction. Others were just getting into the philosophies of the East, and I remember the joy with which I heard for the first time the curious expression, "I'm into Zen some." I shall

At Amherst College, in the late sixties

Daniel Kaufman, New York

never forget the happy year I spent at Amherst.

Nor shall I ever forget Athens, Ohio, with its charming campus, friendly staff, and enthusiastic students. Here, too, there was intense interest in the East and its cultures. But there were also many students of European languages with whom I worked on careful translations of modern European poets and prose writers. We produced some good work, I believe. Towards the end of my stay, I gave a reading of my poetry in the chapel, and it was a deeply moving experience for me. I was sorry to leave Athens, where I spent one of the happiest periods in my life.

From Amherst and Athens I made trips to places all over the United States. I took the delightfully-named Peter Pan Line buses to Boston: I remember there was one bus called "The Lost Boys." I was utterly spellbound by Boston and by the whole of the East Coast. I used to spend weekends there, and in New York, Philadelphia, and Washington, all of which I grew to know and admire.

From Athens, the city of Cincinnati was my favourite destination, a most civilized and endearing place. But it was New York that really fascinated me, so much in fact that after leaving Athens I went to live there for several months in Greenwich Village, in a small apartment on Waverley Place. It was all enchantment. I wrote a number of poems about New York that appeared in my collection *White Shadows, Black Shadows* (Dent), and some of these were about favourite jazz singers—Anita O'Day, Nina Simone and Ella Fitzgerald, for I was a frequent visitor to the Village Gate, the Half Note, and other jazz rendezvous in the Village. One of the greatest thrills of my life was meeting Anita O'Day and talking to her at the Half Note, where she was appearing with Roy Eldridge, another of my old favourites:

> . . . Those little white gloves
> caress the mike. She smiles
> softly (that brown mole
> upper lip left of centre),
> waves at my strobe flash,
> 'They can't take that Away from Me . . .'

I collected my poems about female jazz singers in *The Body Servant* (Dent). But the poems about New York and Los Angeles in *White Shadows, Black Shadows* were my best hymns to the USA. Here is one of the shorter ones:

A Window Cleaner in Wall Street

> On two tenterhooks
> he shores himself up on
> space, then leans on it,
> a wall that gives.

> In the stockstill air
> windows bid for
> fragments of sky
> white as tickertape.

> He leans far out there
> as if on a heeling yacht,
> belted behind a taut
> topsail of windowglass.

> The airconditioners above
> drip spray between
> his feet parted on nothing,
> spit in his eye.

> He does battle
> with the dusts of time,
> and winces only
> at the window-wiping birds.

Of all the cities in the world, New York is the one I should most like to live permanently in, though I grew very fond also of Chicago, Denver, San Francisco and (very especially) Santa Fe and Albuquerque.

But it was time for a return to base. I had lived for a few years in Dublin, one of my ancestral places. But after New York, I returned to Britain, to a Creative Writing post at Sheffield University, and then as Resident Poet and Dramatist at the Sherman Theatre in the University College of Cardiff, Wales. I was not at all happy in either place, and I think perhaps I had been spoilt by the warmth and charm of Amherst and Athens. So I was soon winging my way back to Japan, where I was fortunate to be invited to a very pleasant position at Kyoto University of Foreign Studies, where I have taught comparative literature for the last ten years.

Kyoto is a very mixed sort of city, with exquisite little corners lost among the almost uniform ugliness of new modern buildings. Even those quiet temple grounds are no longer tranquil. They have been invaded by the trampling feet of millions of tourists, and, even worse, by insensitive loudspeaker information that bursts upon the ears just as one wants to sit quietly and contemplate the exquisite placements of rocks and mosses in Ryoanji. There is something stagnant and stifling in the air of Kyoto, with its centuries of traditional arts and crafts: it is very hard for a foreigner to become accepted in such exalted artistic circles. So I return twice a year to my home in Europe, in the small Principality of Andorra, for rest and recuperation, and for a replenishing of my bookshelves with the latest European literature, unavailable in Kyoto, whose bookshops are well behind the times.

But in spite of everything, I love Kyoto, and always hate to leave for Tokyo. I prefer the cities of

Kirkup and his parents in their garden at Corsham

Osaka and Kobe, which are within easy reach of where I live, in the northern hills of cryptomeria and bamboos. As in my childhood, I am trying to detach myself from what are often nerve-wrackingly noisy surroundings and increasingly intolerant and insensitive crowds. I take refuge in Zen contemplation. I should like to end with an extract from my collection *Zen Contemplations* (Kyoto Editions), which was written in Kyoto, in a Zen temple, but which curiously enough brought me back to the place where I was born, to the town of South Shields on the great River Tyne that flows forever into our stormy, romantic North Sea:

> . . . In childhood, I knew
> enlightenment so many times,
> in the best way,
> without knowing it.
>
> That time with my mother and father,
> late at night, in a tiny boat,
> crossing the stormy River Tyne—
> at once I fell into a calm sleep
> in my father's arms.
> I was three years old.
> —When they saw me sleeping,
> breathing so easily and so gently,
> and with a faint smile on my lips

> (I who was always so nervous and timid)
> they felt no more fear.
>
> I had become
> both the boat and the boatman . . .

BIBLIOGRAPHY

Poetry:

Indications, with John Ormond and John Bayliss. London: Grey Walls Press, 1942.

The Cosmic Shape: An Interpretation of Myth and Legend with Three Poems and Lyrics, with Ross Nichols. London: Forge Press, 1946.

The Drowned Sailor and Other Poems. London: Grey Walls Press, 1947.

The Creation, in *Acadine Poets,* No. 2. Hull, England: Lotus Press, 1951.

The Submerged Village and Other Poems. London: Oxford University Press, 1951.

A Correct Compassion and Other Poems. London: Oxford University Press, 1952.

A Spring Journey and Other Poems of 1952-1953. London: Oxford University Press, 1954.

The Descent into the Cave and Other Poems. London: Oxford University Press, 1957.

The Prodigal Son: Poems, 1956-1959. London: Oxford University Press, 1959.

Refusal to Conform: Last and First Poems. London: Oxford University Press, 1963.

Japan Marine. Tokyo: Japan P.E.N. Club, 1965.

Paper Windows: Poems from Japan. London: Dent, 1968.

Japan Physical: A Selection, with Japanese translations by Fumiko Miura. Tokyo: Kenkyusha, 1969.

White Shadows, Black Shadows: Poems of Peace and War. London: Dent, 1970.

A Bewick Bestiary. Ashington, England: The Mid-Northumberland Arts Group, 1971.

The Body Servant: Poems of Exile. London: Dent, 1971.

Broad Daylight. Farnham, England: Sceptre Press, 1971.

Transmental Vibrations. London: Covent Garden Press, 1971.

Many-lined Poem. Sheffield, England: Headland Poetry, 1973.

Zen Gardens. Guildford, England: Circle Press, 1973.

Scenes from Sesshu. Guildford, England: Circle Press, 1977.

Scenes from Sutcliffe. Ashington, England: The Mid-Northumberland Arts Group, 1977.

Enlightenment. Osaka: Kyoto Editions, 1978.

Zen Contemplations (includes prose). Osaka: Kyoto Editions, 1978.

Cold Mountain Poems. Osaka: Kyoto Editions, 1979.

The Tao of Water. Guildford, England: Circle Press, 1979.

Dengonban Messages: One-line Haiku and Senryu. London: Kyoto Editions, 1981; Osaka: Union Services, 1981.

Ecce Homo: My Pasolini. London: Kyoto Editions, 1981.

Fellow Feelings: My Blue Period—Poems Grim and Gay. Osaka: Kyoto Editions, 1982.

Contrasts and Comparisons. Tokyo: Seibdo, 1983.

To the Ancestral North: Poems for an Autobiography. Tokyo: Asahi Press, 1983.

The Sense of the Visit. Bristol, England: Sceptre Press, 1984.

Plays:

Upon This Rock: A Dramatic Chronicle of Peterborough Cathedral, produced in Peterborough, 1955. London: Oxford University Press, 1955.

Masque: The Triumph of Harmony, produced in London, 1955.

The True Mistery of the Nativity. London and New York: Oxford University Press, 1956.

The Meteor, adapted from a play by Dürrenmatt, produced in London, 1956. London: Cape, 1973; New York: Grove Press, 1974.

The Prince of Homburg, adapted from a play by Heinrich von Kleist, produced in New York, 1976. Published in *Classic Theatre 2,* edited by Eric Bentley. New York: Doubleday, 1959.

The True Mistery of the Passion: Adapted and Translated from the French Medieval Mystery Cycle of Arnoul and Simon Grélan, produced in Bristol, 1960. London and New York: Oxford University Press, 1962.

The Physicists, adapted from a play by Dürrenmatt, produced in London and New York, 1963. London: French, 1964; New York: Grove Press, 1964.

Play Strindberg, adapted from a play by Dürrenmatt, produced in New York, 1971; London, 1973. New York: Grove Press, 1970; London: J. Cape, 1972.

Peer Gynt, adapted from a play by Ibsen, produced at the University Theatre, Newcastle upon Tyne, 1973.

The Magic Drum (for children), produced in Newcastle upon Tyne, 1974; London, National Theatre, 1977.

Cyrano de Bergerac, adapted from a play by Rostand, produced in Newcastle upon Tyne, 1975.

The Anabaptists, Period of Grace, and *Frank the Fifth,* adapted from plays by Dürrenmatt, produced in Cardiff, 1976.

An Actor's Revenge, music by Minoru Miki, produced in London, 1979; St. Louis, 1981; Illinois Opera, 1984; Tokyo, 1985.

Television plays:

The Peach Garden. BBC-TV, 1954.

Two Pigeons Flying High. BBC-TV, 1955.

The True Mistery of the Passion. BBC-TV, 1960.

The True Mistery of the Nativity. 1960.

The Prince of Homburg. CBS-TV, n.d.

Radio play:

Ghost Mother. 1978.

Nonfiction:

The Only Child: An Autobiography of Infancy. London: Collins, 1957.

Sorrows, Passions, and Alarms: An Autobiography of Childhood. London: Collins, 1959.

These Horned Islands: A Journal of Japan (travel). London: Collins, 1962; New York: Macmillan, 1962.

Tropic Temper: A Memoir of Malaya (travel). London: Collins, 1963.

England, Now. Tokyo: Seibido, 1964.

Japan Industrial: Some Impressions of Japanese Industries (essays). Osaka: Daishin Printing Co., 1964-65.

Frankly Speaking. Tokyo: Eichosha, 1966.

Japan, Now. Tokyo: Seibido, 1966.

Tokyo (travel). London: Phoenix House, 1966; South Brunswick, N.J.: A.S. Barnes, 1966.

Bangkok (travel). South Brunswick, N.J.: A.S. Barnes, 1968; published as *Cities of the World: Bangkok.* London: Phoenix House, 1968.

Filipinescas: Travels through the Philippine Islands. London:

Phoenix House, 1968.

One Man's Russia (travel). London: Phoenix House, 1968.

Aspects of the Short Story (literary criticism), with commentary by Kirkup. Tokyo: Kaibunsha, 1969.

Streets of Asia (travel). London: Dent, 1969.

Hong Kong and Macao (travel). London: J.M. Dent, 1970; South Brunswick, N.J.: A.S. Barnes, 1970.

Japan behind the Fan (travel). London: J.M. Dent, 1970.

Heaven, Hell, and Hara-kiri: The Rise and Fall of the Japanese Superstate (essays). London: Angus & Robertson, 1974.

America Yesterday and Today. Tokyo: Seibido, 1977.

Mother Goose's Britain. Tokyo: Asahi Shuppanshi, 1977.

The Britishness of the British. Tokyo: Seibido, 1978.

The Guardian of the World. London: Collins, 1980.

No More Hiroshimas. Osaka: Kyoto Editions, 1982.

The Glory That Was Greece. Tokyo: Seibido, 1983.

When I Was a Child: An Autobiographical Interpretation and Appre-ciation of Mother Goose Nursery Rhymes. Tokyo: Taibundo, 1983.

Fiction:

The Love of Others. London: Collins, 1962.

Insect Summer (for children). New York: Knopf, 1971; Tokyo: Hokuseido Press, 1980.

The Magic Drum (for children). New York: Knopf, 1973; London, 1977.

Editor of:

Shepherding Winds: An Anthology of Poetry from East and West. London: Blackie, 1969.

Songs and Dreams: An Anthology of Poetry from East and West. London: Blackie, 1970.

Besides many Japanese works, Kirkup has translated numerous verse and prose selections from French and German writers both contemporary and classical. These translations include fiction and nonfiction, dramas, librettos, and juvenile literature.

Jakov Lind

1927–

DANUBE BLUES

(Translated from the German by Christopher Middleton)

O, let our red flags flutter like a flaming sea.
We're the freedom, we're the future.
Vienna's working class are we.

February 1934. A not very cold February, but a dangerous one. And it had to be on the thirteenth, my birthday, when cannons and machine guns of the militia of the Patriotic Front, the military arm of the Austro-Fascists, rolled up the red flags. Our Goethehof, a housing project built under the Socialist First Republic for workers and other low-income groups, was a prime target for bombardment. Like the Karl-Marxhof, the Goethehof was considered a natural "fortress" of "Red Vienna." We were evacuated in all haste and spent two nights with hundreds of other families in the basement of the Girls' Elementary School on the Schuettauplatz. When we left our shelter the logos of the Socialists (three arrows) had vanished. Vienna was painted all over with the *Krukenkreuz* (also known as the Jerusalem Cross, going back to the Crusaders). No more red songs, no more red carnations, the benign beard of our Socialist mayor Karl Seitz had also vanished. The Socialist salute, the raised clenched fist, was banned (but so was the outstretched hand of the Nazi salute). No more future and freedom. For us, Jewish Austrians, this was the beginning of the end. Five months later, in July, the Nazis tried to overthrow the Patriotic Front. They managed to enter the Chancellor's office and assassinate Engelbert Dollfuss behind his desk. The fact that the murderer could enter the chancellery with such apparent ease and prevent any last-minute medical aid to the dying man indicates, of course, how deep the Nazis (our own Austrian Nazis not the Germans) had managed to infiltrate all levels of our society. The assassin, a certain Schlageter, was caught and executed, mourned in Nazi Germany as a true Austrian martyr made of the stuff of Teutonic heroes. Dollfuss's assassination rang in a new era in middle Europe, similar to what we witness today in the Middle East. Cold-blooded terror dictates political rules. Still, the Nazis had not succeeded and wouldn't until supported by a German invasion in March 1938. Just a little too early, as everyone said.

Jakov Lind

For us schoolchildren there was a new song to be learned:

Line up young men, a dead man leads our way.
For Austria he shed his blood,
A truly German [!] man.
The murderer's bullet which cut him down,

195

Rose our people from sleep and strife.

Equally simple was the refrain:

> Youth stands ready
> With Dollfuss into a new age.

Not in English, but in Austrian-German it all rhymed. Dead rhymes with red. Blood with courage. And the new writings on the wall, "*Jews perish in your own filth*," rhymed as well.

At home we sympathized with Socialists but not with the Communists. We also were open to the appeal of Zionists. It was about time we learned what to do with our Jewishness, as we were neither religious nor particularly affiliated to any Jewish group or cause. We were Austrians, but a special kind of Austrian. Life had become a little more dangerous for us, yet seemingly far from lethal, that's all. We children, my two older sisters and myself, had joined Zionist youth clubs, similar to Boy Scouts, with their love for uniform and outdoor games. We believed at this early age we had a goal, a purpose in life.

In 1917, less than twenty years earlier, before the end of World War I, the British Prime Minister, Lord Balfour, had promised the World Zionist Federation led by the Russian emigré Chaim Weizmann, a top scientist, that Britain would help the Zionists in establishing an autonomous state within the borders of Palestine. This political statement merged with a traditional affinity to the ancestral home of the Bible—a new political awareness harnessed to messianic daydreams—and created an extraordinary rejuvenating energy which soon gripped a large segment of our Viennese Jewish population. Even today this combination of self-assertion and self-sacrifice baffles Israel's numerically superior enemies. Our goal was the implementation of the Balfour Declaration, that is, the establishment of a Jewish State in Palestine. My parents and their generation, used to anti-Semitic outrage by their own or their parents' experience, were maybe a little too philosophical on the subject of emigrating to Palestine. They were Austrians and not Poles or Russians; they had few illusions, yet reasonable confidence in their urban fellow citizens. What could have happened in the East of Europe they could not imagine coming true in the heart of Vienna. Of course they lived to see they were wrong, after the Germans moved into Vienna in March 1938. Our childish enthusiasm for Palestine they accepted as so much childish phantasy. Looking back today I cannot blame them. In the thirties a Jewish State in Palestine seemed a mirage and nothing but that.

For us children there was elementary school which taught us the elementary lessons of the new political situation in Austria in some roundabout way.

Excused from Catholic religious instruction (Austria, like France and Italy, is Catholic) we Jewish children went to Viktor Rosenfeld, who persuaded us to become Zionists (which was positive), but lacked the talent of Father Meinert when it came to illustrating Biblical stories with multiple colours on the blackboard. Meinert, a true artist of the blackboard, conjured forth with coloured chalks a paradise of fruits, trees, animals, flowers, and butterflies. To see his pictures I gladly listened to the mysteries of the Trinity.

To my father the Catholic religion was Christian, the Jewish religion Jewish mumbo jumbo. We rarely went to synagogue but when we did he admonished us to pray quietly. "God is an old man, don't shout into his ears"; or "Never sit in the first row; if God wants to see you, he sees you also in the back rows"; besides "It all comes to nothing anyway."

He was right. My theological speculations only got me into fights.

Our Christian schoolmates claimed it was us, the Jewish children at school (and I believe I was the only one in my class), who had crucified their Lord Jesus. The same legend was spread wherever we met children of our age group who had heard it in church or at home from their parents. Of course, there is no point in denying this sort of accusation, even though they had to admit that it was not we personally but our ancestors who had committed the heinous crime. Going that far back into history, without being able to establish solid evidence to the contrary, weakened our defense.

"If that's the case and our ancestors killed Jesus, you should be happy. We did it for your sake or you would never have become Christians, don't you see!"

With this kind of argument, I occasionally got a bleeding nose or I had to run for it. I preferred, though this might sound weird, the bleeding nose to my fast footwork. A bleeding nose would soon be over, but the humiliation of running away from the gang of Walter Koenig's bullies made me feel miserable, the "coward" they would call me when I ran away remained like a dull pain.

"They are stronger, because there are more of them," my mother warned me.

"But why do they hate us, why do they lie? Are we really so different from 'them'?"

Many questions that could not be answered, or maybe the answers were considered too complicated for children. As far as I could judge, Christians and Jews wore the same clothes, spoke the same language, ate the same things. At least among our assimilated immediate Jewish neighbours I could detect no difference between "them" and "us." The essential difference was demonstrated in our places of worship. In our synagogue you found no ornaments, no statues of saints, no flowers, no incense, and no organ music. Above all no statue of our God. Our God, invisible by definition, gave rise to all sorts of prejudice. Either people said: "What can't be seen, can't be there" or "If you say you can't see your God how do you know he is not a pig or a dog?" Things like that. The abstract idea of the invisible God was obviously beyond them. The idea might have been beyond my conception as well but we had to defend His existence and no time for doubt.

"They are strong, but they have no brains, they can hit but they can't think. And because they are stronger, we have to be smarter, *because* they have muscle we have to show that we have intellect."

And when all these silly and misleading consolations didn't help us, we were treated to fabulous tales of David and Goliath and the pride and the heroic achievements of the Maccabees. And thus every historical or contemporary victory of the weak over the strong, the intelligent over the stupid, and the oppressed over their oppressors, served our "goal." To rebuild our courage and self-confidence we had to rebuild our country, the Land of Israel, and by rebuilding the country we would also ourselves be reborn. This was the ideological ammunition which fired my imagination. A barrel of mixed components: socialism, revolution, anarchy, discipline, fanatical belief in the "cause," and cool and collected self-confidence when facing an enemy.

Certainly, the ideas of socialism and communism were the most current intellectual coin in the thirties in Europe as well as in America, but our particular Jewish deviation from the Christian norm was that we saw in the rebuilding of the Land of Israel a messianic salvation for the entire world. Yet our primary concern was for dignity and self-respect, synonymous with the little word Zion.

When I was eight I received a blow to my right kidney during a friendly boxing match. Instead of water I passed blood. Ambulance. Emergency. Hospital. Even now, on certain wind-still afternoons I may *feel* the sleepy warmth of the hospital ward. I hear the flies on the windowpanes, the street traffic, footsteps crossing gravel in the courtyard, now and then a dead branch breaking off. Through the windows the broad green boughs of the chestnut tree are beckoning. Not a breath of air. Visiting hours between four and five only. Supper not long afterward. Washing and communal evening prayer. ("Father, now I seek repose / and my eyes in sleep I close / Father guard me while I sleep / from all harm Thy servant keep.") After prayers one of these kindly smiling nuns would come over

(all the nurses are nuns) and tie our hands down to the bed with leather straps. "So you won't fall out of bed," they say, but we know better. "So you won't play with yourself." I can't tell whether morals are still as closely watched in Viennese hospitals as they used to be in my time, but we were crucified to our beds like Jesus above the doorpost. There hung Jesus, arms outstretched in agony, head bowed in shame for being caught in the act. That's the way I understood it. My theological theories had found more and very unforeseen nourishment. Not we, but they. They did it, their own nuns, they punished Jesus for his sin. Yet what mystery! He who masturbates might also become divine.

Their own clergy might have put their own God to death for what He did or tried to do, but *I am innocent,* I don't touch myself, yet the curse of Christ, "May my blood come over you and your children," had visited me, had fulfilled itself on me. Blood flows from a wound upon which no hand may be laid. What had I done to deserve this?

Religion was no more important than soccer and soccer no more important than reading. Politics and sports we followed in the newspaper. Yet no kind of knowledge was rated more highly than book knowledge. Study, we were told, is the key to the future. From study comes knowledge, but knowledge cannot be found in schoolbooks only. Most knowledge was supposed to come from the difficult works of fiction by our sages Dostoevsky, Gogol, Gorki, Chekhov, Tolstoy, Zola and Wassermann, Stefan and Arnold Zweig, Morgenstern and Rilke. Our sages were poets and writers, the brilliant brains who knew how to hide "knowledge" in a simple story. Yet to know poems by heart was considered an even greater virtue than the reading of "difficult" books. Mothers urged their children to recite poems and rewarded them for it with cash. My uncle Theodor paid everytime with one or even two ice creams when I managed to recite by heart a little rhyme I had just made up.

Besides reading, writing was highly respected. Anyone who could write a few rhymes was certainly considered a future poet. People (other children especially) respected my mother's judgement because she herself wrote poems. Not surprisingly I wanted to write better poems than she did as long as I could remember.

We considered ourselves altogether an artistic family. My mother loved to write poems, had studied the violin; my father loved music (especially opera and operetta). My oldest sister was considered very talented in drawing fashion designs, my second sister "extremely gifted" in drawing and painting (at school she had the highest grades in the class), and I, of course, was the writer in the family, because I really never stopped writing and reading books (not just the difficult ones but also Edgar Wallace and Karl May). Some close cousins had studied medicine or architecture. We felt elated. Our more remote relatives, who had money, while we were fairly poor after the crash of 1929, were considered to have "nothing but money," hence we disliked or despised them. I am not sure which. Of course, a family blessed with artistic offspring feared for their future. Not art but arithmetic gets you into medical school. Naturally my mother hoped I would become a physician.

Fortunately for me, Hitler thwarted my mother's intentions: first, he closed our school and later sent me packing into exile, or I might have had to torment myself for eight long years with the cumbersome study of man's pathology.

As long as I can recall, we talked at home and with friends about emigrating, leaving, going far away to live. No one I knew planned to remain in Vienna for the rest of his or her life. Our home was only a few minutes' walk from the banks of the Danube and I was either eight or nine years old when I packed three sandwiches into a knapsack, cut myself a walking stick from a bush, and set out for Budapest, which supposedly was a town with golden roofs, only a few kilometers downstream. If not golden roofs I hoped to find there my father, who was never at home. When it got dark I had second thoughts and was happy a stranger brought me back. Yet, "sooner or later," I consoled myself, "I'll get out of here." In 1938 it was nearly too late.

Hell no, we didn't like home. Some of it, of course, but not all of it. It was no Home-Sweet-Home. Far from it. I remember home as rhymes and proverbs, desire and longing, phantasies and idealism, and a lot of anxiety and fear.

Above my parents' bed hung some nineteenth-century monsters in yellows, pinks, light blues, and white: fauns, nixies, elves, and water nymphs bathing, frolicking, and generally having a good time. Little fat cherubs were sailing through the air, little trumpets in their puffy palms. These blonde semi-gods (God only knows what they were doing on our Jewish walls), entertaining themselves in a pond or stream under willows and cypresses, suddenly and menacingly jumped out of their crummy gilded frames. Fauns, nymphs, and even cherubs, dressed in the white shirts and black ties and black velour breeches of the Hitler Youth, wearing daggers and black armbands with a huge black swastika, were now marching down our main street and shattering the peace of our Goethehof with drums and fanfares. And they sang:

Forward, forward!
The fanfares call

Forward! forward!
Youth know no perils!
With Hitler we march,
There is nothing we dread,
Carrying the banners of youth for freedom and
    bread.

And from all windows and not just in the Goethehof and not just in the main street, but also from churches, bridges, and other public buildings, as well from private homes, waved the new flag. No Viennese would have dared not to show his allegiance to the new government. The new red flag had a white circle, and in its center sat a black ugly spider: the swastika.

Now many Viennese say: "You know we had to, we had no choice." But even after all these years I am prepared to swear: "True, you had no choice. Sooner or later a man wears his heart on his sleeve." Sixteen hundred years of Catholic-inspired anti-Semitism were taking their toll in human misery and later in human life, now in twentieth-century quantities. In an age of overpopulation, when human life has become cheap, the life and fortunes of small groups have forfeited all their value.

The swastika, its very symbol, was a declaration of war against all real and imaginary enemies of the Third Reich.

And this Reich had many enemies and not just friends. True liberals, genuine communists, honest socialists, real nobility, loathed and despised the vulgarity and plain evil of the Nazis. In order to weaken and undermine the resolve of decent people to fight the Nazi insanity, Goebbels used "the Jewish spook, the Jewish danger, the Jewish-Imperialist-Bolshevist conspiracy" as a decisive factor in his propaganda campaign. By separating the fate of Jewish citizens from the fate of other citizens, disregarding whether or not the Jews en masse had asked for this role (Who can tell? Many might have even become Nazis, given the opportunity), by declaring THE JEWS as the Number One Enemy of the German people and the Aryan Race, the government ensured that any kind of association or expressed sympathy with the accursed could now be treated as an act of *Landesverrat* betrayal of the Fatherland—and did. Yet, to hate and loathe, accuse and insult in speech and print was evidently not enough to show how seriously they adhered to their convictions. Hence measures and special laws had to be introduced in order to manifest the Hitlerian teachings. The Fuehrer himself, while still in jail as a rabble-rouser in post-World War I Munich, had written in *Mein Kampf* ("My Struggle") in more than one passage that if and when he and his party came to power, he would force all Jews to leave Germany or kill them.

After his successful invasion of the Saarland and the Rhineland and his unhindered invasion of Austria, Hitler had to prove he meant business—to the world at large and to his people at home.

"How could it happen?" people ask me now, meaning the *Shoah*, the Holocaust.

The answer is simple: It could happen because we couldn't and wouldn't even dare to sit on a bench in the park when it said on it (in big black gothic letters) *Fuer Juden Verboten* ("Forbidden For Jews").

We also couldn't do anything against Nuremberg laws that forced people in mixed marriages to divorce, ordered non-Jewish servants to leave their Jewish employers, forbade Jewish doctors to attend to "Aryan" patients (except for Goering who secretly kept on his Jewish physician). It was these slow and gradual, seemingly unimportant anti-Jewish measures aimed at dividing the population as much as intimidating their will to resist that gradually, (as in Kafka's legend of the Metamorphosis) turned men into cockroaches which you may then kill without moral qualms and apparently with impunity.

A few of these special measures are worth remembering. 1) The letter J printed in the ID, 2) the middle name Israel or Sarah added to first names, 3) deportation of all stateless men (those who held no Austrian passports) back to their place of birth. A cruel and senseless decree depriving thousands of families of their breadwinner. The poor men were selected to go back "where they came from" by the whim of their "nationality." Later selections followed quite naturally on the ramps of Auschwitz and Treblinka.

My love, Berta Bella (I had met her in my youth club) vanished at the end of the summer of 1938, bound for Australia with her mother, after her father had been shipped off to Poland. Berta was gone and I restlessly walked the streets, looking at the parades and marches of the Nazis or wasting the little pocket money I had in the pinball machines of the Prater, Vienna's perennial fun fair where the world's fattest ladies, smallest dwarfs, giant Chinese, ghosts, dragons, and two-headed freaks entertained a gullible audience with cheap thrills. Not cheaper than Nazi parades, true, but much more fun.

Vienna Westbahnhof, the central station, cold, the lighting dim in December 1938, and weeping parents on the platform, as if the train had just come back in. A long train, its cargo children of all ages and backgrounds. Children with luggage, large pieces or small, bags and thermos flasks and packages of hard-boiled eggs, sticks of hard sausage. Children leaving for an everlasting holiday. For many of us the first journey abroad, and ourselves accordingly excited. I can still

Jakov Lind

Gerhard Hinterleitner/CONTRAST

hear the harmonica my friend Heinz Mühlrad played; he was "relocated" in 1942 and never came back. Few names and even fewer faces are distinct. It's as if the whole train had drowned in an ocean of tears. From ocean to ocean. From the ocean of bad dreams into an ocean of terror. In a few hours the train would arrive at the German border. A train full of Jewish children traveling through a *Reich* of Black Spiders. How could such a journey end well? Who'd be waiting for us at our destination? Who and what? We had no return tickets on that journey into no-man's-land. I recall nothing of it, except one image. Somewhere in Germany a child was standing—in long woolen leggings, woolen cap pulled down over his ears—at a crossing, and he waved at the train as it passed. That precisely this child, this so very ordinary sight, should have stuck in my mind, must signify something. I've thought about it a lot and never fathomed it. Nothing about this child's clothing, nothing about his behavior, was distinctive; thousands of children still stand at all the crossings in Germany (wearing, exactly as they did almost fifty years ago, woolen caps and leggings). I can offer only one explanation why the image stayed in my mind; it was distinctive because it was ordinary. Perhaps, we'd expected columns of storm troopers to pelt our train with stones all the way to the Dutch border. A German child who can't distinguish a train packed with Jewish children from an ordinary express train proved to me that an adventure need not be as dangerous as our parents would make us believe. Of course the child could be a dummy and the worst was still to come at the next crossing. Not to expect anything but the worst behind a courteous gesture was definitely wise counsel for the uninitiated traveller.

In *Niels Holgerson's Miraculous Journey* by Selma Lagerloeff (a best-selling author in the thirties and a children's favourite), Little Niels, much younger than I, boards the back of a wild goose in Sweden and reaches after many an adventure the Holy City of Jerusalem. If little Niels could, why not us? In Ockenburgh, not far from The Hague, hundreds of these little Holgersons, boys and girls between five and sixteen, waited to board their next ride. Still, too astonished at our own bravery, spoiled and pampered by grown-ups, who, for mysterious reasons loved us Jewish refugee children, we believed we had arrived at the most wonderful summer camp on earth. To be out of the German hell and away from under our parents' mournful looks. What more could one wish for?

Ockenburgh had long ago, it seemed, been the summer residence of a Count of Ockenburgh. The count's salons were now our dining rooms, and in his endless other rooms, we slept in bunks stacked three deep.

We learned to make our own beds. We also learned to ride bicycles and race the wind on the beach of Scheveningen. We learned a new game called *Honkbal* (a Dutch version of American baseball), something we had never heard of in Vienna. Many things were new to us. What still lingers in my mind is the loving yet no-nonsense attitude the Dutch have toward their children. Our special affection was for our sports teacher Mr. Lampe and for Henny Batist, his (and our) best friend. What a wonderful world when refugee children are treated like important personalities. For one: the grown-ups in Holland seemed to listen to what a child had to say, something we were not used to in Vienna, where they treat children to this day like backward midgets. In fact I loved Holland and everything Dutch so much and so spontaneously, I hardly knew *how* I could speak Dutch that quickly, learning it within a few weeks. My first foreign language was Dutch, and Dutch is the language of tolerance and love for our fellowman. The philosopher Erasmus of Rotterdam was both Catholic and tolerant, a humanist who spoke and wrote Dutch. It was getting a little confusing. Christians who do not hate Jews? What next? In Vienna anti-Semitism had been endemic, traditional, and spontaneous, if not always out in the open. In Holland it seemed to be practically the other way round. Most Dutch people loved Jews and said so openly, while those who didn't kept their feelings to themselves, at least for the time being. If gentiles are no longer our enemy, what need is there for a country of our own?

What use was there for my Zionist ideals which had consoled and inspired me over the past few years, strengthened my resolve: "May I forget thee, O Jerusalem, may my right hand wither," just as it said in the prayerbooks, for which I had otherwise no particular fondness. Our anthem was called *Hatikvah*—("Hope"), and what distinguished us from the non-Zionists was just this Hope, "the principle of hope," as Ernst Bloch, the German-Jewish philosopher, called it later.

What would happen to the others who could not get out? What would happen to our parents and the rest of our friends and our family and the parents of our friends and their families? First of all, there was no chance for all to escape. Second, I didn't like the cowardice and the humiliation of running away. I hated myself for having run away, for not having stayed behind to fight the bastards.

From the eyes of our heroes shone strength, courage and self-confidence. Whether they were calling us to fight our enemies with the gun, like Jabotinsky and Trumpeldor, or preached peace, like A. D. Gordon and Arlosoroff, or wrestled in the corridors of world politics, like Ben-Gurion and Weizmann. Self-confidence was in their eyes.

How can one trust gentle Christian humanists? We certainly distrusted our own Jewish agnostic humanists who argued cleverly against both Zionists and Communists that all humans were basically (!) one big brotherhood. Of course all mankind was one big brotherhood, but only after we Jews had become equals among equals. To be just like the others, yet, of course, not exactly the same. This accent on insisting on our difference, just so we may be like everyone else, was the universally applicable teaching of Zionism.

In the marathon of ideologies the humanists had cleverly attempted to steal our prophetic mission by putting the cart before the horse. Universal brotherhood, yes, what else? But first be accepted as a brother in the family of man. To call yourself humane and to serve universal humane interests sounded like deceptive lies. Hitler was then a humanist, too. He tried to save the entire world from what he termed the Jewish-Bolshevist pest. Stalin no less, by getting rid of anyone who ridiculed or denounced his megalomanic utopia of a just world, could claim to speak for all the oppressed people on the globe.

All these grand saviours of humanity were blood-thirsty monsters (though I admit, out of sheer hatred of Hitler, we didn't believe it when Nazis maligned the Communists).

In all earnestness political discussions among us children reflected the current divisions among grown-ups, except that we were more passionate and maybe more honest than they. Our real opponents were, of course, the orthodox kids who loathed us atheists—left, right, or centre. They claimed to know it all or para-doxically to know nothing, leaving all knowledge to the Creator who had spoken to His servant Moses and given him the laws and commandments, which were naturally beyond dispute.

Blessed are the believers, we mocked them, while they called us stubborn and arrogant and predicted that we atheists would be the first to be punished by God. The irony, of course, was that it was the orthodox Jews and their children, defenseless and pacifist as they were, who rallied voluntarily to be slaughtered when called up to do so a few years later, while atheists and Zionists, socialists and communists had no qualms in resisting God's will and His apparent scourge.

The fairly orthodox but not ultraorthodox Zionists were a class apart. They had a point when they claimed Jews had only remained Jews over two thou-sand years of diaspora by adhering to ancient ritual. They also made their point with the non- and anti-Zionists by proclaiming that the physical labour and personal hardship suffered by us Palestine Pioneers de-manded our *voluntary action* "for the love of Zion" and nothing else.

Convinced or not by the importance of Jewish re-ligious ritual, I still wasn't used to eating kosher or avoiding public transport on the Sabbath. I certainly wouldn't let them talk me out of riding a bicycle on Saturday. Genetically conditioned or not, but just like my father, I didn't like spending time in a synagogue, yet suffered these weekly excursions voluntarily be-cause it was the only way of getting extra visits to the city, The Hague.

On one of these visits, it must have been Septem-ber 1, 1939, I saw the headlines in all the newspapers and sensed an excitement in our sleepy, peaceful, new country. OORLOG! ("War"). England and France had declared war after the Germans had begun to in-vade Poland. War! What it meant in reality, not in headlines, we still had to learn. After all borders were declared closed, we barely had a chance ever to see our parents again. Overnight my sisters, fifteen and ten, and I, age twelve, were no longer children.

Responsible for ourselves, from now on, we had also become responsible for the thoughts and deeds of others; maybe even for everything that happened in the world at large. Or so it seemed to me at the time. That's why all our fights from then on were to be even more meaningful, and the linguistic, semantic differ-ences between ourselves and the children from Ham-burg, Cologne, or Berlin even more important. As it became more obvious day by day that we would not soon return to our homes in Vienna or Berlin, if ever, and never again speak German except among our-selves, it now mattered as never before whether or not *Chinese* is pronounced *Kinese* (as we did in Vienna) or *Shinese* (as they did in Germany). These were differ-ences beyond politics and religious traditions.

Instead of *schauen* the Germans said *gucken* (see-ing), and neither threats nor insults (like: Stupid *Piefke*!) could prevent a German child from breaking up laughing when we said *Ananas* to a strawberry and *Ribisel* (redcurrant) and *Ogrosel* (gooseberry) instead of *Stachelbeere*.

Our fights, rarely conducted with fists or sticks, though even that occasionally happened, felt no less serious than the war between England and Germany. Our weapons were passion and sarcasm, fiery speeches and biting irony. Friendly, peaceful arms, compared to what "they" had used against the unfortunate Poles who were overrun by Germans from the West and the Red Army from the East.

Until 1940, until the Germans invaded the Nether-lands, life went on quite normally in this mar-vellous haven of civility. Since November I had been living with a lively and rather cultured Dutch-Jewish-Zionist family, the van Sons, in Bussum, near Amster-dam. I went to school on my bicycle and tried to learn skating on the canals and ponds near our house. Even the first year of German occupation passed fairly un-eventfully for us in the provinces, but then the anti-Jewish laws followed one another in rapid sequence. Public transport, restaurants, shops, and not just the benches in the park. Theatre, cinema, concert halls. For Jews no longer allowed. VOOR JODEN VERBO-DEN. ("Forbidden for Jews.")

The same message—but now in Dutch. What next? Sometime near the end of 1940 I had moved from Bussum to Gouda (world reknown for its cheeses) where I had entered an agricultural preparatory school (*Hachsharah*) modelled on the life of a collective farm, a kibbutz in Palestine. We learned to grow tomatoes and lettuce, prune apple trees, and harvest potatoes, all this with an eye on the future in Palestine. A future barely thinkable, a phantasy, a dream.

The new German laws ordered all Jews to leave the provinces and concentrate in Amsterdam by 1942. Young men had been rounded up earlier, especially those between the ages of eighteen and thirty, and were carted off to Mauthausen, the infamous concentration camp near Linz in Austria, where most arrivals perished in the quarries within a week or ten days. Why learn to grow mushrooms? What one needed now were forged identity papers to turn oneself into a mushroom and vanish underground. Shortly before our school in Gouda was officially closed I moved to Amsterdam. The Jewish Refugee Committee, still feeling responsible for their charges under sixteen, provided me with an address of another family. Just in time to watch the ongoing daily deportations as a spectator, just in time to learn the tricks of escaping a dragnet.

Now life depended on a piece of paper, on the ID. In the beginning even an ID with the big black printed letter "J" on it could extend your life if it carried the stamp "until further notice deferred from work in Germany." But when gradually, week by week and day by day, these lifesaving words were being ignored by the Dutch and German police who did the Gestapo's dirty work, only one last hope was left: the forged ID.

On June 20, 1943, I slipped out and away from what was probably the final big roundup of Amsterdam Jews, most of them having left before when called up by the first letters of their surnames. (A-F report at 8:00 A.M. sharp at the railway stations . . . bring no more than twenty kilos of hand luggage. Non-compliance with the order is punishable by special hard labour, etc.) On June 20 the action started at dawn, and was completed by six or so. With the help of comrades (Palestine Pioneers) working with the resistance, I had a new address the same day. For the first time, as I walked about Amsterdam without the yellow star, making sure my little sister and her foster parents had survived the calamity (my older sister had fortunately left for Palestine three weeks before the German invasion of Holland), I felt the meaning of the word resurrection. To be walking in the sun alive! What other blessings could one possibly pray for?

I had to spend two entire weeks, which seemed excruciatingly long, hiding in five rooms with four other children, until I finally received my new ID. I became Jan Gerard Overbeek, born January 17, 1926, in Aalten, province of Gelderland, by profession: labourer. The new ID was my new set of aqualungs, but they still needed testing. A week or so later I had my major trial with many more to follow. I had received an address where I would work on a farm. The farmer was, of course, not to know anything about my true identity. Anyway, here I was working on the farm near Utrecht. One day, while I was turning the hay, two Dutch policemen on their motorcycle with sidespan came driving up the meadow to check our papers. After they left we (Theo, the other farmhand, and I) had

the following little chat:

Theo: "It's not us these bastards are after. They are sniffing around for Jews."

"You think so, Theo?"

"The poor devils can't help being Jews."

"Right. They can't, Theo."

"If I were a Jew, Jan, I wouldn't let myself be carted off like a sheep."

"What would you do, Theo?"

"Me? I'd get myself a forged ID and I'd go to work on a farm."

"I agree. I'd do the same."

To make a long story short I ended up working in Germany as a deckhand on a Rhine riverbarge and stayed in Germany until the end of the war in May 1945. I'd never thought I would go to Germany of my own free will, but when the alternative was waiting to be picked up and sent to Poland, I knew what I had to do. In November 1944 in Marburg, I had a chance meeting with Mr. H., a German civilian in charge of what he said was metallurgical research for the Reich's Ministry of Aviation. In fact it was nuclear research. My humble job was to deliver brown manila envelopes my employer refused to trust to the haphazard postal services, as he put it. After Hitler had committed suicide and I felt safe to reveal my identity, Mr. H. confessed to me that for several years now he had been passing on the results of their research to the Allies, via a corporation in Switzerland. In fact I had been carrying much of this information with me in those brown manila envelopes I'd been delivering by hand. Without knowing it, I had assisted a German who spied for the Allies and employed a Jewish lad from Vienna, who made believe he was a Dutch bargesailor. We were equals in deception. When British troops occupied Kellinghusen, north of Hamburg on May 10, 1945, a nightmare that had lasted exactly five years had come to an end. In two works of fiction, *Soul of Wood* and *Landscape in Concrete,* and in one work of autobiography, *Counting My Steps,* I wrote about those years in detail. Five years of millions of minutes of fear. Fear of breathing, fear of falling asleep. Fear of using the wrong word, or looking the wrong way.

The war came and went, a natural calamity. In May 1945 entire cities were reduced to ashes, wherever you looked you saw half-demented, walking skeletons emerging from medieval torture chambers and dungeons called concentration camps, shadows in rags had come out into the sun. The fobs of political opportunists who all now denied ever having been Nazis and their despicable collaborators hurriedly shuffled away into hiding, shedding their swastikas and opinions like snakes shed their skin in spring. May 1945 was a beau-

Jakov Lind at the Goethehof in Vienna. The sign to his right reads, "Never Forget"

tiful warm spring. I came back from Germany to Amsterdam and then went to Palestine via France with many survivors from the camps. Their pink cheeks looked strangely healthy until I found out that those with the pink cheeks suffered from TB, while the others were not yet in fit state to travel. There was much

travelling going on in Europe in those days with barely any cars on the road, no air transport, few buses, but many trains. The Nazi fat cats, those who had the right connections and plenty to account for, travelled to Peron's Argentina, to Chile and Brazil, to Franco's Spain, or to the capitals of the Middle East where they could hustle their experience in cold-blooded terror to new masters who fought the survivors of a catastrophe with all the means at their disposal.

BIBLIOGRAPHY

Fiction

Eine Seele aus Holz: Erzählungen. Neuwied, Germany: Luchterhand, 1962. Translation by Ralph Menheim published as *Soul of Wood, and Other Stories.* London: J. Cape, 1964; New York: Grove, 1965.

Landschaft in Beton. Neuwied, Germany: Luchterhand, 1963. Translation by Ralph Manheim published as *Landscape in Concrete.* London: Methuen, 1966; New York: Grove, 1966

Eine bessere Welt. Berlin: Wagenbach, 1966. Translation by Ralph Manheim published as *Ergo.* London: Methuen, 1967; New York: Random House, 1967.

Der Ofen. Translation from the English by Günther Danehl and Jakov Lind. Salzburg: Residenz Verlag, 1973; also published as *The Stove: Short Stories.* New York: Sheep Meadow, 1983.

Travels to the Enu: The Story of a Shipwreck (novella). London: Methuen, 1982; New York: St. Martin's, 1982.

Nonfiction:

Counting My Steps: An Autobiography. New York: Macmillan, 1969; London: J. Cape, 1970.

Numbers: A Further Autobiography. New York: Harper, 1972; London: J. Cape, 1973.

Israel: Rückkehr für 28 Tage ("Twenty-eight Days Return"). Translation from the English by E. Tranger. Frankfurt am Main: S. Fischer, 1972.

The Trip to Jerusalem. New York: Harper, 1973; London: J. Cape, 1974.

Published Plays:

Anna Laub (radio play). Berlin: Luchterhand, 1965.

Die Heiden: Spiel in 3 Akten. Translation from the English by Erich Fried. *Das Sterben der Silberfüchse* (radio play). Neuwied, Germany: Luchterhand, 1965.

Angst und Hunger (radio plays). Berlin: K. Wagenbach, 1968.

Ergo: A Comedy (dramatization; based on *Ergo*). New York: Hill and Wang, 1968.

The Silver Foxes Are Dead, and Other Plays (includes *Anna Laub, Hunger, Fear.*) Translation by Ralph Manheim. London: Methuen, 1968; New York: Hill and Wang, 1969.

Plays—Selected Productions:

Ergo, produced by Joseph Papp at the Public Theater, New York, 1968.

Fear, produced at Workshop of the Players Art, New York, 1973.

Anna Laub, produced in London, 1974.

The Ditch, adapted from *Anna Laub* and directed by Ann Scofied, produced at Theater of the Open Eye, New York, 1982.

Sound Recordings:

The Writing of Jakov Lind. New York: J. Norton, 1974.

Barry N. Malzberg

1939-

NOTES TOWARD AN AUTOBIOGRAPHY

Willam Gaddis was at Fairleigh Dickinson down the block the other evening, speaking to an audience of twenty-two for a well-publicized appearance (I should know better by now but do not; I was bitter about the turnout even if Gaddis seemed perturbed not the slightest), and remembered some lines he had written a long time ago about the silliness of those who wanted to meet writers. "What is any writer but the shambles of his work, who is any writer but the empty shell who follows the work around?" Something like that. I am paraphrasing. I am not taking the time to look this up; we science fiction writers, we commercial toilers in the vineyards of literacy, we learn to cut a few corners here and there.

Not bad, I thought. "The shambles of his work, the empty shell who follows the work around." I take this to be true. Along with Woolrich's "I didn't learn to live; I learned to write." Along with Robert Sheckley's "It is very hard to learn from something you already know." All of these are true. The interesting thing about prose fic, as we like to call it, is that almost *anything* you say about it is true, at least some of the time.

The shambles of the work.

*

In "Corridors" (1982), the last chapter in a book composed of thoughts about science fiction, I put it another way: Ruthven, a fifty-seven-year-old sf writer and pretty bitter about all of it, ends a guest of honor speech at the Cincinnati World Science Fiction Convention (which I did not then but would, I think, now have the wit to call "Sincon"):

"We tried . . . I want you to know that, that even the worst of us, the most debased hack, the one-shot writer, the fifty-book series, all the hundreds and thousands of us who ever wrote a line of this stuff for publication: we tried. We tried desperately to say something because we were the only ones who could and however halting our language, tuneless the song, it was ours.

"We wanted to celebrate, don't you see? We wanted to celebrate the insistent, circum-

Barry Malzberg at the 1980 Philcon
Sci-Fi Conference, Philadelphia

Jay Kay Klein

stantial fact of the spirit itself, that wherever and in whatever form the spirit could yet sing amidst the engines of the night, that the engines could extinguish our lives but never our light and that in the spaces between, we could still thread our colors of substantiation. In childhood nights we felt it, later we lost it, but retrieval was always the goal, to get back there, to make it work, to justify ourselves to ourselves, to give the light against the light. We tried and failed; in a billion words we failed and failed again, but throughout was our prayer and somewhere in its center lived something else, the mystery and power of what might have been flickering.

"In these spaces, in all the partitions,

hear our song. Let it be known that while given breath we sang until it drew the very breath from us and extinguished our light forever."

And then, "in hopeless and helpless fury . . . Ruthven pushes aside the microphone and cries."

Somewhat less sentimentally (but for all I know, therefore less truthfully), I had another opinion in "The Man Who Married a Beagle," a short story written almost exactly a decade ago now, and four years earlier than "Corridors":

> *Life is not an ending; life is a process, I later came to understand, and it was exactly at that moment and in a way ten times worse than the first, that the pain began again.*

Well, yes. Something like that. *Not an ending but a process.* You have to be at a certain age to understand this, and it is an understanding which might well have you pushing aside the microphone and crying. Or would turn you into a fair simulacrum of a washed-up novelist, somewhat before your natural time.

Buried in your work are all kinds of messages, little grenades, timed to go off ten years or more later; buried those little messages to the elder self up the line, down the line, following the work around.

*

In 1975 I embarked upon what I later called "the most relentless self-exposition of any contemporary science fiction writer." Self-pitying bleats in Fanzine X and vengeful rejoinder in professional magazine Y and truly furious gauntlet-throwing in semi-professional magazine Z, reminiscent, nostalgic, high-toned essays in publications A, B, C *and* D. I had a good deal to say about my career or lack of it in science fiction but was also a lot more cunning than ever credited: throughout those tens of thousands of words of ontology and eschatology, musings and recrimination, I managed to say nothing about: a) my childhood, b) adolescence, c) inner life as an adult (if adults have inner lives). No one ever pointed this out, that the ruminative, professorial, frantically confessing M was committing no indecent act.

But then again, my rationalization which might have been no rationalization at all was that childhood, growing up, high school, junior high school, flailing in the waters of Riis Park or Schroon Lake or the hard time that Evelyn Kramer (may she have a mustache!) gave me when I was seventeen was *already* on display; it was in the Collected Works, sometimes in the interstices but often enough (*pace* Girodias) up front: virtually every line was central, internal, and there was no need, then, to take off an already transparent mask

and give the little details which in the nature of things would be less interesting than the fiction anyway. "What is a man compared to his work?" Big Ernie from Ketchum asked somewhere, and I lived by that dictum. I figured I was self-evident as a puppy, anyway, and that it was more important to make my case as a writer and within the terms of my public career. So I had almost nothing to say about Flatbush Avenue, David Bachrach, Syracuse University, Robinson's home run over the wall in the first inning of the first baseball game I ever saw (in 1951) in Ebbets Field. I had nothing to say of Herbert Finney, later entombed in *Beyond Apollo* (1972), Darlene Shapiro, Miriam Grzebenian (three whom I thought I loved as well by seventeen as all the rest to come). I didn't discuss what it was like to play second violin in the Midwood Symphony under a vitriolic and insulting Benjamin S. Chancey (oh my, oh my! as I wrote someone in 1980, *every* writer should be a weak second violinist; it will teach you humility . . . if Heinlein had been a second violin he would have been incapable of most of his later work) or what a truly wretched time Evelyn Kramer (may she have a mustache!) gave me because she was in love with my best friend who didn't even *like* her and regarded me as a friend. As a "friend." She wrote me all that after she got engaged to yet another guy.

I figured that stuff was all to be inferred from the work itself. Maybe I was right, perhaps I was not, but thinking about all this in light of further and further developments has, with a tip of the hat to Dr. Johnson, concentrated the mind most wonderfully.

*

On December 26, 1962, near the dawn, I put a 1956 pink DeSoto Firedome into a guardrail on the Saw Mill River Parkway in Yonkers at fifty miles an hour, and I do believe that if I had lost consciousness as I went gliding through the windshield instead of managing to crawl from that doomed car in the cold or that if I had not been taken back to the toll booth by an anonymous, sainted figure whose headlights had found me crawling on the pavement and over whose back seat I so cheerlessly and rapidly bled, I would have died. No more work, no work at *all* as a matter of fact.

I had had vague ambitions, well a little more than vague for that time: writing workshops with Donald Dike, two stories in *Syracuse 10* in the 1959-60 academic year (pretty terrible, the mannered second not as awful as the tragic first), maybe 150 pages of fiction all told through my twenty-first year but I had written virtually nothing in the years between graduation and the accident, figuring that I would get around to it later or not at all. No problem either way. Life, let alone the commission of fiction, was all too much for me and you know exactly who you are.

So it was rather a shock; I could have died and my absence would have been noted for a little while by parents and sister, maybe a few others would have had gainful employment patching a guardrail but essentially there I would have been, extinguished. "Hey there, Mac, I don't want to be extinguished," the inner voice pointed out, "not quite yet and that was a pretty close one; you better get going because this is Second Chance City. Better do some writing, huh, Mac?"

Yeah, I guess so. I did some writing. It took me two years to get at all good and three years to sell anything and five years to begin to have anything approximating a consistent record of sales, but I was kind of driven by then. Oh yes. I had, like the Common Man in Peter Weiss's *Marat/Sade*, Big Plans.

*

Almost twenty-one years later, lying in the emergency room at Holy Name Hospital, the I.V. tubes in and out of the arms and veins and wrist and nose, just a precautionary measure you understand, but fifteen extra PVCs a minute is kind of, well, *ominous* and if you follow what I'm saying and look at this chart from the EKG you'll note that if this line went up just a little *more*, not much, well your heart could begin to fibrillate and then you'd die: I think you'd better plan to stay with us overnight . . . as I was saying, almost twenty-one years later, I had another excuse to stare at the ceiling of an emergency room and ask questions. You have to understand, Mac, that thanks to you there were this time about eight million words published: seventy-five novels and almost three hundred short stories, some essays too, a book of essays, reviews, even a poem . . . well, you know how it is with us commercial writers, we never quite mean to get that deep into the business but the assignments come and the windows open and they might close any time and there's this and that . . . one kind of proliferates.

Mac had been asked, "Why did you stop? What are you going to do now? How can you get into it?" The questions at Holy Name (*pace* Gaddis) were similar but, as they say, different. "Why did you get into it? What did you think you were doing? Why did you waste your life? Are you out far *enough*?"

Fibrillation.

David Bachrach got me into reading science fiction. It was early 1951 and I was in class 6-3 at Public School 119, the third best reader and the best speller in Miss Hemenway's class. Bachrach brought home a whole bunch of Groff Conklin anthologies from the Flatlands library and back date *Astounding*s from Stephen's Book Service and told me I had better start

reading. It was important stuff. Bachrach's IQ was 162 and he was in the Special Progress class at Cunningham Junior High; I certainly wanted to listen to him. Most of the science fiction was opaque, abstruse, almost impenetrable to my twelve-year-old mind (interestingly, Robert Silverberg writing in *Hell's Cartographers* about his first experiences with *Astounding* in 1948 reported the same response from a thirteen-year-old but seven years later he was *selling* that market; me, I was no prodigy) but every now and then there was a name, a story (Tenn/Kuttner/Padgett were the ones to look for) that would take me bolt upright. David Bachrach was going to be the science fiction writer but in the summer of 1952 he just got too obnoxious and so we never met again, I never even talked to him on the phone after 1953 and I have no idea, unless I am missing a *really* buried pseudonym in the Linebarger class, what happened to him. And by 1952 I was into Horace Gold's magnificent early *Galaxy* which suited me much better indeed.

But I was still the guy who was going to write (if he would write anything) literature. I wasn't scientific enough for science fiction, I said. Didn't even like it. No, it was going to be literature for sure. By 1955 I had found *Look Homeward, Angel* and I had settled it for sure; I was going to be Thomas Wolfe and get laid and die young and make a big name for myself and it was going to be terrifically consequential. I sold out my science fiction collection.

*

Well, that was the first time I sold it out. I sold it again in 1958, having reaccumulated magazines, because I was facing my junior year in college and it was time to get serious. And then in 1964 when I got married and moved to Syracuse to be the Schubert Foundation Playwrighting Fellow, I dumped it for good and real . . . if Schubert's legatees or *The Hudson Review* learned that I had the stuff around, that would be the end.

*

When the younger daughter, Erika (9/16/70) was in the seventh grade, her English teacher assigned a book in every genre for a report. Erika wrote a note: she wouldn't read science fiction. She would substitute an extra mystery or *three* "serious" novels but no science fiction. "I would be happy if every science fiction book and writer were taken away," she said. (As with Gaddis, I am paraphrasing just a little, but you get the idea.) She had to read Madeleine L'Engle, anyway. The teacher was a little surprised to find out—many months later—one of the occupations of Erika's father.

But, then—as I relentlessly maintained in my relentlessly self-expository period—50 percent of my production from the outset had been out of the field of science fiction. So there, Erika.

*

The Schubert Foundation was a fluke. I was no one's playwrighting fellow and had, in fact, never attempted dramatic form until the trust for the two most hated men on Broadway in their time, always excepting Jed Harris, put $2500 into hand and said, in effect, "Pretend you're playwrighting." I had applied to the Syracuse graduate creative writing program and had tried for a fellowship but all four had been committed to the Harvard and Bennington and University of Michigan Hopwood bunch and something else had to be worked out. (The Harvard guy had a kind of semi-academic career with a couple of novels, one of the Bennington girls later became a psychiatrist and the other published one novel, the Hopwood poet was a whole different legend but none of them had a real career.) Without some kind of financial assistance, I could not enroll, I said. This was almost true, I *could* have come but it would have meant taking money from my new wife who had offered to stay in the city and at her job and send weekly checks, but I was not cold-blooded enough then or now to accept that arrangement. If Jack Woodford's advice, "If you must be a writer or die, why don't you just die? millions have every day without permanent aftereffects," was brought to mind, well then surely, I would rather die.

But death or the civil service follies (a tautology!) was not necessary; things worked out because the Schuberts had given Syracuse a graduate fellowship, were handing them out to universities all over the country in that season, and Syracuse in its wisdom had absolutely no one to whom to award it, not a warm body in the drama department who could be persuaded to don a playwright's mask. "Any ideas?" Gerald Reidenbaugh, Chairman of Drama, asked Sanford B. Meech, Chairman of English, in 7/64. "Well," Meech might have said (might not), "maybe one, there's this guy who says he needs a fellowship; he probably can't write plays but then again we've looked at the stories he sent with the application and he can't write fiction either." In any case, they let me have it.

It was a good thing. I liked it. If there had been any credible career in this country for a playwright (and I could not see one if I crawled on my knees with a magnifying glass; there was Kopit and Gelber and Albee; only poets, I thought, had it worse than playwrights in the mid-sixties), I probably would have abandoned fiction before I got so deeply in. The fellowship gave the opportunity to lurk around the Regency Theatre a mile from campus and watch faculty and graduate student-directors fit the student productions together from the beginning. It let me fool around with plays (I wrote five terrible one-acters and one terrible long one, and a pretty good long one and a terrific one-acter) in addition to the fiction that I was working on concurrently. Only the good one-act was produced and that on a weekday afternoon in the workshop theatre, but the good long one, *Stone*, was novelized a year later as *Death to the Keeper* and although that novel was never published, I was able to extract a novelette of the latter which appeared in the 8/68 *Fantasy and Science Fiction* and which was almost as good as the 4/68 "Final War," my first sale to that magazine. Most importantly, most lovingly, it enabled me to know actors.

They are fine people, actors; they are just like the rest of us, only better looking and even more vulnerable, dedicated from the beginning of consciousness to accessibility, and even bad ones are good in the bravest of ways. They are ingenuous, childlike, easily fractured, easily restored, eager to please, at the mercy of directors everywhere, and fearless in their fear. The women, even unto the most beautiful, are shy and wounded and the men are stouthearted, knowing that all of it can be taken so swiftly by audience, so painfully by time. None of the Syracuse actors went on to a major career, but a few of them got into television, regional theatre, the fringes of the New York theatre, and I loved them all, even the ones I did not like. In aggregate, they are the best people I have ever known, excepting only career army noncoms who are extraordinary.

I never wrote a play after 5/65 when *Stone* was completed and never even thought it possible after, say, the summer of that year, but the Schubert loss was my gain; wherever I went from there, whatever I did was easier than playwrighting. It was absolutely liberating in its modest fashion; playwrighting was almost impossible, I fought it every step of the way; it was perhaps the only thing that came hard to me in which I nonetheless persisted to become good. (I never got good on the violin.) Novels were a banquet; short stories were popsicles after *Stone*. Jimmy Breslin asked in 1969 why he was involved in a crazy political campaign for city council president that he would surely lose; he answered, "Listen, *anything* is easier than writing." Writing is easier than playwrighting. Or so I felt, so it seemed in those murderous but somehow comprehensible late sixties when piece by piece, inch by inch, even as the land was falling apart, the writer was finding his material, falling only in place, steady, steady at the helm of self.

*

Oh it is true, how true it is, fast Eddie, I wrote in the afterword to an anthology (*Uncollected Stars*, 1986);

Jay Kay Klein

*A panel discussion at the 1973 Lunacon Science-Fiction Conference in New York: from left,
Harlan Ellison, Barry Malzberg, Lester del Rey, Fred Pohl, and Hans Stefan Santesson*

I do have an affection for losers. But one must understand this, one must always understand: it is possible to learn things from losing that winning will never teach. If all of my work from the outset came from Scott Fitzgerald's "authority of failure" (and I never felt otherwise, was framed by a sense of loss before I had even found the wardrobe of literacy), then that made the work a kind of testimony. I was not only giving voice to the losers but, unlike so many of the naturalistic writers who had taught me, I was not patronizing them. The difference between patronization and truth is the difference between, say, Michael Gold and Nelson Algren: if you could see the difference as I learned, then it was possible to invoke testimony.

Algren, the Man with the Golden Arm, passed briefly through Syracuse in that academic year; he was a pretty good guy. When I learned years later that he had moved to Paterson to write a book on Hurricane Carter, I wanted to get in touch but the number was unlisted so I didn't. They were going to let him into the Academy of Arts and Letters one spring but instead, he died.

*

I think that to write fiction—and despite the essays, the criticism and the scutwork for Scott Meredith which has been my former and latter fate, I have never considered myself anything other than a fiction writer in or out of hiding—is to attempt to organize what is for the writer the otherwise chaotic and uncontrollable surface which he takes as life, Delmore Schwartz's "wound of consciousness," if you will. To find some kind of structure, some order, however arcane, in this, is that impulse which drives the work from inception and to learn to do it at all well is to be able to transmute, to control.

Hence, the composition of an autobiography, that naked, kindly face at last so revealed, is the antithesis of everything I had thought painfully learned in these four decades; to come out and give the facts and data was to attack that control or detachment (but only in print, only in print) to which I had dedicated the working life. If I was able, at least now and then, to get it done right in fiction, how could I be blamed for getting it wrong in life?

Well, it was a question.

In August 1970 I was in the midst of *Underlay* (1974), my metaphysical horse-racing novel, sequel to

Overlay (1972) but oh so much more, really running with the central scenes of what has turned out to be my favorite if least-known good work (Roger Sale in *The Hudson Review* gave the only review; he called the writer "a good paperback hack") when my father called. "Your mother is in the hospital," he said, "they're operating on her gall bladder. It seems she made a bit of a pig of herself up there in the mountains."

The old man (10/25/96–8/10/79) was splendidly matter of fact. "No, I don't think there's anything you can do," he said. This was back at 164 West Seventy-ninth Street in New York; I was typing and phoning and smoking and chattering away in that odorous maid's room which was displayed, *maledetto*, in *Herovit's World* (1973). "I'll be in touch." Michael Malzberg always fulfilled commitments.

I allowed that this would be expected and replaced the phone and as Celia Alice Finebaum Malzberg (4/12/04–10/1/82), lay under the knife, I mirthlessly, busily, wrote another ten thousand words of *Underlay*, first draft right to final, like almost everything else in those years. Mothers come and fathers go, but novels, I felt, were forever, or at least for a larger piece of forever than the other stuff. When my father called a couple of hours later to report a successful outcome, he almost had to remind me of the circumstances.

This intensity can come only at a certain point, usually fairly early, in a working career. It is a meaningful intensity, albeit one fueled by equal parts of self-delusion and self-revulsion and it can lead to fine work. But you pay, you pay for this kind of commitment. You pay then and for the rest of your life in inexplicable and rigorous ways which can barely, like the slurred speech of the brain-damaged fighter reacting to ten thousand forgotten blows, be measured.

*

But of course that phrase is an echo of something the late (1928-1982) science fiction writer Philip K. Dick wrote near the end of his life: "I tell you, wives come and lovers go, but we science fiction writers are forever." On and on, that is true, blood and bile mingled, old times and new times, history and outcome bound; of this community there is no sundering nor is death itself a parting, the consequences and rumors just go on and on; to fail to understand this, to think that one can perpetrate a large body of work and yet stand isolated from the template of "science fiction" is to misunderstand, perhaps dangerously, the course of one's life. What we know, only science fiction writers know, but it is a knowledge not to be communicated through solemn, formal memoir. It is of Ruthven's nights of recollection, it is through that attempt to get back

there, it is through the failing to get back over and again, of which we must construct those approximations of intention which are testimony.

*

In one of the autobiographical anthologies in this series, I read X's statement; he is a writer whom I have always inordinately admired, his earlier novels and short stories influencing me enormously, making me see that a certain kind of glacial control which would admit passion through leaving it out was possible. X is a private, an insular man of whose personal life I know little and of whose professional history I know only simple facts; I was intrigued by the possibility of learning something about him.

Reading attentively, I was intrigued instead by the ability that X showed in his long memoir to seem absolutely forthcoming while telling nothing. His essay was a masterpiece of evasion disguised as confidence, a kind of triumph of technique over material. Of his loves, his losses, his accommodations to career and later decline we could apprehend nothing, so splendidly did X fail to tell. It was as triumphant, as artful as his novel, Y, which had had such effect upon me. (Although now, two decades later, I am kind of on to the trick. You refuse to grant specifics and let the reader, by filling them in on his own, feel the more implicated because of co-authorship. Hemingway talked about it some.)

This was an approach I never learned. I never learned to say much but to reveal almost nothing. The waters didn't run exactly the other way—no, I was not a New England laconic saying little, implying much. Instead, in the best tradition of my life and times, I was the guy from Flatbush who has a Big Mouth; that is to say, I would learn to talk a lot and reveal too much. Brooklyn was full of people like this, probably still is. No wonder Walter O'Malley, a rather more taciturn type, it is understood, took the Dodgers and the oil deeds for Chavez Ravine and stuffed the politicians' promises in their faces, hurtled out of town, hurtled west, took the point of Brooklyn away just when I was trying to figure out how I could get out of the place myself.

*

O'Malley died two or three days after my father, and reading the obituary, I wanted to phone and say, "Look at this, Dad, we survived the bastard," but of course we didn't, not quite. James T. Farrell, a man who had more in common with O'Malley and my father than any of the three could have judged, also died right around then, in his sleep, quickly, the draft of the novel on which he had been working on the desk. Working until the very end. Which is the only way, the only answer, unless it turns out not to be.

Many things turn out not to be in your thirties or forties, as most of us sensitive, artistic types are prone to learn. Also the insensitive, inartistic types. The accretion of chronology, the weight and irreversibility of it, will make philosophers of us all.

*

I took thirty stitches in four places on the forehead and over an eyebrow and despite the doctor's promise that age would smooth them out, I can see those scars any time I want. Seven months after the guardrail, I was in Anatole Broyard's creative writing course at the New School. It was in this class, very near my twenty-fourth birthday, that I met my wife Joyce Nadine (10/21/38) and this was perhaps the lasting consequence, for despite my humility and new dedication I was still not to begin writing at all consistently or well for another year. *The Sense of the Fire* (1/68) was my first good story, written in 9/64. (Something nearly good called "The Epiphanist" was written in April of that year but was never published and probably, since it was ersatz Bruce Jay Friedman crossed with Malamudian obscurity, a good thing.)

Interesting people, none of whom but for Joyce I ever saw again, were in that class. Fred Marcus, the handsome stockbroker, and Claudia Branch who was involved with a novelist whose book had been printed in English in his native India and which he carried around to class, and Bill Hinnant, that wonderful actor. Hinnant later became the original Snoopy in the off-Broadway *Peanuts* revue and did lots of television commercial work; he played the title role in a Broadway musical, *Frank Merriwell*, that gave him the kind of reviews actors fantasize but which were otherwise venomous toward the production and which closed it after one night. Bill Hinnant, drowned and dead at the age of forty-two in the Dominican Republic, almost a decade ago. The summer nights were warm and promising and the fall and winter nights weren't so bad either and the young welfare investigator and the trademark researcher he would marry spent the weekends seeing everything that would open on or off Broadway that season. *The Passion of Joseph D.* by Paddy Chayefsky (the worst play by a writer of reputation I have ever seen or heard of) and *The Milk Train Doesn't Stop Here Anymore* with Tallulah Bankhead on New Year's Eve and *Spoon River Anthology* and *The Bald Soprano* and *The Ballad of the Sad Cafe* and *Oh Dad, Poor Dad* with Hermione Gingold and Barbara Harris.

And Aqueduct and Belmont in the afternoons, many of them on field time, and the drives home from the upper West Side at midnight, a can of beer in the right hand, steering wheel in the left, all possibility a cloak in the night; it was the year of my life, and then

it was the fall of that year and I was the Schubert Foundation fellow and things began, suddenly, to become very serious.

That condition has not yet ceased.

*

Driving on the roads of Rockland County where I worked as a reimbursement agent at the state hospital had its resonance also; it all seemed so palpable in the spring of 1963: everything that I had done, everything that I wanted seemed to meet in the soft density of those nights. In the office I read Foley anthologies and *Seymour: An Introduction* and *A New Life* and *The Thin Red Line* and the O. Henry Awards anthologies and in those evenings before I went out alone to drink and drive and think of the work to come, I did some writing of my own, all Foley-type stories, all of them miserable. *New Yorker* stories, I thought. Science fiction? I didn't know how to spell it. The collection had been sold off for the third time. I was going to be a writing-type writer, not a commercial hack. I could spell and punctuate; I knew an epiphany from a hole in the ground, a peripety from a fast ball thrown right down the middle of the plate that would make you freeze, struck by the arc of the ball, the arc of flight that could, but for fate, impact on the forehead, send slivers through the brain, make the explosion of light annihilate life itself.

None of that work ever got sold, but a few of the stories, slyly presented in the right circumstances, would make a certain kind of woman enormously sympathetic. Women seemed to go for that kind of thing, particularly if you talked about the seriousness of it all. I learned a few lessons then that were to stand by me in difficult stead years down the line.

Places, institutions, people replicate. This seems to be the grand or pathetic theme; it is not a progression, this life, so much as an infinite series of recursions. Syracuse University as an undergraduate and then, four years later, a graduate fellow. The NYC Department of Welfare in 1961-62 and then again, after the reimbursement agenting at Hudson River and Rockland State hospitals, in 1963-64. The Scott Meredith Literary Agency as my first job in publishing, the place where publishing really began for me and then again, from 1981—when I could no longer deal with the consequences of that career.

And science fiction, first as a kid and then as a bigger kid and then as the biggest kid of all . . . but then again, the very first stories I had written were amorphous attempts at science fiction and my first rejection slip in 1952 came from *Amazing Stories*. And I had made serious, pathetic attempts to sell Horace Gold's *Galaxy* when I was thirteen and fourteen years old.

With Robert Sheckley at the 1979 Science-Fiction Writers of America Editors Reception,
New York

And so on and so forth to be known over and again: that spectre of "progress," the iron of recursion. We (or at least I) may think it is different but then again and irrevocably it becomes the same. Perhaps that is the only lesson yet ahead of me, but oh my! I have been through this for a very long time and it would seem I have not yet learned it. To try once more and yet again to let experience and knowledge take the place of further brutalization, and to understand that it never will. "A cynic is a dog who has been kicked once too often," as Oscar Wilde did not say. "Cynicism: that quality in which vulnerability and hope are ineptly disguised as their opposites," as Ambrose Bierce might have.

*

At one time, 1975 was where it ended, I thought that Salinger's course was right; there came a time, finally, when there might be no more and that was all right, that was manageable: you responded with silence. You said nothing, published nothing, had nothing at all to say and your silence, in its eloquence, surpassed anything that one's enemies or critics might offer. The silence became a metaphor; it could contain all of the world.

Catherine L. Moore said at a party in 1974 when asked for comment by the intrepid reporter of the *SFWA Bulletin,* "Oh, I never comment on anything." This seemed an excellent policy.

The world, the stars, the galaxies, the sprawling, arching, busy cosmos itself are filled, simply crammed to bursting, with excellent policies I never observed. This seems to be another example of consistency.

*

"So tell me which years you *weren't* involved with science fiction," my colleague, fellow toiler in the humble fields of the agency asked me a few months ago. "You say you were in and out of it all the time."

"Well," I said, "well, there was 1960 through 1964, and then back in 1955 and then there was my junior year at Syracuse, before the summer—"

And then I had to stop and consider all of this. "All right," I said after a while, "the truth is that I was always involved with science fiction after 1950; it was central to my life, sensibility, all of that. If you want to understand me, not that I could imagine anyone caring, you could see all of it as a series of increasingly frenetic attempts to separate myself from that which was most important, the field of science fiction, and periods when I didn't make the attempts. But I was always fixed; it was central. Couldn't get away from it, all the moves taking me deeper."

*

The recursions, of course, can be seen in the work as well.

The work and the writer are not to be separated. (Although part of what I take to be the tragic circumstance is that all through the late sixties, early seventies, I thought that it could. I thought that I could sit at the typewriter and turn out this stuff on $3000 contracts to deadline, full of cracked voices, stinging pain, urban lunacy, off-center cataclysm, and meanwhile live a perfectly normal suburban life just like a real person. That I could join the temple, pay the bills, make the PTA, own a new Cadillac *and* be the author of *Beyond Apollo*. That I could go from this to that, Ganymede to the marital bed, temple follies to the falling astronauts, without dropping a stitch. This may be dumb, but it took a lot of stupidity to land me on that table with the intravenous equipment.)

I wrote one crazy astronaut story, "Triptych" (1969) and then another, "Making Titan" (1970), and then a whole slew of them, and not one crazy astronaut novel but three or four, of which *Falling Astronauts* (1971) can be seen as rough draft for the later *Beyond Apollo* (1972) or *Revelations* (1972). I wrote a horse-racing story, "Notes Just Prior to the Fall" (1970), which became the first chapter of *Overlay* (1972) and then used that as a set of working notes for *Underlay* (1974), which is worth anyone's gall bladder with Roger Sale a throw-in. Horse racing also appears prominently in *Screen* (1968) and is the central business of "A Bed of Money" (1970) and it is what got *The Spread* (1971) off the ground, even though *The Spread* is really about the death of sexuality to be found in commercial, institutionalized pornography (this too a theme to have been enacted more than once). I wrote so many assassination short stories and novels that they won't even be cited; over and again Zapruder took the photos as the skull exploded in the Southwest noon, an explosion which rocketed on and on, heaving out the fragments of bone—

And my most recent, and for all I know, final novel, *The Remaking of Sigmund Freud*, is based upon material I have been actively considering, brooding about for a quarter of a century. The novel emerged very slowly with a few premonitory short stories in the late seventies, but only got written painfully and through a series of drafts (*not* a characteristic performance) when I was at such distance from the impetus as to be able to control the material. Freud, schizophrenia, dementia praecox, Bleuler, the lunacy commission, hebephrenia,

chronic undifferentiated . . . well, all of this had been on my mind for a long time and to get the novel done finally was to argue the issue yet again. Writers, perhaps, are not very smart people; they do not understand their experience or its significance and they need their work to come to terms, slowly and usually unsuccessfully, with what is really eating at them. Or at least that is what I began to think.

The good part of recursion is that when it is done (if ever) it is truly finished: there have been no racing stories since *Underlay*, no mad astronauts or Zapruder splinters since the mid-seventies, and with the completion of *Freud*, no need to deal with neo-lunacy commissions. It is, as a matter of fact, possible that novels truly banish perplexity although then again—anything you say about this business is likely to be true—maybe not.

*

From a review in a science fiction fan magazine some years ago (I have lost the provenance): "Malzberg has too much irony and self-awareness to be a truly successful writer."

Also, Brian Aldiss: "Malzberg, a master of sex and depression." The *Rutgers Daily Targus* on *Acts of Mercy* (1977) with Bill Pronzini: "The authors should be killed for having written this novel." The *New York Daily News* Sci-Fi roundup on *The Remaking of Sigmund Freud*: "A good idea gone wrong, a wonderful concept ruined—in the best s-f tradition—by a labored, incoherent treatment . . . none of these characters are anything but puppets lip-synching the author's rather self-serving message which involves the destruction of true artists by the crass pressures of the marketplace."

As you go on and on in this business, the "good" reviews are understood to be meaningless; in modern publishing, reviews do not sell books. But the bad reviews increasingly hurt, the knife gets in deeper because the surfaces are narrower. Gaddis at Fairleigh Dickinson read, taking the quotation from a jacket pocket to make sure that he had it word for word, a venomous ten-year-old review of *JR* which appeared in *The New Yorker*, shuddering.

Why did he? Why did this man in front of twenty-two people in a classroom find it necessary to exhume this long-forgotten review and make it new?

Perhaps it is our inability to overcome the belief, planted deep and early, that somehow what we are doing doesn't count, that it is essentially frivolous, that we are really—all against the social will and for no reason at all—managing to get away with something.

*

My parents, like the parents of every science fiction writer of my generation, knew nothing of the field and as they came to terms with the fact that their son was reading quite a bit of it, came to hate and fear the genre. ("Stay away from that jive," I heard a determined lady admonish her twelve-year-old son who had stumbled into a dealer's room in Philadelphia from another gathering in the same hotel, "that jive make you *crazy*.") "I can't follow science fiction, it's too deep for me," my mother would say. My father, the graceful ice skater and long-distance swimmer who used the English overhand, would not—like Catherine Moore—even comment on the issue.

So why, wherefore, this? I am in town from Syracuse for the first time; it is Thanksgiving vacation of 1956 and my parents have met the freshman at Grand Central. We are driving now through lower Manhattan and Bedford Stuyvesant as I chatter about first college experiences (the ones that do not have to do with vomiting or Utica, New York) and chatting too about my confusion: what am I going to do with my life? Writing, maybe, but writing what? Something contemporary, of course, but material is uncertain—

We are at a red light. My father turns to the back where my trunk and I sprawl hunched against one another (but I never sit in the back, that is what makes this scene so strange, so vivid; maybe I never did it again) and says, "What will you write? You will write about that point at which science and humanity meet, at which the consequences of science upon all of us are enacted. That is what you can write and you will do it better than any who ever did it before."

My father turns, the light changes, the DeSoto lurches ahead. "You know what you've described?" I say; "you've just defined science fiction better that I've ever heard it done."

"And why not?" my father says. This is the 1955 DeSoto, near simulacrum of the horrendous pink 1956 I put into that guardrail, his favorite car, almost my favorite car too, the one in which I really learned to drive some years later. He says no more on this. As far as I know, we never discussed science fiction until—well, until 1965 when he wanted to know what I was writing if I had dropped out of the graduate program.

I am not inventing this. This is not retrospective falsification nor the novelist's convenience. It happened. My father who had never heard of science fiction before, say, 1951 and who never read it until I gave him my own wretched early rejects, really did say this. How could he have said it? How could he have known?

"That is what you can write and you will do it better than any who ever did it before."

Stephanie Jill (5/27/66) and I used to go on Sunday afternoons in 1970—the year in Manhattan that I had the car, the last full year in Herovit's World—to

Palisades Park across the river. There she would play ducks-in-the-water ("This is a *nice* game," she pointed out solemnly; the rifles weren't) and eat cotton candy; a little later I would throw a basketball, always rimming, and we would go over the river sternly refreshed, frivolously invigorated. Also, while her mother worked on Saturdays we would go to the slate store on Third Avenue, to the Seesaw Place in Central Park and to the baby bookstore on Broadway and Seventy-ninth.

"Someday," I instructed, "*I'll* have a book in the baby bookstore. Something I wrote."

"Like this?" Stephanie said. She showed me *Bread and Jam for Frances*, co-authored by the author of *Riddley Walker*. "This book?"

"Not exactly. Longer."

"No pictures?"

"Well, maybe one or two."

"Be nice, daddy."

And it came to pass. Two years later, *Screen* (1968) and *Oracle of the Thousand Hands* both got there, even though it was just a courtesy of the franchiser. Even though they appeared in the window, one copy each, for months and at the end when the bank took over the lease and threw the baby bookstore out, I bought them myself at 40 percent discount.

Screen sold 663 copies in its Olympia Press hardcover edition. That was the bestseller. I cannot bring myself, even in the confessional mode, to give the figures on *Oracle*.

*

In July, 1959, on the IRT local, the man beside me in the hot car keeled over, fell gracelessly on my lap, collapsed to the floor, and died. A man in his mid-fifties, *Daily Mirror* in his right hand, pencils in the suit pocket, just a guy on his way to work in the morning like the rest of us. He collapsed at Newkirk Avenue; by the time the cars pulled into Franklin and the passengers were cleared, he had already cyanosed, turned a pale and beautiful purple, lying stately on the floor of the car all alone, people wedged against the doors, against one another, to give death space.

I was a temporary typist at a Wall Street law firm. The first thing I did was to tell them about it and they were interested, but it wasn't enough; then I sat at the electric and wrote it all up, not as an essay or memoir, but as *fiction*, told from the point of view of the dead man. The about-to-be dead man, that is to say. It was all too disturbing, too threatening and terrible until I was able to get that kind of handle, back off, detach, create some distance between myself and the casual event.

The story was not good—cynical even in youth, I certainly had enough perception to know that—but the point was this: after the wretched piece, I felt better. This writing had its good points. It gave you the feeling of control over matters that otherwise, perhaps, were all too much for a simple lad. Just a simple lad from Flatbush.

*

I found James Agee's *Let Us Now Praise Famous Men* in 11/60 in the post library of Fort Dix. Little brief is to be held for the army, even that bumbling, relatively benign pre-Kennedy military in which I so undistinguishedly served, but Donald M. Evans, Capt., USA, did with his cadre entertain me mightily for a while and granted me the first particles of experience which might have been my own (as opposed to "generational" which is how we talked in those days) and it did put me into juxtaposition with Agee.

That was a revelation, the 1960 Houghton Mifflin reissue of a young man's observations of the Depression South. Agee had been only a little older than I was when he and Walker Evans had gone into the back roads of Alabama on assignment for *Fortune* and the book (never published by the magazine which never bargained for what it got) taught me that writing could come out of your own sensibility, your own involvement. You could write something that came from yourself and it would matter; writing did not have to come out of Balzac or Irwin Shaw, Alfred Bester or Thomas Wolfe. It could come out of me, just as the dread and suffering of the poor whites came from James Agee. We had within ourselves the makings of our work.

This does not seem like a large insight and is, in fact, a very slow and shallow perception. (It was noted earlier that writers are truly not very smart.) But it is precisely that kind of epiphany which any of us has to have along the way in order to do work worth leaving. It is possible to publish, and very successfully, without having recourse to one's experience and circumstance. The genres, particularly fantasy and science fiction, are historically receptive to writing by precocious young and old, many of them never to go beyond that. You can go a long way in the genres by a careful and alert reading, just as it is possible to play a fair game of chess, just below grand master level perhaps, simply (well, I shouldn't say "simply"!) by studying and memorizing the progressions of thousands of the classic games, the classic attacks, and knowing how they can be applied. You may not be "creative" that way but only at the level of a Karpov or a Tal does that begin to show up.

But if you are going to do anything that will last or will create the delusion that it will last, you must have what I define as the Agee insight. I owe the man for this and was mortified to learn later on (I knew

nothing of Agee until 1960) that this clear case of self-indulgence and artistic waste had died more than half a decade ago at forty-five in a New York taxi, leaving one nearly completed novel, one novella, a slew of essays on film, a couple of film scripts and more notes and ideas for more never-to-be-written novels and films than any writer of his time. Oh Agee, you taught better than you learned, which is also the case for most of us.

*

By 6/65, I was pretty tired of writing out of experience. Mine or anyone's. The Schubert Foundation Fellow was drowning in rejection slips, sloth, angst, his own growing intimation that *The New Yorker* and Atlantic Monthly Press were a racket more sinister than all offered through the spaces of South Ozone Park or Elmont, Rosecroft or Yonkers. Resigned he, then, the Schubert Fellow, a fellowship even *more* splendid than that which he had held ($5000 a year from the Cornelia Ward Foundation was twice what the Schuberts offered and big money at the time for a graduate student); back to the city the Fellow went with his bride of one year. Arrived they in 6/65 with $400 worth of personal debt, $200 in cash, $800 of outstanding student loans and a 1960 Dodge Dart soon to be proven worth $125. Where he was to end, knew the Schubert Foundation Fellow not. All that he knew—and Wolcott Gibbs too—was that quality lit was not the answer. Quality lit, in fact, was not even the question.

I found work through purest coincidence at the Scott Meredith Agency and observed that among the heterogeneous set of writers represented here were a number who sold science fiction in various quantity to *Analog* and *Galaxy* and so on, even though the stories, mostly, stunk. "I used to read this stuff," I thought cunningly, "maybe I can write it, see if I can sell something. I mean, I ought to sell at least one story before I quit all of this, considering the trouble I went through, the trouble I've seen."

Subsequent events were discussed in the introductions to *Best of Barry N. Malzberg* (1976), *Down Here in the Dream Quarter* (1977), and through much of *Engines of the Night* (1982). *Op. cit.*

*

On 1/11/67, I sold my first science fiction story, and thus the first story that mattered (there were sales to the fifth-rate men's magazine *Wildcat* in 11/65 and 11/66 but no one including the author had ever heard of the place), to *Galaxy*. "We're Coming through the Windows" was published by Fred Pohl in the 8/67 issue. Almost upon learning of the sale from the agent (*not* Scott Meredith who was the center of earlier and later working but never writing life) I called my father at his office to report the remarkable news. Oh, how

With Jack Dann at the 1981 Alphacon, Ithaca, New York

the need for approval beats within the heart of the Jewish son! the difference with *genus Malzbergius* being that it throbbed for the approval of the *father.* "How much did you get?" the old man asked sensibly.

"Thirty-six dollars."

"And how long was it?"

"It was twelve hundred words. Three cents a word, that makes $36."

"I see. Well, *next* time you can sell them twelve *thousand* words and then you'll get $360."

This sane advice from a plywood salesman who could never fathom the son who stumbled around the glaze of the Brooklyn Ice Palace, yet who had bought that son the *Penrod* books in 1949 because "you'll probably like these" and had so infinitesimally changed my life that way too, pretty well became the pennant by which the later career was measured. Twelve hundred words at three cents a word? Don't be a goat; if you're going to write for those rates, you'd better really fill up the pages and a lot of them.

Funny thing, though: "Final War," published in *The Magazine of Fantasy and Science Fiction* in 4/68, my second science fiction sale and the sale which got me noticed . . . that story was almost exactly twelve thousand words.

And it wasn't my fault that I had to settle for $250; those were *F & SF* rates at the time, and the story had fallen through all of the higher paying maga-zines in the field, also out of the field. *Esquire, The Hudson Review, Kenyon Review* had failed to capture. As a matter of fact, the then-entitled "Shoe a Troop of Horse" was called "too grimly realistic" by *Kenyon.*

*

But in the nights, all of the dreaming nights, it had seemed palpable; walking the streets of Coney Island after midnight in the summer after college graduation, driving on the dim roads of Rockland County, staring at the lights of the city from the Palisades; all of this in the early twenties seemed to fuse ambition, desire, possibility in the nights in such a way that I could, if I were to close my eyes and focus with enough intensity, make it happen, make it happen at that very moment. The girls huddled beside me in the 1954 Oldsmobile, the *consummatum est* of change, close enough to be clutched.

Oh, it was true then as Ruthven was to say at the Cincon, and not only for science fiction; it was truer than the poor bastard ever knew . . . for all of it, all of the writing, all of the work was an attempt to get back there, to make it real, to make all of the places come alive again and although one was to try and fail in eight million words sent shrieking against the panels and enclosure of one's life, although one would fail again and again, the cry was there and all of the colors of desire.

For they could take everything from you and as the years ground on, as you ground down, in small and large ways they did, but they could not take the intensity of the work itself or what it had once meant. All we can leave, someone had said, all we can leave are the little markers of our place; for some it would be rooms or possessions, for me—and I knew it then as from the beginning—it would have to be the work itself. Ultimately and one knew it early from a dead man in the subway, one did not need to learn from Gaddis, you were indeed the shambles of the work, the little man bound by ropes who followed the work around. Trotted after it, first slow, then fast, then faster yet until at last you fell. Were dragged then through all the stifling places of the heart.

Of memory.

In 5/62, I took my sister, Ruth Ann (5/8/44) out for her eighteenth birthday, paid for it and everything; it would have been a date except that it wasn't. There had been little between us up until then; this must have been the first time that I can remember being glad that I had a sister, appreciating the fact that I would not, after all, have to carry that parental burden alone.

We went to dinner at Rosoff's, a favorite restaurant gutted in 1981, and then to *An Evening with Nichols and May;* we talked like sensible adults which, perhaps, we were on the verge of becoming. Mike Nichols and Elaine May, more than anyone at the time (except Shelley Berman), seemed to speak to my condition. "You wouldn't respect me if I did *that.*" "Oh, honey, yes I would; I'd respect you like *crazy.*"

"Mommy, how could I call you? the big rocket ship was going to go up, boom in the sky. I'm sorry, mommy, mommy, oh mommy—"

"Now, Al Schweitzer, sure I know Al. Al's a lot of laughs—"

Ruth Ann became Ruth (now I have let her secret into the world again but no one, I truly believe this, reads these memoirs except other writers, and then only to learn if the competition is younger or more successful than they) and married Robert Schlesinger (1/24/45), a good guy, in 12/66 and has two children. She took upon herself the responsibility for dealing with my parents through their terrible, extended decline all through the seventies, all the way through to the end; my debt is great, guilt sufficient, sin as marked as in all of the other places.

"I'd like to read your work," my sister said, some time ago, "but I can't; it's as if I hear your voice whispering to me. When I read *Screen* it was like you were murmuring dirty words in my ear." The world will make telephonic murmurers of us all, it seems.

Replication and recursion: I played the violin in the fifties and sixties, coming to it much too late, fourteen, and self-taught for the first years at that, to ever have a chance of being good, but I was able to hang around the back benches of high school and college orchestras and also something called the Welfare Symphony which played nursing home dates. Then I gave it up to become a major writer, of course.

Not having succeeded in that to my satisfaction or anyone's, and suffering from ever deepening regret, I started to play again in 1976 and lurked around some really awful orchestras and pick-up assemblages. (The not-so-awful bands like the Bergen Philharmonic either wouldn't let me in or threw me out, courteously, as soon as the conductor paid attention.)

I have encountered from these back benches as much folly, greed, arrogance, stupidity, brutality and self-delusion as ever in publishing but publishing never gave me Mendelssohn, the B Minor Mass, Beethoven's Third Piano Concerto, *Die Zauberflote* or K. 488, little things like that; writing novels was a pursuit which paid me (never enough) and involved jackals, but writing was never—as was the music—its own compensation.

That was the difference. Chancey at Midwood High School could throw batons and damn us; Louis Krasner in college (a good conductor and great violinist who had commissioned and premiered the Berg and Schoenberg concerti) could make me a piano mover because, "If you can't play you have to make yourself useful in other ways . . . I can't ask the concertmaster to lift a harp"; Rubin of the North Jersey Symphony could threaten the violins and curse them because they couldn't manage the coda and fugue of the *London Symphony* or could drop all of the back benches in William Boyce . . . but Chancey, Krasner, Rubin, none of them could take away Mendelssohn or Brahms or the Bach Third Suite in D for Orchestra. There was no possibility that they could obliterate or even change the score and that, perhaps, was the source of their rage; even the Krasners would go and the Rubins would come and depart inconsequentially but Bach and Mendelssohn would survive as if Rubin had never been.

I did not take this to be true in the novel where they could, despite all of the homilies of delusion, bury you so deep that you would be out of business well within your lifetime, but it was true in music and so I came back to the violin and put up with the astonishing and ever-interesting debasement of the inept back-bench second and took it cheerfully for quite a long time until it was necessary—Rubin having been simply *too* outrageous—to put it away for a while, anyway, and become a serious student, try to hear repertory and learn it as I should have decades ago. But recursion is inevitable: given time I will come back yet again and should I crawl into the further decades I would hope to sit at the fifth stand and celebrate, be the Juggler of the parable, serve as one to give voice to that which, transcendent, gives voice to us all.

*

I was one of the group that was going to write the Midwood Senior Show back there in 1956 except that there wasn't much writing that March, just a lot of talk. We discussed this and surely there would have to be a scene for that and then we wanted to do a takeoff on the college boards and the admissions racket and as days went by we decided that the play would revolve around this typical senior and a typical day in her life and then of course we would need a curtain number and it was getting pretty close to the time when we had to cast and rehearse, already, but no script and then on a Tuesday, Judy Abrams, class writer and salutatorian, came in at 3:30, just when another meeting was beginning, with a 9 × 12 manila envelope and put it on the desk in front and said, "I wrote this last night. I mean, you can do anything you want with it, change scenes around, add some, but *here* is the script, all right?" And then she left the room and it was true: there was the script.

I found this truly impressive. I decided that if I ever had my way, next time, somehow, I wanted to be the guy who went away while all the others were talking and fooling around, and came back with the script. Put it on the desk. Gave them the work they only fantasized they could do.

*

We were stopped in the *Egmont* Overture just before the presto section so that Ben Chancey could yell at a trumpet and I looked at Miriam Grzebenian to my left, Miriam on the outside of the fourth stand seconds where she belonged, an infinitely stronger violinist, and she was crying; her cheeks were wet. Thirty years later I still want to kiss those tears; thirty years from now it is undone.

"It's so beautiful," she whispered. A Polish accent. "It's just so beautiful."

So beautiful, Miriam.

*

"You son of a bitch," Maurice Girodias said to me in the restaurant, a week after I had delivered *Screen* to his Olympia Press. This was no celebratory lunch, let me tell you. "You son of a bitch, I give you a nice little idea for a dirty book, a guy who imagines himself on the screen in movies fucking famous actresses, this little guy, and you give me the most beautiful opening forty

pages: Elizabeth Taylor, Brigitte, everybody; you even seem to know what color Brigitte's *bush* is . . . and then what happens?

"What happens? You son of a bitch, you give me literature, you give me horse racing and decadence and death and impotence and darkness! So I have, you see, no nice little book of porno-graffee as I wish; I have this *literature*. I cannot publish it in paperback, of course; they would throw it across the room. I publish in hardcover then, and I lose all my money."

"I did it the only way I could, Maurice." The fact that in Girodias's mind there was no question of *not* publishing *Screen* did not astonish as it would have a few years later when I learned how the business worked.

"That is the only way? Then this is your problem. But I am the one who has to pay for this."

"I didn't mean—"

"I said I'd publish it, didn't I? Do you think just once you could write me a nice little dirty book?"

Not quite.

*

First you know very little but intimate a lot and it pours out, then you learn a few things and see shades of meaning and it's a little harder, maybe a *lot* harder, and finally when your knowledge far exceeds any belief in its efficacy or the ability to cause change, it is very difficult to say anything at all. To know everything, perhaps, is to find only silence, which is not the only explanation for the Salinger/Hemingway effect, but it is the one with which I am most satisfied and which seems to foreshadow my circumstance and that of most writers I admire. The more you know, the less you can say. Ignorance, then, is virtue awarded.

*

I have said that *The Sense of the Fire,* written in 9/64, was the first decent story I perpetrated. Actually, I think it is a little more than that; it is an eight thousand-word novelette which somehow managed to focus a great deal of my experience in the Department of Welfare without—and this is crucial—saying too much; its mistakes were those of the old writer rather than the young writer, which is to say that at least it did not over-explain. It did not say too much.

If anything, it said too little. *The Sense of the Fire* was about this welfare investigator named Stein who was going over the edge; he walked up and down the stairs of the tenements, visiting welfare recipients on his caseload and counted backwards by twos, sometimes, fours; dreamed of blowing up the tenements, incinerating the clients. At the end, facing an old man in his doorway, Stein went crazy altogether. (These days we say "lost it.") It's coming to an end, he said. He cursed the old man and imagined the fire, the purifying fire as it leapt from floor to floor, leapt from staircase to roof, then the buildings, the city, the world itself—

The first draft was full of angst and foreboding but never came together. "*Give* him a grenade," Joyce said. "He's thinking of throwing grenades at the clients, make him an ex-army man and give him a dummy grenade in his coat that he squeezes all the time, thinks is real." I thought about that. "It needs a grenade," Joyce said.

"Yes," I said, and wrote the second draft. (In those days I did two drafts, later on I did only one, then with *Freud* it was four or five or six gasping drafts and I needed every one, o Peg of my heart.) *Stein, an obsessive,* it began, *carried a dummy hand grenade in the pocket of his converted fatigue jacket.* At the end, in the end, he threw it at the old man and, dummy grenade or not, it blew up. The fire, leaping flames, no metaphor now, *that* was the sense of the fire indeed. Esther Yntema of the Atlantic Monthly Press said when I sent it to *The Atlantic* (she read over shoulders) that it was a masterpiece, an "anthology piece." They rejected it anyway. So did everyone else. Ted Leighton at *Escapade* bought it for $250 and no one noticed it in that 1/68 issue either. No one noticed the story when it was anthologized in *Out from Ganymede and Other Stories* (1974) either, but that, I maintain, was their mistake. Sometimes, as Delmore Schwartz knew, they really *are* out to get you. Even now, XY number of stories later, it is no worse than the third or fourth best of them all. Maybe it *is* the best. It was certainly the first.

Joyce put the grenade in *The Sense of the Fire.* For years and years I have said this, once or twice in print, more often not. By saying that she put the grenade in that story I meant to say much more but like many other things (writing do rip one up) it got sidetracked. If not everything got done because of her, more than I ever noticed did. Once, Pronzini and I got bogged so deep in a novel whose title I cannot mention, that she had to get us out of it singlehanded, do the first draft from which she built. Two other novels of mine were first-drafted by her. Any time that I gave her something to read before it was turned in, which was not often enough, and she told me to fix something and I listened to her (which was not often enough), it got better.

When I say that she put the grenade in *The Sense of the Fire* I mean to say a lot more but then again— back-bench second violinists will understand this anyway—I am able to play the last movement of the second fiddle part of the Mozart *Jupiter a tempo* only as a simulacrum of itself, only as a representation of what is on the page. *A tempo* I can catch half of it.

And then again, buried in the second violin part

of the Bach Third Suite for orchestra first movement— I was amazed at this when I read through it for the first time in 1979—is an entirely *different* first movement of the Third Suite, a counter-melody which is as powerful as the material which the first fiddles have to play but which is so thoroughly subsumed that it cannot be heard on its own. What it becomes, under the main theme, is the sound against the sound, the sound that informs without itself being heard.

The sound against the sound. The grenade in *The Sense of the Fire.*

In 1977, when Bill Pronzini was in town to work with me on the final draft of *Night Screams,* we decided to throw a party for him, invite the neighbors in. I am not sure exactly why. Perhaps I was still trying to live like a suburbanite, although by then I knew better.

I was still drinking in those days. Late in the evening—well, late in the evening for *me;* call it nine o'clock—we were sitting around, the neighbors and Pronzini not really hitting it off all that well, and I found myself saying to Elaine X, "I'll tell you what *I* think of writing. Being a writer has ruined my life."

Everyone stared. Even Pronzini stared. It takes a good deal to make Pronzini stare, particularly when he was drinking. (Like me, he drinks no more.) "Oh come on, Barry," Elaine X said, "you don't really mean that."

"I do," I said. I put down the glass. (I am not sure that I was holding a glass in the first place. I was very little drunk, if drunk at all.) "I'll repeat that. Being a writer has ruined my life."

"You really mean that?" Elaine X said.

"From the bottom of my heart."

A lot of people were suddenly in the next room, doing this or that. This was a couple of days before we got the envelope from Putnam containing the first bunch of reviews, including the one from Rutgers saying that we ought to be killed for writing *Acts of Mercy.*

By early 1981, I was gasping. Maybe earlier than that. The dread, the angst had set in much earlier; by 1976 I was already scattering retirement essays around the field, "hanging around the coffin waiting for mourners," as one non-fan pointed out publicly. But somehow I was able to go on, at least a little; there were a few collaborative novels with Bill Pronzini which almost made it as suspense but didn't quite; there were some very strange, very pained short stories (as the "Writer's Heaven" series) published as science fiction but even less so than was the norm; there were even a couple of science fiction novels, *Chorale* and *The Cross of Fire,* which were inflations of novelettes written years earlier. (I seemed incapable, after 1977 and including *The Remaking of Sigmund Freud,* of entirely new work, of work done without the crutch of earlier, truncated versions.) But the books were going out of print even as I typed them; the ribbons were invisible ink; the course toward oblivion seemed to be an acceleration of everything that had happened earlier in the decade. From being the most maddeningly prolific writer in the history of the field (I wrote more novels and short stories of ambition in less time than anyone, even the redoubtable Robert Silverberg) I became one of the least but that didn't work either. There was no more demand for less of my work than there had been for more of it.

There was, if I were to continue as a writer, only one route left but it was a very short and dangerous drop and I had given up drinking by that time anyway; I was bored, ultimately, with the hangovers and the dread. So there was, effectively, no route left as a writer and in 1981, recursive recursion, I went back to the Scott Meredith Agency where it had all begun for me more than a decade and a half ago and where, at this writing, I remain and intend to remain for the rest of all our working lives, circumstances permitting. There was a time and it was less than a decade ago when I would have taken this as a defeat but I do not, I do not at all; the *career* has been a defeat but the return to the agency has been a triumph. I am one of the very few writers I know or of whom I have heard who was able in mid-life to admit that the whole thing had been a terrible mistake and had been able to get out, even if it meant going back. In the beginning was the Word and the Word was there and it went on and on but it is possible to understand that in the world without end (amen) the Word itself, once uttered, need not be spoken again and again and that there may be more or less to this, finally, than the endless, the ravening, the teeny-tiny and insistent, the blocked and stuporous, the desperate and necessitous, the prayerful and ravaged, sound of one's own voice.

*

In the toll station, the compresses against my forehead, the toll-taker who stanched the wounds and saved my life looking down at me in astonishment, I raved and ranted a little as shock victims are apt to do, "It must be different," I said, "I *have* to write, don't you understand? I could have thrown it all away and no one would ever know; I have to find out now, I have to get it done." And the state police came and bundled me off to Yonkers General Hospital and I lay on the table as the intern stitched me up under local, pounding and pounding the table with my fist, weeping, not now because I had almost died with work undone (because I was too young to cry for writing; that would take many years and would be for other reasons)

Malzberg, 1983

but because the work undone would have left me obliterated; no one would ever love me. I had to write, get something into print, be my own James Agee because only then would there be—the next time the car hit the guardrail, the fire next time—someone to hold my hand and to whisper that it was all right, that it had been so beautiful, that it was the most beautiful thing they had ever known, that I was known, that I was touched, that I had reached, that I was loved. Testimony. Markers for the man that followed the work around.

BIBLIOGRAPHY

Fiction:

Oracle of the Thousand Hands. New York: Olympia, 1968.

Screen. New York: Olympia, 1968; London: Olympia, 1970.

Diary of a Parisian Chambermaid, under pseudonym Claudine Dumas. New York: Midwood, 1969.

In My Parents' Bedroom. New York: Olympia, 1970.

Confessions of Westchester County. New York: Olympia, 1971;

London: Olympia, 1971.

The Falling Astronauts. New York: Ace Books, 1971; London: Arrow Books, 1975.

The Spread. New York: Belmont-Tower, 1971.

Beyond Apollo. New York: Random House, 1972; London: Faber, 1974.

The Case for Elizabeth Moore. New York: Belmont-Tower, 1972.

Horizontal Woman. New York: Nordon, 1972; also published as *The Social Worker.* New York: Nordon, 1977.

The Masochist. New York: Belmont-Tower, 1972; also published as *Everything Happened to Susan.* New York: Belmont-Tower, 1978.

Overlay. New York: Lancer, 1972; London: New English Library, 1975.

Revelations: A Paranoid Novel of Suspense. New York: Warner Paperback, 1972.

Herovit's World. New York: Random House, 1973; London: Arrow Books, 1976.

In the Enclosure. New York: Avon, 1973; London: Hale, 1976.

The Men Inside. New York: Lancer, 1973; London: Arrow Books, 1976.

Phase IV (adapted from the screenplay by Mayo Simon). New York: Pocket Books, 1973; London: Pan Books, 1973.

The Way of the Tiger, the Sign of the Dragon, under pseudonym Howard Lee. New York: Warner Books, 1973.

The Day of the Burning. New York: Ace Books, 1974.

The Destruction of the Temple. New York: Pocket Books, 1974; London: New English Library, 1975.

Guernica Night: A Science Fiction Masterwork. Indianapolis: Bobbs-Merrill, 1974; London: New English Library, 1978.

On a Planet Alien. New York: Pocket Books, 1974.

Out from Ganymede and Other Stories (short stories). New York: Warner Paperback, 1974.

The Sodom and Gomorrah Business. New York: Pocket Books, 1974; London Arrow Books, 1979.

Tactics of Conquest. New York: Pyramid, 1974.

Underlay. New York: Avon, 1974; New York: International Polygonics, 1986.

Conversations. Indianapolis: Bobbs-Merrill, 1975.

Galaxies. New York: Pyramid, 1975.

The Gamesman. New York: Pocket Books, 1975.

The Many Worlds of Barry Malzberg (short stories). New York: Popular Library, 1975.

The Best of Barry N. Malzberg (short stories). New York: Pocket Books, 1976.

Down Here in the Dream Quarter (short stories). Garden City, N.Y.: Doubleday, 1976.

The Running of Beasts, with Bill Pronzini. New York: Putnam, 1976.

Scop. New York: Pyramid, 1976.

Acts of Mercy, with B. Pronzini. New York: Putnam, 1977.

Lady of a Thousand Sorrows, under pseudonym Lee W. Mason. New York: Playboy Press, 1977.

The Last Transaction. Los Angeles: Pinnacle Books, 1977.

Chorale. Garden City, N.Y.: Doubleday, 1978.

Malzberg at Large (short stories). New York: Ace Books, 1979.

Night Screams, with B. Pronzini. New York: Playboy Press, 1979.

The Man Who Loved the Midnight Lady: A Collection. Garden City, N.Y.: Doubleday, 1980.

Prose Bowl, with B. Pronzini. New York: St. Martin's, 1980.

The Cross of Fire. New York: Ace Books, 1982.

The Remaking of Sigmund Freud. New York: Ballantine, 1985.

Under pseudonym K.M. O'Donnell:

The Empty People. New York: Lancer, 1969.

Final War and Other Fantasies. New York: Ace Books, 1969.

Dwellers of the Deep. New York: Ace Books, 1970.

Gather in the Hall of Planets [and] *In the Pocket and Other SF Stories.* New York: Ace Books, 1971.

Universe Day. New York: Avon, 1971.

Under pseudonym Mike Barry:

Bay Prowler. New York: Berkley Publishing, 1973.

Boston Avenger. New York: Berkley Publishing, 1973.

Night Raider. New York: Berkley Publishing, 1973.

Chicago Slaughter. New York: Berkley Publishing, 1974.

Desert Stalker. New York: Berkley Publishing, 1974.

Havana Hit. New York: Berkley Publishing, 1974.

Los Angeles Holocaust. New York: Berkley Publishing, 1974.

Miami Marauder. New York: Berkley Publishing, 1974.

Peruvian Nightmare. New York: Berkley Publishing, 1974.

Detroit Massacre. New York: Berkley Publishing, 1975.

Harlem Showdown. New York: Berkley Publishing, 1975.

The Killing Run. New York: Berkley Publishing, 1975.

Philadelphia Blow-Up. New York: Berkley Publishing, 1975.

Phoenix Inferno. New York: Berkley Publishing, 1975.

Playing Dirty. New York: St. Martin's, 1983.

Nonfiction:

The Engines of the Night: Science Fiction in the Eighties (essays). Garden City, N.Y.: Doubleday, 1982.

Editor of:

Final Stage: The Ultimate Science Fiction Anthology, with Edward L. Ferman. New York: Charterhouse, 1974; Harmondsworth, England: Penguin, 1975.

Arena: Sports SF, with E. Ferman. Garden City, N.Y.: Doubleday, 1976; London: Robson Books, 1976.

Graven Images: Three Original Novellas of Science Fiction, by Richard Frede et al; edited with E. Ferman. New York: Thomas Nelson, 1977.

Dark Sins, Dark Dreams: Crime in Science Fiction, with Bill Pronzini. Garden City, N.Y.: Doubleday, 1978.

The End of Summer: Science Fiction of the Fifties. New York: Ace Books, 1979.

Neglected Visions, with Martin H. Greenberg and Joseph D. Olander. Garden City, N.Y.: Doubleday, 1979.

Shared Tomorrows: Science Fiction in Collaboration, with B. Pronzini. New York: St. Martin's, 1979.

Bug-Eyed Monsters. New York: Harcourt, 1980.

The Science Fiction of Mark Clifton, edited with M. Greenberg. Carbondale, Ill.: Southern Illinois University Press, 1980.

The Arbor House Treasury of Horror and the Supernatural, with M. Greenberg and B. Pronzini and with introduction by Stephen King. New York: Arbor House, 1981.

The Arbor House Treasury of Mystery and Suspense, with M. Greenberg and B. Pronzini and with introduction by John D. MacDonald. New York: Arbor House, 1982.

The Science Fiction of Kris Neville, edited with M. Greenberg. Carbondale, Ill.: Southern Illinois University Press, 1984.

Uncollected Stars, with Piers Anthony, M. Greenberg, and Charles Waugh. New York: Avon, 1986.

Malzberg has also written several hundred short stories for various mystery, suspense, and science fiction magazines such as *Ellery Queen's Mystery Magazine, Analog,* and *Fantasy and Science Fiction.*

Ted Morgan

1932-

Chance and choice, my old pals, choirmates, and bookends: to begin with, it was because of Bugatti that I was born in Geneva, Switzerland. My father, Gabriel de Gramont, was studying to pass his exams to join the French diplomatic corps. His friend Bugatti made his cars by hand, about eight of them a year, and asked my father to be his Geneva salesman. Since this meant selling two cars a year, it would not interfere with his studies, and my parents moved to Geneva in 1932.

At the age of one, I persuaded them to leave Geneva, and we moved to Paris. The word often used to

At age four in Indian costume, with pretty ballerina

Sanche de Gramont, the author at age three in front of de Gramont castle, Mortefontaine, France

describe my father was "quixotic." Finding it hard to study in a house crowded with a wife, an infant son, a brother, and a mother, he went down to the police station on the corner, picked up a rock, broke the streetlamp in front of the police station, and asked to be arrested so that he might enjoy the privacy of a cell. Because he didn't like to go to the dentist, he had all his teeth pulled out. His passion was golf, and one day when it was raining hard my mother saw him pick up his golf bag. "But it's pouring," she said. "Not in Mortefontaine," he replied.

Mortefontaine was the de Gramont estate about twenty miles outside Paris, with its own golf course, purchased by my grandfather the duke after he married a rich woman. The de Gramonts were an old French ducal family, who started out as Agramonte in a part of France that was once Spanish. The story goes that King Henry IV, the Protestant who converted to

Members of de Gramont family in front of main entrance to castle. From left: Jean, comte de Gramont; Antoine, duc de Guiche; Odile, duchesse de Guiche; comtesse de Miramont; uncle Armand, duc de Gramont; Elsie, comtesse de Gramont; comte de Miramont; Laure, comtesse de Gramont; René, comte de Gramont; mother, comtesse de Gramont; father, Gabriel, comte de Gramont; Charles, comte de Gramont; and Ghislaine, comtesse de Gramont.

Catholicism in order to become king, saying, "Paris is well worth a mass," had as his mistress Corisande de Gramont, otherwise known as "la belle Corisande," at a time when the male line of the family was dying out. Corisande had a son by the king and was thus able to perpetuate the de Gramont name, so that we are all descended from lusty Henry.

In ducal families, primogeniture is the name of the game. The oldest son of the oldest son has a lock on the title. My grandfather's wives kept dying on him, so he married three times, and had children by all three marriages. His third wife, my grandmother, was a lovely Italian girl named Maria Ruspoli. She was seventeen, and my grandfather was fifty-five. On her honeymoon, she called her mother in Rome to say she didn't like being married and wanted to come home. "You didn't like the convent either," her mother said, "but you got used to it."

So she got used to it, and bore her husband two sons, but they were younger sons. It was the sons of the second marriage who would inherit the ducal title, the wealth, and the property. Not being landed or funded,

my father had to go to work, an unusual occurrence in the family. He passed his exams, finally, and his first diplomatic post, as chance would have it, was Washington, where we arrived in 1937. I was five, and when people express surprise that I don't have a foreign accent, the explanation is that if you arrive in a country young enough, you don't have to talk like Henry Kissinger.

At this point history gets into the act. In 1939, when the war broke out, my father took us all back to France—my mother, myself, and my two brothers—and joined the French Air Force, for he had taken flying lessons in Washington. The war between France and Germany was brief, and my father was one of the first to answer the call of General de Gaulle, whom he joined in London. In the meantime, we were in the Basque village of Ustaritz, and I remember being awakened by the sound of marching boots on cobblestones—the German occupying forces.

My mother got us out of France and into Spain and Portugal, where we were able to find passage on a boat back to America, and in the fall of 1940 I was back in my old school, Mrs. Cook's school on Massachusetts Avenue. I spent my spare time going to war movies, identifying each hero with my father, who was in the French escadrille of the RAF and was flying bomber missions over German targets. In one of the movies, Alan Ladd played an OSS agent who was parachuted into France and was posing as a Frenchman. He was picked up by the Gestapo while having lunch in the Champs-Elysées because he used his fork in an American way. The cards of identity might be shuffled but had to be dealt.

In 1943 my father died in a flying accident not far from his base in the South of England. I felt cheated, not only because I wanted him alive, but because if he did die, I wanted him to die in battle. The Free French were bad paymasters, and my mother was left penniless, and went to work for Elizabeth Arden, selling lipsticks in her Connecticut Avenue store. I was doubly dispossessed, for being the son of a younger son, with no claim on the de Gramont estates, and for having lost my father, who, had he remained alive, would have been rewarded by de Gaulle when he came to power after the war.

Now it happened that a Washington friend of my father's, a Belgian diplomat named Jacques de Thier, had been secretly in love with my mother. But being a very proper man, he never said a word about it. Jacques was now posted in Madrid, and when he heard of my father's death, he began courting my mother by letter. The mail in wartime was slow and irregular, and the letters were opened by Spanish censors, but after a couple of years Jacques' message was heard. He proposed, and my mother accepted. Censor no. 266, who had been following the correspondence with interest, wrote *Felicidades* on the envelope of my mother's acceptance letter.

It was chance again, the chance of my father's death and my mother's remarriage, that took us to Madrid in 1946, so that I left Washington, where I had begun to sink roots, even being invited to my classmate Diana Hopkins' birthday party at the White House—her father, Harry Hopkins, lived there. We moved into the Belgian Embassy in the calle Padilla, Jacques being *chargé d'affaires*. It was the proverbial lap of luxury, with servants as numerous as mice. I had a big room with a four-poster bed, and each morning I would be awakened at the sound of metal shutters being opened by a maid wearing a white apron over a starched blue dress, who would then bring me my breakfast tray.

Ah, those Spanish maids . . . the way they looked at you and walked and moved, giving you the sense of flesh under cloth. I was fourteen, and the sap was rising. In the evening, from my window, I could see lovers kissing under the trees. I had my eye on Julia, a red-

The author with parents, 1939

haired Andalusian with lovely hips and a raspy voice, a Carmen with laryngitis. Finding her ironing in the pantry one afternoon, I came up behind her and put my arms around her waist. She laughed and pulled away, saying, *"Sancho no, tu es de massiado joven."* (No, Sancho, you are too young.—I forgot to mention that my first name, Sanche, which actually means Saint Charles, is an old family name going back to the Agramonte days). Julia's rebuff made me think of a home-front movie I had seen in 1943, where Bette Davis sings: "They're either too young or too old, They're either too gray or too grassy green." I was grassy green all right, and went back to solitary pleasures.

Then it was Brussels for two years, gray, drab, pot-bellied Brussels, oily *pommes frites* with *cornichons* and little onions, Gueuze Lambique (beer with some sort of sweet syrup added), the platforms on the backs of streetcars . . . passing, on the way to the French Lycée, the prostitutes near the Gare du Midi, sitting in plate-glass windows at nine in the morning, crocheting or knitting, seldom looking up.

Then the luck of the draw—Jacques was named Consul-General in New York. The summer I was sixteen I went to Camp Sheldrake on Lake Cayuga as a junior counselor. Pat Barlow was four years older, a junior at Cornell, a full counselor, but she liked me.

One of the reasons she liked me was that she was going steady with a senior at Cornell and figured that with me she could get through the summer with her virtue intact, but I didn't know that at the time. I was heady with my good luck, because Pat Barlow was absolutely lovely, with that deeply sweet, demurely sexy, home-coming-queen loveliness, that lack of false worldliness that made European girls seem artificial. Pat Barlow was honey from the honeycomb, in its natural state, with no additives. The older counselors spent their time devising stratagems to ease me out of the way. Once they tried to get me drunk by challenging me to drink a water glass full of bourbon. The only beverage stronger than wine that I had ever tasted was vermouth. I didn't know they were giving me bourbon, but I drank it down, and then, in order not to betray my ignorance, I said: "Say, that's pretty good vermouth." By downing the bourbon and calling it vermouth I had unwittingly one-upped them, and after that they left me alone with Pat. But I was still grassy green, and did not press my advantage, and in spite of many hours spent under a blanket or sharing a sleeping bag, we both ended the summer with our virtues intact. She went back to her Cornell senior, while I mooned about the house playing "The Things We Did Last Summer, I'll Remember All Winter Long." Pat Barlow, where are you today? My God, you'd still be four years older than I am. You're probably a grandmother.

My mother had promised my father that even though I was raised in the United States, she would give me the chance to live in France in the bosom of my family so that I could decide where I wanted to be. In fact I was a mongrel, with a Greek mother (brought up in a shipping family in Germany and France), a French father, and an Italian grandmother. I did not look like the other de Gramonts, being tall and dark, Mediterranean rather than French-looking. I had spent my childhood wandering from place to place and school to school, whereas they were landed and parochial. All I had was the name and the title of count, or as my first wife would later put it, "no-account."

So, at the age of eighteen, I was back on the transatlantic shuttle, staying with cousins in Paris and going to the Sorbonne. My first evening with my family, or more specifically with my cousin Antoine, was a prelude of things to come. Antoine was duc de Guiche, as the oldest son of the duc de Gramont is known while waiting for his father to die. I had not expected the deference accorded in Republican France to titles and family names. One of the guests that night at dinner was a small man with a large bald head and hooded eyes, who spoke with a slight lisp. It turned out that this was Christian Dior, who had been invited because my cousin Antoine wanted some advice on fabrics for curtains. They remained huddled together after dinner for a good half hour examining swatches, and it seemed to me at the time a useful thing to be able to summon up experts in all fields on the strength of one's name.

Antoine took my education in hand. He gave me a copper plate so that I could have *cartes de visite* made—they had to be embossed and not cheaply printed, he explained. When replying to an invitation, it was a mark of special courtesy to fold down the upper right-hand corner of the card. There were various salutations, minutely calibrated to express degrees of deference or lack of it. He upbraided me once for writing *sentiments distingués* to a duchess. "This is the way one addresses tradesmen," he said.

It wasn't such a bad life. I was invited to a great many parties, all because of my name. "Gramont, one *m* or two?" I would often be asked, since there were two distinct families, and the two-*m* Grammonts were upstarts dating back to the recent reign of Napoleon III. The other question to a newcomer such as myself was *"Qu'est-ce que vous êtes par rapport à?"* (Who are you in relation to), and I would have to launch into an elaborate genealogical discourse to establish my bona fide. The idea behind these parties was that one would meet a *jeune fille bien élevée* (well brought-up young lady), whose father might have a bit of *galette* (money), and that one would marry her and live in an apartment or house with a *vue imprenable,* a view that cannot be taken from you, on a park or a cemetery. That is what my cousin René did, making discreet inquiries about his prospective father-in-law's properties and bank account, and making sure of his *vue imprenable* on the Boulevard Maillot, where he lives to this day.

But I was in love with Caroline Child-Villiers, an English girl who was attending Mademoiselle Anita's finishing school. The French girls seemed dessicated before their time, they were already in training to be dowagers, chairpersons of the rose exhibit at Bagatelle or the Bal des Petits Lits Blancs. Whereas Caroline was Tenniel's Alice miraculously grown up, an Alice with tits and ass. My only trump with Caroline was that occasionally I could get her invited to parties, which made me into the pleader I hated to be. One particularly sought-after party was being given for Anne-Aymone de Brantes, whom I called to ask if Caroline could come. "We have enough girls as it is," she brusquely replied. I was brooding over my failed effort when Anne-Aymone called back: *"Maman* says that because she is a foreigner it would be rude not to invite her." Anne-Aymone in later years went on to bigger and better parties as the wife of the President of France, Valéry Giscard d'Estaing.

I never really felt that I belonged to this world to

which my name entitled me. When I announced my name to the *aboyeur* (barker) at the door, who repeated it in stentorian tones, I felt like an imposter, or a passenger on some archaic form of transportation, like a coach-and-four. It was a very handsome coach-and-four, the coachman tipped his hat and the horses were well bred, but what was I doing there? I knew that my mother wanted me to follow in my father's footsteps as a diplomat, but it was not an appealing career. The diplomatic life was one of ceremonies and surfaces, of incessant and boring social obligations, of vacuous tasks meticulously performed. I had seen my stepfather get up at six in the morning in order to greet a Belgian cabinet minister at the airport, and I thought: "This is not for me."

So I made the first major choice of my life, between the old world and the new. It was a liberating thing to turn down the place at table with one's name on it and say, "I think I'll find another eatery." With my two years of Sorbonne behind me, I was admitted into junior year at Yale, where I found that there were different elites, to which I did not belong, but no matter—the lines were fluid enough not to be binding, and I made friends easily.

One of my friends, Hendon Chubb, asked me to take to a Christmas dance a girl he irresistibly described as "beautiful and sad." She was more than that, she was, if such a thing can be imagined, a six-foot-two-inch sprite, and in my eyes an extraordinary beauty, Titania of *A Midsummer Night's Dream* in human guise. I was captivated, particularly when, after a weekend in New Haven, as her train was leaving the station, she mouthed the words, "I love you" from behind the window—a scene I found repeated in a story by J.D. Salinger, to whom the same thing may have happened quite independently.

To please Margo, an ardent admirer of Ezra Pound's early poetry, I arranged for us to visit Pound at St. Elizabeth's insane asylum, where he had been committed to avoid standing trial for treason. I was amazed at how easy it was. All it took was a letter, which he promptly answered. It was my first meeting with a major writer. Pound, although in his seventies, seemed like a hyperactive boy, unable to sit still, jumping up to fetch a book or a pamphlet, talking a blue streak in several languages, and pacing the corridor. He was brilliant, but also a bit daffy, and it seemed to me that the insanity plea was not pure pretense. In spite of his political idiocy, his blind love of Mussolini, and his anti-Semitic diatribes, it was hard not to like his energy and optimism, although in retrospect they seem like forms of self-absorption. He was looking for disciples, not friends. Even so, it was a shock at the end of our visit when this great figure in the literature of our century was led into the hospital dining room to take his seat at a table where two loonies were throwing peas at each other with their spoons. "Probably literary critics," I said to Margo as we left.

After Yale, what? I did not feel I had any particular talent, and only knew what I did *not* want to do. I did not want to be a doctor or a lawyer or a businessman. Something of the de Gramont disdain for being in trade or the professions had rubbed off on me. By attrition, I arrived at journalism, which seemed congenial. My father's death had me wary of commitment and participation. He had rushed off to join de Gaulle and look what it got him, an early grave at age thirty-three. I liked the idea of being an observer of events, of being paid to watch and not take part. It was a profession where you could stand outside the ring of fire, slightly aloof, keeping your distance. I was also impressed by Albert Camus' remark, "the journalist is the historian of the moment."

In 1955 I went to the Columbia School of Journalism, which did its best to duplicate the working conditions of an actual newspaper. The results, however, were unconvincing, and the work I was asked to do did not seem real. When they assigned me to interview Dag Hammarskjöld at the United Nations, I knew I would never get past the security guards, but I naively tried, instead of joining some of my fellow students, who covered their assignments from the initial-carved tables of the West End Bar. I did, I remember, attend a sidewalk press conference outside the UN given by the former President of France, Vincent Auriol. I questioned him in French so eagerly that he replied with a pun: "*La presse est bien pressée ici*" (The press is in a big hurry here).

In those days, the editors of out-of-town newspapers came to Columbia to recruit young reporters at low salaries, and I was hired by the managing editor of the *Worcester Telegram,* Frank Murphy, at $57 a week. Worcester was a dreary factory town, but I loved the work, and would stay long past my shift to see the paper come up. The sight of my byline made me dizzy with joy. In retrospect, it seems silly that such a small thing could have given me so much pleasure. I think I was pleased at being part of a great enterprise, the gathering, writing, and editing of the day's news, the only team effort I have ever been comfortable with.

In the fall of 1955, France was at war in Algeria with nationalists called "fellaghas" who wanted their country to be independent. Half a million French soldiers were serving there. One day there arrived in my mail at Worcester a draft notice instructing me to report at such and such a date to the barracks in Vernon, a town in Normandy. I could easily have abstained, but I felt I owed a debt to my father. Since he had gone off to war, I should go too, even though I was not sympathetic with the aim of keeping Algeria French. Also, it seemed like an adventure, and I was getting a bit bored with Worcester. When I announced the news to Frank Murphy, he shook his head in disbelief and said: "I've lost a lot of men for a lot of reasons, but this is the first time I've lost one to the French Army."

It was a shock to be transported overnight from the city room of the *Worcester Telegram* to a French infantry barracks. At six-foot-four, I was the only private in the regiment who had a made-to-order uniform. In my dormitory, there was a fellow with one leg shorter than the other, which made me wonder just how hard-up the infantry was. I could sense among my bunkmates a certain lack of enthusiasm for military service. One of them claimed to suffer from asthma, and coughed through the night, and was sent home after a week. Another wet his bed, but the sergeant announced one day at roll call: "We know what to do with bed wetters here—we put them in the top bunk."

Since I had been out of France for three years, it took a while to adjust to local custom. One day we were hustled into the courtyard to be reviewed by the general commanding the military region. A portly,

With a noncommissioned officer (right) and mortar equipment in Algeria

white-whiskered old fellow in a képi with burst capillaries in his cheeks looked us over, asking each one of us about our *état civil* (social status). *"Marié, deux enfants, mon général"* (married with two children), the man on my left boomed out. *"Célibataire, mon général"* (bachelor), I proclaimed when he stood in front of me. Then came the turn of the man on my right, who shouted: *"En concubinage, mon général"* (in concubinage), and to keep a straight face, I had to remind myself that concubinage in France was a legal state and that the man's "concubine" was eligible for allotments, like a wife.

The French army had its share of martinets, but generally the atmosphere was relaxed. The expression I remember hearing most often was *"faut pas chercher à comprendre"* (don't try to understand), indicating a fatalism that made all zeal or superfluous effort suspect. Military service was an unfortunate episode one had to get through with minimal damage. Another expression was . . . *"coincer la bulle,"* . . . (squeezing the bubble), which referred to the bubble on a mortar sight that had to be positioned between two markers, and which meant to breathe easy, to sit around in suspended animation. This was the principal aim of every red-blooded French soldier. My favorite expression, however, referred to the incomprehensible and possibly harmful decisions of the high command: *"Quand les baleines s'agitent, les crevettes souffrent"* (When the whales become agitated, the shrimp suffer).

We were supposed to be in for two years, and the idea was to avoid being sent to Algeria as long as possible. Accordingly, I signed up for corporal's training, sergeant's training, and officer's school, and I managed to stay in France for a year before crossing the Mediterranean as a Second Lieutenant in the Colonial Infantry. This was a corps made up of men recruited from France's colonies in Africa and the Far East. My platoon consisted of thirty coal-black Senegalese with tribal marks on their cheeks, Moslems for the most part, who must have wondered why they were fighting their fellow Moslems, the Algerian nationalists. My private priority was not to kill "fellaghas" but to avoid casualties in my platoon, which I was able to do thanks to good luck and assorted stratagems.

In compliance with their religious beliefs, the Senegalese had a special diet, based on rice and hot sauce. In addition, I received a monthly allotment of Cola nuts, a bitter West African nut with a reddish-brown husk, which I kept locked in a chest under my bed, doling them out for acts of heroism and meritorious service, for there was nothing the Senegalese were more fond of.

My most hazardous duty was to take my platoon, according to regulations, once a week to a military brothel in the town of Medea, twenty miles from our bivouac, through a ravine. The regulations specified that as commander of this detachment, I had to stand up during the journey in an armored car, flying the French flag. But there were snipers in them thar ravines, and I soon saw that I was a choice target, and decided I was damned if I was going to be shot while taking my Senegalese to get laid, so I devised a uniformed dummy that stood up in my place and took the fire.

The non-coms in my platoon were heavily decorated veterans of the Indo-China war. Decorations for some reason were called "bananas," and one of my men wore, among the striped ribbons of his French campaigns, a bright blue metal-framed "banana" that was decidedly un-French. I asked him what it was, and he proudly explained that he had served in the French Battalion in Korea and been awarded *"La Deestaingwish,"* the U.S. Distinguished Service Cross. Aside from decorations, the non-coms had brought back from their campaigns a truly awesome array of tropical diseases, including heretofore unknown strains of venereal ones, and were constantly giving themselves shots of penicillin. If the "fellaghas" didn't get them, the clap would.

Our main loyalty, as I have said, was not to France, or to the Army, but to our platoon, and we managed pretty much to walk the line between performance of duty and avoidance of combat. I was released at the end of 1957, after about twenty-seven months of service. With two other released officers, I drove through Morocco and Spain in a battered Citroën. In Seville, the car broke down, and my two friends proceeded without me. The mechanic who was fixing my car introduced me to his pretty cousin, and the annoyance of waiting for the car turned into a romantic interlude. It seemed like a vindication, an Appointment in Seville, all these years after having been spurned by Julia, the Andalusian maid. I remember tiled floors, a brass bed with creaky springs, and jolly sounds in the courtyard of a working-class neighborhood.

A man just out of the army is a man ripe for the plucking, and no sooner had I returned to New York in January 1958 than Margo plucked me. I was in love, but I also had an ulterior motive. With the promise of a job in the New York office of the Associated Press, I needed a green card fast, and would get one by marrying Margo. We were wed in Mexico City, where my stepfather was Belgian Ambassador. The entire embassy staff was invited, and brought presents to a couple they had never met before, an act of blind obedience quite in keeping with the act of blind faith Margo and I had just committed, for we were totally

Sanche and Margo on their wedding day, 1958

unsuited to one another. One of the ironies of our union was that her deceased father, Frank Kinnicutt, had drafted the legislation to restrict immigration into the United States, and now she was marrying—horrors!—an immigrant. Another irony was that she had converted to Catholicism because I was a (lukewarm) Catholic, and presently became, as the converted tend to do, more Catholic than the Pope. Indeed, I believe the high point of our marriage was the ceremony itself, performed by the Papal Nuncio to Mexico City in the baroque Nunciature. Everything after that was anticlimax.

After a year on the Associated Press, I was hired by the *New York Herald-Tribune* as a rewrite man, cranking out C-heads, releases, obits, weather stories, and crime stories phoned in by our police reporters. Once I took a story from our star woman reporter, Marguerite Higgins, who was covering a political convention, and had a demure, little-girl voice. She was called away from the phone for a second, and when she got back someone else had apparently grabbed it, and I was able to understand her reputation for combativeness when I heard her say, in the same little-girl voice, "Get off this fuckin' phone, you goddamn, motherfuckin' sonofabitch."

Bored with rewrite, I longed to get out of the office. The day city-editor, Buddy Weiss, sent me to cover General de Gaulle, who was visiting New York. I managed to infiltrate the official party and accompanied the general to his suite in the Waldorf-Astoria. I called Buddy and said: "What do I do now?" Buddy, a practical joker, said: "Hide in the closet." Green as grass, I hid in the closet, where I was discovered a few minutes later by a security guard.

If I keep returning to the role of chance in determining my life, I have my reasons. One night in the spring of 1960, there were three rewrite men sitting around the city desk with nothing much to do when Jerry Katz, the night city-editor, cupped his hand over the phone and asked: "Any you guys know anything about opera?" I knew nothing about opera, but smelling a chance to get out of the office, I volunteered. "Go over the Met right away," Jerry said. The Met in those days was two blocks away from the paper. It happened that Leonard Warren, who was singing that night in *La Forza del Destino,* had collapsed on the stage with a heart attack in the middle of the third act. The *New York Times* music critic had left after the second act. Our man, Jay Harrison, had also left, but had the presence of mind to leave his wife behind, and it was she who had called Jerry Katz. Leonard Warren died on stage in his wife's arms just as I arrived, and Rudolf Bing, the general manager, made a melancholy announcement that the performance could not go on. It was high drama, and when I got back to the paper, I had an experience I had only heard about—the presses were stopped, the front page was replated, and copy boys tore the pages out of my typewriter paragraph by paragraph.

The next morning, the *Trib* had a full account of Leonard Warren's death, while the *Times* carried a review of a performance that had not exactly taken place as described. For that hour's work, made possible by the proximity of the paper and the opera house, and by the alert Mrs. Harrison, I won the Pulitzer Prize for the best story under the pressure of a deadline. When I saw my plaque in the lobby of the *Trib,* next to Walter Lippmann's, I felt not only the honor that I had been done, but the disparity between our respective achievements, his for a body of work as the most respected columnist in America, mine for a fluke. But as the Spanish say, they can't take away the dances that you've danced.

In 1961, before the Pulitzers were announced, the paper sent me to Paris, and I realized my dream of being a foreign correspondent. Margo stayed behind, being by then involved in fasting and health foods. She once fasted for thirty-two days, taking nothing but distilled water, and the weight on her six-foot-two-inch frame dropped to ninety pounds. I told her we could make a fortune renting her out to protest movements.

From Paris, I covered the Algerian war I had recently served in, which was entering its final phase with the rebellion of part of the French army in a last-ditch effort to keep Algeria French. The renegade generals were egged on by the French settlers, known as *pieds-noirs* (black feet). Every day in Algiers there were bombs and murders. Henry Tanner, the *New York Times* correspondent, got an idiotic query from his foreign desk: "How do you tell a *pied-noir* from an Algerian?" "The *pied-noir,*" he replied, "is holding a smoking gun, and the Algerian is lying in a pool of blood." Sometimes in the morning, in front of the Hotel Aletti, where we were staying, we would see sanitation crews cleaning blood from the sidewalk.

In December 1961 I was sent to the Congo to cover the secession of Katanga province, usually described in dispatches as "mineral-rich," and the intervention of United Nations troops. The capital of Katanga, Elizabethville, was surrounded by the UN and was being defended by Katangese gendarmes and white mercenaries. When UN dive-bombers destroyed the post office there was no way for correspondents to get their stories out. I caught a ride with a British reporter leaving for Northern Rhodesia, who had one other passenger, a Swiss member of Katangese leader Moise Tshombe's civilian staff.

We were heading south on a deserted dirt road leading out of Elizabethville when firing broke out from a patch of woods on our left. A bazooka shell exploded against the side of the car. Sitting in the back, I was flung out and saw the British reporter lying not far from me, his head covered with blood. He reminded me of the Sherwin-Williams paint ad, a can of red paint being poured over a globe, with the message: "Sherwin-Williams covers the world."

Then I saw blue-helmeted soldiers emerging from the woods. They were Swedish UN troops, and had apparently mistaken us for mercenaries. Not entirely mistaken, for the Swiss civilian was in a sense a mercenary, and it was later alleged that he had been fleeing with a shoe box filled with cash, which was never found. After ambushing us, the Swedes called for ambulances to take us to the UN hospital. I was in an ambulance with the badly hit Swiss, whose head was alongside my feet, one of which he clasped with his hand. When the ambulance doors were opened, I heard an Italian voice say: "*E morto*" (He's dead). I thought he was talking about me, and I registered a vigorous protest, but it was the Swiss he was talking about. The medical staff was Italian, and I waited my turn beside Irish and Ghurka troops wounded in the day's fighting, to be operated on. I had shrapnel in my knee and shoulder, light wounds compared to the others. My mishap was given pretty good play in my paper, which carried a headline that said: "De Gramont Under the Knife."

Being shot made me come to terms with a childish notion I had of my own invulnerability. I felt that my dead father, wherever he was, was looking after my interests. I had now been given ample evidence that such was not the case, which caused a slight personality change. I became more wary, more guarded, more suspicious. One of my teachers at the lycée had told me once that I reminded him of Rousseau's Good Savage in my cheerfully ingenuous disposition, but I lost that for good in Elizabethville. A minimum of skepticism was necessary for survival. I should, for starters, have chosen my traveling companions more carefully. As for the Swedes, one of the correspondents who came to see me at the hospital observed: "What do you expect of a people who have not fought a war in three hundred years?"

I returned to Paris with my left leg and left shoulder in a cast. I was then living with a poet and flower child named Nancy Ryan, who had that deep and mysterious woman thing that I had been missing with Margo. Nancy had been for years secretary to the playwright S.N. Behrman, and had left New York to travel through Europe, but interrupted her wandering to stay with me in Paris. As it developed, we were together eighteen years. Sam Behrman, who divided mankind into life-diminishers and life-enhancers, and was clearly one of the latter, came to Paris and gave us his blessing, dubbing Nancy "the barefoot Contessa." She was a free spirit, with a beauty that shone from within, and she sometimes wondered what she was doing with this unlikely offshoot of the French aristocracy.

By the time our son Gabriel was born in November 1962, I had been transferred to Rome, and was still married to Margo, who insisted on a Catholic annulment. My de Gramont relatives were shocked that Nancy had given birth to my child out of wedlock, to which I responded with the Falstaffian cry: "God stand up for bastards!" One of my aunts announced that she was coming to Rome, and wanted to see my son, but could not of course meet Nancy. Gabriel should be playing in the Piazza Navona at a designated time, so that she could observe him without having to be introduced to his mother. I am ashamed to say that I agreed to her request.

I spent a good deal of time covering wars in those days, the *Trib* in its decline being shorthanded. What I saw of the world was its bloody turmoil, in Cyprus, the Middle East, the Congo again, and Vietnam. Life in Rome by contrast was peaceful and easygoing, with from time to time an important story like the death of a Pope. When Nancy was pregnant with Gabriel in 1962 we stopped one Sunday afternoon in a church we liked off the north end of the Navona. It was at the time the custom of John XXIII to make unannounced visits each Sunday to a Roman church, and there he

was. Nancy was on the aisle, and as Pope John came by, backed up by incense-bearers, he spotted her bulging stomach and stopped and blessed her, conferring a "madonna and child" aspect to Gabriel's birth.

When John XXIII died the following year, and I was filing columns of type each day, a visiting friend said with sarcasm, "And what did the 81-year-old Holy Father do today?" It was his way of telling me how formulaic newspaper writing was. Each story led with "Pope John XXIII was reported today, etc. . . .", and continued with a second paragraph that invariably began, "the 81-year-old Holy Father, etc."

I began to think that I was in a rut and should move on to something else, a notion that was reinforced by my having met Alan Moorhead, author of the "Nile" books, who had started his career as a war correspondent. Moorhead encouraged me to leave newspaper work and write books, as he had done. He promised me that I would not regret it.

So in 1964, when I came back to New York on home leave, I quit the *Trib*, which, as it turned out, only lasted two more years. To assure myself a financial base, I contracted to become a Contributing Writer with the *Saturday Evening Post*. I had already started working on a translation of the memoirs of the Duc de Saint-Simon, with whom I felt a sort of kinship, for he was a courtier at Versailles under the reign of Louis XIV, but also an outsider who had the odd compulsion to chronicle what he was observing, with no thought of publication. This quality of witness to a time, of events carefully observed and pungently described, was what I aspired to myself. Saint-Simon seemed to be writing not only for his own pleasure, but from some obscurely felt duty toward history. In my view, he was one of the great French prose stylists, although he had not intended any of his memoirs to be read.

My book on Saint-Simon, called *The Age of Magnificence*, did not bring fame and fortune, and my *SatEvePost* articles were few and far between. In addition, I had bought a huge apartment in Rome. Afflicted by the common folly of wanting to own a piece of the eternal city, I found myself in a financial crisis. Nancy and I hit on the scheme of advertising our apartment for rent complete with a butler and cook—ourselves. We survived this way for a year, as servants to our tenants. The apartment was taken for short rentals by movie people such as the director Joseph Losey and the Franco-Armenian singer Charles Aznavour. It all came to an end when Aznavour fired us after a burglary. How could we be fired? We owned the place. We fired *him*.

After Saint-Simon, I wrote a study of the *ancien régime* called *Epitaph for Kings*. I was becoming typecast

*With second wife, Nancy, in their apartment in Rome
where they served as butler and cook, 1964*

as someone who wrote about French subjects. At this point, I was assigned to interview Luigi Barzini, who had just brought out *The Italians.* We found that we had quite a bit in common, since he too wrote in English and had spent years in the United States. But it seemed to me that he was basically Italian, whereas I was not basically French. He made fun in his book of the ridiculous titles Italians love to use, such as *Profesore* and *Ingeniere* and *Onorevole.* But whenever he called, he always told the maid, *"Che il Onorevole Barzini"* (this is the honorable Barzini). He was a part of what he was mocking.

Barzini urged me to do for the French what he had done for the Italians, a sort of national portrait. Why not, I thought? It would mean moving to France for research, and I had had enough of Rome, a seductive but too indolent lady. I sold the apartment and moved to Paris, where we lived through the student-worker uprising of 1968. Through friends I met André Malraux, himself a one-time political activist, adventurer, and looter of Cambodian temples. But now he was Minister of Culture, on the side of the government, describing the students as "over-agitated dunces" as he talked a mile a minute, his face alive with facial tics. It

was coming home one night from a dinner with Malraux that Nancy and I were caught in a demonstration and chased by the riot police into a courtyard. A policeman looked us both over and then clubbed Nancy as the more inviting target. This personal experience of police brutality made me join the demonstrators, and I spent the next ten days marching and throwing cobblestones and fleeing teary-eyed as the police fired tear gas grenades. The whole movement collapsed, however, when the Communist Party took a law-and-order stand.

Having spent too much time demonstrating instead of writing, I was broke again, or as the French say, *fauché* (scythed). I needed to find someplace cheap to live to write my book on the French, and a friend proposed Tangier, which had an American school where I could obtain a scholarship for my son. We moved there in the fall of 1968, and stayed four years.

Tangier had an expatriate community of writers, chief among them Paul and Jane Bowles. Jane had suffered a stroke and been hospitalized in Málaga, but Paul was there, courteous and low-keyed, drinking his tea and smoking his kif, complaining about the numerous mortifications of life in Morocco but never contemplating a move. He seemed to need to live among a people who made him uneasy. "Be sure never to use a mailbox to mail your letters," he advised. "Mail them only from the post office." I asked him why and he said "because the urchins throw lit rags in the mailboxes as a good joke on the Nazarenes." He saw life in Morocco as a state of war between the locals and the expatriates, or Nazarenes.

Nancy and I were taken up by Lord David Herbert, younger son of the Earl of Pembroke, the social arbiter of Tangier. He often had notables passing through, and being unmarried, asked Nancy to serve as his hostess. It was through David that we met Cecil Beaton and Rex Harrison. For Rex Harrison, David had his Spanish chef prepare his best dinner—a delicious Mediterranean fish known in French as St. Pierre and in English as John Dorry, with Spanish-style fried potatoes. After dinner, David asked me to give Rex and his wife a ride down to their yacht, and as we drove toward the harbor, I heard Rex say in a stage whisper to his wife: "Just like David to give us fish and chips."

Tangier was a good place to work, as there wasn't much else to do, aside from an occasional swim in the Atlantic surf. *The French* came out in 1969 and did quite well. I flew to New York for a publicity tour, feeling like the professional Frenchman which in my heart I knew I was not. But I seemed trapped in the role. Another 1969 production was my daughter Amber, born in Tangier and raised by a Moroccan nurse,

*Gabriel and Amber, on terrace of house in
Tangier, 1972*

so that her first language was Moghrebi. To this day when she is angry she uses a phrase which must be a translation of something she heard from her nurse: "I am not your friend."

With the money from *The French,* and the cheapness of life in Tangier, I could afford to write fiction. My first novel, *Lives to Give,* was the story of a French resistance group in which one of the four leaders has betrayed the other three. My brother Pat, a psychologist, later informed me that the novel's real theme was the futility of commitment, which was tied to my sense of loss at my father's death.

Then I wrote a novel in the form of fictitious memoirs by a Count de Gramont living at the court of Louis XV, called *The Way Up.* The trouble was that, although clearly labeled a novel, some reviewers thought the book was an authentic memoir, and so did some readers, which led to confusion. Looking back, I now see my early books as attempts to write my "Frenchness" and family background out of my system.

One day in Tangier, it occurred to me that although I saw mainly American and English expatri-

ates, I was living on the African continent. I decided to travel to black Africa, and took a boat trip down the Niger River, which left such vivid impressions that I wanted to write the story of the river's discovery. *The Strong Brown God,* in which I endeavored to do for the Niger what Alan Moorhead had done for the Nile, was the first book I wrote that had nothing to do with France or the French. Nancy and I took a two-month trip down the Niger, crossing the Sahara twice, and I can tell you that if you want to find out what a woman is really like, cross the Sahara with her—Nancy was a gallant traveling companion, cheerful in the worst of times, more resilient than I was.

Tangier was beginning to seem like lotus land. The expatriate life was getting me down. The country was beautiful, but I had nothing in common with its people. I didn't want to live in a place where I couldn't understand what people were saying in the street. I felt that I was an American writer, and I wanted to get back to America. I was impressed by a phrase of Joseph Conrad's, "my nationality is the language I write in." Language, it seemed to me, was more important than where you were born or who your parents were.

I resolved to return to New York, become an American citizen, and legally change my name. I was sick and tired of people asking: "Who translates you into English?" By changing my name I could become what Hazlitt called "The Gentleman in the Parlour," anonymous rather than tagged by his name. I would take the letters of my last name and rearrange them, so that it was the same name and yet different. I was writing articles for the *New York Times Magazine* at the time, which I began signing Ted Morgan, and eventually, after I was back in New York, I took out my American citizenship and made my name change legal.

My wife and children were supportive, they didn't mind becoming Morgans, and my French family shrugged, ascribing the change to my well-known *esprit de contradiction.* When Rob Cowley, my editor on the Niger river book, asked me to write an account of what it meant to become an American, I agreed, coming up with a sort of half-memoir, half-editorial called *On Becoming American.* "Sixty Minutes" picked it up, and Mike Wallace went to France and interviewed my cousin Henri de Gramont. I had written that I preferred a General Electric refrigerator to a Louis XIV chair, and Henri stole the show when he told Wallace: "You see zis Louis XIV chair over zere? Wiz zis chair I can buy many refrigerators."

Once again chance intervened in my life, in the form of Patrick O'Higgins, who had been secretary to Helena Rubinstein and was now working on a memoir about Somerset Maugham, which was mostly of his own invention. Patrick had lung cancer, didn't feel he could go on with the memoir, and asked me to take it over. Upon examination, I found that a full-scale biography of Maugham might be attempted, and I stepped into the breach. Patrick had half a lung left, and his doctor told him never to laugh. But when I debriefed him, it was hard not to, as when he said of Maugham's secretary, Alan Searle: "He used to be quite a dish, but now he's quite a tureen," and then started laughing at his own joke, ending up doubled up in pain on the floor.

I liked the idea of biography because it was focused on one man's life rather than sprawling and diffuse. I had started out writing obits on rewrite, and what was a biography but a long obituary? I chose as my models Boswell and Lytton Strachey. I liked Boswell's concreteness, the way he gave the reader not only Dr. Johnson's mixture of intolerance and kindness, but also his brown stockings, his disordered buttons, the dust settling on his wig, the way he cut his nails and talked to his cat. In Strachey I liked the willingness to go against the Victorian suppression of unedifying facts. I made my motto the French phrase, *tout est bon à dire,* (everything is good to say, or it is good to say everything). That was the way Saint-Simon had written his memoirs. It was what Dr. Johnson recommended when he said: "If nothing but the bright side of great characters should be shown, we should sit in despondency and think it utterly impossible to imitate them in anything."

Accordingly, I dealt candidly with Maugham's homosexuality and with the more pathetic aspects of his senility, and was roundly chastized by certain late Victorians still in our midst. I felt that the reader should have in hand *all* the data, and not some cosmeticized or bowdlerized version, in order to make up his own mind. The lives of great men were instructive precisely because of the character flaws they had overcome.

When I wrote *Maugham,* I took the family to live in a ski resort in California's Sierra Nevada, thinking that the combination of mind-work and body-work would be a good thing, and it was. But it was also there that Nancy and I parted company, for when I had finished the book and wanted to return to New York, she elected to remain in California. Just as there is a life expectancy, there is a relationship expectancy, ranging from still-born to life-long. At eighteen years, ours fell somewhere in between. Nancy was better in the Sahara than in the daily routine of family life. She was still adventurous, while I had become sedentary and career-minded.

Author with Gabriel and Amber and fiancée, Mary Donald — Christmas, 1981

My publisher suggested I follow *Maugham* up with *Churchill,* on the grounds that since both men had been born in the same year and had died in the same year, I was already familiar with the period. I realized that a lot had already been written about Churchill, but I thought I could come up with new material and explore a complicated personality. Finding myself unable to fit the whole life into a single volume, I ended up with a book on the first forty years of his life, called *Churchill: Young Man in a Hurry.* My goal was to elicit in the reader this simple response: "Now I know what this guy was like."

After Churchill, I went on to a one-volume FDR, in which again I applied the *tout est bon à dire* rule, which led the fervently pro-Roosevelt New Dealer Ernie Cuneo, who was a source and became a friend, to exclaim: "As a Knight of the Round Table, I don't want to know that Lancelot was diddling Guinevere." My point was that accounts of FDR's mishaps, some of which other historians had ignored as being irrelevant or in bad taste, did not diminish the man but served as a corrective to the plaster-saint image. The personality of a great and complex man has a rainbow-like intangibility, which can only be caught by giving full value to all the colors.

The amount of research I had to dig through for FDR was prodigious. Normally I liked research. It was a form of archeology, like digging up a buried statue piece by piece, putting it together, and breathing life into it. But this time, as I spent month after month in the FDR Library in Hyde Park, I went through my first experience of burn-out. One day the pages blurred, and I got in my car and drove up the Hudson, and sat by the river for hours, wondering whether I could ever finish.

So after FDR, I said to myself, "No more dead statesmen." I wanted to try the biography of someone who was still alive. Imagine being a contemporary of Mozart's and writing his biography and going to see him, and asking: "Listen, Amadeus, how were you getting on with your wife at the time you wrote *The Magic Flute?*" I wanted that kind of access, that kind of direct information.

With William S. Burroughs in Boulder, Colorado, July 1985

Michael White

In Tangier, and later in London, I had made friends with one of the most curious and interesting figures in contemporary American literature, William S. Burroughs. As FDR was "the great insider," somehow in tune with the currents of mainstream America, Burroughs was "the great outsider," who had rebelled against his affluent St. Louis background and become a criminal and a drug addict. His novel *Naked Lunch*

had been stopped by U.S. Customs on grounds of obscenity, and he followed it with other works dubbed "experimental," becoming a leader of the counter-culture and a sort of *éminence grise* to many writers and rock musicians. What he had told me of his life made it sound like a picaresque novel, and I was delighted when he agreed to let me write his biography.

Burroughs was seventy in 1984, and now lives quietly with his cats in Lawrence, Kansas. The first time I went out there to tape what would add up to more than one hundred hours of interviews, I thought to myself that the one drawback of a live subject was that there would be no death scene, so that the book would end sort of hanging in the air. As we sat down to start taping, he seemed to read my mind, giving me a piercing look and saying: "Don't think I'm going to kick off to suit you." I reassured him that I much preferred to have him alive, words that I have in the meantime come to believe.

I don't know what I'm going to do after I finish Burroughs. When people wonder how I could go from FDR to Burroughs, I explain that my whole aim has been to avoid expertise. I never wanted to be a Churchill expert or an FDR expert, and serve on committees, and write prefaces. I was interested in biography as a literary form, and I wanted to see how far I could take it. As a friend of mine said, "Biographers are the only ones today who are writing modernist prose." My instinct tells me that when I learn to do something well, it's time to move on, as I moved away from newspaper writing. I have a hunch that the next step for me will be fiction, and, as I did before, I want to start afresh, not as a biographer who writes novels, but with a new name. I've been playing around with anagrams lately. How does Tom Garden sound?

BIBLIOGRAPHY

Fiction:

Lives to Give, as Sanche de Gramont. New York: Putnam, 1971.

The Way Up: The Memoirs of Count Gramont, as Sanche de Gramont. New York: Putnam, 1972.

Nonfiction:

As Sanche de Gramont:

The Secret War: The Story of International Espionage since World War II. New York: Putnam, 1962.

The Age of Magnificence: The Memoirs of the Duc de Saint-Simon, selected, edited, and translated by Sanche de Gramont. New York: Putnam, 1963.

Epitaph for Kings. New York: Putnam, 1967.

The French: Portrait of a People. New York: Putnam, 1969.

Morgan with Allen Ginsberg (right) in Boulder, Colorado, July 1985

The Strong Brown God: The Story of the Niger River. London: Hart-Davis, 1975; Boston: Houghton, 1976.

As Ted Morgan:

On Becoming American. Boston: Houghton, 1978.

Maugham. New York: Simon & Schuster, 1980; published as *Somerset Maugham.* London: J. Cape, 1980.

Rowing toward Eden. Boston: Houghton, 1981.

Churchill: Young Man in a Hurry, 1874-1915. New York: Simon & Schuster, 1982; also published as *Churchill, 1874-1915.* London: J. Cape, 1983.

FDR: A Biography. New York: Simon & Schuster, 1985; London: Grafton, 1986.

Robert Pinsky

1940-

Long Branch, New Jersey, is an ocean resort, once a famous watering spot painted by Winslow Homer, visited by Abraham Lincoln and Diamond Jim Brady. "The Newport of its day," people said. (My poet friend Bob Hass has discovered, in a history of California, that in its early days the little town of Berkeley styled itself "the Long Branch of the West.")

But in the days when my four grandparents moved to Long Branch, and later when I grew up there, the town was decayed: the beach eroded, the boardwalk on the famous bluffs given over to honky-tonk, many of the immense Victorian "cottages" on Ocean Avenue converted to hotels or to "cook-alones." When I first read in Yeats the name of the Irish hero Cuchulain, the name seemed a perfect spelling of the Yiddish term for such buildings of multiple "kitchenettes." The ethnic coloration of the town, and especially of the beachfront hotels and penny arcades, the bars and restaurants, was Jewish and Italian. In the summer season, everybody played the horses at Monmouth Park, which brought money to the town. High-school teachers worked as cashiers at the pari-mutuel windows.

In this half-dead but still gaudy and once glorious setting, I was born and raised. Downtown, a few blocks from the beach, my grandfather Dave Pinsky owned the Broadway Tavern. My father, Milford Pinsky, was an optician. All of us—my parents, and my aunts and uncles and cousins, and my brother and sister and I—graduated from Long Branch High School. This is what the town was like: I had the same homeroom teacher as my father, Miss Scott, because Miss Scott always took that part of the alphabet.

This kind of fantastic, almost whimsically extreme small-town stagnation blended with the shabby raffishness of an historic, ethnic pleasure-and-gambling spot with fire companies (*e.g.*, "The Phil Daly Ladder and Hose") named for the nineteenth-century gamblers who endowed them. Critics have described the spirit of my poems as "urban" or "suburban"; this startles me, because I know relatively little about cities or suburbs. My first inner landscape is based on the frozen, enchanted microcosm of a small town's family names and street names, the doleful Romance of a honky-tonk oceanfront in winter, streets of shapeless

Robert Pinsky

two-family houses and corner stores, local sports leagues and volunteer firehouse hangouts, the sinister glamour of Mafia bars called Cammarano's, the Paddock, Tee-Tee's Lounge, the Silver Dollar, Mickey B's, the Piano Bar. Long Branch was a kind of Summer White House for certain Mob families, just as it had once been for Garfield and Grant, and my father made the once-famous yellow lenses worn to hearings and trials by the celebrated, insuperable Vito Genovese.

People who have not grown up in a partly closed provincial world, especially such a world connected by intervening water to the larger world, might misunderstand what a certain kind of childhood in such a place is like. The enclosing, lower-middle-class Dublin of James Joyce's pub gossips, the scruffy Odessa of Isaac Babel's porters and dockside toughs, are too self-suffi-

Robert, about 1943

traditional pose. One of the first presents I can remember getting is a pair of boxing gloves from him. His father, my great-grandfather, came to this country from Poland, where Jews sometimes ran taverns, but when asked what Grandpa Dave's father did the family all use the same word, "laborer."

Dave's rowdy confidence and swank were something to admire. In his bar I first saw television (a soccer game). All sorts of town people and racetrack people drank there, and accorded him the peculiar deference that barkeepers sometimes command. Stories about guns, shipments, beatings-up surrounded him. Long Branch's chief of police was a former partner of his from the old days, and Dave knew the detectives and patrolmen well, too. He had big hands and an ape face, a gentile wife (his third), an enormous tree and family dinner at Christmas. Army Ippolito, the Long Branch High football coach when I was in school, once told my Spanish class a long story about being taken to Yankee Stadium by Grandpa Dave when Army was a kid. It had something to do with Army feeling faint, and my grandfather's comic callousness.

I wonder if Dave was a spontaneous or willed assimilationist. Why, for example, did he call his first

cient as communities to know that they are mean or provincial. To be a child where you know that every storekeeper and cop, every bookie and old lady, will recognize your name, is to belong to a world. Such belonging is both good and bad, in ways memorably evoked by writers like Babel and Joyce. But because a few significant parts of that Long Branch world belonged to my family—for instance the bar, my father's optical office, his beautiful sisters, his reputation as an athlete—there was some reflected glory. When you are small, you do not know that you are a child in a lower-middle-class Jewish family living in an economically depressed, culturally low backwater. It feels more like being a Renaissance nobleman's son. Up to a certain age (and I may have been eleven or twelve before I realized that "Give My Regards to Broadway" referred to a street in New York, not Long Branch), I had, in a way, an aristocratic upbringing.

Like some other aristocracies, this one was somewhat stained by crime. My grandfather Dave had been a bootlegger during Prohibition and in a minor way a gangster. My aunt Thelma demurred at this word when I used it once. "He and his friends went into the wholesale liquor business," she said, "and it happened to be during Prohibition." Before that, he was a professional fighter for a time, and there is a picture of him as a young man scowling and putting up his dukes in the

Dave Pinsky "putting up his dukes"

*Grandpa Dave with Robert at 36 Rockwell Avenue,
Long Branch New Jersey*

legs, attended by a second husband about fifteen years her junior—when Aunt Kitty of the other, less gaudy side of the family came over and assumed that Thelma was my wife. And my father was six years old when their mother Rose died after giving birth to Thelma.

Thelma and I walked through the Jewish cemetery on Long Branch Avenue to Rose's grave, a grave I remembered from very early. Around the time of her death, someone had perfected a process for preserving photographs on headstones, under thick glass or mica, and as a famous beauty dead at twenty-four Rose had an oval portrait of that kind on her stone. A few years ago, somebody vandalized the cemetery, knocking stones over and smashing many of these photographs to white blurs. Looking with Thelma for the right row of graves, we fretted for Rose's picture—but it survived. I was also afraid she might not look as amazingly beautiful as I remembered. But the picture still shows a wonderful face, like Thelma's but maybe more delicate and mischievous, girlish poise in the shoulders and straight posture, with just one streak of white across the ribcage where the hammerblow glanced away. Thelma and I sized up the picture together proudly, as if we were preparing a case for a marriage broker.

child Milford? His children by three successive wives all had period names and period nicknames: Milford, Thelma, Evelyn, Dorothy, and Martin, who never address one another except as Sonny, Toots, Babe, Dot, and Bunny. Because of the different mothers, and because they often lived with various relatives while widowed or divorced Dave was off on shady business, some of these aunts and uncles didn't think of one another as brothers and sisters. Sonny and Babe were Jewish, Dot and Bunny were Methodist, and Toots was married to an Italian. But they all came to those Christmas dinners, and gave me terrific presents.

This family had in common good looks—truly unusual good looks—and an obsession with good looks that I have always found slightly off-putting. Among the Pinskys, "How did he look?" and "She looked good" and "He isn't looking good" and "You look good, very good" are not part of the casual, meaningless chat of family life. My father was voted Best Looking Boy in his graduating class, and his sisters have always been knockouts, about whom men of their generation still reminisce with lyrical awe. At a family funeral a few years ago I was chatting with Aunt Thelma (Toots)—high-breasted, tall, stunning in a knit dress, thick hair worn down, cinematic cheekbones, great

*Cousin Florence, Robert, and Milford Pinsky,
about 1942*

Thelma's first husband, my Uncle Italo, was a garrulous, prosperous lawyer, older and shorter than Thelma. He was more conservative than the New Deal Jews in the family, and when at about sixteen I tried to argue some political point with him, Italo told a long, irrelevant story about the humiliation of some young lawyer who combed his hair about the same way I combed mine. Italo's family was in trucking, and he had a legendary, publicized feud with New Jersey's Director of Motor Vehicles, a dour Armenian reformer. When I was in college and about to lose my driver's license because of a few speeding violations, Italo came with me to the hearing. On the way in, he assured me that I'd get off because all of the Motor Vehicle officials hated . . . what was his name? Vartanian? and he, Italo, was a big hero to them. All I had to do was keep quiet while Italo made his appeal to an expressionless, red-faced New Jersey Yankee with his name, Bale, on his black plastic badge. I kept my mouth shut, and Italo made what I felt was a preposterous pitch, and Bale threw the book at me.

The little uncles married the beautiful aunts and acquired the family concern with profiles and hairlines and crowsfeet and shapes. A few years ago, another uncle gave me the once-over that he had married into, the Pinsky check-out. He hadn't seen me in years, and gave me my looks biography as he saw it. "You look good, Robert," he said, in a way that reminded me of the hard, cruel side of this family inclination. "Better," he added, "much better," and brought his face—pop-eyed, fishmouthed, with coke-bottle glasses and a potato nose—up closer to mine. "When you were little," he said, "you were a beautiful baby. But then at about ten years old, Robert, you got *so funny looking.* Teeth and nose too big. Teenager—ugly. But you know, you've been getting better since you were about twenty-five, and now it's amazing, I think you really look good. Really good."

Sometimes an ascetic, almost Puritanical side of my own poems surprises me: Why such mistrust of the human body, in relation to how much I admire and enjoy it? Why impatience with the diverting gavotte or jitterbug of desire? Trying to convey the beauty-snobbery and self-conscious primping of the Pinskys, it occurs to me that perhaps at least in part I am rebelling against that cold, heartlessly carnal scrutiny. In other ways, I suppose it was drummed into me, so that I feel some sheepish recognition of the truth in the comic Billy Crystal's farewell line as the fatuous, coiffed talk-show host Fernando. "Remember," he says, "Ees better to *look* good, than to *feel* good."

My mother, who did not always get along well with these people, sometimes declared during a violent argument with my father that she had been stupid

Sylvia and Milford Pinsky on their wedding day

enough to marry for looks. Her family came to Long Branch when she was in high school, at what turned out to be the end of wandering around the country. She was pretty, articulate, anarchic, and willful, with a mostly thwarted love of books and music. It is awful that she couldn't go to college. She married young, in the Depression, from a family with no money and until Long Branch, no stable way of life. Her father, Morris Eisenberg, would start a business—motorcycle repair in Missouri, haberdashery in Tennessee, Venetian blinds in Manhattan, used plumbing fixtures in Ohio—and quickly sell or abandon it. She was born in Little Rock, Arkansas and felt a fierce, I suspect theoretical loyalty to Portland, Oregon where her grandfather had a big house.

It's worth saying a little about that grandfather, my mother's mother's father, if only because he supplies a tenuous connection with the San Francisco Bay area, where I have spent a fair part of my life. He was a black sheep who abandoned his wife and children. His respectable brothers tracked him down where he was living with a woman, I think in Philadelphia, and gave him money to start a new life, provided he did it far away, very far away, in California in fact. He arrived in time for the Great Earthquake and Fire of

1906, on which he seems to have turned a profit by means of insurance. He had invested in a warehouse, and took the insurance money to Portland where he first made, then lost, a fortune in real estate, including the big house with fruit trees and servants that my mother remembered, and contrasted bitterly with our own house.

Until I was thirteen we rented the downstairs of 36 Rockwell Avenue, a converted two-family house a block away from Broadway and on the border of Little Africa. Monmouth Avenue, around the corner, was all Black, but our street was all Jewish and Italian. In this too, Long Branch resembled a city while remaining utterly small town. (The population was about twenty thousand, doubling in July and August.) It was a semi-respectable street of mostly one-family and two-family houses, with a few rooming houses, the fancier ones catering to jockeys and trainers during the track season.

In the less high-class house next door to us, the roomers were mostly painters and restaurant workers, coming and going in spattered white pants and shirts, with a darkly male air of whiskey, rough language, and turpentine. They gave Mother fuel for sarcasm toward the neighborhood where we lived "temporarily" as she said, pronouncing the quotation marks, for thirteen years. The painters sat on the porch drinking beer and talking on summer evenings. It was a symposium I loved, sitting on the steps in hearing distance with a friend or two. The painters stood in my mother's mind for the swinishness of men, in mine for a beery leisure and independence, a sort of Shakespearean-rustic version of the Tom Collins drinkers at the Broadway Tavern.

Upstairs at 36 Rockwell lived Margaret and Guido (Woodie) Alessi, kind and generous people with, moreover, an intuitive elegance. Their apartment always smelled good. Their beds were made with the pillows creased lengthwise and rolled into luxurious tubes under snowy chenille spreads that Margaret dried in the backyard on special stretchers, hardwood frames with rows of tiny brass pins to grip the spread. Snow fell in paperweights on their dressers, and their one child Alex, two years older than me, had a lamp made out of a model airplane. He wrote his homework assignments with a pen, in the mottled composition books required by the Star of the Sea Academy, a kind of notebook I envied, and which I now use with a little thrill of unauthorized pleasure. The Alessis' car was a Buick roadster, with a rumble seat.

In other words, they had an elegant lower-class life, while ours was inelegant, disorganized, and contentious—and yet, however vaguely, "cultured." My mother somehow found out about an Aeolian baby

Robert and Sylvia Pinsky, Long Branch New Jersey, about 1943

grand piano which could be had free from the studio on a rich woman's estate. We paid only the moving costs. This instrument, which was intended to give me an advantage in life, had been painted pea green. One of the hard-drinking painters next door was also a painter in the other sense, and we hired him to "antique" the piano ochraceous white, with floral ornaments. He had decorated the borders of the big mirrors in the Sanitary Barber Shop with a greeny romantic fringe of reeds, trunks, and foliage.

In my story "Mr. Mintser," I describe the arguments and partial disasters of the piano's decoration, the painter drinking the paint money but finally producing a durable gold-white skin (without flowers). I think for me the incident embodied a contrast between the vulnerable, aspiring, posturing style of my family and the more dependable, assured, contented style of Alex Alessi and his family. This contrast reflects, for me, the contrast between my mother's highbrow aspirations and the thuggish swank of Grandpa Dave's bar. When the story was published in the *Kenyon Review,* the editors highlighted it in their Vulgarity Issue, shocking me a little. I had thought of the story as sweet, nearly pastoral.

Such differences in viewpoint are revealing, like the times one makes, soberly and sincerely, some remark that others laugh at as a joke, a stroke of paradoxical wit. It happened to me when some people asked me about a lie I told to some official agencies for a writer friend—signing some forms that let his son use my address, so that the child could wangle a school transfer that, in the end, he didn't use. How could I lie, some people who heard about it asked me: didn't it worry me? I thought a second—I suppose about the personal networks of Long Branch—and said something like, "I guess it all depends upon how you were brought up," and in context it was a laugh line.

I hated school, and I didn't do well in it, I don't know why—certainly I wouldn't do any better if I had to go back tomorrow; I never "straightened out" or changed my work habits: it's just that as I got older life offered more situations where my habits and methods have been acceptable, even successful. Your father was such a gentleman, your uncle did so well, said the principals and assistant principals and discipline officers at Long Branch Junior High School and Long Branch High School: what is wrong with you?

Even more insulting was the line of questioning that went: is anything wrong at home, do you have a desk lamp and a quiet place to study, are there problems in the family? As a matter of fact, my mother and father were still fighting like hell, throwing furniture and crockery and one memorable time great fistfuls of money, arguing especially about the fact that even after the births of my little sister and brother, five and ten years younger than me, we still lived (as my mother put it) in a slum, next door to a flophouse. Every weekend, year after year, they inspected "model homes," and never bought. Finally, my mother fell through unfinished attic flooring in one of these houses, giving herself a concussion that exacerbated her difficulties for several years. (I think they may have settled with the builder and got enough cash for the down payment they finally made as I entered my teens.)

But it was insulting for Mr. Guzzi or Mr. John "Chief" Beattie to invite me to expose family dirty linen. It was even more irritating to suggest that I might be such a moral and mental twerp that if my mother threw a few dishes around, or my father broke a door slamming it, I would quiver helplessly, unable to do the school's contemptible homework or follow its rules.

In the eighth grade, I was assigned to what was known (I think with some defensive pride on our part)

as the Dumb Class. This had at least two consequences. One is that I was eventually tracked into the group that took Spanish rather than French (presumably because Spanish was considered easier, and maybe less classy). This established a pattern that has lasted all my life: I struggle awkwardly with French, can speak or read Spanish pretty well with the right warm-up. On the other hand, I somehow got into Latin, getting straight "D" from alcoholic Miss Van Breese for two years, except for one six-week marking period when another boy and I made a papier-mâché aqueduct, raising my grade to "C⁻."

A second, and I think more important, consequence of being in the Dumb Class was that for some reason it left a period free to register for Band and learn an instrument. (For some years afterwards, because of this bureaucratic quirk, the Long Branch High School Orchestra and Marching Band was a distinctly rough and "hoody" group, much given to strong language, attrition, and violence.) I had learned to bong tunes and chords on the antiqued Aeolian, using a method of my own invention, a system based on left-hand sixths in the octave just under middle C, ultimately torture to the listener but superficially effective. Now, I took up the clarinet, then the saxophone, and for the first time since early childhood I had what might be called a reason (beyond animal self-preservation) to live.

Until I began playing music, I had been ordinary, with no *kinetic* distinctions, only the passive, static qualities of being extremely smart and terrifically rebellious. This ordinariness was in painful contrast with my fantasy life, which was enriched by *Ivanhoe, Rob Roy,* and the heroic science fiction in magazines like *If, Galaxy,* and *Astounding.* I was a squirt, but not really very small. I was average at sports. I had won two or three fights (among my happiest memories of school years), been knocked around or humiliated in twice as many. We lived in a bad neighborhood, but we weren't really poor—and certainly not rich. In music I found some justification for my deep but barely conscious conviction, as the first son of a clever, thwarted young woman, that I deserved a lot of attention.

The first saxophone was the school's, a gargantuan baritone. The day they let me lug it home, my brother disappeared into the case. Later, playing professionally, I bought used, from a soldier at Fort Monmouth, my tenor, a Buescher Aristocrat. My band was called the Downbeats, the name on business cards printed on pearlized baby-blue paper, with sixteenth notes for the "d" and "b." We played weddings, Bar Mitzvahs, bars, high-school dances. At the Red Bank Catholic High School tea dances, we played show tunes in a Lawrence Welk tempo given us by a nun. At poolside of the Colony Surf Club we played cha-chas and mambos, wearing pink ruffled shirts. At an Elk's Club New Year's Eve dance we played while my mother and father won the mambo contest, and at the Paddock we played while a man whose name I am afraid to write sat at his table with his lieutenants and a white telephone. The drummer was Chris Barbieri, the piano player was Andy Edison, and they played at my wedding.

When I was a freshman at Rutgers, Chris and Andy asked me to come help them audition for a gig playing Friday and Saturday nights at a bar in Atlantic Highlands. The place turned out to be a German restaurant. I can't remember what the manager requested, but I know that I played horribly. I hadn't practiced in months, my imagination was already drifting toward writing, and I wasn't really in shape for anything but rockabilly. I cost them the job, a terrible experience.

The last time I played for pay was in my sophomore year, a party at some WASP fraternity house. Backed by drums and an appalled piano player, I improvised about five hundred choruses of the Symphony Sid theme—I and another tenor player, my classmate Digby Diehl, later editor-in-chief at Harry Abrams Company and the *Los Angeles Herald Book Review*. I stopped playing altogether and stored my horn at my parents' house. In their feckless way they misplaced it or gave it away. They can never remember which, and I can never forgive them.

I liked college. First of all, I was out of my parents' house. Having a roommate, a pleasant boy who liked telling everyone he had graduated last in his class at Mount Hermon, was like having my own room for the first time since I was small. At home, I had to share a room with my brother, ten years younger than me, a small room with a trundle bed—we wanted bunks, but I think my mother liked the *sound* of the words "trundle bed," so that if he was asleep when I came home there was no floor space at all. I had to walk over his bed to get to mine.

Another thing that made me like college right away was that the teachers called me "Mr. Pinsky," just the way I called them "Mr. Weimer" or "Mr. Goodwin." This appealed simultaneously to my snobbery, because it seemed British and old-fashioned, and to my ungoverned side, because it was egalitarian. With one tremendous exception, I got B's and A's freshman year, despite a few stunts that harked back to high-school days. (I was rightly asked to leave a history class because I wouldn't shut up, and showed my contempt for a particularly dull Political Science final by finishing it in twenty minutes out of the allotted three

hours, basking in the gasps when I strolled out.)

The exception was ROTC, required for two years at all Land Grant state universities until Eisenhower decided it was unnecessary. That we had to go to idiotic classes taught by round-shouldered captains, and drill for two hours on Wednesday afternoons, while boys rich enough and obedient enough to find themselves at Princeton could lounge around playing with their stereos, seemed a tremendous injustice. In my ROTC section I made friends with Bob Maniquis, a brilliant, cynical half-Filipino spirit who always wore ultra-dark sunglasses and a black T-shirt. At weekly drill, I marched with the band, blowing blues riffs into Sousa marches and trying to mess up the formations until I got kicked out for wearing a paisley tie with my uniform. I was supposed to report to Company H— "the hump company," a kind of junior-military Dumb Class, but spent the rest of that year's Wednesdays drinking beer or coffee with Maniquis, who had bribed his way out of drill by a series of crooked academic favors. (Bob had scams and capers I won't detail here; he is now an urbane but still sybaritic Professor of English Literature at UCLA.) By the end of the year, we were bold enough to wave hankies and cheer as the sweating, captive freshmen and sophomores trudged down Easton Avenue to Buccleuch Park, screamed at by the scowling, falsetto upperclassman fraternity boys who were their officers.

Second semester, Maniquis and I were both assigned to an Honors Section of Freshman English, taught by Paul Fussell, later author of *The Great War and Modern Memory*. It was an extraordinary group, which went on to produce quite a lot of published writing. Fussell drew expertise on art from Peter Najarian, whose fine novel *Voyages* was published in the sixties by Pantheon. The expert on the Bible was Henry Dumas, a tall, gaunt, intense Black. Henry's collected poems have been published by Southern Illinois University Press; a few years after we left Rutgers, he was shot to death by a policeman in the New York subway system. Ernie Ruckle, who went on to have a career as a painter and satirist—I have lost track of him—was the most meticulous of us. Digby Diehl, my saxophone partner, also had Fussell for English.

Paul Fussell, quite young and not yet well known, ran this gifted and rough-edged crew, so like the stereotypical ethnic Hollywood infantry company, with panache. Mr. Najarian's uncle was a painter who took him from Union City to Manhattan and introduced him to the museums and galleries. Mr. Maniquis, from Edison, New Jersey, spoke wonderful French (and always told girls he was born in Paris to political exiles). Mr. Dumas had a car and an impeccable prose style; in 1958, when the other campus Blacks were more or less Young Republicans, he was interested in the idea of the Afro-American. Mr. Diehl wrote the jazz column for the Rutgers *Targum.* (At first, I thought he was a pseudonym.) Mr. Fussell, patrician and generous, showed us the first poetry by living writers I had read, and used Ezra Pound's *ABC of Reading* as our textbook.

All of us had poems and stories in the Rutgers *Anthologist,* which had a series of covers—all printed on silver stock—by another Rutgers student of that era, Lucas Samaras. *Anthologist* was edited my freshman year by my friend Alan Cheuse (presently book reviewer for National Public Radio) and later by me. None of us took creative writing classes, though they did exist (taught by John Ciardi, whose poems I rather admired though I never met him). I think we felt that writing, and the *Anthologist,* were unofficial, our own property and not part of the world of school and grades and the judgment of teachers. It is a little odd for me now to teach such courses, never having taken one. Many of my poet friends—Bob Hass, Frank Bidart, Jim McMichael, none of whom are products of Creative Writing or M.F.A. programs—are in a similar situation. Maybe we are the last generation (at least for a while) to make this separation between school and writing.

For Maniquis, Najarian, Cheuse, Dumas, and me the idea was more Bohemian—a word, needless to say, that we would never use, though I think there was some pleasure in being identified by fraternity boys or student politicians as "beatniks." Alan Kaprow taught at Rutgers and was staging the first Happenings, ancestors of Conceptual Art. Marijuana was having one of its historic resurgences. On the other hand, Maniquis and I did join a fraternity, though it was an unconventional one, like Honors English an ethnic rainbow—Blacks, Jews, demi-Filipinos, and so forth. Many an afternoon Maniquis and I plotted in detail, and I am sad to say never carried out, our robbery of the Confederate flag from the front balcony of the loathesome, pseudo-Princetonian Delta Phi house.

How mild this beatnik phase was, by later standards, is demonstrated by the fact that I got married, over the Christmas vacation of my senior year. Ellen Bailey was an eighteen-year-old sophomore at the time, maddeningly gorgeous, and at just over twenty-one I felt like an older man, driven against my judgment to cradle-robbing by an erotic frenzy. I suppose that in principle getting married so young was one of the most rash, heedless, stupid things I have ever done, and yet in practice it has turned out to be the wisest.

When asked how I have managed to remain married to the same woman for twenty-four years, I have no idea what to say. When people admire the fact (often awarding extra credit for being a poet), I feel em-barrassed and a little condescended-to, as if remaining in love or growing in kindred directions were a matter of will or deliberate accomplishment. I don't know how to stay married, or how to "work" at marriage. Sexual attraction, love of conversation with a particular person, trust, are not matters of accomplishment the way that establishing a successful business or mastering an art are accomplishments. Most of my writing has been based on marital conversation, and most of the poems in *Sadness And Happiness* are addressed to Ellen. Between the ages of twenty-one and forty-five, I have been very lucky.

Bob Hass and Jim McMichael on the Pinsky porch in Berkeley, California, 1984

This might be a suitable point to mention that I have also been extremely lucky in friendship. Everywhere I have gone, I have had one or two extraordinary teachers and one or two close friends in the art of writing. At Rutgers I was close to Bob Maniquis and then to Peter Najarian. My contemporaries at Stanford included Bob Hass, Jim McMichael, and John Peck. And when I taught at Wellesley, my colleagues included David Ferry, a fine poet and critic who was responsible for my meeting Frank Bidart, whose friendship and advice have had an enormous impact on my life and writing.

When I say "lucky," I mean to acknowledge a debt to fortune—and not merely to preen myself. Luck brought Francis Fergusson to Rutgers, for example.

His classes on Aristotle, his amazing edition of the *Poetics*, his concepts of action and plot, his teaching of Chekhov and Shakespeare, his model of humanity and intellectual excitement, are sources I draw on every day. Sometimes I feel sheepish about being invited to lecture somewhere: I get on an airplane, arrive thousands of miles from home, have dinner, stand before an audience, and in exchange for a check I tell them things I learned from Francis Fergusson when I was twenty. But they are good things, and it seems a fair deal.

Blind luck, too, brought me to Stanford. (Ellen, who was near the top of her class at Douglass, the women's college of Rutgers, transferred to Stanford for her last two years.) We really wanted to go to Berkeley, but there was a kind of mixup about fellowships. I thought of myself as a poet who was going to graduate school to avoid the draft and to sponge off a university for a year or two: someone who already knew all he needed to know. Fergusson told me that there was a man at Stanford named Yvor Winters, who was known mostly as a critic, and a cantankerous critic, but who had actually written quite good poems. (I had seen the name once in my work on Eliot's plays, and thought it was a woman's name.)

Then, my first semester in Palo Alto, taking courses not including any taught by Winters, I read Robert Lowell's review of Winters's *Selected Poems* in *Poetry* magazine. Lowell praises the book passionately. He quotes Winters's wonderful poem on John Sutter and says that he thinks it would pass A. E. Housman's test for poetry: that is, if Lowell should try to shave himself while reciting the poem, he thought he would probably cut himself.

So I decided that possibly Winters was worthy of looking at some of my poems—what I then called my poems—and I had heard that you could get credit for writing poems, and I thought I might as well pick up some academic credit. I knocked on his office door, having with me a manuscript of about twenty-five poems. My plan was that I would leave this manuscript with him, he would read it overnight, and the next day he would call me up and tell me he would be willing to—what? Study at my feet, I guess, help me publish the poems, joyfully give me any amount of credit or number of A's that I might desire.

He asked me to sit down, and he thumbed through the manuscript while I was there. It took him perhaps four minutes, stopping once or twice at certain ones. Then he looked up at me, and said, "You simply don't know how to write."

He added that there was some gift there, but because I was ignorant of what to do with it, he could not estimate how much of a gift it was. If it was blind luck or happy fate or smiling Fortune that must be thanked for leading me to Stanford, let me congratulate myself for having the sense not to leave the room when he said that. Some note of truth or conviction made leaving seem a mistake.

He asked me what I had read, and I said I had read everything by Yeats and almost everything by Frost, that I had read a lot of Williams, a little Pound, everything by Eliot. I wisely omitted my young heroes Allen Ginsberg and Alan Dugan, whose work meant far more to me than, say, Lowell's. He said, "What have you read in the Seventeenth Century?" I said I had read some poems by Donne, meaning the ones in the anthologies, and I had read some poems by Marvell. He said, "What about the Sixteenth Century?" I had read some sonnets by Shakespeare.

He said, "Anybody who has only read that much can never write a good poem, except by a very unlikely accident."

Again I congratulate myself for having the brains or instinct to ask him what I was supposed to do to catch up. He said—all of this in his incredible, hanging-judge *basso*, with careful dentals, and vowels like the inside of a whale—"Well, you're too late to take my History of the Lyric, which is the *study* course for the *practice* of poetry writing." The Lyric course was offered only in the fall, and I hadn't taken it, so I said, "What am I supposed to do, I'll lose a whole year." My thin, New Jersey wise-guy arrogance had wilted that quickly in those cold, booming gusts of confidence and knowledge.

I think he recognized my determination, because he agreed to do the History of the Lyric course with me one-on-one, as an Individual Directed Reading. He gave me the syllabus, and I met with him every week—and most of my graduate education consisted of reading English and American poetry with Winters, as a series of these Directed Readings. I think I did more of them than regular courses with the rest of the faculty. The following year he gave me a writing fellowship—Albert Guerard used to joke that I went from Doesn't Know How To Write to Important Young Poet in about five months—and that helped me have time to do all this reading.

Winters said, and I do not doubt him, that he had read all of the poems of any significance by all of the poets, of any reputation at all, in English. He invited us to do the same if we wanted to disagree with him. He also knew French very well, and read it aloud very beautifully. His recitation of Valéry approached actual hypnotism, the great deep penetrating voice almost palpable and the beautiful, plain Californian consonants supporting the precise French. His many Stanford disciples, the Wintersians—Winters-lets—made this performance even spookier, though less magisterial, when they imitated it, throwing their voices way down and groaning as much as possible like the Master, imitating even the shortness of breath that made him skimp an occasional enjambment when he was old. It was like spiritual possession, and is even more so now that he is dead.

He was my most powerful teacher, magnetic, unfair, and glorious. He preferred people to agree with him. (How some of the Wintersians made me suffer for being soft on Yeats!) I owe him an immense debt. The Old Man in section XXII ("Peroration, Concerning Genius") of my poem "Essay on Psychiatrists" is based on Winters. Or, oddly enough, it is based on Bob Hass's impression of Winters. I knew Winters far better than did Bob, who was never close to being a disciple (Peck went through a period of total conversion, and McMichael came close to that for a while), but it was Bob's ear and memory that gave me that part of the poem.

In these years I published my first poems in national magazines, the *Southern Review* and *Poetry*. Also, Stanford students were organizing in support of the Berkeley Free Speech Movement and against the war in Asia. We were the Graduate Co-ordinating Committee, later to evolve into the SDS chapter. Bob Hass edited the GCC newsletter, the first issue of which contained a film review by him called "Coming Out of Mother" and a very solemn poem by me (with some good lines about snow, however) which led to somebody painting swastikas on my front door one night, an event that filled everybody with great self-satisfaction.

Of the poems I published in this period, only two or three made it into my first book, *Sadness And Happiness*. One that marks an important transition or moment is "Old Woman." The Winters ambience was extremely conservative metrically in a passionate way very different from the East Coast, Audenesque emphasis on witty iambic tetrameters and so forth. The old man had written free verse, had scanned Steven's "The Snow Man" in print, and could be harsh on people about their "ear." (I starred in this area, being very good at hearing variations in quantity and pitch, able to hear or write pentameter without using my fingers, etc.)

In this atmosphere, it was considered quite daring to write syllabics. Syllabics were in a way the official daringness of the Wintersians, usually seven-syllable lines. I didn't like them, didn't think anybody could hear numbers of syllables in English, or that such numbers made any difference, but it occurred to me that maybe you could hear *pairs* of syllables, so you could try writing a poem that avoided iambs but kept varying the patterns of accents over four *pairs* of syllables:

Old Woman

Not even in darkest August
When the mysterious insects
Marry loudly in the black weeds
And the woodbine, limp after rain,
In the cooled night is more fragrant,
Do you gather in any slight
Harvest to yourself. Harsh gleaner
Of children, grandchildren—remnants
Of nights now forever future—
Your dry, invisible shudder
Dies on this porch where, uninflamed,
You dread the oncoming seasons,
Repose in the electric night.

This is not the kind of writing that most interests me any more, for reasons that might begin with the overt lyricism of vocabulary and syntax. Yet I retain affection for the poem, and learned a lot from writing it—and, from its reception by Winters and his other students.

He liked it very much, and even read it aloud (the ultimate honor) for the group of five or six disciples, praising its rhythm particularly. Out of the Stanford-Winters context, it does not seem a daring piece of work, but there it was as if I had gotten away with an immense risk. The standard poem of the group was in

Pinsky, Palo Alto, California, 1965

accentual-syllabic—that is, iambic—lines, often qua-trains with the rhyme pattern of "skill-dust-will-trust." But the main point is that in the technical discussion that followed, Winters described the rhythm he liked as *accentual,* based on the number of accents within the line. When I explained that the lines were all eight syllables long, and that I had tried for a varying, in-tense pattern of accents within that frame, his response was that the poem worked thought of either way. Then he read it aloud again, very beautifully. This instruc-tive little victory—*quite* little in itself—seems worth in-cluding here because it seemed to mark a moment of formal permission. The conclusion I drew was to trust my body's idea of successful lines and rhythms in verse. It was a kind of turning point.

Ellen graduated in 1964, and a year later we left for England, where I was supposed to write my Ph.D. thesis on the poems of Landor, introduced to me by Albert Guerard. Leaving Palo Alto after three years seemed easy to do—our friends would leave soon them-selves, and the sleepy, genteel conservatism of the place was not our speed. Twenty years later, I feel more sen-timental about the place, our tiny house behind a bun-galow behind the main house at 163 Waverly Street, where one of Stanford's first sixties-style political meet-ings met, where I believe I gave John Peck his first alcoholic drink (a gin and tonic), and where, in a way, Ellen and I changed from married kids to married adults.

We sailed across the Atlantic from New York in October, with Bob Maniquis on the pier embar-rassing my mother and everybody else by waving a satirical hanky as we went into the harbor. The ship was a freighter, wonderfully named the *Black Falcon.* She carried ten passengers, all young—a Belgian cou-ple returning from their honeymoon in America, some Dutch students, a German, an Australian with horrible table manners who sat next to me snorting and slurp-ing. On our third night out, the short wave brought the incredible news of the great New York City Blackout of 1965. We all played multilingual scrabble, feeling like the last people on earth.

Our luggage consisted of two large suitcases and an immensely heavy carton containing the sixteen-vol-ume Welby, Wheeler, and Wise edition of Landor's complete works, which I had purchased at Bartfield's for two hundred dollars. I was working on Landor be-cause he was the best poet in English about whom there was virtually no critical work. Moreover, there was an expert, scholarly biography of no literary pre-tention by R. H. Super, and Super's meticulous bib-liography. We set up the Welby, Wheeler, and Wise (Wise was the famous bibliophile and criminal who

stole and mutilated so many rare books in the British Museum) in the front room of our apartment on Foster Road, in Chiswick. On the table I had two typewriters: one for writing poems, one for Landor.

We had met an American couple, David and Caroline Bady, on the *Black Falcon,* and saw a lot in London of them and of Peter Najarian. Peter was liv-ing on Fournier Street in the East End, in unbelievable squalor, doing odd kinds of teaching: a film class for bricklayers and BBC secretaries, and a class in basket-ball for a group of London police cadets. I helped him out once or twice, and we dazzled the junior Bobbies with our third-rate playground moves.

Partly because of Peter, we saw a lot of movies, many of them at the British Film Institute. They were very cheap in those days, as were plays, music, Paki-stani and Greek restaurants. It was the dawn of the age of miniskirts and tights in popsicle colors, Carnaby Street shirts for men. My fellowship went surprisingly far. As a result of all this, the typewriters, especially the Landor one, were not using up immense amounts of ribbon. On the other hand, I was reading a lot, Landor and many other things. I had sent John Peck a sheaf of parodies of all the poems I (and others) wrote during the last year at Stanford, and he responded with news of Donald Davie, who may have just begun teaching at Stanford. I read *Articulate Energy,* Davie's book on syn-tax in English poetry, and then his poems and the rest of his criticism. It turned out that he and Ezra Pound were far and away the most perceptive and cogent readers of Landor as a poet.

I had been offered several academic jobs for the following year, and settled on the University of Chi-cago (turning down an offer from Harvard, to the im-mense but forgiving distress of Albert Guerard, who had wangled it for me). The people at Chicago ex-pected me to have written my thesis, we had paid a deposit on a place in Spain for June, and suddenly it was March. In one of the manic bursts of energy and focus that punctuate my long, lazy stretches, I wrote 225 pages in about six weeks, and sent them off to Palo Alto, where they were accepted. When we arrived at Chicago, an editor at the University of Chicago Press with nothing to do called new faculty out of a direc-tory, asking for manuscripts. He liked it, sent it to Hugh Kenner who liked it, and it was published nearly unchanged as *Landor's Poetry.* I think it is a good book, but because it was written so quickly I am not sure I would have had the nerve to send it out. Anyway, as a result of those panicked weeks in Chiswick and—again—blind luck, I had managed to dispose of the "publish or perish" question at the outset of my career as a professor, before there was time even to think about it.

In Spain, we had a wonderful time, swimming and gawking. I showed off my Spanish to Ellen, who had to translate for me through France. We ate squid and snails and hare in the Barrio Gotico of Barcelona. Walking around there, Ellen would occasionally feel queasy, and vow to lay off the octopus and rich sauces. We flew back home in August, and stayed for a time with Ellen's parents in New Jersey where she would occasionally feel funny. Finally we grew concerned enough for her to visit her mother's doctor, who couldn't stop laughing because Ellen was pregnant. Nicole was born the following February at the Billings Lying-in Hospital on the South Side of Chicago, a mean institution in a mean city. I walked through seven-foot chasms of dirty snow in bitter cold to see Ellen and Nicole, past tough-looking, blubbering young men in jackets that said "Devil's Disciples," sobbing and moaning over their friend, horribly bloody and cut-up and apparently dead.

Many of my Chicago memories are of dirt, a callous university, a city full of racial bad feeling and drenched in cynicism. Yet we made lasting friendships there, and I wrote poems, possibly more poems than during the sweet year in London. But I hated it, and by December we had decided to take another job at Wellesley. Teaching at a single-sex college with an upper-middle-class style, and living in a Republican suburb seemed absurd to us when we moved there, and continued to seem absurd for the twelve happy years that we lived there (with time off for years in London and California).

Wellesley had an extremely distinguished literary tradition: Jorge Guillén and Vladimir Nabokov had taught there, and more recently Richard Wilbur. In David Ferry I had a protective older colleague whose poems and criticism I respected, and through him in 1971—just as we returned from another year in London, this time with Nicole and Caroline, born in 1969—I met Frank Bidart.

Frank is a unique friend. Ellen and I liked him from the start. Even at first meeting, he was clearly both more serious and more capable of play and goofy pleasure than the people one tended to meet at dinner parties around Cambridge, Massachusetts. We became very close almost immediately, and started sharing the writing of poems, often on the telephone because of his strange hours. He would stay up all night working on his stunning, now rather famous long poem "Ellen West," then before going to sleep at around seven or eight in the morning would phone us to read it from the beginning, adding each night's new section at the end. Several days in a row, I heard harrowing, successively longer versions of the beginning of the poem while I dawdled in bed with morning coffee, Ellen lis-

tening on the downstairs extension. Then some discussion of the poem, some kibbitzing and "goodnight" to Frank and the day began. The lines at the end of the first section of "Ellen West":

> But he is a fool. He married
> meat, and thought it was a wife

Frank got from Ellen's retelling at suppertime of a myth she was teaching her students at the Dana Hall School.

Frank's *Golden State* had been accepted when we met him, and was published by Braziller in 1973. I was still trying to publish my first book, called first *Dr. Frolic* and then *Cold Wide River*. "Sadness And Happiness," which came to be the title poem, was written around 1973, the successive sections read to Frank over the phone. We liked working on poems together so well

Frank Bidart with Ellen Pinsky (rear) and the Pinsky children: Nicole, Caroline, and Elizabeth, in Wellesley, Massachusetts

that in one spell when neither of us was writing he sort of coached me through a rhymed translation of Valéry's "Cimetière marin," the two of us sitting with dictionaries and trots, doing one or two stanzas an evening after dinner with Ellen, who graded papers while we strained over Zeno's paradox, the infinite worms, and so forth. This is similar to the way Frank worked with Robert Lowell on the successive revisions of Lowell's unrhymed sonnet books.

Through Frank I met Robert Lowell and Elizabeth Bishop. Both were extremely kind to me, Lowell writing a blurb for *Sadness And Happiness* when it was accepted in 1974 by Princeton University Press for their new poetry series. Though I admired Lowell very much, I had never been devoted to his writing in the way that Frank was, or other brilliant students of Lowell's like Alan Williamson and Lloyd Schwartz. *Life Studies* had never made a big impression on me. It is Bishop's poetry, especially the poems of *Geography III* to start with, that has seemed a model to me. On the other hand, she was a kindly presence but only intermittently willing to talk about poetry: once, almost the first time I met her, to lament that we all—"You Cal, and me, and Mr. Pinsky"—ought to write poems more like a song of Landor's she recited. Lowell, in contrast, was constantly, excitingly, and disconcertingly full of poetry. Being with him, for me, was like taking part in a supercharged, generalized, zany oral examination in poetry from Homer to the present.

During the years when I was impatiently waiting to publish my first book of poems I had been working on a book in prose about contemporary poetry, putting bits and pieces into a folder labelled "The Folly." After the poems were accepted, I went back to work on this book, rewriting every sentence with Frank. After the publication of *Sadness And Happiness,* and its unusually good critical reception, it seemed almost unnecessary to publish the critical book, which was—to be honest about it—largely designed to make

room for the kind of poem I was writing and wanted to read. But I had written it, and it seemed wasteful not to publish it. Princeton wanted to call it something snappy like *Poetry Now* or *Poems for the Present,* but I insisted on the title *The Situation of Poetry.* Because it and *Sadness And Happiness* came out within less than two years of one another, and were fairly successful, I found people treating me as a kind of child prodigy, just as I was preparing to steel myself for the lot of the middle-aged unknown poet. Writers often seem to strike people as too young or too old to be who they are.

I don't think now the way I thought when I wrote *Situation of Poetry.* It is a pleasure, though, to recall that when I wrote in that book at length about the poems of Frank Bidart and James McMichael they were practically unknown, at the beginnings of their careers. There was the risk that I was merely writing about my friends, and overestimating their work and their promise. Since then, what they have written and the respect their work has earned make the sections on their poems seem possibly the most solid in the book.

Princeton (a splendid publisher, despite my mocking their taste in titles) also published my second book of poems, *An Explanation of America,* in 1980. Around this time, I was invited to teach at Berkeley, where I renewed my friendship with Bob Hass, another example of how, in the large moves and decisions in life, incidental good luck is usually more important than

Caroline, Robert, and Elizabeth, Martha's Vineyard

the main outward factors. We now had three children; at the time of the move West in 1980, Nicole was thirteen, Caroline Rose (called Rosey) just eleven, and Elizabeth (Biz) four.

During the period when Bob was introducing me to Berkeley's rather lively cafe life—Stephen Mitchell was just finishing his Rilke translations, and would sometimes meet us in the Cafe Renaissance with various other friends and graduate students—we began talking about helping Czesław Miłosz and his secretary, Renata Gorczynski, with English versions of some untranslated and new poems of his. I had read and admired *Bells in Winter,* and Bob had been affected by Miłosz since reading *The Captive Mind* in high school. We ran into Czesław on Telegraph Avenue one day, and arranged to get together. Renata called and we set a time, but I had to break it for some reason at the last minute. Then we set another date, but Bob had to break it. A few days after that the Nobel Prize in Literature was announced. Bob and I agreed that this was good for the world, and a catastrophe for the Hass-Pinsky work on Milosz: if we called the man up now, it would seem he was only good enough for us after he won the Prize.

But within a few weeks Renata called again, and we began the four-way collaboration that resulted in *The Separate Notebooks,* a volume that provides poems from every stage of Miłosz's varied and spectacular career as a poet. Renata and the poet provided us with trots and indications of form, rhyme scheme, idiom, and so forth, and then criticized the versions we came up with. Usually, Bob and I worked on different poems, conferring at roadblocks and quagmires, but sometimes we worked side by side. The impossible "Hope," "Faith," and "Love" sections of *The World* were done in a very collaborative way, Tin Pan Alley style.

People assume that it was wonderful to work with Miłosz, a great poet, on English incarnations of his work. It *was* wonderful: it is hard to imagine a more effective form of reading. A less obvious benefit of this work was learning about writing by working so closely with Bob. As with Frank, this was an extremely useful kind of postgraduate study, feeling the similarities and differences between my own sense of writing and another. With Bob, it sometimes came down to my desire to make sentences longer, with semicolons and dashes and dependent clauses, when he went for the plain, killer period. There were also discussions of diction, prowling and chewing the differences between "rush" and "hurry," "yell" and "scream," "simple" and "plain," "strength" and "power." And equivalent syntactical questions. Sometimes, I found myself emphasizing what a stylistic choice would do about tone, who

was talking or writing, while Bob emphasized what was shown or indicated. But it wasn't that symmetrical.

Another side effect of working on the Miłosz book was a decision to change publishers to the Ecco Press, Bob's publisher and Miłosz's. I was finishing my third book, *History of My Heart,* often phoning drafts of poems to Frank in Massachusetts (and splurging on Express Mail), and showing them to Bob and Ellen in California. The first summer in California, Louise Glück, another Ecco poet whose poems I admired, came to Berkeley and confirmed that Ecco, under the direction of a poet (Dan Halpern) was pretty much the ideal place to publish a book of poems. Among other things, Dan asked me who I would like to design the book, not a usual luxury of choice. I suggested Bruce Campbell, the designer of *Sadness And Happiness* (and of the Library of America), an extremely sensitive and elegant graphic designer.

Another writing opportunity, quite different from the Miłosz book, seemed to follow from moving West. Two years ago a man called Ihor called me up and said that he worked for a company called Synapse, which was interested in having a serious writer do a computer narrative text game for them. Was I interested, and did I know anything about computers or narrative games? I had been talking vaguely about doing something different, and I had just written and published the first two stories of my life. So my answers were yes to the first, no the second, of Ihor's two questions. Synapse was eventually absorbed by Broderbund Software, which recently issued *Mindwheel,* an interactive computer text entertainment by Robert Pinsky, Steven Hales, and William Mataga (my programmer-collaborators).

This unexpected project, shocking to some acquaintances, inspires some closing reflections. The single most useful gift I brought to writing the computer game, I think, was my ability to play around, to live with uncertainty and the possibility of failure. This capacity to experiment in an optimistic muddle, withholding judgment, seems to come out of my conviction that I am somehow innately lucky. In school, I followed instructions poorly, but in the long run I happened to get away with it. I got married young, but as it turned out to the right person. I blundered into Rutgers, California, New England and was treated kindly by older writers like Fergusson, Winters, Lowell. In my own generation, too, I have been unusually lucky in my friendships within the art.

So if these people I have known and cared about, and who have cared about me, don't necessarily confirm my merit, they certainly indicate my good fortune. Having a bad high-school career followed by good luck in marriage, art, and friendship, I think, has

Elizabeth, Robert, Ellen, Caroline, and Nicole Pinsky, Berkeley, 1984

given me some confidence about suspending prudence for a time—not abandoning it ultimately—while giving commitments of various kinds a try. If I try to learn something from the narrative of my blessed, mild life up to the present, it seems to be something to do with luck and risk: willingness to undergo some embarrassment or failure in the effort to write something good, a willingness based on the possibility of good fortune. I find in myself a little of the conservatism and respect for comfort of the reformed tough, and a lot of the personality type that is suited, not for flying huge planes or performing delicate brain surgery, but rather for work in which making mistakes and following hunches can be essential processes. I like trying things for the hell of it, and I also like polishing things. I am attracted to the aristocratic disdain of perfected forms, and also to the heuristic barbarism of art, the dash and vulgarity of the computer game. There is always, somewhere, more work for a writer to undertake or to reconceive. And one of my favorite writing slogans is, Paper Is Cheap.

BIBLIOGRAPHY

Poetry:

Sadness And Happiness. Princeton, N.J.: Princeton University Press, 1975.

An Explanation of America. Princeton, N.J.: Princeton University Press, 1979; Manchester, England: Carcanet, 1979.

History of My Heart. New York: Ecco Press, 1984.

Nonfiction:

Landor's Poetry. Chicago: University of Chicago Press, 1968.

The Situation of Poetry: Contemporary Poetry and Its Traditions. Princeton, N.J.: Princeton University Press, 1976; Guildford, England: Princeton University Press, 1978.

Translator of:

The Separate Notebooks: Poems by Czesław Miłosz, with Renata Gorczynski and Robert Hass. New York: Ecco Press, 1984.

Other:

Mindwheel: An Electronic Novel, with programmers Steven Hales and William Mataga. Corte Madera, Calif.: Broderbund Software, 1985.

John Rechy

1934-

John Rechy

My beautiful mother fled the City of Chihuahua during the revolution when word reached her family that Pancho Villa was sending one of his lieutenants to kidnap her after having seen her at a ball which he had invaded, and my Scottish father fled his wealthy home in Mexico City as his mother fired a gun at his heels to emphasize her act of banishment. Or so I was to learn throughout accounts of my family history as I inherited ghosts that roamed the memories of others and floated into mine.

My mother bore the grand name of Guadalupe Flores de Rechy, and my father bore the equally grand name of Roberto Sixto Rechy. The "Sixto," or sixth, was attributable not to any sequence of birth—he was an only child—but to a remote lord, the sixth, exhumed in versions of his aristocratic lineage, originating in Scotland but transferring to Mexico City, where my father's father, a respected doctor, was a frequent guest, with his family, of President Porfirio Díaz, the Mexican dictator with European loyalties.

While the revolution raged across the Rio Grande, both my father and mother—still unknown to each

253

other—simultaneously fled their respective threats miles apart and crossed the border into El Paso, Texas, at exactly the same time. In the new city my mother's youngest brother, playing, thrust a ball through the window of my father's house. Chasing the young destroyer, my father encountered my mother—and married her.

In the deep of the Depression, when Texas was swept by poverty, and winds gathered to grind the crops of nearby Oklahoma into dust, I was born into a sea of clashing memories, the youngest of five children, two brothers, two sisters.

Another sister, Valeska, died at age twelve before I was born. I inherited my mother's haunted memory through her daily tears. I had a half-brother named John, too, my father's son, a beautiful boy with curls who died before I was born. When on the somber Day of the Dead we went to decorate with dark flowers the graves of my father's mother and father—who also fled to Texas—I would stare in fascination at the grave which bore my own name.

Now of course my father and mother did not flee at the exact time. Of course they did not cross the border at the same moment. Autobiography creates its own time in rearranged memories. It orders random accidents into inevitability. I am able to reconstruct my life from birth, even before birth through inherited

memories, and so to provide structure to what is shapeless, reason to anarchy—and the only meaning possible, a retrospective meaning, imposed—and the only truth, one's own. That is, autobiography as novel.

Oh, my mother was a conquering beauty, her dance card instantly filled during the balls she reigned over in Chihuahua. Her aunt, my great-aunt, *Tia* Ana (who practiced white magic and converted, through efficacious prayers and holy incantations, my first novel—I believe this—into a top best-seller) loaned me her recollections of my mother as a girl, of her beautiful green eyes, flawless fair skin and hair. My mother denied it all, but in tones which asserted happily, "Yes, it's all true, tell him more." And *Tia* Ana did, gave me such careful memories that in them I become my mother's chosen escort—she draws a line cancelling out all dances with others. And, years later, she did teach me how to waltz! Her skin remained flawless, her hair bright, her eyes truly green—until death attempted to close them; they remain in my mind clear-green.

Death exists only for the living. It is a presence, not an absence, a new presence born at the moment of death. People gone, places left behind continue to grow and change, are resurrected, rediscovered. And die daily.

My father willed me deep memories, too. His were of fortune and fame, then withering fortune, withering

The Rechy family, about 1953: standing, from left, sister Olga, John, brothers Juan and Robert, sister Blanca; seated, mother Guadalupe and father Roberto

fame, finally assaulting loss. There was a tenuous reconciliation between him and his mother. She left me two paintings: One was of their family home in Mexico City, the horse-drawn carriage before it emphasizing their former station in life; for me, years later, that carriage looked like a surrendered relic. The other was a portrait of herself, painted on glass: a handsome haughty woman with stark-black hair and a white lace-ruffled blouse rising to her chin, deliberately isolating the face of the powerful woman who had banished my father with gunshots. Why?

My life-as-novel allows me to supply motives that satisfy me, adhering to autobiography by basing them on subsequent evidence, always allowing for mystery. Reordered memory at times discovers only the shape of mystery.

At dinnertime while oppressed servants silently attended, my father announced, "I oppose the tyranny of the Dictator Díaz!"

"I forbid you to continue," says my grandmother.

My grandfather does not take sides, but quietly champions my father—as do the servants. My father goes on to assert sympathy for agrarian reforms. "And the revolutionaries!" exclaims one of the maids. (She was a pretty Indian woman, and she had introduced my father to sex and the ways of social justice.)

"Yes, and them!" my father asserts. My grandmother grabs her jeweled gun. Yes! That is exactly how it happened; now it is lodged in my memory. I remember it! Reordered time, inherited memories, and imagination allow me to applaud my father's act while my grandmother glares at me, too, and my mother smiles approvingly at it all in adjusted time. The Indian maid's name was—. . .

Maria.

I have based that reconstruction on what happened subsequently: My father was run out of a small Southwest town for opposing municipal corruption by exposing it in a "radical" newspaper he printed by himself. A daring pioneer against injustice, especially in bigoted giant Texas, he was defiant, courageous— and cruel, with the cruelty he inherited from the woman in the glass portrait.

Autobiography changes from moment to moment. It is not what happened but what is remembered, when it is remembered. Its only sequence is that of memory. Alter the order of events and you change meaning.

In my memories I discover this: My father's eyes were always filled with tears!—perhaps unseen tears.

Before that new discovery, I knew only this: He was my father and he hated me. Now that I remember real and invisible tears, I find a new man bearing the same life. Early he became a notable figure in the world of music. He had been a child prodigy, learning

to play "every instrument." The music faded. Aging memories were replaced by those of decline. He is no longer the conductor of his own celebrated orchestra, composer of musical scores, no longer the director of his own touring theater, no longer writes music for the films that occupied him briefly, no longer even tutors untalented Texas children. Now he spends dark hours reorchestrating music no one wants, music filed in an old wooden cabinet, eventually lost. Soon he will no longer be even the caretaker of a public park. Now he is an old gray man, mocked by ghosts. He gets up at dawn to clean the night's debris at a hospital, fragments of accidents and death. When he returns home, he lashes out with threats of fire and violence. Then he screams for recognition: "I am respected, known!" My mother soothes him, agreeing. When he died, telegrams came from important figures all over the country and Mexico, who had ignored his slow dying.

Remembered—or inserted—unseen tears reveal this now. He hated only the reflection of himself in me.

Truth changes with new memories. We do not move into the past, we bring it forward with new life. My mother and father speak words I heard long ago (or heard about) but hear now anew, spoken only to me, spoken through me. Tomorrow, if I find my father's anger in me, I may forget his tears, insist that *I* inserted them, revise today's truth.

Before that happens, I will remember this, which will now color all subsequent recollections: After the rampages of anger, my father would bring me presents. He lavished armsful of fresh flowers on my mother, the flowers splashed the drab house of poverty with astonishing colors. He loved her! Shall I allow myself to believe that she loved him, too?

On her Saint's Day, December 12—the day of Our Lady of Guadalupe—he would serenade her at the tint of dawn, turning up with dashing mariachis to sing *"Las Mañanitas"* outside her window. She, pretending surprise but having gone to bed carefully arranged for her appearance at the window, would then invite everyone grandly to an already prepared breakfast of coffee, chocolate, *pan de dulce*. She reigned with her smile. He continued the yearly serenades even when he was old, turning up at the window with a band of increasingly ragged musicians.

Facts—what someone continues to remember, a live memory—are reshaped by the growing past. Only the past changes.

But for me this is constant: On the steps of a bandaged Texas house that has a tattered screened porch, four-years-old I lie on my mother's lap. The Texas sky multiplies a million stars. I begin to doze as my mother curls with her saliva-moistened finger my eyelashes,

John, about one year old

which were long and thick.

We had moved from a pretty house we could no longer afford. Poverty invaded our lives. Over fire made from wood and propped on bricks, my mother heats tin tubs of water to wash our clothes. I remember white sheets. They hang on a line. Memory washes them again. My mother empties the tub, water carves mysterious shapes on the dry soil. I see her against the blue sky under a white sun.

A sharp memory asserts: In kindergarten Miss Stowe was showing us how to make butter in an old-fashioned churn. But the butter remained curdled liquid. Angered, longing for a vanished frontier, its props (I find this for her in my recollection), she kept us after school while she churned. I stand by the window, knowing my mother is waiting for me. Will she think I've been stolen, go through her life looking for me while Miss Stowe churns? Did the teacher succeed in making butter? I don't know. Right now I'm rushing out of the room, down corridors, out the schoolyard. Now I walk home holding my reward for defiance—my mother's hand.

There was another teacher. Miss Oliver. A Texas Cassandra. In El Paso Junior High she was a dreaded teacher because she was smart and demanded attention in class. Black, black hair, a pale, pale face, she seemed always on the brink of unendurable pain. Someone said that in her clenched fists she clutched secret pins. She walks into the classroom. She looks more pained and angered than ever. I hear her now. She says to me—no, to us, all the children there: "You will always be as unhappy as you are now. Always!" A curse? A projection? A prophecy? A challenge? Her truth?

Years later when I denied God melodramatically, I was certain he was listening and caring. Did he hear Miss Oliver? Still later I cherished the splendid indif-

ference of beautiful cold stars in limitless unseeing darkness and hoped that she did, too.

The Greeks had Gods that intervened on tragedy. Euripides was not sure and so did not win first prizes. Newer Gods were seducible by prayer and offerings and sacrifice. Then there was One, then there was none, and there was no substitute for salvation. Miss Oliver just taught me that.

The despised Texas windstorms begin in February, howling across the desert, thrusting gray dust against hints of spring, budding trees confused into resurrection by brief hours of sun, and the wind hurls tangled masses of tumbleweeds into the city.

We lived near railroad tracks. Hundreds of men and women fleeing the Depression from one state to another would ride through, hidden in freight trains. Police raid the cars, bludgeoning flesh. Tramps sweep across the tracks in search of shelter—and, for me, they sweep into ambiguous memories.

Mystery, too, grows in memory, deepens, reveals clues, only clues, and mystery, sharper mystery—providing only more precise questions, not answers.

Lean men and women often handsome but dirtied, the tattered wanderers would appear at our back door. My mother would seat them at a wooden table kept for that purpose in the back porch. She serves them each a plate of rice and beans, a container of hot coffee.

Slides flash on the scrim of memory, at times unwind images like strips of film. Autobiography contains photographs, faded or sharp. And silhouettes—shadows that exist only when exact light is at the exact angle.

A face. A man among the tramps. He was kind to me, a gentle figure like a dirtied angel. I was six years old. Memory jerks into a dark freight car of twisting shadows where— Is this real? Imagined? Memory invents what it requires for today's truth, or to conceal it, memory's subterfuge—disguising one memory with another. Then why, years later as a youngman roaming America, will I wander into skid rows, filled with rage and terror, and then I will flee, away, anger and terror flowing into sorrow. And, then, sometimes, a brief, warm peace.

When I was nine, I acted with a famous theater company, headed by Virginia Fabrigas (the Ethel Barrymore of Mexican theater). In an allegorical Spanish drama titled *El Monje Blanco*, I played the Christ-child. As my carpenter-father begins to walk away from me and my mother, I lean against an arrangement of boards on stage, converting two into a cross, and I say:

"Why are you abandoning me, father?"

When others were taking curtain calls, I rushed into the audience, to be embraced by weeping women and men—who loved me! Or merely the child in the role?

I will splice two memories, containing others, for a growing meaning: I was poor with borrowed memories of gentility; of "mixed blood"—a *guerro*—Mexican but not looking it, by Texas standards. In Texas discrimination saturates the soil. "Oh," they would say, "you must never claim to be Mexican, you're too fair." As a *guerro*, I was doubly exiled—by other Mexicans, when they knew, and by other "Anglos" when *they* knew. Asserting my unique identity, without overt "allegiance" then to either of the banishing camps, I managed to become "popular" in high school, president of all the clubs I belonged to. But my "popularity" ended when school was over and I fled to secret poverty. Now jump across many years, when two "Anglos" are proposing me for membership in a popular fraternity. We went to visit the ranch of one of their families, in Balmorhea, darkest gothic Texas—where *all* Texas Rangers are bred. A single theater, playing only on weekends, separated Mexicans from Anglos and never allowed Negroes. At dinner, a relative of my would-be "fraternity brother" expressed her dismay at eating while the Mexican maid "is still in the room." It was Maria's daughter! I didn't know it then but I know it now. Yes! And that is in strong part why I walked out of that house and began my ethnic rebellion—furthering my isolation. Now—as I leave that Texan dinner of hatred—I say *"buenas noches"* to Maria's daughter. Her name was— . . . Maria, like her mother. *But why was she still in servitude?*

What is strongly imagined is finally remembered. Maria has become a living ghost, the first Maria—and an influence on my whole life! Yes, and when my father told my mother—and told her with some hesitation—about Maria, my beautiful mother—of course—approved. "Was she pretty?" she asks him. "Yes—but not as beautiful as you," he answers; he had to be truthful. "But why didn't you go back later to say goodbye to her?" my mother chides him. "I did," he tells her, "but she had run away, too; to join the *Zapatistas*."

I edited the college magazine and then was removed because I had turned it into a "radical" literary periodical. Like my father before me! A welcome ambush of memory.

Teaching me independence, my father allowed me to miss school whenever I wanted. A truant officer courageous enough to object was confronted by his enormous wrath and never did it again. My father therefore allowed me—on windy afternoons, when Texas clouds shut the rest of the world out—to go to the Texas Grand Theater for magical hours, splendor of delights, especially during recurrent "revival

Guadalupe Flores de Rechy, about sixty-two years old

week"—"old" movies. Hedy Lamarr! Tyrone Power, Bette Davis! My father made that possible.

Memories of him tangle. Oh, did my mother love him? She stayed with him until he died—and, after, remembered him only as the dashing Scotsman who married her, serenaded her.

A film clip unwinds beautifully on the screen of memory. I'll keep it in slow motion. After my first novel was published, I bought my mother a house; and soon after, we drove to Los Angeles to visit my sister. Halfway there, so she will not grow tired, I rent for overnight a suite in the gaudiest and most expensive motel in Phoenix, Arizona. We collect stares as we enter the pretentious lobby, because I am wearing torn jeans, no shirt; my mother wears a lovely summer hat, white gloves, a faintly violet lace dress. I ask for the best accommodations.

Closeup. Tight focus. The motel pool sprawls across a green lawn under pastel-haloed palm trees, the water is colored silver in the desert night. My mother has taken her sleeping pill. She wears a summer robe, so light it sighs in a breezeless night. We sit by the pool. She tells me she would like a cool soft drink. I order it, and it comes on a platter. She sips it. She smiles her magical smile. "Thank you, my son. Now I'll have a restful sleep. Goodnight, my son." I see her small form moving in and out of tinted shadows. I want that mysterious moment to stay, to halt. If it is true that when you die, images of your life flash by, I hope this one will linger.

Dual Catholicisms, Scottish and Mexican, but more Mexican, because I was raised in El Paso: Splattered colors, ritual, confession, Mass, sin, guilt, and no substitute allowed for salvation. Painted saints with painted tears writhe in gorgeous agony. Christ poses on his cross. Excessive, that religion burrows into roots of superstition, at best white magic.

A memory rustles, stirs, calls, speaks:

"Treasure is buried under the house!"

Tia Ana said that. A spirit has told her that treasure is buried under the crawl space of our house. My mother says nonsense, my father says it's worth a try to find out—his background in opera allowed acceptance of the unseen. *Don* Ben, pope of El Paso's good witches, a tiny root of an old man, is summoned. The late sun waits in suspense on the purple horizon. My brothers, my sisters, my mother, my father, myself, *Tia* Ana, and *don* Ben gather in the yard.

Don Ben becomes rigid. Something *is* buried nearby. "Treasure," my aunt interprets. Only *don* Ben and I—I think I was five years old then—are small enough to crawl into the dank darkness. No treasure, no sign. Coughing from the dampness, and cramped in that prostrate position, *don* Ben is about to crawl out. I will help *Tia* Ana and God. I move ahead, twist two sticks into a hurried cross, and I put it atop a mound of dirt. "Look! *Don* Ben, the sign!" *Don* Ben groans. From beyond, *Tia* Ana issues a relieved "Amen." But in the dusking evening, a weary *don* Ben testily says we must pray twelve novenas before he can proceed. He rubs his back to emphasize the need for a long, long devotional period. My mother loses patience, my aunt has a lapse of faith, and only the Texas dust remains under our house.

But perhaps I didn't make that cross. Perhaps it was there and I found it. Perhaps there *was* treasure. No. Yes. No. Memory and autobiography are affected by the time of day, the month, the season. Winter memories in summer, summer memories of winter. Of spring. Day. Night—light and angles of shadows alter form. When at another time I remember *Tia* Ana's prophecy of treasure, I may imbue it with the sense of sad loss that followed for days: There was, after all, no

treasure. The poverty continued—and new waves of tramps swept across the tracks.

This remembrance asserts: When I was finishing *City of Night* in my mother's home after years of desultory wandering about the country, in the evenings I would translate into Spanish passages I thought appropriate, and I would read them to her. "You're writing a beautiful book, my son," she said.

The longer a distance in time it survives, the more "real" the assertive memory; it has survived the onslaught of new ones. With new power, it may even be borrowed.

My brother Robert. Smart, sensitive, brooding. When he was a child and before I was born, my grandmother, the woman in the glass portrait, asked him as he stared outside the window, "Robertito, Robertito, what are you staring at so hard?" He answered, "I am occupied with life." But in my mind I give myself that fact, link myself even more closely to my brother. I look out the window, and it is my mother who asks me the question.

I answer: "I am occupied with life."

Given another series of accidents, my brother might have become the writer. But being the oldest, he had to sacrifice his education because we could not otherwise survive on what my father was able to earn. My loving brother-father, handsome enough to be Robert Taylor's double, got the only job he could then, in a pool hall. Sometimes he would wake me up when he came home on a hot summer night, and he would take me out to the Spinning Wheel to get a hamburger and a malted milk—magic potions which I never was able to finish.

With his help—and a journalism scholarship—I went to a small college in El Paso. It nestles in the desert; we climbed rocks to get to class. In an English literature class—majoring in English, minoring in French—I wrote a paper "proving" that John Milton was on the side of the rebel angels, and had succeeded in justifying the ways of *man* to God. Emboldened, I wrote a private poem in which at judgment day all humanity, led by Jesus, turns the final trial about and sentences God to hell. If I were writing it now, Miss Oliver would lead the prosecution.

I read a lot, eclectically; Greek tragedies, Margaret Mitchell, Dostoevsky, García Lorca, Ben Ames Williams, Rimbaud, Emily Brontë, Nietzsche, Henry Bellamann, Joyce, Proust, Frank Yerby, Donne, Kathleen Winsor, Swift, Faulkner. And I saw many, many movies.

After classes in college, I often climbed the nearby Mount Cristo Rey, a barren rocky mountain bordered by the Rio Grande, usually waterless—the passageway by which *braceros* make their way into the farms and ranches of Texas. At the top of the mountain is a giant Christ, an Indian Christ, looking down as the Border Patrol rounds up the "illegals." Vast empty desert marked with cactuses. I climbed for hours, sweating. Once I climbed with a beautiful girl I was in love with. Was I? People said we resembled each other. A doomed girl whose beauty never ages in my mind; a strange wounded girl as joined by hatred to her mother as I was by love to mine. Years later she taught my mother—who by then had recurrent fainting spells—how to do a graceful oriental "dance." I see them in my mother's bedroom as they make floating ghost movements.

No, it isn't true that that girl did not age in my memories. I tried to avoid this: She returned to El Paso when I had returned, too. Then only for a few moments was I able to see in that new stark presence the vague resemblance of the girl I had loved. A specter, it glided over her and then was gone. She had returned for her mother's death.

I grasp an earlier memory of her. On Times Square, hustling, I ran into her—beautiful then. But we did not speak, not that night. She understood why I was there as she left a movie theater with another youngman.

Rechy, New York, about 1964

I finished college at an early age. An English teacher offered to recommend me for a scholarship to Harvard, his school; but rather than extending the wait, I allowed myself to be drafted into the army. I didn't tell anyone—except my immediate family—that I was going away.

I get up early. My mother is already up. She has been crying. I hug her. My father is up, too! Is he crying? Yes! I remember it. He has just started to cry. We hadn't spoken to each other for months, locked silence replaced rage and curses—rage I had begun to vent back at him—yes, cruelly, I can't escape that—thrusting his collapse from musical grace back at him as "failure," yes, I see that I did that, but then I knew I was only trying to escape from drowning in his rages.

That morning: He gives me a ring he wore—a ruby mounted in gold, he told us. I take it, put it on my finger and look at him both for the last time and the first time: The man standing before me is a defeated old man, crushed by conflicting memories of what was and what became; his sorrow, hidden before by rampaging anger, is clear now as he looks at me through his tears of loss and regret. In a few weeks he will be dead. I will return to his funeral. I will go on forever finding him within the present of alleviated memories. Memory interprets.

I went into the army a private and came out a private, never staying in one place enough to be pro-

moted, maneuvering to be transferred, feeling a restlessness that will soon take me over. Stationed in Germany, I traveled over Europe. Accepted by Columbia University, I applied for, and got, an early release. I returned briefly to my mother in Texas, telling her that I had to leave now on my own, beginning another pattern—leaving, returning, leaving, returning, always dreading the moment of separation.

I arrived in New York with only twenty dollars and on an electrified late afternoon when a hurricane threatened the island. A cop told me I could find a room at the nearby YMCA. There I met a merchant marine. He buys me hamburgers and tells me I can make quick money on Times Square—"hustling." A new word has opened a new world to me.

Instead of Columbia, I went to Times Square.

Autobiography as novel allows revealing juxtapositions. Out of chronological sequence, events that occurred later in "real time" illuminate what came before.

This happened a year before: In Paris one late night near the Café de Flor the area suddenly assumed a strange clarity for me. I knew why I had remained late on that street. There are only men idling about. And I *know*. No, I may not have known then, exactly. Yes! Memory comes forth. An attractive man talks to me, in French, and then English. I say yes, feeling that

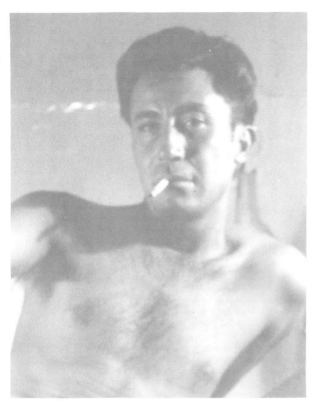

In New York, about 1957, the "Times Square period"

I am in a lucid trance. I go to his nearby apartment. He touches me intimately. I pull away, but I wait. Then I turn away and rush out.

As a child I had crushes on the pretty actresses in my father's theatrical company, and on girls in my classes, especially one, who was chosen to be a "couple" with me, and model grown-up clothes for the PTA! We were both eight. There was a girl named Barbara. I was infatuated with the Wicked Queen in *Snow White,* never insipid Snow White. Later I would hear the queen described as looking like a man in drag. I fell in love with Hedy Lamarr, Veronica Lake, Dorothy Lamour, and I think—I'm not sure now—Lauren Bacall. I wanted to be like Erroll Flynn, Tyrone Power, Alan Ladd—that superb. The demarcation between admiration and desire is thin. Did they intersect even then?

On Times Square, which the merchant marine has told me about—arousing a cacophony of terrified excitement, strange magic—I study other idling youngmen selling their bodies. From them I learn quickly how to stand, look—as if I had *always* known. A middle-aged man approaches me and says, "I'll give you ten dollars and I don't give a damn for you." Two needs of my time then: to be desired powerfully, and not to be expected to care.

This memory comes forward: As a little boy in Texas, I stood in the back yard of our house and looked up at a million stars. God was there. That's where I said nightly prayers, each night adding new ones as the miseries I was increasingly aware of in the world became clearer. (There was so much poverty and hunger in El Paso and Juárez that we did not consider ourselves poor because we ate and had a home.) Finally, the list of violations I thought my prayers would alleviate grew so long, so complex, that I made a unilateral agreement with God: In the future I would merely say, in my thoughts: "You already know why I'm praying."

I hustled in New York, Los Angeles, San Francisco, St. Louis, Chicago, New Orleans—and once—no, twice—in El Paso. If it had been only once, I would have said I did so to banish pursuing ghosts. My journey begun on Times Square led me—"inevitably"—to the epiphany of Mardi Gras, my own Ash Wednesday.

I fled the shrouded city during Lent. New Orleans is always black and white, never in color, in my mind—and I returned to the gentle sanctuary of my mother's house and love. There I wrote a letter to a friend in Evanston, Illinois, about the frantic events in New Orleans—crowded with sex and pills, and casual dope, feeling myself out of control, falling. Unsent, crumpled, found later, reshaped, that letter became my first published "story"—"Mardi Gras" in *Evergreen Review;* it was also the beginning (although it would be incorporated into its last chapter) of my first novel, *City of Night.* As sections of that book continued to appear in literary quarterlies, I had offers from several publishers for a contract. I chose Grove Press, the company I admired most for its quality and courage, and because its senior editor, Don Allen, had been the first to assert belief in the book.

Despite a contract and an advance, I did not write that book for years. I returned to the "nightcities" and to the private, beautiful, and ugly magic of hustling, playing there the then-required role of "paid tourist."

Autobiography as novel allows for a "flashforward" for extended meaning: Soon—not yet—I will start going with certain men because of desire, not for money. The same night will find me hustling once, and then cruising many times in the territory of unpaid sex, mutual desire—finding a refuge for mystery in numbers, countless anonymous encounters.

Hitchhiking in Los Angeles, I met a man who made it possible for me to return to El Paso to finish in a year the novel I had started three years earlier.

From childhood I had wanted to write—and paint. I wrote and illustrated stories always titled "Long Ago"—perhaps I was revising my life to a time when I would become my mother's escort at her triumphant dance affairs. Influenced by the film *Marie Antoinette*, I wrote about 500 pages of a novel about the French Revolution, researched diligently. I abandoned it to write about 200 pages of a novel about a boy of "mixed blood" in Texas. By age sixteen or seventeen, I had written many stories, many poems, including two epics—about war in heaven. Most of my writings were started in pencil and continued on a portable Royal typewriter my father gave me. My father! I discover him anew constantly with new evidence.

I destroyed all those manuscripts when I went into the army, with the exception of a finished novel, *Pablo!*—a "realistic fantasy" framed about the Mayan legend of doomed love between the moon and the sun, separated at the dawn of time. In it, a narcissistic youngman tells the story of a "beautiful woman who died."

City of Night became a best-seller before official publication; and it was bought by about a dozen foreign countries for translation. The initial critical reaction was vitriolic, cruel. My very existence—literally—was questioned in the *New York Review of Books* and *New Republic*. Even restrained critics concentrated on the book's subject. With precious exceptions, its careful

In San Francisco, 1962. Book jacket photo from
City of Night

structure was virtually ignored. (I believe that self-appointed "important" critics should be licensed to practice—like doctors, so that an artist may sue them for malpractice—the recklessness with which they often assault work they know to be good but which disturbs them for private reasons.) It pleases me that today—when I speak to new readers in college courses where it is required reading—they assume that the book was always highly admired. And it continues to be read widely; new foreign editions appear; it is frequently referred to as "a modern classic." (Autobiography allows sensitive journalism.)

I chose not to promote the book, to retain my private life. I did not want my life to change radically while the lives of the people I had written about remained the same; that seemed betrayal. When I had bought my mother her new house but we had not yet moved in, a letter and some telephone calls from a man who admired my novel extended into an invitation to go to Tanglewood to hear the American premiere of Benjamin Britten's *War Requiem*. During the following weeks, perhaps two months, I stayed with this extraordinary caring man—in Riverdale outside New York. (Focus: An eagle appears on the balcony of his fourteenth-storey apartment and peers in through a glass wall.) We went to Puerto Rico, the Virgin Islands. Through newspaper and magazine items placing me in cities I have never been to, the guest of people I have never known, I learned of several imposters.

I returned to El Paso. I will hold this memory, too, in slow motion: My mother shows me through the house I have bought for her. She points out the new furniture. She holds my arm, and I link mine through hers, and she takes me outside to see the magnificent late roses.

Strangers appeared at my house, inventing ruses to be let in. I answered hundreds of letters—good letters—from readers. Increasingly reclusive, I had only two or three friends. I took frequent drives into the Texas desert, or the banks of the Rio Grande. I climbed bluish mountains. I began the transition from "youngman" to "man." I created my own gym in my mother's house and I began body-building fiercely with weights—an activity that continues to be central to my life.

With my mother I took a trip to Los Angeles. Because it belongs by itself, a part of nothing else, I have pulled out for special attention the cherished moments with her by that Arizona motel pool. Autobiography allows separation of memories.

In Los Angeles, my mother stayed with my sister, and I rented a motel room—and I crammed my life with sex again—as if to make up for lost years—in an area of a vast park, a sexual paradise that could become a sexual hell when the hunt became frantic, without surcease.

As I drove out of the city of daily apocalypse—my mother holding a writing pad firmly on the console of my cherished black-and-tan 1965 Mustang as I steered with my left hand—I began my second novel, *Numbers.*

Written in exactly three months, this book, as much about sex as about dying, was strongly influenced by Poe. It has some of my best writing, including a first chapter that introduces all the themes and symbols that illuminate the protagonist's—Johnny Rio's—descent into the dark heart of the sexual park I had discovered. In this novel my attention to structure increased, shaping chaos.

Again, the critical reaction was largely hysterical. Even the photograph of me on the front of the book's jacket aroused anger. Again, only the sexual content was glared at.

Then love enclosed—locked—me and my mother in that new house, the love that occurs, when it does, only between mother and son. Freud was wrong, so wrong. It has nothing to do with sex, incest; only a special love that defines itself. With the money from my books, I would try to make up for all her years of poverty and sacrifice, the demands I and the rest of my

In El Paso, 1966. Book jacket photo from Numbers

family had placed on her love. In wanting to give her everything I thought she needed, did I deprive her of everything she really needed? Her rose garden—I gave to a man to tend for her. Her kitchen—I gave it to a woman to take it over for her. I insisted on giving her a superb vacation to Mexico City, with my sister; I know now she did not want to go back. I insisted she visit distant friends, insisted we go out to lunch, dinner. I did not know she wanted, increasingly, to rest now, just rest; that she was tired; that the unscreamed protests of her life were being screamed at last—but inside, burrowed inward, wearing. What I did was all out of love—and all destroying. And so I raged at her. (The way my father had done when I despised him most! His unwelcome presence asserts that now. No, I refuse to accept that. It was not like that, no.) "What do you want me to do—become young!" she pled once to me. Yes! But she was seventy then. In defense, she retreated to her bedroom, decorated like a doll's room, with delicate filigree, in shades of pastel, white golden-gilded drapes drawn so that the room glowed faintly.

I understand only now. What remains constant from that time is this: Her eyes grew even more beautiful, more luminous than ever. Yes, I remember that. And I know this: I did not realize that my beloved mother, who had waltzed with me in imagination and then in reality—had grown old. I never saw her aging.

This Day's Death—a novel that does not understand the situations it attempts to explore, because I did not understand them—came out of that time. I will return to the subject in another book, the subject of a mother and son trapped by love—only love—so powerful it begins killing both.

During that same period I wrote *The Vampires,* a book that sometimes baffles me. It came out of a central reality—a time I had spent on a private island with a man, his mistress, his ex-wives. Beyond that, it is a strange, exotic creation, a splashy luxurious novel about opulent decay and corruption as beautiful wealthy guests gather on an island mansion to play out a pageant of confessions and judgment. It is written in "Technicolor," employing filmic techniques in prose. It is influenced by the exaggerations of classic comic strips like "Terry and the Pirates"—and, too, again, much influenced by Poe.

It was virtually ignored, in major part because its publisher was in a financial crisis at the time, publication constantly postponed. There was no promotion, no galleys sent out for review.

On October 9, 1970, my mother died.

In the hospital, she had come out of a coma to say: "I understand—we love each other so much, my son, that we hurt because of it." I clasped her hand and she clasped mine. I told her she had to live. And al-

Rechy in Griffith Park, Los Angeles, about 1970

though I would not face that she would—could—die, I had her transferred to a room where a wide window faced the giant Indian Christ atop the Cristo Rey Mountains. There was a brilliant Texas sunset before it all became night.

The ungraspable horror of her death sent me to drugs. But I suppose I chose to live. I stopped the drugs. I return more and more to that time by the swimming pool in Arizona when she asked for a cool soft drink and said she would have a restful night.

Like memory, art falsifies, altering experience, bringing the added artifice of words, symbols. In *The Fourth Angel,* I converted myself into a teenager who cannot cope with his mother's death; I turned other "real" characters into the same age. I added invented situations. I was still keeping away the reality of my mother's death and my involvement with drugs. The teenagers in the book are so wounded that they embark on playing "games" that will teach them to stop feeling, stop hurting. In the process, they almost destroy themselves and each other. For me it is a moving, frightening, powerful book. But it, too, was ignored.

I was broke. Ten years after the huge success of *City of Night* had made me rich and "famous" (I had managed to remain private), I was back in Los Angeles hustling the same streets that first book had described; anonymous again. At first I was terrified that after many years away, that world, relying on physical de-

sirability, would spit me out. Had I unconsciously prepared for this return by my physical conversion through body-building, now that I was no longer a "youngman"? I was able to survive again on those streets.

Then I was invited to be a guest writer at Occidental College. Since then, I have taught at UCLA and USC—and I've lectured at many universities, including Yale and Duke. I am considered to be an excellent "teacher" of writing; that is, I recognize and encourage creativity.

The Sexual Outlaw, which came in part out of my return to the streets, both hustling and cruising, is the literary equivalent of a film documentary—influenced by Robbe-Grillet's theories on the new novel. Plotless, "black-and-white," it is a minute-by-minute accounting of three days and nights of anonymous sex as "Jim" roams the sexual underground of Los Angeles. Many characters appear, only briefly, as their lives intersect with Jim's. All are "pastless." I wanted all the characters, including Jim, to be "defined" only through their sexual journeys. Interspersed throughout the account

In Los Angeles, 1971

of this night odyssey are voice-over essays, multi-media splices of commentary. It is a brooding exploration of a misunderstood world.

It was knocked quickly off best-seller lists when bookstores refused to carry it; major television stations would not advertise it. In England news of its publication drew threatened lawsuits.

While receiving "mixed reviews," it was—again—discussed almost solely on the basis of its content. Its adventurous form was not considered.

Rushes is a "realistic" account of one night in a sadomasochistic leather bar and orgy room. It is also a Catholic Mass. The sleazy bar finds careful paralells in the structure of a church, the pornographic drawings on the walls evoke the stations of the cross. The contemporary dialogue at times paraphrases sections from the Mass. Realistic incidents involving people that would frequent such a bar, find equivalents in the rituals of baptism, initiation, sacrifice, even possible purgation. There are two crucifixions, one symbolic in the orgy room, one real—a brutal murder occurring outside perpetrated by "gay-bashers." It is a dark novel,

Rechy, Los Angeles, 1973

and the structure is central to its meanings.

Again, sexual content was emphasized in even favorable reviews—with a few notable exceptions, and these exceptions encouraged me to believe that my *writing* was now receiving careful attention at least from a few critics.

Bodies and Souls is an apocalyptic view of Los Angeles today as a modern paradise for still-rebelling "angels." Its gallery of characters ranges from a pornographic actress to a Mr. Universe; a bagwoman, a Chicano teenager, a gothic female evangelist, a black maid from Watts, a male stripper, a TV anchorwoman. A youngwoman and two youngmen—"lost angels"—bring about the apocalyptic ending.

The peculiar aspects surrounding the novel's publication created almost insurmountable barriers to its reception, through nobody's deliberation. My talented editor on two earlier books had formed his own publishing house. He made a good bid for *Bodies and Souls*. I withdrew the book from other publishers, feeling that a new company's first original book would bring major attention to it; and I did not want to break an excellent editorial relationship. Too, the book would be brought out in a few months as opposed to the usual almost-year. I was dubious about the book being issued simultaneously in hardback and trade editions; but I became convinced that was, indeed, a trend of the future, with notable antecedents among respected books. Because of pressures endemic to new publishing enterprises, the hardcover edition of the book was makeshift, ugly; it and the trade edition contained dozens of typographical errors, pages askew. I would have demanded publication be stopped until a new edition was printed, but the book was already advertised, galley proofs sent to reviewers. I knew that the shoddy appearance of the book would arouse incorrect suspicions that the book had been widely rejected. That, of course, was not so. Far from so.

Written from advance galleys before the shoddy edition was seen, two fine reviews appeared, one in the *New York Times Book Review*, which borrowed my description of Los Angeles to call the book "a scarred beauty"; and one in the *Los Angeles Times Book Review*, which lauded it as a "memorable feast."

Reviews stopped. Just as I had known, the book's condition had done inestimable damage to the book. I wrote individual letters to book-review editors I respected, calling attention to my novel, letting them know that a new respectable edition was being prepared. In some instances, I knew, my letters would arouse further antagonism, and they did—but excellent reviews eventually appeared in the book sections of the *San Francisco Chronicle*, two Dallas newspapers, the *Los Angeles Herald*, and a few others.

Eventually the publishers did release a good looking limited hardback and a handsome trade edition. There is also a handsome paperback. My relationship with my publishers and my editor is restored to the point that they will publish my next novel. It was a nightmarish situation that had entrapped everyone concerned.

Despite all these obstacles, *Bodies and Souls* continues to draw attention, and praise. It is, I believe, a daring novel in content and form; a grand and lasting artistic achievement.

Now that autobiography has slipped into passionate journalism, I will remain there for a while longer: Today, I find myself a "Texas" writer left out of discussions of Texas writers, a Chicano writer omitted from anthologies of Chicano writers, a "California writer" ignored in books about California. Even though I am excluded from several anthologies of homosexual writers, I am still known as "the homosexual writer." Yet several of my books do not deal centrally with the subject of homosexuality; and for the *Nation, Saturday Review,* the *Texas Observer, Evergreen Review,* and many other publications, I have written essays on poverty among Mexican-Americans, injustice against juveniles in detention homes, discrimination against black athletes, the persecution of dissenting soldiers during the Vietnam War. I have translated the writing of notable Mexican authors, and have written essay-reviews of books by William Golding, William Burroughs, Jean Rhys, Jonathan Swift, André Gide, Elizabeth Bowen. My one-act play *Momma As She Became—But Not As She Was* is widely performed, anthologized.

My books continue in print, gaining readers and attention. *City of Night, Numbers,* and *The Sexual Outlaw* were just reissued in new format, with Forewords by me. New translations appear. My play *Tigers Wild*—which ranks with my best writing—is moving toward Off-Broadway production in 1986. My next novel, *Marilyn's Daughter,* about the legend of Marilyn Monroe, will appear the same year. I want to write two more books: *In the Beginning,* about war in Heaven, and *Autobiography: A Novel.*

If I died tomorrow, I would know that I have written as formidable a body of work as that of any other writer of my generation.

Collision of memories!

One emerges, seizes completely—is followed by a question. I sort through other memories.

This cherished one! A beloved friend and I have been let into the Museum of Modern Art before the doors open to the public. My friend and I and rooms and rooms of the magnificence of Picasso!

This! Miss Stowe changed my name from Juan Francisco Rechy to John, no, Johnny (when she counted to ten and I heard "one," I thought, knowing only Spanish, that she was calling me, "Juan").

And this: Reflecting the grisly determined optimism of that vast State of Texas, Miss Stowe made us change a word in one of the songs we had to sing for her daily: "Home on the Range." "Where seldom is heard a discouraging word" became "where *never* is heard a discouraging word." In the text, she made us draw a dark line through "seldom" and substitute, with blue ink, "never."

What would Miss Oliver have done?

Now the avoided memory flows into the present: I am five years old. I have been told that I must start school. I refuse to go. I do not want to leave my mother unprotected. "What will happen if the robbers come or the house burns? Who will save you?" I ask her. "You will," she tells me. "You will know if anything threat-

On a Los Angeles street, about 1980

ens me and you will save me."

But did I? Years later—after the wandering from city to city—I did return to El Paso, and stayed until her death. In that new house I bought her, she retained this: An old glass case from years back which contained delicate figurines, crystal angels, hand-painted cups and saucers, miniature white statues of the Madonna. Why, in my memories, do those objects seem imprisoned in a beautiful glass cage?

This is an outline of my "autobiography" today. Only today. Even it contains contradictory "truths." Tomorrow it may all change.

With one exception. Perhaps two. And another—

BIBLIOGRAPHY

Fiction:

City of Night. New York: Grove, 1963; London: MacGibbon & Kee, 1964.

Numbers. New York: Grove, 1967.

This Day's Death. New York: Grove, 1969; London: MacGibbon & Kee, 1970.

The Vampires. New York: Grove, 1971.

The Fourth Angel. London: W. H. Allen, 1972; New York: Richard Seaver/Viking, 1973.

Rushes. New York: Grove, 1979.

Bodies and Souls. New York: Carroll & Graf, 1983; London: W. H. Allen, 1984.

Nonfiction:

The Sexual Outlaw: A Documentary. New York: Grove, 1977; London: W. H. Allen, 1978.

Plays:

Momma As She Became—Not As She Was, produced in New York, 1978.

Charles Simic

1938-

IN THE BEGINNING . . .

I

The radio. It sits on the table by my bed. It has a dial which lights up. The stations have names. I can't read yet, but I make others read them to me. There's Oslo, Lisbon, Moscow, Berlin, Budapest, and many more. One moves the red arrow to a spot and hears a strange language or unfamiliar music. At ten o'clock the stations sign off. The war is on. The year is 1943.

The nights of my childhood were spent in the company of that radio. I attribute the insomnia from which I still suffer to its temptations. I couldn't keep my hands off it. Even after the stations went silent, I kept turning the dial and listening to various noises. Once I heard beeps in Morse code. Spies, I thought. Often I'd catch a distant station so faint I'd have to turn the sound all the way up and press my ear against the rough burlap that covered the speaker. Somewhere dance music was playing or the language was so attractive I'd listen to it for a long time, as if on the verge of understanding.

All this was strictly forbidden. I was supposed to be asleep. Come to think of it, I must have been afraid to be alone in that big room. The war was on. Terrible things happened at night. There was a curfew. Someone was late. Someone else was pacing up and down in the next room. Black paper curtains hung on the windows. It was dangerous even to peek between them at the street—the dark and empty street.

I see myself standing on tiptoes, one hand on the curtain, wanting to look but afraid of the light the radio tubes cast dimly through its trellised back onto the bedroom wall. My father is late and outside the roofs are covered with snow.

*

The Germans bombed Belgrade in April of 1941 when I was three years old. The building across the street was hit and destroyed. I don't remember anything about that bomb. The next day we left the city on foot. I remember a beautiful meadow, great clouds overhead, and then suddenly a plane flying very low.

Did we leap into a ditch by the railroad tracks, or was that some other time? How many of us were there?

I remember my mother but not my father. There were strangers, too. I see their hunched backs, see them running with their bundles, but no faces . . . My film keeps breaking. An image here and there, but not much continuity. And poor lighting. I have to strain my eyes, and then the match goes out, so to speak.

Was the world really so gray then? In my early memories, it's almost always late fall. The soldiers are gray and so are the people.

The Germans are standing on the street corner. We are walking by. "Don't look at them," my mother whispers. I look anyway, and one of them smiles. For some reason that makes me afraid.

*

One night the Gestapo came to arrest my father. This time I was asleep and woke suddenly to the bright lights. They were rummaging everywhere and making a lot of noise. My father was already dressed. He was saying something, probably making a joke. That was his style. No matter how bleak the situation he'd find something funny to say. Years later, surrounded by doctors and nurses and in the throes of a heart attack, he asked for pizza and beer. The doctors were afraid that he had suffered brain damage.

I guess I went back to sleep after he was taken away. In any case, nothing much happened that time. He was released. It wasn't his fault his kid brother stole a German army truck to take his girlfriend for a spin. He didn't even get shot, that brother of his. The Germans were astonished—almost amused—by his stupidity. They shipped him off to work in Germany. They tried to, that is, but he wiggled through their fingers.

In the meantime, we kids were playing war. All the kids were playing war. We took prisoners. We fell down dead. We machine-gunned a lot. How we loved the sound of a machine gun!

This kind of playing drove the grown-ups crazy. All the real shooting—and these kids kept firing their imaginary guns. It didn't take much to make our parents fly off the handle. They'd look so serious, so preoccupied, and then all of a sudden—pop! You'd see a woman stop on the street and slap her child, seemingly for no reason at all, and with everybody watching.

You couldn't blame them, really. I had a friend who could imitate an air-raid siren perfectly. Every time his parents locked him in, he'd stand on his sixth-floor balcony and wail. People on the street below would plead with him to stop. He wouldn't. In fact, he'd get even louder, even better. We thought it was very funny and a little scary, too.

*

The building we lived in was in the center of the city on a small side street near the main post office and the parliament. A dangerous place to be. That's what we thought in the spring of 1944 when the English and the Americans started bombing the city.

It was Easter Sunday. The dining-room table was set with our best china when the planes came. We could hear them. The windows were open since it was such a nice spring day.

George and Helen Simic, Belgrade, 1936

"Americans are throwing Easter eggs," my father said. Then, it started thundering. We ran down to the cellar. The building shook. People huddled on the floor. One could hear glass breaking up above. Some kid ran to the stairs to take a look. His mother screamed.

Then it was all over. We came out. The street was dark. All the dust of the city had risen in the air. The buildings in sight were still standing. A man covered with fallen plaster walked by telling everybody that a certain neighborhood had been levelled. That was astonishing. It was one of the poorest neighborhoods in the city. There were no Germans there.

The next day the Allies came again and it was the same. They never hit anything of military importance. A bomb landed on our sidewalk. It didn't explode. My mother was for clearing out immediately; my father was for staying. She prevailed.

The roads out of the city were full of refugees. The planes kept returning. We approved of Americans and the English bombing Germans. I never heard anyone complain. They were our allies. We loved them. Still, with their poor marksmanship, it was dangerous to remain in the city.

My grandfather had a summer house twenty miles from Belgrade. When we arrived there, my father's side of the family had already assembled. They argued all the time. In addition to the German occupation, there was a civil war in Yugoslavia. There were at least half-a-dozen factions made up of Royalists, Communists, Fascists, collaborators, fighting. The family was divided bitterly between the Royalists and the Communists. My grandfather remained neutral. They were all the same, in his opinion.

As for my mother, she said nothing. She disliked my father's people. She came from an old middle-class family while they were blue-collar workers. She was educated in Paris while they spent their time getting drunk in low dives. It's astonishing that she and my father ever got married. My father had gone to the university, was a successful engineer now, but he hated my mother's world.

It wasn't long before he left us. Early one morning my mother and I accompanied him to the small and crowded train station. By the way he looked at me and by the way he hugged me I knew this was no ordinary journey. I was told nothing. Ten years would pass before I would see my father again. People would ask, "Where's your father?" I couldn't tell them. All my mother knew that day was that he was going to try to get to Italy, but there was no news of him for a long time.

We stayed with my grandparents. Summer came. The bombing of Belgrade continued. We could see the

Father with Gypsies at the Red Rooster Tavern, 1935

planes high up over the city. Our house was on a hill overlooking the river Sava and we had a fine view in that direction. Columns of smoke went up as bombs fell. We'd be eating watermelon in our garden watching the city burn. My grandmother would cross herself repeatedly. The dogs would get restless.

The fighting was intensifying. The Russian Army was in southern Romania pushing toward Belgrade along the Danube. Locally, the various factions were settling old scores. There was a lot of indiscriminate killing. After I found some bodies early one morning in a roadside ditch, they did not let me go out any more. Our neighbors were executed in their own home. The people across the street just disappeared. Nothing happened to us. My mother was very pregnant and wobbled around. She had no politics, neither did my grandfather. That doesn't explain it, of course. We were just lucky.

It was a relief when the Russians came. At least now there were only two sides fighting. The Germans had retreated across the river from us. One could see them go about their business. Then they brought some artillery pieces. The Russians had their own big guns. You didn't have to be a genius to figure that if they both start shooting we'd be right in the middle.

Pregnant as she was, my mother decided to flee with me to a village further up beyond the hills, where we had a friend. My grandparents retreated to the cel-

lar.

It was early October 1944. The road to the village was empty and so was the farmhouse of our friend where we found just a very old woman who gave us

Young Charles and his father (right) with grandfather (far left)

goat's milk. The whole of that day we sat and waited in silence. Toward dusk we heard steps. A dishevelled and bloodied peasant told us, without even stopping, that the Germans were coming this way and killing everybody in sight.

There was nothing else to do but hurry back to my grandfather. The old woman stayed behind. We were back on that empty road lined with poplars. It was so quiet we could hear our steps. All of a sudden there were shots. A bullet whizzed by. My mother pulled me to the ground and threw herself over me. Then it was quiet again. Just our hearts beating. No more shots.

After a long, long time, we looked up. The sky was cloudless. The first few evening stars were in place. We got up and stood for a while in the long shadow of a tree. When we entered my grandfather's house, he was at the table drinking a toast with a Russian officer and grinning at us.

*

My wartime adventures really began the day the Russians liberated Belgrade. We had gotten back to our apartment quickly since my mother wanted to be near her doctor. The very next day she managed somehow to get herself a cot in the basement of a private clinic to await the termination of her pregnancy. As it turned out, she stayed there a month. I was entrusted to the care of an aunt of my mother, the only relative we had left in the city.

Nana was the black sheep in that family. It was said that she cheated on her old husband, had spent money recklessly, and used bad language. That's what I loved about her. She would swear often and shamelessly.

I've no idea where Nana's husband was, or why she was still in the city. I suspect she had her own private reasons. This was the second day of the liberation and there was still some street fighting. To my surprise she let me go out on the street alone. There were other children out there, to be sure, but, still, this was strange. Often I'd return home and find no one. Later I'd see her walking down the street, extremely elegant with her gloves and high heels, on the sidewalk strewn with the rubble of recent fighting. She'd be glad to see me, and would have something special for me to eat. I've no memory of what we did in the evenings. Our building was almost empty. The lights were often out. There was nothing to do but sleep a lot. One morning, on waking early, I saw my aunt washing her breasts in a pail of cold water. She caught me watching her and turned around. Then she did a little dance, naked like that.

I was happy. My friends and I had plenty to do

during the day and plenty of time to do it. There was no school and our parents were either absent or busy. We roamed the neighborhood, climbed over the ruins, and watched the Russians and our Partisans at work. There were still Germans holed up in a couple of places. We'd hear shots and take off running. There was a lot of military equipment lying around. The guns were gone, but there was other stuff. I got myself a German helmet. I wore empty ammo belts. I had a bayonet.

One day I was sitting with a friend in front of our building when a column of German prisoners came by escorted by some women soldiers. "Let's go and shoot Germans, kids!" said one cheerily. Well, this was a bit too much. We said no. Actually, I doubt we gave them a straight answer. One learned early to be circumspect and cautious. We followed them as far as the corner and then turned back. I remember one tall blonde German straight as a broomstick. The others looked humpbacked in comparison.

Later we went anyway. There was a large old cemetery nearby with a huge church, and beyond it the fairgrounds where, supposedly, they were shooting Germans. We met some children on the way who said that they were from the circus. It was true. There used to be a circus tent on the fairgrounds, but now only a few trailers were left on its edge. These were odd looking children, barely dressed, and they spoke a foreign language among themselves.

"Show him what you can do," said my friend who had met them before. They obliged. A little boy stood on his hands. Then, he removed one hand, and was left standing on the other. A dark-eyed girl leaned back until her head emerged from between her legs.

"They have no bones," my friend said. The dead have no bones, I thought. They fall over like sacks of flour.

*

The war went on. The Germans had dug-in west of the city on the other side of the rivers Sava and Danube. The Russians had left the fighting to the Yugoslavs while they advanced north toward Hungary. All able men were conscripted and the fighting was fierce. Belgrade was a city of the wounded. One saw people on crutches on every street. They walked slowly, at times carrying a mess kit with their daily ration. There were soup kitchens where such people got their meals.

Once, chased by a friend, I rounded the street corner at top speed and collided with one of these invalids, spilling his soup on the sidewalk. I won't forget the look he gave me. "Oh child!" he said softly. I was too stunned to speak. I didn't even have the sense to help

Mother with Charles, about 1942

him pick up his crutch. I watched him do it himself.

By the time my brother was born, and he and my mother came home, I was in business, selling gunpowder. It worked this way. Many of us kids had stashes of ammunition we had collected after the street fighting. The gunpowder from these rounds was sold to older kids who in turn were selling them to the fishermen on the Danube. This last part I cannot guarantee. "Selling" is also the wrong word. We exchanged gunpowder for old comic books, cans of food, and God-knows-what-else? I remember a particularly tasty can of American corned beef which I devoured all by myself sitting in the winter sunlight behind the great Byzantine church of St. Mark.

I've no idea how long this went on. I had a large laundry basket full of ammunition hidden in the cellar. Removing the gunpowder was a one-man job. I placed the bullet part into the kitchen spigot and yanked the round sideways. Absolute secrecy, of course, was required. My mother had no idea how I spent my time until one of the kids on our block lost his hands. He was trying to remove the long black sticks of gunpowder from some sort of grenade. That's what he told me later, while I tried to avoid looking at his two newly healed and still red stumps.

*

I started school in spring of 1945, but don't remember much of it. My parents taught me how to read early on, and I breezed through the first few grades. The classes that spring were sporadic. My interests, in

any case, were elsewhere. The streets were full of semi-abandoned children. Gangs were being formed. Legendary toughs held whole neighborhoods in terror.

There was so much to worry about. We had no news of my father. Unknown to us, he had been locked up as a spy by the Germans in Italy and was about to be liberated by the Americans. He had no desire to return. He didn't like the Communists and he didn't get along with my mother. Before the war he had worked for an American company, had many American business connections, and had always wanted to see that country.

There were other reasons, too, for concern. The Communists were firmly in power. People were being arrested left and right. In school there was indoctrination.

I remember a young man coming to talk to us about Communism. The subject of religion came up. He said there was no God, and asked if anyone of us believed in God. Everybody kept their mouths shut except one kid who said he did. The fellow asked the kid what can God do? Everything, the kid said. Well, the fellow said, if you were to ask him to help you pick this table up, would he do it? I wouldn't ask him, said the kid, eyeing the heavy table. Why not, insisted the man. It'd be a dumb thing to ask for, replied the kid barely audibly.

That ended that. But there were other, more sinister things. One day the same man asked if our parents at home complained about the new regime. No one said anything. When I described to my mother what happened, she told me, in no uncertain terms, that she would kill me if I ever opened my mouth. In any case, she didn't take any chances. Anytime I walked into a room, the grown-ups would shut up and eye me suspiciously. I had plenty to be guilty about and it must have shown in my face, for there would be a long cross-examination: "What did you say?" "Nothing! I swear it!" And so it went.

My life on the street was also getting more complicated. I hung around with older boys. If I was seven, they must have been ten, twelve years old. Gang territories were being charted. If you left your neighborhood unaccompanied, you could get hurt. Even going to school was complicated since I had to pass through several enemy areas. We travelled in groups everywhere, fists at the ready, glaring, looking mean. I had so many fights then and later on. Mostly I got beat up, since I was the youngest.

Then there was stealing. We stole for profit and for the fun of it. We took things from people's yards mostly. If it was valuable, we sold it to the older boys, if not, we'd throw it away. I was usually the one to make the snatch since I was the smallest and the nimblest. I remember being chased by an ax-wielding man whose bicycle pump I'd stolen. I remember walking into a grocery store, grabbing something from the counter, and running away. This was for practice. There was not much to be had in those stores. Most of the food was rationed. If you took someone's monthly ration of sugar, you were committing an unforgivable crime.

My mother never heard about my exploits. She had a lot on her mind. I don't know when exactly it was that we heard that my father was alive and well in Trieste. She was determined we should join him. The frontier between Yugoslavia and Italy was still open, as the area around Trieste was disputed by the two countries. There was still a chance we could leave, but it was dangerous. One could get arrested. One could get shot in those days for nothing.

We left Belgrade for the coast in the fall of 1945. That train journey took forever. The tracks were still in terrible shape. All along the way one could see the derailed railroad cars and bombed-out stations.

When we reached Opatia-Fiume, that once fashionable Austro-Hungarian sea-resort, we heard the border was closed. Still, if one knew the right people one could cross illegally. We stayed in a near-empty grand hotel for a week. I remember the high ornate ceilings, the crystal chandeliers, and mirrors everywhere. We took our meals in a large, immaculately set and deserted dining room which looked out at the gray sea. I've wondered since, who the few other guests were? They had a secretive air about them, didn't speak to each other, and rarely acknowledged our nods. I could walk for hours down the long hallways without meeting anyone, or hearing a sound. Once I heard sobs, muffled sobs, and even got my eyes on the keyhole, but could see nothing. Just the gray sea through the open balcony door, and the silence of the hotel around me. The woman had stopped crying.

We went back to Belgrade but my mother was stubborn. She found someone who knew someone else who, for a price, could take us across the border into Austria. Again, I was told nothing. I thought we were going on vacation in the mountains of Slovenia since once more we found ourselves in an elegant, half-empty chalet, sleeping late and taking long mountain walks. One evening we walked farther than was our custom. We sat on a couple of rocks in the woods, and my mother told me that that very night we'd be going to my father.

It was almost pitch dark when a man came to take us to a farmhouse where two other men waited. The rest of the night we spent climbing the mountains with my mother carrying my infant brother in her arms. They had given him something so he would sleep.

We couldn't see much for most of the way. The moon only came out when we crossed the border. We were on the side of a hill and Yugoslavia was down below. We sat on the grass talking and the men smoked. That was a mistake, as it turned out. We heard someone shout in German. One of our guides opened fire and the two of them took off in the direction of Yugoslavia leaving us in the hands of an Austrian-American patrol. That wasn't so bad. The Americans treated us well. They took us to their post where we spent the rest of the night. In the morning they fed us and asked no questions.

The problems started when the Americans handed us over to the English Army whose zone of occupation it was. A colonel asked my mother for our passports. My mother laughed. After all that mountain-climbing, our clothes were in tatters, our faces and hands were covered with scratches. My mother even tried a bit of humor. She told him, in the best English she could summon, that if we had a passport we would have taken a sleeping car. The fellow was not amused. What he did then—and it took us a while to grasp his intentions—was to put us in a jeep and deliver us to the Yugoslav border officials. We were back in Yugoslavia and under arrest.

We didn't know, of course, that this kind of thing happened often. The English were deporting the Russian war prisoners and anybody else they got their hands on. They didn't care what happened to these people. Stalin, as everybody now knows, sent them to labor camps where many perished. Our case wasn't so tragic. We were transported from prison to prison for the next two weeks until we reached Belgrade. There, my brother and I were released into the hands of my grandmother, and my mother was kept in prison for another four months. Her defense was that she simply wanted to be with her husband and was not given the legal means to do so. This was true enough, although probably not the reason they let her go so quickly. The jails at that time were full of people with more interesting political transgressions. We were small fry. They slapped my mother around a few times, but that was all.

As for me, I thoroughly enjoyed being in jail. They put me in with the men. The cell doors opened at some wee hour and a little kid stood there. The prisoners were stunned. The cells were packed. They'd have to make room for me, make sure I had plenty of cover. They also wanted to hear my story. I obliged, of course. The bedbugs made it hard to sleep. I embroidered, how I embroidered! At home, too, all our relatives and friends were waiting to hear what happened. I don't remember the details of what I said, but there was a lot of shooting in my reenactment. I cocked my finger and fired for the benefit of all those grim and wary faces.

II

It is raining. It is Sunday . . . late fall. My radio is turned down low. I am on the bed reading. I have a deep sense of well-being. I love the book. I love the rain which prevents me from going out to play.

I no longer remember the name of the book, or what year it was, but the time I spent with books is one of my happiest memories. I started reading early because I was taught to, and because my father had a large library. There were serious books even in my room. They made me curious. First I turned the pages looking for pictures, then I looked at the words. By the time I was twelve I was in love with books.

My friends read, too. We liked westerns, adventure stories, mysteries. Most of these books were published before the war and their supply was limited. It was possible, and this eventually happened to me, to have read all the books available in our circle. They could not be purchased in book stores or taken out of libraries. We borrowed from people we knew. That is, we exchanged them for books in our own possession. There were stretches of time when I had nothing to read. I had to turn to my father's library. I read Zola, Dickens, and even Dostoevsky, out of sheer boredom. Dickens' *Oliver Twist* I liked very much. Thomas Mann's *Magic Mountain* was impossible to read. I loved the medieval Serbian ballads, but poetry anthologies left me cold.

That need to read a lot has never left me. I still read everything. All kinds of books on all kinds of subjects. Consequently, I know about a great many things only a little. I could live and die in a good library, and I don't even respect great learning. That is, I'm suspicious of the single-mindedness that kind of learning is prone to. Still, it seems impossible that one wouldn't want to know what's inside books.

The movies, however, didn't leave such a strong impression on me. By today's standards we saw very few films. The Communists didn't approve of westerns, and that's all I cared for. By the time they started showing American movies again, we had already left Yugoslavia.

I listened to music a lot. My radio was always on. I discovered jazz, couldn't get enought of it. Late at night, the radio would pick up the American Armed Forces stations in Germany and Italy. I read and listened.

During the day, my mother, who was a voice teacher, an opera singing-teacher, often had her conservatory students over to the house for lessons. I knew, by an early age, most of the major operatic arias. I even sang them as a joke, which gave my mother the idea that I was destined to be a musician. The consequences were terrible. I had two years of piano lessons followed by two years of violin lessons, until, one lucky day, my brother jumped on the violin which I had carelessly left on the couch. Violins were expensive in those days, and everybody realized by then that my heart was not in it, so there was no mention of getting me another one.

In the meantime, I was in big trouble. Without anyone knowing, I had stopped going to school. The school which I attended and liked suddenly turned me away. Unknown to us, they had changed the school districts, and on the first day of classes in my sixth grade, I was told to go to another school on the other side of town. When I presented myself there the next day, they had no record of me. I was advised to stay home a couple of days and return on Monday when my file should have arrived and I could be placed. Well, I never went back. At first I only wanted to prolong my summer vacation, but I kept postponing the day until it became impossible to go back. My mother knew nothing. I'd leave in the morning for school, and return in the afternoon. It was the middle of January before somebody figured out that I was unaccounted for, and sent the cops after me.

While the weather was still balmy it was rather pleasant to roam the streets and parks of Belgrade. But then the rains came. If I was lucky and had money, I went to the movies. Otherwise, I shivered in doorways. The cold weather was decidedly preferable. In the cold I paced the city from one outskirt to the other to keep warm and time passed quickly. At times, I'd be so lost in thought, I'd walk past the outskirts and far into the countryside. I remember one such terrifying moment, turning around and seeing the city far off in the distance.

I was miserable. I couldn't even talk about it to my friends. For some reason they were still in the old school. They had no idea what I was doing. I had to pretend and invent elaborate lies about school. It was a relief when it was all over, and the school officially expelled me for truancy.

Still, all and all, the city was so interesting. I knew every corner of it well. I examined every store window with the leisure of one who has infinite time on his hands. I can still visualize each dusty item in a poor shoe-repairer's window. It was the only store in a quiet residential neighborhood, so I would stop in front of it often. One time, looking into the window, I saw my mother reflected in it, hurrying on the other side of the street. I held my breath and continued to examine the wooden shoe trees and the empty cans of shoe polish which somehow I knew were empty. They had a foreign brand name, "Kiwi," which I liked saying to myself.

"You're going to America to live with your father," is what I told myself. I never believed it for a moment. It didn't seem possible that one could leave this life forever.

In retrospect, it's lucky that I did go. Had I stayed, I would have ended up in a reform school. Not many of my friends finished school. Sooner or later, they all got into trouble of some sort and ended up learning a trade. I was certainly no better. By the time I returned to school, one year behind my old classmates, I hated the place.

*

There was a time in 1947 or 1948 when we had almost nothing to eat. My mother didn't yet have her job at the conservatory and we had difficulties making ends meet. I remember coming from school one afternoon, telling her I was hungry and watching her burst into tears. The only thing we had in the house that day were some onions which I cut up. There was no oil, just some dry bread and salt. I remember thinking, this is pretty good.

My mother, who is an awful cook under any circumstances, used to make a kind of meatless stew consisting of potatoes, onions, and perhaps a few carrots. This is what we ate all the time. By the third day, after all the reheating, the thing tasted foul. I'd gag with every mouthful, and would have to drink big gulps of water in between to get it down. The bread was rationed. There would be only a large slice of black bread which I ate last, as a dessert.

The kids on the street talked about food all the time. Whatever food one happened to have had to be shared. I mean, if I had an apple, I was obliged to give everybody present a bite. When there was nothing to eat, there was talk.

I remember one cold winter evening, all of us with hands deep in our pockets, sheltering ourselves from the wind behind a boarded-up kiosk. Someone described a salami he once had, in great detail. We listened and asked questions about the fine points of taste. Someone else discussed the advantages and disadvantages of fried versus roasted chicken. My own contribution was on the subject of pigs' ears. In my opinion, there was nothing tastier than roasted suckling pigs' ears. I gave the particulars, reminded them how the little ears tend to get burnt and can be easily broken off. Then, there was the crunch the ear made as one bit into it and the delicious taste that followed.

There were other views, of course. Some of my buddies liked only sweets. They rhapsodized about ice cream, Swiss chocolate, various kinds of cakes and sweet pies. "You forgot the whipped cream, you stupid shit," somebody would interrupt. We'd get delirious with craving. Eventually someone would say, without much conviction, "I hope there's something good to eat at home."

There were days when there was. Everybody feasted on the holidays. Belgrade is surrounded by farming country, and if one knew the right people one could get just about everything for a price. A peasant woman would come to see us on the sly, and after bargaining with my mother, would remove her top garments to reveal long strips of bacon wrapped around her waist.

Most of the time we didn't pay with money. We'd barter. A pair of my father's black dancing shoes went for a chicken. Sometimes the yokels couldn't make up their mind what they wanted. We'd let them look around. They'd walk from room to room with us in tow, looking things over, shaking their heads when we suggested a particular item. They were hard to please. At last, they'd make up their minds. An old gypsy man wanted a top hat we had. It didn't bother him that it was too big for him. With that hat way down over his eyes, he handed over a duck.

In the summer I was usually sent to my grandfather in the country to fatten up. This was my mother's father who had a house and an orchard some hundred miles south of Belgrade. He lived there most of the time, making only infrequent trips to the city to visit his family. Long ago, as an ambitious young officer, he had participated in the assassination of a king which brought him rapid promotion in the ranks. He fought bravely in the First World War and was even the military commander of Belgrade for a brief period after the war. Then the new king forced him to retire. He didn't trust him and the other hotheads who had conspired to bring him into power.

When I knew him, my grandfather had been in retirement almost thirty years. He was a dour, self-centered, and humorless man. He was also a hypochondriac. It was torture staying with him, observing his many rules and listening to the catalogue of his imaginary maladies.

I couldn't wait to get back to my friends in the city. The absence of two months was interminable. There were always important changes in the pecking order to worry about upon return. Then there were new slang expressions to learn. I'd be afraid to ask what they meant. I'd hear them, even use them, but it took a long time before I figured out what they meant. I felt like a foreigner, as I was to feel so many times in

*Charles (center) with his maternal grandparents, his brother, and a cousin
in Belgrade, about 1947*

my life.

What my secretive mother didn't tell me was that shortly we would be leaving Yugoslavia. She had applied for a passport. The relationship between Yugoslavia and United States had improved enough for the Communists to permit a few people to leave. The problem was that there was an American quota, a long waiting list for Yugoslavs applying to immigrate to the United States. One had to wait, but my mother was afraid to wait in Belgrade since the authorities occasionally changed their minds and took the passports away. The moment she had ours, she decided to leave for Paris the same night. Her brother was living there and my father, who had been in America since 1950, was going to send us money and support us during our wait.

I was playing basketball in the neighborhood that day in June 1953 when my mother summoned me and informed me that we were going on vacation immediately. This was very strange. There had been no talk earlier of a vacation on the coast. She was packing feverishly. Why are we taking so many suitcases, I wanted to know? Why were all the relatives coming to see us with tears in their eyes? Why is it that I'm not permitted to say goodbye to my friends? I was upset.

My mother's gone crazy, I thought. That whole family was nuts, as far as I was concerned. We had uncles and aunts we used to visit once a year who were clearly lunatics. Like my aunt Marina. She wore old-fashioned dresses, sung to herself, never went out. By the time I was ten, I knew there was something wrong with these people.

Our train left at ten, but only the next day as we were approaching the Italian border did my mother reveal to me the true destination of our journey. I was stunned. Soon enough, we were in Trieste—that almost mythical Trieste for us—eating ice cream and hearing Italian being spoken as the train made its way toward Milano.

It took us almost two days to reach Paris. My uncle met us at the station. We were taken to a small, modest hotel where we took a small, narrow room with one bed and a tiny window. My mother and brother slept on the bed, and I slept on the suitcases. That's how we lived for one full year. It was a shock. We were poor, I realized. That first evening strolling along the Champs-Elysées, I saw that our clothes were absurd. People stared at us. My pants were too short. My jacket was ugly.

My mother wasn't going to buy us any new

clothes. "You'll get everything new in America," she kept saying. That took much longer than we expected. By the end of the summer, it was clear we might remain in Paris for a while. It was decided then that my brother and I should attend school to learn French. I had studied the language for three years in Yugoslavia and knew just enough to feel embarrassed every time I opened my mouth. My brother was only eight years old and had just learned to read.

The school we were enrolled in was for children who were not planning a higher education. The French weed out the dummies at an early age and consign them to a permanent inferiority status. I felt pretty inferior myself. I couldn't do the schoolwork even on this level, and I couldn't communicate well. The teachers were not friendly. It's as if they really didn't believe I couldn't speak French. Perhaps I was just pretending, trying to make a fool of them! As for my classmates, most of them took no interest in me. The few who did were the troublemakers, the class idiots. I made friends with that bunch. In the eyes of the teachers, I was now one of the hopeless.

One of the advantages of being in school, as far as my mother was concerned, was that we ate lunch there. The rest of the time we cooked in my uncle's tiny apartment, or we ate sandwiches in our hotel room. We almost never ate in restaurants. My mother didn't like to spend money, and she never cared for food enough to risk spending money. The only experience of French cooking that I had was at school. I held a high opinion of our cooks which my classmates didn't share. They thought the food was slop fit for pigs, which meant I got to eat their portions too. This made it difficult to stay awake after lunch. I kept falling asleep in class. "Simic! Simic!" I still hear Monsieur Bertrand yelling.

The school ended at five. We ate early dinner and then went for a walk. Our sole entertainment was walking. Sometimes on weekends, after studying the map of Paris, we'd take the metro to a far and unfamiliar neighborhood, and then walk back to our hotel. If we were hungry, we'd buy some bread in the bakery and chew on it as we walked and looked at Paris.

I studied the clothes stores. My father had sent me money to buy a jacket and I had my eyes on a blue corduroy one. My mother was of the opinion that the one I had was perfectly fine. I insisted, and finally she gave in. I stood before the store mirror transfixed by the elegance of my new jacket. It fit perfectly. I could walk into the Paris evening with a new sense of confidence. It didn't last long. The very next day I noticed that one of our Algerian garbagemen wore the same jacket. All the garbagemen in Paris, it seemed, wore that kind of jacket. It was a terrible disappointment. I

Charles, about 1952

said nothing of this to anyone, of course, but from then on, I wore that jacket only at night.

My mother was beginning to allow me to go out at night to the movies with friends from school. At first it was to the movies we went. Afterwards we only pretended to do that, and went instead to Pigalle and Place Blanche to look at the hookers. We began to dress up too. I wore a tie, kept my hair slicked down, and smoked cigarettes in the French manner, with the butt hanging from the corner of my mouth. Nobody took us seriously. We sat in little dives, drinking beer and smirking. We had no money for the girls. We were hoping for charity, love at first sight. The problem was that we had to be home by a certain hour. Whatever opportunities offered themselves after midnight, we were never to find out.

*

The best thing we did in Paris was to study English. My mother found out that there were free night classes, twice a week, given by the World Church Service. All three of us went. Previously, I don't believe I knew ten words of English. My mother knew some, but not much. In any case, here we were in a class with a bunch of refugees from all over Eastern Europe and a very nice American minister as a teacher. I worked hard. I liked the language immediately.

I began buying the *Saturday Evening Post* and *Look* magazine to practice reading. I understood very little of what I read but looking at pictures and advertisements was very interesting. The American colors were so bright. One didn't see such yellows and oranges in Europe. The pictures of children terrified me. They looked so clean, so happy. The girls often had freckles. They smiled a lot. Everybody smiled. The grandparents, the movie stars, the politicians, all had their mouths stretched from ear to ear. In France nobody smiled like that. Certainly not the barbers. I remember a Norman Rockwell-like cover of a little redheaded kid in a barber's chair with a smiling barber hovering over him with scissors. The barbers I went to didn't care for young people. They knew there wouldn't be much of a tip coming.

When we went to the American Embassy for the obligatory physical examination, I expected the doctor to be smiling. He wasn't. He looked glum throughout the examination. I must be very sick, I told myself. None of these Americans smiled. It was clear, I'd be rejected. My brother and my mother would go to the United States, and I'd stay in France dying from an incurable disease in some state sanatorium.

Weeks passed before we got the results of the examination. In the meantime, we turned the pages of American magazines, studying the cars, the baked hams, the rich desserts. The summer was approaching. It was hard to stay in our small, airless hotel room. We walked all the time. One evening, just after dusk, on the fashionable Avenue Victor Hugo, we saw Prince Paul, the brother of the dead Yugoslav king. My mother went up to him to say who we were. I remember a tall, impeccably dressed elderly man bowing stiffly and asking me my name. I had a clear sense that he didn't care one way or the other.

In those days, both in Paris and in America, you ran into famous personages, people who were responsible, if anyone was truly responsible, for Yugoslavia's downfall. Here would be a face you remembered from a newspaper, signing something with Hitler, now sitting at somebody's kitchen table, eating salami. It was hard to believe that they were the same people. They looked ordinary, had nothing especially interesting to say. They hoped to go back soon. Their villas would be waiting. Great crowds would welcome them. "You were right! You were always right," the people would say. They didn't like what my mother and I had to say about Yugoslavia. They insisted that nothing had changed since they left.

In June of 1954, or thereabouts, we received our American visas. It took a few more weeks to book passage. The World Church Service paid our trip and in style. We were to sail on the *Queen Mary* on August 5. What excitement! "You'll be starting a new life," everybody said.

The remaining days in Paris dragged on. My mother took us to museums so we'd remember the great art treasures of France. We also started eating in modest neighborhood restaurants. We now went to the movies every day watching American films with new interest and apprehension.

III

The *Queen Mary* was all lit up the night we boarded. It was huge, and a veritable labyrinth on the inside. We were travelling in the cheapest class but the accommodations looked luxurious to us. It took a couple of days to discover that we were not supposed to leave our class. There was a door with a sign which spelled that out. I snuck through it once, walked through the Cabin Class, and made my way to the First Class. There were shops and restaurants as

In Paris, 1953: Charles (right) with his mother and brother

swanky as those in Paris. I saw ladies in evening gowns cut so low their breasts were about to fall out, men in long-tailed dark suits, little children who wore neckties and looked snotty. I remember a bejeweled old woman in a wheelchair pushed by a very beautiful nurse in white. It didn't take long before some steward spotted me ogling and directed me back to the Tourist Class.

We had no complaints about our facilities. Far from it. Our cabins were small and windowless but otherwise comfortable. The food was excellent and there was a new film shown every day.

A day or two after we left Le Havre there was a storm. It started during the night. The ship heaved and creaked. Sleeping was hard and many people got seasick. In the morning there were only a few people at breakfast. By the afternoon, with the storm still raging, the movie theatre was empty. They showed the movie anyway. The boat rocked, the waves pounded its sides, but the people on the screen remained perfectly calm.

My mother was back in the cabin throwing up, but my brother and I refused to stay in bed. We liked the food so much, we didn't allow ourselves to get sick. We roamed the ship. It was difficult to walk, of course. We had to hold on to things. It never occurred to us to be scared. We sat for hours in the empty lounge watching the waves crest and slide under the ship.

The next day the storm had subsided. The sky was cloudless. The chart outside the purser's office indicated the progress of our voyage. We were half-way across. The next day we were even closer. We kept asking the crew when we would be able to see land.

The sighting occurred at night. By the time we rose in the morning the land was clearly visible. We were speeding into the New York harbor. After breakfast, everyone was on deck. We began to make out details on land. There was a road on which a car was travelling. Amazing, I thought! There were neat white houses. One even had laundry hung to dry. Then a fishing boat came by. There were a couple of black men on deck, waving. Pretty soon there were boats everywhere. We could see the Statue of Liberty. I think a cheer went up.

What stunned me, left me speechless with excitement, was the first sight of Manhattan with its skyscrapers. It was just like the movies, this enormous city before us. The docks with the big ships, the traffic on the outer highways, and the crowds of people everywhere. My father was out there somewhere waiting for us. I kept trying to spot him. We didn't realize it would take many hours to clear the immigration. With our past experience of border crossings, we still had worries. What if they surprise us and send us back to Yugoslavia!

George Simic, Chicago, 1954

My father waited on the other side of the customs. A tall man. We recognized him. We waved. He waved back. He was wearing a white suit and a sky-blue shirt. A handsome man. He smoked a long thin cigar which made him look very American in our eyes.

Then, the confusion of embraces and kisses, the emotion of him seeing my brother for the first time, the search for a porter, the wait for a taxi, and everybody talking at the same time. It was all incredible and wonderful! The garbage on the streets, the way people dressed, the tall buildings, the dust, the heat, the yellow cabs, the billboards. It was nothing like Europe. It was wonderfully ugly and beautiful. I liked America immediately.

In the hotel another surprise awaited us. There was a television set. While my mother and father talked in the other room, my brother and I sat on the floor and watched a Dodgers-Giants game. I remember who was playing because my brother fell in love with baseball that afternoon and with the Dodgers in particular, and insisted on being outfitted immediately with a baseball cap and a glove.

That evening, after a stroll around Times Square and Broadway, we went to a restaurant where we dined on hamburgers, french fries, and milk shakes, followed by banana splits. I don't know what my mother thought of the meal, but we loved it. American cuisine is kid's cuisine and no child in the world can resist it. "Remember this day," my father kept saying. Indeed, it was August 10, 1954. Tomorrow he was going to buy us American clothes and shoes and all sorts of other things.

Who could possibly sleep? My brother and mother did. My father and I watched TV and talked. It was still early. "Let's go out," he said. The hotel was only a couple of blocks from Times Square. We found ourselves there again, walking, watching the crowd. I felt comfortable with my father right away. He never treated any kid as a kid. He talked to everybody the same way. He'd shoot the breeze with a five-year-old selling lemonade on the street as if he were a head of a major corporation.

We ended up in a jazz club that night. It was called the Metropole, used to be on Broadway around Forty-eighth Street. A long narrow room with a bar on one side and small booths on the other. The bandstand was just above the bar. There were six black musicians blasting away.

We took a booth and my father ordered some whiskey for himself and ginger ale for me. This must have been some day for him too. I was all absorbed in the music. This was definitely better than my radio. It was heaven.

We stayed a long time. My father even gave me a few sips of his whiskey. Between sets we talked. I told him about my life, and he told me about his. This was just the beginning. We spent many nights together like that. My father loved the night life. He was happiest in bars and restaurants. In company of a friend and with something good to eat and drink, he'd glow. It was pure joy to be around him then. He was full of life and interesting talk. Let this night never end, I silently hoped.

*

My father was still employed by the same telephone company he worked for in Yugoslavia. Their headquarters were in Chicago, but my father was on the road most of the time, travelling around the country. Whenever one of their client companies needed more telephone lines, my father would examine their facilities, draw up the blueprints, and often stay to see the job through. As it was, he had spent the years 1950-54 moving from place to place, staying in each town anywhere from two months to a year, and then moving on. He had no home. At the time we came, he was working in Middletown, New York. After his vacation was over, and he had found an apartment for us in Jackson Heights, he went back to Middletown. Shortly

after, I joined him.

The idea was, I would stay with him, study English on my own, and not enroll in school till the second semester. We would spend the week in Middletown and come on weekends to New York. That's what we did. I stayed in our furnished room while my father worked. In the evenings we ate out, then went to the movies or came back to our place to talk and drink wine.

My father, as was his custom, had a lot of books, two trunks full. At that time his ambition was to write a critical history of Marxism. He read and took voluminous notes. He even told me a little about his project when he was not telling me about his life.

The first book I read in English was Whittaker Chambers' *Witness*. I don't remember a thing about it today, but at the time it gave me the confidence necessary to attempt others. When in New York, my father would spend Saturday mornings going through bookstores. He bought books, and it was understood I could pick some for myself. I remember reading Hemingway and Twain, but can't recall the others.

My return to school worried me. It had been a long time since I was properly a student. I had no confidence in my ability. I also had no idea what grade I would be in. I would see young people my age going to school and I would feel terrible. My spoken English was still very poor. The moment I said one word, anybody could tell I had just gotten off the boat.

The closer we got to the holidays, the more miserable I became. My father was still a lot of fun, but the mood at home was tense. It was clear my parents were not getting along. They had such different personalities. Whatever one liked, the other didn't. My mother, for example, had no interest in things American. She had already found some Yugoslavs, was seeing them, and aside from wanting to improve her English so she could get a job, had no curiosity about this country. Since my brother and I were siding with my father, there were difficulties. She was jealous. "You don't love me anymore," she'd blurt out. "We have more fun with him," we'd make the mistake of saying.

The high school I was supposed to be attending was in Elmhurst, Queens. We had gone there to make inquiries. I was invited to come shortly before the classes resumed after the New Year, and take some tests so that I could be placed.

I was worried the day my mother and I went to keep that appointment. My father was in Middletown. It was windy and bitter cold, and the walk from our place to the school was very long. I was numb with cold and terror when we arrived.

As it usually happens in life, things turned out quite differently from what I anticipated. First of all, there was no question of writing for a transcript to Belgrade. The Yugoslav education system is very different and it would be very difficult to interpret such a document whenever it arrived. So, they made it simple. They gave me an IQ test and as for the rest, they just asked me to write down the subjects I had studied in Europe. That was easy. I wrote down things like Algebra, Physics, French, Russian, World History, Biology. They asked me a couple of questions in each area and in the process found out that in Paris we had read Homer and Virgil in school. That did it. I was made a second semester junior on the spot. The whole thing didn't take much more than half an hour.

I was tremendously relieved. I still had some apprehensions about actually doing the schoolwork, but this was a miraculous beginning. I loved America. No more Monsieur Bertrand and his crummy jokes at my expense. Even the Yugoslav teachers gave me a hard time after I stayed back. School was not for dummies like me. Years later I heard that they were genuinely surprised when told that I was at the university. "That bum!" It was hard to believe.

The school itself was amazing. Newtown High School may have been the model for the movie *Blackboard Jungle*. The teachers had their hands full maintaining discipline. If you kept your mouth shut, as I did, you passed.

I remember a large class in something called "Hygiene." I sat in the last row playing chess with a black boy. Up front the teacher was arguing with a couple of punks in leather jackets. That's the way it was every day, half of the class was harassing the teacher while the other half daydreamed. I never did any work. Nobody called on me. I don't think I even had a clue what I was supposed to do. I received a B for my effort.

The other classes were more or less the same. In English, the old lady who was our teacher kept trying to read aloud to us one of Edgar Allan Poe's short stories. The class, against her objections, provided the sound effects. There were creaking doors and coffin lids, the chimes at midnight, the wind blowing through the ruined tower. She pleaded with us to stop. When we were reading *Julius Caesar*, it was the same. More sound effects.

I came to see her once after class to ask for an extension on my paper, pleading my ignorance of the English language. "Don't worry," the poor woman told me. "I know you're good boy." I certainly was. I behaved in class and did my homework. The girls interested me, but I was too shy to speak to them in my heavily accented English. As for the boys, I could see that most of them were trouble-bound and I had had enough of that. Also, I had no time. I was working after school and all day Saturday.

It was a great job as far as I was concerned. I worked in a small company that sold spare parts for airplanes. I helped the stock clerks. What I remember best is counting screws. These screws were very expensive and one had to count them carefully. It wasn't difficult and I got paid. I bought a cheap phonograph and my first jazz records. On Sundays I went to Manhattan and the movies. I was beginning to feel very comfortable.

The big event that spring was our buying a television set. It was a huge twenty-one inch model, and my father and I had a hell of a time lugging it from the store. Once we turned that set on, it stayed on. We watched television every chance we got. "It was good for our English," everybody said. It certainly was. I stopped reading and just watched TV. I remember Sundays spent in front of it from early morning till midnight. Everything was so interesting. I think that it was while watching television that my brother and I started speaking English to each other. We heard certain phrases on TV and we wanted to use them.

I'm surprised how quickly we felt at home in the United States. My father's attitude had a lot to do with it. He loved America, thought it was the most exciting place on earth, and he wanted to share his excitement with us. He had no desire to go back to Yugoslavia. He wanted us to be Americans. My mother, on the other hand, had always retained the notion that Europeans were superior. She missed Europe. We did not. I was a flop there. Here I had managed to finish a grade. I had a job and summer was coming.

We had another shock then. My father's request for a transfer to the company's headquarters in Chicago had come through. We were moving to Chicago. From now on we would live together, see him all the time, and have a normal life.

I wasn't entirely happy about being uprooted again, nor was my mother. She worried about leaving New York where there were more opportunities to find work in the music business. She was trying to resume her career as a voice teacher, but had had no luck. Still, she too desired some kind of normal family life. There was no choice. It was decided that my father and I would go first, find a place, and they would follow.

*

It was in late June of 1955 that we travelled to Chicago on the Twentieth Century Express. We were going in style, sleeping in Pullman berths and taking our meals in the fancy dining car. In Chicago we took a room at the elegant Hotel Drake on Michigan Avenue. The lake was right outside the hotel. There was a beach we could go to and many fine restaurants and

In Chicago, 1956

nightclubs in the area. We spent two weeks like that, enjoying life and not making the slightest effort to look for an apartment. When my mother called, we told her it was difficult to find the right place, the city was so big, and so on.

Again my father and I talked and talked. I was beginning to have a much clearer picture of our family background from these endless conversations.

My great-grandfather Philip, for example, was a blacksmith in a small village in southern Serbia. My great-grandmother had died in childbirth and he himself took care of his son and daughter. It seems he didn't have any relatives in the area. Earlier on, his own father, or his grandfather, had migrated to Serbia from Montenegro. My father didn't know for sure.

I especially liked one story about my great-grandfather. Apparently, he had not been paying taxes for some time, and eventually one day the cops came to arrest him. He pleaded with them not to take him away and make his children orphans. He even had a suggestion. What if they were to give him a part-time job at the police station, make him a deputy or something, so he could earn some extra money and pay his taxes?

Well, the cops being local fellows and knowing Philip, took pity on him. At the police station arrangements were made. He was issued a rifle and was even given a small advance on his pay for other purchases. There were tears of gratitude on his part, everyone was

moved, and after many handshakes Philip left. He made his way straight to a tavern where he proceeded to get soused. When he was thoroughly drunk, he made the waiters carry four tables outside. This he did at riflepoint. Then he ordered that the tables should be stacked, one on top of the other, with a chair and a bottle of brandy at the very top. There he climbed. A crowd had gathered by then. There were gypsies, too, fiddling on their violins and banging on their tambourines. When he started shooting his rifle and shouting that no Simic was ever going to be a stupid cop, the cops themselves came. They beat the daylights out of him and threw him in jail.

Philip's son, my grandfather Zika, went to Vienna and Prague while still a very young man to learn the tool-and-die trade. Upon his return (in 1903 or 1904), and over the years, he became the best craftsman in that trade in Belgrade. Following the First World War, his skills were in such demand that he even became quite wealthy for a while. Temperamentally, though, he was like his father. He couldn't keep money. He hated all the middle-class values and institutions. Politicians, priests, and schoolteachers were on his list of contemptible beings. "I only love waiters," he used to say.

Nevertheless, he married a schoolteacher's sister. Radojka, my father's mother, bore Zika four children and died from a lung ailment when my father was twelve. As he was the oldest, my father took care of his two brothers and a sister. Even in the last days of his life while he lay dying in the hospital, my father often spoke of his mother. She sang beautifully and played the accordion. He still remembered the songs she taught him and would try to sing them with tears in his eyes:

Three meadows and no shade anywhere,
Three meadows, just an old bare pear tree . . .

He never got over her death. His grief for her and her unhappy life was greater to him than the thoughts of his own imminent extinction.

My mother, on the other hand, comes from an old Belgrade family. They were Greeks originally who had settled in the city as tradesmen. The Turks, who occupied that part of the Balkans for five centuries, did not allow Slavs to conduct business. Eventually, there was intermarriage with Serbs, and the family, which was very rich up to the middle of the nineteenth century, began to decline. Many of its male members, instead of going into trade, entered the church and the military. There are many high-church dignitaries in my ancestry, which always struck me as funny since neither my mother nor anybody else in that family is very religious. They never go to church and when the subject of priesthood comes up, there's plenty of scorn.

Two of my mother's sisters and one of her brothers died under mysterious circumstances. The sisters, I believe, were schizophrenic, and at least one of them ended her days in an institution. The brother was supposed to have died from pneumonia. Nobody knew for sure. The whole energy of that family went into keeping up appearances. They never talked about the past. If I asked a question, I received no answer. For example, it seems that my mother's father, as a young officer, gambled away my grandmother's dowry. I got most of this from my father. It's fair to say he wasn't objective. It's also true that he didn't know very much and was just repeating what my mother had blurted out once.

Be that as it may, my father and I were continuing to live it up. Every night we told ourselves that tomorrow we would start looking for an apartment, but we never did—not, in any case, till my mother informed us that she was coming to help us look. In the meantime, my father was running out of money. He was supposed to start working soon, but the paycheck would not be coming for a while and his savings were gone. One morning he visited a loan company where he finagled a huge loan. We still had a few days before my mother's arrival and we spent them in the usual way. The way my father tipped waiters and bought things I was afraid we would have nothing left again. He'd give a waiter ten dollars upon entering a fine restaurant, order him to bring us a bottle of wine and not bother us until we called him.

That recklessness of his both attracted me and drove me crazy. Years later in New York, we once spent our monthly rents for a meal in a French restaurant. It was an expensive and fashionable place. We were ushered to a tiny table in the darkest corner where we polished off our appetizers, main course, and a couple of bottles of wine rather quickly and unconsciously while arguing over god-knows-what? When the snotty waiter presented us with a bill, we realized all at once that: a.) The service was lousy. b.) We talked too much and didn't really remember what we were eating and drinking. c.) We were in no rush to go anywhere. Without exchanging a word we understood each other perfectly. My father informed the waiter that instead of a dessert we'd like to have the whole meal repeated starting with the appetizers and the white wine. "The whole thing once again," I told him too. The waiter went away and came back, flustered, to ask us to repeat what we said. So we told him, and resumed our talk. In time they brought the food which we ate with an even greater appetite. By then the place was emptying. The waiters stood across the room watching us. The boss and the cook finally came over with a bottle of fine cognac. "Do you always eat like this?" they wanted to know. "Only when we are hungry," my father assured them.

*

Three days after my mother arrived in Chicago we had found an apartment in Oak Park, a suburb west of the city. My mother got in touch with some Serbians she knew and they told us that Oak Park was a nice place to live. We took the El there one morning, bought the local papers, and by the afternoon had our place. It was on the top floor of a three-story tenement-like building, and had two bedrooms, a living room, and a fairly large kitchen. The neighborhood with its tree-lined streets and one-family homes was a good one, but the apartment was crummy. In their impatience to find a place, my parents didn't realize that there were railroad tracks just outside our back windows. All the trains leaving Union Station for the West Coast rattled our pots and pans, and just about everything else. We could see the people in the dining car being expertly served by black waiters. We could almost make out what they had on their plates. It didn't occur to my parents to move. I guess they were sick and tired of moving. We stayed and made the best of the situation.

I was enrolled in Oak Park's River Forest High School. It's the one Hemingway attended. The teachers reminded us of that. My mother found a job in the Marshall Field's department store as a seamstress. My brother was in third grade. Life could have been normal, except my parents were arguing more and more when they were not silent for days. I had the unenviable task of passing messages between them. As far as I was concerned, they were both right and both wrong. I loved them, but I hated having them in the same room.

My new school was no joke. One had to study, do homework, and be prepared to answer intelligently in class. My classmates were mostly children of professional people and had the confidence and ability of the privileged. They were very nice to me. I think I was the only foreigner in school and so I was a curiosity. Soon enough I was leading the life of a typical small-town teenager. I went to football games, and hung around the drug stores and hamburger joints frequented by other students.

I had some interesting teachers too. My English teacher, a man whose name was Dolmetsh, took time with me. He gave me Joyce's *Portrait of the Artist as a Young Man,* and a number of other contemporary classics to read. A French teacher gave me contemporary French poets. In addition to the books I got in school, I discovered the public library. I couldn't believe that one could take home all those wonderful books and records. I went almost every day, and brought something home. Even later on, while I was living in Chicago, I kept coming back to that library.

I was also beginning to be interested in painting. I drew, did water colors, and even some oil paintings. This was an important activity. I discovered modern art and its aesthetic. I never had any illusion that I had much talent, and I stopped painting when I was twenty-six years old, but some of the things I did show a fairly sophisticated knowledge of the modern idiom.

In school, of course, I gravitated toward students who were interested in the arts. One day, two of my friends confessed that they wrote poetry. I asked them to show it to me. Well, I wasn't impressed. I went home and wrote some poems to show them how it's supposed to be done. To my astonishment my poems were as stupid as theirs. I couldn't figure it out. It made me read poetry. I went through a couple of anthologies and then tried again. Still, it was no good. I mean, it seemed fine while I was writing it, but the next day I was disappointed.

*

I graduated in August of 1956 after my class did. I was missing some credits and had to take classes in summer school. I was supposed to go to college but there was no money. My father spent everything he earned, and he even managed to get into a large debt.

At the end of the summer I found a job as an office boy at the *Chicago Sun Times,* and started attending night classes at the University of Chicago. I took the El to the city early in the morning and returned late at night. It was a lonely period. All my school friends were in college. My parents were fighting all the time. It was hard to be at home.

At the *Sun Times* I met a young writer, a fellow a little older than me, who had a furnished room on the North Side. That gave me the idea. I got a room, too. It was in a basement of a tenement next to the hot-water boiler. I went home early that night and told my parents I was moving out. They were stunned. For once, they ganged up on me. I was too young, too irresponsible, and so on.

I couldn't be budged. I ended up by telling them that I hated their fighting, couldn't bear the sound of their voices any more. The next morning I was gone. Shortly after, my parents came to visit me, individually. They were appalled by the squalor I was living in. I didn't notice it. I was happy.

At work I made just enough money to get by. I had my books, my paints, and my jazz records. When I was broke, I went home or my father took me out to eat.

I made friends in the neighborhood saloons and

Charles Simic, New York, 1957

got to know some girls at the university. The people I saw were all into arts and that encouraged my own efforts. I painted more than I wrote, but poetry was my secret ambition. I was getting obsessed with it. I read it all the time. A friend introduced me to the works of Lowell and Jarrell. Another gave me the poems of Stevens and Pound. At night when I was not attending classes I went to the Newberry Library where I read the French Surrealists and literary magazines.

It all still felt unreal. Even today I'm amazed by the change I underwent in that four or five-year period. One moment, so to speak, I was an unremarkable Yugoslav schoolboy, and the next moment I was in Chicago writing poetry in English.

*

My first poems were published in the 1959 winter issue of the *Chicago Review.* They were written about a year and a half earlier. The two poems published differ a great deal. They don't seem to be written by the same poet. I liked so many different kinds of poetry at that time. One month I was a follower of Hart Crane, the next month I was writing like Walt Whitman, or so I imagined. I wrote, for instance, an eighty-page long poem on the Spanish Inquisition in the manner of Ezra Pound. It was awful but the effort I put into it was tremendous. I'd work all night, go to work half asleep, and then attend night classes. I probably produced more poetry in that period of 1956-61 than in all the years since. Except for a few poems, it was all bad, and one day I destroyed them all.

I was in the Army, had been in the service for six months when in the winter of 1962 I asked my father to send me the folder with my poems. I sat down one evening in the barracks and read them. Everybody else was shining shoes, playing cards, listening to their radios, and I was reading my collected works. Perhaps it was being away from it so long and in such different circumstances that made my head so clear. I could see all the influences and all the awkward writing. There were at least a couple of hundred pages. I ripped them up and threw them in the garbage. It was like my eyes were opened. I still wanted to write poetry, but not that kind.

Now I look more affectionately on that early Chicago period. Had I gone to college like everybody else, had I stayed at home with my parents, it wouldn't have turned out quite the same way it did. Being alone I had to justify my existence in my own eyes. It was obvious I wasn't going to succeed in life in the usual way, so I wrote and painted.

Otherwise, I had no idea where I was going. My previous life had taught me that plans and decisions don't mean much. My father used to ask me jokingly, "Where are we going to immigrate next?" Anything was possible in this century. The experiment was still in progress. We were its laboratory animals. Strangest of all, one of the rats was writing poetry.

BIBLIOGRAPHY

Poetry:

What the Grass Says. San Francisco: Kayak, 1967.

Somewhere among Us a Stone Is Taking Notes. San Francisco: Kayak, 1969.

Dismantling the Silence. New York: Braziller, 1971; London: J. Cape, 1971.

White. New York: New Rivers Press, 1972.

Return to a Place Lit by a Glass of Milk. New York: Braziller, 1974.

Biography and a Lament: Poems 1961-1967. Hartford, Conn.: Bartholomew's Cobble, 1976.

Charon's Cosmology. New York: Braziller, 1977.

Brooms: Selected Poems. Barry, Wales: Edge Press, 1978.

School for Dark Thoughts. Pawlet, Vt.: Banyan Press, 1978.

Classic Ballroom Dances. New York: Braziller, 1980.

Austerities. New York: Braziller, 1982; London: Secker & Warburg, 1983.

Shaving at Night. San Francisco: Meadow Press, 1982.

Chicken without a Head: A New Version. Portland, Ore.: Trace Editions, 1983.

Weather Forecast for Utopia and Vicinity: Poems 1967-1982. Barrytown, N.Y.: Station Hill Press, 1983.

Selected Poems 1963-1983. New York: Braziller, 1985.

Nonfiction:

The Uncertain Certainty: Interviews, Essays, and Notes on Poetry. Ann Arbor: University of Michigan Press, 1985.

Translator of:

Fire Gardens, by Ivan V. Lalic. New York: New Rivers Press, 1970.

Four Yugoslav Poets: Ivan V. Lalic, Branko Miljkovic, Milorad Pavic, Ljubomir Simovic. Northwood Narrows, N.H.: Lillabulero Press, 1970.

The Little Box: Poems, by Vasko Popa. Washington, D.C.: Charioteer Press, 1970.

Selected Poems of Ivan V. Lalic, translated with C.W. Truesdale. New York: New Rivers Press, 1970.

Another Republic: 17 European and South American Writers, edited with Mark Strand. New York: Ecco Press, 1976.

Key to Dreams According to Djordje, by Djordje Nikolic. Chicago: Elpenor Books, 1978.

Homage to the Lame Wolf: Selected Poems, 1956-1975, by Vasko Popa. Oberlin, Ohio: Oberlin College, 1979.

Atlantis, by Slavko Mihalic, translated with Peter Kastmiler. Greenfield Center, N.Y.: Greenfield Review Press, 1983.

Sound recordings:

School for Dark Thoughts. Washington, D.C.: Watershed Tapes, 1978.

Louis Simpson
1923-

Louis Simpson in the Scottish Highlands, 1984

I am sitting on the drawing-room floor looking through a record album. I grasp the handle of the gramophone and wind it. I put a record on the turntable, and the music begins. One of the compartments of the gramophone holds a book, the *Victor Book of the Opera.* I take it out and turn to the pages on *I Pagliacci.* The music proceeds: the chorus of villagers, the chorus of the bells, and Caruso's aria. The theatre of my imagination is as splendid as La Scala in Milan with its chandeliers and lighted balconies. I do not know what Nedda and Silvio are up to, and why Canio is angry, but I do not have to understand. It is enough for them to utter these passionate words and for the orchestra to produce these melodies. It is not the sense that matters but the music.

The house I am in is named "Volyn," after Volhynia Province in Russia where my mother lived as a child. She travelled from Russia to the United States when she was a girl. Then she came to Jamaica and met my father, and so they were married. But when she was living in New York with her mother, sisters, and brother, she dreamed of being a singer like the great opera stars, and took singing lessons. Her days were passed in the garment district, working in a hat shop. Then she managed to find work with a motion-picture company. She was only an extra, but one day an actress refused to jump into a tank of water and act as though she were drowning, and Rosalind jumped in her place. As she couldn't swim she gave a convincing performance. This led to her being hired as one of Annette Kellerman's Bathing Beauties. They came to Jamaica to make a movie, *Neptune's Daughter*. My father, Aston Simpson, was a lawyer, a native Jamaican of mixed background. He fell in love with my mother and went to New York to meet her family. They were married and lived at Cross Roads in the suburbs of Kingston. Two sons were born, five years apart. I was the younger, born on March 27, 1923.

My mother retained her love of singing and hired a singing teacher. I loved the gramophone with its "gems" from operas and musical comedies, Sousa marches, fox-trots, the music people danced to in the twenties. That music still haunts me. The melody of "Dancing in the Dark" evokes a world that no longer exists: the lane outside our house, shadowed with bamboos, and cars parked in the lane—Aston and Rosalind are giving a lawn-tennis party. Or it is Sunday and we are at Bournemouth, the big swimming pool where the white people go. There is a dance floor overlooking the pool. When you are through swimming you sit drinking a Delaware Punch while people in flannels and frocks dance to a fox-trot. The splashing and shrieks of the swimmers come up from the pool.

This white world was precariously balanced—most of the population was black or "colored." The white people looked down on the rest, and their manners were copied by the people of lighter color. At the bottom of the pyramid were the descendants of slaves who labored in the cane fields and banana plantations and broke the stones to make roads. On the other hand, there were no absolute barriers of race—a clever man of color could work his way up in society. There were colored lawyers, doctors, and engineers.

Besides the British colonists and descendants of African slaves there were East Indians who worked in the cane fields and Chinese who kept grocery shops. They were the targets for outbursts of violence by the black population. There were some Syrians who owned stores, and a small number of Jews.

My mother was Jewish but she did not tell me so. Her early life among the immigrant Jews of New York had given her a dislike of such associations.

Every middle-class house had black or colored servants. But they were more than servants—for a small boy they were companions. I followed the garden boy around listening to his stories about Brer Nancy, the long-legged spider, Brer Crow, Brer Alligator, Brer Tiger, and Brer Donkey. Brer Nancy was the folk-hero, the cunning one. I sat by the garden boy watching him cook his lunch in a pan, cornmeal rolled in a leaf and fried in coconut oil, with maybe a piece of codfish. He made me a slingshot with which I went around aiming at lizards and birds.

My love of stories came from our mother's telling stories about her childhood and reading to us. She read fairy tales—Oscar Wilde's *The Happy Prince* was a favorite—and we had a set of books, *Journeys through Bookland*, that began with nursery rhymes and became progressively more advanced.

When she talked about her childhood in Russia she would be carried away and relive the fears of that time. She told about the rats that invaded the cellar where she slept. Her bedding was on the floor but she slept on a chair so as to be out of the reach of the rats.

Rosalind De Marantz, the poet's mother

Rats had brought the typhus that killed her sister Lisa. Rosalind fell sick at the same time, and would have died but for a neighbor, a woman who took care of her. When she came back to her senses and looked in a mirror they had cut off all her hair. They had burned her doll, the only one she had, made of rags and a stick.

The family sent her to Odessa to stay with relatives. She remembered the broad streets and the harbor with ships. When she was about to return to Lutsk she saw some plums in a window. She bought them with her last kopecks to take back to the family. But the journey by train took three days and the plums were beginning to spoil. So she ate them, one by one. She had a stomach ache but she continued to eat the plums rather than let them go to waste. When she arrived home they were all gone.

Forty years after hearing these anecdotes I put them into poems. The world my mother described was a place in which sadness and comedy were mixed. The people who lived there were poor, but they were at-

it may speak of, the voice itself
tells of love and infinite wonder.
             "Why Do You Write about Russia?"

My mother must have felt deprived as a child: the family was poor and there were other children to be cared for. So when she grew up she determined to make a life all of her own. She went into the movies, then married a gentile—to marry a gentile was the worst thing a Jewish girl could do—and went to live in

Aston Simpson, the poet's father

Louis Simpson (front) and his brother, Herbert, in Kingston, Jamaica

tached to one another. They had a community, the sense of living a shared life that I could not find in my own surroundings.

These stories were told
against a background of tropical night . . .
a sea breeze stirring the flowers
that open at dusk, smelling like perfume.
The voice that spoke of freezing cold
itself was warm and infinitely comforting.

So it is with poetry: whatever numbing horrors

a country no one had ever heard of. At the same time she felt abandoned and alone.

This was the cause of the trouble between my parents that would give my life the direction it has taken. My mother would make trips back to New York to see her mother and sisters and brother, and she would be away for weeks at a time. In one of her absences my father embarked on an affair with a stenographer. The upshot was that my mother divorced my father. As he was a lawyer he was able to arrange matters so that, though he was in the wrong, the children were to stay with him. My mother, no longer having a position in society, had to leave Jamaica.

I could not have been more than seven when this happened. No one explained it to me—one day I had a mother, the next she was gone. There had been quarrels, screams and tears, but these were not explained.

Once I went with my father to look at a house he was thinking of buying. We were standing in a room that was still unfinished, just bare boards, when a woman appeared in the doorway. It was my mother. She was holding a revolver and pointing it. "Now, Rosalind," he said. He walked over and took the revolver out of her hand. She shrieked, fell to the floor, and became unconscious. Her face was pale, her mouth flecked with foam.

At this time my brother was away at boarding school. I was sent to live with relatives, my father's sister Edith and her family. Edith was married to the Postmaster. Another of my father's sisters, Aunt May, lived in the same house—the burden of taking care of me fell upon her. There were four children in the family, two boys and two girls, and always some activity, unlike the silence or hysterics of our life at home. The younger son, Douglas, would be practising with a soccer ball or hitting a tennis ball against the garage. He collected stamps and collected the tram tickets that took him to school every day. Once Douglas had to memorise lines of Macaulay's *Lays of Ancient Rome* for his homework. He recited them aloud vigorously:

> Lars Porsena of Clusium
> By the nine gods he swore . . .

This was the first time I heard poetry recited—it was much more exciting than nursery rhymes. Years later Douglas became a lawyer, and was appointed Jamaican ambassador to the United States.

I went to day school and did my homework in the afternoon sitting on the floor of the drawing room, helped by my cousin Sybil. When I had finished my task I would ask her to tell me a story, and then, "Tell me another." In order to keep me supplied with stories she began writing them. She is an old lady now. In her letters she tells me she has been writing stories all her life, that some have been published, and that she owes her start as a writer to our sessions on the floor.

As I write, the atmosphere of a time and place returns. It is late in the afternoon; Aunt Edith and Aunt May are rocking and fanning themselves on the veranda. A tram goes by on the South Camp Road, clanging its bell. A john crow drifts in the sky, making slow circles. A bugle sounds from the encampment of British soldiers.

It is a great occasion when a British regiment

Simpson as a boy in Jamaica

leaves Jamaica and a new one marches in, dressed for the tropics in pith helmets and khaki shorts. Afterwards, lying on my stomach in the drawing room I arrange shotgun shells in ranks. Whenever my father goes on one of his bird-shooting expeditions he brings back these empty shells that make good soldiers. I line them up and aim with my cannon. My father, who is handy with tools, made me a cannon out of a length of pipe. It has a bolt powered by elastic bands. Drop a projectile down the pipe, pull the bolt back till it clicks, aim, and fire. The ball flies through the air and knocks a hole in the ranks.

"Steady, the Guards!"

A drumming shook the ground. A line of helmets appeared above the curve of rising ground, then cuirasses and horsemen. The guns in front of the square fired a volley, and horses and men were seen to go tumbling.

"Come on, Frenchy," shouted a voice in the ranks, "over here!"

These cavalry charges, impressive though they appeared, were a welcome relief to the men standing in square. Anything was better than standing still to be shot at.

When I was nine I was sent to boarding school with my brother. Munro College was a hundred miles to the west—over the mountains this seemed a great distance. The red-roofed buildings overlooked an empty plain and empty sea.

Our masters were Englishmen and the school was a colonial imitation of an English public school. There was one difference: many of the boys were "colored." There was no race prejudice at Munro, though the boys of English or Scottish parentage had a certain glamor. The headmaster, "Wagger" Harrison, believed in flogging, and the masters beat the students for misbehaving, not knowing their lessons, or any other reason. This system was copied by the boys, the bigger boys bullying the smaller. In my first term I happened to glance in the Sixth Form window as I passed. A Sixth Form boy named Weller, who was a notorious bully, called me in, the other Sixth Formers lined up, some looking rather sheepish, and I had to run a gauntlet of kicks. It is a wonder that some boy was not crippled under this regime.

We studied Latin, still considered to be the core of a public school education. We studied the history and geography of England as if we were going to live there. We studied mathematics, science, French, Scripture—both the Old and New Testaments—and English grammar and composition. Later on we studied English Literature.

I loved to read. My mother would send from Canada, where she was living, books for boys such as Booth Tarkington's Penrod books and Edgar Rice Burroughs's Tarzan stories. I read *Gulliver's Travels* and *Tom Sawyer*. In my father's study were books of all kinds, ranging from stories by Kipling to novels of the 1920s—when he and my mother were divorced. After that it seemed that he read nothing but law books. I read books of travel and adventure with illustrations of wild beasts, and looked through the *Times History of the Great War*, with its pictures of German howitzers, Greek troops in ballet costume, Zouaves, and "Tommies" in tin hats. Every year my father gave me the big red *Chums* annual with its serial adventures of English seamen, soldiers, flyers, and racing drivers. There were serials about boys named Tom Merry and Dick Cherry who had a wonderful time at school playing pranks, confounding the school bully, and winning at games. For colonial readers there would be an Indian, Canadian, or Australian boy who had the right school spirit.

I had no particular liking for poetry. It was taught by the sportsmaster, and the poems we read were simple lyrics by Robert Bridges, John Masefield, and other minor English poets. In the upper forms we read poems

The Meccano Club (a hobby club), Munro College, Jamaica. Simpson is in the second row, center.

by Keats and Shelley and Tennyson. Then a master named H. J. Andrews taught us Shakespeare and I was gripped with a thrill of discovery.

There is a great difference between the poetry of Shakespeare and the poetry of the Georgians. But our teachers, even one as sympathetic as Andrews, did not attempt to show us why one kind of writing was superior to the other. They themselves were products of a British education, the point of which was to uphold British traditions. If one began being critical, where would it end? With criticizing the Empire and the Monarchy.

Our naiveté may not have been a bad thing—it is dangerous to be a critic before one has been wholeheartedly a reader. A few years later when I went to the university I would meet young men who had been taught at an early age to be critics. This seemed to go hand in hand with a contempt for imagination. They were preparing to be doctors, lawyers, engineers, or professors, and had no time to waste. They did not read for pleasure but for information.

At Munro we were required to write in all subjects except science, and an English essay every week. Reading novels made me want to write stories of my own, and Shakespeare led to writing my own blank verse. Two or three of these efforts were published in *The Munronian* alongside the cricket scores. One day our English master told us to write an essay on the coronation of George VI. I based mine on an account of the coronation in the Kingston newspaper, *The Daily Gleaner.* The essays were submitted to a competition being held by the *Gleaner;* mine won the first prize and was printed in the *Gleaner.* The next year I entered a *Gleaner* short-story competition and won second prize. The story, "Back to Earth," was about a black boy from the country. He came to Kingston looking for work and was caught in an earthquake. He saved a man's life; the man gave him some money, and he went back to his village. But his mother was dying, and the story ended with the words, "Too late, too late!" I was profoundly moved by this ending.

During school vacations my brother and I lived with our father and his new wife, formerly his stenographer. We had moved to a new house at Bournemouth on the sea. There was none of the social activity of his marriage to our mother, no lawn-tennis parties. He went to his office on Duke Street, or drove to Spanish Town to argue a case, and in the evenings he worked in his study. On Sundays he would take us out in the motorboat he had made out of a ship's lifeboat. We travelled across the harbor to Port Royal and back. He steered and did not ask my brother or me to take the wheel—I suppose it never occurred to him. The only diversion in these monotonous outings was to go

around a freighter or ship anchored in the harbor.

My brother and I lived in the house almost as strangers. My brother resented this second marriage—or my father thought he did. My brother failed his school examinations; after leaving school he was articled to my father, and failed his law exams. The atmosphere at home became very strained. And yet I was quite happy, swimming every day and bicycling on the "Hercules" I had bought with the prize money from my essay.

I swam in the big pool at Bournemouth. One day when I came out of the locker room I was facing a girl with grey eyes and long golden hair. It was like a blow to the heart; I had been invaded by a creature that moved as she did with every movement of her limbs, every toss of her head, or glance of her eyes. From that day until I left the island I thought about Gloria Roberts. I took her out once or twice, to go swimming or to a movie. We were chaperoned by her brother and hardly ever spoke.

I think that the wish to create beauty begins with some such experience; reading Dante or looking at paintings of the Renaissance, one sees that it is so. The hero of James Joyce's *Portrait of the Artist* sees a young woman at the edge of the sea, and understands that he is to write about the beauty of the world. Poetry begins with a vision, a pattern of beauty in the mind.

I was inspired to write, and some of my poems and stories were published in *Public Opinion.* This was a weekly newspaper that argued for Jamaican independence, that it was time for Jamaica to break with England and have its own government. This was in the late 1930s; there were riots and the troops were called out to keep order. My contributions, however, were nonpolitical. I wrote a poem about the willows that lined the driveway at my school; another about passengers on a Kingston bus. I published a story that was a rhapsody about my love for Gloria Roberts—I called it, "In Love and Puberty." My Aunt May read it and sniffed—sex was never mentioned by middle-class Jamaicans. The lower classes, however, had no such inhibitions, and when you went to the movies the cheaper seats were filled with people who made remarks during the love scenes and uttered whoops of appreciation.

As I have said, my brother and I were outsiders in our house, definitely *de trop* in our stepmother's eyes. She had a child of her own, a girl child, and another, a boy. Then our father died. He had diabetes and was being transported to Panama for medical treatment. He never arrived; he died on board ship with our stepmother in attendance. When the will was read my brother and I were virtually disinherited. Our stepmother inherited house, law office, property, everything—she was a rich woman. A few days after the reading of the will my brother and I left the house and went to live in a furnished room. There was some talk of the injustice that left us just enough money to live on—not enough for me to go to a university. But our stepmother had the best legal assistance money could buy—the barrister Norman Manley—and no one seemed to care very much.

I returned to school. Then my mother wrote asking if I would like to come to New York for a visit. I left Jamaica, and have never gone back.

I was expected back, to sit for an examination. If I did very well I might win a scholarship to Oxford. But I had already taken that examination twice without winning anything. Besides, England was at war with Germany—if I returned to the island, I might be stuck there for the duration.

I applied to Columbia College and was accepted. That summer I began learning about the new country. The canyons of Manhattan, the rush of traffic, the way people talked, the billboards . . . everything struck me as new and significant.

At Columbia I came to know the hypercritical young men I have mentioned, readers of Marx and Freud. My taste for novels by Jane Austen, Thackeray, and Joseph Conrad struck them as quaint. In poetry, however, I was modern—my favorite poets at this time were T. S. Eliot and W. H. Auden. Auden's mocking verses with their hints at some esoteric knowledge—Marxist, Freudian, or existential—seemed attractive. Nothing is so appealing to the adolescent mind as the idea of belonging to an inner circle speaking a private language. With the passing of time I would find Auden's verse increasingly shallow. But the poetry of Eliot has lost none of its power; he will be remembered as a great poet, for he wrote out of necessity.

In my first year at Columbia I drew Lionel Trilling as my instructor in a course called Humanities. We read and discussed Homer, Herodotus, Thucydides, the Greek playwrights, Aristotle, Plato, Virgil, Dante, and other authors of western civilization. In another course, Contemporary Civilization, we studied writers on political economy and did bits and pieces of philosophy. We had to read a book by John Herman Randall called *The Making of the Modern Mind*. It was written in a compacted prose that was practically unreadable and made the modern mind seem constipated.

There was no poetry in Humanities. If we studied Homer or Dante with Lionel Trilling it was for the useful ideas, not for the feeling or style. Trilling had no interest in poetry for its own sake; some social or psychological theories seemed to lurk in his mind, though they were never explicit. A good description of his attitude is the one he used for the title of a book, the

"liberal imagination."

Mark Van Doren, with whom I studied the poetry of Hardy and Yeats, and Shakespeare's plays, was at the opposite pole from Trilling. Poetry was all Mark cared about, the imagery, sounds of words, and their associations. A line by Shakespeare would start him speculating about the motives of the character who was speaking, and, beyond that, the nature of tragedy or comedy . . . universal questions. Mark was an impressionist; his teaching would not have pleased a critic who believed in sticking to the text, but it pleased us and set us wondering. We looked forward to his classes as though we were going to a play.

He was an inspiring teacher but, I am sorry to say, his writing was not as memorable as his teaching. He did not "make it new" when he wrote verse, but used the meters and language of English verse. I think he was too much influenced by Shakespeare. In every age it is necessary to find a new language and new forms of poetry. The newness is what makes a work classic, that is, likely to last.

As a foreign student I was not subject to the draft—I could return to Jamaica. But I preferred to be drafted, and entered upon active service in the U.S. Army in January 1943. I took basic training in an armored regiment in Texas, but did not see combat with the tanks—I went overseas as an infantry replacement and was assigned to the 101st Airborne Division in England. I was a rifleman in G Company of the 327th Glider Infantry Regiment. We were trained to be launched in gliders behind enemy lines.

How did I feel about this? I loved my country. There was nothing of the conscientious objector in my makeup—conscience said it was my duty to fight. After going into combat I felt a bond with my companions, and, looking back, I am proud to have been a soldier in the 101st.

The division fought in Normandy, Holland, Belgium, and Germany. I have written about the fighting in poems and a few pages of prose. But writing had to wait until after the war—it was not possible to write in a foxhole, and the division was kept almost continually on the line.

I was discharged in 1946, and went back to Columbia and resumed my studies. Then I had a breakdown. I had been wounded in Holland, and in the fighting at Bastogne my feet were frozen and I was sent back to Paris in an ambulance with what was called combat fatigue. Now, under the pressure of study and, it seems, an indifference to eating and sleeping, I cracked entirely. One symptom of my illness was amnesia—the war, and much of my previous life, was blotted out.

In the 101st Airborne Division, U.S. Army, 1944

I was kept in Kings Park Hospital for six months. There was very little care of the patients and the ward attendants were given a free hand. I saw one patient, a young man, kicked to death in front of me. The attendants who did it warned me that if I gave evidence at the inquiry they would see to it that I spent the rest of my life in the hospital. I was not called upon to give evidence.

After my release I finished my B.S. degree at Columbia—the College would not have me back but General Studies would—supporting myself by working on the night shift of the *New York Herald-Tribune* as a copyboy. I worked as a packing clerk for an import-export firm. Then I received a pension from the government for my service-connected disability. This, together with the "GI Bill," added up to a tidy sum. I travelled to France—my glimpse of Paris in wartime had whetted my appetite—and attended the University of Paris. But I soon got fed up with the rules and the quality of the teaching. Our French professors placed great emphasis on perfect command of the French language; and as American students did not have it, they treated us like schoolboys.

I was living on the Left Bank. One night I

dreamed I was in combat, and when I woke wrote a poem about it. It was no dream, but memory breaking to the surface. "Carentan O Carentan" tells of an American infantry platoon ambushed by the Germans. This was G Company's first contact with the enemy. We were pinned down by machine guns and mortars on a canal bank outside Carentan.

> The watchers in their leopard suits
> Waited till it was time,
> And aimed between the belt and boot
> And let the barrel climb.

The meter and tone of Heinrich Heine, whom I had been reading, helped to give the poem its vivacity of a *danse macabre*.

I wrote other poems about the war, one of which, "The Battle," describes the fighting at Bastogne.

> Helmet and rifle, pack and overcoat
> Marched through a forest. Somewhere up
>   ahead
> Guns thudded. Like the circle of a throat
> The night on every side was turning red.
>
> They halted and they dug. They sank like
>   moles
> Into the clammy earth between the trees.
> And soon the sentries, standing in their holes,
> Felt the first snow. Their feet began to freeze.
>
> At dawn the first shell landed with a crack.
> Then shells and bullets swept the icy woods.
> This lasted many days. The snow was black.
> The corpses stiffened in their scarlet hoods.
>
> Most clearly of that battle I remember
> The tiredness in eyes, how hands looked thin
> Around a cigarette, and the bright ember
> Would pulse with all the life there was within.

I was also writing love poems. Before the war I had met a girl on Riverside Drive with whom I fell in love. After the war I saw her again and we began a passionate affair. Then she went away to college in another city and I wrote about the fickleness of women. For these poems my model was the Tudor lyricists, especially Wyatt. My early poems were modeled on someone or other—Wyatt, Marvell, Byron, Eliot. I ranged like a magpie stealing other men's styles, but the feelings were my own.

While in Paris I gathered my poems and had a book made by a French printer. It cost only $500 to make 500 copies, and they were attractively printed. I arranged with a small publisher in New York, a man named Gustav Davidson, to distribute the books. Two dozen were sent out for review, others I gave away, and a few were sold. *The Arrivistes* was reviewed favorably by Randall Jarrell in *The Nation*. He said I was one of the most promising poets he'd read though there wasn't a perfectly realized poem in the book. Then no more was heard of it. A few years later Gustav Davidson denied having any copies in his possession. After his death, however, copies began surfacing, as new as the day they were printed, and a copy that originally sold for two dollars is now worth several hundred.

I returned to New York and studied for the M.A. at Columbia with a view to teaching. I also married, and that year my first child was born, Louis Matthew. But I did not go into teaching immediately, for positions were scarce—instead I became a reader in a publishing house. For five years I worked for Bobbs-Merrill in their New York office, reading and editing manuscripts. The work was pleasant, undemanding, and underpaid.

I would do my writing at night. Taking Jarrell's criticism to heart, I concentrated on perfection of language and form. When I had a book-length manuscript of poems I submitted it to publishers. It came back with letters of rejection.

I entered it for a competition called the Borestone Mountain Poetry Award. I received a telegram from Gustav Davidson, whom I have already mentioned, informing me that I had won the award. This meant book publication and $1,200. It made me very happy—for a few days I walked on air. Then I received a phone call from Davidson saying there had been an error, a "miscount," and the award was to go to someone else. He asked me not to tell people about what had happened as it would reflect badly on the Borestone Mountain Award. The judge who had changed his mind was the poet Robert Lowell.

I was persuaded by some people I knew not to raise any objection. I was foolish enough to take their advice, and even accompanied them to a meeting of the Poetry Society of America where I saw the award given to a woman named Leah Bodine Drake who was a prominent member of the Society.

This was a painful experience. I could have stood rejection, but to be given a prize and then have it taken back! Book publication would have meant a great deal to me. Moreover, I was quite poor—my marriage had broken up and I was paying alimony and child support. The prize money would have been very welcome.

This experience left me suspicious of prizes and those who gave them. In later years when I served on Pulitzer Prize juries I tried to be scrupulously fair, and saw that the underdog was not passed over. It sometimes happens that there is an unspoken agreement among critics that a certain author is to have an award; on a few occasions I have had to deal with this

situation and stand up for an author, against the odds. Had I not been on the jury, Anne Sexton, James Wright, W. S. Merwin, George Oppen, and Gary Snyder, would not have won a Pulitzer Prize.

A writer has to hold fast and persevere in the face of "the spurns / That patient merit of the unworthy takes." If he cannot do this he may as well give it up. One must have faith in one's work and believe that readers will see what is there.

My second book, *Good News of Death and Other Poems*, was published by Scribner's in a series, *Poets of Today*, edited by John Hall Wheelock. Three books were published together in one volume. Though better than no publication at all, you did not feel that you had a book of your own, and the reviewers treated the three poets as though they were competing with one another.

During my years in publishing I met some of the leading new writers: Styron, Mailer, Bellow, and a dozen others. At that time the word "writer" was synonymous with "novelist." Some of the glamor of novel-writing has been lost—young people today are more likely to dream of directing movies and becoming another Coppola or Kubrick. Bobbs-Merrill brought out a number of first novels. With the exception of Styron's *Lie Down in Darkness*, they have all vanished without a trace.

Sometimes I was delegated to edit a book or rewrite an author's bad sentences. One novel by a Frenchman, an enormous medieval romance, had to be shortened drastically. Then I had to write a few chapters to link up the plot fore and aft. I wrote these pages with a manic energy; I had the heroine gambled away by her husband, and for this I invented a medieval game of dice. I described the siege of a castle. I could have written hundreds of such pages in which no atom of my real interests was engaged.

One day I read a manuscript that gave advice on finding a mate. You were to put your prospective mate in a chair with an electrical device. A pointer would swing to a certain number. Then you were to put yourself in the chair and see if the numbers correlated. After this you were to consider such matters as temperamental affinity, habits, and tastes in food. I wrote a letter of rejection. Then the author turned up, a slender, fair woman in her thirties. She sat down and addressed a question to me: "What did they tell you about me in San Francisco?" I had just returned from a vacation in San Francisco and apparently she thought I had gone there to check on her. I explained patiently the reasons why we could not publish her book. She was leaning on my desk and her elbow began to rap on the wood—she was trembling all over. I got her out of there without a scene; the incident, however, stayed in my mind; it was the kind of stuff of which poems are made. Some years later I wrote a poem about it.

> People who read a deeper significance
> into everything, every whisper . . .
> who believe that a knife crossed with a fork
> is a signal . . . by the sheer intensity
> of their feeling leave an impression.
>
> And with her, tangled in her hair,
> came the atmosphere, four walls,
> the avenues of the city
> at twilight, the lights going on.
>   "The Hour of Feeling"

I was supplementing my income by teaching, first at the New School for Social Research, then in General Studies at Columbia. When the head editor at Bobbs-Merrill, Hiram Haydn, left for another job, I decided to leave too. I had no future as an editor—I was not driven to create best-sellers. On the other hand, teaching came easily—in any case, I liked reading the books I had to teach. So I began studying for the Ph.D. at Columbia and teaching in General Studies on a half-time basis. Then I switched to the College.

In 1955 I married again, and a year later I had another child, a daughter, Anne Borovoi. What with teaching, studying, writing, and being a parent, I was very busy in these years. Instructors at Columbia were underpaid but I was always able to make ends meet; just when the larder was bare a check would arrive from some magazine for a poem I had submitted.

In 1958 my writing was rewarded with a Prix de Rome and a fellowship from *The Hudson Review.* I took my family to Rome for a year. We lived outside the walls of the American Academy on Janiculum, the hill with a view across the Tiber. During this year I wrote my dissertation, a critical study of the Scottish writer, James Hogg, who flourished at the beginning of the nineteenth century. Hogg had written a novel of the supernatural that caught my fancy, *The Private Memoirs and Confessions of a Justified Sinner.* I made a journey to Scotland to see where he lived and to carry out research in the National Library at Edinburgh. On my return to New York I submitted the finished dissertation to my committee. It was accepted by two members of the committee, then it went to Lionel Trilling who wanted to reject it—he thought that Hogg was not an important enough figure. But he had approved of my writing on this subject in the first place. His attitude struck the other members of the committee as unjust—the dissertation was accepted and I was given the degree. I decided, however, to leave Columbia since Trilling was there, and when I was offered a position by the University of California at Berkeley, I accepted.

I moved with my wife and children to California in the summer of 1959. We now had a second child, Anthony Rolf. We bought a house in the Berkeley hills.

Universities are much the same everywhere, and I have not found much in my life as a teacher that could be written about in poems. I turned inward for my subjects. In the years that followed I published a third book of poems, *A Dream of Governors;* a novel, *Riverside Drive; James Hogg: A Critical Study;* and, in 1963 another book of poems, *At the End of the Open Road.*

One afternoon after teaching I returned to my office to find a stranger waiting by the door. He identified himself as a reporter and asked what I thought about the Pulitzer Prize. I said I thought it was a good thing on the whole. He seemed puzzled by my answer, then he told me I had won a Pulitzer Prize. I said that he ought to check back with his paper, there must be some mistake. My previous experience of prizes had made me skeptical. But there was no mistake, and in the days that followed I was a celebrity. The Pulitzer Prize for poetry is no great thing, but something about my winning it attracted attention, perhaps because I was a professor who had been in the 101st Airborne Division.

Strangers telephoned me wanting to borrow money. A poet in San Francisco wrote saying that he was giving me the opportunity to help him write his manuscript, and when I refused he wrote me another letter in which he hoped I would not have a heart attack like Theodore Roethke's. A poet I had thought of as a friend wrote to say that no one who won a Pulitzer Prize ever again wrote anything worth a damn. Since then I have come to know how envious poets can be. "In heavenly breasts do such fierce passions dwell?" The answer is, emphatically, yes.

At the End of the Open Road marked a change in my writing. My early poems were in meter and rhyme. This was typical of the 1940s and 1950s—everyone praised Robert Lowell and Richard Wilbur who wrote in meter and rhyme. But at the end of the 1950s I felt a need to express my thoughts more intimately, and began writing in free forms and a conversational style. Other poets, James Wright and Robert Bly for example, were going through a similar change.

At this time I was reading the poems of Whitman intensely. Wright and Bly went to the poetry of other countries for their models: poems translated from the Chinese, from the German, from the Spanish of García Lorca and Pablo Neruda. Bly, Wright, and I were referred to as poets of the "deep image"—it was said that our poems depended on images that had some extra meaning. The ending of Wright's "A Blessing" would be cited as an example:

Suddenly I realize

Left to right: Louis Simpson, James Dickey, and James Wright in Washington, D.C., following a reading at the Library of Congress. (Reprinted by permission of The Library of Congress.)

That if I stepped out of my body I would break
Into blossom.

Or the ending of my "Walt Whitman at Bear Mountain":

The clouds are lifting from the high Sierras,
The Bay mists clearing.
And the angel in the gate, the flowering plum,
Dances like Italy, imagining red.

I was frequently asked to give readings of my poetry. I travelled widely, and once, I recall, gave nine readings in a row. I needed the money and also to make my poems known, for books of poetry do not sell.

When the Americans began their invasion of Vietnam I took part in group readings protesting against the war. Seeing poets on the platform, if not hearing their poetry, encouraged people in the audience to oppose the war. I had no axe to grind—I felt compelled to take a stand on a question that was changing all our lives. But I did not relish criticizing the United States, and felt an aversion for those people who obviously enjoyed doing so.

To escape from the political atmosphere of the 1960s I turned to the past and wrote about my mother's people, the Jews who lived in southern Russia. I wrote about Dvonya:

In the town of Odessa
there is a garden

and Dvonya is there,
Dvonya whom I love
though I have never been in Odessa.
                    "Dvonya"

I wrote about Isidor who hid from the police under the mattress on which his pregnant wife was lying; Avram the cello-mender who served in the Tsar's army, and other characters based on stories I had been told. Volhynia Province with its family affections, its mixture of pathos and humor, was a refuge from the sun-baked emptiness of California.

In 1967 I accepted an offer from the State University of New York at Stony Brook, and moved back East. Stony Brook is situated on the north shore of Long Island, sixty miles from New York City. The housing developments and shopping areas that make the middle of Long Island indistinguishable from the urban sprawl of Los Angeles have not reached the north shore. It is possible to walk along a beach and encounter no other human being; the seabirds and tall green reeds are the same that Whitman knew. When night falls you can imagine Gatsby on his lawn, stretching his arms out to the green light on Daisy's dock.

In 1970 I received a grant from the Guggenheim Foundation that took me to England for a year, and I stayed on for another year. I published two books in England: a book of poems, *Adventures of the Letter I,* and an autobiography, *North of Jamaica.* They received favorable notices in England, but the American editor's decision to print *Adventures of the Letter I* only in paperback resulted in the book's not being reviewed.

In London we lived in Primrose Hill, an area favored by writers—the novelist Fay Weldon lived next door. I met some English poets, gave poetry readings, and made three programs for the BBC. The English attitude to poetry was different from the American: to the English, poetry was an amusement, a "giggle." They had no interest in experimental writing and one could understand why English poetry had become so unimportant. The trouble with English poets was brought home to me once when I gave a reading with one of them. Before we went up to the platform he talked in an easy, unaffected manner. When he stood up to read he adopted an Oxford accent and his poems were essays in standard English. When an Englishman speaks or writes he wishes to show that he is a gentleman. Moreover, English poets do not understand that, as Charles Olson said, "Art does not seek to describe but to enact." That is to say, poetry is mimetic—but English poets write essays in verse. My two years in England showed me that I was fortunate to have gone to New York rather than London when I was a young man.

When I returned to Stony Brook I found myself isolated. American poets are separated by hundreds of miles, and I had no one to talk to about the thing that interested me most. There was no one in the Department of English; after a brave beginning the Department had hired a number of "solid" scholars who were just like the people one would find in any other Department of English. At the end of the day they retired into their houses. If I was going to talk to someone about poetry it would have to be the dead. I plunged into writing literary criticism and wrote about the poets Ezra Pound, T. S. Eliot, and William Carlos Williams, the founders of modern American poetic theory. *Three on the Tower* received wide attention when it was published, though not from university scholars. They were offended by the style—I wrote in the familiar style Hazlitt recommends—and they complained that I had not brought any new information to light. My aim, however, had not been to "make an original contribution to scholarship," the ambition of professors, most of whom are profoundly unoriginal, but to enter into the thinking of the poets and show why they wrote as they did.

In the following years I published other books of criticism: *A Revolution in Taste: Studies of Dylan Thomas, Allen Ginsberg, Sylvia Plath, and Robert Lowell;* a collection of reviews, essays, and interviews, *A Company of Poets;* and a second collection, *The Character of the Poet.* With

the exception of *Three on the Tower*—which gripped me so that when I sat at the typewriter I trembled, ideas were flowing in so fast—I have not liked writing prose. I rewrite a great deal to make my ideas clear, and the work is exhausting. In writing poems, on the other hand, the poem takes over and seems to be writing itself.

While in London I had become interested in Buddhism and attended meetings of the Buddhist Society presided over by Christmas Humphreys. I learned a technique of meditation. This was reflected in a book of poems, *Searching for the Ox,* published in 1976. The title was taken from a series of Chinese drawings in which a boy sets out to find a lost ox. He finds it, leads it, and rides it home. In the final drawing the boy, the ox, and the hut have vanished—all that remains is a circle. The parable describes the vanishing of self in the search for ultimate reality. Though I have not continued my exercises in meditation, this experience of Buddhism has helped me to rid my mind of distractions and concentrate on what is actually there. It has shown me that, as the Buddhist Nansen said, "Your ordinary mind, that is the way."

I have written a number of poems about matters that engage the ordinary mind—about people one might meet and everyday occurrences. In 1983 I published a collection of these poems, *The Best Hour of the Night.* At the same time I published a selection of poems from all my books. *People Live Here* is arranged so as to show the themes of my writing: "The Fighting in Europe," "A Discovery of America," "Modern Lives," and "Volhynia Province." The book includes a few poems I wrote about Australia following a visit to that country.

I think that all good writing springs from the hope of bringing a community into being. Joyce's Stephen said that he wished to forge in the smithy of his soul the "uncreated conscience" of his race, and Yeats said that he wrote "for the race and the reality." I too have written for a race, the people who live in houses, drive to shopping centers, and commute to the city. They are not poets and intellectuals. This is what readers who are intellectuals cannot understand—they think that everyone must think as they do. But I am attempting to show life as it is. There is no need to improve on life—it is deep enough, and it touches a mystery at each end.

To write about the banal does not require one to subscribe to it. On the contrary, in order to see clearly one has to preserve a distance from one's surroundings. My writing is based in things I have seen and heard, but they are rearranged, added to, or subtracted from, so that the finished product may bear little resem-

The poet and his dogs—Willa (left) and Custis Lee

blance to the original person or event that furnished me with ideas. I am most pleased with my writing when it goes beyond realism—which may appear to be satirical—and conveys the sympathy one must feel for human beings when one considers their lives as a whole. When I read aloud from "The Beaded Pear" about a family settling down for the evening and reading *TV Guide:*

> Delightful family fare,
> excellent melodrama of the Mafia.

the audience laughs. But when I read from "Quiet Desperation" about a man suffering an attack of anxiety, the audience is moved, and this seems more important.

> A feeling of pressure . . .
> There is something that needs to be done
> immediately.
>
> 　　　　But there is nothing,
> only himself. His life is passing,
> and afterwards there will be eternity,
> silence, and infinite space.

There is a kind of writing that is both humorous and moving, like life itself, a mixture of happiness and sad-

ness. Such is Chaucer's poetry and Chekhov's plays and stories. I would like to write poems about the life around me that would affect people in this way.

In an account of this kind much has to be omitted. I have not spoken of many things that give life its pleasure—dogs, for example. In the first generation there were two beagles—Tippy and Lady; now Miriam and I have three dogs: Willa, Custis Lee, and Veronica.

I have said very little about my private life. I am not a confessional writer—I am not so avid for money or fame. But I have some ideas about marriage and having children, especially where the husband and father is a writer.

The writer usually works at home; his family knows that he is there, but are told they must not disturb him. If he went to an office every day and did not reappear until evening, they could accept it. But it is hard to accept his unavailability while he is writing or perhaps just daydreaming. It may come to seem that the time spent in writing is time taken from the family. I have sometimes thought that my children would have had a more cheerful upbringing if I had been a businessman. But suppose I had been the kind of businessman who embezzles company funds? Perhaps it is just as well that their father is a poet. Poetry is a strange occupation, but it is harmless.

In the 1950s when I became a parent, parents relied on books on child care that told them how to prepare for and control every eventuality. We assumed

Louis Simpson and Miriam Bachner at their wedding, Setauket, New York, June 23, 1985

Miriam Simpson in Paris, July 1985

a responsibility for our children that previous generations had shared with God. Ten years later this illusion was shattered; in the 1960s it was what the "peer group" thought that mattered—parents counted for very little, and this way of thinking was encouraged by the industries that sold fashions in clothing, music, and drugs. I think that we no longer feel responsible for everything our children think and do.

To round off this account I must step back and tell what happened to my mother after she left Jamaica. She lived in Toronto, supporting herself by doing a small business in cosmetics. From time to time she would return to Jamaica for a few weeks to be with her children. She travelled for the Helena Rubinstein Company, demonstrating cosmetics. Her travels took her to South America, and she persuaded Rubinstein to assign her a franchise for Venezuela, then an unimportant market. She built up the business in Caracas until it was very profitable. She married again, retired from business, and moved with her Italian husband to Italy. They bought a villa and estate at Lucca in the heart of Tuscany, and lived there until, a few years ago, it became impractical to keep the "Villa Rosalinda."

I have omitted to mention that my second marriage ended in divorce. In June of 1985, with my marriage to Miriam, my life as a man and poet entered a new phase. The substance and manner of poetry depend on the character of the poet and character is determined by the choices the man or woman makes. The poetry I shall write in the future will reflect my life with Miriam—as the feeling with which it is written, not directly as the content. The people I have known appear in my poems as characters in a story. When I myself appear it is as a character in a story.

SELECTED BIBLIOGRAPHY

Poetry:

The Arrivistes: Poems, 1940-1949. New York: Fine Editions Press, 1949.

Good News of Death and Other Poems, in *Poets of Today II.* New York: Scribner, 1955.

A Dream of Governors. Middletown, Conn.: Wesleyan University Press, 1959.

At the End of the Open Road. Middletown, Conn.: Wesleyan University Press, 1963.

Selected Poems. New York: Harcourt, 1965; London: Oxford University Press, 1966.

Adventures of the Letter I. London: Oxford University Press, 1971; New York: Harper, 1971.

Searching for the Ox. New York: Morrow, 1976; London: Oxford University Press, 1976.

Armidale. Brockport, N.Y.: BOA Editions, 1979.

Out of Season. Deerfield, Mass.: Deerfield Press, 1979; Dublin: Gallery Press, 1979.

Caviare at the Funeral. New York: F. Watts, 1980; London: Oxford University Press, 1980.

The Best Hour of the Night. New Haven, Conn.: Ticknor & Fields, 1983.

People Live Here: Selected Poems, 1949-1983. Brockport, N.Y.: BOA Editions, 1983; London: Secker & Warburg, 1985.

Fiction:

Riverside Drive. New York: Atheneum, 1962.

Nonfiction:

James Hogg: A Critical Study. New York: St. Martin's, 1962; Edinburgh: Oliver & Boyd, 1962.

North of Jamaica (autobiography). New York: Harper, 1972; also published as *Air with Armed Men.* London: London Magazine Editions, 1972.

Three on the Tower: The Lives and Works of Ezra Pound, T.S. Eliot, and William Carlos Williams. New York: Morrow, 1975.

A Revolution in Taste: Studies of Dylan Thomas, Allen Ginsberg, Sylvia Plath, and Robert Lowell. New York: Macmillan, 1978; also published as *Studies of Dylan Thomas, Allen*

Ginsberg, Sylvia Plath, and Robert Lowell. London: Macmillan, 1979.

A Company of Poets (literary criticism). Ann Arbor: University of Michigan Press, 1981.

The Character of the Poet (literary criticism). Ann Arbor: University of Michigan Press, 1986.

Editor of:

The New Poets of England and America, with Donald Hall and Robert Pack. New York: 1957.

An Introduction to Poetry (anthology). New York: St. Martin's, 1967; London: Macmillan, 1968.

Sound recordings:

Physical Universe. Washington, D.C.: Watershed Tapes.

Spoken Arts Treasury of 100 Modern American Poets Reading Their Poems, Volume XV. New Rochelle, N.Y.: Spoken Arts.

Today's Poets, Volume I. New York: Scholastic.

Yale Series of Recorded Poets. Carillon.

R. S. Thomas

1913-

Cardiff, 1913. Pain, and a woman bearing it; the child, too, but only half-aware. A difficult birth; the child too large. Then meningitis; the photographs show one only half-sane. All forgotten. How far back can one remember? I am on the floor by a door. The nursemaid opens or closes it too suddenly. Next I am on someone's lap with adults fussing about me. "It's ridiculous. You can't possibly remember as far back as that." But why shouldn't one remember a dislocation? In any case childhood is composed of memories. My father was a sailor. We followed him from port to port. We were in Liverpool for most of the first World War. There was gas in the bedroom. One night it sank to the size of a maggot. We learned next day that a zeppelin had approached. Liverpool was smells and ships' sirens and parks, the one escape from streets and houses into something like country. I bent to smell a flower and an insect went up my nose. Panic. The park resounded to my bellowing, as I sought my mother. There were ferries over the Mersey to the Wirral. As we disembarked at New Brighton, there would be a one-legged man climbing to a platform from which to plummet into the water for the coins thrown to him.

One day on the sands at Hoylake my father pointed southwest to where some blue-green hills loomed. "That's Wales," he said. Prophetic words. Sometimes when his boat was in, my mother would go down to the quay to dine with the other officers, and I would be taken and put to bed in my father's cabin. Occasional faces would appear at the door, inquiring whether I was all right. In between, to my horror, a cockroach or two would run across the floor. How can grown-ups realise what such things mean to a child?

At the end of the war my father found employment on the cross-channel boats between Caergybi (Holyhead) and Ireland. The day we arrived it was raining. I stared without interest through the taxi window upon the bleak, wet streets. But on the morrow, ah! The sun shone, the sky was blue, the sea bluer. I ventured out into a world whose like I had not seen before. I was supposed to be delicate. I had a reprieve from school on condition that I was taught at home. I learned to copy marks which was supposed to be a lesson in writing. Such tasks over, I was free to explore our new surroundings. I linked up with other children

Father, T. H. Thomas

who taught me to go bird-nesting. The pale, china-like eggs lying in the mud's cup fascinated me.

When school could no longer be avoided, I went to a "refined" kindergarten, where I met, among others, two boys who lived with an elder sister and their widowed mother on the west coast about two miles out of town. Their house, Bryn Awel, became the place I loved most to go to with the sea wind blowing around it, secret tunnels through the gorse bushes and a view of the Welsh mountains from the upstairs windows. Sometimes I would stay the night there, and in the morning, before anybody was up, I would steal to the window and stare out over the fields at the sea, grey and cold in the dawn light. It was this family who taught me the joys of Guy Fawkes' night. Len, a year older than I, and Colin, the same age, would spend much time beforehand dragging in dead gorse to make a bonfire, and on the evening of the fifth I would arrive to help to put the finishing touches to the guy. My parents would arrive before dark with their fireworks to put with the others. After letting off a few we would light the fire and off it would go belching thousands of sparks into the air. The guy would ignite and collapse, and after the last and biggest rocket had gone hissing into the darkness, we would go indoors to play at bob-apple and ducking apple, until it was time to walk home with the gorse bushes in the hedges squeaking and fidgeting in the night wind.

When it came time for us to leave the kindergarten for the secondary school, none of us was up to standard, so two teachers had to be engaged to coach us. The one who taught us English was surprised at my vocabulary. Is it fair to criticise one's school in retrospect? Think what a Philistine I was, my head full of games and the open air. But I would opine that it was not a very good school. Caergybi was famous ornithologically for its cliff-nesting birds; but no one ever drew our attention to the fact, much less took us to see them. There was little interest in games and no coaching. It was also very un-Welsh in accordance with the climate of the day. Once a year on St. David's Day there was a concert, and in the evening a Welsh play, when, to our surprise, we discovered that quite a few of the staff could speak Welsh. The number of Welsh speakers in Wales has declined disastrously since then; and yet there is more Welsh and Welsh history in the schools now. And there are secondary schools where Welsh is the medium of instruction, a thing unheard of, when I was a boy.

The school was coeducational. I was conscious of the girls and their attractions, but shy. The idea that I should walk out with one would have been dismissed by my mother anyway, and she was the boss. My father being much of the time at sea, it was to her I was answerable. As I reached the top-form, there were background debates as to what I was to do. My father, a former sailing-ship apprentice in the bad old days, was against the sea. My mother, early orphaned and brought up by a half brother who was a vicar, fancied the Church. Shy as I was, I offered no resistance. Is this also how God calls? The only change in my curriculum was the introduction of Greek into my course. I had already been reading Latin for years. I have suggested that it was a poor school; but in one thing I was fortunate. The headmaster, Derry Evans, was an excellent Latin teacher. It was surely to him I was indebted for passing the senior examination and proceeding to University to take a not very good degree in Classics. Little ability and a poor memory were responsible for the latter, not he. But the occupation with words and their meanings, and the translating from one language into another were surely laying the foundations of the practice of poetry that was ahead.

Before I was ready for University my father had had to give up the sea as a career owing to deafness. This deprived him of becoming captain of a ship and led to subsequent stomach trouble because of worry. Money was scarce at home, and I was entered for a Welsh Church scholarship, which I secured. (No one ever failed!) When the time to go up to college arrived, my mother accompanied me to Bangor, ostensibly to see that my lodgings were all right, but really loth to relax her hold until the last moment. Mercifully being a nonentity, I was unnoticed, and by evening she had departed, leaving me really on my own for the first time. The following day I registered, and later in the week found myself standing undanced with at the Freshman's Ball. This was actually the beginning of a series of unsuccessful flirtations. I knew little of girls, less of the so-called facts of life. Whoever agreed to consort with me very soon dropped me. But the heartbreaks were short-lived. There were other excitements: the first breath of freedom; the managing of my small allowance—those were the days when sixpence mattered; the attempt to get into the Rugby teams, although I never made it beyond the Second Fifteen, and I was in and out of that. But above all there was new territory to explore. One moonlight night I slipped out after supper down through the town and out along a track beside the stream that came from Felin Esgob. The way led beneath the trees. Tawny owls called; the water flashed and rippled under the full moon; a feeling of exhilaration at being out in the country at night, young and free, possessed me. Not that my mother had ever prevented me from going where I would by day. She only expressed occasional doubts about the advisability of my being so much alone. On this night I returned late to my lodgings to be let in by the landlady. If she thought about it at all, she, no doubt, took it for granted that I had been out with a girl.

I discovered the mountains. The peaks which had been visible thirty miles to the southeast of Caergybi were now within reach. I would catch a bus to a certain point, then, leaving the road, climb the nearest of them and walk along the ridges of Carnedd Llywelyn and Carnedd Dafydd and down into Bethesda to catch another bus back. The first time I did this and was confronted by the whole sweep of the mountains, I stood on a hillock and shouted "Mae hen wlad fy nhadau," the Welsh national anthem, for no reason I knew.

The second year the Church Hostel had been enlarged and there was room for twenty-one of us, so I left my lodgings and became a boarder. There was a

Photo taken by Thomas as a young student. Shadows of hills on horizon are those of the Lleyn peninsula where the author now lives.

pleasant little modern chapel with a sanctuary light burning. As the Warden was a high churchman, there was generally a smell of incense there. From the window of my bed-sitter I could look out over the Menai Strait to Ynys Môn, Anglesey. My approach to my course was quite wrong, but knowing that my parents would have difficulty in supporting me until I was twenty-three, my one thought was to pass my degree examination, so apart from much unintelligent swotting, I took such time off as I could to go my unproductive way. One sacrifice I made; I did not play cricket. I was moderately good at it, but it is a slow game and would have taken too much out of the summer term. But that worry about passing left its mark. For many years I had a recurring dream that I was about to face an examination and was not ready.

It was reported that a faith-healer was to visit Bangor. With a mixture of vocational trust and youthful enthusiasm I persuaded my father to attend a session. Never had I prayed so hard. Kneeling in the Hostel chapel, I lifted my eyes time and again to the large wooden crucifix that hung before the altar. The evening arrived. The large marquee was full. My father's turn to go up

came. The healer put his fingers in his ears, said something and dismissed him. Outside afterwards my father declared that he could hear a bird singing, something he had not done for years. There was a feeling of well-being and gratitude. Later I saw him and my mother to the train. Alas, within a week or so his newly recovered hearing had ebbed away. My mother was foolish enough to accuse him of having lost his faith.

There were holidays spent away from Caergybi. My parents would choose some place and off we would go, ostensibly for my father to fish for trout, but as my mother was unwilling to go in the spring, we rarely caught much. The first time, we changed trains at Llandudno and went up Dyffryn Conwy. As the glorious scenery of hill and stream and woodland unfolded, I rushed from side to side of the carriage to admire it. It was so different from the flat, rocky bareness of Caergybi. Another time we went to Llanwrtyd, a village in South Wales. One morning I set off on my own to discover the cave of Twm Siôn Cati, an eighteenth-century outcast, who had a hideaway in the hills. On the top of one of these a little man with a black beard rode towards me on a mountain pony. "From this spot here," he said, "you can toss a stone into three counties."

Having, after a lot of worry and hard work, graduated, I prepared to attend the theological college at Llandâf outside Cardiff. There were four terms a year here, which meant leaving Caergybi in July to go down to the stickiness and dust of a city. I was unhappy there. The students, being mostly South Walians were, of course, friendly, but the atmosphere was constricting. Worse still, there was nowhere to go for a walk. To reach such country as there was meant walking along a busy main road. There were two parts of a General Ordination Examination to pass, entailing a stay of two years. But a certain Canon Lloyd of Chirk, near Wrexham, wanted a curate, and being a man of influence he persuaded the Bishop to ordain me at the end of my first year at theological college, having passed only Part One of the examination. So to my relief and the disgust of the staff I was spared Part Two, and left Llandâf with no tears shed. Two pleasant memories of that year remained. I saw Wales defeat New Zealand at Rugby in 1935, and heard Kreisler give a recital in the city.

In the autumn of 1936 I entered upon my first post as curate of Chirk, a mining village right on the Welsh border, and adult life began. I had to preach sermons, which I had shirked doing until then, and I had to begin visiting a fairly stratified parish from two earls at the top through a residential class down to the miners at the bottom, as it were. I soon realised that I was under an obligation to read outside my course to equip myself better for my responsibilities. The first thing was to begin building a small library, for I had nothing in the way of books but a few left over from my terms at college. There was a book firm in London, which ran a hire-purchase system, and from them I ordered some fifty books, which, having arrived, made me feel I was both a scholar and well on the way to being a man of letters, too.

It was October. I went for a long walk up the Ceiriog valley, following the river of that name. The sun shone, the leaves glowed. I wrote a lyrical description home, which made my father say that I must be going to be a poet. It was exciting to be on my own and receiving a small salary, although rent took half of it. It took my mind temporarily off what I had done. But with November the weather changed to the damp, sunless cold so characteristic of the border country, and I realised how far I was from the sea, where, if it rained one day, the sun broke through the next and piled the clouds in white masses above the hills of Eryri, Snowdonia. Still, there was work to do. I had to get to know the parishioners. The miners had to be visited; the residential class invited me to a meal. One day two of the girls from a neighbouring house on their way to play golf stopped the car and invited me to join them. I was

off to catch a train to the neighbouring town. The daughter of the house was driving, but my eyes were on her passenger. I gave her that look which a man gives to the woman of his choice. As we got to know one another, I discovered that she was a recognised painter, and this made me wish to become recognised as a poet.

I had been writing verse since school days, conventional, sentimental stanzas about nature based on Palgrave's *Golden Treasury*. Even after reaching Chirk, Yeats, Hopkins, Eliot did not exist for me. What had we been taught in school? The Georgians mainly, but hardly Edward Thomas. Discovering him, I tried to write about the hills about Chirk, as he had written about the English downs. I discovered Fiona Macleod, and lost my head completely. His re-creation of the Gaelic scene reminded me vividly of my island home. I became sick for the sea and the west coast, even transferring my longing to the Hebrides. My painter friend, Elsi, abetted me. She shared my inner dissatisfaction with modern society. We dreamed of breaking away, and going to live in a cottage "on water and a crust." Yeats, too, had now entered my life; the Yeats of the Celtic twilight, of course, as I was too immature to be aware of the significance of his later work.

Elsi had an Austin Seven, which was ready for anything. Early one morning in August we set out for Scotland with vague plans in our minds. By half-past two we were crossing the border and stayed that night well up in the Highlands. We had decided to catch the MacBrayne steamer for the outer isles, but the road to Mallaig was under reconstruction and by the time we came in sight of the quay the boat was fast drawing away. We wandered the dockside rather at a loss. I saw a fishing boat moored there. "Are you going to the islands?" I asked a rough-looking man in an old sailor's jersey.

"Which islands?" he asked, somewhat dauntingly.

I took breath. "Barra" I said hopefully.

"Nay; I come from Soay," he answered. Then with a canny look he said:

"I'll take you there, if you like."

And so it was. Bidding Elsi "good-bye" and leaving her rather ungallantly to her resources, I went aboard, and presently we were on our way to the island of Soay by Skye. After an hour or so a small island under the Cuillins began to draw near. There was a beach with four or five crofts lining it, and a few dingies drawn up on the shore. Two or three children were playing by the water.

The boatman took me to his cabin, where I was given a meal by his wife, who was none too pleased at what her husband had brought from the mainland. The upshot was that I was billeted with a family a few doors away. Their cabin contained a husband, wife, two large sons and a daughter. I was treated as a guest and put in the parlour, from where I could hear the soft swish of their Gaelic in the kitchen. I was put to sleep in a feather bed over which the ceiling sagged. As one by one the family climbed to their beds, wherever those were, the whole house creaked and swayed. Unfortunately it rained most of the time and I had no suitable clothes. The reality of a Hebridean island began to dilute my dream. As soon as the next Mac-Brayne appeared off-shore, I left my kind hosts and returned to Mallaig, where I learned that Elsi had gone to Canna. Selfishly I telegraphed for her, begging her to return with me to Wales for the rest of our holiday. So ended my infatuation with the Hebrides.

I was more fortunate with the west of Ireland. Having heard that Seamus O'Sullivan, the editor of the *Dublin Magazine,* was sympathetic to young writers, I had already had a poem or two accepted by him as well as meeting him while he was visiting his brother in North Wales. One Christmas Day after morning service the Vicar told me that I was free for a week or so, if I wished. I jumped on my bicycle, made for Caergybi, and within a day or so was visiting O'Sullivan in Dublin. Armed with an introduction to a professor at Galway University, I caught an early morning train from Dublin and before mid-day presented myself at the house of Liam O'Briain, Professor of Celtic and former Irish rebel imprisoned in Wales after the 1916 rising. He had a great love for and knowledge of Connemara, and insisted on accompanying me a few miles on my walk west, talking all the time. Presently he turned back, and I walked on through the dying light with the smell of peat heavy and sweet about me. It was now that the kelp carts, which I had seen in the square in Galway, began overtaking me with the drivers calling out in Irish, as they passed. That night I stayed at a house recommended by O'Briain, and in the morning found that I was looking over the sea to the Aran Islands. I continued my walk through an increasingly beautiful and wild landscape of blue loughs and small, white cabins, each with its stack of turf as large as itself, until I came to the other house recommended to me, that of the painter, Charles Lamb. Here I was kindly entertained for a night or two, by which time it was New Year's Eve. There was a girl staying with the Lambs, and after supper we went out to see the hundreds of candles shining from the windows of the cabins around the loughs and beaches. This was the crofters' way of seeing the New Year in and of indicating to whatever spirits were abroad that there was a welcome within. The next day, it being time to return, I caught a bus back to Galway. Everyone in the bus was speaking Irish.

Alas, unheeded by me the European situation was deteriorating fast. After settling down in Chirk I was approached by one of the members of Toc H, who informed me that my predecessor had been their chaplain, and they hoped that I would follow suit. This entailed among other things giving them an occasional talk. As the threat of war increased, I had been reading a booklet by Hewlett Johnson, the "red" Dean of Canterbury, about the evils of capitalism and its wars. Fired by this, I gave Toc H a talk based mainly on this booklet, which was enthusiastically received. A day or two later happening to mention to my vicar how much I agreed with Johnson, I was met with the curt command: "Don't you preach that stuff here." This was my awakening to the general attitude of the Church to war between states, an attitude completely contrary to the teaching of Christ, who was that most unpopular creature in most circles, a pacifist.

The war came, and in 1940 Elsi and I decided to marry. I now learned that the Vicar did not want a married curate, so I had to look for a curacy with a house attached. I became Curate in Charge of Tallarn Green in the parish of Hanmer, and woke up one morning to see the Welsh hills fifteen miles away over the flat country of Flintshire. I was now farther away from the real Wales than ever.

It was while we were in this house that the Luftwaffe attacks on British cities began. Every evening after dark on suitable nights the droning of approaching aircraft would be heard, to be followed later by the sound of bombs being dropped on Merseyside, some fifteen to twenty miles away. I'm afraid I didn't set my new wife a fine example of male steadfastness. Apart from the physical apprehension of having these killers overhead, the thought that they were going to drop their loads on defenceless people in the towns and the senselessness of it all worried me. Standing in the doorway with Elsi one night, looking towards the red glow over Merseyside, I felt the wind from the bomb blast move through my hair and saw her skirt stir. Another night, unwilling to face the barrage to the Mersey approaches, the planes began circling overhead, and some released their bombs and land-mines. Happening to look out of an upstairs window, I heard a bomb whistling down quite close, but there was no explosion. The next day it was discovered that it had plunged into the ground within a couple of yards of a corrugated iron cabin, where two old people were asleep, without going off or so much as waking them.

Partly from a cowardly wish to get away from this in a place where I did not belong, but more from a desire to have the whole of Wales open to me, I began to take Welsh lessons. I discovered a teacher in Llangollen, and used to go over once a week, while Elsi was

Rectory at Manafon where Thomas was appointed Rector in 1942

holding an art class nearby. Still progress was slow, and I was quite unready to take over a Welsh parish. Presently, however, a benefice in the Montgomeryshire hill country fell vacant, and through the influence of my former vicar, I was appointed Rector of Manafon at the age of twenty-nine.

During my return by train from theological college to Caergybi I used to pass through the Welsh border country. Since it was an evening train, I used to see the Welsh hills outlined darkly against the after-glow in the west. My imagination was stirred, and I thought of lonely farms and dark-faced people, and a past of strife and bloodshed. Although it was no longer Welsh-speaking, Manafon was situated among such hills. It was in a river valley, with a church, a school, a pub, and a post office, and farms scattered along the hillsides. The rectory was on the banks of the stream, the Rhiw, which rose in the moorland about ten miles to the west. It was thick with trout, which gladdened my father's heart, when I told him. Seeing the clouds at dusk scudding along the edge of the hill made me feel that at least I was back within reach of where I wanted to be. The farms nearly all had Welsh names, as did the parishioners, but the language had not been used in church since the first World War.

The harsh simplicity of the life fascinated me. In 1942 it was still largely unmechanised. One grey autumn afternoon, coming away from a hilltop farm I had been visiting, I saw the farmer's brother in the fields, docking swedes. I came back home and wrote "A Peasant," the first of my poems about Iago Prytherch, my symbol of the hill farmer. During the war Keidrych Rhys had revived his magazine *Wales*. The Anglo-Welsh movement had come to life again as a result of Welsh people's experiences in the forces. Thrown together with English and other servicemen, some of the Welsh became very conscious of their difference, and the writers among them articulated these feelings. Under the stimulus of this movement I wrote several poems, deliberately choosing Welsh names and places to emphasise the fact that, although I wrote in English, I was really Welsh.

The parishioners had more to teach me than I them. They were hard, hard-working and narrow, with the crude wisdom of workers on the land. Theirs was mixed farming, so they had little time for cultural pursuits. The Vicar of Chirk had warned me against preaching at them about cruelty to animals and such like. Any of my enthusiastic expressions about the beauty of the surrounding country were met with faint smiles, half-amused, half-cynical. Yet they loved the land in their way, and were prepared to talk about it for hours, when I visited them of an evening. One of the subjects to avoid was religion! They liked to entertain the Rector and his wife to supper, and after a farm meal and a talk by a wood fire, it was an adventure to walk back down over the fields to the Rectory below, where the river glittered under the moon or stars, and murmured of other things, or surged wildly by in full spate. "I wonder if it comes into the cellar?" I asked one day during flood water. I opened the cellar door, as I spoke, and there it was almost to the top of the steps. I shut the door quickly on it, as though it were a wild beast.

March was the time for lambing, and from the house at night I could see lights in the fields, as the farmers moved about with their lanterns among the ewes. Sometimes, visiting them, I would find an orphan lamb in a box by the kitchen fire, white as fresh snow. The war was far away, and being farmers the men had not been called up. I preached about farming as an innocent vocation, and of nature as part of the economy of God. I became obsessed with the importance of small communities and the worth of the individual, however insignificant; that is, with the small farmer in his few acres. They listened to me or half nodded off to sleep.

Llangollen was too far away for me to continue my Welsh lessons. I discovered there was a Welsh chapel on the hill between Manafon and the next valley to the north. I began visiting the minister, H.D. Owen, and his wife Megan. They were kind and put up with my stumbling efforts to speak Welsh. Gradually I improved, but progress was still slow. I attended meetings and concerts and preaching festivals to gain practice, but it meant that I always had to leave the parish to do so, and as petrol was rationed, it meant many journeys on foot. No wonder it took years.

As the end of the war came in sight, Elsi expressed her desire to bear a child. I had never really given the possibility much thought, but so it was, and in 1945 a son, Gwydion, was born. "Now Gwydion was the best storyteller in all the world," as the Mabinogion has it. In order that I should go on writing and Elsi painting, a nurse-help was obtained, and Elsi started art classes in the neighbouring towns to help pay her. But Gwydion proved to be a poor sleeper; so, unable to expect the nurse to be with him day and night, Elsi and I took it in turns to sleep with him. By the time he was three he had improved, and the nurse departed. But she had been a help, more so through her little boy, who though somewhat older than Gwydion, often minded him and played with him. The proximity of the unfenced river was a worry, and when it was running

Elsi with Gwydion, age two and a half, beside Afon Rhiw at Manafon, about 1947

high, carrying all manner of debris by like goods trains, we had many anxious moments.

Manafon was a cold place. Five hundred feet up and yet down in a valley bottom, it incurred severe frosts. Most memorable was the bad winter of 1946–47. It began suddenly on 23 January 1947. The wind changed and it began to snow. The east wind drove up the valley, and since the drive to the Rectory ran north and south, it was soon full of six feet of snow. When the snow stopped, I began digging my way to the village, while some of the villagers dug from their end, so that I had a narrow passage to the main road. But for nine weeks I was unable to take the car out. The east wind blew tirelessly, and the poor farm women had to battle into it over the fields to give the hens their food. There came tales of the moorland farmers walking miles down to the nearest village to buy bread. At night, out visiting some of my own farmers, I nearly got lost sometimes on my way home owing to the uniform whiteness and absence of landmarks. Sometimes on clear nights with the stars sharp as glass, the temperature fell dramatically, one night reaching −10° Fahrenheit, 42 degrees of frost, which was as cold as anywhere in Britain. That night I was aware of the house cracking and grieving as the frost tightened its grip. Gwydion was still not two, and much time was spent

Thomas with Gwydion, about three years old, at Manafon Rectory

entertaining him, since it was too cold for him to go out. The arrival of Roy, the nurse's little boy home from school, signalled by a snowball thrown at the window, was always a welcome event. Needless to say the river froze pretty well solid, and when the thaw came there were loud cracks as large sheets of ice reared up before being carried away like large pieces of masonry on the surging brown flood.

Being far from the sea, Manafon was not affected by salt winds, so the leaves often stayed long on the trees in autumn. With the red of the cherries, the russet of the birches and the yellow of the ash, the valley could be very colourful in late October, provided no severe frosts occurred prematurely, as they could do. At·the entrance to the Rectory drive there was an enormous ash. One year the leaves stayed longer than usual; but at last a sharp frost came during the night. Next morning, as the sun reached them the leaves began to fall. This they did for about two hours, so that it

was like a huge golden fountain continually playing.

The years passed. I kept an eye on the Church in Wales papers to see what Welsh-speaking parishes were vacant. Some vacancies happened from time to time, of course, but somehow they were never quite what suited both of us. Then in 1953 I saw a notice in a daily paper to the effect that a bird observatory was being opened on Ynys Enlli, Bardsey Island. The name of the secretary was given as William Condry of Eglwysfach. We went over to visit him and his wife, Penny, and a friendship began. We arranged to visit the observatory the following August. We were warmly advised to call on the Keatings on our way to Aberdaron. These were three unmarried sisters, who lived in Rhiw in the Lleyn peninsula. This we eventually did, and made new friends.

After our stay on Bardsey, we had not been long back, when Bill Condry wrote to say that their vicar was retiring, and why not be the new one? I wrote to the Bishop, indicating my interest in the parish, and somewhat to my surprise received a letter back offering me the benefice. So in October 1954 after twelve-and-a-half years among the Montgomeryshire farmers, we moved over to Eglwysfach, a small roadside parish just inside the Ceredigion border. This was rather inconvenient for Elsi, who was halfway through an extensive mural painting for the Orthopaedic Hospital in Gobowen. But she coped in her usual competent way. Although I had not known beforehand, Eglwysfach was a very different parish from Manafon. It was rural and had farms, but there were also a number of residential houses containing retired tea-planters, ex-army officers, a small preparatory school as well as a village school, and the villagers themselves, mostly Welsh, but many of them married to English women. There were Welsh services every Sunday and Welsh was spoken in the parish, but the emphasis was on the English Sunday morning service, which was far better attended. The River Dyfi flowed down the northern boundary of the parish and was tidal bringing salt water in daily from the sea about five miles to the west. All this, I felt, had been a step in the right direction. The country was very beautiful. The hills came close to the main road, and valleys ran up into them down which clear torrents poured over the boulders. The whole district was excellent for birds, and because of the estuary and its salt marsh provided species which there had been no hope of seeing in Manafon.

The different congregation called for different approaches. Many of them especially parents visiting their children at preparatory school, were better educated than the Manafon farmers. But as at the English services I always had thirty-or-so young boys, I had to make myself interesting and intelligible to them, too. So twelve years in Manafon and twelve-and-a-half in Eglwysfach trying to make myself clear had its effect on my poetry. That also was straightforward; rarely clever or obscure; perhaps overexplicit at times.

Before leaving Manafon I had met James Hanley, the novelist, who was living in the north of the county. Finding that I had not yet been published in London, he undertook to correct this and introduced my work to Rupert Hart-Davis. By the time we moved, Rupert had accepted a collection of verse, got John Betjeman to write an introduction to his new poet, and invited me up to London to meet John, that engaging man-about-town, who invited me to breakfast at his flat in Cloth Fair.

One of the attractions in prospect at Eglwysfach had been its proximity to the National Library of Wales and the University at Aberystwyth. But after one or two perfunctory visits to the former, and a dull lecture at the latter, I reverted to my old habits of preferring to be out-of-doors rather than in the stale air of library or lecture room. Bill Condry was a naturalist and a member of the Kite Protection Committee. After a while I, too, became a member, which meant going out and about the lower end of the county in April to find as many nests as possible, and keep a record of their progress. It was a real joy to explore the small oak woods in spring, with tree-pipits, redstarts and pied-flycatchers singing in them, and to discover a large, fork-tailed raptor sailing in the sky above. Through the activities of the Kite Committee the birds built up from only two or three pairs after the first World War to over a hundred birds on the wing by the 1970's. There was for me the added attraction that Wales was their only breeding area in Britain.

Eglwysfach was a parish of factions, and I had to be careful to keep a balance. There were two landowners, dividing the parish between them, Hubert Mappin and a retired major general, Lewis Pugh. Then there was the preparatory school. All employed parishioners, and all had their following. They were self-interested, but Mappin was generous and a good friend of the Church. But they tended to be jealous of each other, and there was always the possibility of friction, especially at meetings. Pugh, like many of his kind, could never forget his rank, and made a nuisance of himself. In Manafon I had grown tired of the crudity and narrowness of farmers, but at least they were extenuated by their lack of education. They had also provided me with material for poems. Some of the Eglwysfach people had had the advantage of education and travel, so there was less excuse for their jealousy and small-mindedness. They were material for slight novels rather than poetry, so I tended to revert to the Montgomery-

shire background for poetic inspiration. The only variation was a period of Welsh political unrest, which induced me to write several more explicitly patriotic poems.

Hubert Mappin's estate, Ynyshir, contained many interesting bird habitats including the Dyfi salt marsh, so Bill Condry and I persuaded him to declare it a sanctuary with no permission for shooting over it. His wife was my churchwarden, which was a help. Unfortunately he became terminally ill and our plans for getting him to covenant his estate with the National Trust were endangered. With the help of a kind friend, David Ormond, we were able to expedite matters, and Hubert signed the document within a day or two of his death. Bill and I had also been trying to interest the RSPB (Royal Society for the Protection of Birds) in the estate, and later Mrs. Mappin sold it to that society as Ynyshir Nature Reserve. Bill Condry, now well-known for his books on natural history, became its first warden.

In 1966 Bill and I went to Spain. I had been reading Guy Mountfort's *Portrait of a Wilderness,* a description of the Coto de Doñana in south Spain, and fascinated by the numbers of birds to be seen there, I persuaded Bill to accompany me. One morning in late April we said farewell to our wives and set off in my Mini Estate van bulging mainly with Bill's equipment; he was also a photographer. We had decided to skip culture by avoiding the towns and camping out in the country. I was fascinated by Spain, which had great atmosphere. Bill had already been to Africa and had seen many of the birds which were new to me. But southern Spain reminded him of that country. There was still no proper road to the Coto, so it was, indeed, a wilderness with its myriads of birds and mosquitos, wild cattle and wild boars, and sand gradually encroaching from the Atlantic coast. The time went all too quickly, and it hardly seemed that nearly a month had passed when we arrived back safely in Eglwysfach, having luckily experienced no trouble with the Mini after a journey of nearly three-thousand miles.

We had been in the habit of spending holidays in the Lleyn peninsula in one of the cottages on the Keatings' estate, and eventually they gave us a long life-tenancy of one of them. They were enthusiastic supporters of the National Trust and had already bequeathed this cottage, so that actually we became tenants of that body. When I heard that the parish of Aberdaron at the end of Lleyn had become vacant, it seemed a good idea to move there, if we could. But by now it was clear that Hubert Mappin was seriously ill, and I did not feel it would be right to leave. Luckily for me no candidate for the parish offered himself, so after

Mappin's death, I intimated my desire to the Bishop of Bangor, a different diocese, and again had my wish granted. I was offered the benefice, and in May 1967 moved into the vicarage, a large house on the slope above Aberdaron and only four miles from the cottage at Y Rhiw. The house was in the sun from morning till evening, but was consequently exposed to every wind that blew. The sea was visible half a mile away, and the summit of Bardsey island could be seen from my study window. With the wind and the sea and the strong sun and the herring gulls calling from the chimney pots, it was like a return home.

This move more or less coincided with a new direction for me in poetry. The last of my books from Hart-Davis' old firm came out the year following my move to Aberdaron. Rupert had retired and sold his firm, which had changed hands more than once since. I became dissatisfied with the new publishers, and was advised by Rupert to offer my next book to Macmillan, to whom several of the Hart-Davis staff had repaired. So my next book in 1972 came from that firm. In Eglwysfach I had continued to write about the Montgomeryshire hill country and its farmers, but having moved to Aberdaron I did not then write about Eglwysfach.

I began writing many different poems. I had said more or less all I had to say about hill farms, as well as about the Welsh situation. Manafon was un-Welsh. Eglwysfach, although more Welsh, was very much dominated by the English people who lived there. As a member of the so-called Anglo-Welsh school I had indulged in a certain amount of attitudinising, a kind of beating the breast and declaring: "I'm Welsh, see." But after reaching Aberdaron I found myself among a simple but kindly people, who had never spoken anything but Welsh, until the English visitors began arriving. In moving among them and speaking Welsh daily, I gradually lost any need to emphasise my Welshness, but settled down to be what I had always wished to be: a Welsh-speaking Welshman in a thoroughly Welsh environment. True, as a seaside parish Aberdaron was visited by an increasing number of English visitors, some of whom had cottages there. English services had long been provided for these, and unfortunately several of the Welsh came to these morning services and neglected their own evening service, as was the case in so many of the churches throughout Wales. The nonconformists were more loyal to their language. However my Sunday school was Welsh as was the primary school, and my two other churches in the district were monoglot Welsh.

Aberdaron was a twelfth-century church, situated uniquely on the seashore, with a sea wall to protect it from the high tides. In the period of Celtic Christianity it had been one of the mother churches of Wales, and had connections with the abbey on Bardsey, which was a place of pilgrimage in mediaeval times, three visits there being considered equal to one to Rome. At the Holy Communion service in the early morning the sea could be heard breaking on the sand outside, as it had done long before there was any church.

This was the atmosphere of the place, then: an area pervaded by memories of Celtic Christianity and pilgrims and still inhabited by Welsh speakers. But as if to introduce a tension there were the English tourists with their ice cream and newspapers and transistors, and as another emphasis of the twentieth century there was the roar of planes overhead as the Royal Air Force practised for the next war. But beyond this I became aware of a much older time-scale. It was, of course, satisfying to think of those early Christians, and to look at the Romanesque arch over the church door and the Pre-Reformation water stoup. But out at the end of the peninsula opposite Bardsey there were Pre-Cambrian rocks, which were anything up to a thousand million years old. The mind reeled. As I stood in the sun and the sea wind, with my shadow falling upon those rocks, I certainly was reminded of the transience of human existence, and my own in particular. As Pindar put it: "A dream about a shadow is man." I began to ponder more the being and nature of God and his relation to the late twentieth-century situation, which science and technology had created in the western world. Where did the ancient world of rock and ocean fit into an environment in which nuclear physics and the computer were playing an increasingly prominent part? Or how did the traditional world of Lleyn harmonise with the latest in technology?

Corresponding to the above subject matter, my poetry underwent a change of style. I broke up the lines and introduced more scientific or technological terms into my verse. It appeared that many of my readers, accustomed to thinking of me as a Welsh country poet, were unable to adjust to the new work, and, for all I know, still are. There was, of course, the occasional poem that reverted to former themes, but this was a tendency which could lead only to repetition and an appearance of exhaustion, so I found myself throwing the poem away, when I saw myself going back over old ground.

As long as I was a priest of the Church, I felt an obligation to try to present the Bible message in a more or less orthodox way. I never felt that I was employed by the Church to preach my own beliefs and doubts and questionings. Some people were curious to know whether I did not feel some conflict between my two vocations. But I always replied that Christ was a poet, that the New Testament was poetry, and that I had no difficulty in preaching the New Testament in its poetic context. The puzzlement comes in viewing what the so-called Christian makes of the message. In my first two parishes I felt a certain bitterness at the failure of the people to be worthy either of the beauty of their surroundings or of the Bible insights. In Aberdaron, with the growth of nuclear rivalry between the major powers and the increasing power of the multinationals, there was a growing feeling that the few inhabitants of the peninsula could hardly be blamed for the world situation. Apart from the need to preach Sunday sermons, therefore, the tendency was for me to become more absorbed with my own spiritual and intellectual problems and to see what poetry could be made from them. And the ever-present background was the sea. Beneath that smiling surface, what horrors! And as if conscious of the grotesques within it, the sea would sometimes become wildly agitated. With the wind west-nor-west often the spray would be whipped up higher than the summit of Bardsey, which was 548 feet. I became obsessed with the mirror image, comparing the sea now to a window, now to a looking-glass. Several poems were on this theme.

Elsi became seriously ill in 1969, and there followed a long convalescence, never back to full health unfortunately. In an effort to give her something to look forward to after a spell in hospital in 1972, I arranged for us to visit Mallorca in the autumn. I had never seen the Mediterranean before, and looking at its blue waters against the honey-coloured rocks, I was reminded that this was the sea that Aeneas and Odysseus had sailed, and my years of not very successful study of the Classics came back to me. I was impressed with a feeling of being back near the cradle of western culture.

In 1973 my mother died. Since my father's death in the Sailors' Hospital in Caergybi, she had lived alone, although surrounded by kind neighbours. I knew that she had hoped after my father's death to come and live with us. But I knew also that it would never work, so it was a case of being cruel to be kind. I used to go over to see her fairly regularly. Sometimes on the way back I would call on Charles Tunnicliffe, the bird painter, always to find him hard at work in his bungalow at Malldraeth on the Cefni estuary. Friends told me that although he had become blind before he died, he kept painting right up to the end without knowing what he was doing.

We had a large, roomy, if draughty, house at Aberdaron, and I loved the feeling of being right at the end of the peninsula, where I could slip out to the headland and watch the sea-birds migrating in spring and autumn, and sometimes the cetaceans, too. I was conscious that the cottage at Rhiw would be very con-

fining after the vicarage, and made inquiries about future plans for the parish, but nobody seemed to have any. There were other movements afoot in the Church in Wales at this time. The services were being revised and there were vague plans for reunion with the Nonconformists. Neither of these did I like, but would have been prepared to cope with them reluctantly in return for staying on in the Vicarage. So with my sixty-fifth birthday in sight, I wrote to the Bishop to say that, if he did not intend appointing a successor, I would be prepared to stay on and do voluntary duty for the sake of the house. Receiving only an inconclusive reply, I wrote back giving the necessary six-months' notice of resignation, and immediately after Easter 1978 we retired to the cottage at Rhiw.

I had, of course, been making some sort of contingency plans, and with the consent of the National Trust had added a room to the original cottage to act as a bed-sitting study for myself, leaving Elsi in her small room at the other end of the house. But we had to get rid of most of our things. The walls of the vicarage had been covered with Elsi's paintings; but the cottage walls, consisting mainly of boulders, made this impossible. Of our three-thousand-plus books, we gave over half to Gwydion, keeping what we hoped would be most needed by us. The Rhiw stone is a dolerite outcrop and very heavy. Some of the boulders in the walls of the cottage are enormous and must weigh about a ton. One wonders how the original builders got them into place. The cottage itself is approaching four-hundred-years old, and stands on a slope overlooking Porth Neigwl, or Hell's Mouth, as the English maps have it because of its bad reputation in the last century. Once running in before a south-westerly gale, sailing ships found it very difficult to get out again. It was out over this bay I now found myself gazing day and night. Sometimes, when it was calm, there would be a sudden crackling, followed by a long rush of water, as the swell from the far-off Atlantic came in and spent itself on the sand. On clear days to the southeast Cadair Idris could be seen, and from a few paces down the garden, Yr Wyddfa, Snowdon, was visible forty miles to the northeast.

There was now more time than ever to read and to ponder some of the themes of my later poetry: the being and nature of God as presented to the twentieth century; the mystery of time, and the assault of contemporary lifestyles on the beauty and peace of the natural world. Apart from the overindustrialised south, Wales, though small, is of a beauty to bring tears to the eyes, and I am familiar with most of her special places, her moorlands and mountains and rushing torrents. I have always claimed that, if someone blindfolded me in some other country and brought me back by night and

R. S. Thomas outside Sarn-y-Plas

removed the bandage, I would know I was in Wales by the dark shape of a hill looming up before me and the sound of running water. But if pressed to name the pick of Welsh scenery, I think I would always choose the country between Beddgelert and Maentwrog for its hills and rocks, its birch trees and hurrying streams.

The problem I have always had difficulty in coming to terms with is the majesty and mystery of the universe and the natural world as a kind of symbol of God over against the domesticating urge in man. To kneel in my furnished room with its chairs and books, and then to look out and see Orion and Sirius rising above the bay makes it difficult to hold the two in proportion. I know that mind in the case of exceptional human beings is capable of a range beyond Orion. I know also that my experience of human nature has been restricted both intellectually and emotionally, so that it is man's urge to domesticate and exploit nature that I have been most conscious of. I acknowledge the validity of the mystics' claim to know God immediately; but it would seem that the deity has chosen to mediate himself to me via the world, or even the universe, of nature. I realise, therefore, that, because I have chosen the love of created things, I may not have reached the highest state possible to a human here on earth, but must be content with the fact that that is the sort of poet I am.

Although I live in a secluded and beautiful part of Wales, the peace is shattered most days by jet aircraft practising overhead. But it is not just they that disturb my peace. They are a reminder of the uneasy peace that exists between east and west, and of the fact that if war were to break out, it would inevitably deteriorate into nuclear holocaust, which really makes it impossible to sit back and contemplate one's navel. This is not just from fear for my own skin, but I have a son and a grandson, like most other people. And there is the thought of all the wonderful and innocent forms of life that would be charred to ashes, if the worst should happen.

Soon after I retired, a branch of the Campaign for Nuclear Disarmament was started in Pwllheli to embrace the peninsula and beyond. I joined and soon became a committee member and representative to the county movement. With Wales as a supposedly nuclear-free country, this has involved me in considerable activity, and much ground has been covered with, alas, too little fruit. But once in, one can scarcely withdraw from a cause which seems so categorically sane and just. We seem to be winning the argument and losing the struggle.

This has been a dull autobiography. To have dealt

more with the Welsh side of my life would not have been possible through the medium of English. It is kitchen talk. I have moved in unimportant circles, avoiding, or being excluded from the busier and more imposing walks of life. I was rarely happy in numerous company, and kept out of literary circles. I have always had a bad memory for what I have read, and in the presence of better and more knowledgeable talkers would have had to remain silent. It appears that some people are always anxious to meet poets, but in most cases they will be disappointed by the contrast between the man and his work. If I remember rightly it was Keats who warned that a poet is the most unpoetic of men. Was it a slight gift of Keats' negative capability that made it often so difficult for me to believe in my separate, individual existence? Certainly it has come to me many times with a catch in the breath that I don't know who I am. I do know, however, more from intuition than experience, that there are countless more intelligent, more able, better travelled people in the world than I, whose autobiographies would be a thousand times more interesting. It is just that I developed a small talent for turning my limited thoughts and experience and meditation upon them into verse that caused me to be asked to tell you something about my life.

BIBLIOGRAPHY

Poetry:

The Stones of the Field. Carmathen, Wales: Druid Press, 1946.

An Acre of Land. Newtown, Wales: Montgomeryshire Printing Co., 1952.

The Minister. Newtown, Wales: Montgomeryshire Printing Co., 1953.

Song at the Year's Turning: Poems 1942-1954. London: Hart-Davis, 1955.

Poetry for Supper. London: Hart-Davis, 1958; Chester Springs, Pa.: Dufour, 1961.

Judgement Day. London: Poetry Book Society, 1960.

Tares. London: Hart-Davis, 1961; Chester Springs, Pa.: Dufour, 1961.

Penguin Modern Poets 1, with Lawrence Durrell and Elizabeth Jennings. Harmondsworth, England: Penguin, 1962.

The Bread of Truth. London: Hart-Davis, 1963; Chester Springs, Pa.: Dufour, 1963.

Pietà. London: Hart-Davis, 1968.

Not That He Brought Flowers. London: Hart-Davis, 1968.

Pergamon Poets I, with Roy Fuller, edited by Evan Owen. Oxford, England: Pergamon, 1968.

The Mountains. New York: Chillmark House, 1968.

H'm: Poems. London: Macmillan, 1972; New York: St. Martin's, 1972.

Young and Old (for children). London: Chatto & Windus, 1972.

Selected Poems: 1946-1968. London: Hart-Davis, MacGibbon, 1973; New York: St. Martin's, 1974.

What Is a Welshman? Llandybie, Wales: Christopher Davies, 1974.

Laboratories of the Spirit. London: Macmillan, 1975; Boston: Godine, David, 1976.

The Way of It. Sunderland, England: Ceolfrith Press, 1977.

Frequencies. London: Macmillan, 1978.

Between Here and Now. London: Macmillan, 1981.

Later Poems: A Selection. London: Macmillan, 1983.

Poet's Meeting. Stratford-upon-Avon, England: Celandine, 1983.

Ingrowing Thoughts. Bridgend: Poetry Wales, 1985.

Nonfiction:

Words and the Poet. Cardiff: University of Wales Press, 1964.

Selected Prose, edited by Sandra Anstey. Bridgend: Poetry Wales, 1983.

Editor of:

The Batsford Book of Country Verse. London: Batsford, 1961.

The Penguin Book of Religious Verse. Harmondsworth, England: Penguin, 1963.

Selected Poems, by Edward Thomas. London: Faber, 1964.

A Choice of George Herbert's Verse. London: Faber, 1967.

A Choice of Wordsworth's Verse. London: Faber, 1971.

John Wain

1925-

John Wain, 1985

The invitation to write this essay comes at an auspicious time, since I signed the contract to do so on my sixtieth birthday, very much a point at which people take stock. When I look back over my life and work, the strongest overall impression I get is one of unity amid diversity. I have pursued certain goals and valued certain qualities very consistently; my basic opinions have been modified and adjusted here and there but never altered out of recognition; my interests at the age of twenty, and for that matter at the age of ten, were chiefly literary, and so they are today. I still have many of the friends I made forty or even fifty years ago, and still go often to the same places to which I went often then. On the other hand, within that framework, I have gone for diversity. My friends do not all come from the same social class or the same nationality or the same psychological type. I try to keep an open texture to my life so that the wind may blow through it from many quarters.

Above all, as a writer I have regarded my basic material as the word rather than as this or that literary form. I am the opposite of those novelists who write only novels, those poets who write only poetry and the criticism of poetry, those playwrights who write only plays, those biographers who write only biographies. The first book I published was a book of poems. The first that brought me to public attention and provided me with a reputation by means of which I could make a living was a novel. The most successful work of my middle life, which saved me from bankruptcy in my late forties, was a biography. The only question I decline to answer in interviews (and it always comes up) is what I consider myself to be "primarily." I am always primarily what I am doing at the moment. Are Thomas Hardy's novels better than his poems? Which part of his output is "primary"?

I was born in the spring of 1925 in the city of Stoke-on-Trent, Staffordshire, England. Both season and place were significant. I have always been happier and more energetic in the spring than in any other season of the year, and have a preference for fresh green shoots and new beginnings; I detest autumn with its continual reminder that yet another year is going down into the morass of winter. As for the city of Stoke-on-Trent, it has played such a part in my life that it is very much a character in my story, and perhaps should be introduced first.

Young John with teddy bear, about 1928

Stoke-on-Trent, with some quarter of a million inhabitants, is one of the big cities of the English Midlands, nothing like so big as Birmingham, but about on a level with Nottingham or Leicester or Derby. Like them, it is devoted to manufacture, being the centre of the British pottery industry, but it lags behind them in social and historical prestige. Most people there have always been poor (wages in the pottery trade have traditionally been low) and it has in consequence been poorly served with the arts and amenities, except for music, of which there is a strong local tradition. It has

very little history. Up to the end of the eighteenth century, when the genius and energy of Josiah Wedgwood inaugurated the pottery industry, it was a string of six insignificant villages, and even in my father's boyhood, after growing at the pace of a Klondike for a hundred years, it still consisted of six smallish towns—Longton, Fenton, Stoke, Hanley, Burslem, and Tunstall—each with its Mayor and Corporation and its Town Hall. Federation finally came in 1910 and was, as readers of Arnold Bennett's *The Old Wives' Tale* will recall, a cataclysmic event in local history.

Situated at the point where the Pennine Hills run out into a rash of little bumps, the city is full of steep gradients, so that one is very often standing at a vantage point. The landscape is nowadays no more interesting than that of any other industrial town, but in my boyhood it still had its traditional appearance. The ware was fired in bottle-kilns that looked like giant burgundy bottles, and because the industry had grown up without any planning these were dotted about at random among the rows of terrace houses. The only source of energy, or for that matter of domestic heating, was coal, and smoke hung in clouds everywhere or travelled slowly across the sky. The result was ugly, but ugly in a dynamic, almost apocalyptic way ("dark Satanic mills") rather than the merely dispiriting monotonous ugliness of modern industrialism. There was also a dramatic juxtaposition of the industrial at its most undisguised and the countryside at its most idyllic. North Staffordshire is a fertile farming area, and since the city was not prosperous enough to have suburbs the country came very close to the factory walls. One could stand amid a scene of unbelievable dirt and ugliness and know that within a couple of miles there were tranquil fields and lanes, dotted with patches of woodland, a couple of miles on either side, what was more, because the city was a long narrow streak measuring some ten miles by two. If one had the humblest means of transport, such as a bicycle or even a stout pair of legs, the city was never claustrophobic.

These circumstances fixed in my mind before I was ten years old two notions that are not entirely absent from it today: (1) that town life is physically unpleasant and jarring, though not necessarily boring, and that country life is pleasant and comely; (2) that the best place for anyone who wishes to live a full and satisfying life is somewhere that maintains a balance between the two. This is the reason why today I make my home, and have done so for the past quarter-century, at Wolvercote, on the edge of the City of Oxford and overlooking Port Meadow and the River Thames.

In Stoke-on-Trent, as in other hilly cities, the better houses tend to be at the tops of the hills and the worse ones at the bottom. I was born at 44 James

Stoke-on-Trent, industrial background

Street, a house still very much as it was then, standing halfway up an extremely steep hill. My father had been born in the depressing huddle of houses down at the bottom; his first home with my mother had been there, but soon they had bought a house in one of the streets that began to creep up the foothills of the city's high ground. The James Street house was their next stage, and when I was three years old they moved all the way up the hill and bought the large and well-situated house, on the brow of a hill looking out over the countryside, that remained their home until they were near the end of their lives and I was in my later thirties.

Both my father and my mother were very influential on me, and the reason lay partly in their personalities and partly in their social origins. Both were born in the 1890s before society became mobile under the influence of new kinds of economic freedom and the changes brought about by the motor-car, and so each represented the attitudes of a social class and type in a pure, clearly outlined form, which would not be the case if they had been born twenty years later.

My mother came from a background of artisan wage-earning and small trade. Her father, who had been brought up in dire poverty in Mow Cop, a hillside village in South Cheshire, had managed to get himself apprenticed as a printer and this was the occupation he followed. He spent most of his working life in the employ of G.T. Bagguley, an internationally known bookbinder. (Some of Arnold Bennett's letters are to G.T. Bagguley, who supplied him with specially

bound notebooks.) The printing side of the firm had no such high reputation, being merely a local jobbing printing press very much of the kind described by Bennett himself in *Clayhanger,* but no doubt the same decent standards of craftsmanship applied in the one part of the business as in the other. My grandfather, at all events, developed that precise, careful attention to detail that was in those days the mark of the printer who handled the type with tweezers and corrected the proofs of what he set up. This generally thoughtful and reflective approach also came out in certain habits which I am tempted to call "scholarly," though he was quite uneducated. When he read a book, for instance, he wrote in a clear, careful hand a few lines summarizing his opinion of it, which he then slipped between the pages. For many years afterwards I used to happen on these slips of paper in books that had been part of our household, and thus came to know his opinion of many books that I did not have the opportunity of discussing with him, for he died when I was eighteen. He was interested in local history and used to take me for walks in my boyhood and point out local landmarks. His name was Edwin William Turner.

His wife, my grandmother, whose maiden name was Mary Beckett, was also Cheshire but rural where he was—not exactly urban, but coming from the depressed and impoverished fringe of an urban area. She came from healthy, rich farming country and grew up on a farm where, though the acres were few and money scarce, the food must have been good, for she was a hale, pink-cheeked woman far more robust than her rather gnomelike husband, whom she outlived by many years. She was cheerful and fond of company, enjoyed a good meal, and was at her best when sitting at a well-stocked table with her children and grandchildren about her. The more is the pity that she spent most of her life in fear of extravagance. My grandfather was very careful with money and never allowed his wife to spend even the smallest amount for which she could not account. To prevent her from living in idleness he bought a little shop, selling food and general groceries, and this became the family home. Every week he would sit down with my grandmother and go carefully through the expenses and earnings of the shop and, for good measure, the household accounts as well. This dour regime forced my grandmother to be more strict than she would have been by nature, not only with herself but with her children, who were not, for example, allowed to put both butter and syrup on a piece of bread; it had to be one or the other. Once when my mother was a toddler, perhaps aged three or four, she had been out with her mother to get some milk in a can (it did not, in those days, come in bottles or cartons) and on the way back she was allowed to carry the can, but unfortunately she stumbled and upset the milk on the pavement. My grandmother, in her agitation at the thought that those few pence would have to be spent again and that the inevitable unpleasantness would follow at the weekly bookkeeping, lost her temper and smacked the child severely, which left to herself she would never have done.

My mother's background, then, was cautious, disciplined, rather drably respectable, and with no sunlit dimension except what came from her mother's rural origins, which were a source of anecdotes and personalities and seemed to point to a larger, more bountiful (though still hardworking) way of life. In particular my grandmother would speak fondly of a family named Beech, to whom she was in some way related. They were in a better way of business than her own parents, their farm was larger and employed a fair number of hands, and my grandmother harked back often in nostalgic love and yearning to certain times when they had all—cousins, uncles and aunts, old and young—been assembled at the hospitable board of "Aunt Beech"; she made Aunt Beech's house sound like Dingley Dell, not that she ever read *Pickwick*.

The Beech family even had a branch that transcended the ordinary Cheshire yeomanry and abutted on the minor aristocracy; it included someone called Sir Barrington Beech, though whether he was a knight or a baronet I do not know. My grandmother was very proud to be related to someone who could put "Sir" before his name, but it was an innocent, childlike pride, totally free of ordinary snobbishness, and I never re-

Infant John, age five months, with his mother, Anne, and her parents, Edwin and Mary Turner

member her saying anything that could be taken as meaning that she actually knew this luminary or had ever set eyes on him. But the reason why my middle name is "Barrington" is because in 1925, after I was safely born and had been equipped for life with the plain, straightforward name of "John," my parents thought I ought to have a middle name but nothing suggested itself, so my grandmother filled the gap by pointing out that "Barrington" would testify to the fact that I was related, however distantly, to a good family. I was accordingly given that name, which has been quite useless to me; no one has ever called me by it, and I have had to fill it in on thousands of official forms at an incalculable waste of time and energy; needless to say I never met Sir Barrington Beech or any member of the Beech family, who are unaware that for sixty years I have portaged the name of one of their number through the world because of my grandmother's admiration for them and her happy memories of the kindly Victorian figure of "Aunt Beech."

I realize that in writing of my mother I have tended to approach her through her parents, but that is because they were both people of decided personality and she, as a girl, is shadowy and indeed remained somewhat shadowy always. She was sensitive, easily wounded, bewildered and daunted by the harsh discipline under which she had to live, as if by coming into the world she had committed a crime and had been sent to prison in consequence. Photographs show a beautiful, delicate face with a flowing abundance of dark brown hair, but the effect is made sad by the frightened eyes that look out. She was clever, but no one took much trouble to encourage her cleverness or make her feel glad of it. She won a scholarship to secondary school when she was eleven, and happily set about absorbing everything they put in front of her, rapidly taking her first steps in French and Latin and mathematics; but in less than a year her twelfth birthday came along, and at twelve it was no longer legally binding to keep one's child at school, so my grandfather withdrew her. It was time for her to go out and work at a job and bring some money into the house; she ate food, didn't she, and wore out clothes, and sat by fires that cost money? So she closed her books and went to work, and the only work they could find for her was as nursemaid in a large unruly family, not the best work for a shy, sensitive girl, and after that she was a shop-assistant and had to work till seven o'clock every night except Saturdays, when she worked till ten; and after a year or so of this she became debilitated and anaemic and fell ill and the doctor came and attended to her, and after she was well enough to get up and go to work her father deducted the amount of the doctor's bill from her poor little wages.

When she was seventeen or eighteen she fell in love, and that strong magic might have irradiated her life and changed everything, but the 1914-18 war broke out, and her sweetheart was taken from her to a place of mud and blood and barbed wire and there turned into a corpse and finally to a name on a memorial; and in some deep sense I believe that was the end of my mother's life. She did not actually die till she was sixty-nine years old, but for much of that time she seemed to be not so much living as going through the motions.

A lifetime thus spent was made possible, largely, by the fact that she married a man of unusual vitality who coped zestfully with life and made it possible for her to sink into the background and have very little contact with people. My father deserves an essay to himself, and indeed I have devoted one to him in my book *Dear Shadows,* where he is featured under his first name, "Arnold," in a chapter of that title. My account here will be more objective, less concerned with the essence of the man than with the lesser matter of his influence on myself.

It will be seen that my mother's parentage and ancestry contributed markedly to that mixed, variegated quality which in my opinion has characterized my life and work. It put me in touch—if only by presenting them as realities to my nascent mind—with the world of Cheshire smallholding and dairy-farming and all that it stood for, with the world of G.T. Bagguley and all that that stood for, with Mow Cop and everything that that stood for (it was the scene, in the early nineteenth century, of the biggest camp meeting ever known in English popular religion, when a character named Hugh Bourne launched Primitive Methodism,

a form of Christianity that still survives), and, at the other extreme, with the exalted Sir Barrington Beech. But it was dull, uniform, and regular compared with the violent contrasts that my father brought with him into our family tradition.

My father's profession was dentistry, and he was successful at it if we are to judge from the fact that he built up his practice, starting from nothing, into one of the biggest in the English Midlands, with himself and two assistants working full blast. But it would be a mistake to try to form an impression of him by starting from what dentists tend to be like nowadays. A modern dentist has to undergo a long and arduous period of training which is, *mutatis mutandis,* the same as that of any other medical man. His step-by-step climb towards qualification is much the same as that of any other middle-class professional. My father, by contrast, battled his way up from barefoot poverty and learnt the skills of dentistry in the school of experience. His rise from poverty to comparative affluence was very rapid. At ten years old he was a poor boy in the slums, at twenty a rising young professional man, and at thirty, by our local standards, prosperous and solidly established.

It will be asked how my father, who did not retire from dentistry until 1958, was allowed to practise without the necessary qualifications. The answer lies in the humane application of a law which was passed by Parliament in 1921. This decreed that although from that time on no one could enter the profession who was not at least a Licentiate of Dental Surgery, an unqualified dentist who had been in practice continuously for seven years would be permitted to go on; the idea being, evidently, that if the man had been reliable and harmless enough to attract patients who came back to him regularly and kept him in business for seven years, he was unlikely to be doing much harm. These dentists were known as The 1921 Men, and there were still a few about in my twenties and thirties, though not many; the rule that a 1921 Man had to have been in practice for seven years in a straight line was enough to eliminate most of the younger men who had been called for service in 1914-18. My father was rejected for military service; the malnutrition and wretched housing of his childhood years had severely damaged his health, and, though he later recovered it fully, the recruiting doctors in 1914 did not consider him likely to make a fit soldier. He chose that year to set up his own dental practice, which, as it turned out, gave him the magic seven years in 1921.

He did not, of course, simply take it into his head to set up as a dentist and go out and buy a brass plate. He had served an apprenticeship, starting at the age of seventeen, with a local dentist who ran an unpretentious side-street practice. Every English grocery shop stocks a condiment called Sarson's Malt Vinegar, and every time I buy a bottle of this stuff I think of my father's early years, for the dentist who employed him bore that name. My father had three elder brothers and one of them, Maurice, had already been taken on as an apprentice by Sarson; Maurice put in a word for his younger brother and my father followed him, first into Sarson's practice and then into independence.

Such instruction as Sarson offered his apprentices was evidently quite rudimentary: how to extract a tooth, having first injected the patient with a cocaine-based drug called No-Pain; how to fill a tooth, doing the drilling with a foot-operated "dental engine"; that would be about it. At the age of seventeen my father was sent to run a branch surgery some miles away. There was no telephone. Whatever emergencies arose, he was on his own. He had to grow up quickly, to find confidence from somewhere, to inspire confidence in his patients, to cope with the unforeseen. It must have been a fiendishly difficult life, but the alternative was to go back to poverty and a dead-end job (he had been an errand-boy at Minton's factory, carrying messages from workshop to workshop). He had to manage somehow in his new situation. He managed.

At the time of my birth my father was thirty-one, so that he had been established in his own practice for twelve years, any threat of disqualification had long receded, and he was a respected local figure, already embarked on multitudinous activities in religious work (he was a lay preacher) and local government. He was an exceptionally able man and no one who came into contact with him failed to see him as such, whether they liked him or not. (Most people, in fact, did like him.) Over most of his life his income and standard of living were much higher than anything I have ever managed; he lived in a spacious, comfortable house with a large garden and as the years went by came to occupy in Stoke-on-Trent, which after all is a city of a quarter of a million inhabitants, a senior and respected position. He was a magistrate, and it still happens to me to meet police officers who remember his humane but no-nonsense manner in court. On the other hand he never shook off, nor made any particular effort to shake off, some attitudes characteristic of the poorest of the working class, attitudes he had formed in his first fifteen years or so. Nor did he ever quite overcome the disadvantage of being almost entirely uneducated—for the schooling that in the early years of this century came the way of boys like him was a wretched business and in any case ended at twelve. In argument, he never learned to state his position in a logical way, gaining assent at each step; he was dogmatic and assertive, battering down the opposition by the sheer

force of his personality, and this tended to spoil his case even when, owing to his good natural intelligence, he had understood the matter correctly and was in the right.

Another result of my father's upbringing among the very poor was that he had great sympathy with them. He was the exact opposite of those self-made men who say, "They can always do what I did," and despise them if they don't. He knew that poverty and bad housing and bad education drag people down, and

Father, Arnold A. Wain, age twenty-six

that it takes exceptional strength as well as exceptional ability to get up from the depths. His attitude towards the poor and unfortunate was a beautiful model of compassion, unsullied by any tincture of self-consciousness or self-congratulation. The obverse of this was his suspicious attitude towards anyone in authority and towards higher-ups generally. In childhood and youth he had had to suffer a good deal of cavalier treatment—brusqueness, impatience, half-attention—from people in authority in his world, such as hospital doctors, and to the end he was suspicious of, and potentially hostile to, anyone whom he considered to have had it easy, and been put in a position of power over their humbler fellow creatures merely because of their social origins. Though a Christian and a member of the Church of England, he disapproved of bishops and thought they ought not to live in palaces. Though a law-abiding citizen and a magistrate, he disapproved of the monarchy and always denied that the Royal Family worked hard or did anything useful.

Though not interested in politics and bored by its technicalities and intrigues, he was at heart a fairly standard type of working-class Socialist, and for years his favourite foreign country was the Soviet Union. This preference was not based on anything much in the way of knowledge of that country. In his busy life he had not read much history and was unacquainted with its complexities. All he knew was that the U.S.S.R. was a large country that had got rid of its aristocracy and royalty and called itself a workers' state, and this was enough for him. He read one book on Russia, Hewlett Johnson's *The Socialist Sixth of the World.* This came out at the height of the pro-Soviet wave of sentiment which began in 1941 when the Russians, finding themselves attacked by the Germans, were forced to defend themselves, and this made them technically our allies, though up to that point they had been selling oil to the Germans. My father believed what he read in Hewlett Johnson's book, which was simply a recycling of Stalinist propaganda, because Hewlett Johnson was a Christian clergyman (he was Dean of Canterbury) and also because of his own emotional need to admire the Soviet Union. In my mid-teens I went along with all this, and at seventeen my politics were a carbon copy of my father's, but since unlike him I was subjected to the inevitably disillusioning process of education, and in particular was taught to examine a man's evidence rather than his conclusions, I soon came to see that Hewlett Johnson would not do, and as revelation followed revelation about the actual nature of Soviet society, my enthusiasm for it cooled until the coolness was perceptible even to my father, from whom I would willingly have concealed it. Finally, in my mid-thirties, by which time he himself was well into his sixties, I dropped the mask and made a serious effort to convert him to what had become my view of Communism as practised in the Soviet Union and throughout its empire—that is, as a system that is not only a failure in itself, bringing its people no nearer to happiness and prosperity, but a threat to the rest of the world. I succeeded in dimming the blaze of his totally uncritical admiration for the U.S.S.R., but I doubt if it ever went out.

Uneducated as he was, my father respected books and bought a great many of them. There were many well-filled bookshelves in the house and, though the books were a mixed bunch, there was enough to provide a pasture for my young mind. My father tended to buy a book if he had heard of the author, and he had heard of Shakespeare, Dickens, Tennyson, R.L. Stevenson, the historian John Richard Green, Kenneth Grahame, Arnold Bennett, and, oddly enough, Bertrand Russell.

From my father, then, I derived a materially comfortable background (one of the reasons why I have never been obsessed with money is that I did not feel the bite of poverty in my formative years) and the presence of a powerful and original mind that was at once conventional and rebellious, at once respectable and subversive. Our level of income, and standard of living generally, were high, but in some ways our cultural and social expectations were very modest. I felt myself, as I grew up, to belong to the solid bourgeoisie and yet not to belong to it. Our household was liberally provided, and yet in some ways my parents never abandoned the frugal habits of the very poor. Though my father was always ready to give money away to charity or to anyone who had a hard-luck story, he considered it an impossible luxury to take a taxi if the buses were running, or to telephone long-distance without waiting for the cheap time, however urgent the call might be.

Another factor that during my growing years contributed to my sense of being suspended in mid-air, of not really having a social class to which I naturally belonged, was the simple fact of *where* we lived. Stoke-on-Trent is very much a working town and the overwhelming majority of its inhabitants belong to the traditional working class; that is, whatever their degree of skill and mastery, they tend to work with their hands and to perform physical tasks, and their work is less well paid than the work of those in the professions and business. This is true even now, in spite of the incessant social change of the last fifty years, but in the 1930s it was true in a very simple and levelling fashion. It was effectively a one-class town and if you did not belong to that class and signify your belonging by speech, clothing, preferences in food and amusements, and so forth, you were made to feel very strange and unwanted. Of course at the other end of the scale were the employers of this work-force, some of whom were very rich and most quite comfortable, but they tended to live out of town in country houses or in outer-suburban districts which they had virtually colonised, and belonged to a few clubs where they met their own kind. They sent their sons to fashionable boarding schools and in general lived in their own enclave which was difficult for outsiders to get into, not that my family ever tried. I could not identify with them in any way, but if I tried to identify with the working-class bulk of the population, I was brought up short by obvious differences that made them suspicious and hostile. Because we lived in a big house with a large garden, and ran two cars at a time when only a minority of the nation possessed even one, we were regarded in our neighbourhood as rich people, and this did not make my life any easier when it came to trying to find companionship in the world of local boys, a world to which I naturally needed to belong and which from the age of nine or ten onwards I made persistent efforts to penetrate. These efforts were sometimes met with active hostility and sometimes with what I might call passive hostility, an assumption that it was a kind of law of Nature that I could not be worth getting to know because I was a different sort of animal. I remember one boy telling me quite calmly, not particularly attacking me for it but merely stating an objective fact, that he went past our garden fence on his Sunday afternoon walks and considered that we had too much land for one house. This seemed to me even at the time—I was about ten—a neat example of the way I was tried and found wanting by a set of standards from which most people were exempted in one way or another. If the boy thought our house had too much land, what would he have thought of the estates of the Duke of Devonshire? But the fact is, of course, that people like the Duke of Devonshire did not come within his standards of measurement. They were too remote. I was not remote, and I suffered in consequence.

These problems diminished as I grew bigger, and finally disappeared altogether by the time I was about sixteen. This was because my range of acquaintanceship widened; in my teens I knew a good many youths whose background was similar to mine, and within this wider circle I found to my relief that people were accepted for what they were and that it was possible to behave naturally. Nevertheless, those early years were lonely and often difficult. The journey home from school each day, a large part of which I had to make on foot because of the inadequacies of the bus service, took me through a working-class district whose streets were always crowded with boys also on their way home from school, but a different kind of school from mine, with no telltale uniform and no school cap, and they were bursting with the pent-up energy and aggression of boys who have had to sit still in school for most of the day. Threading one's way through this territory was not a pleasant experience, and even if I had been a pugnacious boy with hard fists and plenty of fighting spirit, one pair of hard fists would have been no use against hundreds. Perhaps worst of all was that I had to bear the problem in utter silence. No boy likes to

admit to being bullied and persecuted because it involves the admission that others are stronger than he, and at home every boy likes to project himself as a success, invincible, and on the winning side.

Experience of any kind is rarely altogether useless, and those difficult years—between, say, eight or nine and thirteen—have left some marks on me that are not merely scars. The many friendly overtures I made towards boys of my own age, and the many rebuffs I had to endure, may be one reason why throughout my subsequent life I have valued friendship so highly and enjoyed it so much. Having friends, spending time with friends, sharing experiences with friends, building up a trusting and cordial relationship with friends, these things have been strong and abiding sources of pleasure to me and perhaps I enjoy them all the more because there was a time when it seemed to be impossible to make friends with anyone.

Other benefits are traceable too. Those horrible journeys home from school, dodging from one patch of shadow to the next on dark winter afternoons, hoping desperately to reach the sanctuary of our quiet cul-de-sac before the yell of the pack rose up, did at least instil in me a certain realism in social matters. Though over much of my life my opinions have been in many areas left-wing, I have never been tempted to share that sentimental idealization of the working class so common among middle-class Socialists, particularly those who

At the summit of Welsh hill, 1934

consider themselves "intellectuals" and usually come from a background in which direct contact with a working-class person was very rare, and then usually in some sanitized setting such as a political meeting. Long before I heard of Socialism or the class struggle, my experiences had made it impossible for me not to recognize that the working class, being human beings like any other, had their unpleasant and vindictive side and that this did not become any less true because they were being economically exploited, as in the 1930s was undeniably the case.

A third result of those early glimpses of violence and animosity has been my lifelong recoil from the notion of mob rule. Ardent theoretical revolutionaries who are always urging "the people" to take to the streets and claim their "rights" by a display of naked violence have never received any backing from me, nor, I suspect, from anyone who has met mob rule even in the mild and juvenile form in which I met it. To be so sentimentally attached to the notion of a yelling and stone-throwing mob, you have to be brought up in places where such mobs are never met with.

It was difficult, then, for me to make friends with boys of my own age until I grew bigger and more mobile, and the result was that my childhood properly so considered—from, say, five to twelve or thirteen—was rather solitary. I had, indeed, an elder sister, but there were seven years between us, and a twelve-year-old boy and a nineteen-year-old girl seldom have much to say to each other. When I was nine my parents presented me with a younger brother, but, once again, any kind of dialogue was years into the future. And so I was thrown very much on my own imaginative resources. I read a great deal, indiscriminately: Stevenson and

Dickens at one end, and at the other the ordinary boys' papers and adventure stories of the time, with a sprinkling of popular works on natural history, since I was very interested in animals and particularly in wildlife. Television, mercifully, had not been invented; I regard a childhood free from its baneful influence as one of the advantages I have enjoyed. Like all lonely children, I liked to tell myself stories, and as soon as I could write I began to sit at the kitchen table and write what were in effect novels—not romances of knights errant with giants and dragons, but realistic stories with contemporary settings and dialogue that was at any rate intended to sound like the way real people actually talk to each other. Some of them were school stories, others adventure stories whose hero was a detective called Smellum Owte.

But I am running a little ahead of my story, since, in order to write, I must have started school. My school education followed a normal pattern for my class, generation, and region. First I went for a year to a one-room school kept by the two daughters of the local vicar, who used a large room in the vicarage and no doubt did it to help with expenses. They were called the Misses Deacon, though of course we called them the Miss Deacons. They taught us to read and write in completely traditional fashion ("The cat sat on the mat"), and to do simple sums. This was what in earlier periods of English history would have been called a Dame School, and I am glad to have been at one. It links me with many generations of my forebears. The next school I went to, between the ages of six and nine, was a more up-market preparatory school favoured by the somewhat more prosperous local citizens. Here I

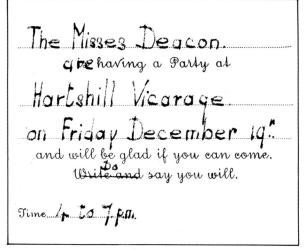

To John from the "Miss Deacons," 1930

had another experience that linked me with past generations, namely, being caned on the palm of the hand. It was done by the headmistress, using a slender cane, probably of hazel, from which the bark had been painstakingly stripped with a penknife. It made a thin red line at each stroke, which remained sore for a day or two; where two lines crossed there was a spot of more painful soreness which took longer to go. My offence was that I had made a disturbance on the bus on the way home.

I only have one happy memory of my three years at this school, and that was one dark afternoon towards the end of 1933. A freak blizzard swept across the British Isles, bringing phenomenal snowfalls. The road outside disappeared under a thick white layer, flakes whirled excitingly down, and a full hour before school was due to finish my father turned up in the car to take me home. He had with him his dental technician, Charles Heath, a willing young man who tended to get roped in for emergency service of any kind. Charles had brought a shovel in the boot of the car in case during the five-mile journey we had to dig ourselves out of drifts. It was wonderfully exhilarating, as if our humdrum urban life had suddenly been confronted with untamed Nature on the rampage. It also meant an hour less of school, and this was always to be welcomed. I was not happy there. My life was made miserable by the relentless persecution of a trio of bullies whose names were David Wild, Martin Graham, and Jim Baines. With the unerring instinct shown by boys of that kind, they had divined at once that my mental landscape was different from theirs and had singled me out as a victim. I do not remember that any of them was ever caned on the palm of the hand, or indeed punished in any way, but then their sadism, unlike my harmless rowdyism on the bus, was not on view to the potential fee-paying public.

At nine I went to a Grammar School, spending the first three years in its Preparatory Department and a further five in its main structure. I call it a Grammar School though it actually called itself a High School. The terms were virtually interchangeable in the 1930s. Here again I was very much in a tradition. The Grammar Schools were a creation of the sixteenth century, designed to produce an educated class capable of filling administrative posts and recruiting the professions. They existed side by side with the expensive and fashionable "Public Schools," which were so called because the oldest of them dated from a time at the end of the Middle Ages when well-to-do families had private tutors and only the sons of poor families needed to be sent to school. They had soon ceased to be "public" in that sense, and the bulk of them, founded in the nineteenth century to service Imperialism, had never been so. A

boy who went to a Grammar School studied the same curriculum as he would have done at a "Public School," while having a more natural life, rooted in his own local community and seeing his own parents in his own home for most of the twenty-four hours. However, among people who had the requisite income, the Public Schools were almost always preferred, and the reason for this was the all-pervading English disease of class-consciousness. If I had gone to Rugby or Shrewsbury, to name two Public Schools that were close to home and which my father did in fact consider seriously, I would have been removed as if surgically from ordinary North Staffordshire life and drilled into a set of attitudes and manners that would have placed a barrier between me and my family. Thank Heaven I escaped this fate. On the other hand the Public School system, at one remove, exerted a bad influence on the school I actually did attend. I happened to strike the school at a bad period. The headmaster was a snob who judged people on social grounds, and under his influence the school was riddled with empty snobbery that undermined its real potential for good. It was an "Endowed School", i.e., it was not funded entirely from public money but contributed some funds of its own, and we were never allowed to forget this, as if we cared. Every effort was made to brainwash us into the attitude that we were a cut above boys very similar to ourselves who went to schools very similar to ours in the locality. We were supposed to be little gentlemen, and this showed itself in countless irksome ways. It also wasted energies that should have gone into our intellectual improvement. For example, the English master spent as much time trying to drill us out of our North Staffordshire accent as he did on teaching us to use the language correctly in its written form or to appreciate literature. He was forever correcting our pronunciation, into which we lapsed back as soon as we got home at half-past four. The eight years I spent in this atmosphere did not turn me into a gentleman, but they did something that has perhaps stood me in better stead—gave me a distaste for snobbery that has persisted throughout my life.

To concentrate on the positive side, the school did at least educate me, however patchily, to the point where I was able to satisfy the minimum requirements and scrape into Oxford University. I was ready for this by the end of 1942; since I was seventeen at the time, and the normal age for entering the University was at least a year older, I would normally have stayed on at school, but I expected to be taken into the Army, and the advice always given to boys in my situation was to get to Oxford while they could, stay there for however short a time they were allowed, and look forward to starting in earnest after the war.

To Oxford, then, I went in January 1943—a time of year in which there would normally be no intake of students. Two months later I was called up and presented myself for my medical examination. I knew that I could see very little out of my left eye, since I had had an accident, the result probably of some foolish piece of recklessness in attempting stunts on a bicycle, and had detached the retina of that eye, a condition for which the treatment was at that time very slow and uncertain. I have in fact never recovered the sight of that eye and have done my entire professional work with the other. It turned out that detachment of the retina was one of the conditions that led one to be put in Grade IV, from which no men were taken for active service. Suddenly, one year earlier than I had any right to be there, unschooled, very ill-read, largely bewildered about what was expected of me, I was at Oxford and the way was clear for me to stay there till I graduated. I had become so habituated to the idea of going away and doing some kind of war service that I still took a few months to give up the idea entirely; I wrote various letters offering to do agricultural work, but the general opinion seemed to be that if I wasn't fit for the Army I wasn't fit for the land either. I settled down to a studious life.

I expressed no regret, nor did I feel any, at not being involved in the actual fighting of the war. I would have been trained in time for the Normandy landings, which involved fierce fighting and heavy losses, and I am the kind of person who usually gets killed in a battle; I am too slow, too hesitant, too inefficient, and no doubt under fire would be too terrified, to survive in that kind of situation. Many of the boys I went to school with, and many of the undergraduates who were my contemporaries during that first year at St. John's and were exactly my age to a month or two on either side, were killed, and I have no grounds for thinking that I would have been a better soldier, or luckier, or braver, than they were. So the damage to my eyesight, which has inconvenienced me every day that I have lived since the age of sixteen, and has become a very acute problem since, in my fifties, my remaining eye began to go wrong for other reasons, may quite possibly be the reason I have had a life at all. I feel humble when I think of my contemporaries who died in the war, and respectful towards men of my generation who fought in it and survived. There are few examples in history of a totally just war, but I believe the Allied action in World War II is one such example, and I have never been tempted to go along with the self-indulgent pacifist line that the men who fought were dupes and only did it because they were too stupid to see that it was all for nothing. It was very decidedly not all for nothing, as the Allied armies

proved beyond doubt when they overran the Nazi concentration camps in 1945.

From the time I was seventeen years and ten months, then, the University of Oxford became my world. I had learnt a great deal in Stoke-on-Trent and I am convinced that growing up in an industrial town, especially one in contact with the countryside and its practical concerns, was a good preparation for life; after all, I have spent my life in an England which has tried, latterly with decreasing success, to earn its living by industry, and even Oxford, where I have lived longer than anywhere else, has been a large industrial city during all the years I have known it.

For the time being, however, my youthful attention was narrowed to the University of Oxford. This is a place of such wide cultural resources, and draws its student body from such wide social and geographical areas, that a good student can survive a bad teacher. But it is a fact that during my time there I was fortunate not only in my unofficial but in my official teachers. My first tutor was A.M.D. Hughes. He was in his early seventies when I knew him, and of course I considered this a venerable age; it would have astonished me to know that he still had another three decades to live, ending as a centenarian and making a splendid speech, with only a few lapses of continuity, to his assembled friends on his hundredth birthday. Hughes had always suffered from bad eyesight and in compensation he had cultivated a prodigious memory; since it was a trouble to him to look things up, he simply quoted from his immense stock of knowledge and very rarely made a mistake. This was particularly impressive to me, because I knew full well, even at eighteen, that I was embarking on the life of a man of letters with eyesight that would never be of normal effectiveness, and Hughes's examples helped me to see that memory could to some extent substitute for repeated reference to print. I began to cultivate my verbal memory and have always done so, with the result that my friends are often surprised by the amount of verse, and sometimes even of prose, that I have by heart.

Hughes was a man of the nineteenth century and contained within himself many of its finest qualities. He took it for granted that scholarship, literary and historical study, and the elucidation of ideas, were self-evidently valuable and worthy of a lifetime's devotion. He was not tormented by modern doubts as to the "relevance" of what he was doing or fears that the world would change so totally that it would have no need of the great literature and philosophy of the past. Such ideas would merely have puzzled him. He had come up to St. John's as an undergraduate in 1890 and received his early training in the Victorian age—he used to go to hear Benjamin Jowett's sermons, for instance, on Sunday mornings in the chapel of Balliol College—and when he spoke of Carlyle or Matthew Arnold, T.H. Green or Newman, Tennyson or Browning, he did so with the ease and inwardness of one who shared their civilisation. His own chosen topic was rather earlier—the life and work of Shelley—but he could discourse from a full mind on any topic within six centuries of English literature, and always in a perfectly rounded phraseology. I used to think that everything he said could have been taken down by a stenographer and sent immediately to the printer. I knew Hughes at the beginning of my life and did not realise, because I had no standard of comparison, how extraordinary he was, but with every year I have lived I have looked back on him with more admiration.

He never had a teaching post at Oxford, and the reason I ever met him was that the English tutor at St. John's, Gavin Bone, had died some months before I arrived there. The war, then entering its fourth year, had left Oxford very short of tutors, and St. John's, his old College, invited Hughes to spend a couple of days a week there and look after the few remaining students of English. At the end of the academic year 1942-43 there were only a handful of us left; two of us had finished their three years and took their Finals, and the rest, except for myself, disappeared into the Services. That left only myself for the next autumn, and Hughes's visits ceased, to my regret.

When I returned to Oxford after the summer vacation the College made arrangements for me to be taught by C.S. Lewis, who was a Fellow of Magdalen. Lewis was not only a star of the English Faculty, whose lectures were packed to the doors and whose books sold in large editions; he was also one of the few Oxford dons who was a household name in the country generally. The millions who had never heard of his work as a literary historian knew him as an extremely effective propagandist, if that is the right word, for the Christian religion. He gave regular talks on the radio at a time when radio occupied the same place in people's lives as television does now: it made celebrities. He had also recently published a highly successful book combining Christian apologetics with satire and humour—*The Screwtape Letters*—which had had an enormous sale. When I trod the stairs to Lewis's rooms in Magdalen for the first time, I knew that I was about to confront, and if possible to find some workable relationship with, a man who was a celebrity not only in the inward-reflecting world of Oxford but in the larger world outside. Under the pressure of wartime with its constant themes of separation, disruption, suffering and death, people had been forced out of their comfortable, hedonistic routines to stand face to face with ultimate reali-

ties, and as always at such times they had turned to religion in its various forms and to philosophy, which also enjoyed a vogue in those years.

Lewis's Christianity was totally sincere and his (highly successful) attempt to woo a mass audience was simply the effort of an honest man to serve his religion. His books and broadcasts on religious subjects brought in a substantial income and he gave every penny of it away, managing his domestic responsibilities, which were not inconsiderable, on his modest salary as an Oxford don plus what he earned by writing on non-religious subjects. He was a forthright, outspoken man and this alone would have been enough to make enemies for him, but of course his popularity with a wide public worked very much against him in Oxford, where the prevailing assumption is that anything that can be understood by a majority of people must be shallow and probably harmful. In general matters, Lewis had more than a touch of this Oxford attitude himself—he was far from a democrat or an egalitarian, and having acquired his vast knowledge by many years of hard work he saw nothing to be gained from telling people that they could achieve wisdom without paying a price for it. Even to his mass audience what he offered was not easy snippets of wisdom but a *discipline*, which, if they followed it, might bring them to Heaven. In his work as a tutor he applied the same principle but more overtly and with absolutely no concessions. He remorselessly trampled out of his pupils any notion that they could become connoisseurs of literature merely by striking a few attitudes and thinking themselves superior. Judgement had to be founded on knowledge, and knowledge on application. Hughes, in his graceful and ceremonial way, had already begun to make me see these truths, but Lewis enforced them more briskly and sharply. I shall always be grateful to the two of them. To be tutored by such men, particularly after the unsound education I had received at school, was the first great piece of good fortune in my life.

During my late teens and early twenties, my energies were mainly absorbed in the study of literature, in the attempt to understand it and to allow my mind to be permeated by its magic and wisdom. I always knew that I intended to write; being a writer is not a profession but a condition, and I had known that I was in that condition ever since I had sat at the kitchen table writing and illustrating my stories of Smellum Owte and his adventures. But from about 1943 to 1950 my aim was to be a scholar-poet. I thought that my original work would consist of poetry and that I should accompany it with a steady output of critical works about the major English and European writers. I had before me a number of examples of writers who had worked in this way and achieved impressive results, from Lewis himself and his friend Charles Williams to T.S. Eliot, W.H. Auden, and (a special idol of mine) William Empson. It seemed to me that their criticism took fire and depth from the imagination that produced their poetry, which itself gained in complexity and range from the reading and thinking that went into their critical work. In the thirty-five years since then I have not so much abandoned this programme as added to it, as a tree adds new rings. I still write as much poetry as I did then, and if I write less in the way of criticism it is partly because I have increasing trouble with my eyesight, which puts me behind with any possible programme of reading, but mainly because of a change in the literary climate. For thirty years I wrote formal critical essays, side by side with my other work, and when I had written enough of them to make a volume, which usually took four or five years, my publisher brought out the volume without hesitation. These collections of critical essays never made any money, but they were an essential part of my work and contributed, for good or ill, to the way I was generally regarded in the world of letters, and my publisher was willing to balance out the accounting and take the rough with the smooth. Towards the end of the 1970s, however, the firm I had been with for thirty years underwent a major shake-up, new people appeared at the top, the accountants began to give orders and the literary personnel to obey them, and literary criticism, and *belles-lettres* generally, disappeared from their publishing programme, closely followed by poetry. At the same time the crop of new fashions in criticism (Structuralism, propaganda for the Women's Movement, *und so weiter*) made me even less saleable as a literary critic even if I had taken the trouble to move to another publisher. So that part of my work has tended, like the State in Marxist theology, to "wither away." I thought it was worth taking a few lines to explain the situation because I am sometimes asked whether I have ceased to take an interest in classical English literature. On the contrary, I am as passionately interested in it as ever, and would still be writing about it if I could find a market for what I write.

When I was a student, then, I was conscious of no wide gap between a life of literary study and the life of a practising writer which I hoped one day to lead. I did not foresee a time when I should change, rather like an insect undergoing its metamorphosis, from a student to a writer. Nor has such a time ever happened. Of course the interest in writing fiction, the conscious decision to add the novel to my armoury, did a great deal to upset this balance, if only because novel-writing is immensely more time-consuming than the writing of poetry. To plan a novel, and to embark on it with any hope of finishing it within a year or eighteen months, is a matter of making it one's main occupation and doing everything else round the sides. It is perfectly possible to write poetry round the sides of other things—if it were not, T.S. Eliot would not have been able to have a career as a publisher or Wallace Stevens as an insurance lawyer—and in fact I have been able to do so, but my main nine-to-five profession has had to be that of a novelist, and even so I have only managed, by the age of sixty, to produce ten novels, though I have a very long one half-finished which has already run to the length of the average novel and will necessarily be very long because it has a wide historical sweep.

Substantially, then, my youthful vision of the kind of life I wanted to live was perfectly reasonable and in essentials I have lived it. Discussion of literature has always seemed to me a natural accompaniment to producing it. When I served the University of Oxford from 1973 to 1978 as Professor of Poetry (it is a five-year appointment whose holder is elected by vote rather than appointed by a Faculty Board) the change in my way of life was minimal, though the obligation to give

Wain, age twenty-six

fifteen lectures on poetry to an academic audience did mean that I had to give more attention to criticism during those five years and consequently less to fiction, which is probably why I did not bring out a novel from 1970 to 1978. It also explains why great teachers like Lewis and Hughes were so important in my life and why they bulk so large in this account; it was they who prepared me for the life of a man of letters, a very different thing from merely helping me to qualify as a College teacher.

This brings me back to Lewis, as it was intended to do. His work and personality have continued of course to attract attention since his death in 1963, and to this day there are people who seek my acquaintance for no other reason than that I knew Lewis and, in 1946-49, sometimes attended gatherings of the circle of friends who called themselves the Inklings. That Lewis should have invited me to join this circle (it was he who took this initiative; the others had never met me) was (it would be false modesty to deny) a considerable compliment and a measure of the interest he had come to take in me during the years of tutoring. Certainly he did everything to encourage me to make the study of literature my profession as it was his; and after I got my First in the summer of 1946 he supported with his recommendation my application for a research post at my College, St. John's. To cap it all he invited me to join his *cénacle*, who met twice a week, to drink beer in a pub on Tuesdays at noon and more formally in Lewis's rooms at Magdalen on Thursday evenings, where they read to one another from work in progress. The regular members were Lewis, his brother W.H. Lewis who was a retired Army major, a doctor named R.E. Havard who was in general practice in the town and looked after the health of the society, and two other dons, J.R.R. Tolkien and Hugo Dyson. The circle was entirely middle-aged; there were no junior members except myself, saving an occasional visit by Christopher Tolkien, the son of J.R.R. and at that time an undergraduate.

Lewis's motive in bringing me into this set was, I conjecture, a mixed one. Partly, I am sure, it was pure friendliness. He had often said that he enjoyed teaching me and looked forward to my weekly appearances. Now that I had graduated he did not want to lose touch, so what more simple way than to enrol me as one of the people he could count on seeing twice a week? But beneath this straightforward kindliness there was, I conjecture, another reason. Lewis was a man who felt himself very deeply at odds with the world he lived in. His Christianity was not of the Catholic variety, but he was deeply interested in, and affected by, mediaeval scholastic theology and the imaginative

writers such as Dante and Chaucer whose world-view was based on it. He disliked the modern world for being rationalistic and material in its preoccupations. He was not such a fool as to disapprove of science where science was simply the disinterested pursuit of truth, but he felt that the modern mind had about it an atmosphere of stale scientific complacency which ought to be challenged. (One of the books he hated most, I remember, was C.H. Waddington's *The Scientific Attitude,* which seemed to him to preach a shallow rationality.)

In all this he drew ready assent from me. I was already halfway towards such an attitude, and if some of it was what I picked up from Lewis and his master G.K. Chesterton, I had independently arrived at an attitude to literature and the arts generally which appealed to Lewis. He disliked "modern" poetry (cf. his endless sniping at T.S. Eliot) and must have been depressed to find that most of the young accepted it quite uncritically. Personally I did not so accept it. I have never been content to swallow modernity in large gulps. The iconoclastic quality of modern painting, music, and literature, which must have seemed so wonderfully liberating to the generation just picking themselves up after the disaster of World War I, often aroused my antagonism. I preferred Mozart to Stravinsky, Titian to Picasso, Hardy and Yeats to the latest drivel I read in the modish avant-garde literary magazines, and in broad outline these have remained my opinions throughout life. I preferred the mainstream of the European arts, then, to the "experimental" phase that had been dominant since the decade or so before I was born. Lewis probably saw this as an innate conservatism and may have built hopes on it, but my own view of the matter is that I was merely being contemporary, responding to the *Zeitgeist* in the particular form in which it impinged on a person born in the 1920s. One of my fellow undergraduates at St. John's—he was three years my senior, but we overlapped for a few months—was Philip Larkin, in my (and not only my) opinion the finest poet to handle the English language in the period since 1945. (Tragically, the news of his death, after months of illness, has come to me now, as I am writing these pages.) Part of Larkin's importance, historically, is that he quietly turned his back on the whole solemnly *recherché* paraphernalia of the modern arts and in particular on the notion that because modern life is complex, therefore the art that interprets that life must itself be complex, to the point where it cannot be understood by the ordinary public unless they have submitted to instruction by a corps of "experts." All his life Larkin made incisive fun of the notion that the ordinary person mustn't expect to understand the arts without prior study ("You don't expect to understand anything as important as art *straight off*, do you?"), and in his practice he brought poetry back to the ordinary reader by writing directly about universal experience in language that was marked out as poetry by its subtlety and precision rather than by any esoteric qualities.

Though I accepted Larkin as an authority from the moment I first met him, he did not need to inculcate this doubt about modernism in me as a matter of novelty. I was, at the age of eighteen, already instinctively ready for it. Within a few days or weeks of meeting Larkin I met another poet, John Heath-Stubbs, with whom I have also kept in touch through the years, and it is a fact that Heath-Stubbs's poetry, though it often refers to myth and legend and is not so realistic and colloquial as Larkin's, is also perfectly straightforward in its language, with none of the puzzle-element that was *de rigueur* for twenty years among those who were afraid of being thought old-fashioned. There may be a few references that one needs to look up in a dictionary (and always the handiest and cheapest dictionary will do, for he never uses arcane material) but, that once done, there is never any difficulty in understanding a poem by Heath-Stubbs.

In other words, both Larkin and Heath-Stubbs belonged, as I, slightly their junior, did myself, to the post-modern generation; we were, in fact, the first wave of it. None of us has ever seen any need for the mystification, the sheer difficulty of digging out what the author is saying, that characterizes Eliot or Valéry, nor for the colossal elaboration of method that led James Joyce from the effective simplicity of *Dubliners* to the ritual observances of *Finnegans Wake*.

In all this I must have seemed to Lewis a natural ally and *protégé*, since he had remained true to the tastes he had formed in youth and was thus a survivor from the age before modernism came in. Premodern met postmodern, and the recognition was a happy one. But the similarities ended there. My literary tastes, and my attitudes in general, were not really similar to Lewis's, much as I liked him.

In particular, my approach to fiction—always a major part of the literary output of any age, and a huge part of my own output and of Lewis's—was and is realistic. The books I most admire are those that take human life as I know it and live it from day to day, and describe it honestly and lovingly, and illuminate it fearlessly. As a novelist I have always seen myself as contributing to the central tradition of the novel, the tradition that grew up in the eighteenth century, which means recognisable human beings in familiar settings, doing the kind of things that you and I do, with all the usual consequences. To me, there is no need to go off into the realms of fantasy with dream-settings and non-

human characters. Everything important, everything lyrical and tragic and horrifying and uplifting and miraculous, is there in our ordinary lives if we can open our eyes and see it. The realistic novel is committed to the proposition that the casual stranger who gets onto the bus and occupies the seat beside you is worth writing a great novel about: and it is a true proposition. Sometimes, in poetry or in radio drama, I have ranged in imagination into historical time and far settings, but as a novelist I have found enough interest in realism—contemporary settings, familiar circumstances, and the surprises coming from the human soul and the human body, rather than from "invention."

It will be seen that, since I start from this premise, Romance is the kind of literature that I appreciate least, and this accounts for the shiver of dread that comes over me when some stranger at a party, having heard that I was reasonably well acquainted with Tolkien and often sat through his readings from *The Lord of the Rings* while it was in progress, bears down on me with the look of one determined not to let slip a golden opportunity. I know I am going to be asked what I think of that opus. The fact is that I don't think anything of it. It has, and had, nothing to say to me. It presents no picture of human life that I can recognize. All it does is remind me of Samuel Johnson's remark, "A story is a picture of life. If it is false, it is a picture of nothing." By "false," of course, Johnson meant not false to the facts of a police-court narration, but false to the nature of things.

When Tolkien came through the door at a meeting of the Inklings with a bulging jacket pocket, I winced because I knew we were in for a slab of Gandalf and Bilbo Baggins and the rest of it. I wished him no harm, but would have preferred him to keep his daydreams within bounds and not inflict them on us.

In the end, then, if Lewis had hoped that I might form the cornerstone of a new generation that would carry on the tastes and preferences and attitudes of the Inklings, he must have been disappointed. But if so he never allowed this disappointment to appear. He continued to be a good friend to me and though my life, particularly after I left the academic profession, must have seemed a strange one to him and some things in it deeply regrettable, he continued to feel the same friendly interest in me that he had felt when I was his pupil, and we kept in touch until his death. The nearest he ever came to alluding openly to the gulf that had gradually opened out between us was when he said to me one day in about 1955, "I think you and I had better have an agreement not to read each other's fiction." It was an agreement I would more readily have entered into with Tolkien, for Lewis's romances, which like all his works are in fact Christian apologetics, con-

John and Eirian Wain with their firstborn, 1960

tain many fine things.

I have mentioned that I left the academic profession. The rest of my story is soon told, and the basic facts are in the usual reference books. My marriage in 1960 brought me a Welsh wife, Eirian, and three half-Welsh sons; since Eirian has a cottage in the Welsh mountains, the effect was to bring me into contact with that beautiful and enigmatic country. I spent much of the 1960s finding out about Wales and building into my life a whole new circle of Welsh friends, and the first results of this are in some of the poems in *Letters to Five Artists* (1969) and the novel *A Winter in the Hills* (1970). I am glad I had something as absorbing as this to do in the 1960s, because on the wider scene it was a decade I disliked. Under the influence of a soap bubble of prosperity that was soon to burst, the world—or at any rate the "developed" world—went mad and false doctrines, rank self-indulgence, and sheer foolishness raged unchecked for ten years. Since then, a lot of painful unlearning has had to go on as step by step humanity has retreated from the blind alley of the sixties. Deeply immersed in the early years of my sons and deeply immersed in discovering Wales, I was too busy to go down this alley, and though at the time it was uncom-

fortable to feel, and very often to be told, that I was out of touch with the times and forgotten by the young, I can now see that not having been caught up in that unhealthy *Walpurgisnacht* was another of the pieces of good fortune I have enjoyed.

Finally: there is in this essay a gap which I have purposely made so glaring that it cannot escape attention. I have said nothing about the vicissitudes of my emotional and sexual life. Every human being has an emotional and sexual life and everyone is preoccupied with it for much of the time. There may be people who achieve completely tranquil relationships and a perfect emotional balance early in life and never waver from them, but I have never met such a person. Everyone I have ever known, and I have known a very wide range of people, has had an emotional life which more or less resembles a fever chart shooting rapidly up and down, under which the patient lies in a state of alternating comfort and discomfort. Obviously I am no exception. I am heterosexual, and women have always been important in my life. I have been married, formally, twice, and the second marriage, to Eirian, has lasted a quarter of a century and produced three sons. I have also another son, slightly older than the other three, whose mother and I did not, for a complex of reasons, get married. I am equally and deeply fond of all my four sons and they have done a great deal to enrich my life, as also have their mothers and the various women with whom I have been closely involved.

That is as far as I am willing to pursue the subject. Everyone has a right to some privacy, and the mere fact that I am a writer does not oblige me to set out the details of my innermost personal life to gratify the casual curiosity of total strangers. As for readers who take a serious interest in my work, who have read what I have written and would like to know more about me, they will already be aware of the obvious fact that a writer *always* uses his or her emotional life as material. Some do so very directly, others at a much deeper level of metaphor, but in the end the diagram of every artist's emotions is there for anyone to see who knows how to look. The sketch I have just written is intended, among other things, to enable the reader to know how to look.

Wain, about 1980

BIBLIOGRAPHY

Fiction:

Hurry on Down. London: Secker & Warburg, 1953; also pub-lished as *Born in Captivity.* New York: Knopf, 1954.

Living in the Present. London: Secker & Warburg, 1955; New York: Putnam, 1960.

The Contenders. London: Macmillan, 1958; New York: St. Martin's, 1958.

A Travelling Woman. London: Macmillan, 1959; New York: St. Martin's, 1959.

Nuncle and Other Stories. London: Macmillan, 1960; New York: St. Martin's, 1961.

Strike the Father Dead. London: Macmillan, 1962; New York: St. Martin's, 1962.

The Young Visitors. London: Macmillan, 1965; New York: Viking, 1965.

Death of the Hind Legs and Other Stories. London: Macmillan, 1966; New York: Viking, 1966.

The Smaller Sky. London: Macmillan, 1967.

A Winter in the Hills. London: Macmillan, 1970; New York: Viking, 1970.

The Life Guard (short stories). London: Macmillan, 1971; New York: Viking, 1972.

King Caliban and Other Stories. London: Macmillan, 1978.

The Pardoner's Tale. London: Macmillan, 1978; New York: Viking, 1979.

Poetry:

Mixed Feelings. Reading, England: Reading University School of Art, 1951.

A Word Carved on a Sill. London: Routledge & Kegan Paul, 1956; New York: St. Martin's, 1956.

A Song about Major Eatherly. Iowa City: Qara Press, 1961.

Weep before God. London: Macmillan, 1961; New York: St. Martin's, 1961.

Wildtrack. London: Macmillan, 1965; New York: Viking, 1966.

Letters to Five Artists. London: Macmillan, 1969; New York: Viking, 1970.

The Shape of Feng. London: Covent Garden Press, 1972.

Feng. London: Macmillan, 1975; New York: Viking, 1975.

Poems for the Zodiac. London: Pisces Press, 1980.

Poems, 1949-1979. London: Macmillan, 1981.

Thinking about Mr. Person, Kent, England: Chimaera Press, 1980.

The Twofold. Somerset, England: Hunting Raven Press, 1981.

Mid-week Period Return: Home Thoughts of a Native. Stratford-upon-Avon: Celandine Press, 1982.

Plays:

Harry in the Night, first produced in Stoke-on-Trent, 1975.

You Wouldn't Remember (radio play, first aired on BBC), 1978.

A Winter in the Hills (radio play; adapted from the author's novel), 1981.

Frank. (radio play, first aired on BBC). Oxford: Amber Lane Press, 1984.

Good Morning Blues. (radio play, first aired on BBC), 1986.

Nonfiction:

Preliminary Essays. London: Macmillan, 1957; New York: St. Martin's, 1957.

Gerard Manley Hopkins: An Idiom of Desperation. London: Oxford University Press, 1959; Folcroft, Pa.: Folcroft Editions, 1974.

Sprightly Running: Part of an Autobiography. London: Macmillan, 1962; New York: St. Martin's, 1963.

Essays on Literature and Ideas. London: Macmillan, 1963; New York: St. Martin's, 1963.

The Living World of Shakespeare: A Playgoer's Guide. London: Macmillan, 1964; New York: St. Martin's, 1964.

Arnold Bennett. New York: Columbia University Press, 1967.

A House for the Truth: Critical Essays. London: Macmillan, 1972; New York: Viking, 1973.

Samuel Johnson. London: Macmillan, 1974; New York: Viking, 1975.

Professing Poetry. London: Macmillan, 1977; New York: Viking, 1978.

Dear Shadows: Portraits from Memory. London: J. Murray, 1986.

Juvenile fiction:

Lizzie's Floating Shop. London: Bodley Head, 1981.

Young Shoulders. London: Macmillan, 1982; also published as *The Free Zone Starts Here.* New York: Delacorte, 1982.

Translator of:

The Seafarer, from the Anglo-Saxon. Warwick, England: Grenville Press, 1982.

Editor of:

Contemporary Reviews of Romantic Poetry. London: Harrap, 1953; New York: Barnes & Noble, 1953.

Interpretations: Essays on Twelve English Poems. London: Routledge & Kegan Paul, 1955; New York: Hillary House, 1957.

International Literary Annual. London: J. Calder, 1958; New York: Criterion, 1959.

Fanny Burney's Diary. London: Folio Society, 1961.

Anthology of Modern Poetry. London: Hutchinson, 1963.

Pope. New York: Dell, 1963.

Selected Shorter Poems of Thomas Hardy. London: Macmillan, 1966; New York: St. Martin's, 1966.

The Dynasts, by Thomas Hardy. London: Macmillan, 1966; New York: St. Martin's, 1966.

Selected Stories of Thomas Hardy. London: Macmillan, 1966; New York: St. Martin's, 1966.

Shakespeare: Macbeth; A Casebook. London: Macmillan, 1968; Nashville: Aurora Pubs.: 1970.

Shakespeare: Othello; A Casebook. London: Macmillan, 1971.

Johnson as Critic. London and Boston: Routledge & Kegan Paul, 1973.

Lives of the English Poets, by Samuel Johnson. London: Dent, 1975; New York: Dutton, 1976.

Johnson on Johnson: A Selection of the Personal and Autobiographical Writings of Samuel Johnson. London: Dent, 1976; New York: Dutton, 1976.

An Edmund Wilson Celebration. Oxford: Phaidon Press, 1978; also published as *Edmund Wilson: The Man and His Work.* New York: New York University Press, 1978.

Personal Choice: A Poetry Anthology. Newton Abbot, England, and North Pomfret, Vt.: David & Charles, 1978.

The New Wessex Selection of Thomas Hardy's Poetry, with Eirian Wain. London: Macmillan, 1978.

Anthology of Contemporary Poetry: Post-War to the Present. London: Hutchinson, 1979.

Everyman's Book of English Verse. London: Dent, 1981.

The Old Wives' Tale, by Arnold Bennett. Harmondsworth, England, and New York: Penguin, 1983.

The Private Memoirs and Confessions of a Justified Sinner, by James Hogg. Harmondsworth, England and New York: Penguin, 1983.

Sound Recordings:

Modern Poetry, with Ted Walker. Santa Monica: BFA Educational Media, 1972.

The Poetry of John Wain. Guilford, Conn.: Norton, Jeffery, 1976.

Jon Manchip White

1924-

Jon Manchip White, about 1979

One of life's principal ironies, it has been said, is that it has to be lived forwards but can only be understood backwards. Even so, how much understanding can we actually bring to bear on our lives, even when, as now, the viewer is about to look back on it from the ripening age of sixty-one?

Not much, after all. The mainsprings of our lives appear to be hidden somewhere down there in the inner darkness, obscure and inaccessible. And certainly you can't understand the important moments of your life while you're actually living through them. Nowadays, as an ageing man, I often find myself leaping bolt upright in the middle of the night, remembering something I'd once said or done, and asking myself:

"My God, did I really say or do something as stupid as that? Could I really have missed the whole meaning of what was actually going on?" And it's then I remember the terrible words of Yeats: "I lie awake night after night / And never get the answers right."

On the whole, understand it or not, and in spite of the inevitable disappointments and griefs, I have very greatly enjoyed my life. On the other hand, it's only very recently that I've come to discern in a hazy way what must have been some of the main threads in the pattern. Probably you have to grow old and start to lose your momentum before you're ready to look back over your shoulder. When you're young you're much too busy living your life to have the time to stop and examine it. It's only in comparatively recent years, for instance, that I've come to appreciate how deeply my outward and social existence was marked by the fact that I was born only six years after the end of the First World War and fifteen from the start of the Second. This also makes me, though I couldn't be expected to realize it at the time, very much a child of the Depression, and also a member of what was even then becoming Britain's post-Imperial generation. Nor could I have known how deeply I was marked by what I've since come to see as an odd parallel between the events of my own birth and childhood and those of Ibsen and Strindberg.

It would be absurd to compare myself with those great figures if the parallel weren't close and hadn't at one time or another given me considerable food for thought. Also, their work has always given me much pleasure: my later novels, for example, show a definite affinity with Strindberg (the references to *The Ghost Sonata* and *The Dream Play* in my *Death by Dreaming* are in fact quite explicit and deliberate). They were both born well-to-do, the sons of prosperous provincial businessmen whose affairs soon suffered a spectacular collapse. My father Gwilym (the Welsh for William) was born on the esplanade of Cardiff Docks, where my grandfather was the harbormaster. Cardiff at that date was one of the most flourishing ports in Europe, rivalling Liverpool, Hamburg, or Rotterdam. It thrived on the export of tinplate, nitrates, and coal, especially the Number One Welsh Steam Coal that kept most of the world's greatest navies at sea. Twenty years before my father's birth in 1887 Cardiff had been suddenly transformed by the construction of giant docks and dry docks from a tiny fishing village into a teeming city, with grandiose public buildings that would eventually qualify it for the status of the capital of Wales.

My father came of old seafaring stock. Among his ancestors was Rawlins White, owner of a fishing fleet, who was burned at the stake during the Marian persecutions in 1555. The story of his "Protestant martyrdom" is dramatically related in Fox's *Book of Martyrs*. The old fellow could easily have avoided his horrid fate, if he hadn't been as proud and pig-headed as all the Whites. As for the Manchips, there is a family tradition that they were the stewards or Manciples of the Fitzhamons, the Norman lords of Cardiff Castle. They too proliferated as a seafaring breed around the shores of the Bristol Channel, where Manchips can be found in such ports of call as Swansea, Llanelly, Barry, Penarth, Newport, and Bristol.

My mother's family came from farther afield. Her father, Thomas Ewbank, was a native of the gritty little town of Shap in Westmoreland (now part of the new county of Cumbria) and was related to Nicholsons in Scotland. Her mother was a Keenan from Cork. Thus I can claim Scottish and Irish in addition to Welsh blood; and since Westmoreland too was originally a Celtic realm (it was the heart of the ancient kingdom of Strathclyde, linking Wales with Scotland), I can claim to be, if not exclusively Welsh, at least completely Celtic. There were romantic stories about the Ewbanks. Thomas was a cousin by descent of the huntsman John Peele, and his family home in the village of Bampton is now buried beneath the artificial reservoir of Hawsewater. There are the usual legends, widespread throughout the Celtic West, of the bells of Bampton sounding beneath the waves. To my sorrow, I never knew my maternal grandfather, long remembered in Glamorganshire as the enlightened headmaster of Barry County School. He anticipated my own history in two interesting ways. He was an antiquary and an historian, and also the first writer in the family. His *History of Barry* is still a sought-after little volume.

My father, the only one of a large brood of brothers who didn't go to sea, nevertheless amassed his considerable fortune in Cardiff's Bute Street. This was the main artery of what was known as Tiger Bay. He broke ships and he built ships, becoming the part-owner and managing director of the Taff Vale Shipping Company. His brothers were tough, hard-case sailors. Many of my most vivid memories are connected with my uncles Evan and Isaac (the Whites, as staunch Nonconformists, favored Old Testamentary names; my grandfather was Moses White, a famous skipper of his day). Evan and Isaac had master's certificates in both sail and steam, and after retirement

Father, Gwilym Manchip White

both became head of the Bristol Channel Pilotage Board. They could be gentle and dangerous by turns. There was a whiff of Captain Ahab about them. My step-grandfather, whom they hated and who hated them cordially in return, was the rakehelly Captain Trott, the captain of *The Marguerite*, one of the fastest and trimmest cutters of the day.

In 1924, when I was born, the Depression (or the Slump, as it was known in Britain) overtook my father just as he was reaching the the apogee of his fortunes. It was especially severe in South Wales and on its shipping industry. My father tried hard to keep his business going and to protect his employees; but when I was about three or four he contracted tuberculosis, and for the next ten years was condemned to die by inches in hospitals and sanatoriums or confined to a bed at home. He confronted his cruel illness, which overshadowed my childhood, with gallantry and tenacity and with the fierce and caustic humor characteristic of the males of my family. He was a gifted, courageous, unfortunate man.

He was a man of wide and varied interests, a provincial autodidact. He collected china, silver, and pictures. He cultivated orchids and had a species of dahlia named after him. He owned a Bugatti painted in French racing blue, with a huge ratchetted brake on the outside of the fuselage. In this I sat by the hour, wearing the old gas mask which an uncle had brought back from Flanders, winning many an imaginary Grand Prix. Above all my father was a reader. Reading was his solace in the years when he was almost completely immobilized. One of the grimmer accompaniments of his illness was that he had been forbidden by the doctors to speak, so I would sit on his bed and we would talk about books and other matters by scribbling messages in notebooks. Some of these I still retain. This was my introduction to literature.

Until I was seven, while my father was away in a sanatorium, I lived at home and went to local board schools, walking three miles to school each morning and back again in the evening. These were schools in which caning and other punishments were common, and where I soon learned to look after myself and keep my own end up. I rejoiced in such juvenile British pastimes as tag, marbles, conkers, and five-stones. Then the contagious nature of my father's disease made it unsafe for me to remain too close to him, so I was sent to live for a year with an aunt in Barry. There, at Cadoxton School, I made my first systematic acquaintance with the Welsh language, spoken sporadically by members of my family. While I never became a really proficient Welsh speaker, in my earlier years I read Welsh a great deal, and I'm sure that some of its inflections can be detected in the style and texture of the books I was to write later.

Although uncertainty and distress were the background of my childhood, in the self-absorbed manner of children I was not unhappy. Many of my memories seem to be connected with the sea. I ranged the then relatively unpopulated and undiscovered beaches of Penarth, Nash Point, Sully; I caught skate and congereel with my uncles off Flat Holme and Steep Holme, aboard the pilot-boats; I roved around the wharves and quays of Cardiff Docks. My mother understood that this urge to wander, which was to become habitual with me, was an antidote to the gloom and anxiety that shrouded our household. She would give me a sixpence or an occasional shilling and I would pass whole days on my own, walking the streets, spending afternoons in the National Museum of Wales, watching Glamorganshire play cricket, in the days when its captains were J. C. Clay and Maurice Turnbull (later killed in the Welsh Guards). I watched Wales and Cardiff play football, in the great era of Wilfred Wooller and Cliff Morgan. I also averaged three or four movies a week by learning how to climb through the lavatory windows of most of the cinemas in St. Mary's Street and City Road.

Abruptly, when I was eight, this freedom among the streets and rockpools came to a jarring halt. As my father's illness neared its culmination and the risk of infection increased, my parents felt they had no alternative but to send me to a school in England that had offered me a place. It was to be a shattering break with my previous life. Three times a year, for the next eight years, a huge green steam locomotive of the Great Western Railway would carry me from Wales to Paddington, whence the red carriages of the Metropolitan Line would bring me to my place of exile twenty miles north of London. In eight years I never ceased to think of the school as a prison. In fifty years I have never revisited it. For years after I left it I would dream I'd been sentenced to return there, in the way Dickens would dream he was back in the blacking factory.

For all that, it was an excellent school. It contained four hundred boys, divided between a junior and a senior school. It was capably run and on the whole well staffed. I received a first-class education. My running battle with the school can probably be traced back to three sources. First, during my earliest years there, I was devastated by homesickness. In spite of my solitary wanderings around Cardiff and its environs, I'd been a member of a large, warm, emotionally demonstrative family, managed, because of my father's indisposition and the natural Welsh tendency towards matriarchy, principally by its women. My mother, a woman of a singularly sweet and gentle disposition, was one of eight sisters. Most Welshmen are brought up by women, spoiled by them, admire and understand them, and know how to love and be loved by them. In a sense, too, to be Welsh is to belong to one big extended family, and all Welsh people think of themselves as related to one another. You can therefore picture my sense of bewilderment when these comfortable props were kicked away and I was suddenly plunged among the English, imbued with their Spartan creed of duty and discomfort and tending to practice a polite hatred towards each other. Unlike the Celts, who are by instinct democratic, the English are democratic only by law. I found myself unaccountably immersed in a callous little society whose rigidity was a microcosm of English society at large. It was impressed on me in a brutal manner what it meant to be a lone Welsh boy in a schoolhouse of fifty English boys. In the 1930s, before it dawned on most of us that the imperial jig was up, the English had no hesitation in including the Welsh, Scots, and Irish among the lesser breeds. Fortunately my experiences in the board schools of Cardiff, allied to a notorious Welsh temper that the English hadn't yet taught me to control, came to my rescue. It was judged prudent to leave me alone.

In a year or two, already a curious mixture of the inveterate loner and the gregarious Welshman, I contrived to get on well enough with the English youngsters who were after all my fellow prisoners. My father had been a director of the Cardiff rugby club, so football was in my blood; I was a passable batsman and medium-paced bowler; I learned to play squash and handball, and was a member of the fencing team; and I scored well on the rifle range. However, I don't think I ever quite managed to fit in with most of my schoolmates, though I formed close and lasting friendships with a number of them. As for my schoolmasters, my determination to go my own way put me at odds with most of them, relying as they did on the subservience traditional in English schools of that epoch.

Fortunately, there existed a coterie of other masters, a group of young Turks and tigers who were also at constant loggerheads with their elders. I recall with immense gratitude those of them who took me up, lent me the newest fiction and poetry, and introduced me to the work of the latest artists and composers. Equally important, whenever they were away for the weekend they lent me their rooms to lounge about in, to read, and to listen to music for hours on end.

Most of these young men, like most young men at the time, were political left-wingers. They thought they could recognize in me a fellow rebel. However, my own rebelliousness took a different turn from theirs—inward and private, rather than public (though of this more later). My craving for a measure of personal freedom took the shape, once I'd achieved the status of head of my house and school prefect, of seizing any and every opportunity to steal away from the school premises in order to savor the forbidden delights of the suburbs of northern London. This was the current expression of my habitual wanderlust. In this way I whiled away many afternoons in the local bookstores and movie houses, or attending the matinees of the local repertory company. I would than creep back to school after enjoying a glass of bitter in some out-of-the-way pub, its taste rendered more delicious by the risk of being spotted and reported to the headmaster by one of the more censorious members of the staff.

I think I already knew I might become an author. My father had given me a good grounding with my reading, and I now gobbled down books at a fantastic rate. One of my more enlightened teachers supplied me with the works of the novelists who dominated the scene or were coming to the fore in the 1930s, such as Hemingway, Dos Passos, Caldwell, O'Hara, Farrell, Faulkner, Maugham, Greene, Waugh, Isherwood, and (in the translations by the Muirs which had begun to appear) Kafka; while another familiarized me with such classical authors as Fielding, Balzac, Dickens, Stevenson, Kipling, and Rider Haggard. However, like most juvenile writers, I first thought of myself as a poet, and here the reigning names were Eliot, Pound, Auden, Day Lewis, MacNeice, and above all, Yeats, whose collected poems and *Oxford Book of Modern Verse* were constant companions of mine. I was also making my first acquaintance with French and Spanish literature. In the light of what was to happen to me later, I was particularly fortunate in that my school was one of the first in England to offer Spanish as a subject. This was a novel departure in the 1930s, when the Spaniards were still lumped together by the English under the general heading of dagoes.

I can see myself filling page after page of my notebooks with poetry—huge clotted masses, a large proportion of it dedicated to girls, either girls whom I encountered fleetingly in the holidays or girls who were entirely imaginary. Like many of my companions I had become obsessed by the idea of girls, a condition exacerbated by the monastic rituals of an English public school. Perhaps I might also add that my other obsession at this time was music. My mother was an excellent pianist, and our household had been intensely and uninhibitedly musical in the Welsh fashion. At school I was tutored by two first-rate teachers: and the end result was a passion for music that has been one of the greatest passions and consolations of my life, and which has had a palpable effect on the tone and execution of my books.

Halfway through school, when I was thirteen, my poor father was finally released from his sufferings. Looking back, trying to make sense of things, it seems to me that it was this event that made me settle into a more sober and determined frame of mind. It was definitely in early adolescence that I began to develop an obsessive ambition to retrieve the family fortunes and restore them to their original condition. This was an ambition it would take me thirty years to work my way out of. It was also at this time, when I was developing what Donne called "an hydroptique, immoderate thirst for human learning and languages," that I was prompted to get down to my books in earnest. My first step on the road to obtaining any sort of professional advantage and distinction was dependent on obtaining one of the scholarships to Oxford or Cambridge for which a handful of boys at my school were regularly entered. It was a cut-and-dried case of no scholarship, no university. Scholarship candidates were pampered by the masters, for winning a place at a senior university shed luster on the school: and I think my otherwise headstrong behavior was largely tolerated because I happened to be strongly fancied in the scholarship stakes.

Preparing to sit for a scholarship was not easy in those last years of the 1930s. As war with Germany became inevitable, masters came and went, either into the territorials or into the regular forces. When war came in September 1939 most of the younger masters vanished overnight, to be replaced by temporaries and dug-outs. It was the haphazard character of my instructors at this period, coupled with the loss of my father, that helped to foster a sense of self-discipline and a conviction that I must learn how to concentrate and how to employ my talents systematically. It was the Englishness of the school, the hard-headed pragmatism of the Anglo-Saxon, which began a process that would be continued during my years at university. I have always sensed that I am somehow a product of Welsh nature and English nurture, the heart of the Celt with the head of the Saxon.

I fell in love with Cambridge the instant I arrived there as a scholarship candidate in 1941. I hadn't been prepared for the impact that its sovereign appearance and special atmosphere would make on me. I knew immediately that this was a crisis in my young life: to be turned away from Cambridge would represent a terrible and irreversible defeat. I remember pacing the banks of the Cam filled with dread at the prospect of flunking. My preparations had been, as I've said, distinctly spotty—strong in some subjects, weak in others. I was apprehensive. But thanks to the don who conducted my final interview, Hugh Sykes Davies (fellow Welshman and author, incidentally, of Britain's first Surrealist novel), I was awarded an Exhibition in English to St. Catharine's College. Immense relief and huge rejoicing. Presumably he was amused by my brashness and precocity, perhaps intrigued by the odd reaches of my knowledge.

The odd instruction I'd received in my last months at school was only a minor fraction of the larger dislocation that had followed the outbreak of war. At night the staff and students bedded down in the cellars and tunnels that ran beneath the school, our sleep interrupted by the crash of anti-aircraft guns and the bursting of bombs, one of which—a land-mine—scored a very narrow miss. During the holidays, while the Luftwaffe pounded Cardiff and the other Bristol Channel ports, I sat with my mother under the stairs of our house, translating Villon and Rimbaud by flashlight. I did my stints as an air-raid warden, and also remember how, during one particularly vicious raid, I ran down Duke Street after a New Year's Eve dance frantic to dive into the gutter and take cover but prevented from doing so because I was wearing a borrowed overcoat and dinner jacket. Showers of glass from the shop window were flying all around me, but I was more afraid of ruining my clothes than I was afraid of the bombers.

Wartime Cambridge, when I reached it, was in the same state of chaos. Sandbags, stirrup pumps, tanks of standing water were everywhere. I only had a year before I was due to be called up, and I was automatically enrolled (following family tradition) in the Naval Training Unit. There I spent a couple of days a week, in addition to regular spells of fire-watching on the college roofs. In common with most other seventeen-year-olds, I regarded these home-front activities, once the Battle of Britain was over and the threat of invasion was receding, as a bit of a lark: but we were all well aware that we weren't in for a joyride once we'd joined up and been drafted overseas. If World War Two wasn't quite the devourer of youth that World War One had been, it was deadly enough. Before it was over, the three heads of my schoolhouse before me, all close friends, had been killed in action, one in the North Atlantic, one over Berlin, one in the Western Desert. As an eventual survivor of four years in uniform, I would have a feeling, one that would remain with me throughout my life, that every day I lived was a marvellous free gift. I think often, for some reason more frequently as the years go by, of those dead young men, and of the many others I served with who were not destined to return.

That wartime year at Cambridge, because of its heightened character, had a powerful effect on me. To begin with, there was the overwhelming sense of freedom, the sense of throwing off the shackles. I can see myself standing on the cobbles of the quadrangle watching a sign-painter inscribe my name outside the sixteenth-century staircase where I had my rooms. *MR. J. E. M. WHITE.* There were the traditional liberties of the university: freedom to follow your own inclinations; to devise your own method of study; to attend lectures or not attend them, as you wished; to get up as late as you liked; to read far into the night. There was boating on the Cam; there were restaurants and coffee shops and pubs. And there were also the unique features of the university as it existed at that period: caps and gowns; being chased through the blacked-out streets and alleys by the "bullers" or proctor's "bull-dogs" if you were out of college after ten at night; climbing into college when the porter locked the college gates. I must have known a dozen ways to negotiate the broken glass and circumvent the iron spikes that topped the college walls.

One of the more agreeable things that happened to me during the course of this crowded year was to make the acquaintance of a lively flock of ATS and WAAFS, girls in khaki or airforce blue who acted as drivers for British and Allied staff officers. They possessed the transport and gasoline to take us for delectable jaunts into the countryside: and it was one of them, whose flat in Jesus Lane I used to frequent, who introduced me to the writer in the flat above who was to be my first important literary contact. Martin Boyd, an Australian novelist, was then in his late forties or early fifties, and was the author of *Lucinda Brayford, The Lime Tree,* and *Nuns in Jeopardy.* A small, neat man, he lived very simply in two tiny rooms. I spent many afternoons with him, huddled over his meager gas fire, talking over tea and buttered toast. He was the first writer I had encountered since, while still a schoolboy, I had been taken up by a wonderfully eccentric temporary master, Brian Lunn, who had published two or three biographies. It was Brian who introduced me to Boris de Chroustchoff, a whimsical and reclusive Russian émigré who would act for much of my life as my chief confidant and almost a surrogate father. Brian also introduced me to his elder brother, the even more eccentric man of letters who wrote under the name of Hugh Kingsmill. The snag was that Brian Lunn and Hugh Lunn were dedicated monologists, whereas my conversations with Boyd were genuine exchanges, affording me my first glimpses into the intricacies of the novelist's craft and into the penalties and rewards of the literary life. Like most Australians, he had the invigorating openness and directness of character which I was later to encounter in America, and I remember him with great affection.

Although I still regarded myself as a poet, I must have had intimations even then that my principal concern would be prose. Although I have written prose consistently, and my books of poetry have been sporadic, I have sometimes speculated about whether it is a help or a hindrance to a prose writer to have started out as a poet. In some ways it makes him too self-conscious, too aware of the individual resonance of each word; prose tends to be a looser, blunter medium. On the other hand, if one has any pretensions to style, a concern for the individual word is essential, and the way one cultivates this is by being a poet. At any rate, it was while I was at school and at Cambridge that I amassed the material for my first two books. These were published in 1943 and 1944 by the Fortune Press, a concern run by a fly-by-night character called Caton, who cadged or filched his stock of paper from bombed-out print shops. All the same, he had an eye for a coming writer, and many of his books are today of considerable value (e.g., Dylan Thomas's first collection, *18 Poems*). These early books of mine are juvenilia and I try not to include them in my list of publications. When I find them on someone's shelves, I follow Thomas Lovell Beddoes' practice of taking out my penknife and cutting out the leaves. Later, at long in-

tervals, I would publish two further collections—but . . . "Rarely, rarely comest thou, Spirit of Delight . . . ."

The author, in the Royal Navy, about 1942

After twelve glorious months, I hurried off to Portsmouth to join the lower deck of the Royal Navy. In short order, because of my previous training, I found myself at sea, taking part in the convoys that ferried troops and war materials backwards and forwards across the Atlantic. The Battle of the Atlantic, which has been described as the most bitter and perhaps the most vital battle of the war, was at its height. I was quickly disabused of any romantic notions about seafaring and the sea. In fact, for several years after the war I was reluctant to go anywhere near the sea, and if I found myself on a beach I would turn my back on the ocean and try to blank out its senseless roaring. It had killed too many ships and shipmates.

Then occurred one of those unforeseen and slightly farcical interludes that make up one's life in wartime. All of a sudden I was told that I was to be seconded to the Indian Army as an officer-cadet; even the regiment, Hodson's Horse, was specified. I was

In the Welsh Guards

transferred to a holding unit, excited at the prospect of spending the remainder of my service in the heat and sunlight of the subcontinent. However, just at that moment the Indian Army, recognizing that the end of the war was coming and that independence for India couldn't be long delayed, stopped recruiting. Whereupon I was given a choice: return to the Navy or help fill a gap in the ranks of the Welsh Guards. Not everyone is offered the privilege of becoming a member of the Brigade of Guards: so it was as a soldier in the junior of the five regiments of His Majesty's Foot Guards that I ended my time in the armed forces.

I wish I had more space to describe my experiences during the war: obviously the war affected in a radical fashion my attitude towards the world and towards my writing. If eight years at an English school and a year at Cambridge had fostered a sense of per-

sonal and intellectual discipline, the process was undoubtedly furthered by the strict regime of a fighting-ship and the comparable severities of the Brigade. Even today I keep my room, my clothes, my possessions in the immaculate order in which I once kept them on the mess deck and in the barrack room. Once a sailor always a sailor; once a Guardsman always a Guardsman.

Looking back over my writing career, I regret that with the exception of a few movies—never a significant part of my output—I have never made direct use of the Second World War or of my own unusual career as a member of two distinct branches of the armed forces. By the time I began to write the war was still too recent; I was too young to evaluate what I'd gone through; there were too many other writers exploiting their own martial splendors and miseries. Nevertheless I can see, looking back, that I am ineluctably a child of the 1930s and 1940s, the most violent decades of what Churchill called "the Terrible Twentieth." They were the decades in which humanity revealed itself in all its nobility and all its squalor. Just as it had taken me many years to appreciate the impact on my life of the First World War, it would take me many years to appreciate the effect on me of what Churchill might have called the Fearful Thirties and the Frightful Forties. Nevertheless the mark which those decades made on my young mind is clearly shown, I think, in the style and approach of both my fiction and nonfiction. My books tend, as reviewers have pointed out, to possess a certain hardness, even harshness, a certain existential lack of sentiment. Since sentiment is the key to popular success, this may partially explain why my books have not obtained the widest appeal: there is something forbidding about them. I had most of the sentiment ground out of me very early on.

On the actual day when the end of the war was being celebrated, VE Day, I met my future wife. I was in military uniform, she was in the uniform of a nurse. In that vortex of cheering, inebriated crowds that on that evening packed the center of Cardiff we were brought together by some mysterious power of attraction. It was very much a moment of instantaneous recognition: and eight months later, at the moment when we were signing the marriage register, I discovered that her mother's maiden name was Manchip, thus making us members of the same uncommonly named family. If there hadn't been this sense of immediate attraction, I would have been attracted to her in any case, because, though Cardiff is famous for its beautiful girls, Valerie Leighton was one of the most beautiful of them all. It seemed appropriate that, with her Manchip and even some White blood, she was also the daughter of a sailor, a Chief Engineer, Gibson Leighton, who lost his life during the sea trials of a new ship. She has been my stay and anchor, in easy days and not-so-easy ones, for forty years. Our fortieth anniversary occurred shortly before the day on which I write these lines. Sadly, she had then been lying for three months in intensive care, following the rupture of an artery in the brain. It has resulted in two operations and in almost total paralysis. All I could do on our anniversary was to moisten her lips with a drop of Veuve Clicquot.

Our first months of marriage, while I was still in the Guards and after my return to Cambridge on demobilization, were an acute scramble. Our worst problem was housing. Three generations of servicemen had all descended on Cambridge at once. We lived in several sets of miserable lodgings before finding refuge at Saffron Walden in Essex, several miles south of Cambridge, to which I commuted each morning on one of the trains of the newly nationalized railways. There we passed a splendid summer before the wretched winter of 1947 drove us back into the city. By a great piece of good fortune, we then settled down in a house on Grange Road, in the home of Sir Frederick and Lady Gowland Hopkins. Gowland Hopkins (a cousin of Gerard Manley Hopkins) was a biochemist and Nobel Prize winner; he was the first man to develop vitamins, which he named. Their daughter was Jacquetta Hawkes, the archaeologist and writer. The house, designed by Sir Edwin Lutyens, had interiors by the *art nouveau* ceramicist and author William de Morgan, and was to be our own home for the next three years.

Valerie Manchip White

I began my second spell at Cambridge by studying English: but after completing my course I changed over to prehistoric archaeology and anthropology. I knew that one day I would become a professional writer, and I wanted to prepare myself by extending my range of interests and subject matter. Besides, we Celts are a time-haunted breed, a race of ancestor worshippers, so it wasn't surprising that I should have been drawn to the study of the past. My supervisor was also a Welshman, the celebrated and genial Glyn Daniel, later Disney Professor of Archaeology. At that time the Cambridge department of archaeology boasted many notable names. I was instructed by such scholars as Miles Burkitt, Grahame Clark, Dorothy Garrod, and T. C. Lethbridge. Archaeology also had the advantage of getting me out of the classroom, and I made many forays into East Anglia in the venerable Armstrong-Siddeley of Tom Lethbridge, the Dark Age specialist, who became a close friend and with whom I dug up many of Sir Thomas Browne's Urn Burials. I also undertook field trips and excavations father afield with Glyn Daniel and Grahame Clark. At the same time that I was preparing myself for a degree in archaeology

I was also pursuing the university diploma in anthropology with such teachers as Reo Fortune: and it was curiously prophetic of events then still far in the future that I should have elected to write my thesis on the pueblo peoples of the American Southwest, a corner of the world I never dreamed I might one day visit, let alone inhabit.

Unexpectedly, I also embarked on a regular career as a writer somewhat earlier than I might have anticipated. One of my wartime friends on the lower deck of the Navy was Gale Sieveking (later himself a distinguished archaeologist), whose father was the writer Lance Sieveking. Lance was head of scripts for the BBC Drama Department (this was three years before BBC Television would be instituted). Over our dinner table at Grange Road he suggested that I might like to try my hand at a radio play. Like most other students I was hard up, eking out my ex-serviceman's grant with my college Exhibition. My wife was working as a nurse at Addenbrooke's Hospital. Under Lance's wise and expert tutelage I wrote a series of brief original radio plays, heard them produced, and during the next five or six years branched out to become one of the BBC's most prolific providers of short plays, long plays, serials, and documentaries. Hardly had I run myself in as a radio dramatist when television programming was established, and I was lucky to find that I was equally adept at that genre too.

It would be very difficult, almost impossible, for a novice writer to enjoy the sort of steady and well-paid apprenticeship which was available then. In my case, however, though in the next twenty years I would write a great many radio and television plays and films, I would never come to consider myself as primarily a dramatist. I regarded my dramatic activity as the financial underpinning of my main activity as a writer of books—novels, biographies, histories, travel books. Yet the fact that my first intensive efforts as a writer were in the dramatic mode had an inevitable impact on my work as a novelist and even as an author of nonfiction. It determined that my approach to a subject would be essentially dramatic. This has been a commonplace of twentieth-century fiction, of course, in much of which the influence of the cinema in particular has become paramount and can be seen in the adoption of new technical devices and in the increasing leanness and swiftness of the narrative. If my literary initiation had been different, the build and atmosphere of my books would probably have been quite different too.

In my final years at Cambridge I found myself involved more deeply than I was really prepared for in what I had originally regarded, after all, as an adjunct to a future career as a writer. The university appointed Stephen Glanville to its first chair of Egyptology, and a press-gang was despatched to the department of archaeology to rope in suitable candidates for its new Egyptological tripos: whereupon Lalage Pulvertaft, Harry Smith, and I became the three original guinea pigs. At first I envisioned this new departure as an amiable winding down of my university studies: but the more I immersed myself in Ancient Egypt the more fascinating and compelling I found it. I thought then, and I think now, that the Ancient Egyptians were one of so-called civilization's few genuinely civilized peoples: wise, gifted, tolerant, good-humored, humane. After I took my degree, Stephen Glanville arranged an interview for me with C. J. Gadd, the Keeper of the Egyptian and Assyrian Department at the British Museum. To my surprise, I was offered a position there. This put me in a quandary. How could I afford to turn down a job in a prestigious department of the civil service? On the other hand, did I really want to spend the rest of my days as a scholar, shuttling every day between a house in the suburbs and Bloomsbury? Moreover, I had reservations about my potentialities as a scholar. Cambridge had implanted in me an intellectual toughness and discipline: but the whole slant of

my mind still seemed to remain far too wayward, imaginative, volatile to meet the austere demands of scholarship. Flattered as I was, I decided in the end to refuse the offer. Stephen Glanville always remained one of my particular friends, and his premature death, shortly after his election as Provost of King's, was a blow to me. The hours I spent with him in his rooms in Gibbs Building, drinking sherry, gossiping, going through the exercises in Gardiner's *Egyptian Grammar*, are among my most pleasant memories of Cambridge. Thanks to him, I retained my passion for Egypt, travelled extensively there, and have kept up conscientiously with developments in the field.

My decision not to enter the British Museum was reinforced by a personal loss my wife and I suffered at this time. Our firstborn, Gwilym, died suddenly after a few months of life. The sight of the small grave and the small white coffin touched off my Celtic impulsiveness: all at once it was time to be done with Cambridge: it was time to move on. Cambridge is a place for the very young or the very old: it had nourished me for six years of my life: now I must strike out on my own. And yet I left it with a sense of huge regret. We had been happy there. I had formed many friendships and received much encouragement from a series of inspiring tutors and directors of studies. Among these I must single out the late Tom Henn of my own college, a man who united an outstanding range and power of mind with an Anglo-Irish warmth and generosity of temperament. I am glad that he accepted the dedication of what is certainly one of the best of my books, and my own personal favorite, my biography of Maurice de Saxe.

I made a complete break. I arrived in London with no prospects and no resources. For the first few months we inhabited a dismal subterranean flat off the King's Road in Chelsea. Then, in the course of a single week, fortune once more turned her wheel and once more seemed to vindicate me for having faith in my star. I was asked to become story editor of the new BBC Television Service, established in that year of 1950: and at the same time I was offered the lease of a spacious and handsome flat in Hamilton Terrace, St. John's Wood.

I reported to the BBC in Lime Grove, Shepherd's Bush. It was a crazy warren of a converted terrace, the headquarters of TV at that date. I found I had a secretary, but no furniture. My single colleague was Wolf Rilla, and between us we read scripts, made adaptations, and wrote original dramas of our own. This was television's Heroic Age, otherwise known as the Age of Improvisation. Every play went on the air live, using at most four cameras, two of which would be shooting a scene in one corner of the studio while the others were being trundled across to set up for the next scene in another corner. If a camera failed, or an actor dried, everyone scurried about and did their best to cover. It was all very hectic and a great deal of fun, and certainly it taught me how to write tightly and economically.

As for our new flat in Hamilton Terrace, it was situated in a wide thoroughfare in Edwardian London's most elegant development. The rent was ridiculously low, thanks to rent restrictions. Life looked up again. My first book, a history of Ancient Egypt, did well, and has remained in print for more than thirty years. *Mask of Dust,* my first novel, was published in America as well as in England, appeared in the then fledgling paperback format, and was made into a film. I thought it was all really rather too easy, and that things would always be like that. I was wrong. However, my newfound affluence enabled me to buy the car in which my wife and I began to make the trips to the Continent which started in the 1950s and early 1960s and which took us increasingly further afield. Astonishing to reflect that we were able to do so on the derisory travel allowance of the time—I think it was fifty pounds—and come home with a pound or two in our pockets. More important, the loss of our first child was soon followed, three years apart, by the births of our two daughters, Bronwen and Rhiannon. Their names were taken from the Welsh epic, *The Mabinogion:* but it is emblematic of my Anglo-Welsh stance that I also provided them with a second, English name— Rosemary in one case, Rosalind in the other. In a

Daughters, Bronwen (left) and Rhiannon, in Hamilton Terrace

Janus-like way, I have always tended to feel rather English when I'm in Wales, and rather Welsh when I'm in England. This combination of Wales and England shows as much in my books, I believe, as in my own character.

I was well launched on a career in the BBC, and also as a writer, when in the spring of 1952 I received out of the blue an invitation to attend an interview at the Foreign Office. I complied, and was astounded to find myself emerging from it as a Senior Executive Officer in Her Majesty's Foreign Service. To this day I have never discovered who had put my name forward. It must have been some don with whom I'd come into contact during my university days. After all, if Cambridge produced its recruiters for spies and traitors, it must also have possessed its recruiters for loyal and reliable candidates as well. This was the year in which the Foreign Office was called upon to cope with the defection of Maclean and Burgess, and security requirements, especially for the department to which I was assigned, had become particularly searching. I am proud that I was deemed to have passed the test: indeed, as proud that I was selected to serve my country during the next five years as a member of the Foreign Service as I was proud to have served it during the war as a member of the Navy and the Guards.

Behold me, then, transformed into a full-fledged denizen of Whitehall, bowler hat, umbrella, spongebag trousers, and all. After luncheon I would play a game of chess at the Athenaeum, drink a glass of port at the Traveller's, or browse in the library of the Oxford and Cambridge Club, before strolling back through St. James's Park to my office in Carlton House Terrace. Nonetheless my work grew increasingly exacting, and ultimately brought me into daily contact with some of the leading diplomats and politicians of the day, as well as affording me periodical trips abroad.

Then why, in the mid-1950s, should I have chosen to give up, for the second time in half-a-dozen years, what was surely an enviable occupation? Looking back, I can now see that a slight puzzlement had set in with regard to the job itself. It is troublesome to belong to a department that is situated fairly close to the center of power and the making of policy and to see its recommendations more or less consistently ignored, or at best substantially watered down. Of course, government functionaries rarely understand the compromises and complications which are of necessity the lot of politicians: but it is frustrating nonetheless. This was also a period of bitterness and disappointment for the young men of my generation who had emerged from the war with high hopes for Britain. During the 1950s we were gradually compelled to face the fact that Britain, so far from recovering something like its former standing, was actually entering a period of seemingly irreversible decline. At the very least we had pinned our faith to the idea that our old Empire might somehow be miraculously transformed into a new and vibrant Commonwealth. It didn't happen. We had been mistaken: more wounding, we had been naive. In spite of the fact that Harold Macmillan's Britain was ostensibly booming, we grew increasingly disillusioned. Suez loomed ahead.

There was also the increasing pressure of my career as a writer. On reaching home at seven, and after eating dinner and playing with the children, I would settle down and write deep into the night. I set myself a rigorous schedule. For relaxation, on my days off, I would visit the galleries and museums, go to concerts and the theatre, or saunter around the corner of Hamilton Terrace to Lord's cricket ground to watch Compton and Edrich and Jack Robertson do their stuff for Middlesex. Another of my prominent interests was motor-racing, the subject of my first novel. I attended all the major meets and knocked around a good deal with the members of the British Racing Drivers Club. My enthusiasm for the sport has never abated.

Altogether in the 1950s I published five novels, a book of poems, a book on Ancient Egypt, and one on anthropology. I was also writing my radio and television plays and had become an industrious screenwriter and screenplay doctor. I was in the more or less regular employment of two British screen companies, for one of which I acted for a year as a sort of freelance story editor, commissioning scripts, getting them written, licking them into final shape. On my frequent trips to visit my family in Wales, I worked up a special connection with Welsh radio and television—and in fact I

gradually developed two distinct sets of literary, musical, and artistic friends, Welsh and English. In Wales, there were Emyr Humphreys, Alun Hoddinott, Saunders Lewis, Gwyn Thomas, Clifford Evans, John Cowper Powys; in England, there were James Hanley and his son Liam, Roy Campbell, E. J. Moeran, James Barlow, Trevor Bates, Hugh Scorer, John Tyrer, Peter Hall, John Scott. John Scott, at that time the literary editor of *The Spectator,* became a very close friend, in Britain and after we had both settled in America. His early death is a continuing grief to me. "For no one in our long decline / So spiteful, dusty and divided / Had quite as many friends as mine / Or loved them half as much as I did . . . ."

I prospered. Increasingly, during the weekends, I would run my family down to Wales, taking the old road through Gloucester. We would often spend weekends in Gloucestershire itself, mainly with friends from Cambridge days, Noel and Barbara Currer-Briggs; and it was in the heart of the Forest of Dean that I found the Speche House Hotel, its oak-panelled dining room the seat of the Verderers' Court, the oldest continuing court or parliamentary body in England. Here I came whenever I had to write a screenplay or do some other piece of work in a hurry. Thus it was more or less inevitable that, after seven years in London, we should have discovered for ourselves a country house in Gloucestershire, a county not only alluring in itself but, practically as well as symbolically, offering equal access to the two spheres of my activity, Welsh and English.

Minsterworth Court, where we took up residence in the autumn of 1958, was no ordinary country house.

Minsterworth Court, Gloucestershire, England

Its main structure was William and Mary. At some date it had been stuccoed and its woodwork painted a subtle and imaginative shade of turquoise. It consisted of two floors each containing three spacious rooms, high-ceilinged, with Adam fireplaces. Its unique feature, tacked on to the main house, was an Elizabethan library with a great brick fireplace. Beyond the library was an even more ancient portion, dating from the late fourteenth century, with massive walls and doorways. The Court (in the West Country the Courts were once its courthouses, seats of the magnates and magistrates) stood on land which was nominally still owned by the Duchy of Lancaster. The original house had been built by John of Gaunt and given by him to his wife, Blanche of Lancaster. What pleased me even more, it had also been given, two centuries later, by Elizabeth I to her personal Tudor genealogist, Gwilym the Herald, whom she created the first Rouge Dragon Pursuivant. It was Gwilym who had bodged up for her one of those splendidly bogus Welsh pedigrees that went back through Uther Pendragon and Charlemagne to the Seven Worthies and the Trojan War. One of my first actions, on assuming ownership, was to seek out an early edition of Gwilym's classic *Heraldrie* and set it in a place of honor in what had once been his own library.

This jewel of a house was enhanced by its setting. On the library side were the tack room, the stables and the coach house, together with an orchard and vinery containing four mature vines, from which in due course I made a wine called (what else?) Blanc de Blanc de Blanc. On the other side was a vegetable garden and an enclosed Italian garden with an eighteenth-century gazebo. Beyond the main lawns, with their lily pool and dovecotes (which eventually housed forty white fantails) were the ha-ha and the paddock. The latter, graced by a towering Wellingtonia, ran down to a broad reach of the river. It was at this precise spot on the River Severn that, every spring and autumn, the celebrated Severn Bore, biggest in the world with the exception of the Red River, would come crashing past, a huge brown wall of water, sweeping along with a tremendous roar and a mighty swash of spume.

The Court was to be our home for the next nine years. We amassed horses, donkeys, doves, geese, dogs, and cats. We gave memorable parties. I became an ardent fisherman and flogged the waters of the Severn and the Wye. My wife became a notable authority on gardening. I collected glass, books, pictures, furniture. It is apparent to me now that this phase of my life, though one can't know such things at the time, represented its peak and apogee ("Life must be lived forwards but can only be understood backwards"). The pain of my father's decline and fall was assuaged. The boy from Wales had beaten the English at their own

A party at the Court: Valerie and the matador
César Girón

game. He had not only become something the English envy and admire, a man of leisure and independence, but something they admire even more—a country gentleman.

It had now become obvious that I was committed to the profession of writer and was in it for the long haul. In the 1960s I would publish seven more books. The general direction of my career was becoming clearer to me. From the outset, I think I had a definite resolve to create something of a personal *oeuvre*. When my books were finally examined, assuming that anyone was interested enough in doing so, I intended a general pattern, an overall shape and balance, to be discernible. I was also aware, at the outset, that their hardness and lack of an ingratiating quality would be a drawback. An even bigger drawback would be their variety and the wide scope of their subject matter. At a time when there are so many claims on a reader's attention, a writer who refuses to turn out a series of readily identifiable artefacts is taking an enormous risk. Still, I felt that it might be worthwhile trying to become something of an *uomo universale*. I didn't want to be condemned, over a career that might extend for forty or fifty years, to performing the same little trick over and over again. I wanted my work to reflect something of life's real span and scale—and just as my own life bade fair to be a varied one, I wanted my work to be varied too. I wanted to resist the shrinkage of subject matter, the onset of timidity, the retreat from wider concerns that was characterizing so much of British writing. I wanted to avoid becoming provincial or parochial. For all that, as I've said, I can't help feeling that, when they're looked at carefully, my books, whatever their superficial differences, reveal a fundamental unity. They possess close correspondences with regard to theme. Their protagonists tend to resemble each other and to be faced with the same kind of dilemmas and moral choices. Above all, if I had to make a personal statement, I would say that one of my chief preoccupations has clearly been to create plots or choose subjects that have been imbued with a sort of tragic vitalism, a desire to take life by the throat, to wring out of it everything that it has to yield. "Energy," said Blake, "is Eternal Delight"—and in a society like modern Britain's, which showed signs of exhaustion of the will and of lowered intellectual vitality, I realized early on that I was probably writing against the grain.

Not, as the years went on in London and Gloucestershire, that I seemed able to remain in Britain for many months at a time. When my wife and I weren't travelling together, I was travelling in connection with the Foreign Service, or later some film or other—

Rome, Berlin, Vienna, or elsewhere. Now, in 1960, there came another major upheaval. I was asked if I would like to work under contract for the Samuel Bronston company, then making a series of screen epics in Europe. The result was that, of the next five years, I would spend one year in Paris and the other four largely in Madrid.

This was without any doubt the most entertaining and outrageous epoch in my life. A full account of it would make hilarious reading. Who would not appreciate the opportunity to live a year in Paris with all expenses paid? I assure you I made the most of the time I spent as the resident of a hotel in the Avenue Victor Hugo. In Madrid, between bouts at the Castellana Hilton, I occupied apartments in various parts of the city.

Spain was a country I had not visited before. I felt instantly and utterly at home there. The Bronston company was in process of making *El Cid* and would go on to make *55 Days at Peking* and *The Fall of the Roman Empire*, so the pressure of work was considerable. However, on most afternoons I managed to slip away to the Prado or the bullfights, and on most evenings to the theatre, the concert hall, the *zarzuela,* the flamenco clubs. I explored Spain diligently, alone or with my wife and daughters, who came out frequently from Minsterworth. Much of this exploration was done in Siegfried, a vintage Mercedes 540K that I bought in Madrid and which would carry me during the next ten

"The Desert Fox": with Siegfried, in Canutillo, West Texas

years all over Europe and much of North America. When I bought him, he was in such poor shape that when I first drove him back to England I had to drive him backwards in reverse gear across the Pyrenees; but my blacksmith in Gloucestershire very soon put him to rights. Originally painted the drab *feldgrau* he had worn since his arrival in Spain during the Civil War, I gave him a resplendent new livery of black and yellow. I loved that car. Hand-built for the chief engineer of the old Untertürkheim works in 1937, he sported luxurious upholstery and a generous range of equipment, including radio and cigar lighter. I made a foolish mistake when, on a sabbatical in Spain twelve years later, I allowed myself to be talked into parting with him. My grandson was born shortly thereafter; I should have kept Siegfried for him.

Sam Bronston, after riding high for several years, finally came a cropper when he fell out with Dupont, his chief backer. Ultimately he lost his shirt on a last and totally misconceived epic. During the painful period when his empire was disintegrating, I was for the most part seconded to a British film company that was working in South Africa. There, in due course, I seized the chance to make an extended tour of South West Africa (Namibia), one of the most memorable journeys of my entire life, and about which I wrote my first travel book. It was now becoming obvious that my career as a screenwriter, such as it had been, was drawing to a close. It would soon be time to take a closer look at my general situation.

I was glad to say goodbye to the cinema. I'd always thought of it as a young man's game: and I was forty. The cinema and television are profligate not only with time and money but with talent. They have a nasty habit of squeezing people dry and throwing them away. Fortunately, I'd never regarded them as much more than a diversion. I'd had my fun and I was ready to depart. I needed to save my energies for more important things. Yet I left with a nagging sense of dissatisfaction. Ought I to have taken the movies more seriously than I did? Perhaps I should have made a greater effort to have my name put on the better films and taken off the worse ones. Perhaps I should have tried harder to write the really good movie I feel I had it in me to write. I wrote some interesting radio and television plays: but I'm conscious, now it's too late, that I never came anywhere near approaching my potential as a screenwriter. It's not much consolation that most screenwriters, especially most novelists turned screenwriters, feel the same way. To some extent my failure stemmed from the chaotic nature of screenwriting itself, since films are usually the product of committees rather than individuals. But I was also never lucky enough to form a close working relationship with some

In South West Africa (Namibia)

sympathetic producer or director who might have brought out the best in me. I don't want to make excuses. In the end, my failure was chiefly due to the way in which—even if from an instinct for personal and creative self-preservation—I deliberately held myself back. Where my books are concerned, I have no such dubious feelings: I gave each of them an honest try. In the 1960s, while still working in the cinema, I would publish another three novels and four books of nonfiction, including a biography of Velázquez, followed by one of Cortés, that were the fruits of those sessions in the Prado and the trips around the peninsula.

Yet side by side with my desire to extricate myself from the movies, I had also begun to sense the growth of a desire to extricate myself in a much more general and drastic sense. *Et in Arcadia ego:* how was it that the serpent could have crept into the paradise of Minsterworth? Had it become too paradisal? Perhaps I was beginning to suspect that, though I was only just turning forty, I might be in danger of growing middle-aged too quickly, a latter day lotus-eater on my West Country bed of amaranth and moly. Or perhaps I was simply undergoing one of my habitual fits of change and restlessness. My wanderings abroad may have contributed to this, as they may have contributed to my increasing distaste for what struck me as the cramped and claustrophobic atmosphere of Britain. This mood grew more acute after my return from Southern Africa; perhaps I had come to resemble Kipling's "English Irregular," brooding on his impending return to England after the Boer War:

Me that 'ave been what I've been,
Me that 'ave gone where I've gone,
Me that 'ave seen what I've seen—
　　'Ow can I ever take on
With awful old England again? . . .

I will arise an' get 'ence—
I will trek South and make sure
If it's only my fancy or not
That the sunshine of England is pale,
And the breezes of England are stale,
An' there's somethin' gone wrong with the lot . . .

Unmistakably, England was entering upon an ever more diminished era. This was the 1960s, a decade of intellectual confusion and muddled social change. The country's troubles had been compounded by the accession to the premiership of Harold Wilson. I didn't want to live in Harold Wilson's England.

White, at Minsterworth Court

In a personal essay I don't want to dwell too much on the subject of politics. Briefly, while I have never been active politically, I have always been distrustful of

and antipathetic to socialism, and by extension to communism. Individualism and individual liberty might really be the paramount theme in my writing. The state has its legitimate claims, but they ought to be strictly delimited and never pressed too hard. Though I was grateful to that younger generation of masters who had made my life at school bearable, I had never shared their left-wing opinions. With the advent of Mr. Wilson I knew we were in for another bout of what British Socialists call "social engineering." I didn't want to be engineered. Even the British Society of Authors, an old and up till then independent institution, had elected at about that time to become a trade union, officially affiliated to the British Trades Union Congress, a dubious body at best. I felt that, of all people, authors ought to resist being regimented and ordered about. I suppose I'd grown tired, like most of my fellow countrymen, of the boring and sterile confrontation between the Left and the Right that has characterized British politics since the end of the First World War. In the 1960s it was at its height. It was time to find a place where one's own vitality and the vitality of its inhabitants weren't numbed by negative and unimaginative confrontation. But please make no mistake about it: British I am and British I shall always remain. However many years I am destined to live away from it, however far it goes on falling in the material league tables, I shall always revere Britain for its enduring love of decency, its championship of common sense and fair-dealing, its imperishable lion's heart. The authoritarians, the opportunists, the Harold Wilsons can never destroy or even greatly damage that. *Civis Britannicus sum.*

Just as I was growing disenchanted with the social scene, so I was beginning to realize that I was also becoming uncomfortable with the pattern I had evolved for myself in Gloucestershire. True, I could jog along, year after year, earning an adequate income by turning out an annual book, a play or two, maybe the occasional movie, a quota of book reviews and other odd bits of literary journalism. But such a routine would put me in real peril of becoming a hack. The free-lance writer is often the last person to appreciate that he isn't really free at all. He reaches a point where he daren't turn down any piece of work that is thrown his way: and inevitably much of it is a waste of his time—which, after all, is his most precious possession and the one that he ought most jealously to preserve. I felt I must sooner or later be faced with the very real possibility of stagnation. Also I was beginning to realize that I'd finally got rid, at last, of that compulsion to put the family fortunes to rights of which I've spoken. Honor was satisfied. I'd liberated myself. I could shed the burden—though the pity of it was that the burden had turned out to be the exquisite one of owning Minsterworth Court.

I'd already formed a clear idea of where it was I intended to head for—America. I'd already been several times to the United States during my time in the cinema. I'd found the atmosphere of America exciting and stimulating. Unlike some of my British friends, I'd never harbored silly and tiresome feelings of animosity towards America, not even in its customary mildly spiteful guise. After all, unlike them, I had actually been there. I liked America and Americans. I even liked New York. American literature and American jazz had been among my earliest enthusiasms in school and college. I liked the confidence of Americans, their capacity for sustained work, their easy manners, their contempt for the restrictions, pretensions, and inanities of the class system, their absence of pomposity, their lack of the malice and suspicion with which Europeans habitually regard each other. Above all I was drawn to the size and to the sheer beauty of the North American continent. That was a place where a man could spread himself and take stock.

It was also fortunate that around this time I had met the critic and biographer Mr. Cleanth Brooks. His work had long been familiar to me, and it was with surprise and delight that I discovered that he was living in London as Cultural Attaché at the American Embassy. It was this kind and distinguished man who suggested that I might look out for a position at an American university, and who undertook to recommend me. A Tennessean and an Easterner, he was rather taken back, however, when I expressed an inclination to head out to the Far West. I thought there was very little point in exchanging England for New England, or Gloucester, Gloucestershire, for Gloucester, Massachussetts. I wanted a thorough change of tempo, a complete change of scene.

A preliminary trip brought me offers of posts in California and Arizona. In the end, after a preliminary visit, I accepted an invitation to become writer-in-residence at the University of Texas at El Paso. The music of its name—El Paso del Norte—enchanted me, and I was enchanted too by its situation on the Rio Grande and the fact that it was a twin-city with Juárez, one of the largest of Mexican cities, and was half-Hispanic and Spanish-speaking in population. At this time I had been commissioned to write a biography of Cortés. Where better to do so than on the border of Mexico?

And so I "arose an' got 'ence." Even so, when the

At the Palace of Hernán Cortés, in Cuernavaca, Mexico

moment of departure came, I set off in Siegfried, loaded to the Plimsoll line, with decidedly mixed feelings. I suffered a frightful pang as I drove, in a blinding rainstorm, out of the gates of Minsterworth Court for the last time. My consolation was the thought that I'd purchased it when it was forlorn and dilapidated, and had steadily improved and refurbished it. Now it had become a truly notable small estate. So I could comfort myself with the reflection that at least before taking leave I'd managed to relinquish a little corner of England in better heart than when I'd found it.

Then, as I disembarked from the *France* (a piquant contrast to my Atlantic crossings in the Navy twenty years before) my spirits rose. I set out on the five-day drive from New York to Texas. The sun came out. I put down the hood. Siegfried bestirred his two-ton weight and hit his stride. When I reached the tawny expanses of West Texas I experienced the same sensation of immediately belonging that I'd felt on first arriving in Spain. This was a place where I was meant to be. In fact it would be the place where I would spend the longest stretch of my life so far.

My wife and I were to spend ten full years, between 1967 and 1977, in Texas. And at least two of those years, reckoning in weeks and months, we must have spent in Mexico, to every corner of which we ultimately penetrated. I also explored every city, village, pueblo, cliff-dwelling, and ghost town, every archaeological site and natural feature of the Southwest. As for Texas itself, I flourished there: but then it is not difficult to flourish in a part of the world that enjoys three hundred days of sunshine a year. In that ample and radiant landscape I found the sense of release and the room to breathe that I had been seeking. Moreover the campus on which I worked, with its seventeen or eighteen thousand students, was one of the most original and striking of all the campuses in America, not unworthy of a Frank Lloyd Wright and with more than a touch of his Taliesin West. From my room on the top floor of the tower, I could lift my head and take in an incomparable view. To my left lay Juárez, dominated by the bulk of Cerra Bola, with the vast plain beyond that reached down towards Chihuahua. In the center were the hills of Anapra, in New Mexico, with a colossal statue of Christ planted on the summit. And on my right, across the valley of the Rio Grande, rose the Franklins, their flanks branded with the prodigious natural image of a Thunderbird with its scarlet wings outspread. A man would have to be very hard to please not to thrive in such surroundings.

If I'd had to uproot myself from Minsterworth Court with groans and sighs, you can imagine the lamentations and breast-beatings with which I had eventually to wrench myself away from El Paso and our

Valerie, with grandson, Antony, in El Paso, Texas

charming house in Kern Place. True, another fit of that damnable restlessness was threatening to take hold of me again: and I'd made the mistake of writing a book about my travels in the Southwest and Mexico. When one has written about a place, it always seems to signal the fact that it may be time to move on. I'd also been feeling something of an itch to take a look at the American South, as once I'd had an itch to take a look at the American Southwest. But my chief reason for forsaking West Texas was that, in 1972, my wife and I had made ourselves responsible for bringing up a grandson, Antony, and I foresaw that, though by this time I'd long been promoted to a full professorship, I couldn't afford to turn down a very promising job that had been offered me elsewhere. Nonetheless I like to think that I remain a Texan, and it is in Texas that I shall in all probability lay my bones (unless I have them transported to Salamanca or to the Black Mountains in South Wales). As the ballad says: "O little did my mother know / The day she cradled me / The lands I was to travel in / The death I was to die . . . ."

In 1976 I took up a position at the main campus of the University of Tennessee, at Knoxville in the eastern part of the state. The college is larger than my college in Texas, enrolling between twenty-five thousand and thirty thousand students. At first my wife and I felt utterly lost without our deserts, our sunshine, our friends in Texas and Mexico, our salpicón and margaritas. It was some solace to recall that after all there has always been a symbiotic link between Tennessee and Texas, and that Sam Houston had been the governor of both: it didn't make Texas seem so far away.

The windows of my home in Knoxville yield as remarkable a view as the one I once enjoyed in El Paso. I gaze out over the leafy hillside with its trackway that I have named Rebel Ridge, in honor of the Confederate troops who advanced along it during Longstreet's bloody and unsuccessful attempt to capture the city, a railroad center that held one of the keys to the eastern and western theatres of the Civil War (or War Between the States, as we Southerners prefer to call it). On Rebel Ridge I walk my dogs, who will occasionally scratch up a buried Minie bullet or a bit of shell. In a clearing at the end of the Ridge, where it falls away into the Tennessee River, stands a dogwood to whose trunk, when it puts out its creamy florets in the spring, I pin a piece of paper with the inscription: *To the God Unknown.* On its roots I pour a libation of wine, milk, blood, and water: just as once upon a time, in our lost realm of Gloucestershire, my little daughters and I would strew the early daffodils on the waters of the Severn, reciting as we did so Milton's lines in praise of the goddess Sabrina. Beyond the Ridge unfolds, mile upon mile, the forest canopy of the Appalachians, in appearance as dense and virgin as in the days of the Cherokee, the mountain-men, the pioneers, or the redcoats on patrol from distant Fort Loudon. And crowning the whole scene, dominating the hazy ridge of the Great Smoky Mountains, are Clingmans Dome and Mount LeConte, the highest points in Tennessee.

Since my arrival in the South I have published a further half-dozen books, following my general practice of trying to alternate a book of fiction with a book of nonfiction. As I've said, I don't really differentiate in my own mind between fiction and nonfiction, though of course the style and tactics are bound to vary between one form and the other. Both, however, seem to me to be very much the same kind of undertaking in most essential respects. And, in accordance with that notion I originally had to create an *oeuvre,* I hope that, now my writing career is inevitably nearing its end, I can somehow find within myself the will and energy to

round it out with a final novel or two, a last biography, maybe a final book of poems, and above all a travel book about the American South, on which I've been working sporadically for some time, called *A Long Road South.* This is intended to complete a trilogy of travel books under the overall title of *My Souths.*

In 1980 I was unexpectedly elevated to a professional plateau at which I couldn't have guessed when I drove Siegfried through the gates of Minsterworth thirteen years before. My university appointed me to a newly founded chair in the humanities. It would be utterly beyond my powers to list the names of the students and members of my departments in Texas and Tennessee who have become my friends. America and the Americans have been generous to me beyond anything I could have wished or expected. Perhaps, since this is a professional memoir, I might simply mention a few of the fellow writers or people concerned with writing to whom I've grown especially close. They would include George Garrett, Richard Dillard, Richard Elman, Nicholas Delbanco, Alan Cheuse, Peter and Marlene Herald, Cynthia Vartan, Leland Sonnichsen, Peter Jennison, James Stowe, Dale Walker, Marilyn Kallet. My relationship with Nicholas Delbanco, with his English and European background and sympathies, has been of particular depth and value.

I have labored reasonably hard at my chosen *métier*—or at the *métier* which chose me, when I was a wild Welsh boy at an English school. On the other hand, I was determined from the outset not to allow my professional activities to devour the whole of my life. Part of

Bronwen and Rhiannon, as young women

it I intended to keep for myself. There is, after all, or should be, an art of living, just as there is an art of writing. From the beginning I resolved to enjoy my life: and, as I said at the opening, on the whole I have contrived to do so; my lines, as the fishermen put it, have fallen in pleasant places. There surely ought to be a good deal more to one's existence than sitting at a table putting words on paper.

In my diary, whenever I want to celebrate a day that has turned out especially well, I write at the top of the page a small sign that represents what the Romans meant when they declared that they "marked this day with a white stone." I've been fortunate in that the borders of my meandering path have been ornamented with a great many of those shining stones. I've enjoyed writing, yes: but I've enjoyed living, too. My motto has been Robert Herrick's: "Live merrily and trust to good letters." What is it to live merrily? To love with a passion and to be loved with a passion in return. To drink a bottle of good wine. To eat a good dinner accompanied by some lively conversation, and concluded with some music, or perhaps a little singing. To drop a fly into a mountain stream. To walk the woods and mountains and deserts, or to drive to the beach, or along unfamiliar roads in search of antiquity, or history, or some majestic spectacle.

"The gods themselves cannot recall their gifts." It is for this among other reasons that the gods can be jealous. In recent months, with my wife paralyzed and in hospital, my luck seems largely to have run out. One must summon up one's courage. One must soldier on. Writing is a prime consolation.

Who knows, one day I may finish that book on the American South and ramble on further down the road.

Heureux qui, comme Ulysse, a fait un beau voyage.

*White with his grandson, at Oak Ridge,
Tennessee, 1981*

BIBLIOGRAPHY

Fiction:

Mask of Dust. London: Hodder & Stoughton, 1953; published as *Last Race.* New York: Mill, 1953.

Build Us a Dam. London: Hodder & Stoughton, 1955.

The Girl from Indiana. London: Hodder & Stoughton, 1956.

No Home but Heaven. London: Hodder & Stoughton, 1957.

The Mercenaries. London: Long, 1958.

Hour of the Rat. London: Hutchinson, 1962.

The Rose in the Brandy Glass. London: Eyre & Spottiswoode, 1965.

Nightclimber. London: Chatto & Windus, 1968; New York: Morrow, 1968.

The Game of Troy. London: Chatto & Windus, 1971; New York: McKay, 1971.

The Garden Game. London: Chatto & Windus, 1973; Indianapolis: Bobbs-Merrill, 1974.

Send for Mr. Robinson. New York: Pinnacle Books, 1974; London: Panther Books, 1974.

The Moscow Papers. Canoga Park, Calif.: Major Books, 1979.

Death by Dreaming. Cambridge, Mass.: Apple-Wood, 1981.

Fevers and Chills (includes *Nightclimber, Game of Troy,* and *Garden Game*). Woodstock, Vt.: Countryman Press, 1985.

The Last Grand Master. Woodstock, Vt. Countryman Press, 1985.

Nonfiction:

Ancient Egypt. London: Wingate, 1952; New York: Crowell, 1953.

Anthropology. London: English Universities Press, 1954; New York: Philosophical Library, 1955.

Marshal of France: The Life and Times of Maurice, Comte de Saxe, 1696-1750. London: Hamish Hamilton, 1962; Chicago: Rand McNally, 1962.

Everyday Life in Ancient Egypt. London: Batsford, 1963; New York: Putnam, 1964.

Diego Velázquez, Painter and Courtier. London: Hamish Hamilton, 1969; Chicago: Rand McNally, 1969.

The Land God Made in Anger: Reflections on a Journey through South West Africa. London: Allen & Unwin, 1969; Chicago: Rand McNally, 1969.

Cortés and the Downfall of the Aztec Empire. London: Hamish Hamilton, 1971; New York: St. Martin's, 1971.

A World Elsewhere: One Man's Fascination with the American Southwest. New York: Crowell, 1975; also published as *The Great American Desert: The Life, History and Landscape of the American Southwest.* London: Allen & Unwin, 1977.

Everyday Life of the North American Indian. London: Batsford, 1979; New York: Holmes & Meier, 1979.

Poetry:

Dragon. London: Fortune Press, 1943.

Salamander. London: Fortune Press, 1946.

The Rout of San Romano. Aldington, England: Hand & Flower Press, 1952.

The Mountain Lion. London: Chatto & Windus, 1971.

Editor of:

Life in Ancient Egypt, by Adolf Erman. New York: Dover, 1971.

The Tomb of Tutankhamen, by Howard Carter. New York: Dover, 1971.

Manners and Customs of the Ancient Egyptians, by E. W. Lane. New York: Dover, 1972.

Egypt and the Holy Land: 77 Historic Photographs, by Francis Frith, edited with Julia Van Haaften. New York: Dover, 1981; London: Constable, 1981.

White has also written numerous scripts for films as well as radio and television plays produced in Great Britain and the United States.

Elie Wiesel

1928-

(Translated from the French by Stephen Becker)

Let us begin at the beginning. But that is not easy, as I know too well. A novel fails or succeeds by its opening: the first page implies the whole. For me the challenge lies in the first sentence: if it rings true it carries me all the way to the book's climax. Sometimes I hunt it down for weeks, months. Once I've caught it, I never let it go. So, where do we start?

At least I know the time and place. Born 30 September 1928 in Sighet: so state my official documents. My parents—Shlomo and Sarah—owned a grocery. We, their four children, helped out as best we could. My two older sisters waited on trade; my younger sister solemnly played the cashier's role.

Sighet: my home town, a special place, an inhabited setting that haunts the memory. I return to it often in my imagination. A search for landmarks? Perhaps for certainties? This permanent obsession nourishes my writing.

Literature, said François Mauriac, is a bridge between childhood and death. I don't agree. For me, literature abolishes the gap between them. In evoking the one, I call upon the other. If, in my books, I return so often to my childhood, my purpose is to describe its death. I return to Sighet to confirm the disappearance of its Jews, myself included. Yes: Sighet no longer exists except in the memory of those it expelled.

I see it with the eyes of a child: a small Jewish town with its synagogues and workshops, princes and beggars, porters and their clients. The official language was Rumanian, with Hungarian second. The peasants of the neighboring villages also spoke Russian, Czech, Ruthenian. At home and at the yeshiva we spoke Yiddish. One consequence of incessant geopolitical convulsions: every Jewish child knew five languages before learning even the first.

When I was three my father draped me in his ritual shawl—the *tallith*—and led me off to the *cheder*. My new comrades were weeping, and so was I: we were appalled by this separation from our parents. And the teacher with his white beard frightened us. And the letters of the alphabet frightened us. The *cheder*, my first exile. I still hear the old teacher's crooning

Elie Wiesel

Boston University Photo Service

voice as he described the wonders that study promised to reveal.

And I hear my mother's voice in the evening, singing me a lullaby, the most beautiful of all, the one I would in turn sing to my own son to calm him:

> *Oifn pripitchik brent a faierl* . . . A fire burns on the hearth, and the room is warm. And the

Rabbi teaches his students the aleph-beit. . . .
When you are grown, he says to them, you
will understand how many tears and sobs live
in those letters. . . .

So I learned that for us in our exile words conceal
a secret that goes beyond their meaning. And a power
too. The Talmud attributes the power of the word to
the first act of all: God himself caused the word to
precede creation. For man, the contrary is true: for
man, the word comes afterward. Even so, it retains its
creative quality. Evocation, invocation: the word, religious in essence, partakes of mystery. It was by naming
beasts and things that Adam imposed himself on history. To know the names of the angels is to rule them.
To pronounce the ineffable name is dangerous: one
risks spoiling all in the attempt to perfect all.

Under the influence of a Teacher steeped in mysticism, I discovered the path of silence. I marveled at
its density, its depth, its possibilities. With a schoolmate—Yerakhmiel—who lived across the street from
me, I practised the "*Taanit hadibour*," the asceticism of
language: we kept silence throughout the Sabbath. My
poor parents never knew whether to be angry or to
laugh: I would not answer their questions except by a
nod. How could I explain to them that one might, by a
single profane word, violate the sanctity of the Sabbath? and that by silence one could enhance its beauty
and prolong its reign? But mystical experience, precisely, unfolds above and beyond explanation.

Now I abridge my account, for I have written of
this at length in certain of my novels. My interest in—my passion for—silence dates from those years.
Sometimes I tell myself that my Master, thanks perhaps to unique powers, was trying to prepare me for
the post-war years. Did he know, did he feel that silence would dominate my work as an obsessional
theme, indeed as a refuge? Did he guess that after we
were separated I would come to struggle against the
word, considering it too limited, too restrained, to communicate a question far more vast and burning? Did
he suspect that language itself would fall mute before
the Auschwitz that was to consume him?

Auschwitz marks the decisive, ultimate turning
point, on more than one level, of the human adventure.
Nothing will ever again be as it was. Thousands and
thousands of deaths weigh upon every word. How
speak of redemption after Treblinka? and how speak of
anything else?

During the ordeal within the accursed kingdom,
our language was reduced to a few primitive words,
elemental, taken from the vocabulary of all occupied
countries. Eat, sleep, work, wake, wash. A crust of
bread was worth all the past's abstract ideas. A gesture

expressed what the poet's word could not reflect. There
was the enemy's triumph, as it seemed to us then: even
if we lived through it, we would be incapable of bearing witness. Yet if our desire to live, or rather to survive, persisted, it was so that we could inscribe our
deaths in the memory of the living.

And yet at the core of our being we knew that the
wish would not be granted. Living side by side with
death, we walked in its shadow. We were all dead, but
did not know it. But we knew that we would never be
alive again, that no return was possible from where we
were now. Our torturers drummed it into us: "This
camp is the last lap." They used more brutal terms,
more lacerating, sharper images. Their purpose? To
demoralize us by depriving us of all hope. As we were
dead in any event, why fight back? why should we try
to remain human, and therefore outside the concentra-
tion-camp system, if not to actively resist it? I abandon
my use of the plural. Others were perhaps stronger and
more confident; but not I. I never succeeded in imagining myself free, happy, whole; I never managed to
think myself, to project myself, beyond the barbed
wire. The night around us and the night within us
merged in an opaque black curtain.

As far as I could hope at all, I counted on some
friend, a comrade known or unknown: let him bear
witness. For me and for all of us. I did not envy him;
on the contrary, I pitied him. "They'll take you for a
lunatic," the killer would say to the last survivor, in
one of my novels. "You'll talk and no one will believe
you. You'll tell the truth, but it will be a madman's
truth." Like the Talmudic sage who, describing the
time of apocalypse, declares that the Messiah will come
but that he, the sage, has no desire to be there to welcome him, I reflected: Surely there will be one last
survivor, but I hope it is not I.

The Liberation saved a few of us—and we did not
know why. Why me and not another? I had done nothing to escape death, just as the others had done nothing
to suffer it. Was I better than they? Surely not. Had I
more merit? No. Luck. That was the answer. Luck
alone was responsible. I believe I said so in my first
account: I might perfectly well have found myself in
another group on 10 April 1945. And someone else
could be here now, before this blank page, to recall
those times.

An absurd and yet painful conviction: for me to
survive, another had to die. Who was it? Often as I
write, my thoughts dwell upon him. Have I the right to
speak in his name? Better: have I the right to speak at
all knowing that I will never succeed in stating the
essential?

Ten years of doubts, wavering, preparations, ten
years of silence followed my return to life. Of course I

was busy; I maintained connections, friendships, I listened, learned, talked and wrote; but I never referred to my experience in the concentration camp. I bore it within me like an obsession that must never be revealed.

I recall picking up the broken thread of life in the first year: the parenthesis barely closed, I resumed my religious practice and studies with a redoubled fervor which, at the time, I never questioned.

In a convoy of four hundred orphaned children and adolescents, I had traveled directly from Buchenwald to France. General de Gaulle himself had issued orders to take us in and shelter us. A Jewish charitable organization—the OSE—assumed responsibility for us. Delivered to a château at Ecouis, we were immediately divided into two groups, the religious and the non-religious. I was among the former. So was the future Rosh-Yeshiva Harav Menashe Klein. And the future professors, scientists, architects. We organized services and classes. I remember well: morning and night, we all recited the Kaddish in chorus. On the Sabbath we chanted. On Rosh-Hashana we wept, praying to God to forgive us our sins—as I had wept years before, in the Rabbi of Borshe's house of study.

Writing these lines now, I am amazed: Whatever became of protest? whatever became of the revolt against creation and the creator? how could I shift with no transition from Buchenwald to the faith and prayers of my childhood?

This is the only possible explanation: we were too rudely awakened. We needed several months to believe that we were truly out of danger; and alive. In the meantime we let ourselves be carried along by old habits revived, habits of body as well as of mind.

An example: on the day, or the day after, liberation, an American soldier offered me a can of food: it was Spam. A week earlier, I'd have devoured it with pleasure; now too, or so I thought. I raised the meat to my lips and . . . passed out. My body, even before my mind, was aware of my liberation and refused, in my name, non-kosher nourishment.

With the war over we reinserted ourselves into our former identities. In one way it was a kind of protest: to show the enemy that he had not won the battle. The test: we insisted on being Jews, bound to our traditions, faithful to our laws. He had not succeeded in permanently interrupting our prayers.

The agonizing reappraisal only came later. Loss of faith? That was something else again. Precisely because I had not lost my faith I felt ineffectual, disoriented, seized in a stranglehold. The tragedy of the believer is incomparably more dolorous, more profound, than that of the unbeliever. The latter is satisfied with his answer, the former not. The believer is condemned

not to understand. "And where is God in all this?" asks one of my characters, staging a show, after a pogrom, in Shamgorod. How can God and his silence be justified? One cannot conceive of Auschwitz with God or without God.

Settled in Paris in 1947, I undertook the study of philosophy. Thanks to classes with the young university professor François Wahl, I managed quite well in French. Racine and Descartes, Stendhal and Montaigne: we read the French texts much as I habitually read a page of the Talmud.

It was a period of anguish and exaltation: philosophical argument, as transmitted and amplified through the ages, became a passion that absorbed my whole being. The ancients, Maimonides, Spinoza, Kant, Achad-Haam: I devoured them, to the point of making a fool of myself in the eyes of my friends. As a choral instructor in a children's home, I bored the young women I liked telling them about the *Critique of Pure Reason* or insisting on the purpose of life, Good and Evil, or the infinite values of phenomenology.

In my Jewish studies I was under the sway of Harav Mordechai Shoushani, that mysterious, intriguing personality who, at the same time but separately, was teaching Talmud to the future Husserlian philosopher Emmanuel Levinas.

In two accounts I have detailed Harav Shoushani's influence on me. With staggering erudition, the Teacher loved to disarrange, to shake up if not demolish the verities before assembling them again, as if in a puzzle the rules of which were known only to him. By happy accident, his volcanic abundance was neatly balanced by François Wahl's sensitivity and rigor. Oscillating between these two extremes of intellectual inquiry, I experienced intensely the confrontation of ideas as well as epochs. Rabbi Akiba and Bergson, is that possible? Yes, it is possible. Nahmanides and Albert Camus, can they be reconciled? Why not? All beings are reconciled in being itself.

But a third element suddenly unbalanced the equation: Palestine. An ancient and unquenchable dream was finally about to come true; one had to be a part of it. Some found their way illegally: I had friends aboard the *Exodus*. Others lived in preparation. I followed current events with high excitement. Those agents of the *Brikha* who chased about Europe helping forgotten Jews to cross borders; those officers of the Haganah who chartered ship after ship in every Mediterranean port; those fighters in the Irgun and the Lehi who made the British Army tremble: we all lived to the rhythms of Jerusalem. The romantic within inspired me to opt for action; I, who have never shown any interest in violence, suddenly found myself fascinated by it. To my surprise, I felt great admiration for the two young revolutionaries name Eliahu who, condemned to death, found a way to cheat the hangman by taking their own lives; and for Dov Gruner, who refused to beg for mercy. . . . I could have wished to join an underground movement in Palestine, but knew no way to do so; it was impossible to establish contact with the Haganah. To tell the truth, I did yield to an infantile (because naive) impulse and went to knock at the door of the Jewish Agency; the doorman received me. He asked the purpose of my visit; I answered, blushing, that I wanted very much to become a member of the clandestine Haganah; he dismissed me with a lack of courtesy that distressed me more than the dismissal itself. Because I could not become a part of the Jewish underground in Palestine in those days, I later wrote a novel about it.

Still, after many inquiries I managed to find a lead not to the Haganah but to the Irgun. A student friend knew someone working for a Yiddish newspaper published by Irgun sympathizers; a meeting was arranged and suddenly I became a journalist. My first article was devoted to the tragedy of the *Altadena,* the ship that David Ben-Gurion's government sank not far from the Tel Aviv beach, to punish Menachem Begin's soldiers. I then wrote several features totally unrelated to the war, underground or open, that the Jewish army had to wage against its enemies; these articles were on Spinoza as well as the Koran and Beethoven.

So I learned none of the skills of insurgents fighting in the shadows; but on the other hand I did learn the journalist's trade, which I plied for twenty years. Thanks to that, I was finally able to embark for Israel. How? It was simple. A French magazine agreed to promote me to "war correspondent." The Jewish Agency offered me passage on a ship carrying North African immigrants. It was an uneventful voyage: I spent my nights on the bridge, staring at the sea and infinity. I loved the sound of the waves. On the morning of our arrival, when I saw Mount Carmel beneath a glimmering red sky, I gave way to violent emotion. My tears flowed freely; I had become as a child again.

Stunned, marveling, delirious, I set off roving through the country. Safed and its mystical resonance. Tel-Aviv and its bohemians along Dizengoff Street. The kibbutzim full of idealists. Jerusalem . . . . I loved Jerusalem even before knowing her; I knew her even before seeing her. When was I first smitten by this city unlike any other? As I drew closer to her gates my heart beat faster, and I fell silent. I remember well: the first time, I had the impression that it was not the first time. And yet each time I have the impression that it is—even today—the first time.

After some months I returned to Paris. Israel was

no longer at war, and my professional activity settled a bit above or a bit below zero. A feature on a camp for recent immigrants, an essay on the election campaign, a study of the unified army: I no longer recall which of my pieces saw the light of day—perhaps none did. That did not keep me from dreaming of a journalists's career. If I could work as a foreign correspondent in Israel, why shouldn't I do the same in France? But I had to dig up an Israeli newspaper that needed a stringer in Paris. The only one without was the evening paper *Yedioth Ahronoth,* and for good reason: it was too poor to allow itself that kind of luxury. The editor-in-chief, cultivated and astute, welcomed me with the courtesy due to a colleague, but insisted on warning me, "Our paper was once the richest and most widely read in the whole country, but those days are over because of a political split. If you want to free-lance at space rates, the job is yours." I could hardly conceal my enthusiasm.

To that newspaper I owe years of fervid activity. They let me travel often and afar. Spain, Morocco, India, Brazil: when a chance came along I jumped at it. I hardly earned a living—$20 a month to start with, eventually $500—but I was young and my needs were not great.

Years of exploration and apprenticeship: I wrote in Yiddish, in Hebrew: in India I learned English. I "covered" international conferences and spectacular events; I learned to condense news and commentary, to work under pressure in stations and waiting rooms, to go without sleep and even food: to score a "beat" filled me with joy, and with pride too. Only interviews rattled me. I was shy, and felt awkward if not paralyzed before the personalities I had to question. Yet I prepared assiduously. Each such confrontation was an exam I was afraid of flunking. Of course I tried to reason with myself; I told myself what everybody knew, namely that men and women whose pronouncements interested readers courted reporters, that the real power lay with the latter and not with the former—but it was no use: with me it was pathological. As a result I believe I am the only journalist alive who, sitting in on hundreds and hundreds of press conferences, never once raised a hand to ask a question; on the contrary, I shrank, I strove to make myself invisible. Politicians, career (and even careerless) diplomats, tycoons and movie stars, temporary or less than temporary celebrities, beauty queens, real and phoney adventurers: I did my job, and interviewed them face to face, trying not to let my stage-fright show.

But there followed, in 1954, an interview that marked a turning point in my life. I met François Mauriac, whose novels and political stand I admired.

Elsewhere I have described that first meeting. My impatience at his passion about Jesus. My childish and discourteous remark that ten years earlier I had known Jewish children who suffered more than Christ, and yet we never spoke of them. His humane reaction, his silent tears. His answer: "But you ought to speak of them." Without a word from me about my experience in the concentration camps, he sensed it. I had no need to go into detail; he felt it. Incidentally, throughout our long friendship, which ended only with his death, that theme remained all but taboo. At first because I do not like to speak of it; it is too intimate. And later because he, discreet and clear-sighted, refused to embarrass me. Nevertheless, I took his advice.

My meeting with Mauriac coincided with the tenth anniversary of my deportation. I sensed clearly that the time had come to begin translating ten years of patient silence into words. In Yiddish it was *And the World Kept Silent,* which was to become *Night.* Why had I chosen Yiddish? Sentimentality? Fidelity? Both. I felt an obligation to make my first book an offering to a culture, an atmosphere, a climate which were those of my childhood.

My first draft was long, too long, about 850 pages. I cut; I cut two-thirds if not more. The French version was cut even further. In Yiddish I began my tale in the ancient Biblical manner: "In the beginning was faith, confidence, illusion. . . ." And I concluded it with an inquiry on the value and meaning of survival.

Why this obsessive cutting? In the first place, I distrust useless words. And then I am much influenced by the chroniclers of the ghettoes and camps. They wrote short choppy sentences, blurted as if by a man out of breath, like scraps of paper slipped through the skylight of a prison or a train clacking toward death. A sentence is worth a page, a word is worth a sentence. The unspoken weighs heavier than the spoken. Each period is perhaps the last. Unconsciously I drove myself to adopt a similar style. No literature; above all do not produce literature. Nor try to please by flattering the reader or critic. Say only the essential—say only what no other could say. And obey the edict of the Hasidic rabbi of Worke: transform the cry to a murmur. A style sharp, hard, stony, in a word, pared. Suppress the imagination. And feeling. And philosophy. Speak as a witness on the stand speaks. With no indulgence to others or oneself.

The Yiddish version appeared in Buenos Aires, while the French version made the rounds in Paris. Despite a preface by Mauriac, the manuscript roused no interest whatever in publishing circles. I remember a comment by an editor who handled Mauriac's novels: "People don't want to read this kind of story any more." Finally the aged Catholic writer and Nobel laureate took matters into his own hands and himself bore my manuscript to Jérôme Lindon, who was head of Editions de Minuit. A lucky break: Lindon said yes. The book came out in 1958 and, invited by my publisher, I returned from New York for publication day, which frankly could have taken place without me: not for nothing was I Mauriac's protégé, and it is unquestionably owing to him that my book won what support it did. I was happy to be back in Paris; I could renew my friendship with Mauriac.

In the meantime I had settled in the United States. Since 1956 I had represented my newspaper there . . . with a few involuntary interruptions. Let me explain: only weeks after my arrival in New York, I was knocked down by a taxi in the middle of Times Square. I came to ten days later in a hospital room. Afterward, I laughed about it: to have survived Auschwitz and Buchenwald only to be half killed in America was after all fairly funny. . . . There were two consequences: I used the accident as a backdrop for a novel, and I postponed my return to France. In fact, I decided to stay in the United States for good.

I could not make ends meet on my salary from *Yedioth Ahronoth,* so was easily persuaded to take a job as editor on the *Jewish Daily Forward.* In time I did a little of everything and a little of nothing: political articles, literary criticism, reporting. I slept less and less, and never took a vacation, because in addition to my professional duties, and along with my novelist's tasks, I continued my studies of the Jewish tradition's sacred texts. Harav Saul Lieberman, the greatest Talmudist in many generations, professor at the Jewish Theological Seminary in New York, consented to give me private lessons: all that I know, all that I wish to pass along, I received from him.

I met him by chance at the home of a colleague, a Russian-born Israeli. I had just returned from my first trip to the Soviet Union, and my friend had invited several guests with an interest in the matter. I made my report to them—in effect a brief survey of what was later published as *The Jews of Silence.*

An unforgettable journey: on the one hand the frightened old people in the Kiev synagogue, on the other the courageous joy of young people on a holiday evening in Moscow. An incredible discovery: the young Jews, sons and daughters of communists, educated in schools where Marx had supplanted the Prophets of Israel, were openly returning to the source of their collective memory. How to explain this Jewish revival after fifty years of atheistic government? I saw them, these young Jews who wanted to learn Jewish history, literature, philosophy, and risked their security, even their lives, to do it. Let us not forget this:

before Solzhenitsyn, before Sakharov, before the dissidents we admire, it was young Jews who dared defy the Kremlin's dictatorial police state; it was they who, even as early as 1965, had the audacity to declare themselves free and sovereign, a few steps from Lubyanka Prison . . .

I came to love the Russian Jews with an exalted yet deeply personal love: their cause became mine. I went back to the USSR the next year; once more I spent the high holidays with them. Some recognized me, and a gleam of gratitude rose in their eyes: "You haven't forgotten us." No, I had not forgotten them. I tried to rouse public opinion so the world would not forget them either.

One personality above all was a constant inspiration: the Chief Rabbi of Moscow, Harav Yehuda-Leib Levin. Twice I found myself in his company on the night of Yom Kippur, during the opening Kol Nidre. The second time I gazed intently at him, begging him silently to interrupt the service, to hammer the pulpit with his fist and shout the truth of his people's tragedy—but I gazed in vain. He was already too feeble and exhausted for that sort of gesture. Then, back in New York, I had an idea: to bring him to life on stage. And I wrote a play: *Zalmen; or, The Madness of God.* This is the story: a madman called Zalmen does his best to provoke the last rabbi to fury in some Soviet city—and finally the rabbi yields to anger, because of his grandson Misha, who has come to visit him on the eye of Yom Kippur. Misha, almost at the age of bar-mitzvah, knows nothing of Judaism; he does not even know what the term "bar-mitzvah" means. His father Alexei is a communist and insists that Misha forget his roots. He explains to his father-in-law: "My father suffered so greatly for being a Jew, and his father before him—how long do you want that to go on? Somewhere we have to break the chain of suffering, and with Misha it will be broken. . . ."

A remarkable coincidence: I thought I was dreaming up that family, but it was a reality, it existed. The Chief Rabbi's daughter, passing through New York, years later, confirmed that. Every character in the play—except perhaps the madman—had lived out a similar destiny behind the scenes. As in the play, the Chief Rabbi was miserable because his daughter had married a communist Jew; as in the play, Misha's parents quarreled about his education; as in the play, Misha was torn between his grandfather and his father.

But there is nothing really remarkable in all that: Jewish history is full of such situations. As King Solomon said, there is nothing new under the sun. And the Talmud, in a poetic flight, reaffirms this: All that a disciple may ask of his Master, Moses received on Sinai.

All? What I was asking of Lieberman too? Yes, all, absolutely all. That is the essential principle of the Talmud. All questions have a past that binds us to our ancestors.

The Talmud binds me to my childhood. I resume a debate two thousand years old and see myself again in a little room lit by an oil lamp or flickering candles; I am only one shadow among so many others that sway to and fro chanting the phrase that asks a question, or that which answers it, as if to absorb them better, to comprehend them better.

I know: in certain circles it is fashionable to denigrate Talmudic discourse. That is not new. How many times has it been condemned to the stake in the name of a fanatical faith? In the name of reason they have ridiculed it. Even in our time they make fun of the "Talmudic spirit." They do not understand the beauty, the profundity, the stimulation in Talmudic thought. I understand it better thanks to the lessons I learned from Saul Lieberman.

At first he was a bit suspicious of me. He never admitted that, but I felt his glance upon me: he was watchful. I came to his rooms, I showed him difficult passages in this or that tractate, I asked him to explain them, which he did masterfully; but even so I sensed a certain reticence on his part. And then one day he said, "I hear you're giving a talk on a Talmudic theme. . . ." I confessed that the subject of my lecture at the "Y" was indeed, well, Talmudic. . . . "Very good," he said. "I'd like to come." I protested: "No, please, please don't come." "Why not? I have a certain interest in the Talmud, you know." All right: I set to work. Sources, references, analyses; I worked for weeks to make it an exemplary lecture. He came to the "Y" and, naturally, was much noticed in the auditorium. He waited for me afterward in the lobby, and paid me compliments in a loud voice; then, more quietly, he invited me to come and see him the next day. He greeted me with a smile: "Am I mistaken, or did two or three original insights come to you during the lecture?" Yes, yes indeed . . . "Come here," he said, opening an old volume that seemed to limp along the table. "Read," he said. "Here." What I had thought original was already there, set down at least a thousand years before. "What do you think of that?" asked Harav Lieberman. "Thank you," I said. "Thank you from the heart. It makes me very happy to think that even in my stumbling I followed the path of my ancestors." Taken aback, he stared at me to be sure I was not being hypocritical. Three times he set me the same test; each time I thanked him for disproving the originality of my insights. Finally he realized that my thirst for study was real. Only then did he accept me as a disciple.

Twice a week I came to spend hours in his library.

Together we studied half the Talmud and the apposite commentaries. I could repeat the *"Midrash kohelet"* even today: every page he guided me through was a wonder to me.

Our ties grew stronger; we became close personal friends as well. I did nothing without his advice. I published nothing without his opinion and his agreement. Mastering French as I had, he read my novels in manuscript and returned them annotated. I owe my works on the Bible entirely to him.

One evening as we left the "Y" he turned to me and said, "I intend to officiate at your wedding." I did not yet know that I was going to marry; nor did my future wife. Indeed he married us in the Old City of Jerusalem on Passover eve 1969. When our son reached the age of three, Harav Lieberman gave him his first Hebrew lesson.

In April 1983 our discussions ran on longer than usual. My Teacher refused to let me leave; but I was due at Yale, where I was teaching that year. I was already at the door when he called me back. We took up the text where we had left off. An hour later I shook his hand and wished him bon voyage; that afternoon he was to board a plane for Jerusalem. I was in the corridor when he called me back once more. Again we took up the text. I was melancholy when we finally parted. I said to my wife, "He's old, so old." That very night he died in the airplane.

I miss him. No Teacher—not even Harav Shoushani—made so deep a mark on me; no Master kept me at his side for so long: seventeen years is a lifetime, more than a lifetime.

The eminences he introduced me to, at the Seminary and at his home, will remain pillars of Jewish studies. Louis Finkelstein, the great philosopher of history; Shlomo Spiegel, author of an exceptionally beautiful and penetrating work on the near-sacrifice of Isaac; Gershom Scholem, who made a science of Jewish mysticism; Gerson Cohen, a young scholar and future president of the Seminary . . .

I had friends at the Seminary whom I had known long before. David Halivni and I both came from Sighet. We were childhood friends and have remained friends. He teaches Talmud. Lieberman was Teacher to us both.

And there was one professor at the Seminary to whom I grew close, while he and Lieberman did not get on well. This was Abraham Joshua Heschel, descendant of the illustrious Rabbi of Apta. We were bound by many ties: a love of Hasidism, activism on behalf of the Russian Jews, the struggle for the rights of man everywhere. . . .

Why were Lieberman and Heschel at odds? I tried to negotiate a rapprochement. Wasted effort. It was perhaps a question of temperament, or of education, or even of ideology. They inhabited two different universes. Perhaps there was some other factor. I only know that to their friends, their breach was always a distressing enigma.

Still, before dying, they . . . No, some other time. I will be forever grateful to both. True, Heschel was not my Master, but he was a sort of older friend for whom I will always feel a special affection and tenderness.

I remember one ceremony they both attended: On June 4, 1967, the Seminary awarded me my first honorary Doctor of Letters. No doubt Lieberman's idea. Knowing my affection for Heschel, he showed generosity and invited the latter to make the formal presentation. The "Six Day War" broke out next morning and I left for Israel, not as a correspondent this time but as a witness. Like so many Jews, I feared that Arab propaganda might result in a real catastrophe for the Jewish state, in which case I wanted to be there. On the plane from Paris to Lydda I met my friend André Schwarz-Bart, who had come for the same reason. To witness. Next day we went up to Jerusalem. A crowd was packed tightly at the Wall. What I felt then, I tried to express later in a novel. Sometimes I reread it and see myself as a beggar, hand outstretched, throat constricted.

The Beggar of Jerusalem is a topical novel, circumstantial and timely, but it is crucial to the body of my work. In 1967 I glimpsed the horrors of war, even if it was a war that meant liberation if not security for my people. The corpses of Egyptian soldiers in the Sinai, the frightened Arab children in the Old City: I cannot forget those, any more than I can forget the sadness and humility of the Jewish soldiers. Were they conquerors? They did not behave like conquerors. May I once more quote my favorite source, the Talmud? The only victory is that which man wins over himself.

Nevertheless there was something metahistoric in that war. It could not be explained either by politics or by strategy. A character in a novel said it: "Israel won because in addition to its soldiers, the army could count on six million men, women and children."

If the Jewish state almost lost the next war, the Yom Kippur War, it is because in 1967 the terms of reference were 1939-1945, while in 1973 the terms of reference were 1967.

The year 1973 was difficult for the Jewish people, a year of assorted upheavals. By coincidence, the most despairing of my novels appeared during that period.

It tells the story of a pogrom somewhere in Eastern Europe at the turn of the century. A Christian boy has disappeared, and the Christian community accuses the Jews of having kidnapped and killed him for ritual purposes. The classic false indictment, which persisted for generations. Vainly the Jews defend themselves, crying that they have no right to use blood, that they are forbidden to kill—even for religious purposes; their blindly fanatical enemies believe what they want to believe. From cruelty to cruelty, from one heinous stroke to another, the mob burns down the Jewish quarter, not realizing that the flames must inevitably spread, attack and in the end destroy the whole town. Seeing the streets and houses ablaze, one character is seized by dread. Later he will understand the meaning and extent of his fear: he has glimpsed the future.

Simply stated: we cannot delude ourselves that the massacre of any group will not affect the whole of civilization. We cannot wish for the extermination of one people without placing all of humanity at risk. The final solution, aimed at the Jewish people, was an outline for the death of all peoples. Auschwitz was perhaps a warning. To refuse to see it as such is to run a supreme risk; to deny the lesson of the '40s is to minimize the nuclear threat.

So I started new work: against the atomic menace. I speak against it often. Certainly I do not compare Treblinka and Maidanek to other tragedies past and those yet to come; I believe, and I shall continue to believe, that Auschwitz defies all analogy. But we must see essential terms of reference in it. We must link everything to that Event without comparing it to anything. One consequence of this new activity of mine was Ted Koppel's invitation to participate in the debate that followed the film *The Day After*.

I believe I was the only participant to confess his ignorance of facts and techniques. I know nothing and understand nothing of nuclear strategy, and I said so before the hundred million viewers watching the program. All I know is that in view of the growing threat, one gets the impression that the whole world has become Jewish. For two thousand years the Jewish people lived in permanent uncertainty, and now we can say that of society in general; for two thousand years the Jewish people endured on the threshold of the unknown, and now that is true of all people everywhere. In other words, the Jewish condition has become the human condition. Where then is the solution? In memory. It remains our only refuge, our only shield. To deny it is to deny oneself.

Communism has tried and failed. Oriented toward the future, it repudiates the past. Whatever is old is bad and therefore to be rejected; hope can thrive only at the expense of memory. They must abolish the divisive past in favor of the unifying future: that is the simplistic message, the pattern of communist dialectic as it was handed down to the exploited and persecuted "masses." It is diametrically opposed to the Jewish tradition, which constantly insists on the centrality of memory. Yet there were many Jews in the communist movement, particularly in the early days. Some came out of orthodox circles, out of the yeshiva. How could they? Long consideration—years and years of it—leads me to a plausible explanation: for them communism was a sort of Messianism without God. So it was "to hasten the redemption" that a David Bergelson or a Der Nister or a Peretz Markish joined the revolution.

Markish and Der Nister fascinated me. The former, a great Yiddish poet, if not the greatest, returned to Soviet Russia after a series of sojourns in the West: for what reason? Der Nister, a Yiddish novelist without peer in the literature of that beautiful language, chose to write of the Hasidim of Bratislava but remain in the Soviet Union: to prove what? These two creative geniuses served as models for Paltiel Kossover, the assassinated Jewish poet, to whom I devoted a novel.

(One day in Geneva, after a lecture on a Talmudic topic, a young professor approached and said, "Where did you meet my father? You speak of him as if you knew him well." It was Peretz Markish's son Shimon.)

Before that novel was published, I had returned to Soviet Russia. It was my third trip. This time, if I may say so, I moved about quite openly. I went wherever I liked, said what I thought, had nothing to fear: I was on an official mission.

Named by President Jimmy Carter to head his Presidential Commission on the Holocaust, I had undertaken a pilgrimage, first to the death camps in Poland, and then to Kiev and Moscow. Kiev, to visit the monument at Babi-Yar, Moscow to renew my ties with the Jews.

I provoked a scandal in Kiev. The monument at Babi-Yar makes no mention of the Jews for whom it was erected. Before the municipal officials I could not contain my anger: "Are you not ashamed?" I shouted. "Have you forgotten the sixty or eighty thousand Jews killed here in the center of the city, in September of 1941? Why were they killed? Because they were Soviet citizens? or communists? No, and you all know it perfectly well: the Jews were massacred only because they were Jews—and now you deprive them of their Jewishness, their identity?"

In Moscow I asked permission to address the synagogue during the Saturday services. I rarely had a more attentive audience. An old man whispered a startling confidence into my ear: "You promised once not to forget us; and you kept your word."

A meeting with high-ranking officers of the Red Army figured on the official agenda. One of them, General Petrenko, had commanded the unit that liberated Auschwitz in January of 1945. He told us how his officers and men had mounted the assault on the death fortress, and I told him about our wait: "Why did you delay so long? You could have prevented the Germans from evacuating us." While the general was talking, an idea struck me: He was among the first to see us, he was one of the first free men to discover our ordeal, our humiliation and our death; he too must witness. Back in Washington we decided to convoke an international colloquy of liberators. To compare their impressions, their memories. Russians and Englishmen, Norwegians and Czechs, Americans and Poles and Frenchmen and Belgians created a warm atmosphere of camaraderie that the capital had not recently been accustomed to.

A meeting with survivors in Jerusalem, and then in Washington; a meeting with the children of survivors in New York; unforgettable moments that loom large in my life.

I have never liked public appearances and I still do not. But for the sake of the survivors and their children—that's something else again. With them, there is an air of the miraculous.

Abandoned, denied, humiliated for long years, the survivors feel the need for one another's company. To prove to one another that they are still alive. And that they are capable of happiness. And above all of humanity.

Logically, they should have given up on mankind. Kept their distance, and spat on society and its idols. Had they chosen, after the war, nihilism or violence or dementia, no one would have been surprised. But they chose faith and compassion. In that, they show us the path to follow. In that, they are all deeply moving. The secret they bear within isolates them forever, and yet they smile at us, they sing, they exchange banter. How can we explain the absence of hatred among them? It is surely that they simply cannot reduce an event of that order to a few spasms of hate. It would be too absurd.

Their children also touch my heart. There were many in my classes. They came not so much to study medieval philosophers as to draw closer to their parents. Later, their parents would come to see me, to draw closer to their children. So I became a bridge, a bond, for all of them.

A young woman student, in tears, asked me: "Will my father ever stop being a survivor?" And a young male student confided, "My father was married, and had children; my mother was married, and had children. My father lost his wife and children in the camp; my mother lost her husband and children in the camp. My father and my mother met after the liberation, and were married, and had a child, me; but when they look at me I know it isn't me they see."

What could I say to these young people? I wrote a novel. For them.

When all is said and done, I know no other way. I set down words and do my best to make them speak the truth, or at least to let them tell no lies.

When I take stock, I see that I have written twenty-five books on a variety of subjects, and yet it often seems to me that I have not yet begun to write.

I can't complain. Some of my works are read and others sell fairly well, and they are not always the same ones. They are taught in elementary schools, high schools, universities, and I am proud of that: I love young people. Very few have read all my books, and that doesn't matter: I am satisfied with what has been offered me. With the years comes a skeptical serenity that helps us carry on. Praises do not turn my head and blame does not disturb my rest. With the years comes a desire to concentrate on the essential.

There was a time when I listened for an echo in answer to my voice; I no longer seek it. I have learned to accept a truth: there will always be readers who like what I write, and others who do not. A writer's purpose should not be to please, but to unsettle, and I might even say, to unsettle himself.

Personally I am rarely satisfied. Is that why I am always venturing into new territory? When no one was paying attention to the Holocaust, I was talking about it; now that everybody is talking about it, I say little. When no one would speak of the Russian Jews' tragedy, I tried to alert public opinion; now that the subject has become an institution, I keep my distance.

What have I learned since I began to write? I have learned that the literature of the Holocaust has this in common with the Holocaust: they do not change people, they only intensify them: the good become better and the bad worse. But there are exceptions, happily. There are surprises, and then words become prayers.

I am still waiting.

BIBLIOGRAPHY

Nonfiction:

La Nuit, with foreword by François Mauriac. Paris: Editions de Minuit, 1958. Originally published in Yiddish as *Un di velt hot geshvign* ("And the World Kept Silent"), Buenos Aires, 1956. Translation by Stella Rodway published as *Night.* New York: Hill & Wang, 1960; London: MacGibbon & Kee, 1960.

Le Chant des morts. Paris: Editions du Seuil, 1966. Translation by Frances Frenaye published as *Legends of Our Time.*

New York: Holt, 1968.

Les Juifs du silence. Paris: Editions du Seuil, 1966. Translation by Neal Kozodoy published as *The Jews of Silence: A Personal Report on Soviet Jewry*. New York: Holt, 1966; London: Vallentine, Mitchell, 1968.

Entre deux soleils. Paris: Editions du Seuil, 1970. Translation by the author and Lily Edelman published as *One Generation After*. New York: Random House, 1970; London: Weidenfeld & Nicolson, 1971.

Célébration Hassidique: Portraits et légendes. Paris: Editions du Seuil, 1972. Translation by Marion Wiesel published as *Souls on Fire: Portraits and Legends of Hasidic Masters*. New York: Random House, 1972; London: Weidenfeld & Nicolson, 1972.

Célébration Biblique: Portraits et légendes. Paris: Editions du Seuil, 1975. Translation by M. Wiesel published as *Messengers of God: Biblical Portraits and Legends*. New York: Random House, 1976.

Un Juif aujourd'hui: Récits, essais, dialogues. Paris: Editions du Seuil, 1977. Translation by M. Wiesel published as *A Jew Today*. New York: Random House, 1978.

Four Hasidic Masters and Their Struggle against Melancholy. Notre Dame, Ind.: University of Notre Dame Press, 1978.

Images from the Bible. New York: Overlook Press, 1980.

Five Biblical Portraits. Notre Dame, Ind. and London: University of Notre Dame Press, 1981.

Somewhere a Master: Further Hasidic Portraits and Legends. Translated from the French by M. Wiesel. New York: Summit Books, 1982.

Against Silence: The Voice and Vision of Elie Wiesel, selected and edited by Irving Abrahamson. New York: Holocaust Library, 1985.

Fiction:

L'Aube. Paris: Editions du Seuil, 1960. Translation by F. Frenaye published as *Dawn*. New York: Hill & Wang, 1961; London: MacGibbon & Kee, 1962.

Le Jour. Paris: Editions du Seuil, 1961. Translation by Anne Borchardt published as *The Accident*. New York: Hill & Wang, 1962; London: Robson Books, 1974.

La Ville de la chance. Paris: Editions du Seuil, 1962. Translation by Stephen Becker published as *The Town beyond the Wall*. New York: Atheneum, 1964; London: Robson Books, 1975.

Les Portes de la forêt. Paris: Editions du Seuil, 1964. Translation by F. Frenaye published as *The Gates of the Forest*. New York: Holt, 1966.

Le Mendiant de Jérusalem. Paris: Editions du Seuil, 1968. Translation by the author and L. Edelman published as *A Beggar in Jerusalem*. New York: Random House, 1970; London: Sphere Books, 1971.

Le Serment de Kolvillàg. Paris: Editions du Seuil, 1973. Translation by M. Wiesel published as *The Oath*. New York: Random House, 1973.

Le Testament d'un poète Juif assassiné. Paris: Editions du Seuil, 1980. Translation by M. Wiesel published as *The Testament*. New York: Simon & Schuster, 1981; London: Allen Lane, 1981.

Paroles d'étranger. Paris: Editions du Seuil, 1982.

Le Cinquième fils. Paris: B. Grasset, 1983. Translation by M. Wiesel published as *The Fifth Son*. New York: Summit Books, 1985.

The Golem: The Story of a Legend. Translated from the French by A. Borchardt. New York: Summit Books, 1983.

Plays:

Zalmen; ou, La Folie de Dieu. Paris: Editions du Seuil, 1968. Translation by Lily Edelman and Nathan Edelman published as *Zalmen; or, The Madness of God*. New York: Holt, 1968. Stage adaptation by M. Wiesel. New York: Random House, 1975.

Le Procès de Shamgorod tel qu'il se déroula le 25 février 1649: Pièce en trois actes. Paris: Editions du Seuil, 1979. Translation by M. Wiesel published as *The Trial of God (as It Was Held on February 25, 1649, in Shamgorod): A Play in Three Acts*. New York: Random House, 1979.

Other:

Ani Maamin: A Song Lost and Found Again (cantata). Libretto by Elie Wiesel; music by Darius Milhaud. Translated from the French by Marion Wiesel. New York: Random House, 1974.

The Haggadah (cantata). Libretto by E. Wiesel; music by Elizabeth Swados. New York: Samuel French, 1982.

Cumulative Index

CUMULATIVE INDEX

For every reference that appears *in more than one essay*,
the name of the essayist is given before the volume and page number(s).

INDEX

INDEX

INDEX